MORBIUS

PRELUDES AND NIGHTMARES

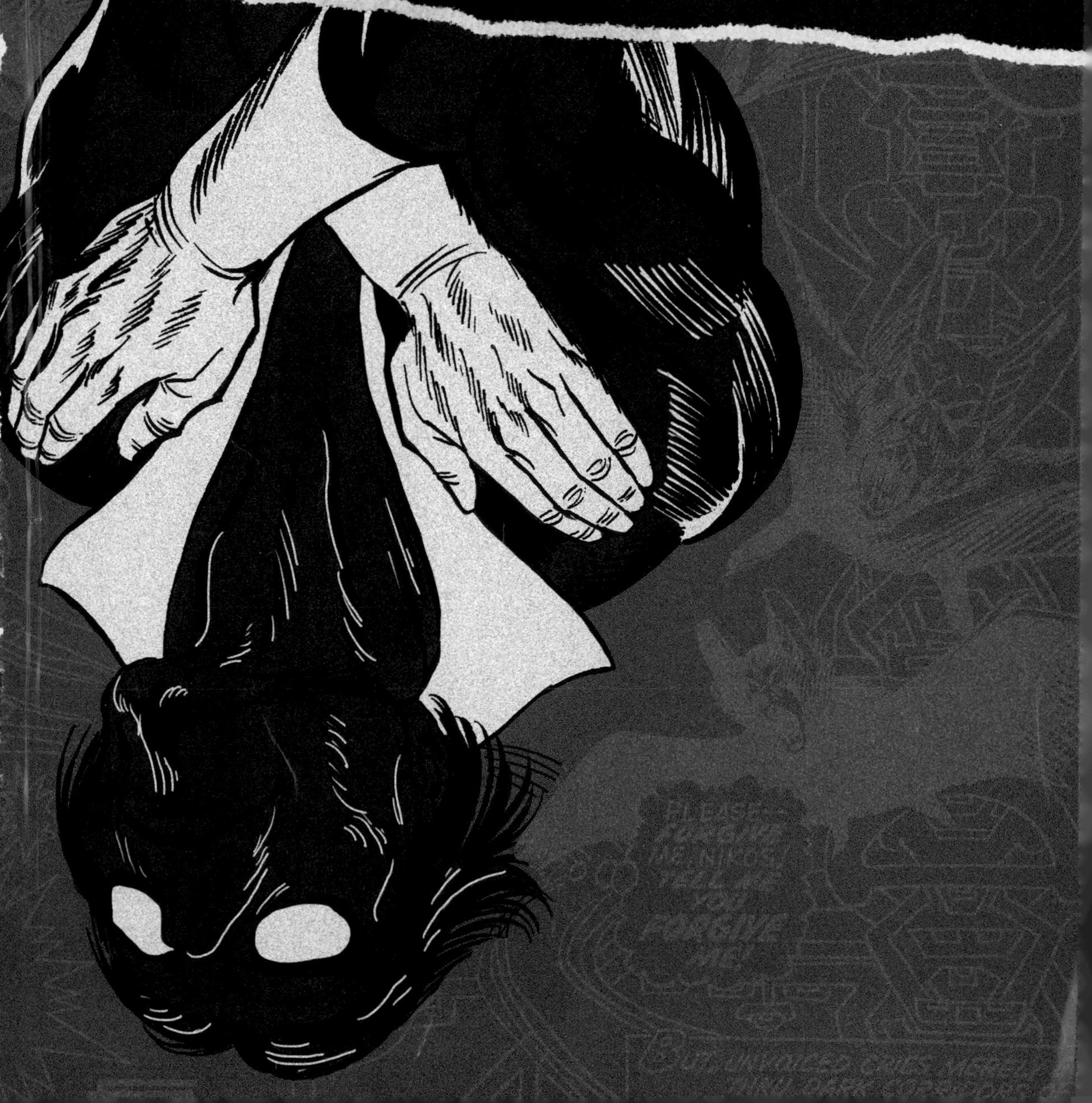

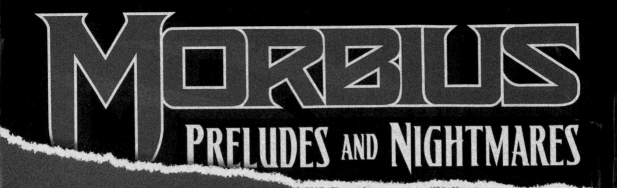

MORBIUS
PRELUDES AND NIGHTMARES

ROY THOMAS, GERRY CONWAY, MIKE FRIEDRICH & JOE KEATINGE with **DAN SLOTT**
WRITERS

GIL KANE, ROSS ANDRU, PAUL GULACY & VALENTINE DE LANDRO with **MARCO CHECCHETTO**
PENCILERS

FRANK GIACOIA, STEVE MITCHELL, JACK ABEL & VALENTINE DE LANDRO with **MARCO CHECCHETTO**
INKERS

GEORGE ROUSSOS & ANTONIO FABELA
COLORISTS

ARTIE SIMEK, JOHN COSTANZA, TOM ORZECHOWSKI & VC'S CHRIS ELIOPOULOS
LETTERERS

ELLIE PYLE
ASSISTANT EDITOR

SANA AMANAT
ASSOCIATE EDITOR

STAN LEE, ROY THOMAS & STEPHEN WACKER
EDITORS

INHYUK LEE
FRONT COVER ARTIST

STEFANO CASELLI
BACK COVER ARTIST

COLLECTION EDITOR **MARK D. BEAZLEY** • ASSISTANT MANAGING EDITOR **MAIA LOY** • ASSISTANT MANAGING EDITOR **LISA MONTALBANO**
ASSOCIATE MANAGER, DIGITAL ASSETS **JOE HOCHSTEIN** • MASTERWORKS EDITOR **CORY SEDLMEIER** • SENIOR EDITOR, SPECIAL PROJECTS **JENNIFER GRÜNWALD**
VP PRODUCTION & SPECIAL PROJECTS **JEFF YOUNGQUIST** • RESEARCH **BRIAN OVERTON** • LAYOUT **JEPH YORK** • BOOK DESIGNER **STACIE ZUCKER**
SVP PRINT, SALES & MARKETING **DAVID GABRIEL** • EDITOR IN CHIEF **C.B. CEBULSKI**

MORBIUS: PRELUDES AND NIGHTMARES. Contains material originally published in magazine form as AMAZING SPIDER-MAN (1963) #101-102, MARVEL TEAM-UP (1972) #3-4, FEAR (1970) #20 and AMAZING SPIDER-MAN (2003) #699.1. First printing 2020. ISBN 978-1-302-92592-5. Published by MARVEL WORLDWIDE, INC., a subsidiary of MARVEL ENTERTAINMENT, LLC. OFFICE OF PUBLICATION: 1290 Avenue of the Americas, New York, NY 10104. © 2020 MARVEL No similarity between any of the names, characters, persons, and/or institutions in this magazine with those of any living or dead person or institution is intended, and any such similarity which may exist is purely coincidental. **Printed in Canada.** KEVIN FEIGE, Chief Creative Officer; DAN BUCKLEY, President, Marvel Entertainment; JOE QUESADA, EVP & Creative Director; DAVID BOGART, Associate Publisher & SVP of Talent Affairs; TOM BREVOORT, VP, Executive Editor; NICK LOWE, Executive Editor, VP of Content, Digital Publishing; DAVID GABRIEL, VP of Print & Digital Publishing; JEFF YOUNGQUIST, VP of Production & Special Projects; ALEX MORALES, Director of Publishing Operations; DAN EDINGTON, Managing Editor; RICKEY PURDIN, Director of Talent Relations; JENNIFER GRÜNWALD, Senior Editor, Special Projects; SUSAN CRESPI, Production Manager; STAN LEE, Chairman Emeritus. For information regarding advertising in Marvel Comics or on Marvel.com, please contact Vit DeBellis, Custom Solutions & Integrated Advertising Manager, at vdebellis@marvel.com. For Marvel subscription inquiries, please call 888-511-5480. **Manufactured between 12/11/2020 and 1/12/2021 by SOLISCO PRINTERS, SCOTT, QC, CANADA.**

10 9 8 7 6 5 4 3 2 1

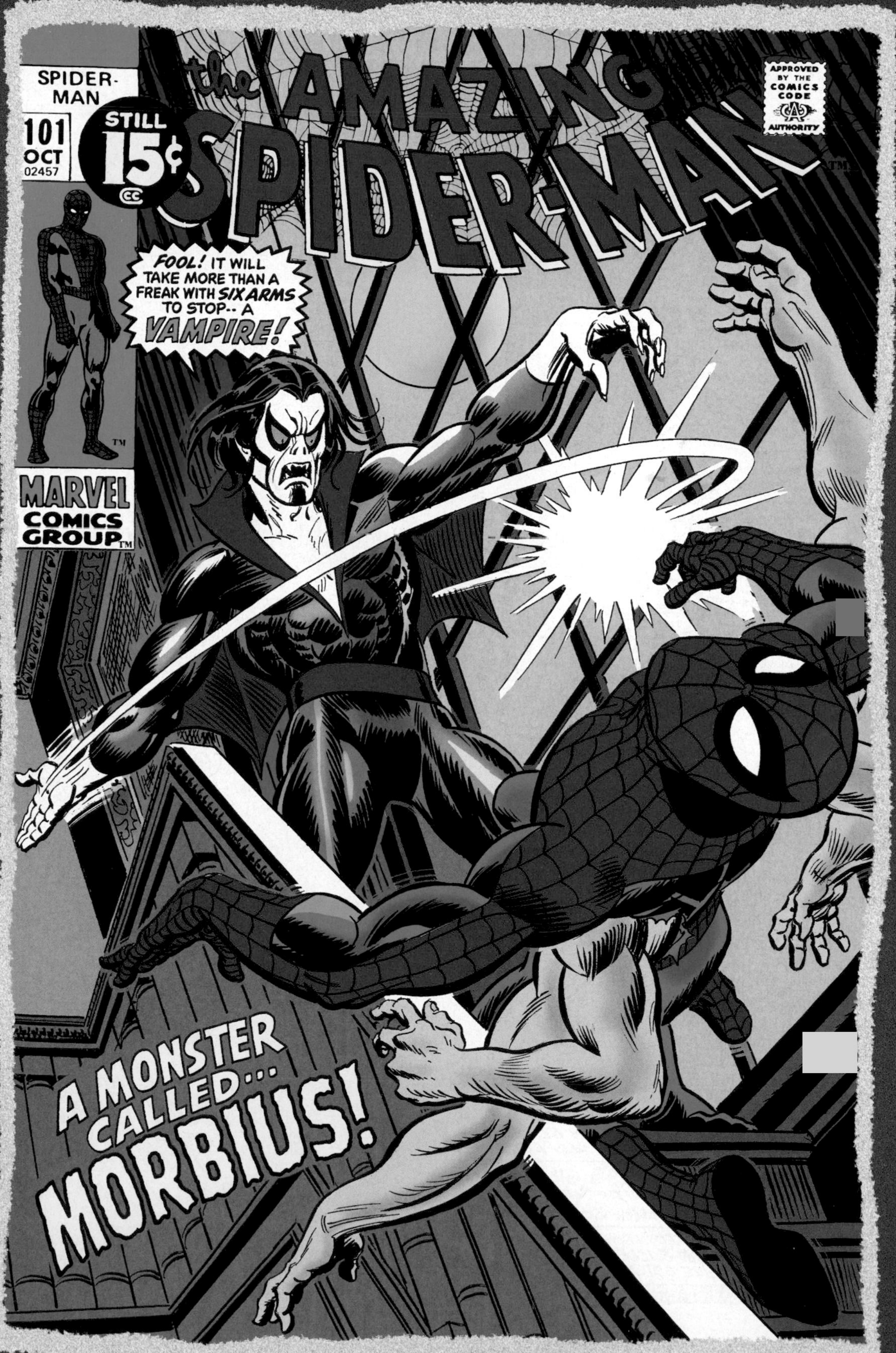

SPIDER-MAN
101
OCT
02457
STILL 15¢
CC
the AMAZING SPIDER-MAN
APPROVED BY THE COMICS CODE AUTHORITY
FOOL! IT WILL TAKE MORE THAN A FREAK WITH SIX ARMS TO STOP-- A VAMPIRE!
MARVEL COMICS GROUP
A MONSTER CALLED... MORBIUS!

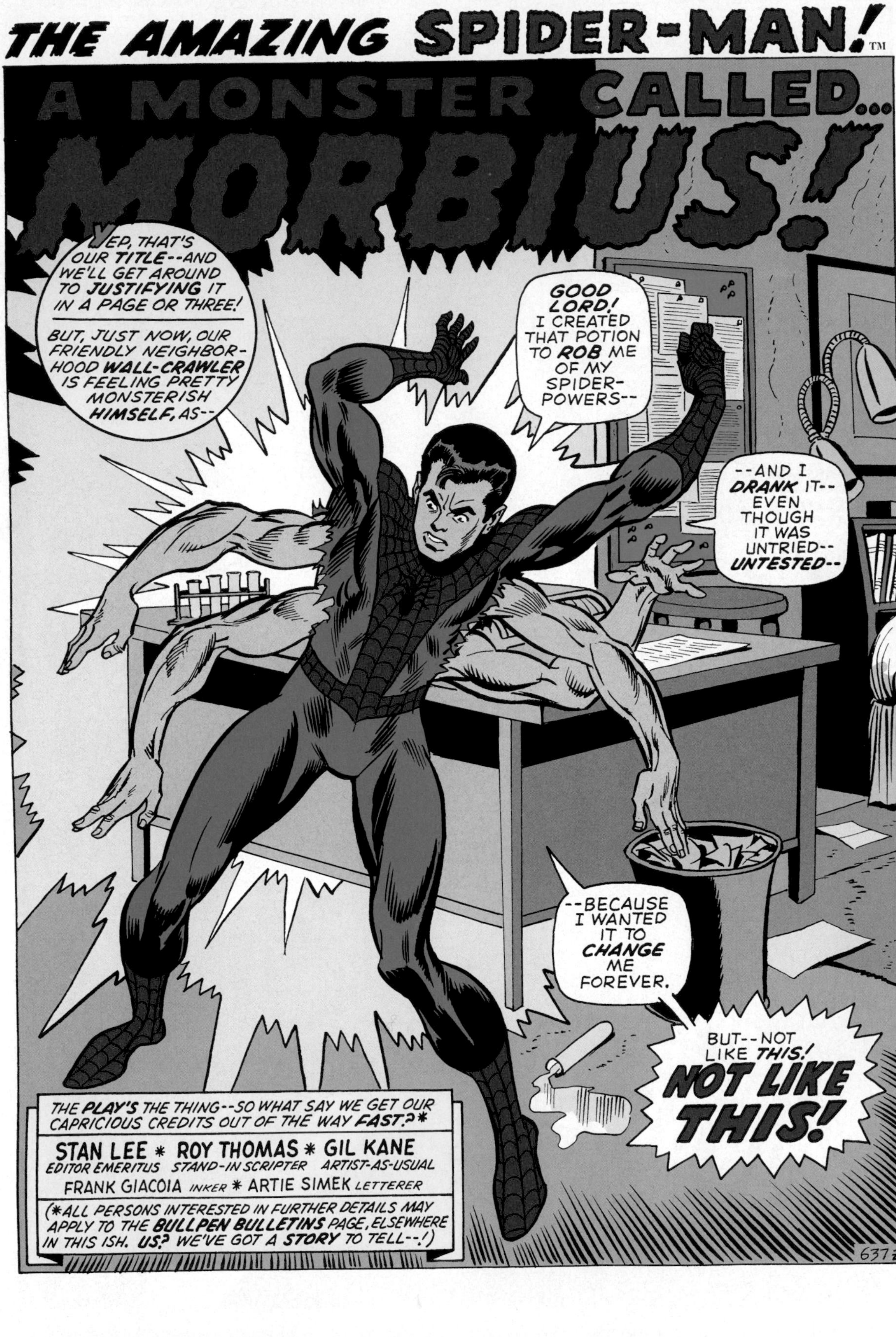
THE AMAZING SPIDER-MAN!™
A MONSTER CALLED...
MORBIUS!
YEP, THAT'S OUR TITLE--AND WE'LL GET AROUND TO JUSTIFYING IT IN A PAGE OR THREE!
BUT, JUST NOW, OUR FRIENDLY NEIGHBOR-HOOD WALL-CRAWLER IS FEELING PRETTY MONSTERISH HIMSELF, AS--
GOOD LORD! I CREATED THAT POTION TO ROB ME OF MY SPIDER-POWERS--
--AND I DRANK IT--EVEN THOUGH IT WAS UNTRIED--UNTESTED--
--BECAUSE I WANTED IT TO CHANGE ME FOREVER.
BUT--NOT LIKE THIS! NOT LIKE THIS!
THE PLAY'S THE THING--SO WHAT SAY WE GET OUR CAPRICIOUS CREDITS OUT OF THE WAY FAST?*
STAN LEE * ROY THOMAS * GIL KANE
EDITOR EMERITUS STAND-IN SCRIPTER ARTIST-AS-USUAL
FRANK GIACOIA INKER * ARTIE SIMEK LETTERER
(*ALL PERSONS INTERESTED IN FURTHER DETAILS MAY APPLY TO THE BULLPEN BULLETINS PAGE, ELSEWHERE IN THIS ISH. US? WE'VE GOT A STORY TO TELL--!)
637Z

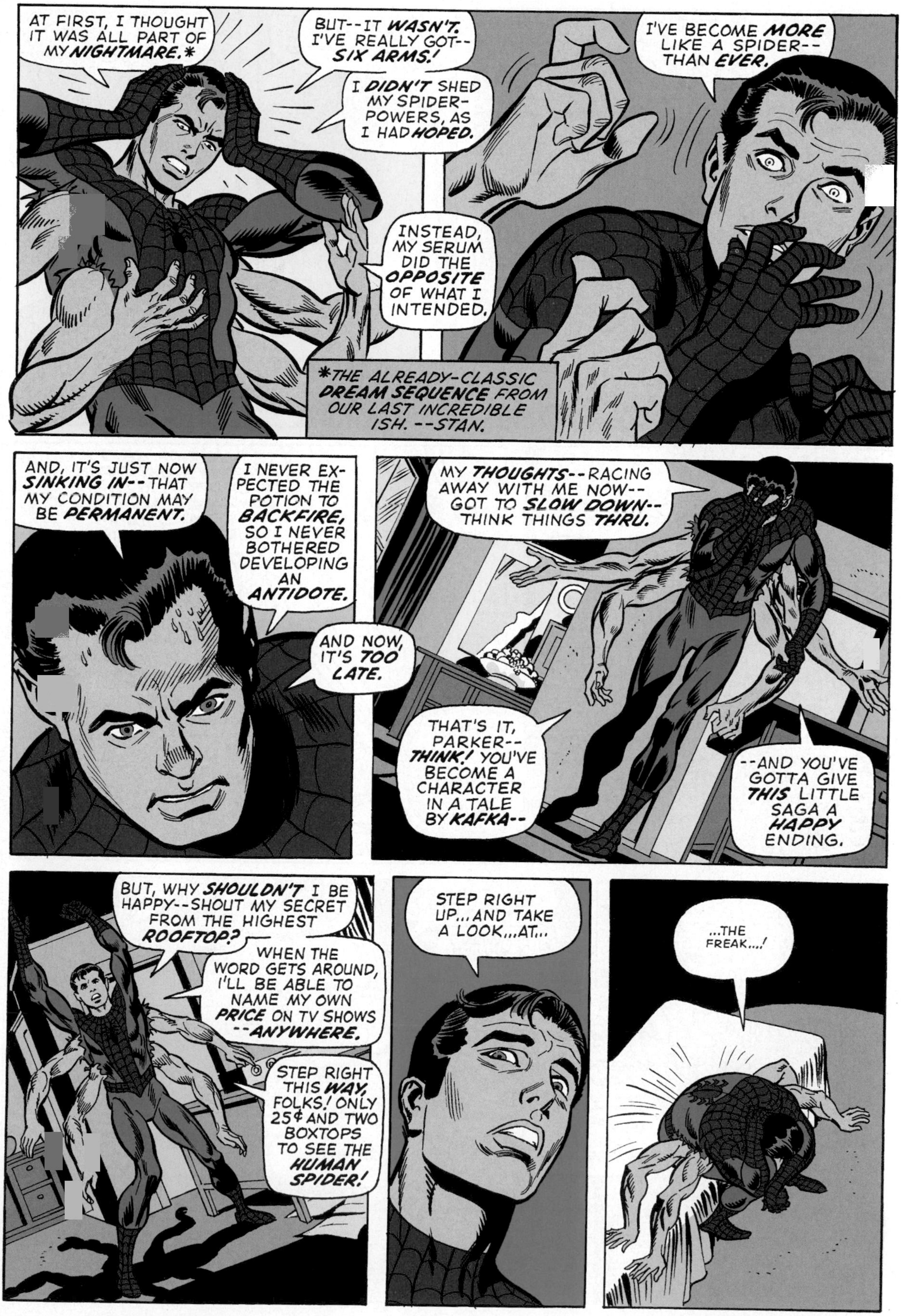
AT FIRST, I THOUGHT IT WAS ALL PART OF MY NIGHTMARE.*
BUT--IT WASN'T. I'VE REALLY GOT--SIX ARMS!
I DIDN'T SHED MY SPIDER-POWERS, AS I HAD HOPED.
INSTEAD, MY SERUM DID THE OPPOSITE OF WHAT I INTENDED.
*THE ALREADY-CLASSIC DREAM SEQUENCE FROM OUR LAST INCREDIBLE ISH. --STAN.
I'VE BECOME MORE LIKE A SPIDER--THAN EVER.
AND, IT'S JUST NOW SINKING IN--THAT MY CONDITION MAY BE PERMANENT.
I NEVER EXPECTED THE POTION TO BACKFIRE, SO I NEVER BOTHERED DEVELOPING AN ANTIDOTE.
AND NOW, IT'S TOO LATE.
MY THOUGHTS--RACING AWAY WITH ME NOW--GOT TO SLOW DOWN--THINK THINGS THRU.
THAT'S IT, PARKER--THINK! YOU'VE BECOME A CHARACTER IN A TALE BY KAFKA--
--AND YOU'VE GOTTA GIVE THIS LITTLE SAGA A HAPPY ENDING.
BUT, WHY SHOULDN'T I BE HAPPY--SHOUT MY SECRET FROM THE HIGHEST ROOFTOP?
WHEN THE WORD GETS AROUND, I'LL BE ABLE TO NAME MY OWN PRICE ON TV SHOWS --ANYWHERE.
STEP RIGHT THIS WAY, FOLKS! ONLY 25¢ AND TWO BOXTOPS TO SEE THE HUMAN SPIDER!
STEP RIGHT UP...AND TAKE A LOOK...AT...
...THE FREAK....!

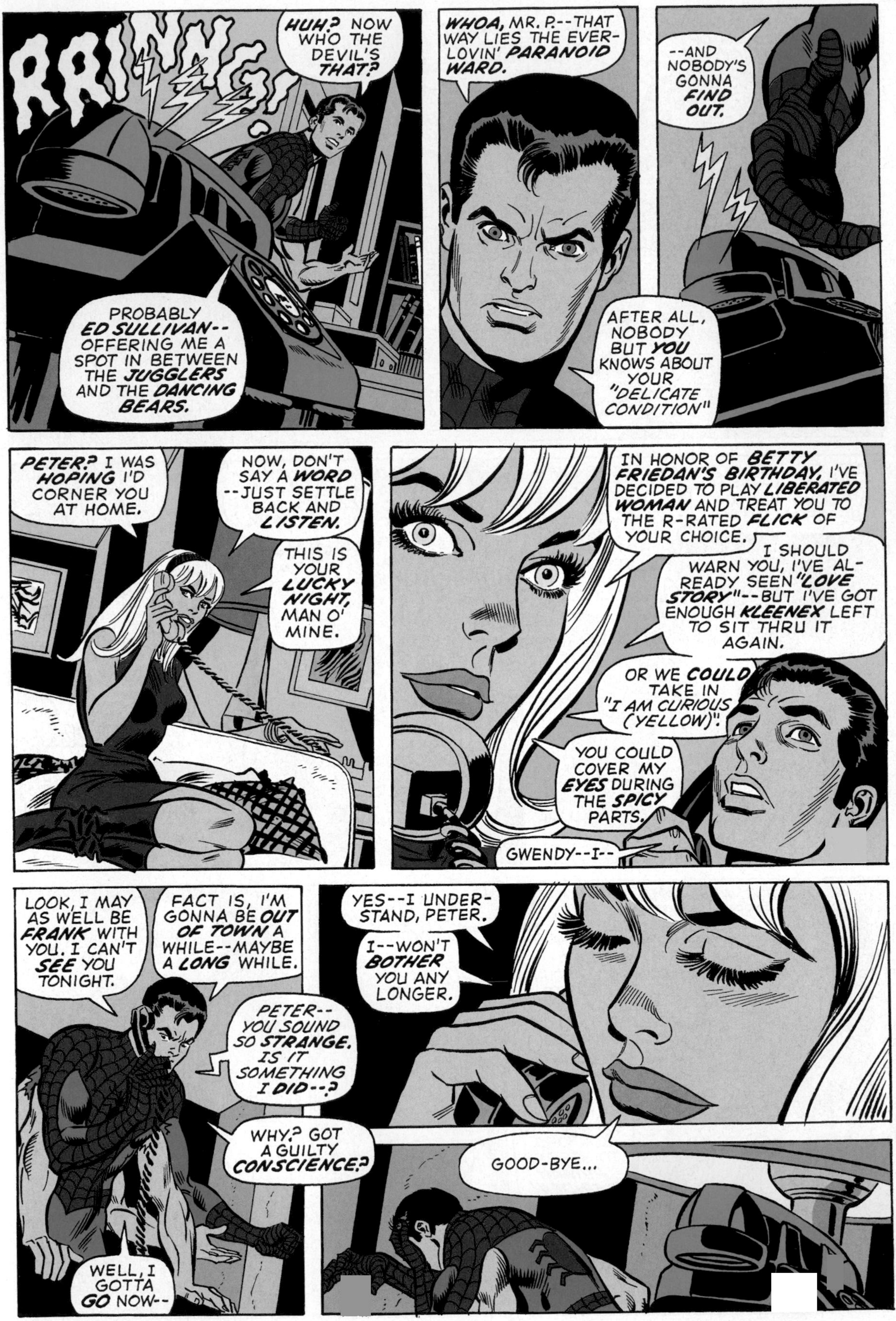
RRINNG!!
HUH? NOW WHO THE DEVIL'S THAT?
PROBABLY ED SULLIVAN--OFFERING ME A SPOT IN BETWEEN THE JUGGLERS AND THE DANCING BEARS.
WHOA, MR. P.--THAT WAY LIES THE EVER-LOVIN' PARANOID WARD.
AFTER ALL, NOBODY BUT YOU KNOWS ABOUT YOUR "DELICATE CONDITION"
--AND NOBODY'S GONNA FIND OUT.
PETER? I WAS HOPING I'D CORNER YOU AT HOME.
NOW, DON'T SAY A WORD --JUST SETTLE BACK AND LISTEN.
THIS IS YOUR LUCKY NIGHT, MAN O' MINE.
IN HONOR OF BETTY FRIEDAN'S BIRTHDAY, I'VE DECIDED TO PLAY LIBERATED WOMAN AND TREAT YOU TO THE R-RATED FLICK OF YOUR CHOICE.
I SHOULD WARN YOU, I'VE ALREADY SEEN "LOVE STORY"--BUT I'VE GOT ENOUGH KLEENEX LEFT TO SIT THRU IT AGAIN.
OR WE COULD TAKE IN "I AM CURIOUS (YELLOW)".
YOU COULD COVER MY EYES DURING THE SPICY PARTS.
GWENDY--I--
LOOK, I MAY AS WELL BE FRANK WITH YOU. I CAN'T SEE YOU TONIGHT.
FACT IS, I'M GONNA BE OUT OF TOWN A WHILE--MAYBE A LONG WHILE.
PETER--YOU SOUND SO STRANGE. IS IT SOMETHING I DID--?
WHY? GOT A GUILTY CONSCIENCE?
WELL, I GOTTA GO NOW--
YES--I UNDERSTAND, PETER.
I--WON'T BOTHER YOU ANY LONGER.
GOOD-BYE...

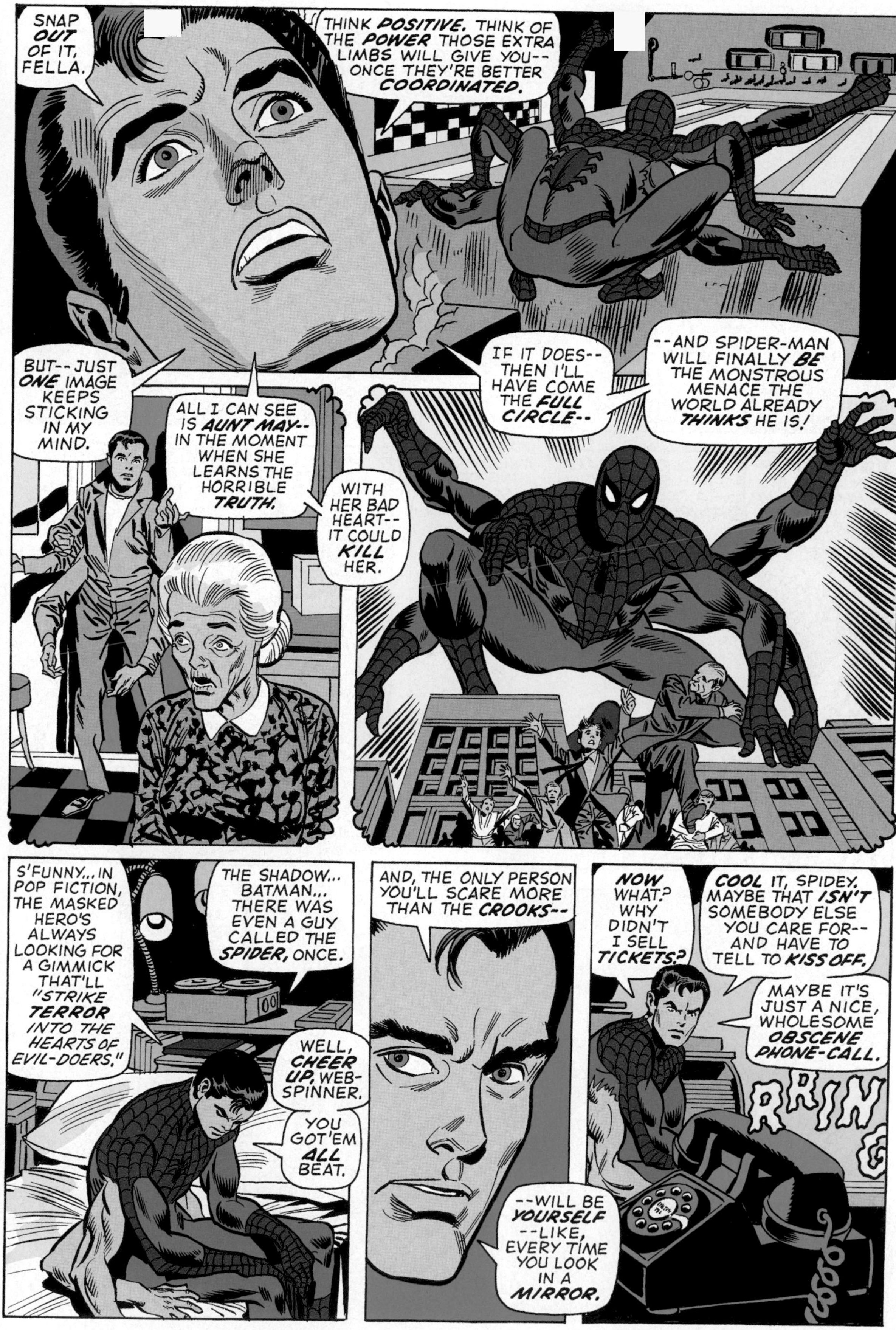
SNAP OUT OF IT, FELLA.
THINK POSITIVE. THINK OF THE POWER THOSE EXTRA LIMBS WILL GIVE YOU-- ONCE THEY'RE BETTER COORDINATED.
BUT-- JUST ONE IMAGE KEEPS STICKING IN MY MIND.
ALL I CAN SEE IS AUNT MAY-- IN THE MOMENT WHEN SHE LEARNS THE HORRIBLE TRUTH.
WITH HER BAD HEART-- IT COULD KILL HER.
IF IT DOES-- THEN I'LL HAVE COME THE FULL CIRCLE--
--AND SPIDER-MAN WILL FINALLY BE THE MONSTROUS MENACE THE WORLD ALREADY THINKS HE IS!
S'FUNNY... IN POP FICTION, THE MASKED HERO'S ALWAYS LOOKING FOR A GIMMICK THAT'LL "STRIKE TERROR INTO THE HEARTS OF EVIL-DOERS."
THE SHADOW... BATMAN... THERE WAS EVEN A GUY CALLED THE SPIDER, ONCE.
WELL, CHEER UP, WEB-SPINNER.
YOU GOT'EM ALL BEAT.
AND, THE ONLY PERSON YOU'LL SCARE MORE THAN THE CROOKS--
--WILL BE YOURSELF --LIKE, EVERY TIME YOU LOOK IN A MIRROR.
NOW WHAT? WHY DIDN'T I SELL TICKETS?
COOL IT, SPIDEY. MAYBE THAT ISN'T SOMEBODY ELSE YOU CARE FOR-- AND HAVE TO TELL TO KISS OFF.
MAYBE IT'S JUST A NICE, WHOLESOME OBSCENE PHONE-CALL.
RRING

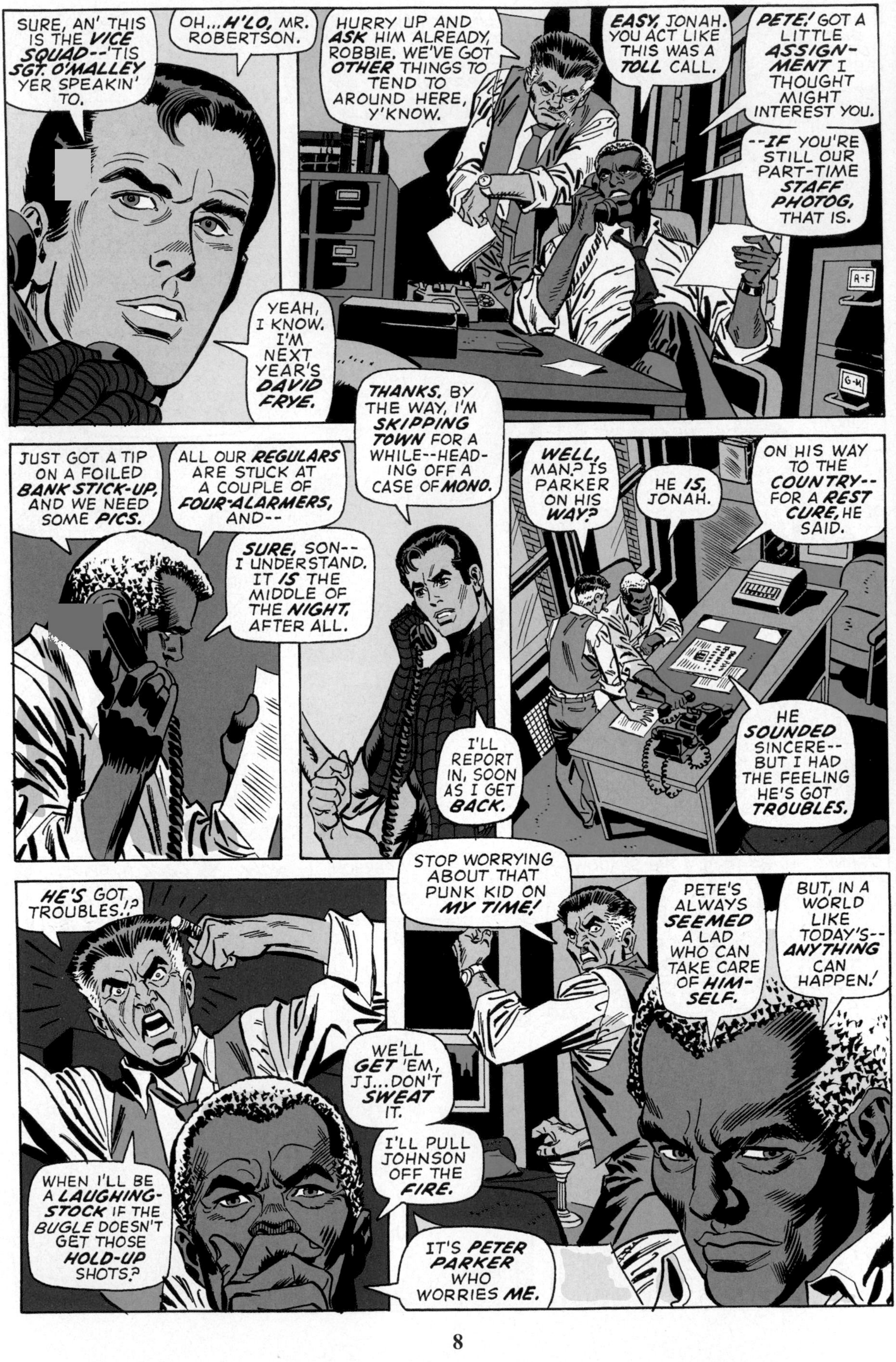

SURE, AN' THIS IS THE VICE SQUAD--'TIS SGT. O'MALLEY YER SPEAKIN' TO.
OH...H'LO, MR. ROBERTSON.
HURRY UP AND ASK HIM ALREADY, ROBBIE. WE'VE GOT OTHER THINGS TO TEND TO AROUND HERE, Y'KNOW.
EASY, JONAH. YOU ACT LIKE THIS WAS A TOLL CALL.
PETE! GOT A LITTLE ASSIGNMENT I THOUGHT MIGHT INTEREST YOU.
--IF YOU'RE STILL OUR PART-TIME STAFF PHOTOG, THAT IS.
YEAH, I KNOW. I'M NEXT YEAR'S DAVID FRYE.
A-F
G-M
JUST GOT A TIP ON A FOILED BANK STICK-UP, AND WE NEED SOME PICS.
ALL OUR REGULARS ARE STUCK AT A COUPLE OF FOUR-ALARMERS, AND--
THANKS. BY THE WAY, I'M SKIPPING TOWN FOR A WHILE--HEADING OFF A CASE OF MONO.
SURE, SON--I UNDERSTAND. IT IS THE MIDDLE OF THE NIGHT, AFTER ALL.
I'LL REPORT IN, SOON AS I GET BACK.
WELL, MAN? IS PARKER ON HIS WAY?
HE IS, JONAH.
ON HIS WAY TO THE COUNTRY--FOR A REST CURE, HE SAID.
HE SOUNDED SINCERE--BUT I HAD THE FEELING HE'S GOT TROUBLES.
HE'S GOT TROUBLES!?
WHEN I'LL BE A LAUGHING-STOCK IF THE BUGLE DOESN'T GET THOSE HOLD-UP SHOTS?
WE'LL GET 'EM, JJ...DON'T SWEAT IT.
I'LL PULL JOHNSON OFF THE FIRE.
STOP WORRYING ABOUT THAT PUNK KID ON MY TIME!
IT'S PETER PARKER WHO WORRIES ME.
PETE'S ALWAYS SEEMED A LAD WHO CAN TAKE CARE OF HIMSELF.
BUT, IN A WORLD LIKE TODAY'S--ANYTHING CAN HAPPEN!

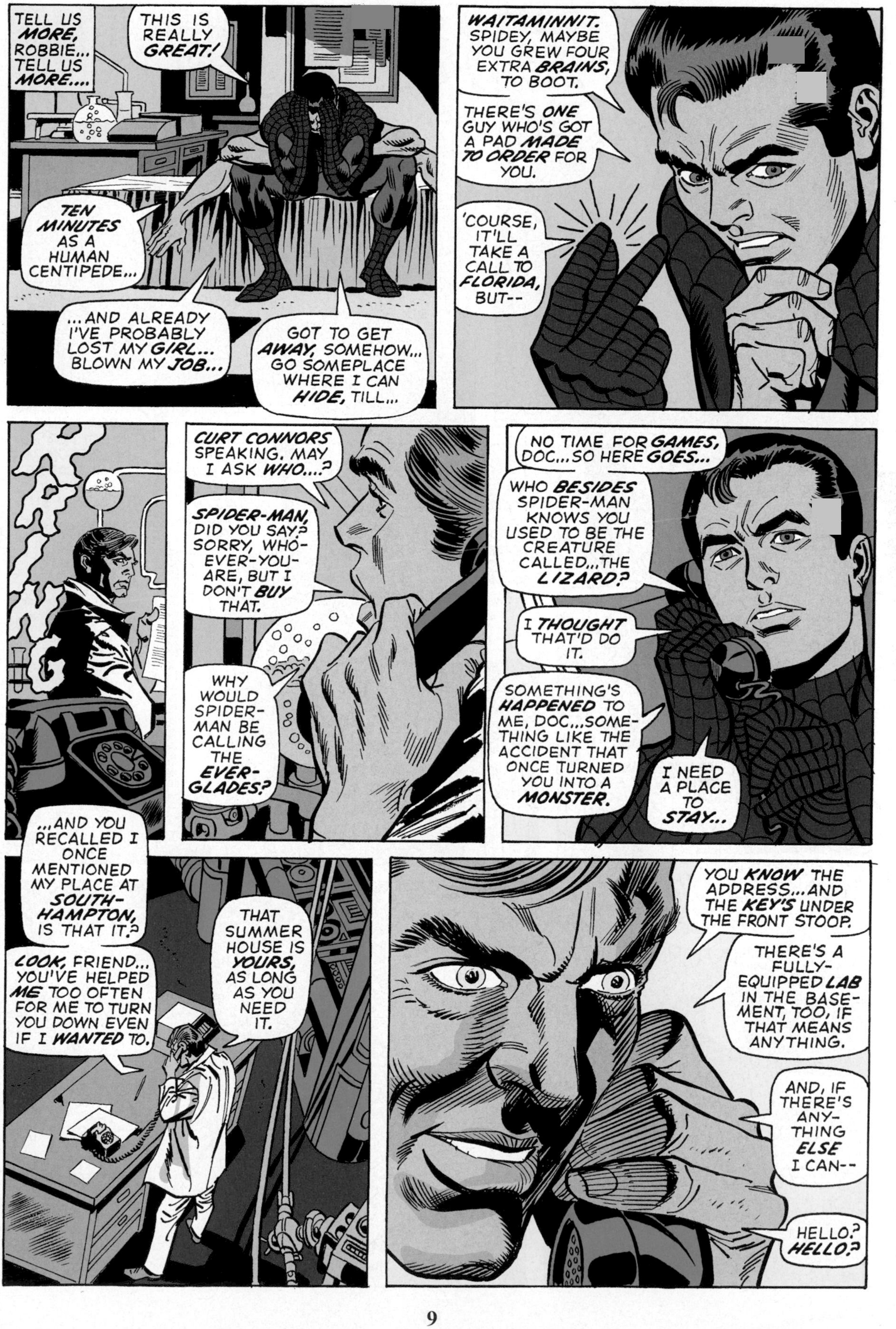
TELL US MORE, ROBBIE... TELL US MORE....
THIS IS REALLY GREAT!
TEN MINUTES AS A HUMAN CENTIPEDE...
...AND ALREADY I'VE PROBABLY LOST MY GIRL... BLOWN MY JOB...
GOT TO GET AWAY, SOMEHOW... GO SOMEPLACE WHERE I CAN HIDE, TILL...
WAITAMINNIT. SPIDEY, MAYBE YOU GREW FOUR EXTRA BRAINS, TO BOOT.
THERE'S ONE GUY WHO'S GOT A PAD MADE TO ORDER FOR YOU.
'COURSE, IT'LL TAKE A CALL TO FLORIDA, BUT--
CURT CONNORS SPEAKING. MAY I ASK WHO...?
SPIDER-MAN, DID YOU SAY? SORRY, WHO-EVER-YOU-ARE, BUT I DON'T BUY THAT.
WHY WOULD SPIDER-MAN BE CALLING THE EVER-GLADES?
NO TIME FOR GAMES, DOC...SO HERE GOES...
WHO BESIDES SPIDER-MAN KNOWS YOU USED TO BE THE CREATURE CALLED...THE LIZARD?
I THOUGHT THAT'D DO IT.
SOMETHING'S HAPPENED TO ME, DOC...SOME-THING LIKE THE ACCIDENT THAT ONCE TURNED YOU INTO A MONSTER.
I NEED A PLACE TO STAY...
...AND YOU RECALLED I ONCE MENTIONED MY PLACE AT SOUTH-HAMPTON, IS THAT IT?
LOOK, FRIEND... YOU'VE HELPED ME TOO OFTEN FOR ME TO TURN YOU DOWN EVEN IF I WANTED TO.
THAT SUMMER HOUSE IS YOURS, AS LONG AS YOU NEED IT.
YOU KNOW THE ADDRESS...AND THE KEY'S UNDER THE FRONT STOOP.
THERE'S A FULLY-EQUIPPED LAB IN THE BASE-MENT, TOO, IF THAT MEANS ANYTHING.
AND, IF THERE'S ANY-THING ELSE I CAN--
HELLO? HELLO?

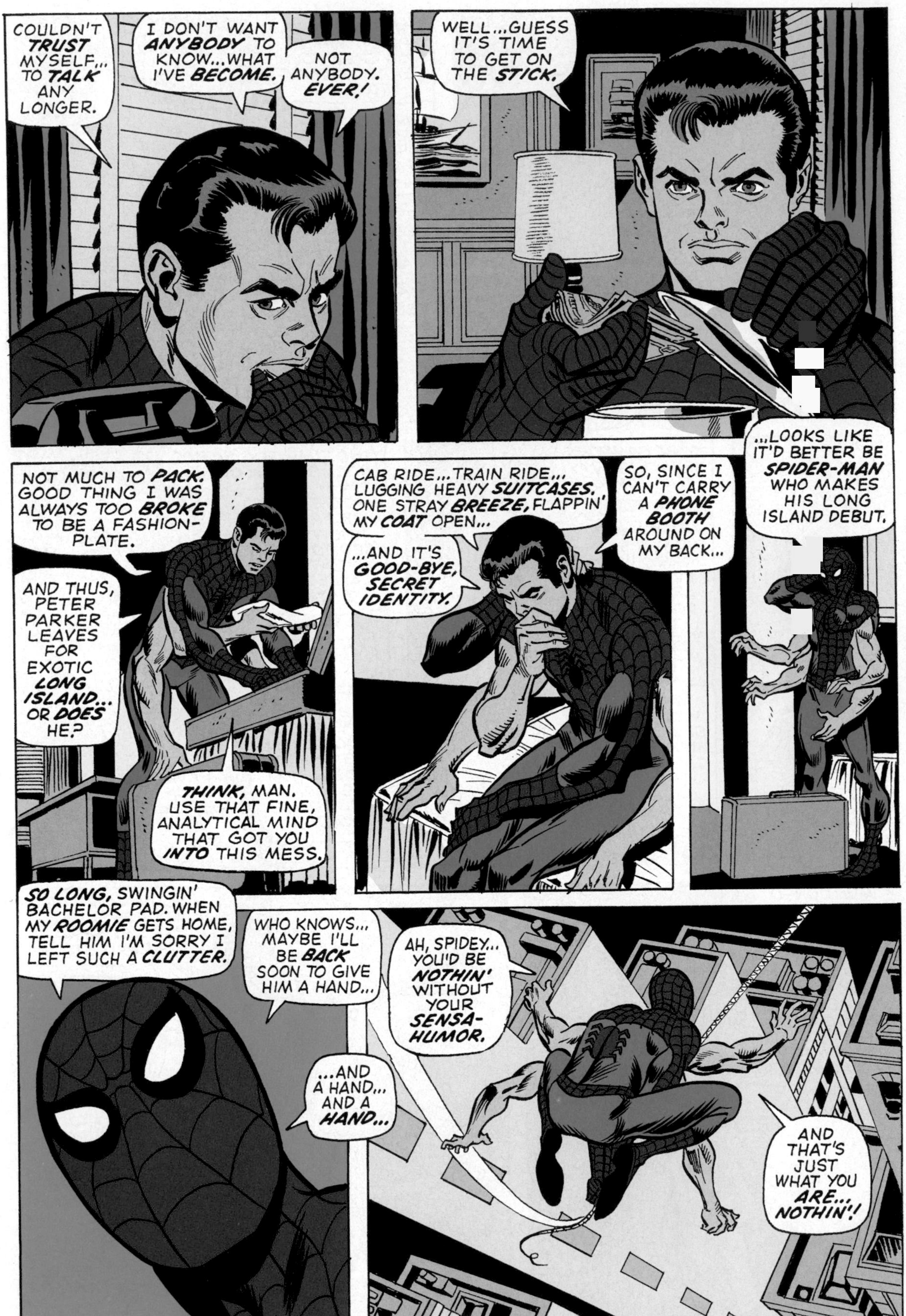
COULDN'T TRUST MYSELF... TO TALK ANY LONGER.
I DON'T WANT ANYBODY TO KNOW...WHAT I'VE BECOME.
NOT ANYBODY. EVER!
WELL...GUESS IT'S TIME TO GET ON THE STICK.
NOT MUCH TO PACK. GOOD THING I WAS ALWAYS TOO BROKE TO BE A FASHION-PLATE.
AND THUS, PETER PARKER LEAVES FOR EXOTIC LONG ISLAND... OR DOES HE?
THINK, MAN. USE THAT FINE, ANALYTICAL MIND THAT GOT YOU INTO THIS MESS.
CAB RIDE...TRAIN RIDE... LUGGING HEAVY SUITCASES. ONE STRAY BREEZE, FLAPPIN' MY COAT OPEN...
...AND IT'S GOOD-BYE, SECRET IDENTITY.
SO, SINCE I CAN'T CARRY A PHONE BOOTH AROUND ON MY BACK...
...LOOKS LIKE IT'D BETTER BE SPIDER-MAN WHO MAKES HIS LONG ISLAND DEBUT.
SO LONG, SWINGIN' BACHELOR PAD. WHEN MY ROOMIE GETS HOME, TELL HIM I'M SORRY I LEFT SUCH A CLUTTER.
WHO KNOWS... MAYBE I'LL BE BACK SOON TO GIVE HIM A HAND...
...AND A HAND... AND A HAND...
AH, SPIDEY... YOU'D BE NOTHIN' WITHOUT YOUR SENSA-HUMOR.
AND THAT'S JUST WHAT YOU ARE... NOTHIN'!

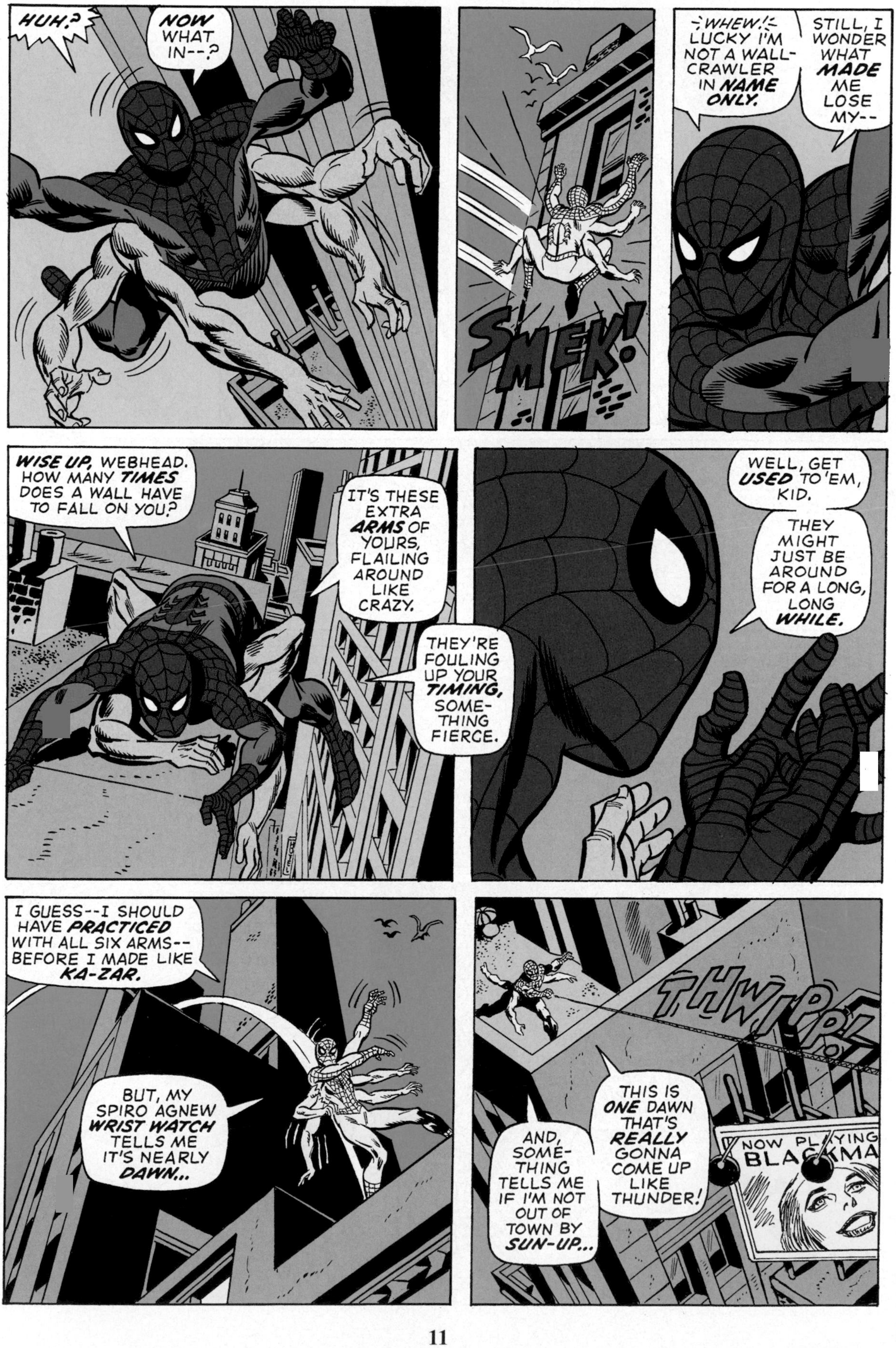
HUH?
NOW WHAT IN--?
SMEK!
WHEW! LUCKY I'M NOT A WALL-CRAWLER IN NAME ONLY.
STILL, I WONDER WHAT MADE ME LOSE MY--
WISE UP, WEBHEAD. HOW MANY TIMES DOES A WALL HAVE TO FALL ON YOU?
IT'S THESE EXTRA ARMS OF YOURS, FLAILING AROUND LIKE CRAZY.
THEY'RE FOULING UP YOUR TIMING, SOME-THING FIERCE.
WELL, GET USED TO 'EM, KID.
THEY MIGHT JUST BE AROUND FOR A LONG, LONG WHILE.
I GUESS--I SHOULD HAVE PRACTICED WITH ALL SIX ARMS--BEFORE I MADE LIKE KA-ZAR.
BUT, MY SPIRO AGNEW WRIST WATCH TELLS ME IT'S NEARLY DAWN..
THWIPP!
THIS IS ONE DAWN THAT'S REALLY GONNA COME UP LIKE THUNDER!
AND, SOME-THING TELLS ME IF I'M NOT OUT OF TOWN BY SUN-UP...
NOW PLAYING BLACKMA

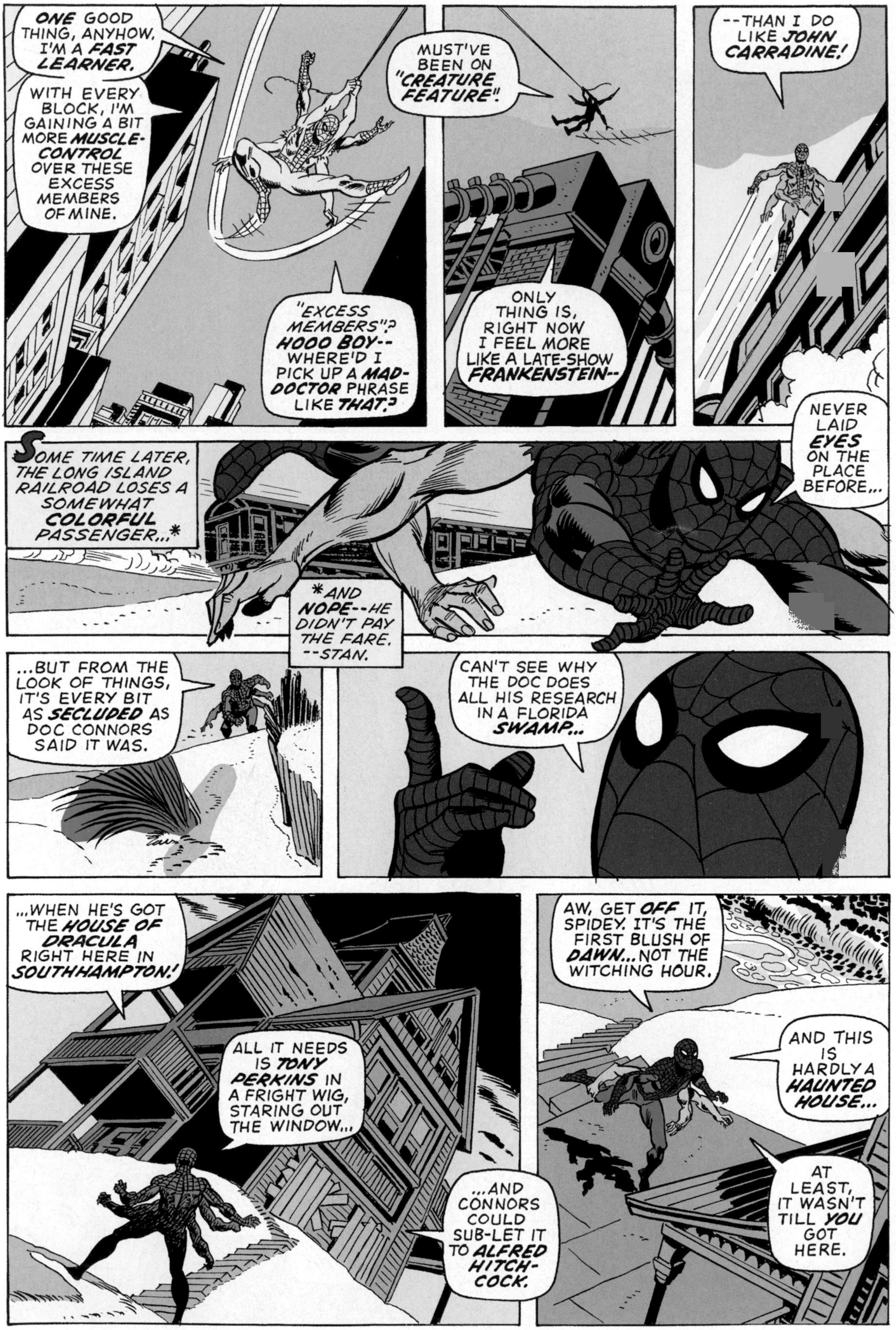
ONE GOOD THING, ANYHOW. I'M A FAST LEARNER.
WITH EVERY BLOCK, I'M GAINING A BIT MORE MUSCLE-CONTROL OVER THESE EXCESS MEMBERS OF MINE.
"EXCESS MEMBERS"? HOOO BOY-- WHERE'D I PICK UP A MAD-DOCTOR PHRASE LIKE THAT?
MUST'VE BEEN ON "CREATURE FEATURE".
ONLY THING IS, RIGHT NOW I FEEL MORE LIKE A LATE-SHOW FRANKENSTEIN--
--THAN I DO LIKE JOHN CARRADINE!
SOME TIME LATER, THE LONG ISLAND RAILROAD LOSES A SOMEWHAT COLORFUL PASSENGER...*
NEVER LAID EYES ON THE PLACE BEFORE...
*AND NOPE--HE DIDN'T PAY THE FARE. --STAN.
...BUT FROM THE LOOK OF THINGS, IT'S EVERY BIT AS SECLUDED AS DOC CONNORS SAID IT WAS.
CAN'T SEE WHY THE DOC DOES ALL HIS RESEARCH IN A FLORIDA SWAMP...
...WHEN HE'S GOT THE HOUSE OF DRACULA RIGHT HERE IN SOUTHHAMPTON!
ALL IT NEEDS IS TONY PERKINS IN A FRIGHT WIG, STARING OUT THE WINDOW...
...AND CONNORS COULD SUB-LET IT TO ALFRED HITCH-COCK.
AW, GET OFF IT, SPIDEY. IT'S THE FIRST BLUSH OF DAWN... NOT THE WITCHING HOUR.
AND THIS IS HARDLY A HAUNTED HOUSE...
AT LEAST, IT WASN'T TILL YOU GOT HERE.

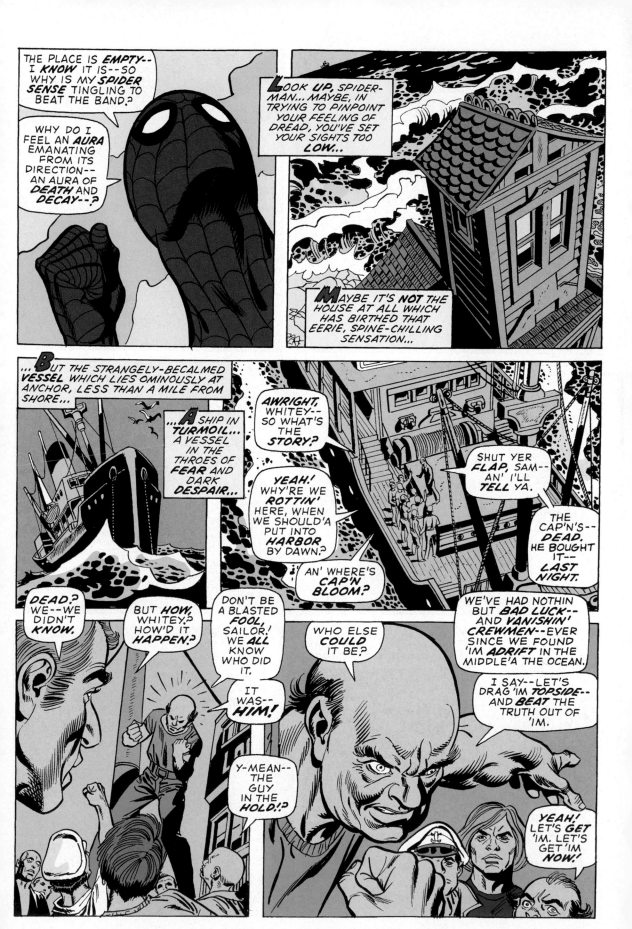

THE PLACE IS *EMPTY*-- I *KNOW* IT IS--SO WHY IS MY *SPIDER SENSE* TINGLING TO BEAT THE BAND?

WHY DO I FEEL AN *AURA* EMANATING FROM ITS DIRECTION-- AN AURA OF *DEATH* AND *DECAY*--?

*L*OOK *UP*, SPIDER-MAN...MAYBE, IN TRYING TO PINPOINT YOUR FEELING OF *DREAD*, YOU'VE SET YOUR SIGHTS TOO *LOW*...

*M*AYBE IT'S *NOT* THE HOUSE AT ALL WHICH HAS BIRTHED THAT EERIE, SPINE-CHILLING SENSATION...

...*B*UT THE STRANGELY-BECALMED *VESSEL* WHICH LIES OMINOUSLY AT ANCHOR, LESS THAN A MILE FROM SHORE...

...*A* SHIP IN *TURMOIL*...A VESSEL IN THE THROES OF *FEAR* AND *DARK DESPAIR*...

AWRIGHT, *WHITEY*-- SO WHAT'S THE *STORY*?

YEAH! WHY'RE WE *ROTTIN'* HERE, WHEN WE SHOULD'A PUT INTO *HARBOR* BY DAWN?

AN' WHERE'S *CAP'N BLOOM*?

SHUT YER *FLAP*, SAM-- AN' I'LL *TELL* YA.

THE CAP'N'S-- *DEAD*. HE BOUGHT IT-- *LAST NIGHT*.

WE'VE HAD NOTHIN BUT *BAD LUCK*-- AND *VANISHIN'* CREWMEN--EVER SINCE WE FOUND 'IM *ADRIFT* IN THE MIDDLE'A THE OCEAN.

I SAY--LET'S DRAG 'IM *TOPSIDE*-- AND *BEAT* THE TRUTH OUT OF 'IM.

DEAD? WE--WE DIDN'T *KNOW*.

BUT *HOW*, WHITEY, HOW'D IT *HAPPEN*?

DON'T BE A BLASTED *FOOL*, SAILOR! WE *ALL* KNOW WHO DID IT.

IT WAS-- *HIM*!

Y-MEAN-- THE GUY IN THE *HOLD*!?

WHO ELSE *COULD* IT BE?

YEAH! LET'S *GET* 'IM. LET'S *GET* 'IM *NOW*!

13

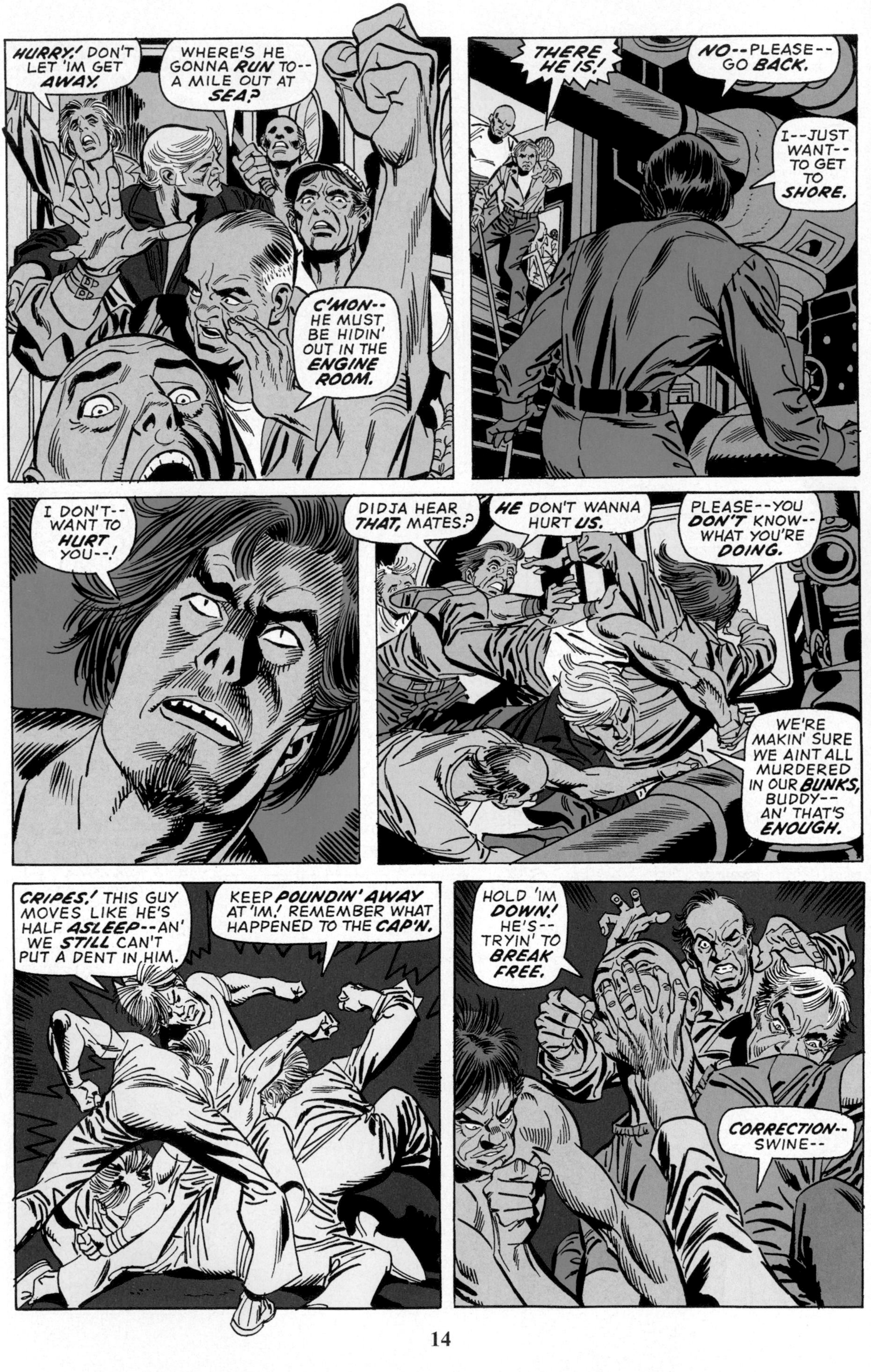
HURRY! DON'T LET 'IM GET AWAY.
WHERE'S HE GONNA RUN TO-- A MILE OUT AT SEA?
C'MON-- HE MUST BE HIDIN' OUT IN THE ENGINE ROOM.
THERE HE IS!
NO--PLEASE-- GO BACK.
I--JUST WANT-- TO GET TO SHORE.
I DON'T-- WANT TO HURT YOU--!
DIDJA HEAR THAT, MATES?
HE DON'T WANNA HURT US.
PLEASE--YOU DON'T KNOW-- WHAT YOU'RE DOING.
WE'RE MAKIN' SURE WE AINT ALL MURDERED IN OUR BUNKS, BUDDY-- AN' THAT'S ENOUGH.
CRIPES! THIS GUY MOVES LIKE HE'S HALF ASLEEP--AN' WE STILL CAN'T PUT A DENT IN HIM.
KEEP POUNDIN' AWAY AT 'IM! REMEMBER WHAT HAPPENED TO THE CAP'N.
HOLD 'IM DOWN! HE'S-- TRYIN' TO BREAK FREE.
CORRECTION-- SWINE--

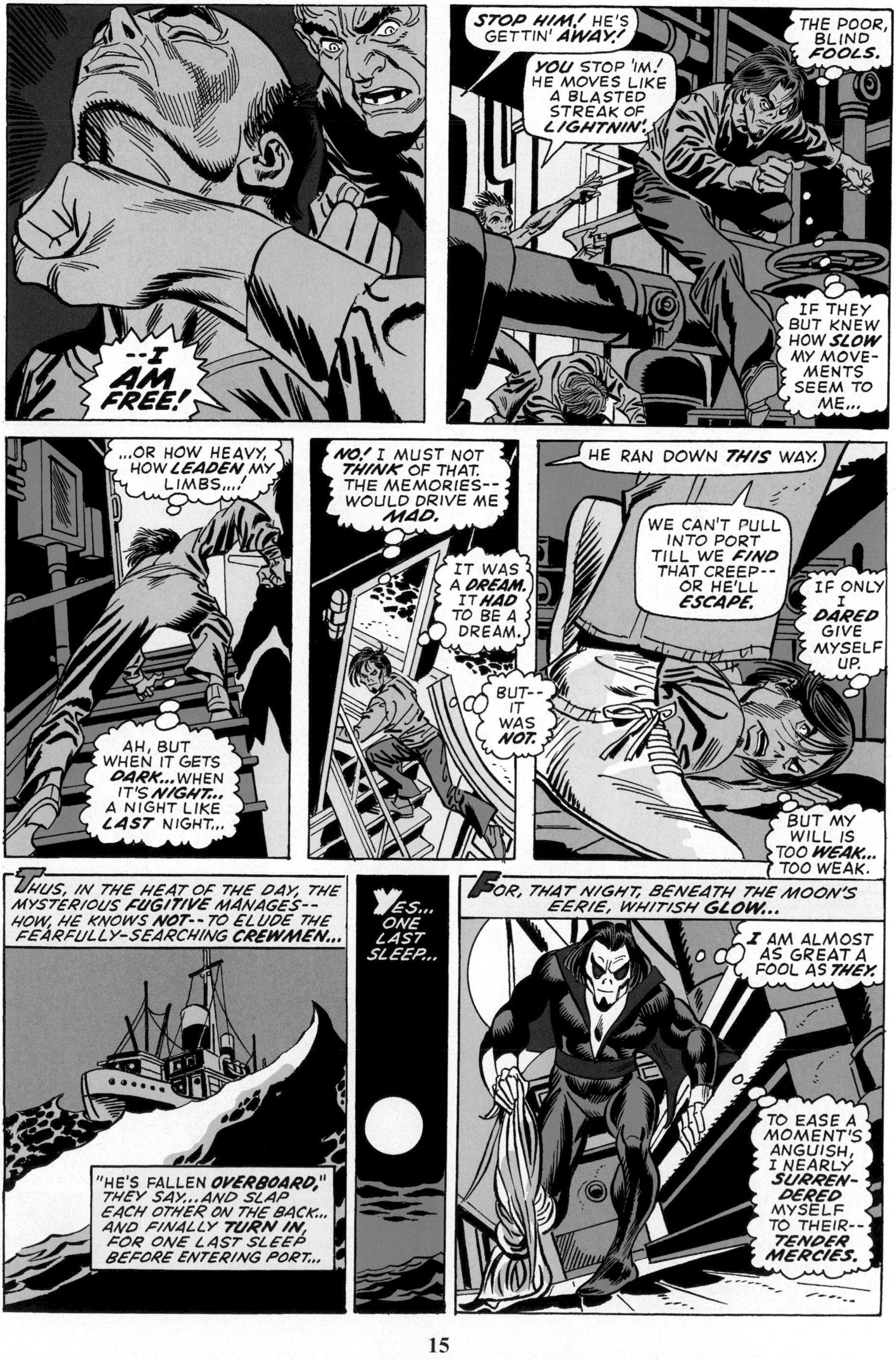
--I AM FREE!
STOP HIM! HE'S GETTIN' AWAY!
YOU STOP 'IM! HE MOVES LIKE A BLASTED STREAK OF LIGHTNIN'!
THE POOR, BLIND FOOLS.
IF THEY BUT KNEW HOW SLOW MY MOVEMENTS SEEM TO ME...
...OR HOW HEAVY, HOW LEADEN MY LIMBS...!
AH, BUT WHEN IT GETS DARK... WHEN IT'S NIGHT... A NIGHT LIKE LAST NIGHT...
NO! I MUST NOT THINK OF THAT. THE MEMORIES--WOULD DRIVE ME MAD.
IT WAS A DREAM. IT HAD TO BE A DREAM.
BUT--IT WAS NOT.
HE RAN DOWN THIS WAY.
WE CAN'T PULL INTO PORT TILL WE FIND THAT CREEP--OR HE'LL ESCAPE.
IF ONLY I DARED GIVE MYSELF UP.
BUT MY WILL IS TOO WEAK... TOO WEAK.
THUS, IN THE HEAT OF THE DAY, THE MYSTERIOUS FUGITIVE MANAGES--HOW, HE KNOWS NOT--TO ELUDE THE FEARFULLY-SEARCHING CREWMEN...
"HE'S FALLEN OVERBOARD," THEY SAY... AND SLAP EACH OTHER ON THE BACK... AND FINALLY TURN IN, FOR ONE LAST SLEEP BEFORE ENTERING PORT...
YES... ONE LAST SLEEP...
FOR, THAT NIGHT, BENEATH THE MOON'S EERIE, WHITISH GLOW...
I AM ALMOST AS GREAT A FOOL AS THEY.
TO EASE A MOMENT'S ANGUISH, I NEARLY SURRENDERED MYSELF TO THEIR--TENDER MERCIES.

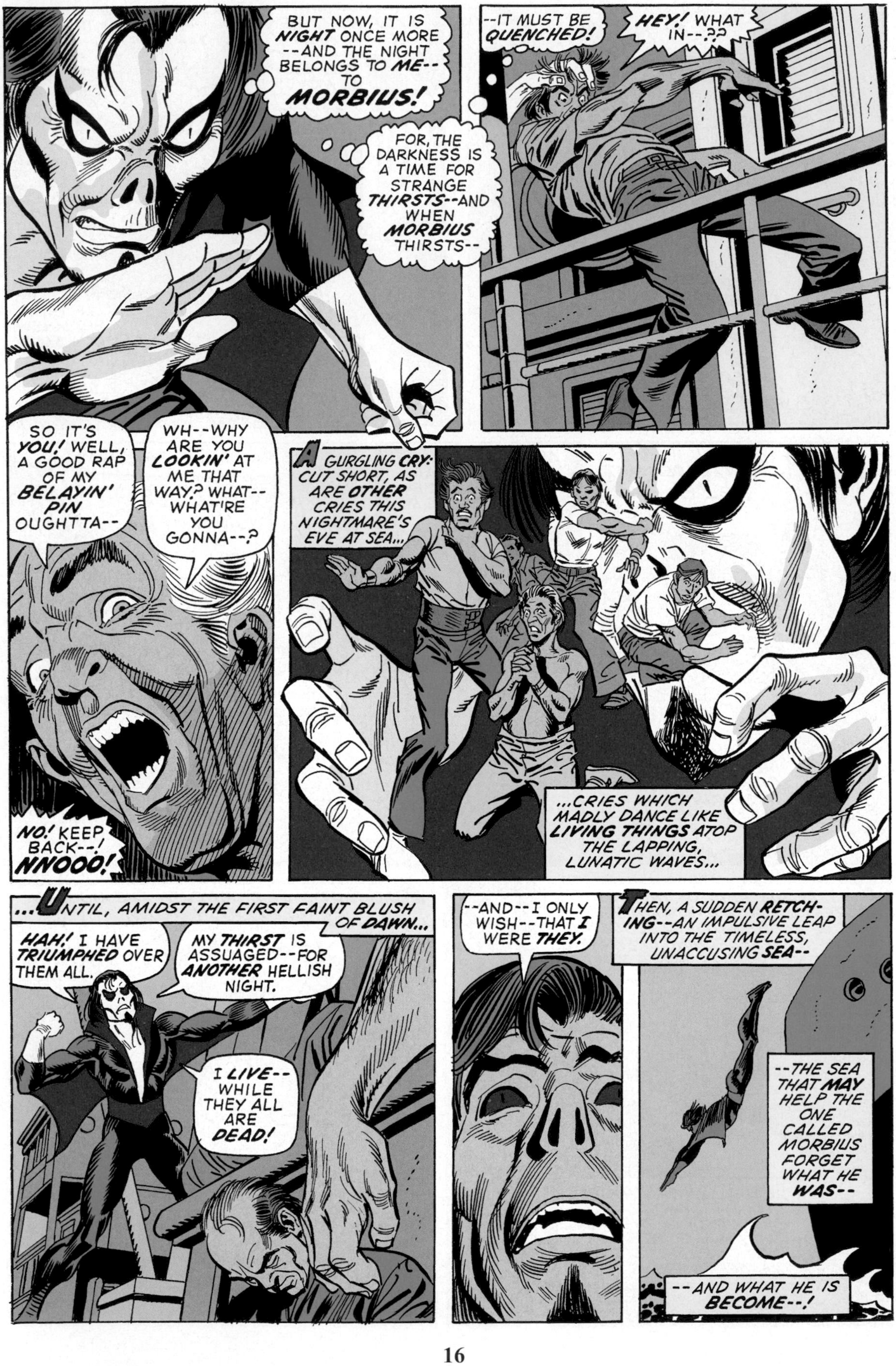

BUT NOW, IT IS NIGHT ONCE MORE --AND THE NIGHT BELONGS TO ME-- TO MORBIUS!
FOR, THE DARKNESS IS A TIME FOR STRANGE THIRSTS--AND WHEN MORBIUS THIRSTS--
--IT MUST BE QUENCHED!
HEY! WHAT IN--??
SO IT'S YOU! WELL, A GOOD RAP OF MY BELAYIN' PIN OUGHTTA--
WH--WHY ARE YOU LOOKIN' AT ME THAT WAY? WHAT--WHAT'RE YOU GONNA--?
NO! KEEP BACK--! NNOOO!
A GURGLING CRY: CUT SHORT, AS ARE OTHER CRIES THIS NIGHTMARE'S EVE AT SEA...
...CRIES WHICH MADLY DANCE LIKE LIVING THINGS ATOP THE LAPPING, LUNATIC WAVES...
...UNTIL, AMIDST THE FIRST FAINT BLUSH OF DAWN...
HAH! I HAVE TRIUMPHED OVER THEM ALL.
MY THIRST IS ASSUAGED--FOR ANOTHER HELLISH NIGHT.
I LIVE--WHILE THEY ALL ARE DEAD!
--AND--I ONLY WISH--THAT I WERE THEY.
THEN, A SUDDEN RETCH-ING--AN IMPULSIVE LEAP INTO THE TIMELESS, UNACCUSING SEA--
--THE SEA THAT MAY HELP THE ONE CALLED MORBIUS FORGET WHAT HE WAS--
--AND WHAT HE IS BECOME--!

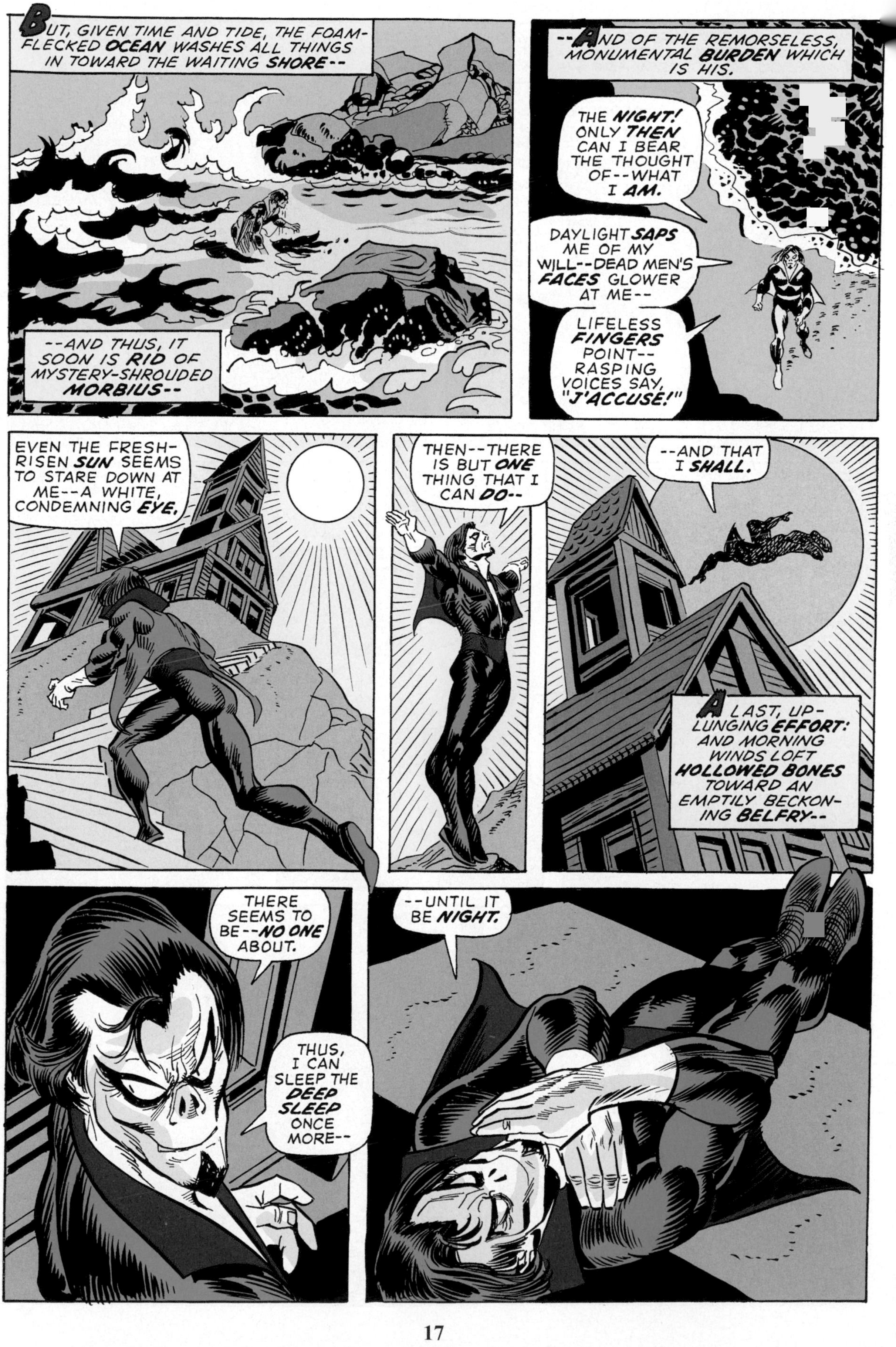
BUT, GIVEN TIME AND TIDE, THE FOAM-FLECKED OCEAN WASHES ALL THINGS IN TOWARD THE WAITING SHORE--
--AND THUS, IT SOON IS RID OF MYSTERY-SHROUDED MORBIUS--
--AND OF THE REMORSELESS, MONUMENTAL BURDEN WHICH IS HIS.
THE NIGHT! ONLY THEN CAN I BEAR THE THOUGHT OF--WHAT I AM.
DAYLIGHT SAPS ME OF MY WILL--DEAD MEN'S FACES GLOWER AT ME--
LIFELESS FINGERS POINT--RASPING VOICES SAY, "J'ACCUSE!"
EVEN THE FRESH-RISEN SUN SEEMS TO STARE DOWN AT ME--A WHITE, CONDEMNING EYE.
THEN--THERE IS BUT ONE THING THAT I CAN DO--
--AND THAT I SHALL.
A LAST, UP-LUNGING EFFORT: AND MORNING WINDS LOFT HOLLOWED BONES TOWARD AN EMPTILY BECKON-ING BELFRY--
THERE SEEMS TO BE--NO ONE ABOUT.
THUS, I CAN SLEEP THE DEEP SLEEP ONCE MORE--
--UNTIL IT BE NIGHT.

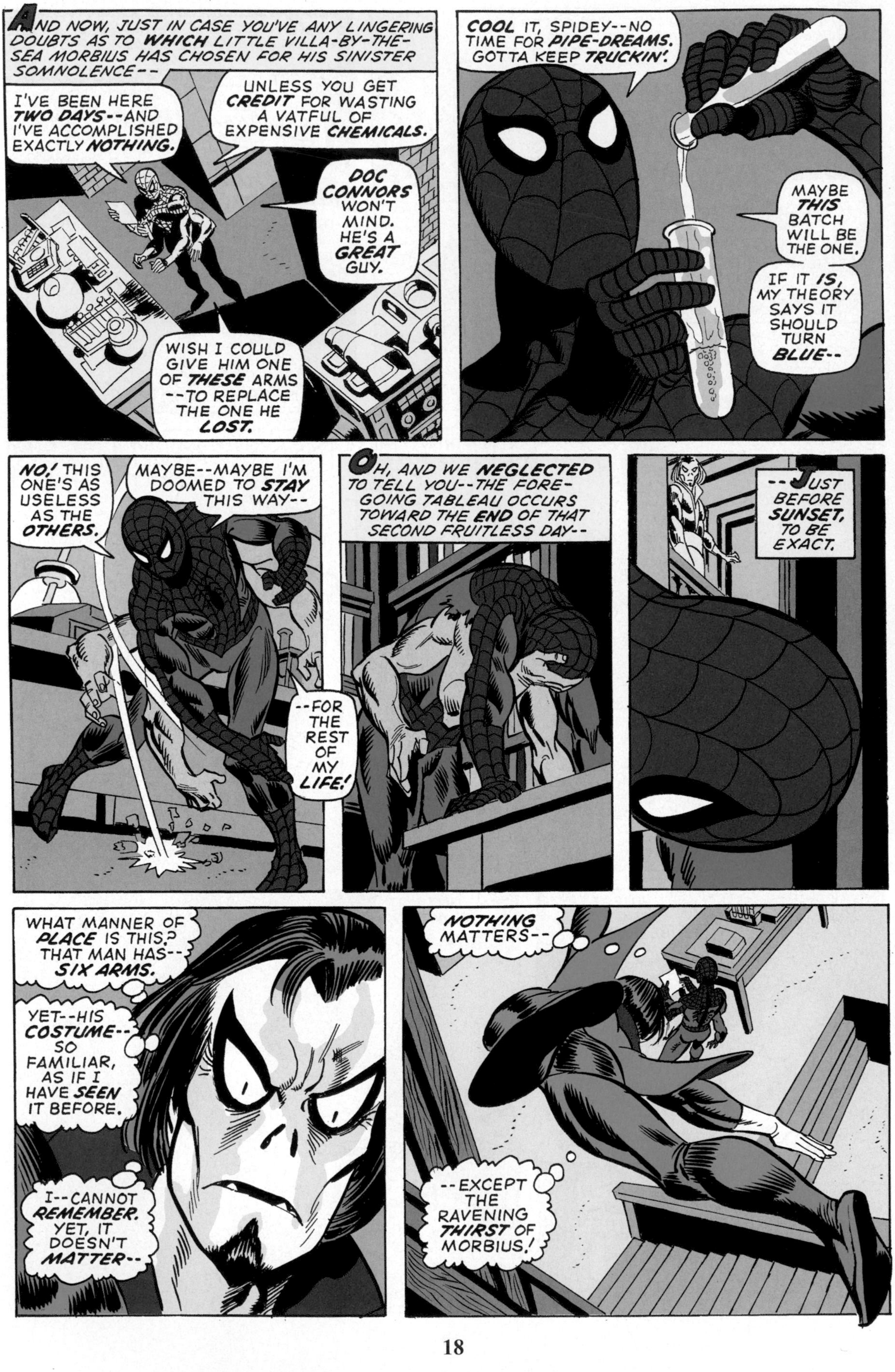
AND NOW, JUST IN CASE YOU'VE ANY LINGERING DOUBTS AS TO WHICH LITTLE VILLA-BY-THE-SEA MORBIUS HAS CHOSEN FOR HIS SINISTER SOMNOLENCE--
I'VE BEEN HERE TWO DAYS--AND I'VE ACCOMPLISHED EXACTLY NOTHING.
UNLESS YOU GET CREDIT FOR WASTING A VATFUL OF EXPENSIVE CHEMICALS.
DOC CONNORS WON'T MIND. HE'S A GREAT GUY.
WISH I COULD GIVE HIM ONE OF THESE ARMS --TO REPLACE THE ONE HE LOST.
COOL IT, SPIDEY--NO TIME FOR PIPE-DREAMS. GOTTA KEEP TRUCKIN'.
MAYBE THIS BATCH WILL BE THE ONE.
IF IT IS, MY THEORY SAYS IT SHOULD TURN BLUE--
NO! THIS ONE'S AS USELESS AS THE OTHERS.
MAYBE--MAYBE I'M DOOMED TO STAY THIS WAY--
--FOR THE REST OF MY LIFE!
OH, AND WE NEGLECTED TO TELL YOU--THE FORE-GOING TABLEAU OCCURS TOWARD THE END OF THAT SECOND FRUITLESS DAY--
--JUST BEFORE SUNSET, TO BE EXACT.
WHAT MANNER OF PLACE IS THIS? THAT MAN HAS--SIX ARMS.
YET--HIS COSTUME--SO FAMILIAR, AS IF I HAVE SEEN IT BEFORE.
I--CANNOT REMEMBER. YET, IT DOESN'T MATTER--
NOTHING MATTERS--
--EXCEPT THE RAVENING THIRST OF MORBIUS.!

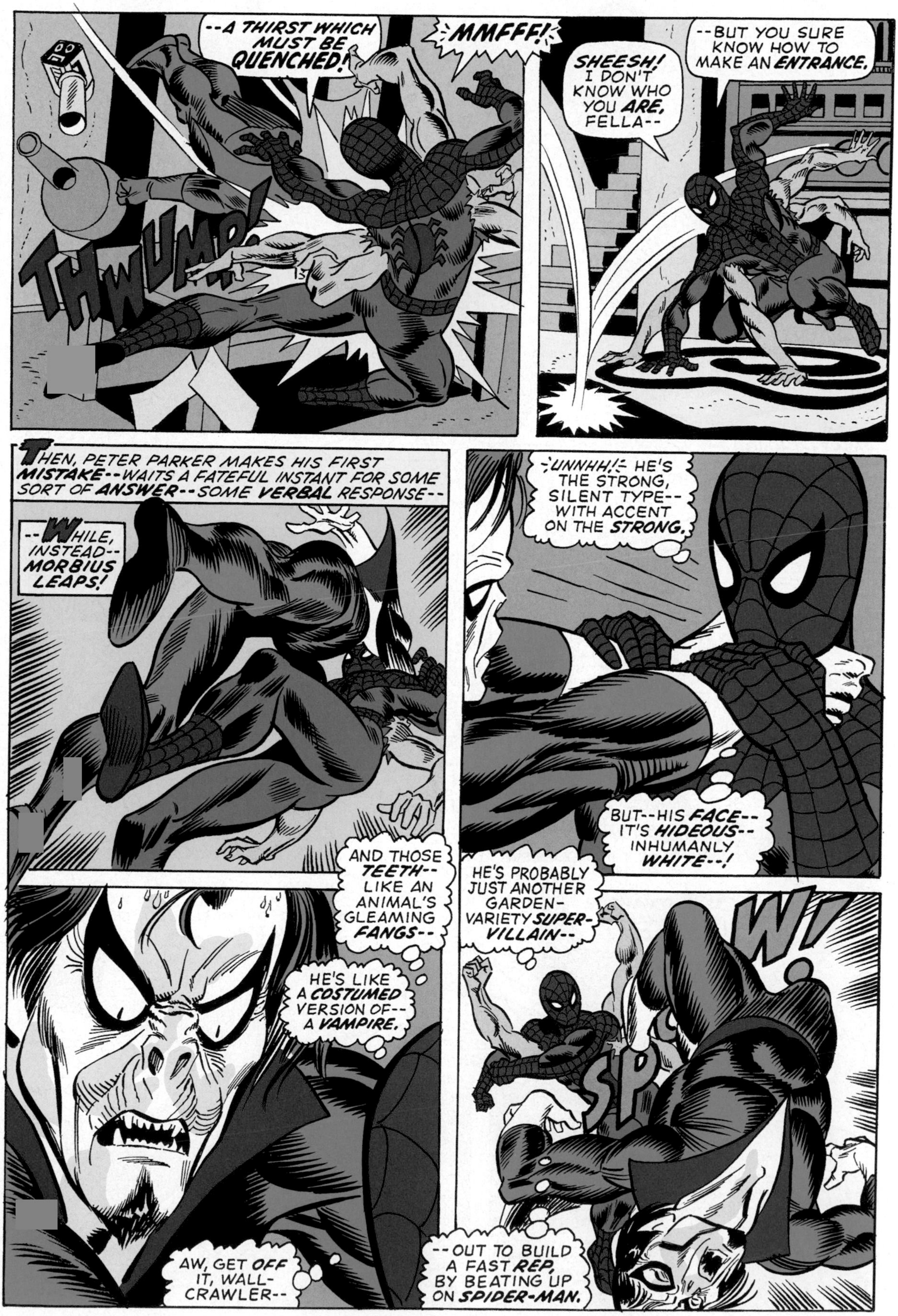
--A THIRST WHICH MUST BE QUENCHED!
MMFFF!
THWUMP!
SHEESH! I DON'T KNOW WHO YOU ARE, FELLA--
--BUT YOU SURE KNOW HOW TO MAKE AN ENTRANCE.
THEN, PETER PARKER MAKES HIS FIRST MISTAKE--WAITS A FATEFUL INSTANT FOR SOME SORT OF ANSWER--SOME VERBAL RESPONSE--
--WHILE, INSTEAD--MORBIUS LEAPS!
UNNHH! HE'S THE STRONG, SILENT TYPE--WITH ACCENT ON THE STRONG.
BUT--HIS FACE--IT'S HIDEOUS--INHUMANLY WHITE--!
AND THOSE TEETH--LIKE AN ANIMAL'S GLEAMING FANGS--
HE'S LIKE A COSTUMED VERSION OF--A VAMPIRE.
AW, GET OFF IT, WALL-CRAWLER--
HE'S PROBABLY JUST ANOTHER GARDEN-VARIETY SUPER-VILLAIN--
--OUT TO BUILD A FAST REP, BY BEATING UP ON SPIDER-MAN.
SPW!

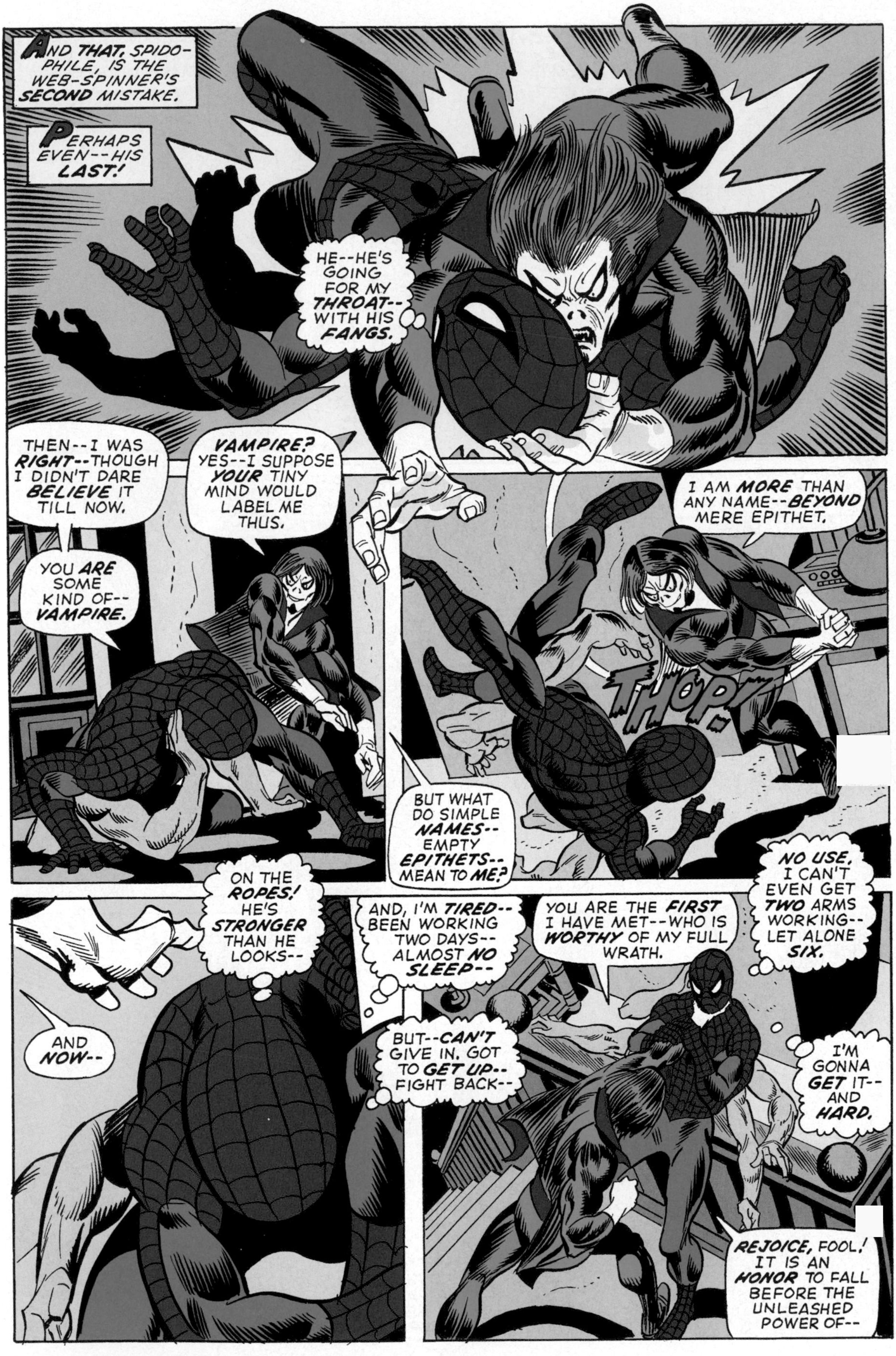
AND THAT, SPIDO-PHILE, IS THE WEB-SPINNER'S SECOND MISTAKE.
PERHAPS EVEN--HIS LAST!
HE--HE'S GOING FOR MY THROAT--WITH HIS FANGS.
THEN--I WAS RIGHT--THOUGH I DIDN'T DARE BELIEVE IT TILL NOW.
YOU ARE SOME KIND OF--VAMPIRE.
VAMPIRE? YES--I SUPPOSE YOUR TINY MIND WOULD LABEL ME THUS.
I AM MORE THAN ANY NAME--BEYOND MERE EPITHET.
THOP!
BUT WHAT DO SIMPLE NAMES--EMPTY EPITHETS--MEAN TO ME?
ON THE ROPES! HE'S STRONGER THAN HE LOOKS--
AND NOW--
AND, I'M TIRED--BEEN WORKING TWO DAYS--ALMOST NO SLEEP--
BUT--CAN'T GIVE IN. GOT TO GET UP--FIGHT BACK--
YOU ARE THE FIRST I HAVE MET--WHO IS WORTHY OF MY FULL WRATH.
NO USE. I CAN'T EVEN GET TWO ARMS WORKING--LET ALONE SIX.
I'M GONNA GET IT--AND HARD.
REJOICE, FOOL! IT IS AN HONOR TO FALL BEFORE THE UNLEASHED POWER OF--

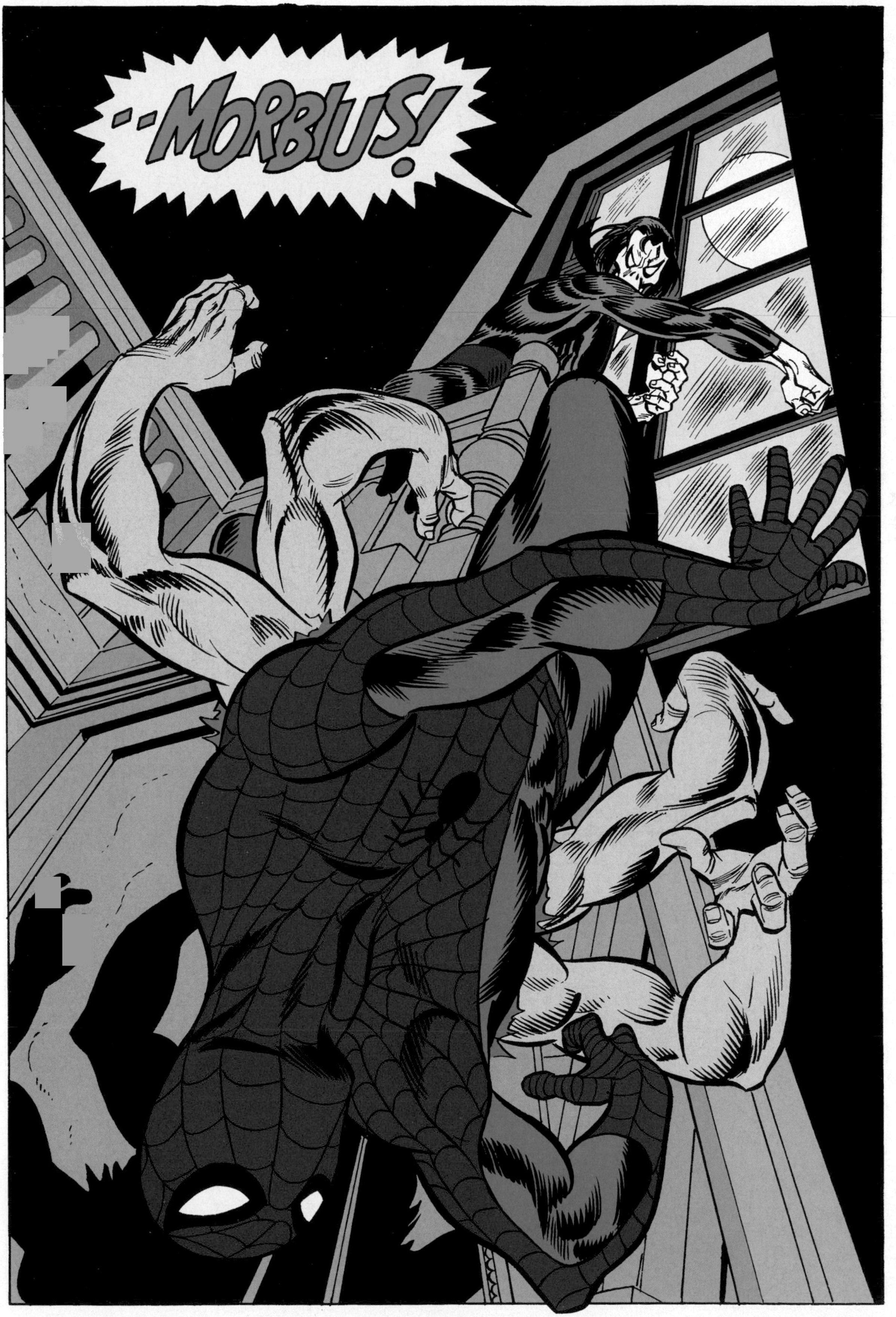
--MORBIUS!

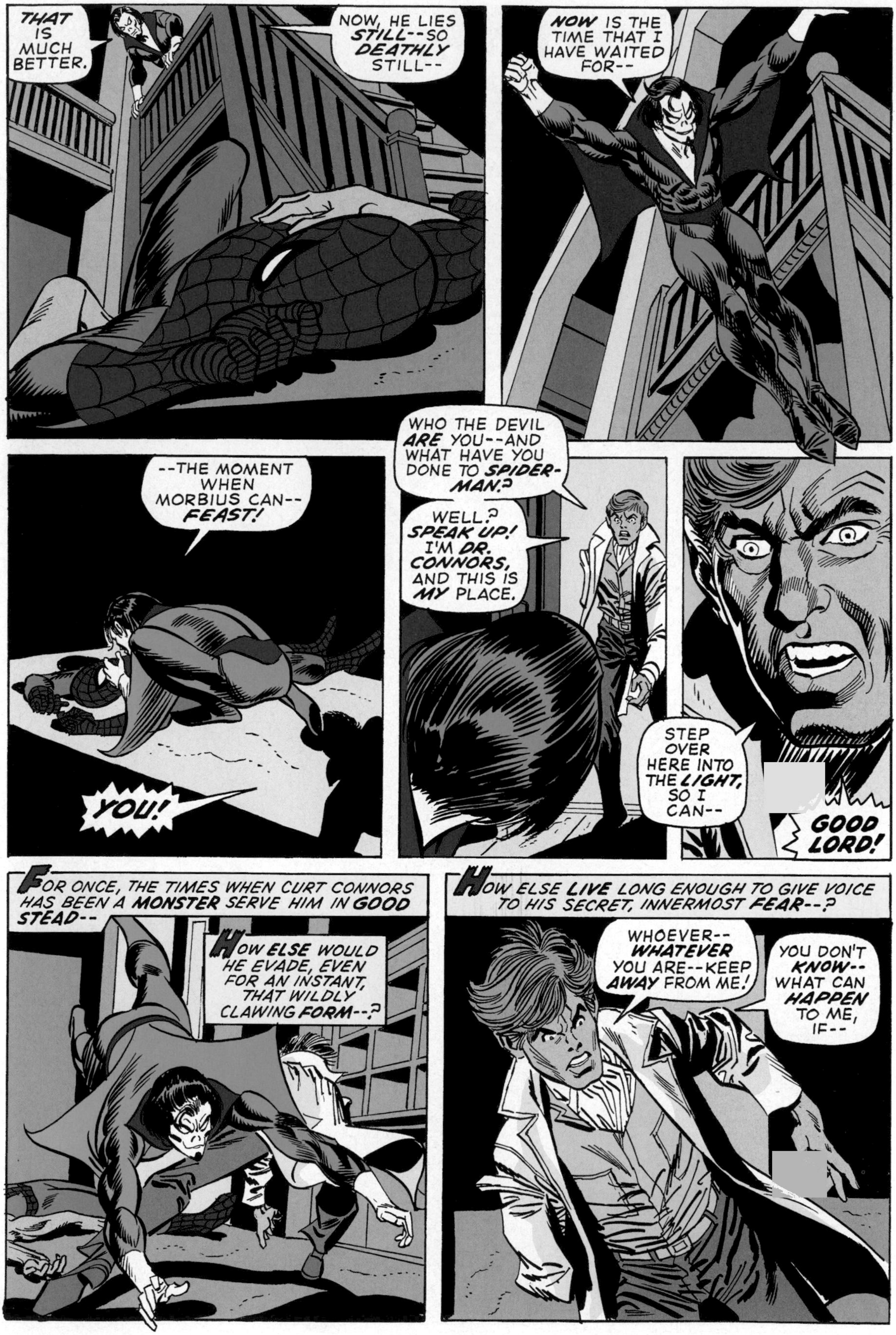
THAT IS MUCH BETTER.
NOW, HE LIES STILL--SO DEATHLY STILL--
NOW IS THE TIME THAT I HAVE WAITED FOR--
--THE MOMENT WHEN MORBIUS CAN--FEAST!
YOU!
WHO THE DEVIL ARE YOU--AND WHAT HAVE YOU DONE TO SPIDER-MAN?
WELL? SPEAK UP! I'M DR. CONNORS, AND THIS IS MY PLACE.
STEP OVER HERE INTO THE LIGHT, SO I CAN--
GOOD LORD!
FOR ONCE, THE TIMES WHEN CURT CONNORS HAS BEEN A MONSTER SERVE HIM IN GOOD STEAD--
HOW ELSE WOULD HE EVADE, EVEN FOR AN INSTANT, THAT WILDLY CLAWING FORM--?
HOW ELSE LIVE LONG ENOUGH TO GIVE VOICE TO HIS SECRET, INNERMOST FEAR--?
WHOEVER--WHATEVER YOU ARE--KEEP AWAY FROM ME!
YOU DON'T KNOW--WHAT CAN HAPPEN TO ME, IF--

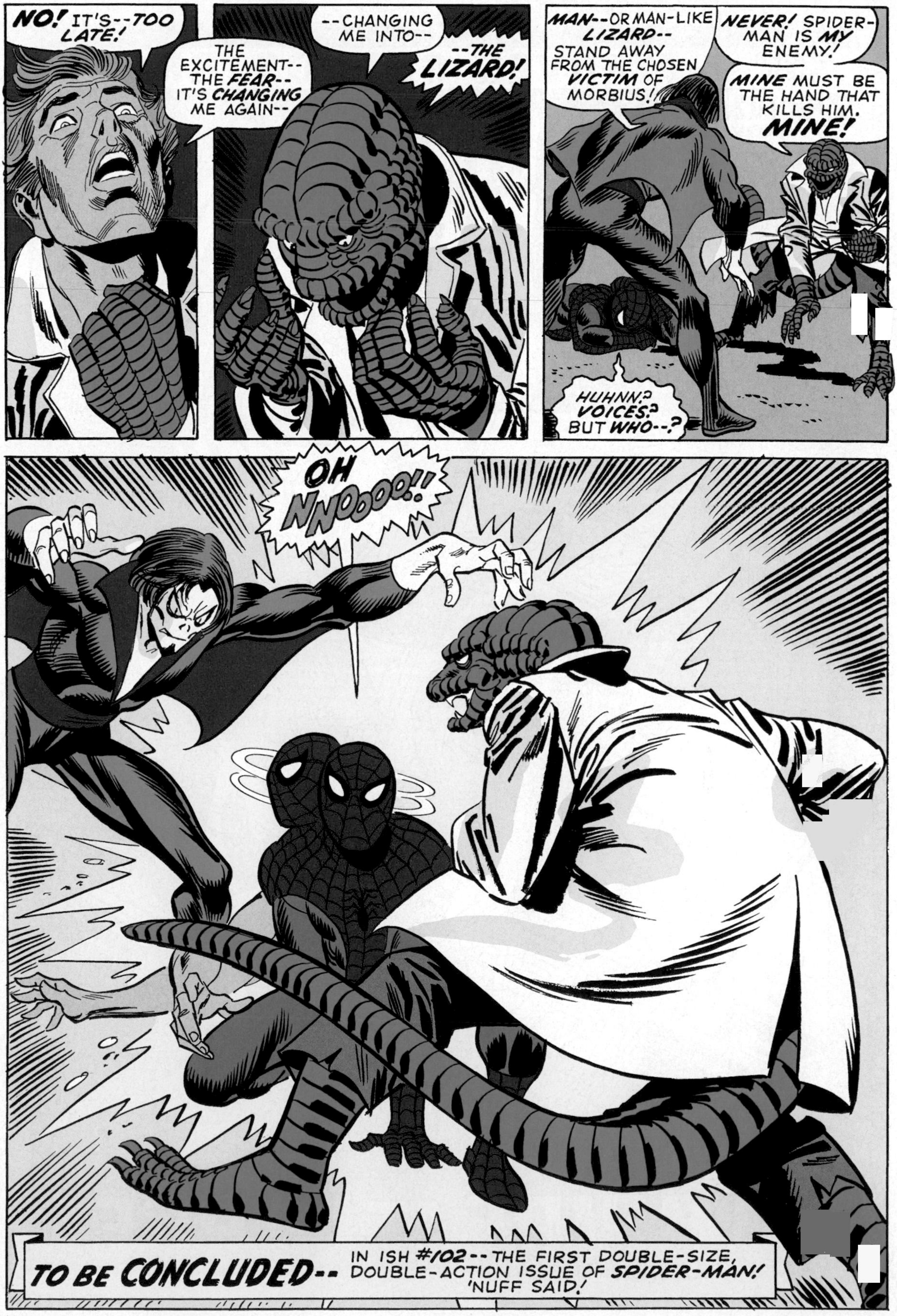

NO! IT'S--TOO LATE!
THE EXCITEMENT-- THE FEAR-- IT'S CHANGING ME AGAIN--
--CHANGING ME INTO--
--THE LIZARD!
MAN--OR MAN-LIKE LIZARD-- STAND AWAY FROM THE CHOSEN VICTIM OF MORBIUS!
NEVER! SPIDER-MAN IS MY ENEMY!
MINE MUST BE THE HAND THAT KILLS HIM. MINE!
HUHNN? VOICES? BUT WHO--?
OH NNOOOOO!!
TO BE CONCLUDED-- IN ISH #102--THE FIRST DOUBLE-SIZE, DOUBLE-ACTION ISSUE OF SPIDER-MAN! 'NUFF SAID!

SPIDER-MAN
MARVEL COMICS GROUP™
25¢ 102 NOV 02457
the AMAZING SPIDER-MAN™
APPROVED BY THE COMICS CODE AUTHORITY
IF MORBIUS DOESN'T KILL SPIDEY-- THE LIZARD WILL!
ALL NEW 'NUFF SAID!
VAMPIRE AT LARGE!

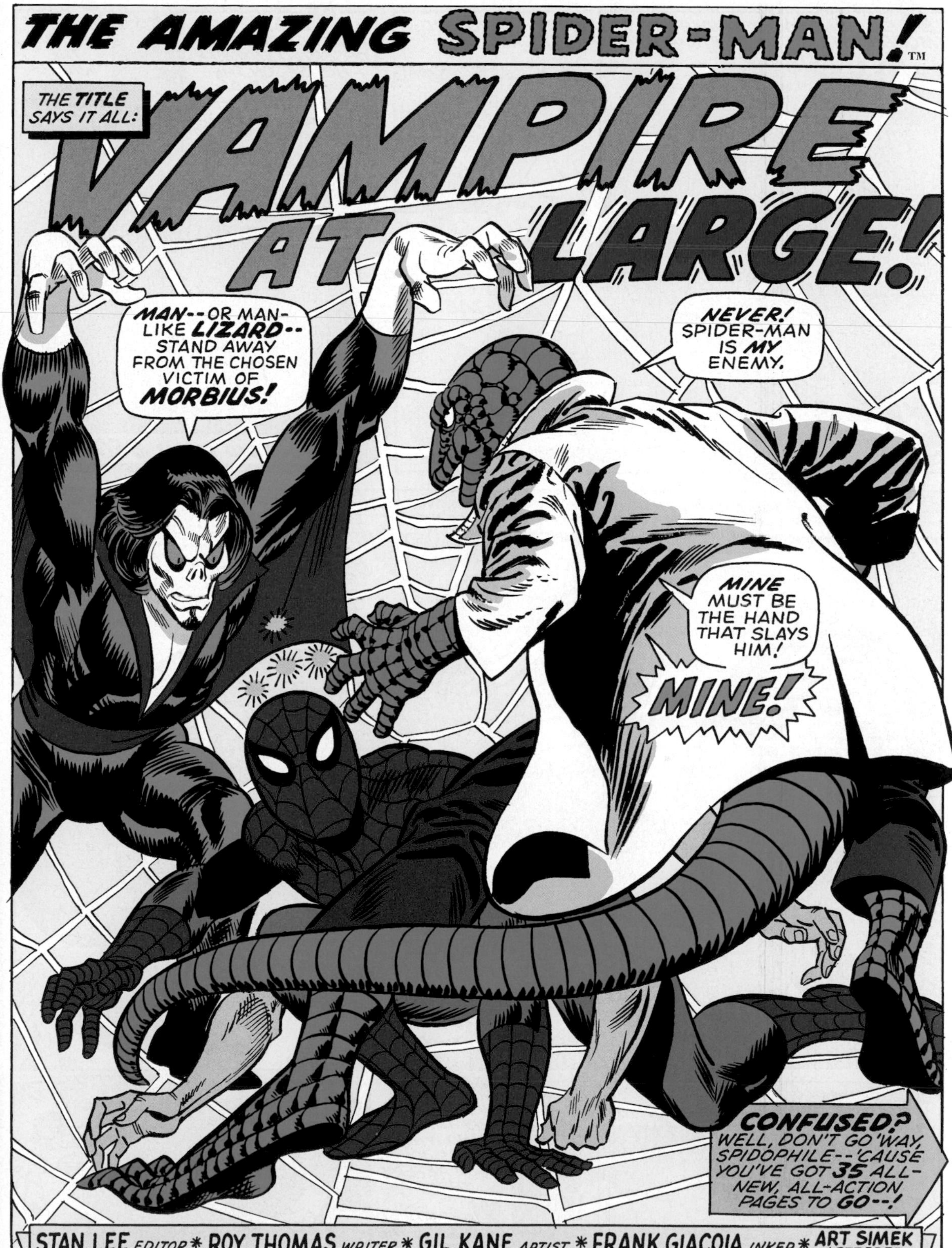
THE AMAZING SPIDER-MAN!™
THE TITLE SAYS IT ALL:
VAMPIRE AT LARGE!
MAN--OR MAN-LIKE LIZARD--STAND AWAY FROM THE CHOSEN VICTIM OF MORBIUS!
NEVER! SPIDER-MAN IS MY ENEMY.
MINE MUST BE THE HAND THAT SLAYS HIM!
MINE!
CONFUSED? WELL, DON'T GO 'WAY, SPIDOPHILE--'CAUSE YOU'VE GOT 35 ALL-NEW, ALL-ACTION PAGES TO GO--!
STAN LEE EDITOR * ROY THOMAS WRITER * GIL KANE ARTIST * FRANK GIACOIA INKER * ART SIMEK LETTERER
662 Z

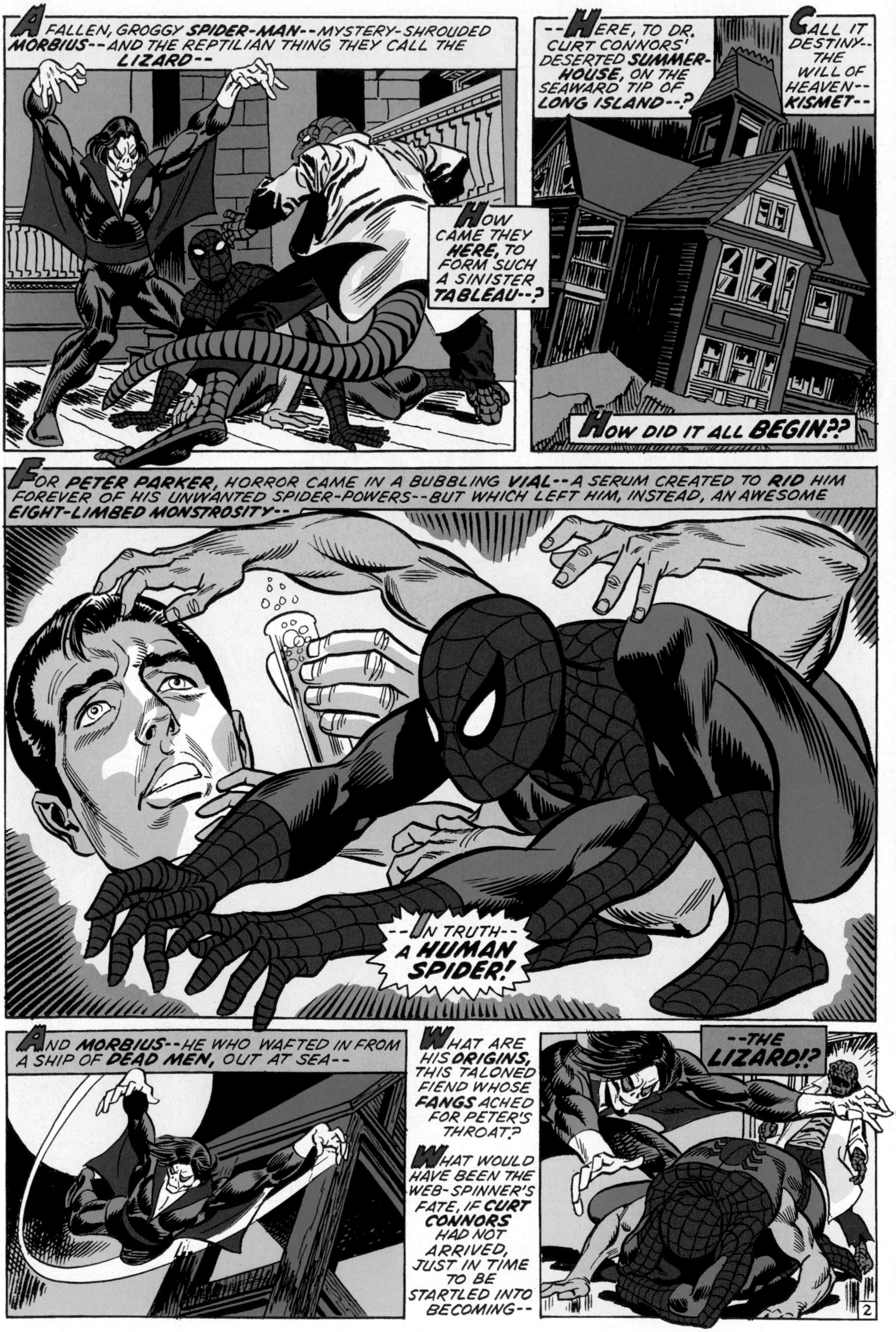
A FALLEN, GROGGY SPIDER-MAN--MYSTERY-SHROUDED MORBIUS--AND THE REPTILIAN THING THEY CALL THE LIZARD--
HOW CAME THEY HERE, TO FORM SUCH A SINISTER TABLEAU--?
--HERE, TO DR. CURT CONNORS' DESERTED SUMMER-HOUSE, ON THE SEAWARD TIP OF LONG ISLAND--?
CALL IT DESTINY--THE WILL OF HEAVEN--KISMET--
HOW DID IT ALL BEGIN??
FOR PETER PARKER, HORROR CAME IN A BUBBLING VIAL--A SERUM CREATED TO RID HIM FOREVER OF HIS UNWANTED SPIDER-POWERS--BUT WHICH LEFT HIM, INSTEAD, AN AWESOME EIGHT-LIMBED MONSTROSITY--
--IN TRUTH--A HUMAN SPIDER!
AND MORBIUS--HE WHO WAFTED IN FROM A SHIP OF DEAD MEN, OUT AT SEA--
WHAT ARE HIS ORIGINS, THIS TALONED FIEND WHOSE FANGS ACHED FOR PETER'S THROAT?
WHAT WOULD HAVE BEEN THE WEB-SPINNER'S FATE, IF CURT CONNORS HAD NOT ARRIVED, JUST IN TIME TO BE STARTLED INTO BECOMING--
--THE LIZARD!?
2

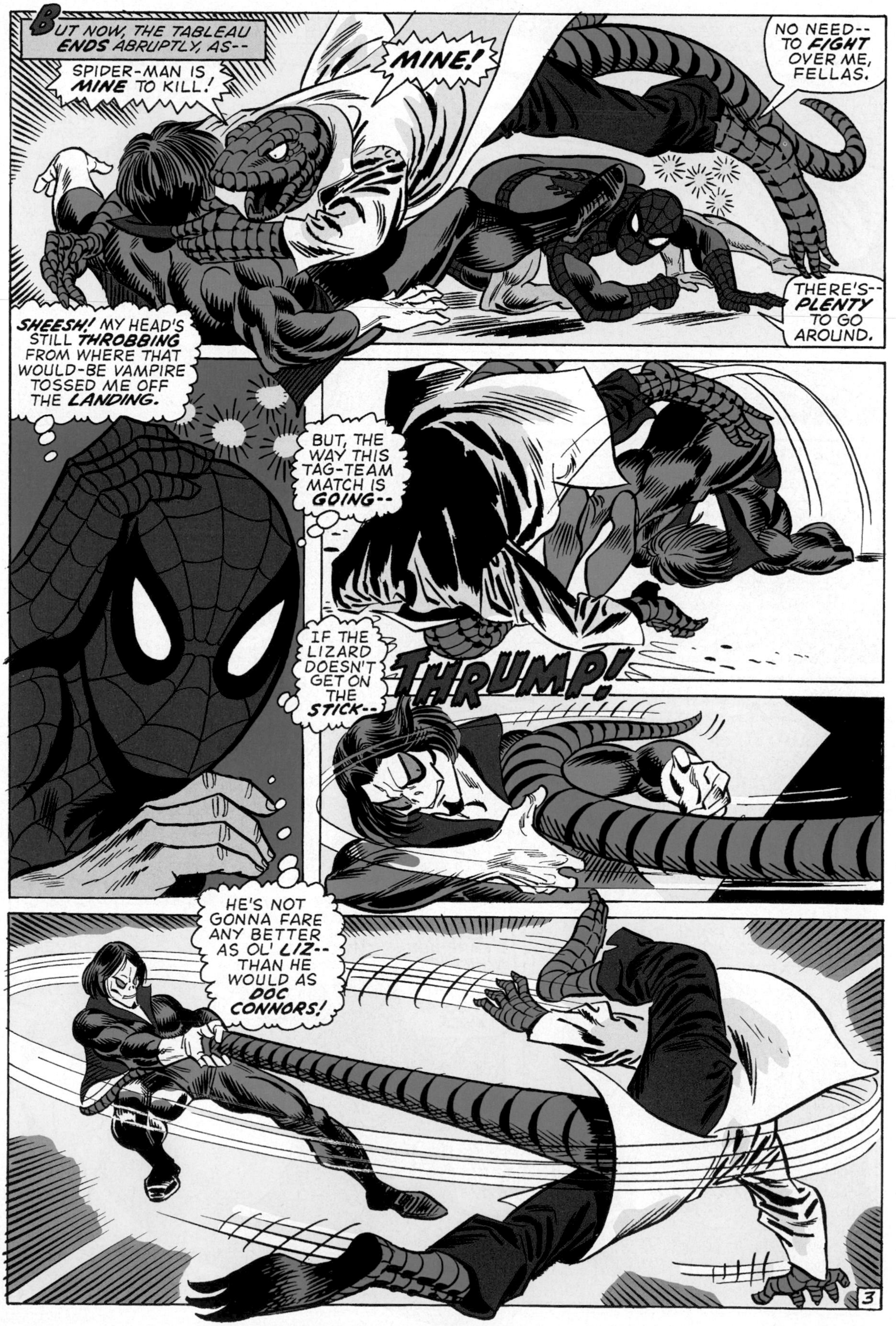
BUT NOW, THE TABLEAU ENDS ABRUPTLY, AS--
SPIDER-MAN IS MINE TO KILL!
MINE!
NO NEED-- TO FIGHT OVER ME, FELLAS.
THERE'S-- PLENTY TO GO AROUND.
SHEESH! MY HEAD'S STILL THROBBING FROM WHERE THAT WOULD-BE VAMPIRE TOSSED ME OFF THE LANDING.
BUT, THE WAY THIS TAG-TEAM MATCH IS GOING--
IF THE LIZARD DOESN'T GET ON THE STICK--
THRUMP!
HE'S NOT GONNA FARE ANY BETTER AS OL' LIZ-- THAN HE WOULD AS DOC CONNORS!
3

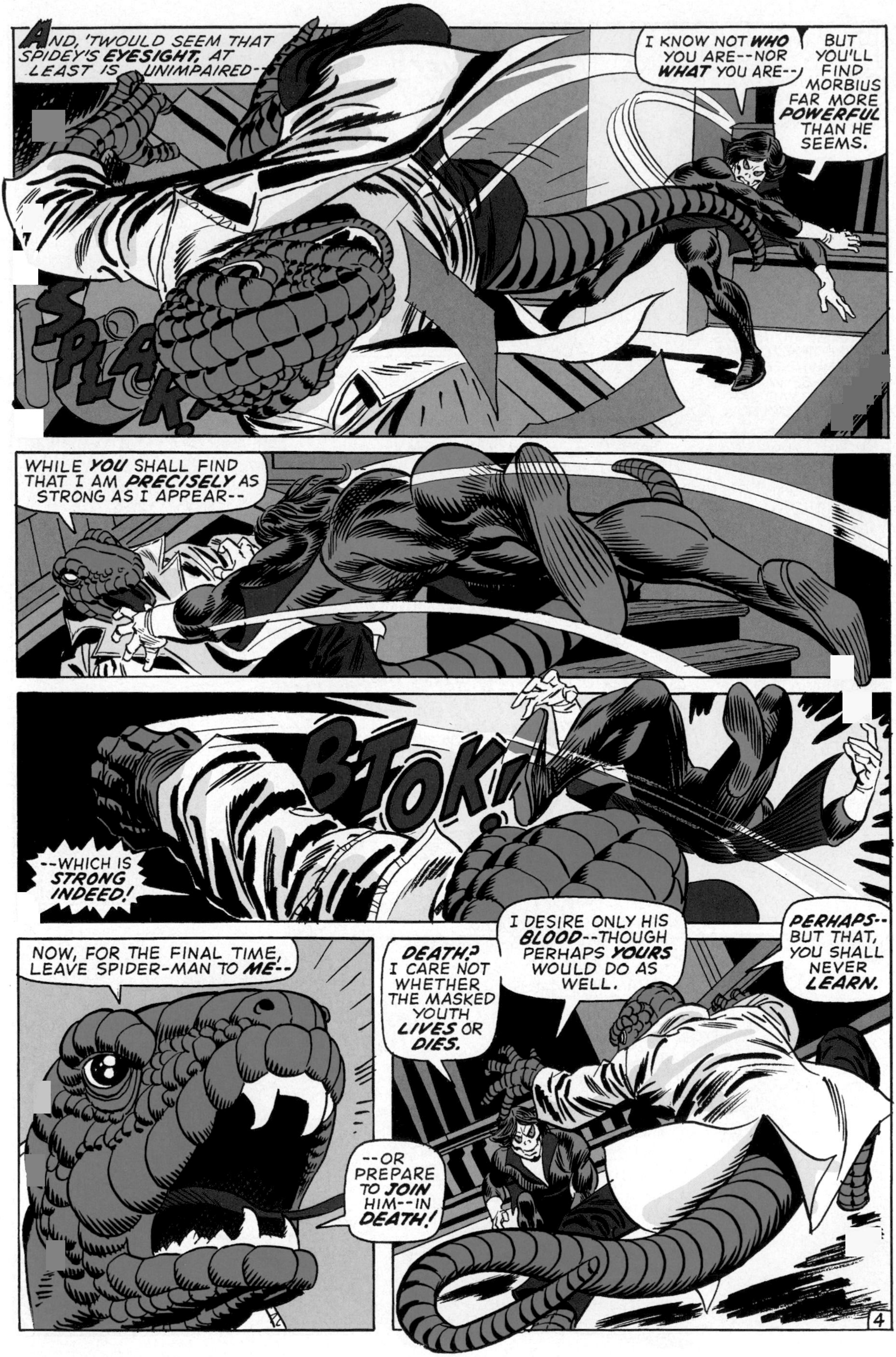
AND, 'TWOULD SEEM THAT SPIDEY'S EYESIGHT, AT LEAST IS UNIMPAIRED--
I KNOW NOT WHO YOU ARE--NOR WHAT YOU ARE--
BUT YOU'LL FIND MORBIUS FAR MORE POWERFUL THAN HE SEEMS.
SPLAK!
WHILE YOU SHALL FIND THAT I AM PRECISELY AS STRONG AS I APPEAR--
BTOK!
--WHICH IS STRONG INDEED!
NOW, FOR THE FINAL TIME, LEAVE SPIDER-MAN TO ME--
--OR PREPARE TO JOIN HIM--IN DEATH!
DEATH? I CARE NOT WHETHER THE MASKED YOUTH LIVES OR DIES.
I DESIRE ONLY HIS BLOOD--THOUGH PERHAPS YOURS WOULD DO AS WELL.
PERHAPS-- BUT THAT, YOU SHALL NEVER LEARN.
4

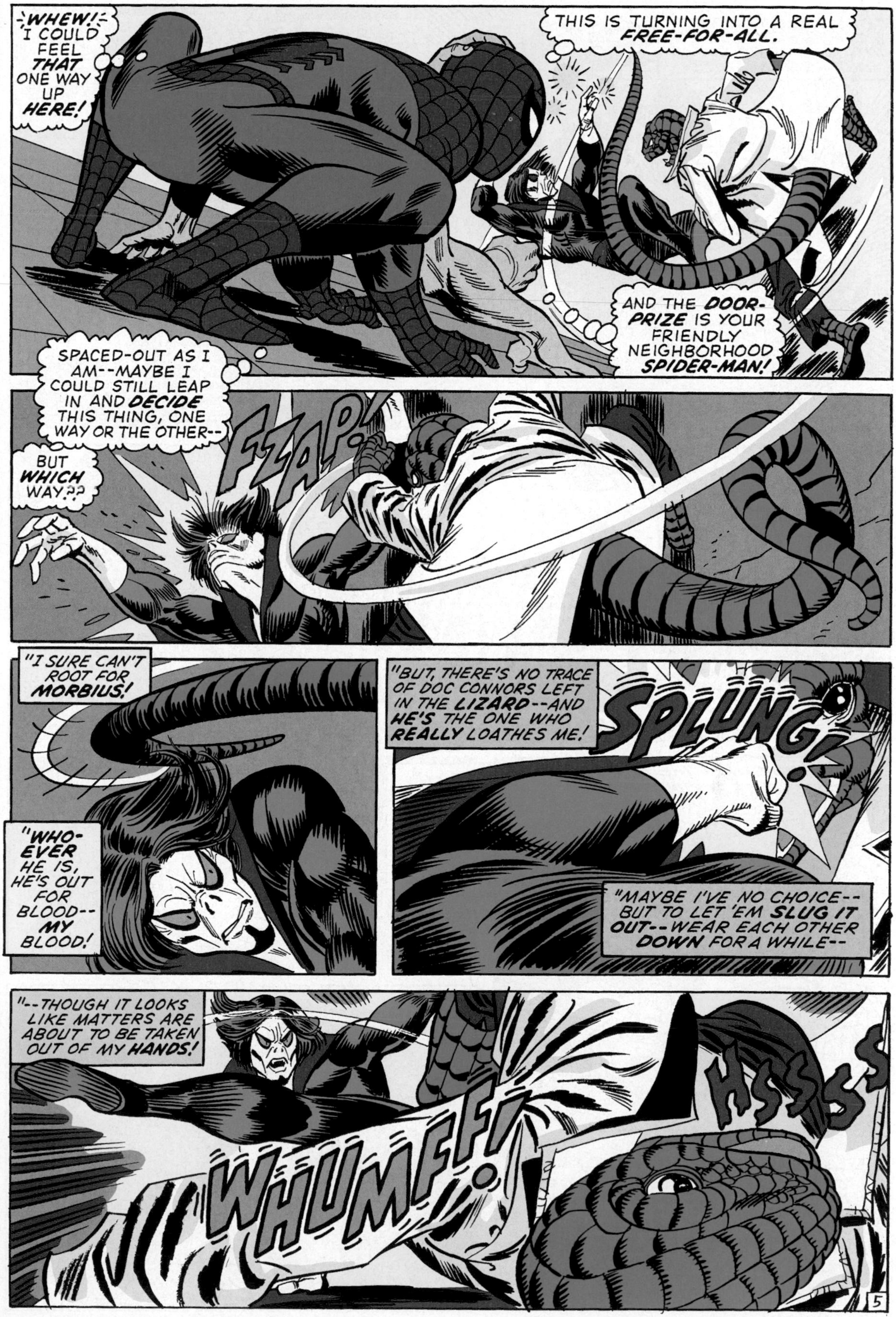

WHEW! I COULD FEEL THAT ONE WAY UP HERE!
THIS IS TURNING INTO A REAL FREE-FOR-ALL.
AND THE DOOR-PRIZE IS YOUR FRIENDLY NEIGHBORHOOD SPIDER-MAN!
SPACED-OUT AS I AM--MAYBE I COULD STILL LEAP IN AND DECIDE THIS THING, ONE WAY OR THE OTHER--
BUT WHICH WAY??
FZAP!
"I SURE CAN'T ROOT FOR MORBIUS!
"WHO-EVER HE IS, HE'S OUT FOR BLOOD--MY BLOOD!
"BUT, THERE'S NO TRACE OF DOC CONNORS LEFT IN THE LIZARD--AND HE'S THE ONE WHO REALLY LOATHES ME!
SPLUNG!
"MAYBE I'VE NO CHOICE--BUT TO LET 'EM SLUG IT OUT--WEAR EACH OTHER DOWN FOR A WHILE--
"--THOUGH IT LOOKS LIKE MATTERS ARE ABOUT TO BE TAKEN OUT OF MY HANDS!
HSSSSS
WHUMFF!
5

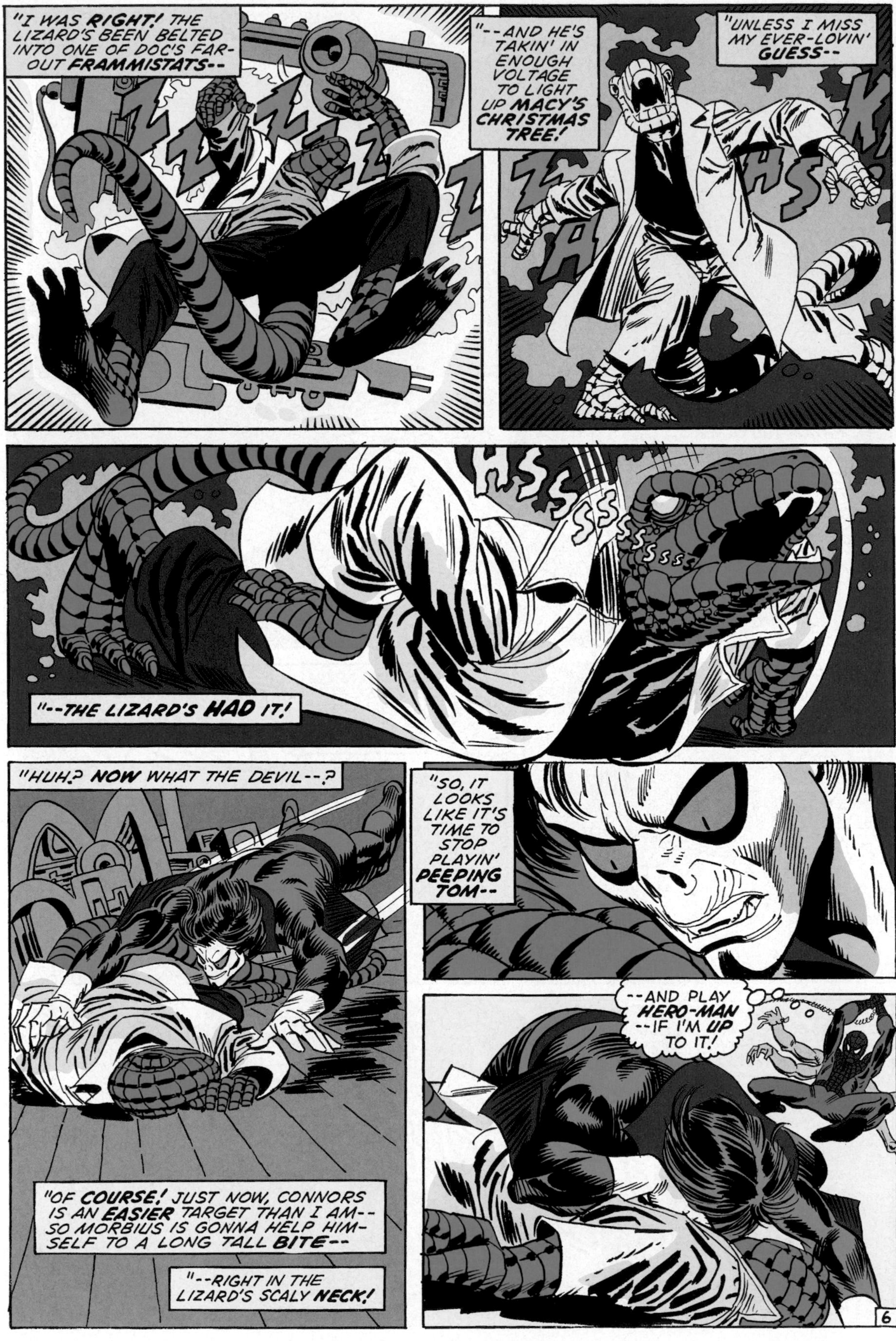
"I WAS RIGHT! THE LIZARD'S BEEN BELTED INTO ONE OF DOC'S FAR-OUT FRAMMISTATS--
"--AND HE'S TAKIN' IN ENOUGH VOLTAGE TO LIGHT UP MACY'S CHRISTMAS TREE!
"UNLESS I MISS MY EVER-LOVIN' GUESS--
"--THE LIZARD'S HAD IT!
"HUH? NOW WHAT THE DEVIL--?
"SO, IT LOOKS LIKE IT'S TIME TO STOP PLAYIN' PEEPING TOM--
"OF COURSE! JUST NOW, CONNORS IS AN EASIER TARGET THAN I AM--SO MORBIUS IS GONNA HELP HIMSELF TO A LONG TALL BITE--
"--RIGHT IN THE LIZARD'S SCALY NECK!
--AND PLAY HERO-MAN --IF I'M UP TO IT!
6

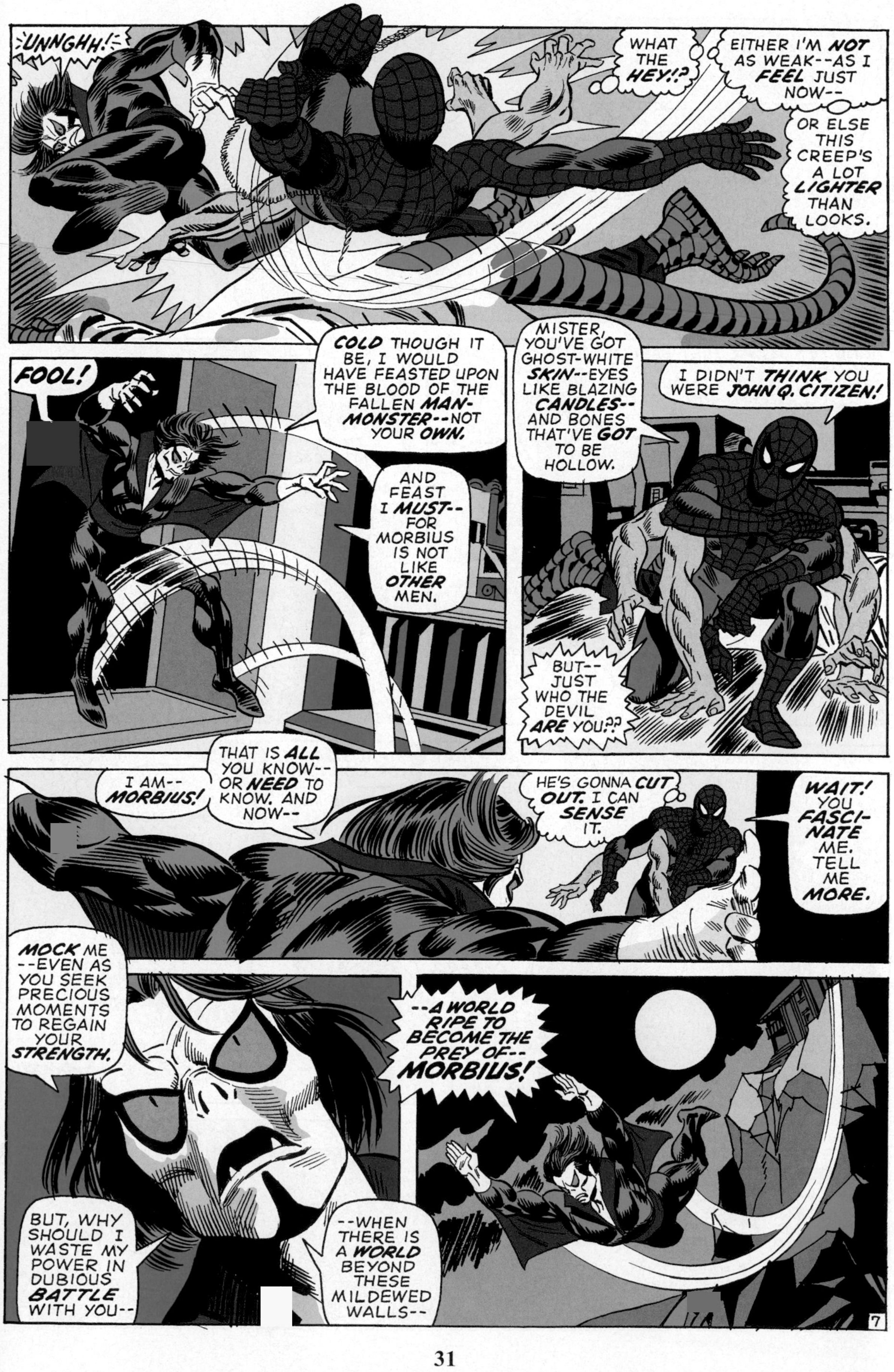
UNNGHH!
WHAT THE HEY!?
EITHER I'M NOT AS WEAK--AS I FEEL JUST NOW--
OR ELSE THIS CREEP'S A LOT LIGHTER THAN LOOKS.
FOOL!
COLD THOUGH IT BE, I WOULD HAVE FEASTED UPON THE BLOOD OF THE FALLEN MAN-MONSTER--NOT YOUR OWN.
AND FEAST I MUST--FOR MORBIUS IS NOT LIKE OTHER MEN.
MISTER, YOU'VE GOT GHOST-WHITE SKIN--EYES LIKE BLAZING CANDLES--AND BONES THAT'VE GOT TO BE HOLLOW.
I DIDN'T THINK YOU WERE JOHN Q. CITIZEN!
BUT--JUST WHO THE DEVIL ARE YOU??
I AM--MORBIUS!
THAT IS ALL YOU KNOW--OR NEED TO KNOW. AND NOW--
HE'S GONNA CUT OUT. I CAN SENSE IT.
WAIT! YOU FASCINATE ME. TELL ME MORE.
MOCK ME--EVEN AS YOU SEEK PRECIOUS MOMENTS TO REGAIN YOUR STRENGTH.
BUT, WHY SHOULD I WASTE MY POWER IN DUBIOUS BATTLE WITH YOU--
--WHEN THERE IS A WORLD BEYOND THESE MILDEWED WALLS--
--A WORLD RIPE TO BECOME THE PREY OF--MORBIUS!
7

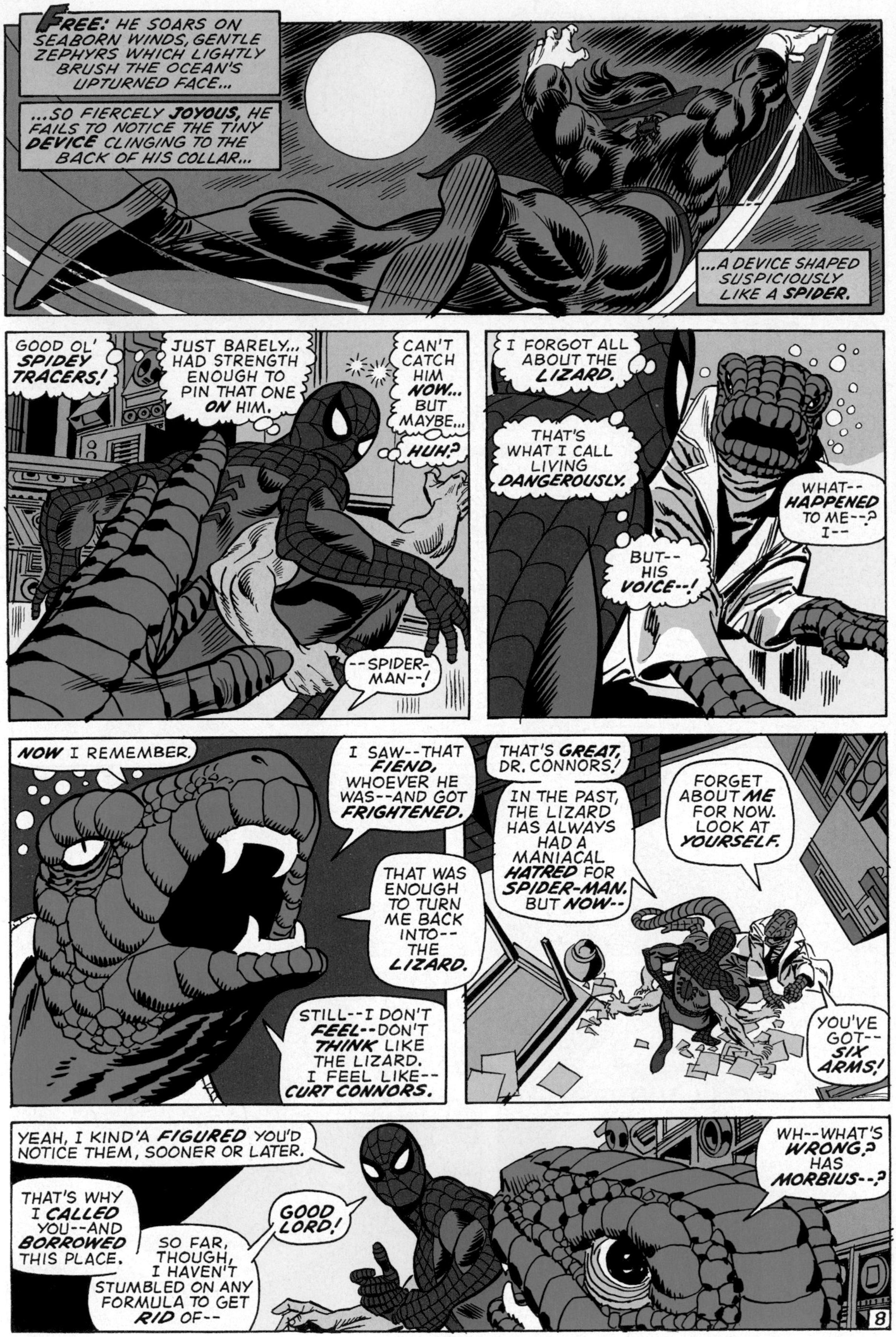
FREE: HE SOARS ON SEABORN WINDS, GENTLE ZEPHYRS WHICH LIGHTLY BRUSH THE OCEAN'S UPTURNED FACE...
...SO FIERCELY JOYOUS, HE FAILS TO NOTICE THE TINY DEVICE CLINGING TO THE BACK OF HIS COLLAR...
...A DEVICE SHAPED SUSPICIOUSLY LIKE A SPIDER.
GOOD OL' SPIDEY TRACERS!
JUST BARELY... HAD STRENGTH ENOUGH TO PIN THAT ONE ON HIM.
CAN'T CATCH HIM NOW... BUT MAYBE...
HUH?
--SPIDER-MAN--!
I FORGOT ALL ABOUT THE LIZARD.
THAT'S WHAT I CALL LIVING DANGEROUSLY.
WHAT--HAPPENED TO ME--? I--
BUT--HIS VOICE--!
NOW I REMEMBER.
I SAW--THAT FIEND, WHOEVER HE WAS--AND GOT FRIGHTENED.
THAT WAS ENOUGH TO TURN ME BACK INTO--THE LIZARD.
STILL--I DON'T FEEL--DON'T THINK LIKE THE LIZARD. I FEEL LIKE--CURT CONNORS.
THAT'S GREAT, DR. CONNORS!
IN THE PAST, THE LIZARD HAS ALWAYS HAD A MANIACAL HATRED FOR SPIDER-MAN. BUT NOW--
FORGET ABOUT ME FOR NOW. LOOK AT YOURSELF.
YOU'VE GOT--SIX ARMS!
YEAH, I KIND'A FIGURED YOU'D NOTICE THEM, SOONER OR LATER.
THAT'S WHY I CALLED YOU--AND BORROWED THIS PLACE.
SO FAR, THOUGH, I HAVEN'T STUMBLED ON ANY FORMULA TO GET RID OF--
GOOD LORD!
WH--WHAT'S WRONG? HAS MORBIUS--?
8

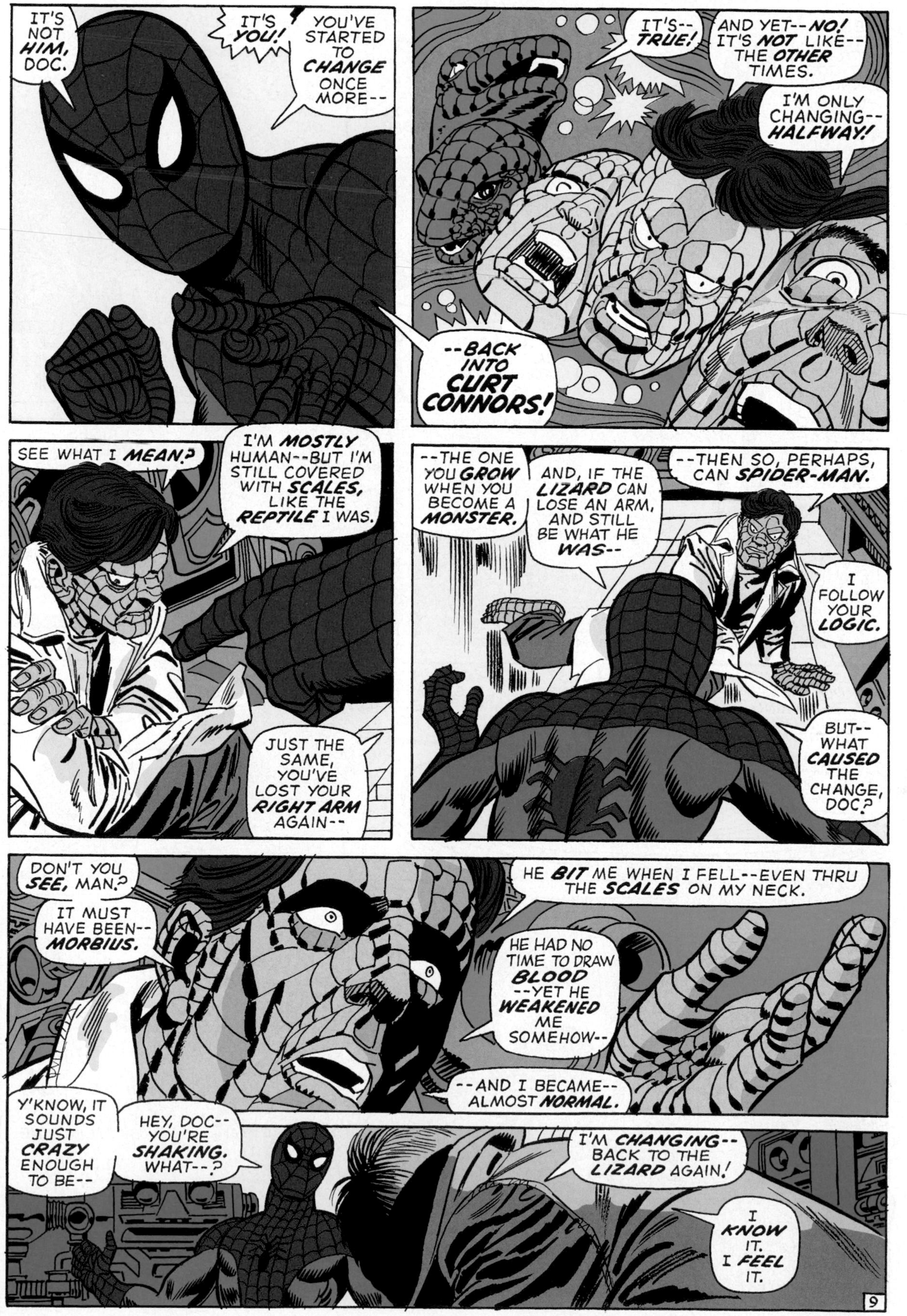

IT'S NOT HIM, DOC.
IT'S YOU!
YOU'VE STARTED TO CHANGE ONCE MORE--
--BACK INTO CURT CONNORS!
IT'S--TRUE!
AND YET--NO! IT'S NOT LIKE--THE OTHER TIMES.
I'M ONLY CHANGING--HALFWAY!
SEE WHAT I MEAN?
I'M MOSTLY HUMAN--BUT I'M STILL COVERED WITH SCALES, LIKE THE REPTILE I WAS.
JUST THE SAME, YOU'VE LOST YOUR RIGHT ARM AGAIN--
--THE ONE YOU GROW WHEN YOU BECOME A MONSTER.
AND, IF THE LIZARD CAN LOSE AN ARM, AND STILL BE WHAT HE WAS--
--THEN SO, PERHAPS, CAN SPIDER-MAN.
I FOLLOW YOUR LOGIC.
BUT--WHAT CAUSED THE CHANGE, DOC?
DON'T YOU SEE, MAN?
IT MUST HAVE BEEN--MORBIUS.
HE BIT ME WHEN I FELL--EVEN THRU THE SCALES ON MY NECK.
HE HAD NO TIME TO DRAW BLOOD--YET HE WEAKENED ME SOMEHOW--
--AND I BECAME--ALMOST NORMAL.
Y'KNOW, IT SOUNDS JUST CRAZY ENOUGH TO BE--
HEY, DOC--YOU'RE SHAKING. WHAT--?
I'M CHANGING--BACK TO THE LIZARD AGAIN!
I KNOW IT. I FEEL IT.
9

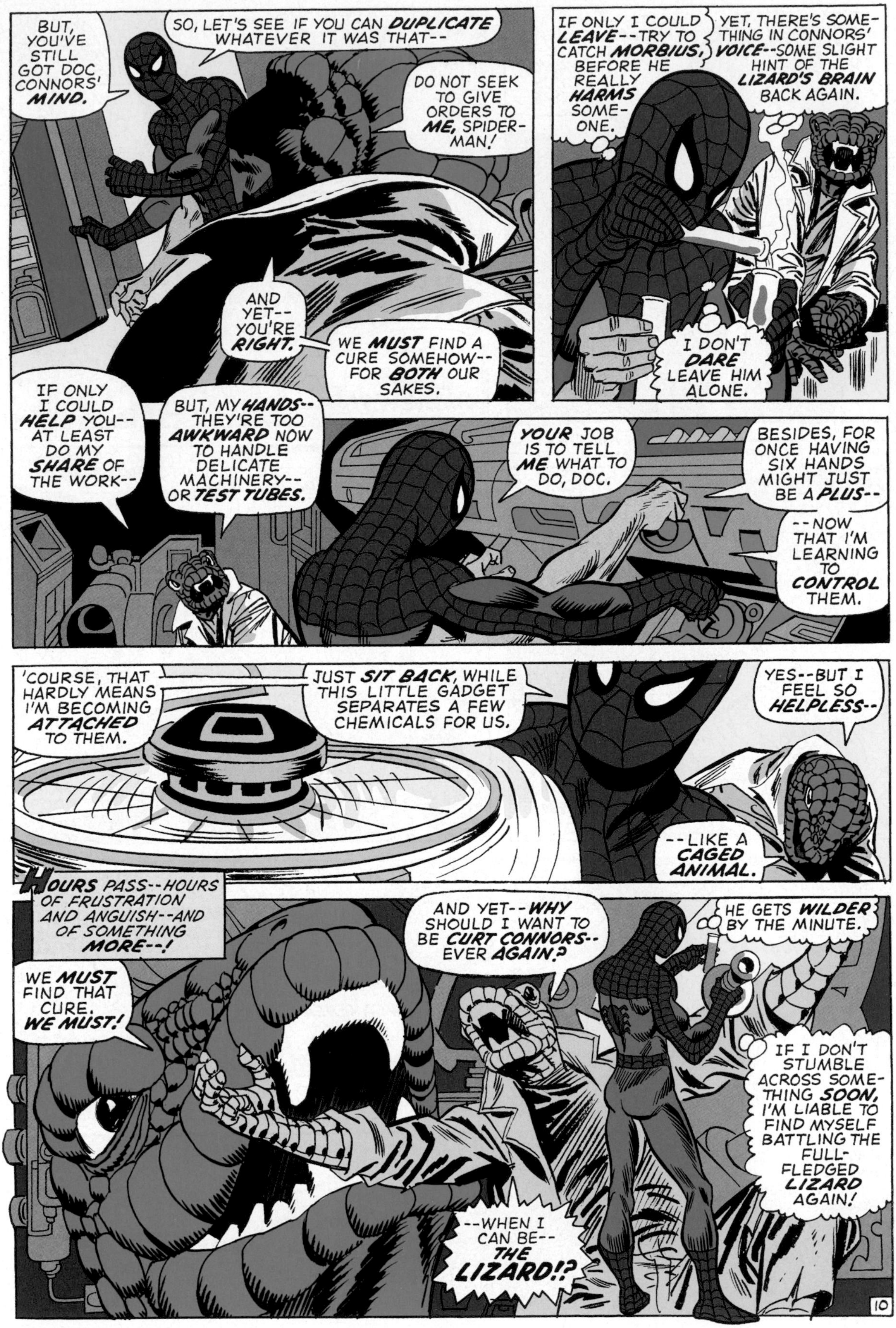
BUT, YOU'VE STILL GOT DOC CONNORS' MIND.
SO, LET'S SEE IF YOU CAN DUPLICATE WHATEVER IT WAS THAT--
DO NOT SEEK TO GIVE ORDERS TO ME, SPIDER-MAN!
AND YET-- YOU'RE RIGHT.
WE MUST FIND A CURE SOMEHOW-- FOR BOTH OUR SAKES.
IF ONLY I COULD LEAVE--TRY TO CATCH MORBIUS, BEFORE HE REALLY HARMS SOME-ONE.
YET, THERE'S SOME-THING IN CONNORS' VOICE--SOME SLIGHT HINT OF THE LIZARD'S BRAIN BACK AGAIN.
I DON'T DARE LEAVE HIM ALONE.
IF ONLY I COULD HELP YOU-- AT LEAST DO MY SHARE OF THE WORK--
BUT, MY HANDS-- THEY'RE TOO AWKWARD NOW TO HANDLE DELICATE MACHINERY-- OR TEST TUBES.
YOUR JOB IS TO TELL ME WHAT TO DO, DOC.
BESIDES, FOR ONCE HAVING SIX HANDS MIGHT JUST BE A PLUS--
--NOW THAT I'M LEARNING TO CONTROL THEM.
'COURSE, THAT HARDLY MEANS I'M BECOMING ATTACHED TO THEM.
JUST SIT BACK, WHILE THIS LITTLE GADGET SEPARATES A FEW CHEMICALS FOR US.
YES--BUT I FEEL SO HELPLESS--
--LIKE A CAGED ANIMAL.
HOURS PASS--HOURS OF FRUSTRATION AND ANGUISH--AND OF SOMETHING MORE--!
WE MUST FIND THAT CURE. WE MUST!
AND YET--WHY SHOULD I WANT TO BE CURT CONNORS--EVER AGAIN?
HE GETS WILDER BY THE MINUTE.
IF I DON'T STUMBLE ACROSS SOME-THING SOON, I'M LIABLE TO FIND MYSELF BATTLING THE FULL-FLEDGED LIZARD AGAIN!
--WHEN I CAN BE-- THE LIZARD!?
10

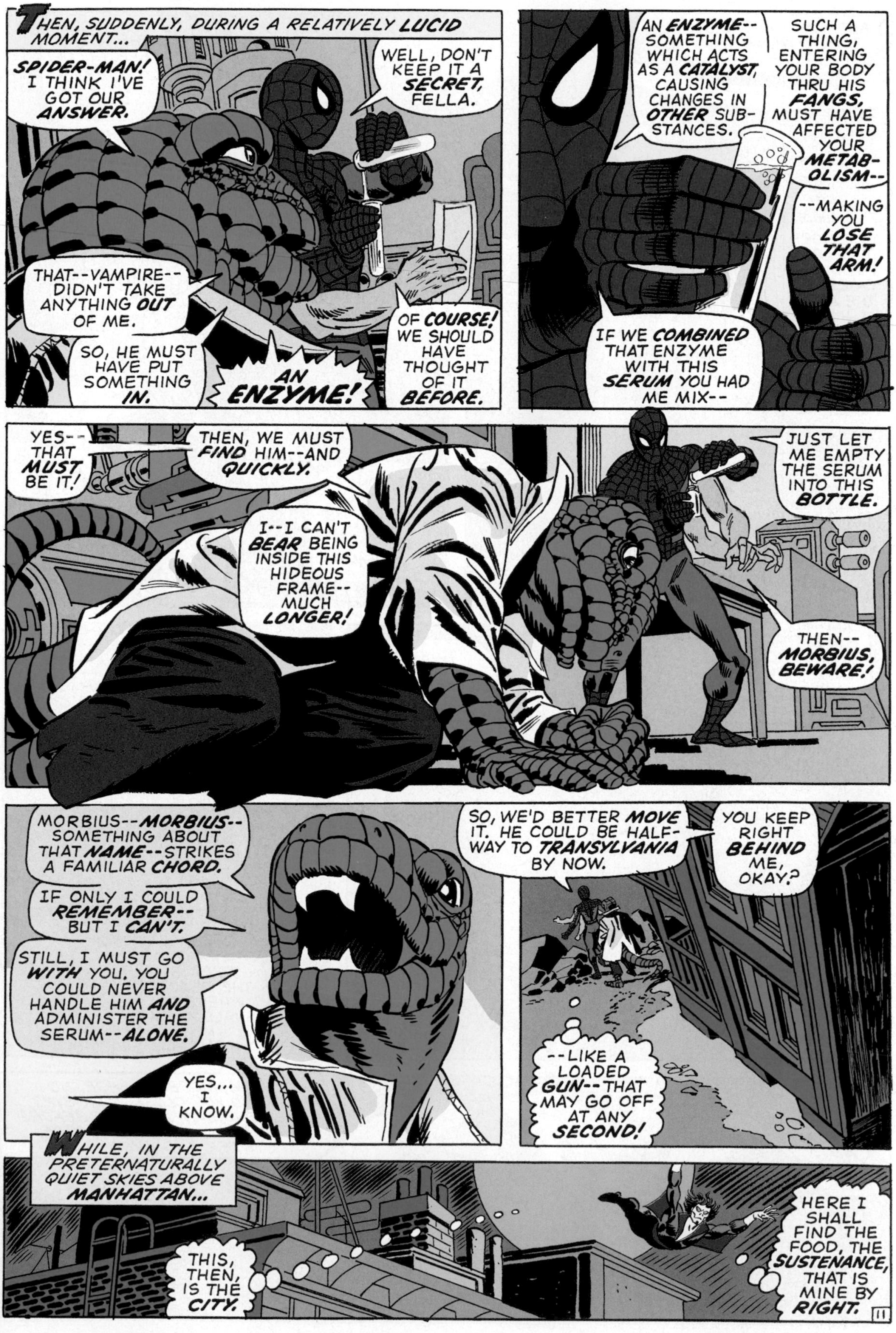
THEN, SUDDENLY, DURING A RELATIVELY LUCID MOMENT...
SPIDER-MAN! I THINK I'VE GOT OUR ANSWER.
WELL, DON'T KEEP IT A SECRET, FELLA.
THAT--VAMPIRE--DIDN'T TAKE ANYTHING OUT OF ME.
SO, HE MUST HAVE PUT SOMETHING IN.
AN ENZYME!
OF COURSE! WE SHOULD HAVE THOUGHT OF IT BEFORE.
AN ENZYME--SOMETHING WHICH ACTS AS A CATALYST, CAUSING CHANGES IN OTHER SUBSTANCES.
SUCH A THING, ENTERING YOUR BODY THRU HIS FANGS, MUST HAVE AFFECTED YOUR METABOLISM--
--MAKING YOU LOSE THAT ARM!
IF WE COMBINED THAT ENZYME WITH THIS SERUM YOU HAD ME MIX--
YES--THAT MUST BE IT!
THEN, WE MUST FIND HIM--AND QUICKLY.
JUST LET ME EMPTY THE SERUM INTO THIS BOTTLE.
I--I CAN'T BEAR BEING INSIDE THIS HIDEOUS FRAME--MUCH LONGER!
THEN--MORBIUS, BEWARE!
MORBIUS--MORBIUS--SOMETHING ABOUT THAT NAME--STRIKES A FAMILIAR CHORD.
IF ONLY I COULD REMEMBER--BUT I CAN'T.
STILL, I MUST GO WITH YOU. YOU COULD NEVER HANDLE HIM AND ADMINISTER THE SERUM--ALONE.
YES... I KNOW.
SO, WE'D BETTER MOVE IT. HE COULD BE HALF-WAY TO TRANSYLVANIA BY NOW.
YOU KEEP RIGHT BEHIND ME, OKAY?
--LIKE A LOADED GUN--THAT MAY GO OFF AT ANY SECOND!
WHILE, IN THE PRETERNATURALLY QUIET SKIES ABOVE MANHATTAN...
THIS, THEN, IS THE CITY.
HERE I SHALL FIND THE FOOD, THE SUSTENANCE, THAT IS MINE BY RIGHT.
11

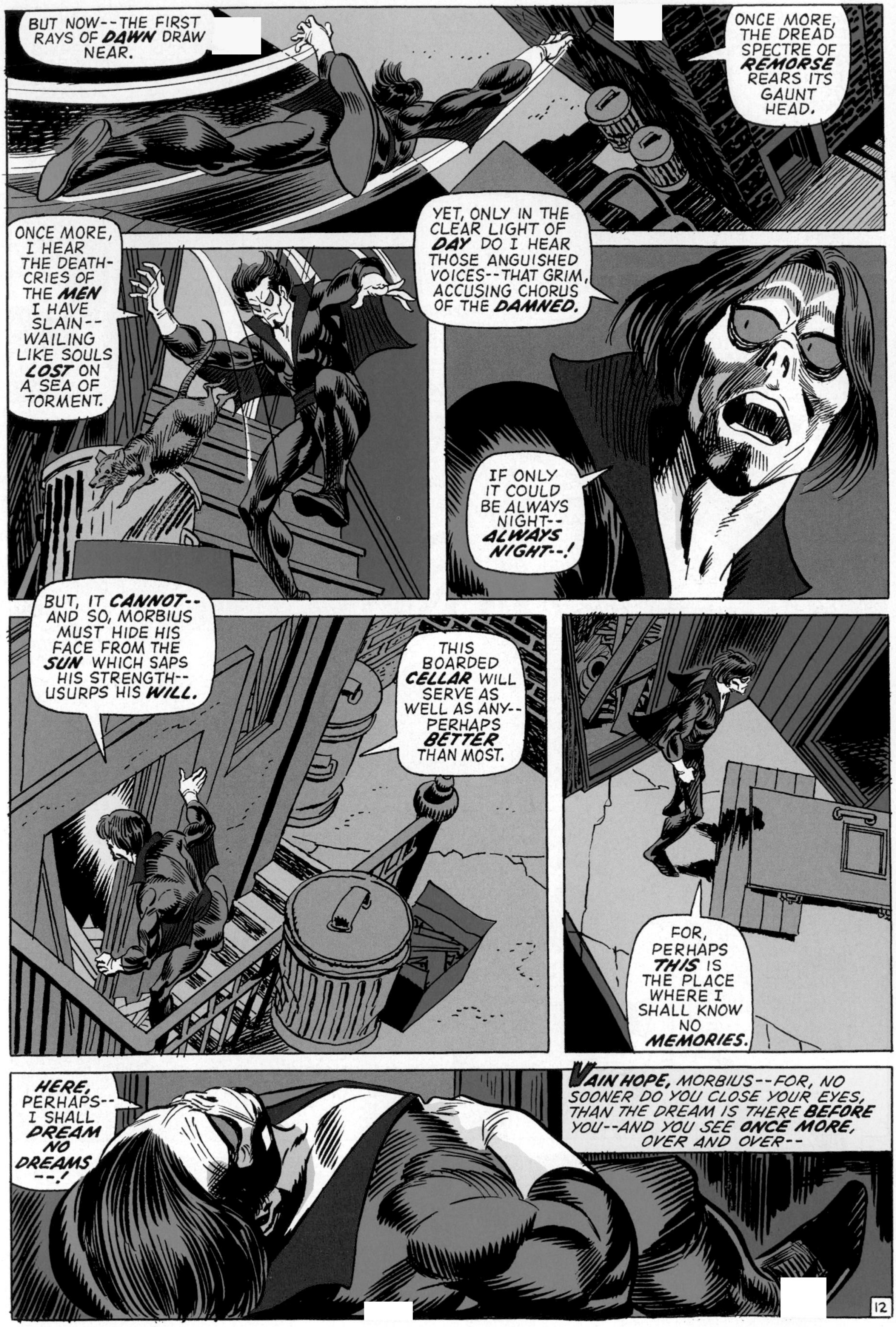

BUT NOW--THE FIRST RAYS OF DAWN DRAW NEAR.
ONCE MORE, THE DREAD SPECTRE OF REMORSE REARS ITS GAUNT HEAD.
ONCE MORE, I HEAR THE DEATH-CRIES OF THE MEN I HAVE SLAIN--WAILING LIKE SOULS LOST ON A SEA OF TORMENT.
YET, ONLY IN THE CLEAR LIGHT OF DAY DO I HEAR THOSE ANGUISHED VOICES--THAT GRIM, ACCUSING CHORUS OF THE DAMNED.
IF ONLY IT COULD BE ALWAYS NIGHT--ALWAYS NIGHT--!
BUT, IT CANNOT--AND SO, MORBIUS MUST HIDE HIS FACE FROM THE SUN WHICH SAPS HIS STRENGTH--USURPS HIS WILL.
THIS BOARDED CELLAR WILL SERVE AS WELL AS ANY--PERHAPS BETTER THAN MOST.
FOR, PERHAPS THIS IS THE PLACE WHERE I SHALL KNOW NO MEMORIES.
HERE, PERHAPS--I SHALL DREAM NO DREAMS--!
VAIN HOPE, MORBIUS--FOR, NO SOONER DO YOU CLOSE YOUR EYES, THAN THE DREAM IS THERE BEFORE YOU--AND YOU SEE ONCE MORE, OVER AND OVER--
12

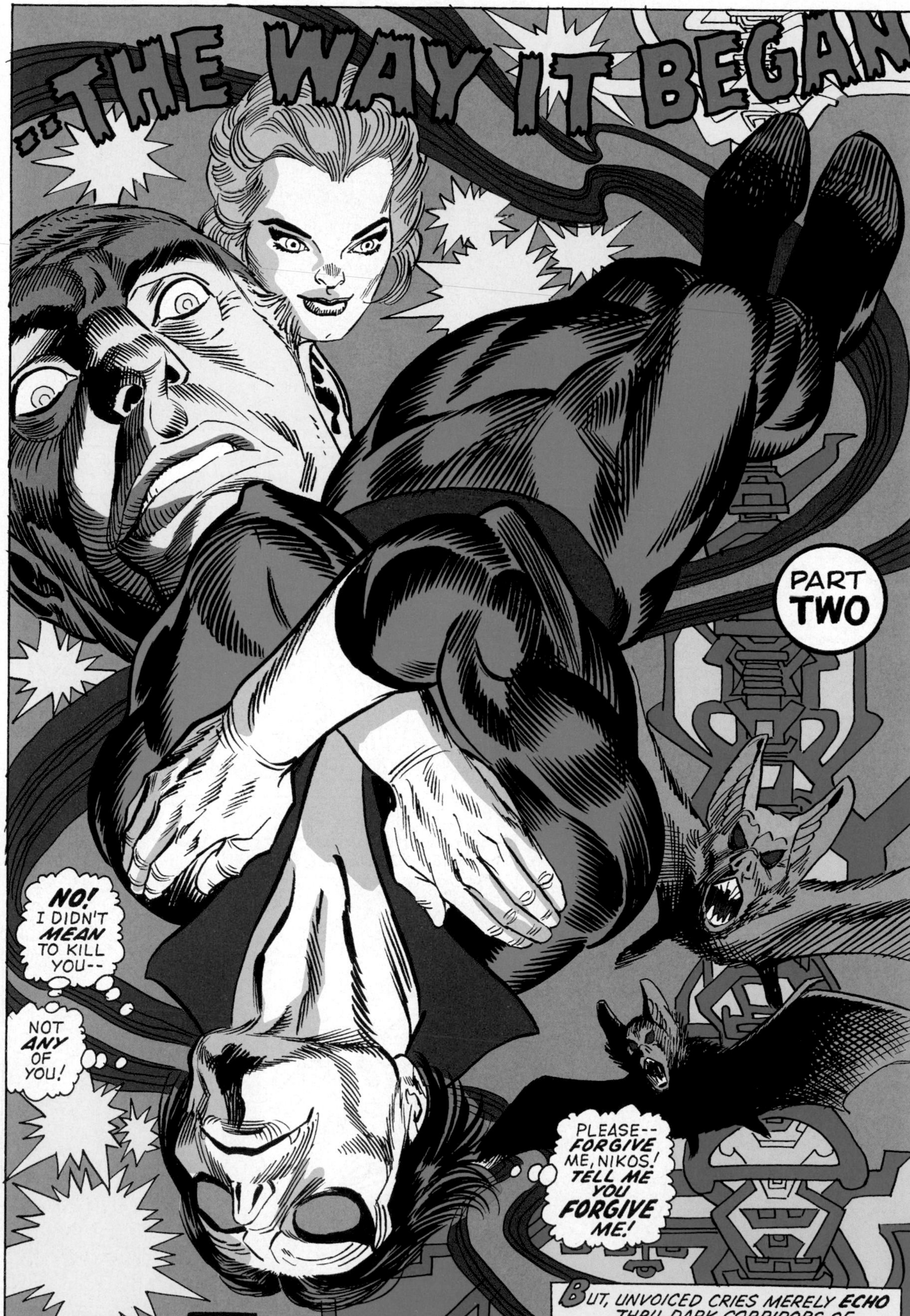

..THE WAY IT BEGAN
PART TWO
NO! I DIDN'T MEAN TO KILL YOU--
NOT ANY OF YOU!
PLEASE-- FORGIVE ME, NIKOS! TELL ME YOU FORGIVE ME!
BUT, UNVOICED CRIES MERELY ECHO THRU DARK CORRIDORS OF UNRELENTING THOUGHT--
13

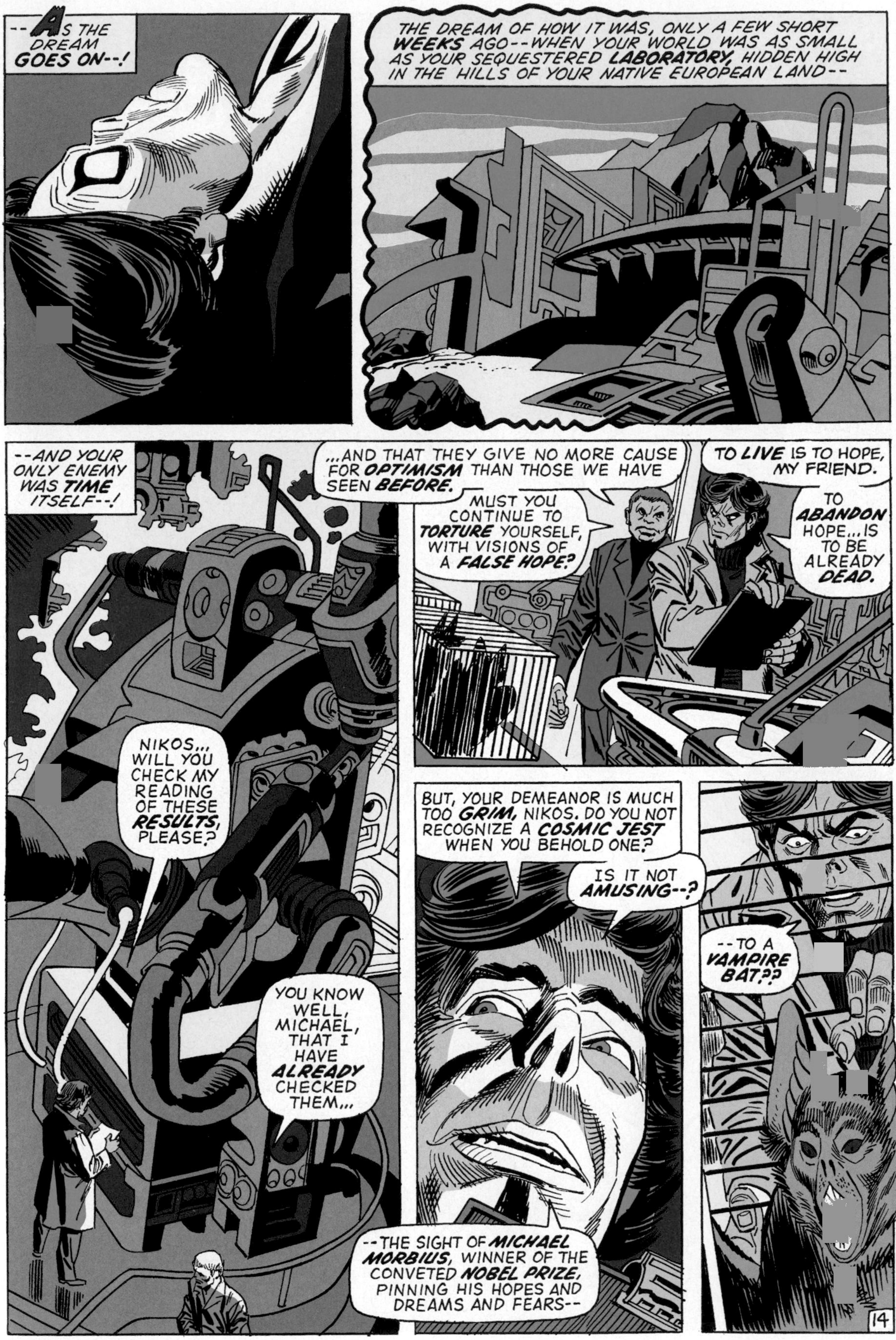
--AS THE DREAM GOES ON--!
THE DREAM OF HOW IT WAS, ONLY A FEW SHORT WEEKS AGO--WHEN YOUR WORLD WAS AS SMALL AS YOUR SEQUESTERED LABORATORY, HIDDEN HIGH IN THE HILLS OF YOUR NATIVE EUROPEAN LAND--
--AND YOUR ONLY ENEMY WAS TIME ITSELF--!
NIKOS... WILL YOU CHECK MY READING OF THESE RESULTS, PLEASE?
YOU KNOW WELL, MICHAEL, THAT I HAVE ALREADY CHECKED THEM...
...AND THAT THEY GIVE NO MORE CAUSE FOR OPTIMISM THAN THOSE WE HAVE SEEN BEFORE.
MUST YOU CONTINUE TO TORTURE YOURSELF, WITH VISIONS OF A FALSE HOPE?
TO LIVE IS TO HOPE, MY FRIEND.
TO ABANDON HOPE... IS TO BE ALREADY DEAD.
BUT, YOUR DEMEANOR IS MUCH TOO GRIM, NIKOS. DO YOU NOT RECOGNIZE A COSMIC JEST WHEN YOU BEHOLD ONE?
IS IT NOT AMUSING--?
--THE SIGHT OF MICHAEL MORBIUS, WINNER OF THE CONVETED NOBEL PRIZE, PINNING HIS HOPES AND DREAMS AND FEARS--
--TO A VAMPIRE BAT??
14

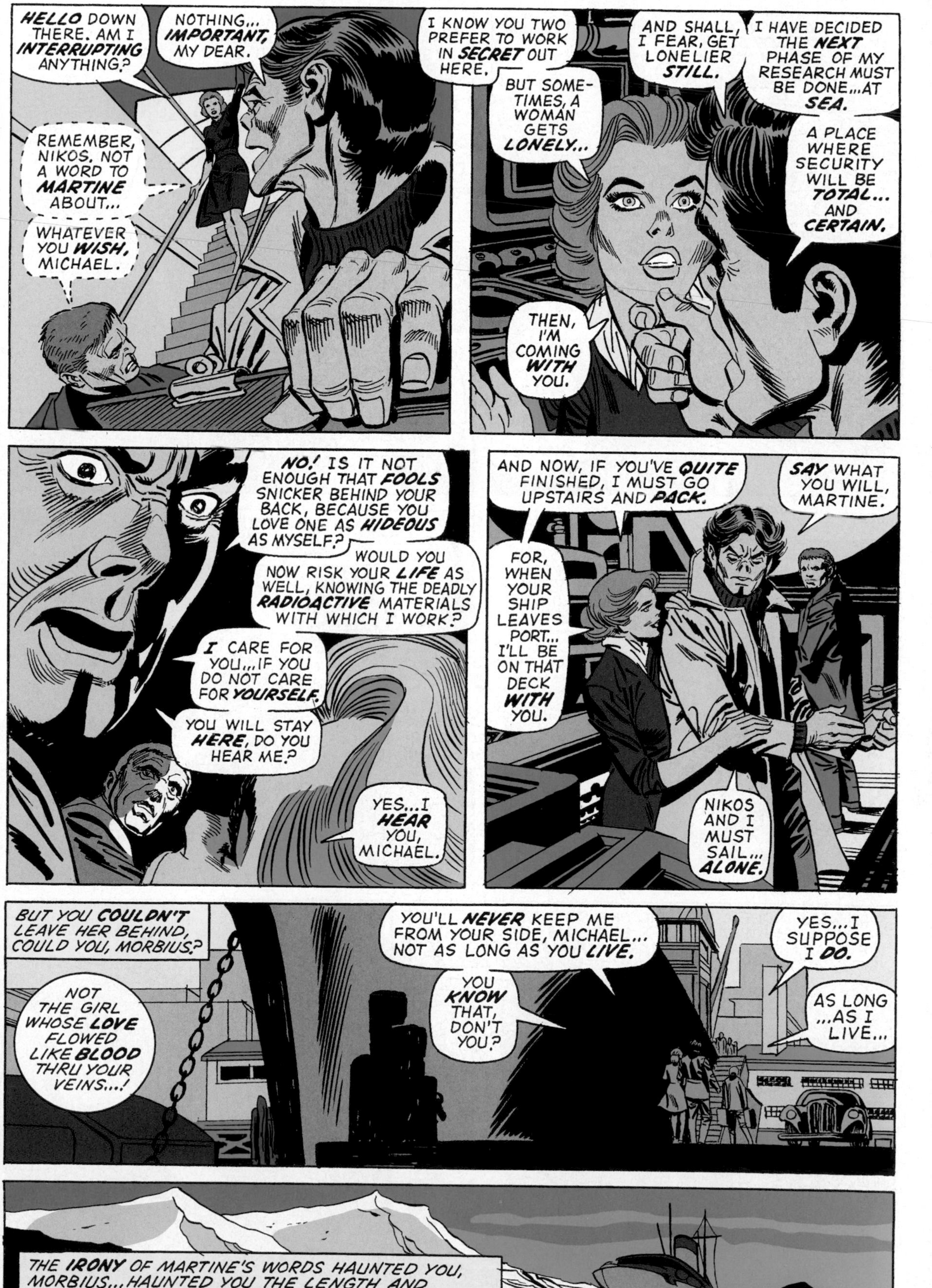
HELLO DOWN THERE. AM I INTERRUPTING ANYTHING?
NOTHING... IMPORTANT, MY DEAR.
REMEMBER, NIKOS. NOT A WORD TO MARTINE ABOUT...
WHATEVER YOU WISH, MICHAEL.
I KNOW YOU TWO PREFER TO WORK IN SECRET OUT HERE.
BUT SOMETIMES, A WOMAN GETS LONELY...
AND SHALL, I FEAR, GET LONELIER STILL.
I HAVE DECIDED THE NEXT PHASE OF MY RESEARCH MUST BE DONE...AT SEA.
A PLACE WHERE SECURITY WILL BE TOTAL... AND CERTAIN.
THEN, I'M COMING WITH YOU.
NO! IS IT NOT ENOUGH THAT FOOLS SNICKER BEHIND YOUR BACK, BECAUSE YOU LOVE ONE AS HIDEOUS AS MYSELF?
WOULD YOU NOW RISK YOUR LIFE AS WELL, KNOWING THE DEADLY RADIOACTIVE MATERIALS WITH WHICH I WORK?
I CARE FOR YOU...IF YOU DO NOT CARE FOR YOURSELF.
YOU WILL STAY HERE, DO YOU HEAR ME?
YES...I HEAR YOU, MICHAEL.
AND NOW, IF YOU'VE QUITE FINISHED, I MUST GO UPSTAIRS AND PACK.
SAY WHAT YOU WILL, MARTINE.
FOR, WHEN YOUR SHIP LEAVES PORT... I'LL BE ON THAT DECK WITH YOU.
NIKOS AND I MUST SAIL... ALONE.
BUT YOU COULDN'T LEAVE HER BEHIND, COULD YOU, MORBIUS?
NOT THE GIRL WHOSE LOVE FLOWED LIKE BLOOD THRU YOUR VEINS...!
YOU'LL NEVER KEEP ME FROM YOUR SIDE, MICHAEL... NOT AS LONG AS YOU LIVE.
YOU KNOW THAT, DON'T YOU?
YES...I SUPPOSE I DO.
AS LONG ...AS I LIVE...
THE IRONY OF MARTINE'S WORDS HAUNTED YOU, MORBIUS...HAUNTED YOU THE LENGTH AND BREADTH OF THE SUN-DRENCHED MEDITERRANEAN...
15

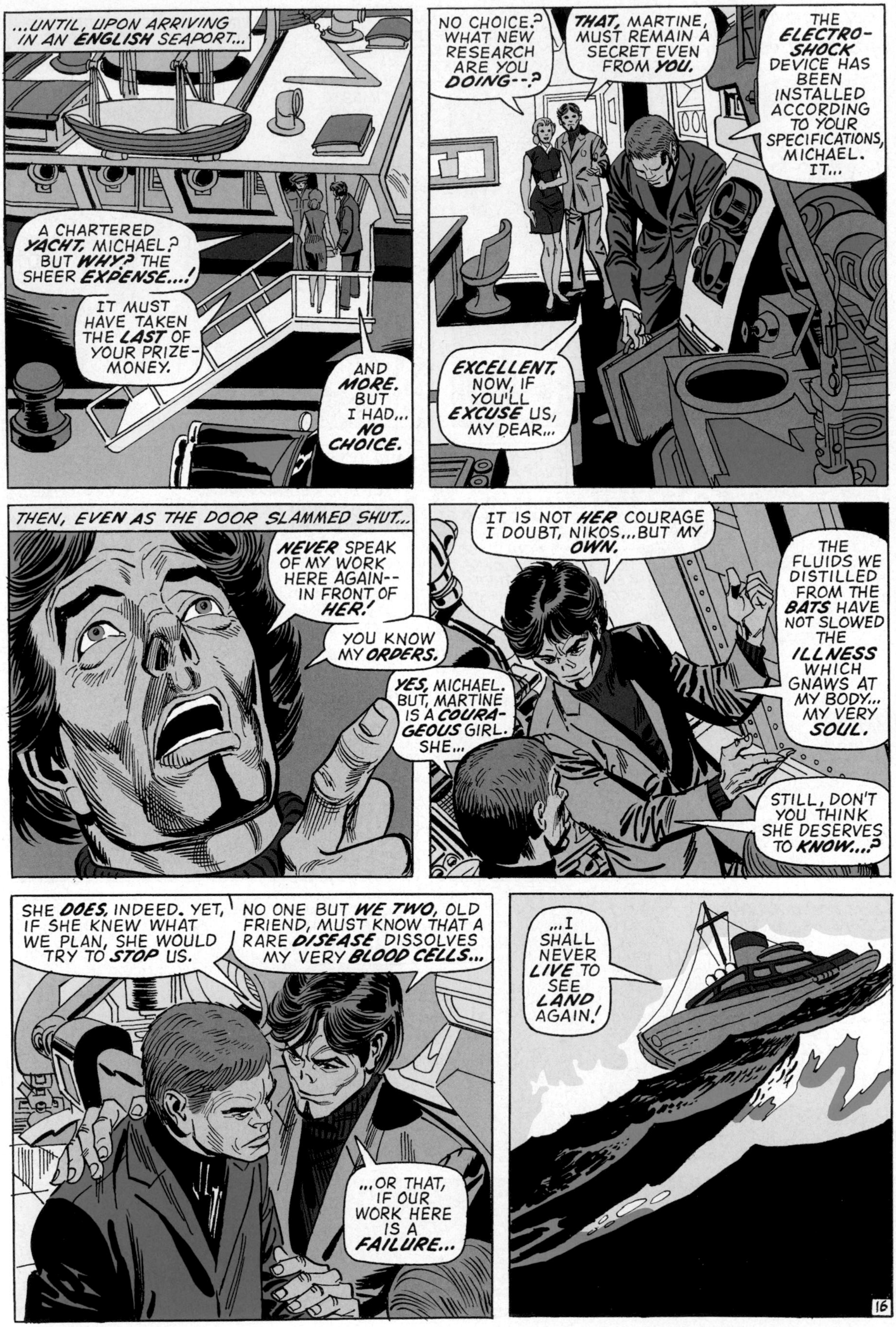

...UNTIL, UPON ARRIVING IN AN ENGLISH SEAPORT...
A CHARTERED YACHT, MICHAEL? BUT WHY? THE SHEER EXPENSE...!
IT MUST HAVE TAKEN THE LAST OF YOUR PRIZE-MONEY.
AND MORE. BUT I HAD... NO CHOICE.
NO CHOICE? WHAT NEW RESEARCH ARE YOU DOING--?
THAT, MARTINE, MUST REMAIN A SECRET EVEN FROM YOU.
THE ELECTRO-SHOCK DEVICE HAS BEEN INSTALLED ACCORDING TO YOUR SPECIFICATIONS, MICHAEL. IT...
EXCELLENT. NOW, IF YOU'LL EXCUSE US, MY DEAR...
THEN, EVEN AS THE DOOR SLAMMED SHUT...
NEVER SPEAK OF MY WORK HERE AGAIN--IN FRONT OF HER!
YOU KNOW MY ORDERS.
YES, MICHAEL. BUT, MARTINE IS A COURAGEOUS GIRL. SHE...
IT IS NOT HER COURAGE I DOUBT, NIKOS... BUT MY OWN.
THE FLUIDS WE DISTILLED FROM THE BATS HAVE NOT SLOWED THE ILLNESS WHICH GNAWS AT MY BODY... MY VERY SOUL.
STILL, DON'T YOU THINK SHE DESERVES TO KNOW...?
SHE DOES, INDEED. YET, IF SHE KNEW WHAT WE PLAN, SHE WOULD TRY TO STOP US.
NO ONE BUT WE TWO, OLD FRIEND, MUST KNOW THAT A RARE DISEASE DISSOLVES MY VERY BLOOD CELLS...
...OR THAT, IF OUR WORK HERE IS A FAILURE...
...I SHALL NEVER LIVE TO SEE LAND AGAIN!
16

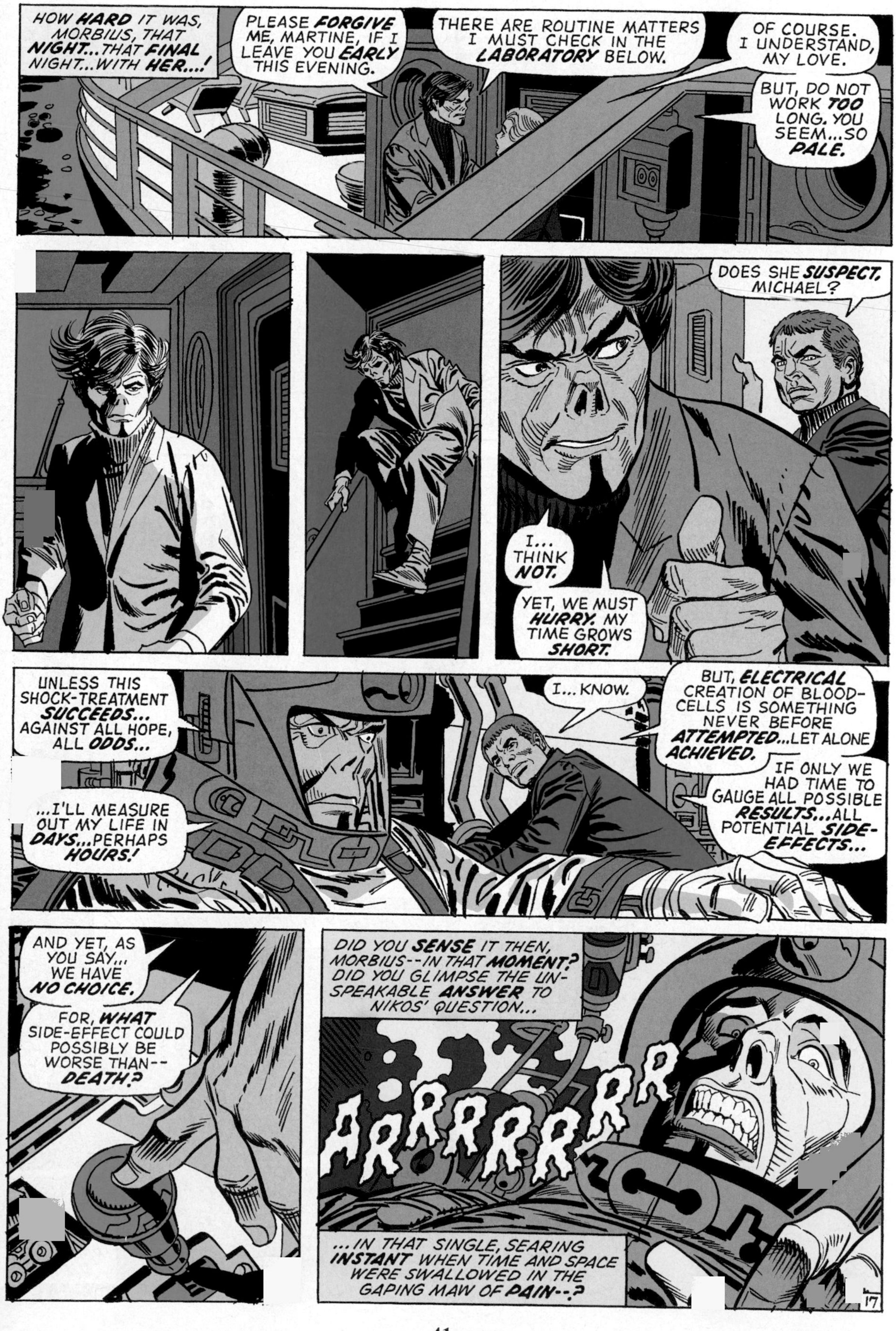
HOW HARD IT WAS, MORBIUS, THAT NIGHT...THAT FINAL NIGHT...WITH HER...!
PLEASE FORGIVE ME, MARTINE, IF I LEAVE YOU EARLY THIS EVENING.
THERE ARE ROUTINE MATTERS I MUST CHECK IN THE LABORATORY BELOW.
OF COURSE. I UNDERSTAND, MY LOVE.
BUT, DO NOT WORK TOO LONG. YOU SEEM...SO PALE.
DOES SHE SUSPECT, MICHAEL?
I... THINK NOT.
YET, WE MUST HURRY. MY TIME GROWS SHORT.
UNLESS THIS SHOCK-TREATMENT SUCCEEDS... AGAINST ALL HOPE, ALL ODDS...
...I'LL MEASURE OUT MY LIFE IN DAYS...PERHAPS HOURS!
I... KNOW.
BUT, ELECTRICAL CREATION OF BLOOD-CELLS IS SOMETHING NEVER BEFORE ATTEMPTED...LET ALONE ACHIEVED.
IF ONLY WE HAD TIME TO GAUGE ALL POSSIBLE RESULTS...ALL POTENTIAL SIDE-EFFECTS...
AND YET, AS YOU SAY... WE HAVE NO CHOICE.
FOR, WHAT SIDE-EFFECT COULD POSSIBLY BE WORSE THAN--DEATH?
DID YOU SENSE IT THEN, MORBIUS--IN THAT MOMENT? DID YOU GLIMPSE THE UNSPEAKABLE ANSWER TO NIKOS' QUESTION...
ARRRRRRRR
...IN THAT SINGLE, SEARING INSTANT WHEN TIME AND SPACE WERE SWALLOWED IN THE GAPING MAW OF PAIN--?
17

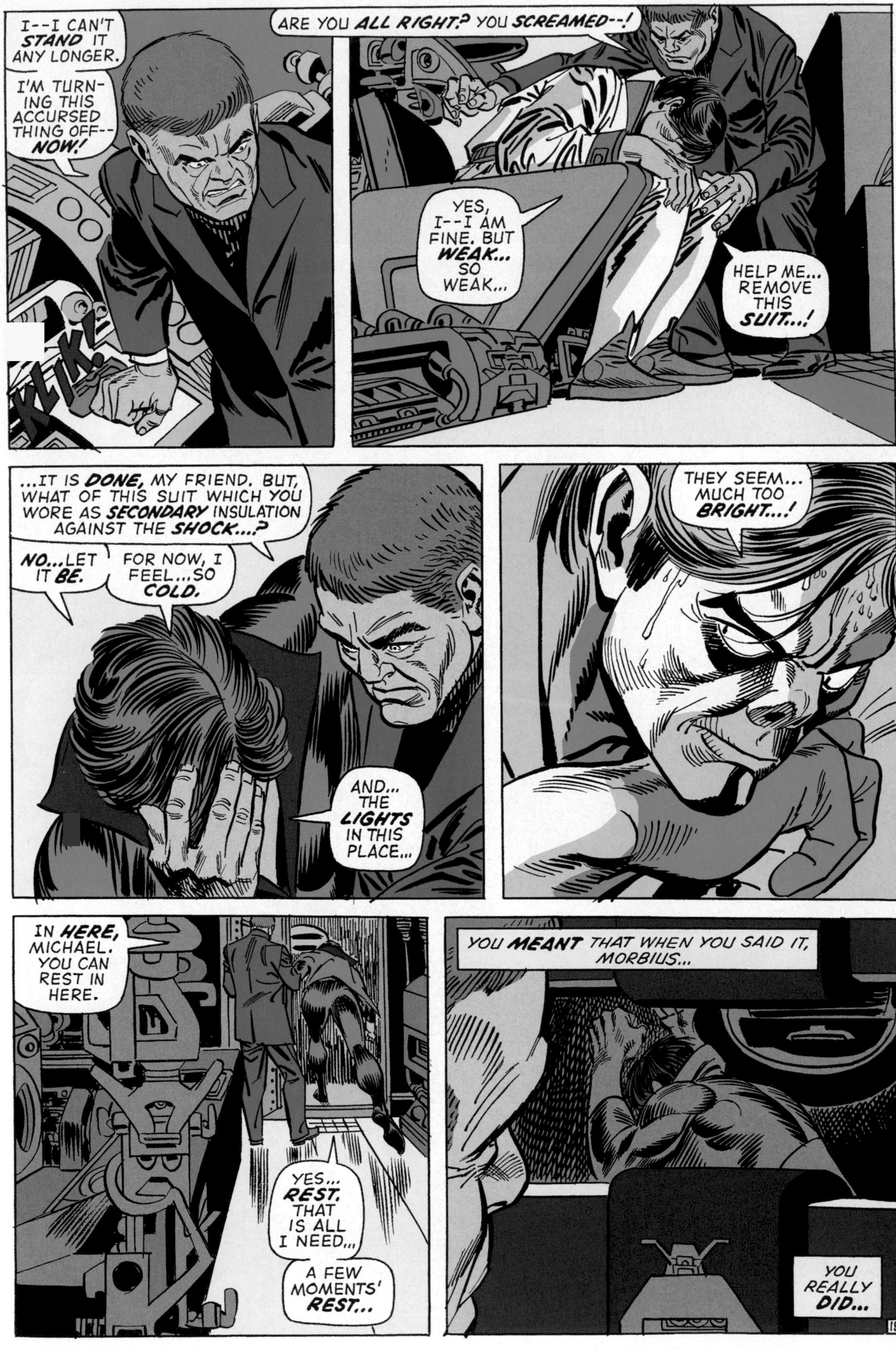
I--I CAN'T STAND IT ANY LONGER.
I'M TURNING THIS ACCURSED THING OFF-- NOW!
KLIK!
ARE YOU ALL RIGHT? YOU SCREAMED--!
YES, I--I AM FINE. BUT WEAK... SO WEAK...
HELP ME... REMOVE THIS SUIT...!
...IT IS DONE, MY FRIEND. BUT, WHAT OF THIS SUIT WHICH YOU WORE AS SECONDARY INSULATION AGAINST THE SHOCK...?
NO...LET IT BE.
FOR NOW, I FEEL...SO COLD.
AND... THE LIGHTS IN THIS PLACE...
THEY SEEM... MUCH TOO BRIGHT...!
IN HERE, MICHAEL. YOU CAN REST IN HERE.
YES... REST. THAT IS ALL I NEED...
A FEW MOMENTS' REST...
YOU MEANT THAT WHEN YOU SAID IT, MORBIUS...
YOU REALLY DID...
18

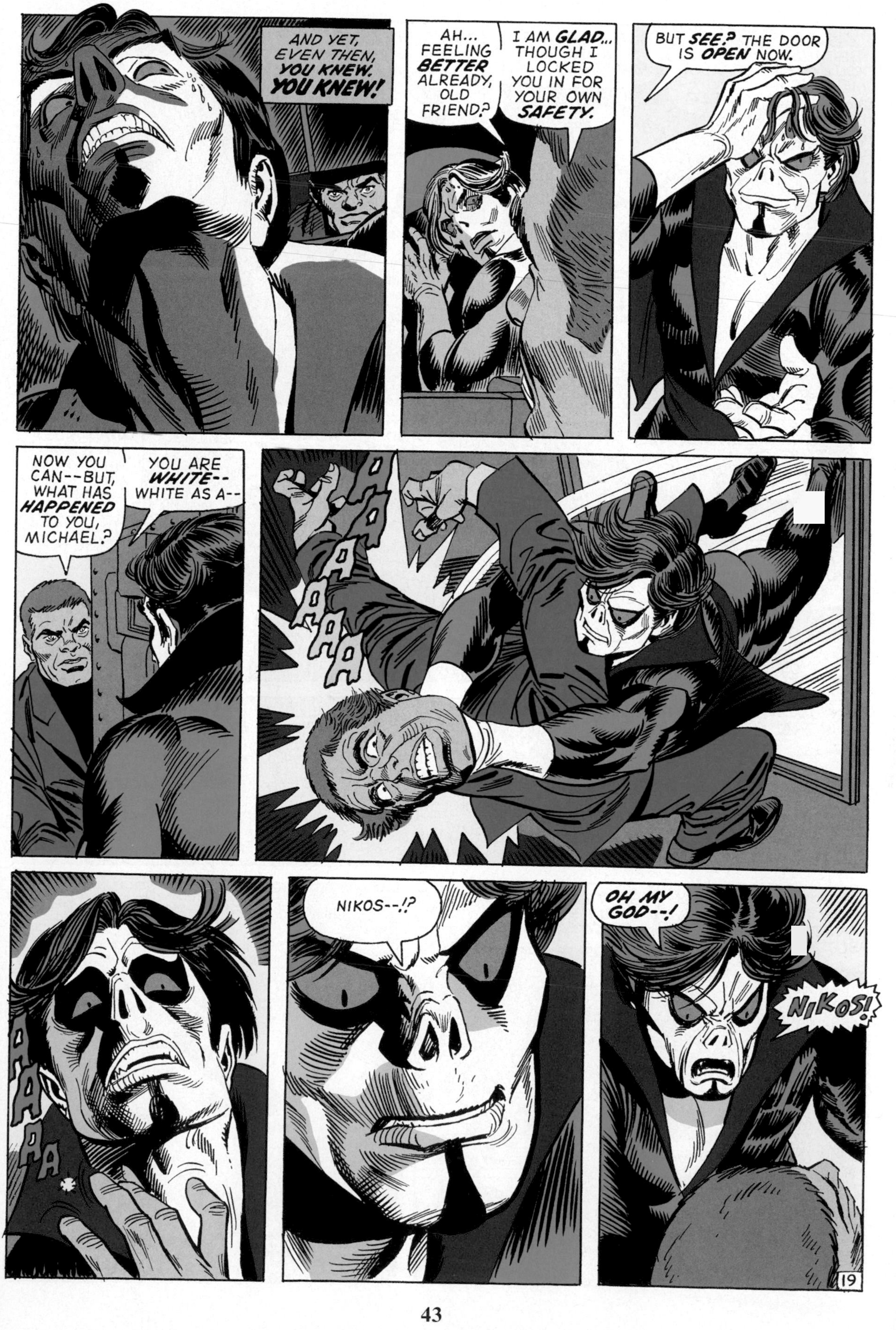
AND YET, EVEN THEN, YOU KNEW. YOU KNEW!
AH... FEELING BETTER ALREADY, OLD FRIEND?
I AM GLAD... THOUGH I LOCKED YOU IN FOR YOUR OWN SAFETY.
BUT SEE? THE DOOR IS OPEN NOW.
NOW YOU CAN--BUT, WHAT HAS HAPPENED TO YOU, MICHAEL?
YOU ARE WHITE--WHITE AS A--
NIKOS--!?
OH MY GOD--!
NIKOS!
19

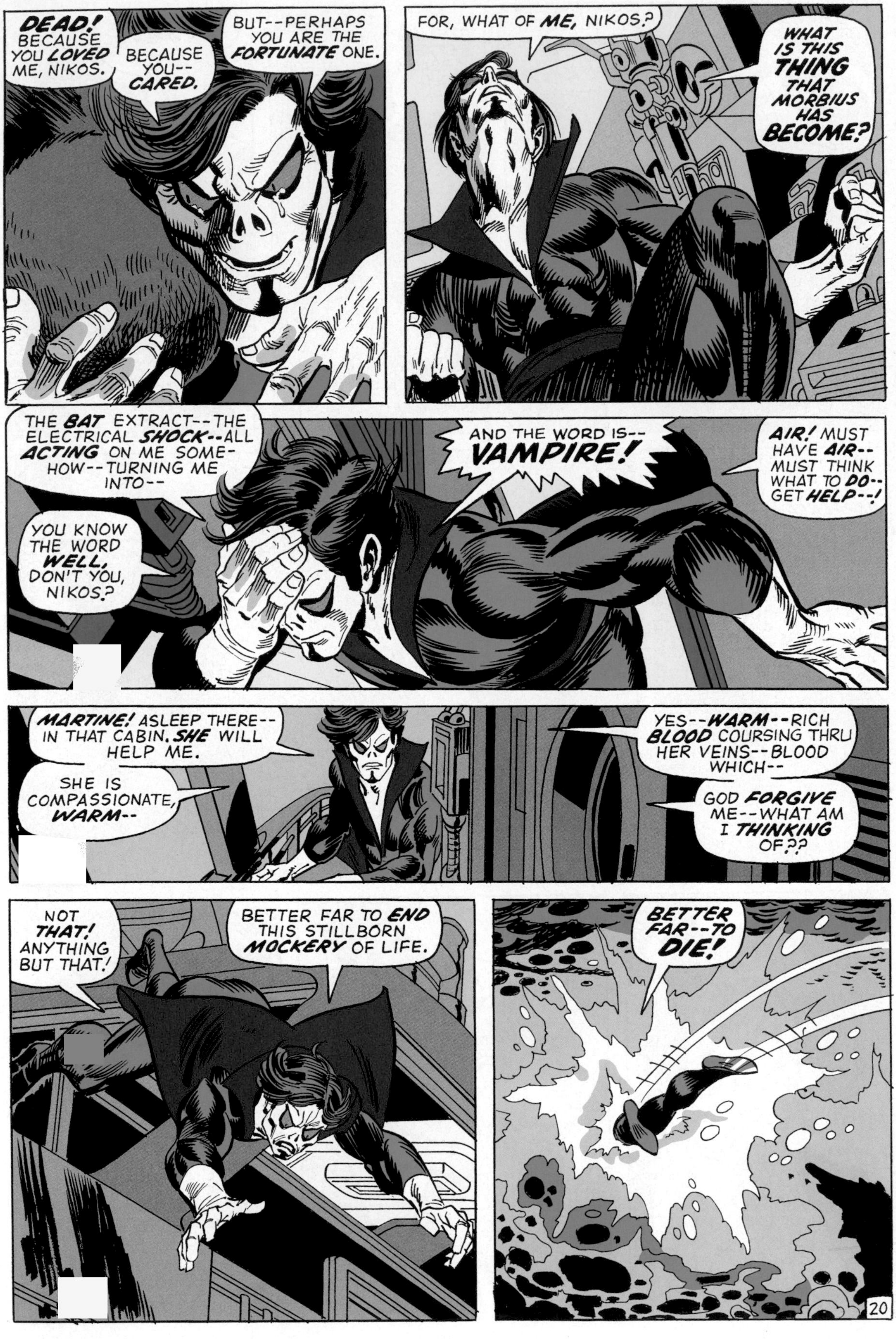
DEAD! BECAUSE YOU LOVED ME, NIKOS.
BECAUSE YOU--CARED.
BUT--PERHAPS YOU ARE THE FORTUNATE ONE.
FOR, WHAT OF ME, NIKOS?
WHAT IS THIS THING THAT MORBIUS HAS BECOME?
THE BAT EXTRACT--THE ELECTRICAL SHOCK--ALL ACTING ON ME SOMEHOW--TURNING ME INTO--
YOU KNOW THE WORD WELL, DON'T YOU, NIKOS?
AND THE WORD IS--VAMPIRE!
AIR! MUST HAVE AIR--MUST THINK WHAT TO DO--GET HELP--!
MARTINE! ASLEEP THERE--IN THAT CABIN. SHE WILL HELP ME.
SHE IS COMPASSIONATE, WARM--
YES--WARM--RICH BLOOD COURSING THRU HER VEINS--BLOOD WHICH--
GOD FORGIVE ME--WHAT AM I THINKING OF??
NOT THAT! ANYTHING BUT THAT!
BETTER FAR TO END THIS STILLBORN MOCKERY OF LIFE.
BETTER FAR--TO DIE!
20

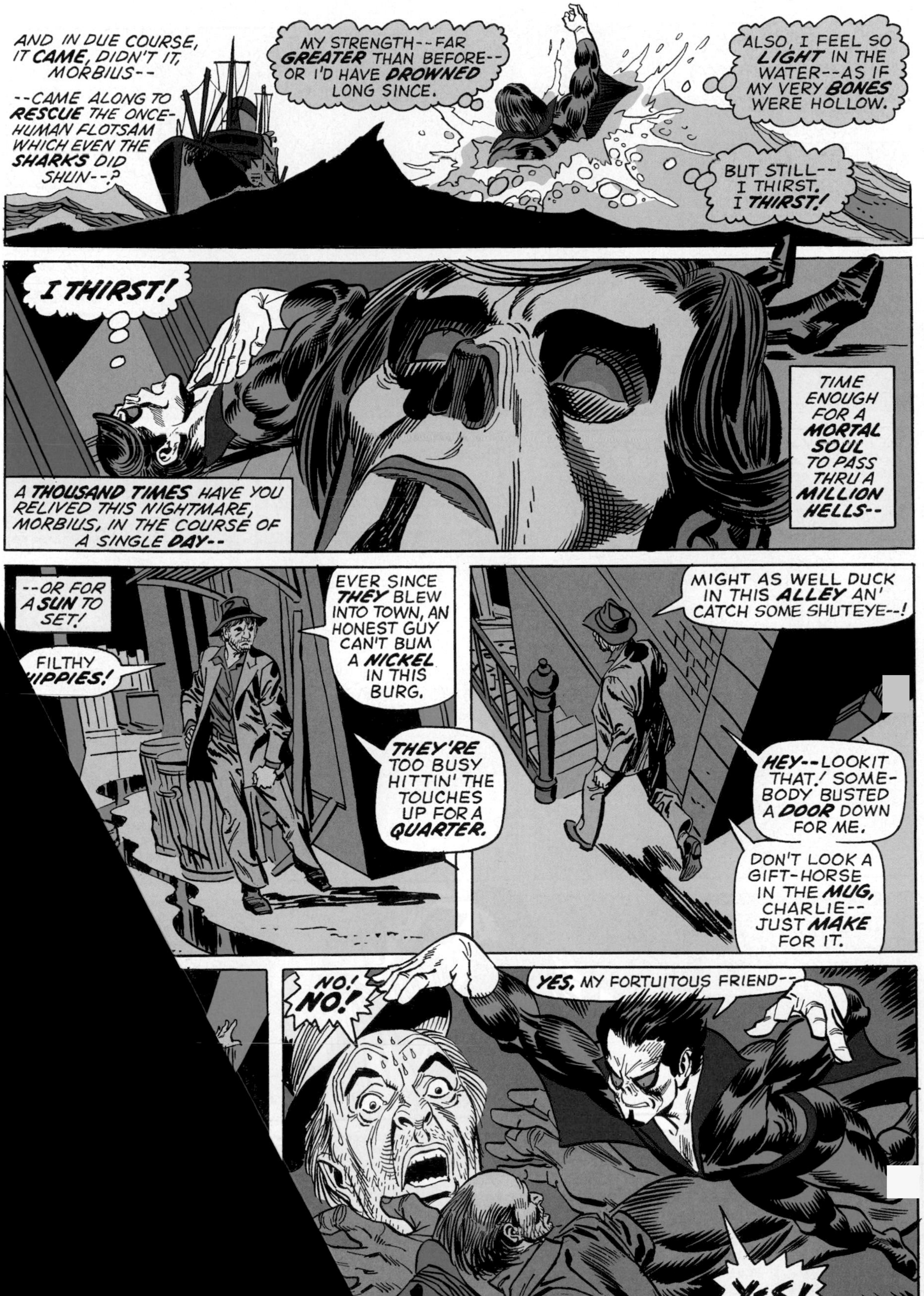

AND IN DUE COURSE, IT CAME, DIDN'T IT, MORBIUS--
--CAME ALONG TO RESCUE THE ONCE-HUMAN FLOTSAM WHICH EVEN THE SHARKS DID SHUN--?
MY STRENGTH--FAR GREATER THAN BEFORE--OR I'D HAVE DROWNED LONG SINCE.
ALSO, I FEEL SO LIGHT IN THE WATER--AS IF MY VERY BONES WERE HOLLOW.
BUT STILL--I THIRST. I THIRST!
I THIRST!
TIME ENOUGH FOR A MORTAL SOUL TO PASS THRU A MILLION HELLS--
A THOUSAND TIMES HAVE YOU RELIVED THIS NIGHTMARE, MORBIUS, IN THE COURSE OF A SINGLE DAY--
--OR FOR A SUN TO SET!
FILTHY [redacted]IPPIES!
EVER SINCE THEY BLEW INTO TOWN, AN HONEST GUY CAN'T BUM A NICKEL IN THIS BURG.
THEY'RE TOO BUSY HITTIN' THE TOUCHES UP FOR A QUARTER.
MIGHT AS WELL DUCK IN THIS ALLEY AN' CATCH SOME SHUTEYE--!
HEY--LOOKIT THAT! SOMEBODY BUSTED A DOOR DOWN FOR ME.
DON'T LOOK A GIFT-HORSE IN THE MUG, CHARLIE--JUST MAKE FOR IT.
NO! NO!
YES, MY FORTUITOUS FRIEND--
YES!
22

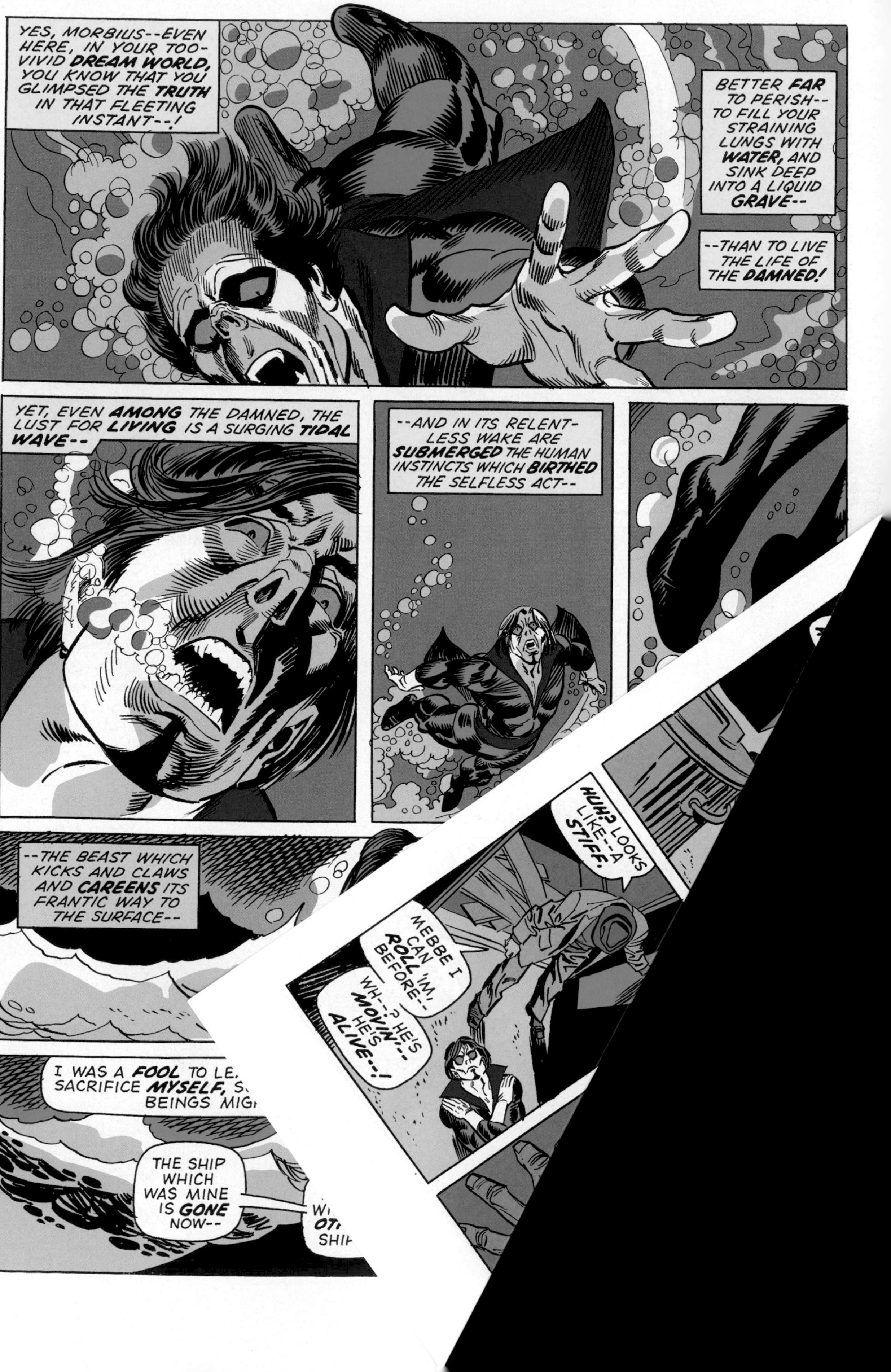
YES, MORBIUS--EVEN HERE, IN YOUR TOO-VIVID DREAM WORLD, YOU KNOW THAT YOU GLIMPSED THE TRUTH IN THAT FLEETING INSTANT--!
BETTER FAR TO PERISH--TO FILL YOUR STRAINING LUNGS WITH WATER, AND SINK DEEP INTO A LIQUID GRAVE--
--THAN TO LIVE THE LIFE OF THE DAMNED!
YET, EVEN AMONG THE DAMNED, THE LUST FOR LIVING IS A SURGING TIDAL WAVE--
--AND IN ITS RELENTLESS WAKE ARE SUBMERGED THE HUMAN INSTINCTS WHICH BIRTHED THE SELFLESS ACT--
--THE BEAST WHICH KICKS AND CLAWS AND CAREENS ITS FRANTIC WAY TO THE SURFACE--
I WAS A FOOL TO
SACRIFICE MYSELF,
BEINGS
THE SHIP WHICH WAS MINE IS GONE NOW--
HUH? LOOKS LIKE--A STIFF.
MEBBE I CAN ROLL 'IM, BEFORE--
WH--? HE'S MOVIN'--HE'S ALIVE--!

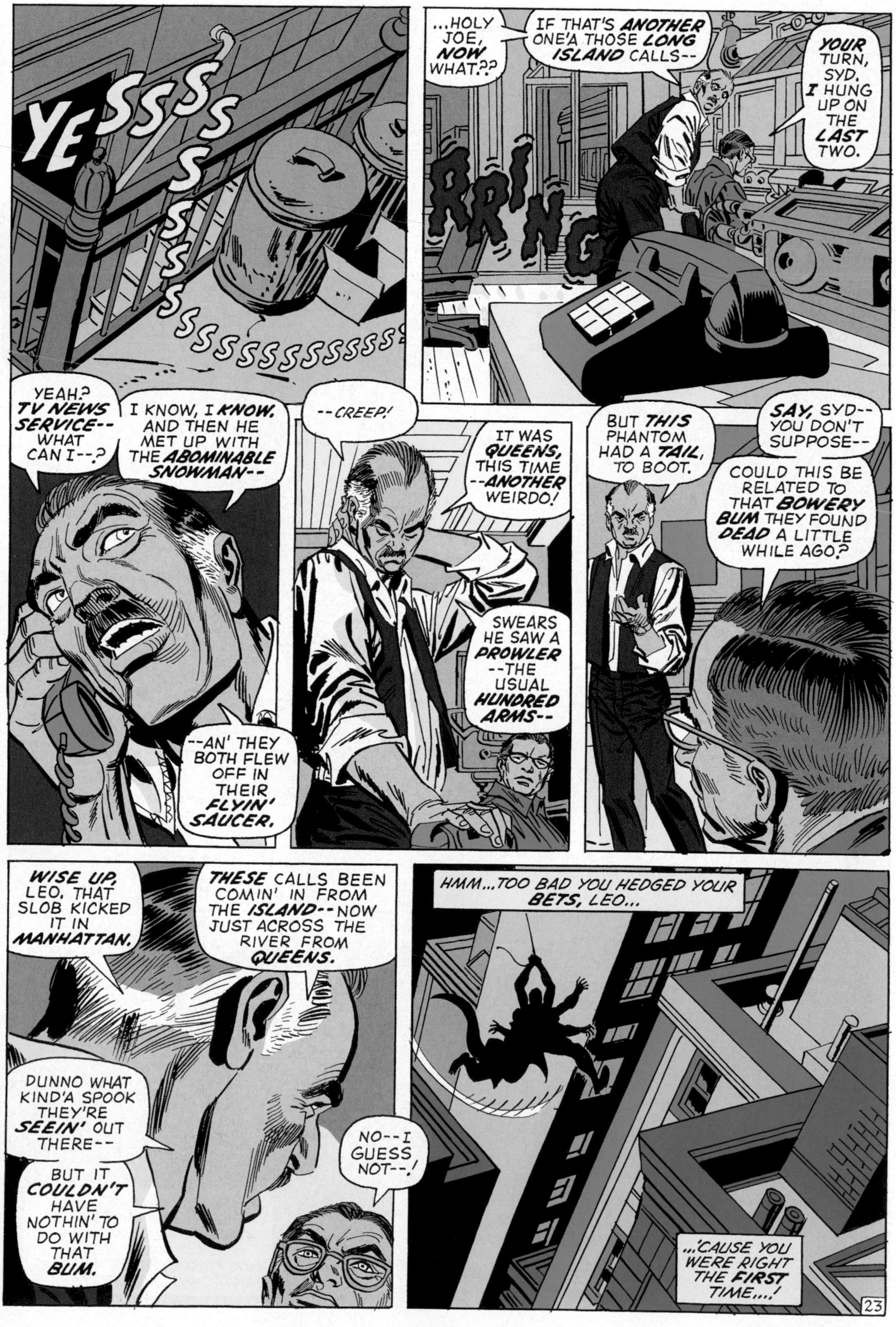
YESSSSSSSSSSSSSSSSSSSSSSSS
...HOLY JOE, NOW WHAT??
IF THAT'S ANOTHER ONE'A THOSE LONG ISLAND CALLS--
YOUR TURN, SYD. I HUNG UP ON THE LAST TWO.
RRING
YEAH? TV NEWS SERVICE-- WHAT CAN I--?
I KNOW, I KNOW. AND THEN HE MET UP WITH THE ABOMINABLE SNOWMAN--
--AN' THEY BOTH FLEW OFF IN THEIR FLYIN' SAUCER.
--CREEP!
IT WAS QUEENS, THIS TIME --ANOTHER WEIRDO!
SWEARS HE SAW A PROWLER --THE USUAL HUNDRED ARMS--
BUT THIS PHANTOM HAD A TAIL, TO BOOT.
SAY, SYD-- YOU DON'T SUPPOSE--
COULD THIS BE RELATED TO THAT BOWERY BUM THEY FOUND DEAD A LITTLE WHILE AGO?
WISE UP, LEO. THAT SLOB KICKED IT IN MANHATTAN.
THESE CALLS BEEN COMIN' IN FROM THE ISLAND--NOW JUST ACROSS THE RIVER FROM QUEENS.
DUNNO WHAT KIND'A SPOOK THEY'RE SEEIN' OUT THERE--
BUT IT COULDN'T HAVE NOTHIN' TO DO WITH THAT BUM.
NO--I GUESS NOT--!
HMM...TOO BAD YOU HEDGED YOUR BETS, LEO...
...'CAUSE YOU WERE RIGHT THE FIRST TIME...!
23

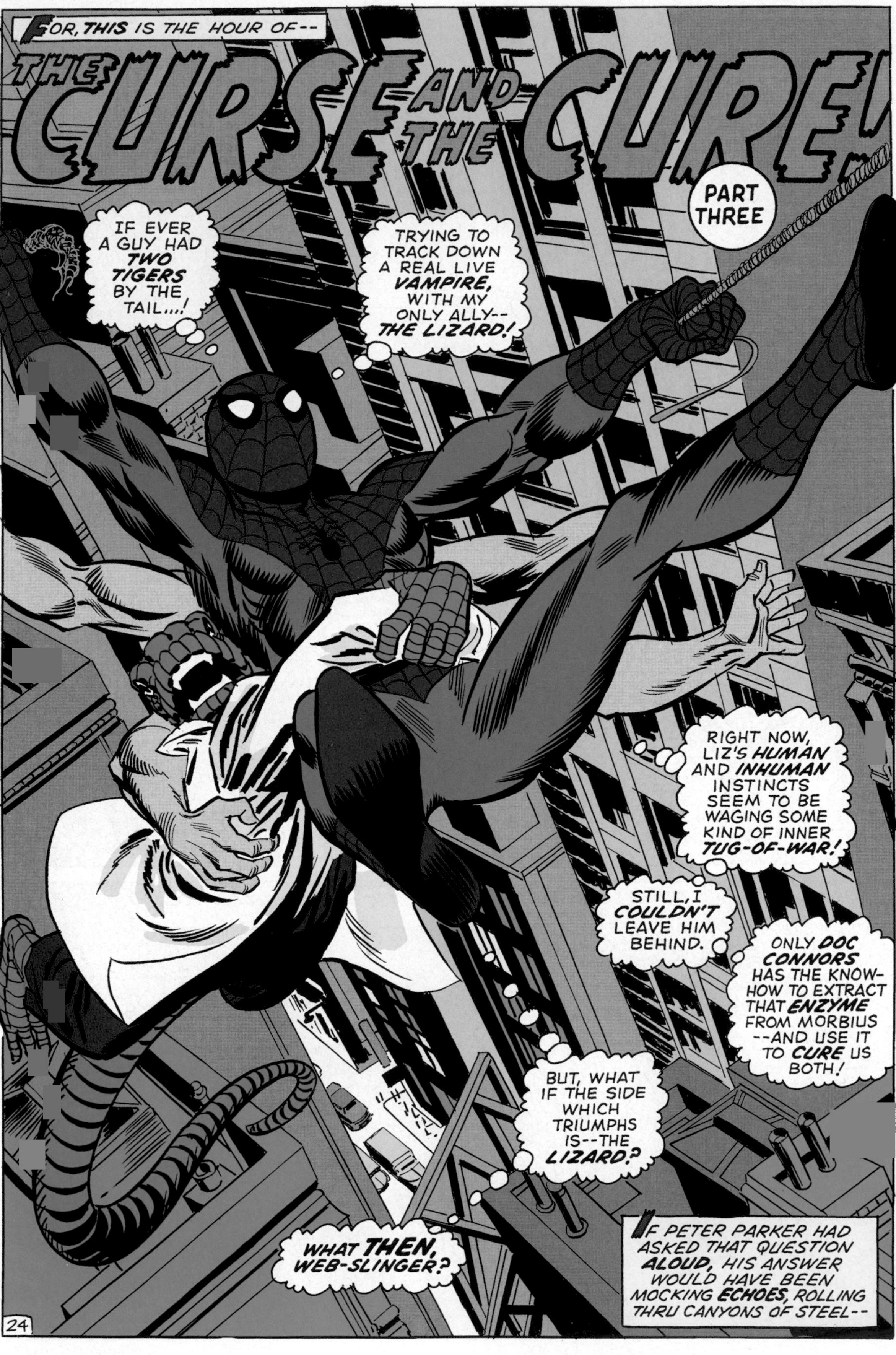

FOR, THIS IS THE HOUR OF--
THE CURSE AND THE CURE!
PART THREE
IF EVER A GUY HAD TWO TIGERS BY THE TAIL....!
TRYING TO TRACK DOWN A REAL LIVE VAMPIRE, WITH MY ONLY ALLY--THE LIZARD!
RIGHT NOW, LIZ'S HUMAN AND INHUMAN INSTINCTS SEEM TO BE WAGING SOME KIND OF INNER TUG-OF-WAR!
STILL, I COULDN'T LEAVE HIM BEHIND.
ONLY DOC CONNORS HAS THE KNOW-HOW TO EXTRACT THAT ENZYME FROM MORBIUS --AND USE IT TO CURE US BOTH!
BUT, WHAT IF THE SIDE WHICH TRIUMPHS IS--THE LIZARD?
WHAT THEN, WEB-SLINGER?
IF PETER PARKER HAD ASKED THAT QUESTION ALOUD, HIS ANSWER WOULD HAVE BEEN MOCKING ECHOES, ROLLING THRU CANYONS OF STEEL--
24

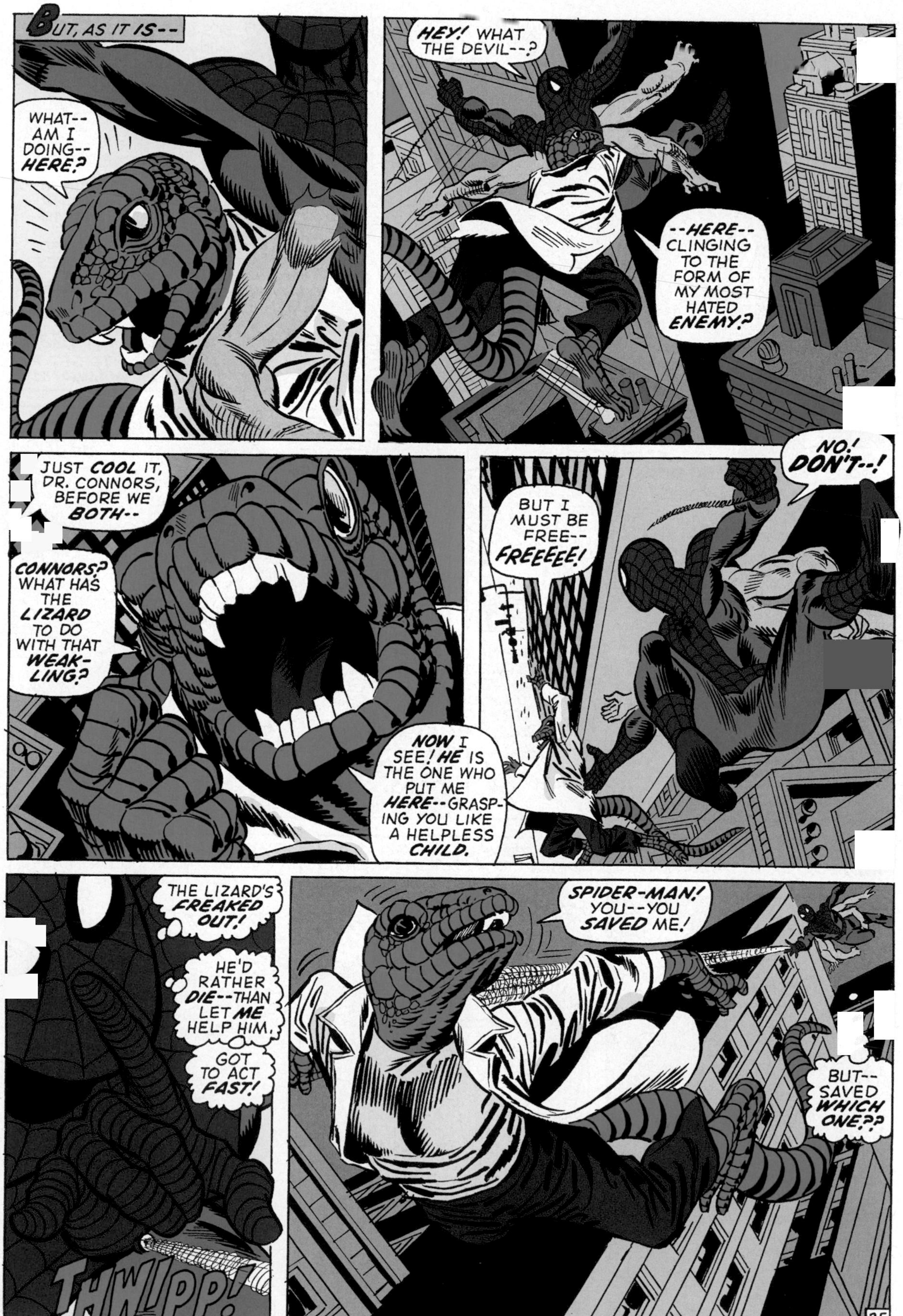
BUT, AS IT IS--
WHAT--AM I DOING--HERE?
HEY! WHAT THE DEVIL--?
--HERE--CLINGING TO THE FORM OF MY MOST HATED ENEMY?
JUST COOL IT, DR. CONNORS, BEFORE WE BOTH--
CONNORS? WHAT HAS THE LIZARD TO DO WITH THAT WEAK-LING?
BUT I MUST BE FREE--FREEEEEE!
NO! DON'T--!
NOW I SEE! HE IS THE ONE WHO PUT ME HERE--GRASP-ING YOU LIKE A HELPLESS CHILD.
THE LIZARD'S FREAKED OUT!
HE'D RATHER DIE--THAN LET ME HELP HIM.
GOT TO ACT FAST!
THWIPP!
SPIDER-MAN! YOU--YOU SAVED ME!
BUT--SAVED WHICH ONE??
25

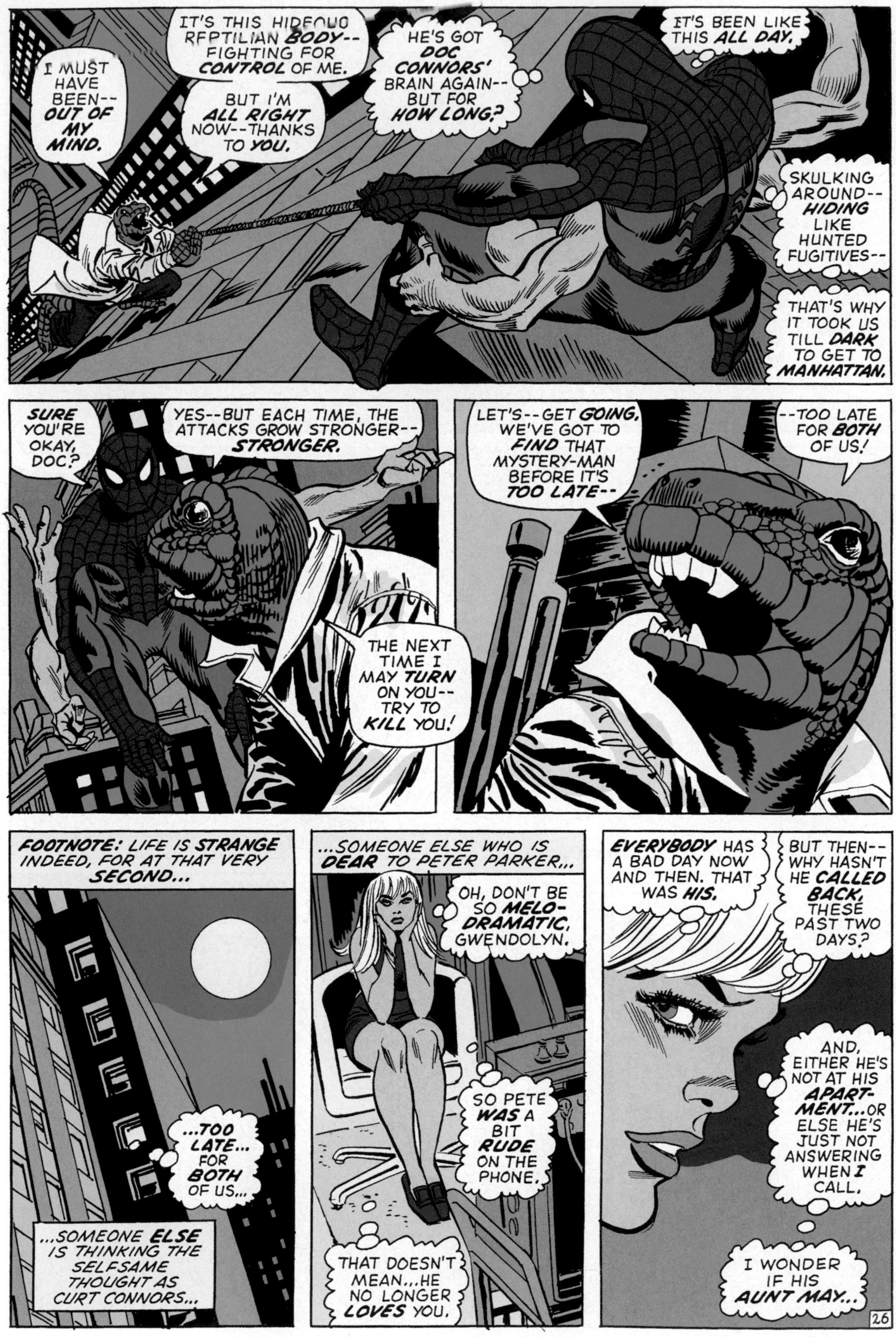
I MUST HAVE BEEN--OUT OF MY MIND.
IT'S THIS HIDEOUS REPTILIAN BODY--FIGHTING FOR CONTROL OF ME.
BUT I'M ALL RIGHT NOW--THANKS TO YOU.
HE'S GOT DOC CONNORS' BRAIN AGAIN--BUT FOR HOW LONG?
IT'S BEEN LIKE THIS ALL DAY.
SKULKING AROUND--HIDING LIKE HUNTED FUGITIVES--
THAT'S WHY IT TOOK US TILL DARK TO GET TO MANHATTAN.
SURE YOU'RE OKAY, DOC?
YES--BUT EACH TIME, THE ATTACKS GROW STRONGER--STRONGER.
THE NEXT TIME I MAY TURN ON YOU--TRY TO KILL YOU!
LET'S--GET GOING. WE'VE GOT TO FIND THAT MYSTERY-MAN BEFORE IT'S TOO LATE--
--TOO LATE FOR BOTH OF US!
FOOTNOTE: LIFE IS STRANGE INDEED, FOR AT THAT VERY SECOND...
...TOO LATE... FOR BOTH OF US...
...SOMEONE ELSE IS THINKING THE SELFSAME THOUGHT AS CURT CONNORS...
...SOMEONE ELSE WHO IS DEAR TO PETER PARKER...
OH, DON'T BE SO MELO-DRAMATIC, GWENDOLYN.
SO PETE WAS A BIT RUDE ON THE PHONE.
THAT DOESN'T MEAN...HE NO LONGER LOVES YOU.
EVERYBODY HAS A BAD DAY NOW AND THEN. THAT WAS HIS.
BUT THEN--WHY HASN'T HE CALLED BACK, THESE PAST TWO DAYS?
AND, EITHER HE'S NOT AT HIS APART-MENT...OR ELSE HE'S JUST NOT ANSWERING WHEN I CALL.
I WONDER IF HIS AUNT MAY...
26

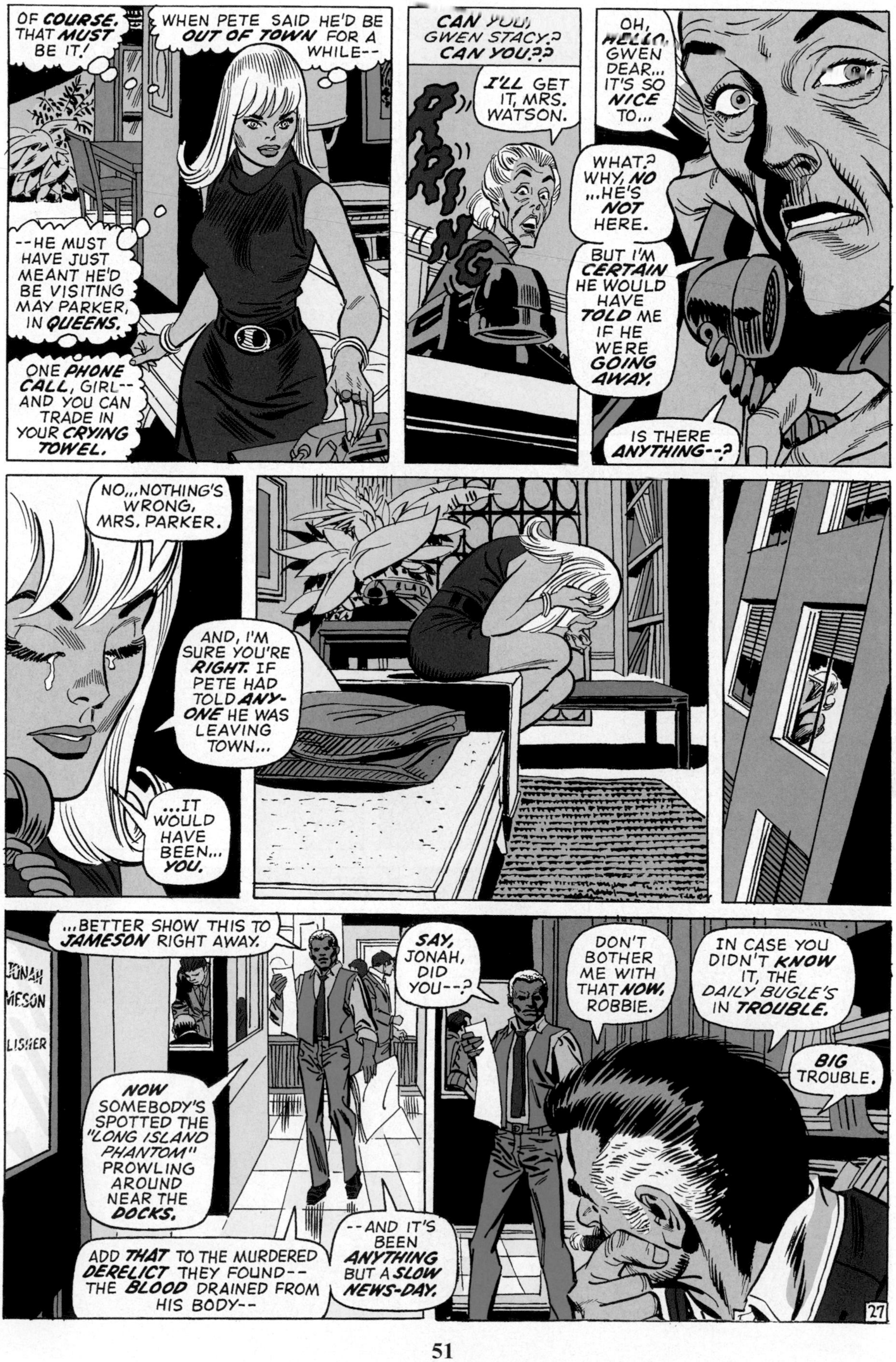
OF COURSE. THAT MUST BE IT!
WHEN PETE SAID HE'D BE OUT OF TOWN FOR A WHILE--
--HE MUST HAVE JUST MEANT HE'D BE VISITING MAY PARKER, IN QUEENS.
ONE PHONE CALL, GIRL-- AND YOU CAN TRADE IN YOUR CRYING TOWEL.
CAN YOU, GWEN STACY? CAN YOU??
I'LL GET IT, MRS. WATSON.
RRING
OH, HELLO, GWEN DEAR... IT'S SO NICE TO...
WHAT? WHY, NO ...HE'S NOT HERE.
BUT I'M CERTAIN HE WOULD HAVE TOLD ME IF HE WERE GOING AWAY.
IS THERE ANYTHING--?
NO... NOTHING'S WRONG, MRS. PARKER.
AND, I'M SURE YOU'RE RIGHT. IF PETE HAD TOLD ANYONE HE WAS LEAVING TOWN...
...IT WOULD HAVE BEEN... YOU.
...BETTER SHOW THIS TO JAMESON RIGHT AWAY.
NOW SOMEBODY'S SPOTTED THE "LONG ISLAND PHANTOM" PROWLING AROUND NEAR THE DOCKS.
ADD THAT TO THE MURDERED DERELICT THEY FOUND-- THE BLOOD DRAINED FROM HIS BODY--
SAY, JONAH, DID YOU--?
--AND IT'S BEEN ANYTHING BUT A SLOW NEWS-DAY.
DON'T BOTHER ME WITH THAT NOW, ROBBIE.
IN CASE YOU DIDN'T KNOW IT, THE DAILY BUGLE'S IN TROUBLE.
BIG TROUBLE.
27

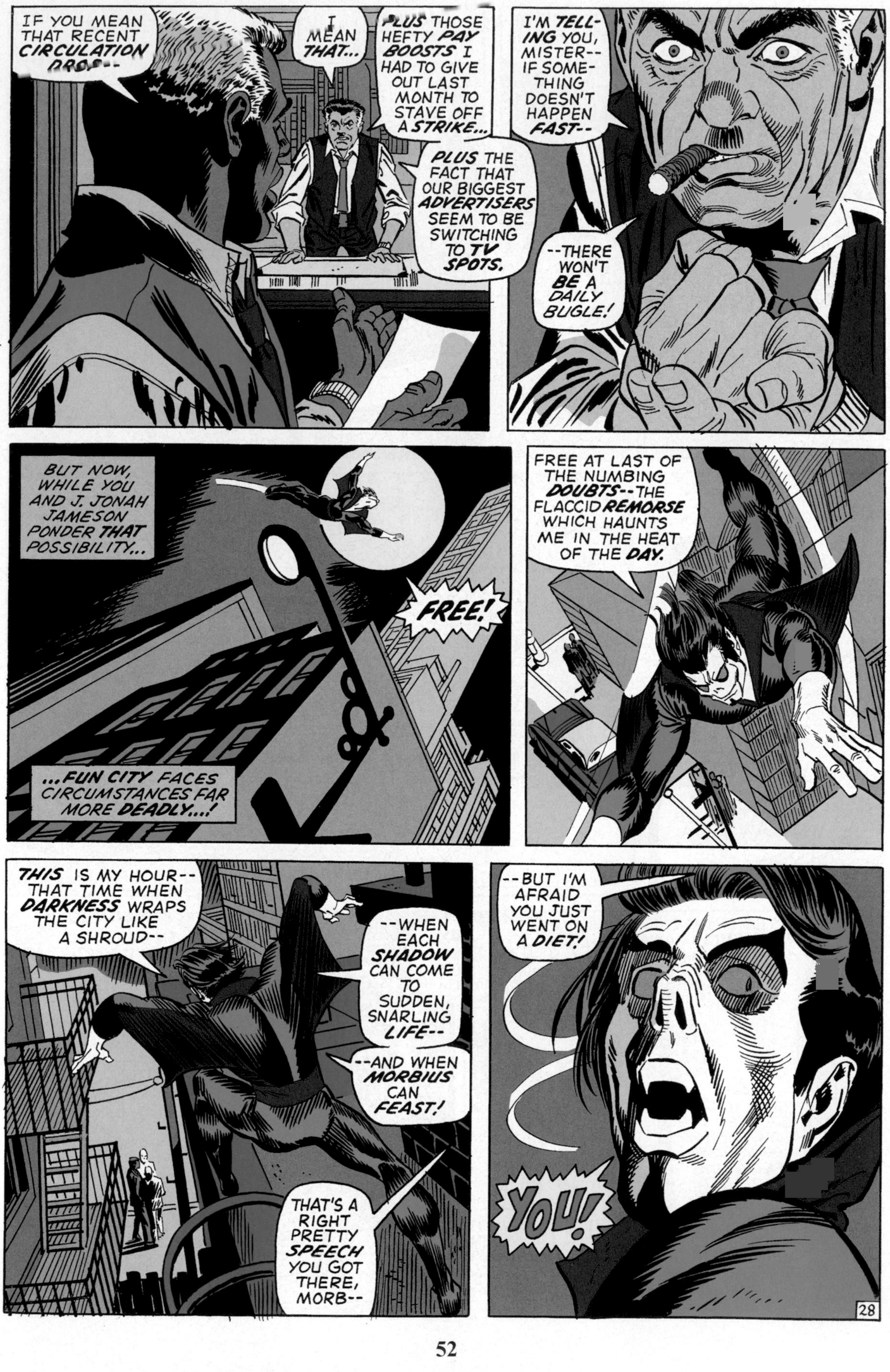
IF YOU MEAN THAT RECENT CIRCULATION DROP--
I MEAN THAT...
PLUS THOSE HEFTY PAY BOOSTS I HAD TO GIVE OUT LAST MONTH TO STAVE OFF A STRIKE...
PLUS THE FACT THAT OUR BIGGEST ADVERTISERS SEEM TO BE SWITCHING TO TV SPOTS.
I'M TELLING YOU, MISTER--IF SOMETHING DOESN'T HAPPEN FAST--
--THERE WON'T BE A DAILY BUGLE!
BUT NOW, WHILE YOU AND J. JONAH JAMESON PONDER THAT POSSIBILITY...
FREE!
...FUN CITY FACES CIRCUMSTANCES FAR MORE DEADLY...!
FREE AT LAST OF THE NUMBING DOUBTS--THE FLACCID REMORSE WHICH HAUNTS ME IN THE HEAT OF THE DAY.
THIS IS MY HOUR--THAT TIME WHEN DARKNESS WRAPS THE CITY LIKE A SHROUD--
--WHEN EACH SHADOW CAN COME TO SUDDEN, SNARLING LIFE--
--AND WHEN MORBIUS CAN FEAST!
THAT'S A RIGHT PRETTY SPEECH YOU GOT THERE, MORB--
--BUT I'M AFRAID YOU JUST WENT ON A DIET!
YOU!
28

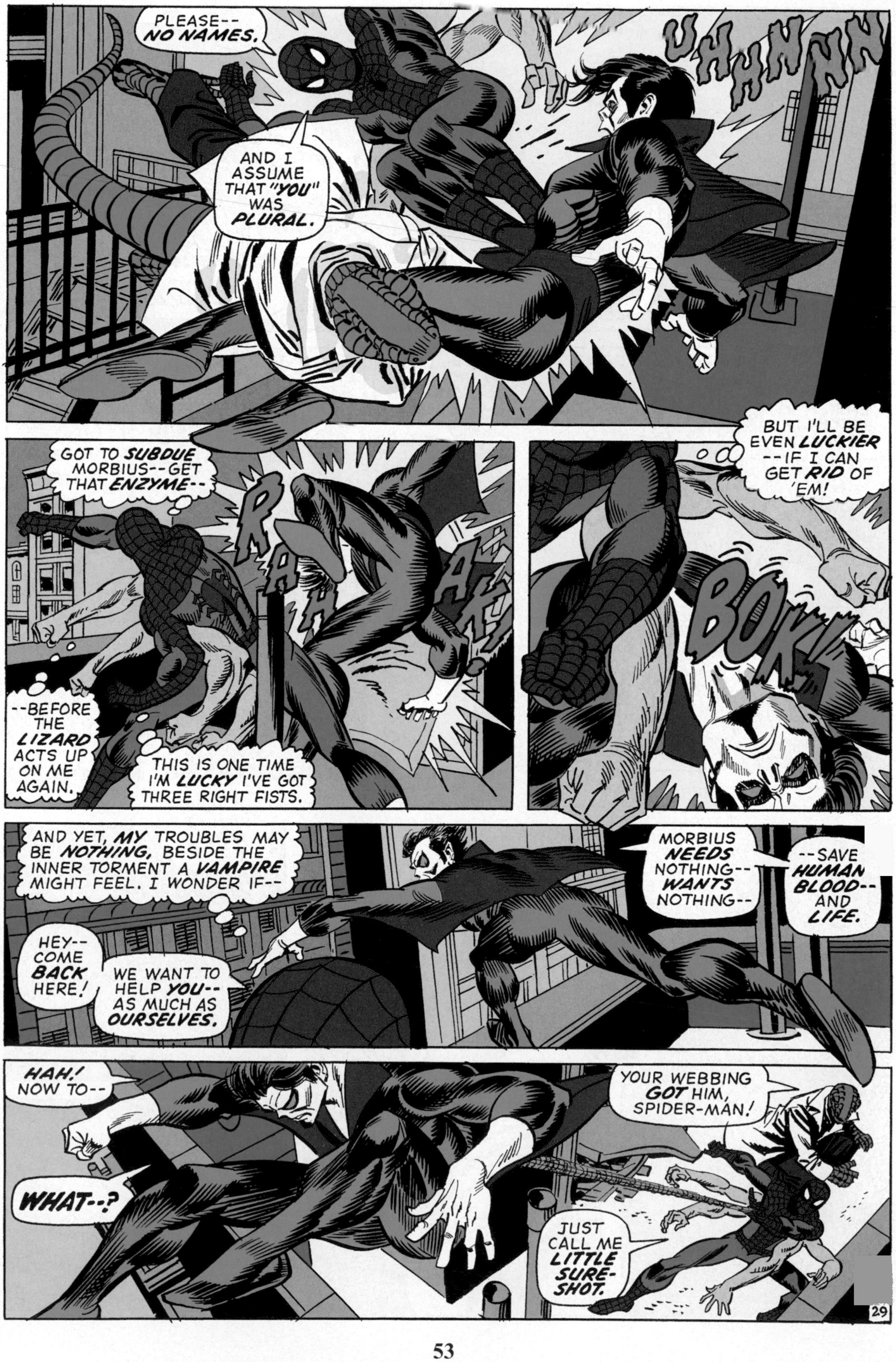
PLEASE-- NO NAMES.
AND I ASSUME THAT "YOU" WAS PLURAL.
UHHNNN
GOT TO SUBDUE MORBIUS--GET THAT ENZYME--
--BEFORE THE LIZARD ACTS UP ON ME AGAIN.
THIS IS ONE TIME I'M LUCKY I'VE GOT THREE RIGHT FISTS.
RAHHAK!
BUT I'LL BE EVEN LUCKIER --IF I CAN GET RID OF 'EM!
BOK!
AND YET, MY TROUBLES MAY BE NOTHING, BESIDE THE INNER TORMENT A VAMPIRE MIGHT FEEL. I WONDER IF--
HEY-- COME BACK HERE!
WE WANT TO HELP YOU-- AS MUCH AS OURSELVES.
MORBIUS NEEDS NOTHING-- WANTS NOTHING--
--SAVE HUMAN BLOOD-- AND LIFE.
HAH! NOW TO--
WHAT--?
YOUR WEBBING GOT HIM, SPIDER-MAN!
JUST CALL ME LITTLE SURE-SHOT.
29

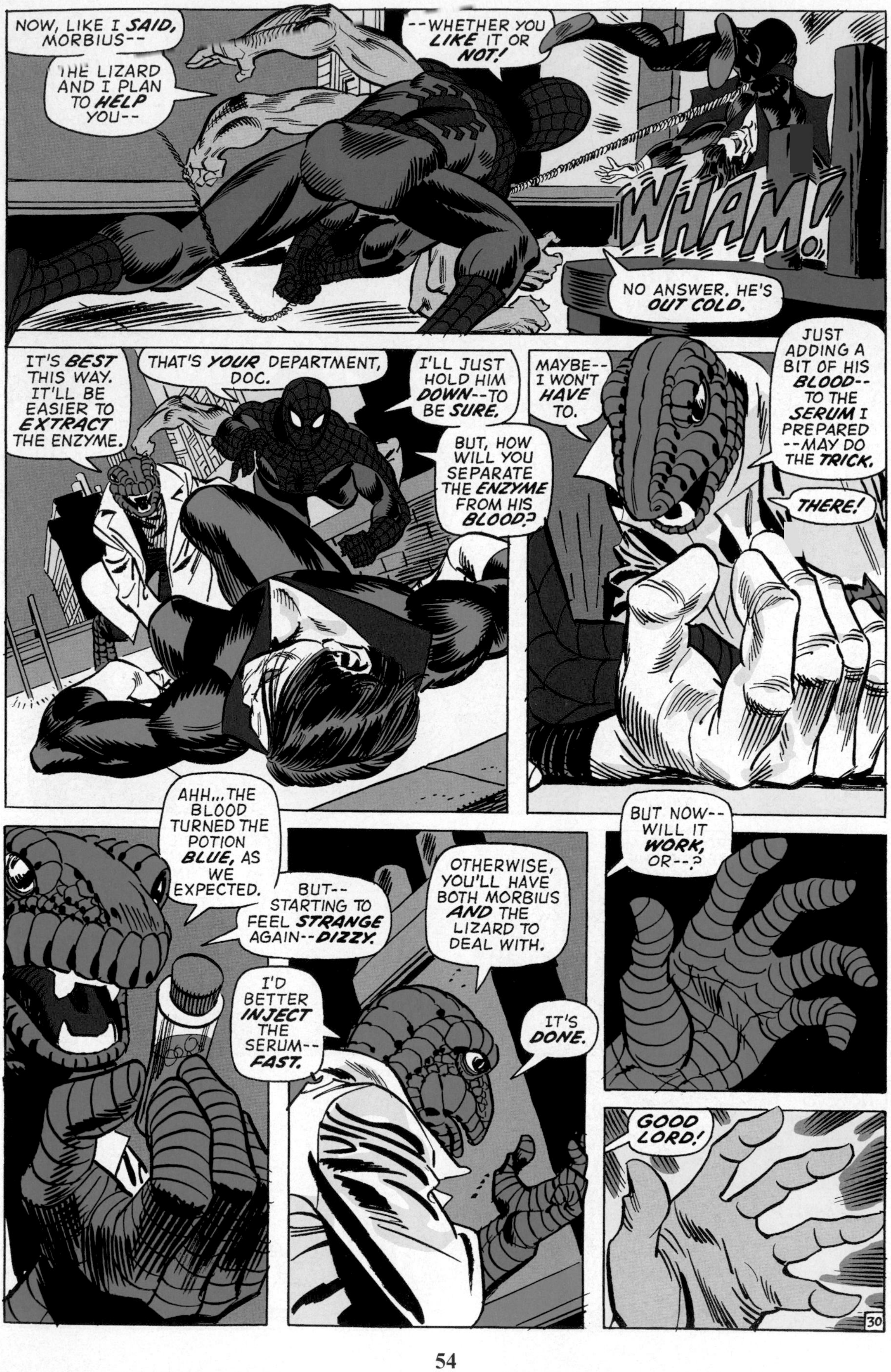
NOW, LIKE I SAID, MORBIUS--
THE LIZARD AND I PLAN TO HELP YOU--
--WHETHER YOU LIKE IT OR NOT!
WHAM!
NO ANSWER. HE'S OUT COLD.
IT'S BEST THIS WAY. IT'LL BE EASIER TO EXTRACT THE ENZYME.
THAT'S YOUR DEPARTMENT, DOC.
I'LL JUST HOLD HIM DOWN--TO BE SURE.
BUT, HOW WILL YOU SEPARATE THE ENZYME FROM HIS BLOOD?
MAYBE-- I WON'T HAVE TO.
JUST ADDING A BIT OF HIS BLOOD-- TO THE SERUM I PREPARED --MAY DO THE TRICK.
THERE!
AHH... THE BLOOD TURNED THE POTION BLUE, AS WE EXPECTED.
BUT-- STARTING TO FEEL STRANGE AGAIN--DIZZY.
OTHERWISE, YOU'LL HAVE BOTH MORBIUS AND THE LIZARD TO DEAL WITH.
I'D BETTER INJECT THE SERUM-- FAST.
IT'S DONE.
BUT NOW-- WILL IT WORK, OR--?
GOOD LORD!
30

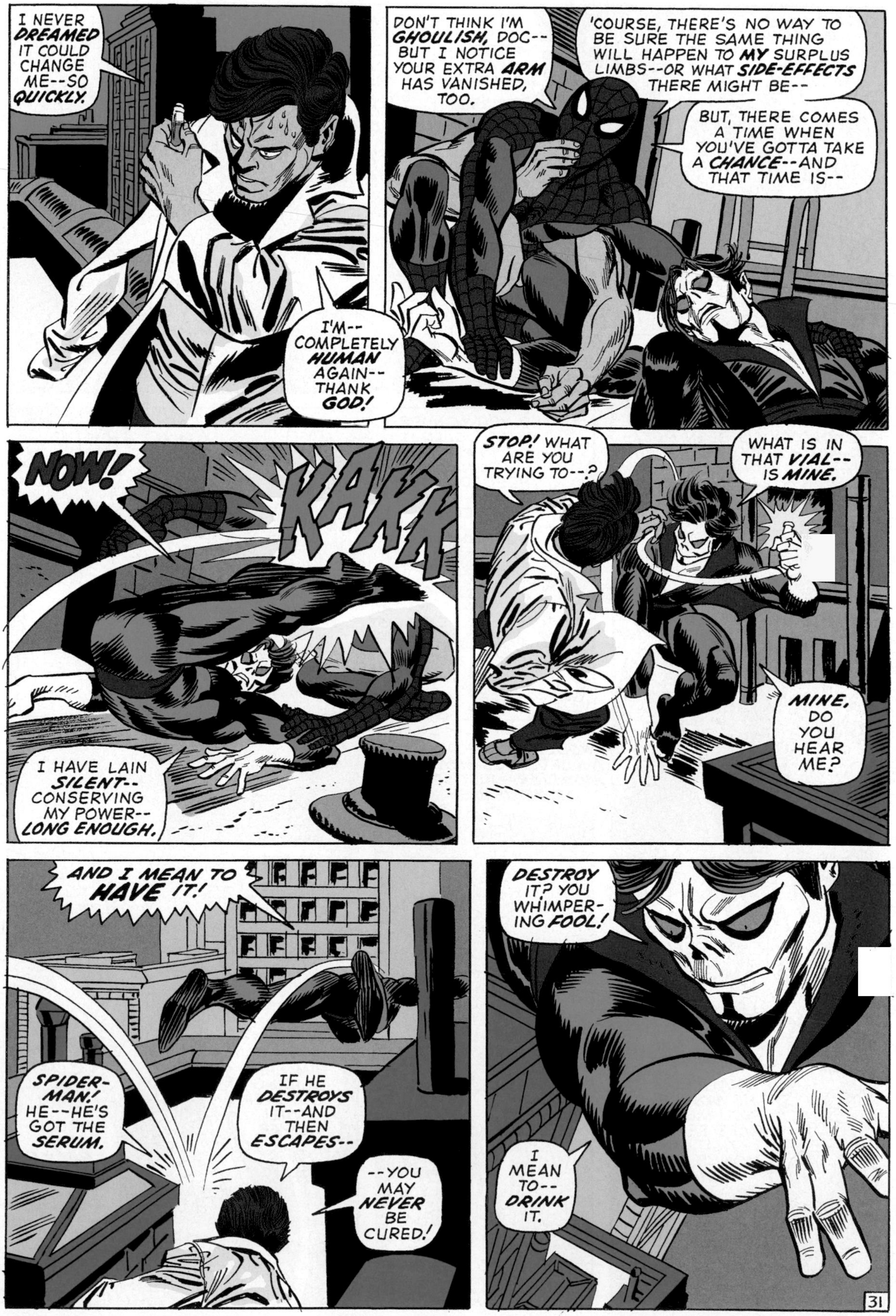
I NEVER DREAMED IT COULD CHANGE ME--SO QUICKLY.
I'M--COMPLETELY HUMAN AGAIN--THANK GOD!
DON'T THINK I'M GHOULISH, DOC--BUT I NOTICE YOUR EXTRA ARM HAS VANISHED, TOO.
'COURSE, THERE'S NO WAY TO BE SURE THE SAME THING WILL HAPPEN TO MY SURPLUS LIMBS--OR WHAT SIDE-EFFECTS THERE MIGHT BE--
BUT, THERE COMES A TIME WHEN YOU'VE GOTTA TAKE A CHANCE--AND THAT TIME IS--
NOW!
KAKK
I HAVE LAIN SILENT--CONSERVING MY POWER--LONG ENOUGH.
STOP! WHAT ARE YOU TRYING TO--?
WHAT IS IN THAT VIAL--IS MINE.
MINE, DO YOU HEAR ME?
AND I MEAN TO HAVE IT!
SPIDER-MAN! HE--HE'S GOT THE SERUM.
IF HE DESTROYS IT--AND THEN ESCAPES--
--YOU MAY NEVER BE CURED!
DESTROY IT? YOU WHIMPERING FOOL!
I MEAN TO--DRINK IT.
31

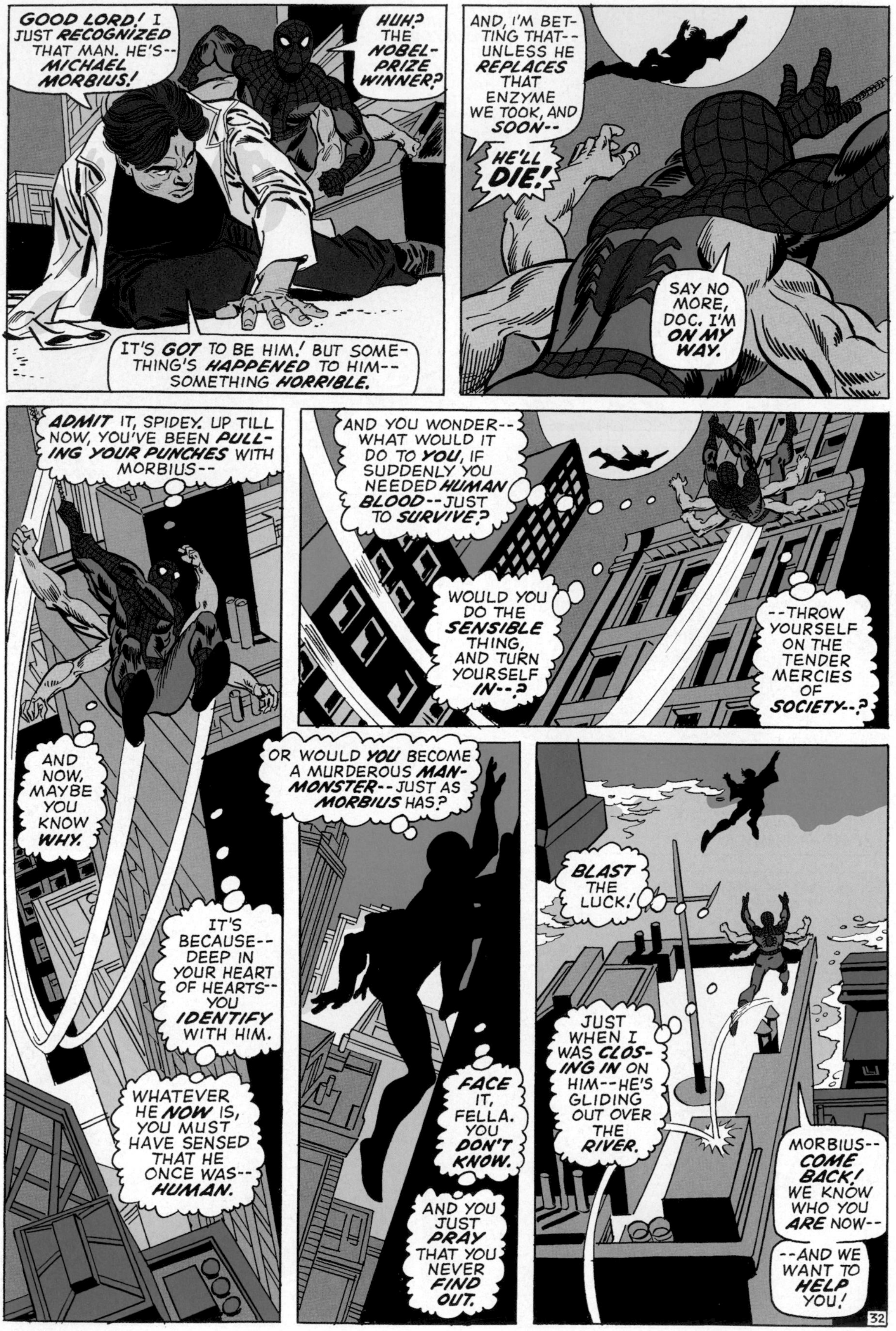
GOOD LORD! I JUST RECOGNIZED THAT MAN. HE'S-- MICHAEL MORBIUS!
HUH? THE NOBEL-PRIZE WINNER?
IT'S GOT TO BE HIM! BUT SOME-THING'S HAPPENED TO HIM-- SOMETHING HORRIBLE.
AND, I'M BET-TING THAT-- UNLESS HE REPLACES THAT ENZYME WE TOOK, AND SOON--
HE'LL DIE!
SAY NO MORE, DOC. I'M ON MY WAY.
ADMIT IT, SPIDEY. UP TILL NOW, YOU'VE BEEN PULL-ING YOUR PUNCHES WITH MORBIUS--
AND NOW, MAYBE YOU KNOW WHY.
IT'S BECAUSE-- DEEP IN YOUR HEART OF HEARTS-- YOU IDENTIFY WITH HIM.
WHATEVER HE NOW IS, YOU MUST HAVE SENSED THAT HE ONCE WAS-- HUMAN.
AND YOU WONDER-- WHAT WOULD IT DO TO YOU, IF SUDDENLY YOU NEEDED HUMAN BLOOD--JUST TO SURVIVE?
WOULD YOU DO THE SENSIBLE THING, AND TURN YOURSELF IN--?
--THROW YOURSELF ON THE TENDER MERCIES OF SOCIETY--?
OR WOULD YOU BECOME A MURDEROUS MAN-MONSTER--JUST AS MORBIUS HAS?
FACE IT, FELLA. YOU DON'T KNOW.
AND YOU JUST PRAY THAT YOU NEVER FIND OUT.
BLAST THE LUCK!
JUST WHEN I WAS CLOS-ING IN ON HIM--HE'S GLIDING OUT OVER THE RIVER.
MORBIUS-- COME BACK! WE KNOW WHO YOU ARE NOW--
--AND WE WANT TO HELP YOU!
32

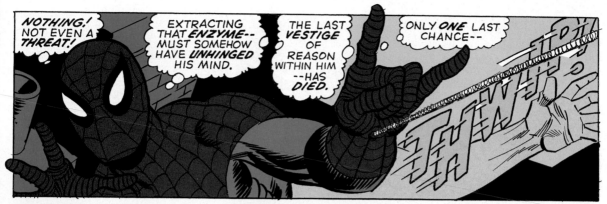

NOTHING! NOT EVEN A THREAT!

EXTRACTING THAT *ENZYME*-- MUST SOMEHOW HAVE *UNHINGED* HIS MIND.

THE LAST *VESTIGE* OF REASON WITHIN HIM --HAS *DIED.*

ONLY *ONE* LAST CHANCE--

THWIP

IF THAT NUTTY *SUB- CONSCIOUS* OF MINE-- MAKES ME *MISS*--

NO! I'VE *GOT* HIM!

NOW TO REEL HIM *IN,* AND--

WH--? HE HAD MORE *MOMENTUM* THAN I THOUGHT.

HE'S *PULLING* ME--*OFF* THE LEDGE!

YOU *WON'T* CAPTURE ME --PUT ME ON *DISPLAY,* LIKE SOME SORT OF *FREAK.*

I WANT TO BE *FREE-- --FREE* TO *LIVE--*

DO YOU *HEAR* ME-- TO *LIVE!!*

HE'S *LOSING ALTITUDE--* DIPPING TOWARD THE *WATER.*

I SHOULD BE ABLE TO *OVERPOWER* HIM THERE.

JUST A LITTLE *FARTHER--* JUST--

OH NO! NO!

I WAS LOOKING *DOWN,* DIDN'T SEE --THAT *BRIDGE!*

WHOM!

AND-- THE *WEBBING* BROKE!

33

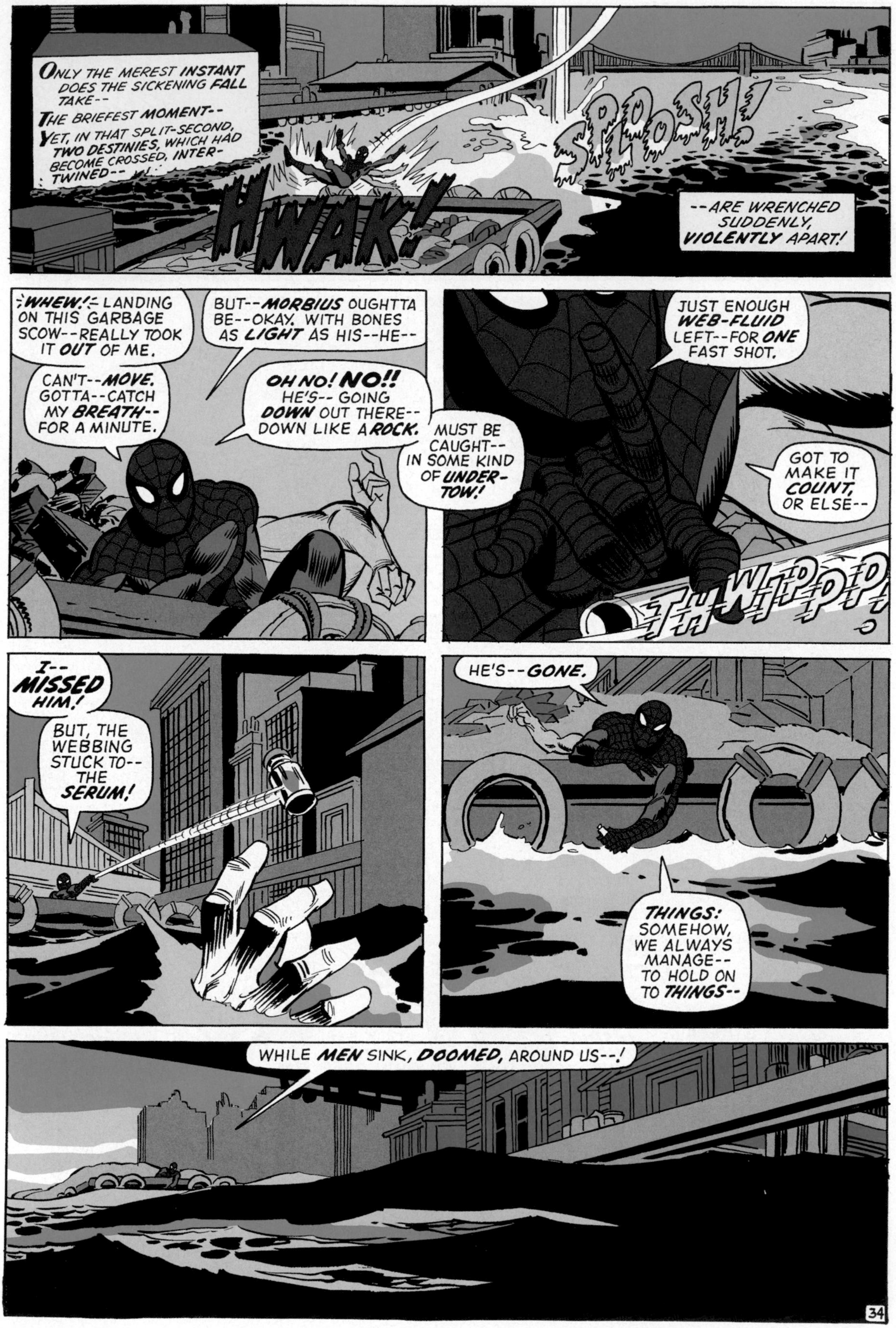
ONLY THE MEREST INSTANT DOES THE SICKENING FALL TAKE--
THE BRIEFEST MOMENT--
YET, IN THAT SPLIT-SECOND, TWO DESTINIES, WHICH HAD BECOME CROSSED, INTER-TWINED--
SPLOOSH!
HWAK!
--ARE WRENCHED SUDDENLY, VIOLENTLY APART!
WHEW! -- LANDING ON THIS GARBAGE SCOW--REALLY TOOK IT OUT OF ME.
CAN'T--MOVE. GOTTA--CATCH MY BREATH--FOR A MINUTE.
BUT--MORBIUS OUGHTTA BE--OKAY. WITH BONES AS LIGHT AS HIS--HE--
OH NO! NO!! HE'S-- GOING DOWN OUT THERE-- DOWN LIKE A ROCK.
MUST BE CAUGHT-- IN SOME KIND OF UNDER-TOW!
JUST ENOUGH WEB-FLUID LEFT--FOR ONE FAST SHOT.
GOT TO MAKE IT COUNT, OR ELSE--
THWIPPP
I-- MISSED HIM!
BUT, THE WEBBING STUCK TO-- THE SERUM!
HE'S--GONE.
THINGS: SOMEHOW, WE ALWAYS MANAGE-- TO HOLD ON TO THINGS--
WHILE MEN SINK, DOOMED, AROUND US--!
34

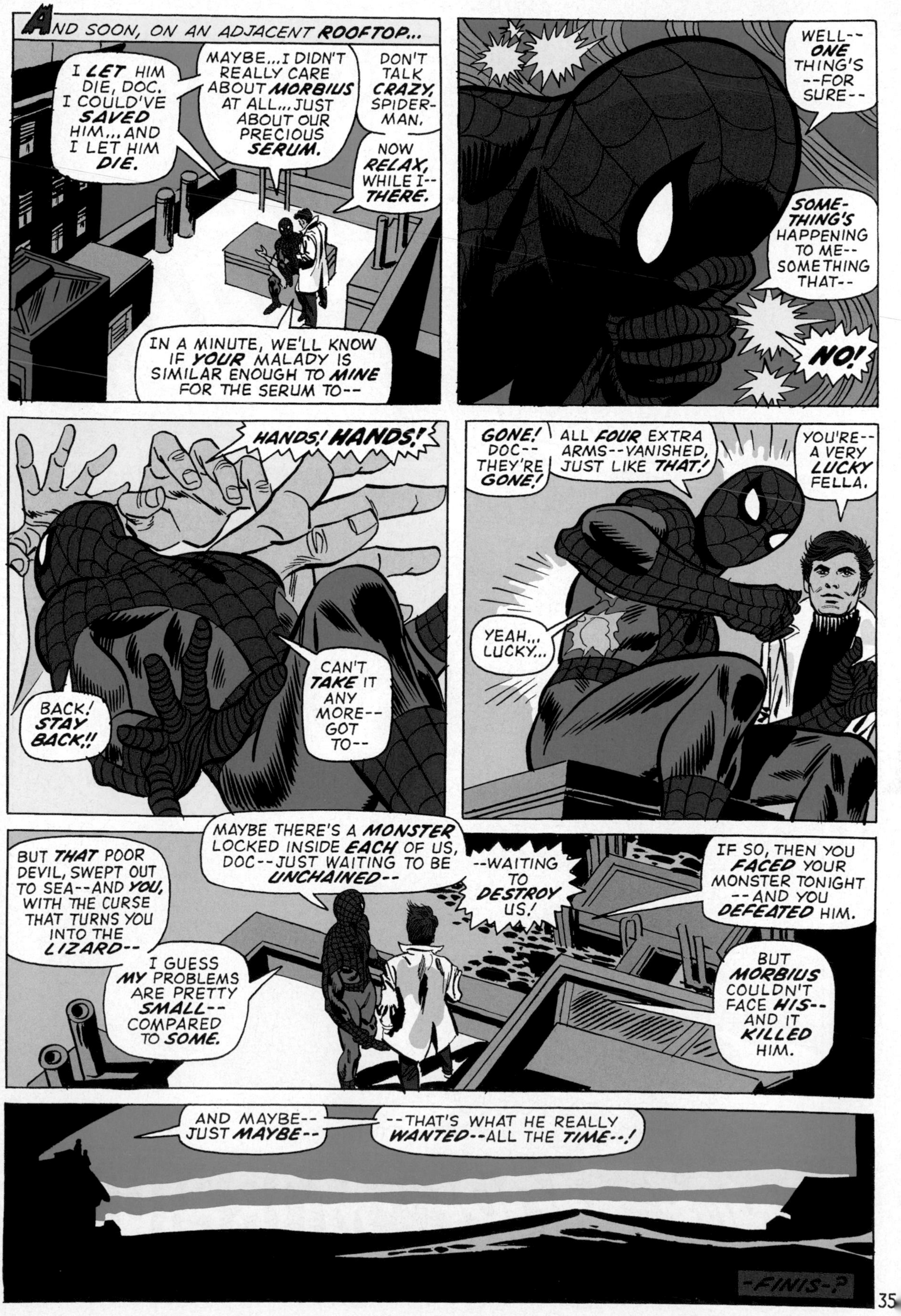
AND SOON, ON AN ADJACENT ROOFTOP...
I LET HIM DIE, DOC. I COULD'VE SAVED HIM... AND I LET HIM DIE.
MAYBE... I DIDN'T REALLY CARE ABOUT MORBIUS AT ALL... JUST ABOUT OUR PRECIOUS SERUM.
DON'T TALK CRAZY, SPIDER-MAN.
NOW RELAX, WHILE I-- THERE.
IN A MINUTE, WE'LL KNOW IF YOUR MALADY IS SIMILAR ENOUGH TO MINE FOR THE SERUM TO--
WELL-- ONE THING'S --FOR SURE--
SOME-THING'S HAPPENING TO ME-- SOMETHING THAT--
NO!
HANDS! HANDS!
CAN'T TAKE IT ANY MORE-- GOT TO--
BACK! STAY BACK!!
GONE! DOC-- THEY'RE GONE!
ALL FOUR EXTRA ARMS--VANISHED, JUST LIKE THAT!
YOU'RE-- A VERY LUCKY FELLA.
YEAH... LUCKY...
BUT THAT POOR DEVIL, SWEPT OUT TO SEA--AND YOU, WITH THE CURSE THAT TURNS YOU INTO THE LIZARD--
I GUESS MY PROBLEMS ARE PRETTY SMALL-- COMPARED TO SOME.
MAYBE THERE'S A MONSTER LOCKED INSIDE EACH OF US, DOC--JUST WAITING TO BE UNCHAINED--
--WAITING TO DESTROY US!
IF SO, THEN YOU FACED YOUR MONSTER TONIGHT --AND YOU DEFEATED HIM.
BUT MORBIUS COULDN'T FACE HIS-- AND IT KILLED HIM.
AND MAYBE-- JUST MAYBE--
--THAT'S WHAT HE REALLY WANTED--ALL THE TIME--!
-FINIS-?
35

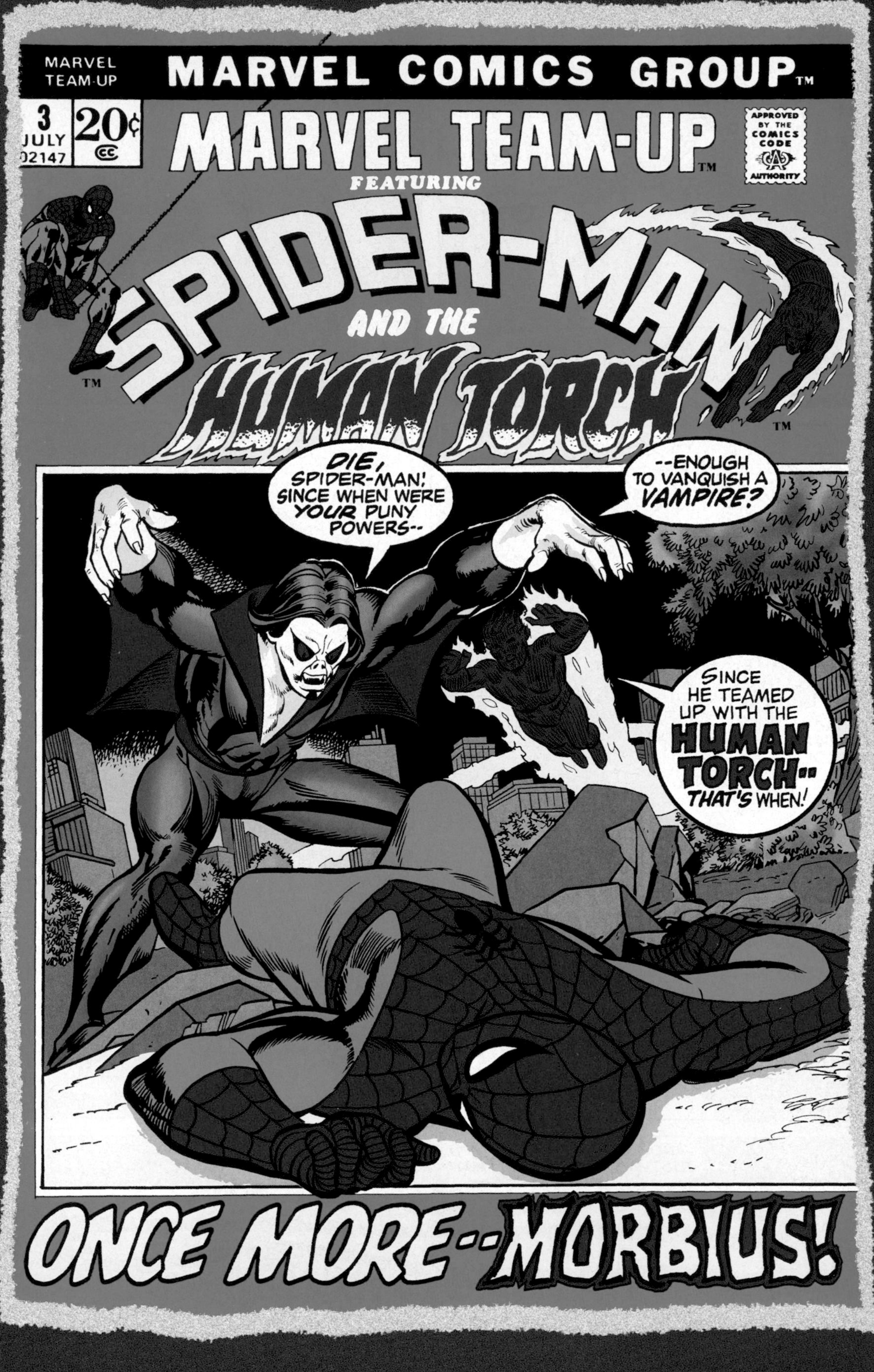
MARVEL TEAM-UP
MARVEL COMICS GROUP™
3 JULY 02147
20¢ CC
MARVEL TEAM-UP™
APPROVED BY THE COMICS CODE AUTHORITY
FEATURING
SPIDER-MAN™
AND THE
HUMAN TORCH™
DIE, SPIDER-MAN! SINCE WHEN WERE YOUR PUNY POWERS--
--ENOUGH TO VANQUISH A VAMPIRE?
SINCE HE TEAMED UP WITH THE HUMAN TORCH-- THAT'S WHEN!
ONCE MORE--MORBIUS!

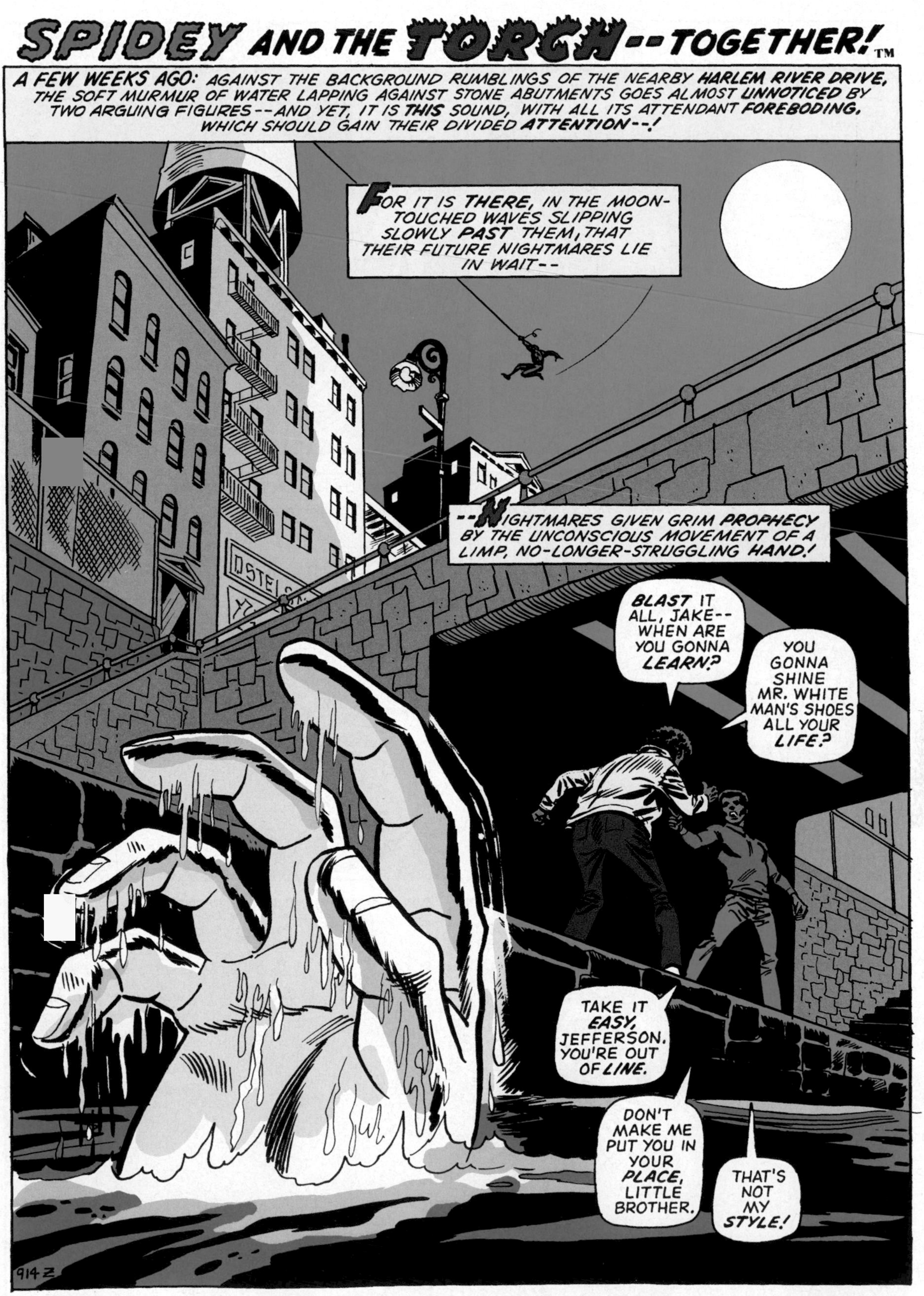
SPIDEY AND THE TORCH--TOGETHER!
A FEW WEEKS AGO: AGAINST THE BACKGROUND RUMBLINGS OF THE NEARBY HARLEM RIVER DRIVE, THE SOFT MURMUR OF WATER LAPPING AGAINST STONE ABUTMENTS GOES ALMOST UNNOTICED BY TWO ARGUING FIGURES--AND YET, IT IS THIS SOUND, WITH ALL ITS ATTENDANT FOREBODING, WHICH SHOULD GAIN THEIR DIVIDED ATTENTION--!
FOR IT IS THERE, IN THE MOON-TOUCHED WAVES SLIPPING SLOWLY PAST THEM, THAT THEIR FUTURE NIGHTMARES LIE IN WAIT--
--NIGHTMARES GIVEN GRIM PROPHECY BY THE UNCONSCIOUS MOVEMENT OF A LIMP, NO-LONGER-STRUGGLING HAND!
BLAST IT ALL, JAKE--WHEN ARE YOU GONNA LEARN?
YOU GONNA SHINE MR. WHITE MAN'S SHOES ALL YOUR LIFE?
TAKE IT EASY, JEFFERSON. YOU'RE OUT OF LINE.
DON'T MAKE ME PUT YOU IN YOUR PLACE, LITTLE BROTHER.
THAT'S NOT MY STYLE!

YOUR STYLE? DON'T MAKE ME LAUGH.
COLLEGE BOY ISN'T GONNA MUSS HIS HANDS ON THE LIKES OF ME.
JACOB, WHY DON'T YOU WISE UP?
TELL ME ABOUT WISE, JEFFERSON.
TELL ME ABOUT THOSE CREEPS YOU HANG OUT WITH.
EASY, BIG BROTHER. YOU'RE TREADIN' ON SOFT ICE.
TACKER AN THE OTHERS ARE RIGHT DUDES--
DON'T GET DOWN ON THEM, JAKE!
FUNNY-- I DON'T RECALL THEM GETTIN' SAINTED--
--BUT THEN, I DON'T PLAY GAMES WITH SCU--
UNNNHHH!
I SAID SHUT UP!
BROTHER, YOU JUST WENT TOO FAR!
NO, JEFFERSON...NOT ME.
I'VE HAD IT WITH YOU, LITTLE MAN...
...YOU AND THOSE GOONS YOU CALL FRIENDS.
YOU WANNA BURN SOME BUILDINGS, GO AHEAD.
JUST DON'T BOTHER COMIN' HOME WHEN YOU'RE DONE!
SURE... COP OUT, BROTHER.
ISN'T THAT WHAT YOU'VE ALWAYS DONE?
HAVEN'T YOU ALWAYS... COPPED OUT...? YOU...AND DAD?
SOMETHING STINGS THE EYES OF JEFFERSON BOLT... FISTS UNCLENCHING AT HIS SIDES, HE BEGINS TO TURN AWAY...
GEEEEZUS!
THEN, HE HEARS A SOUND...THE MURMUR OF WATER 'GAINST STONE, A SHUDDERING MOAN...
2.

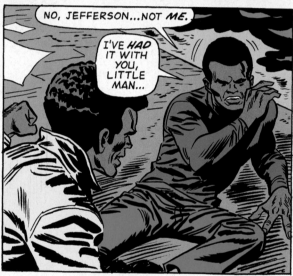

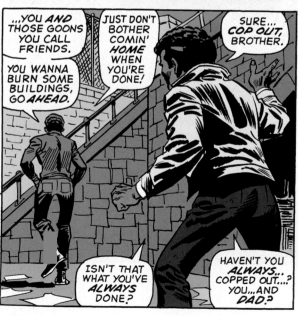

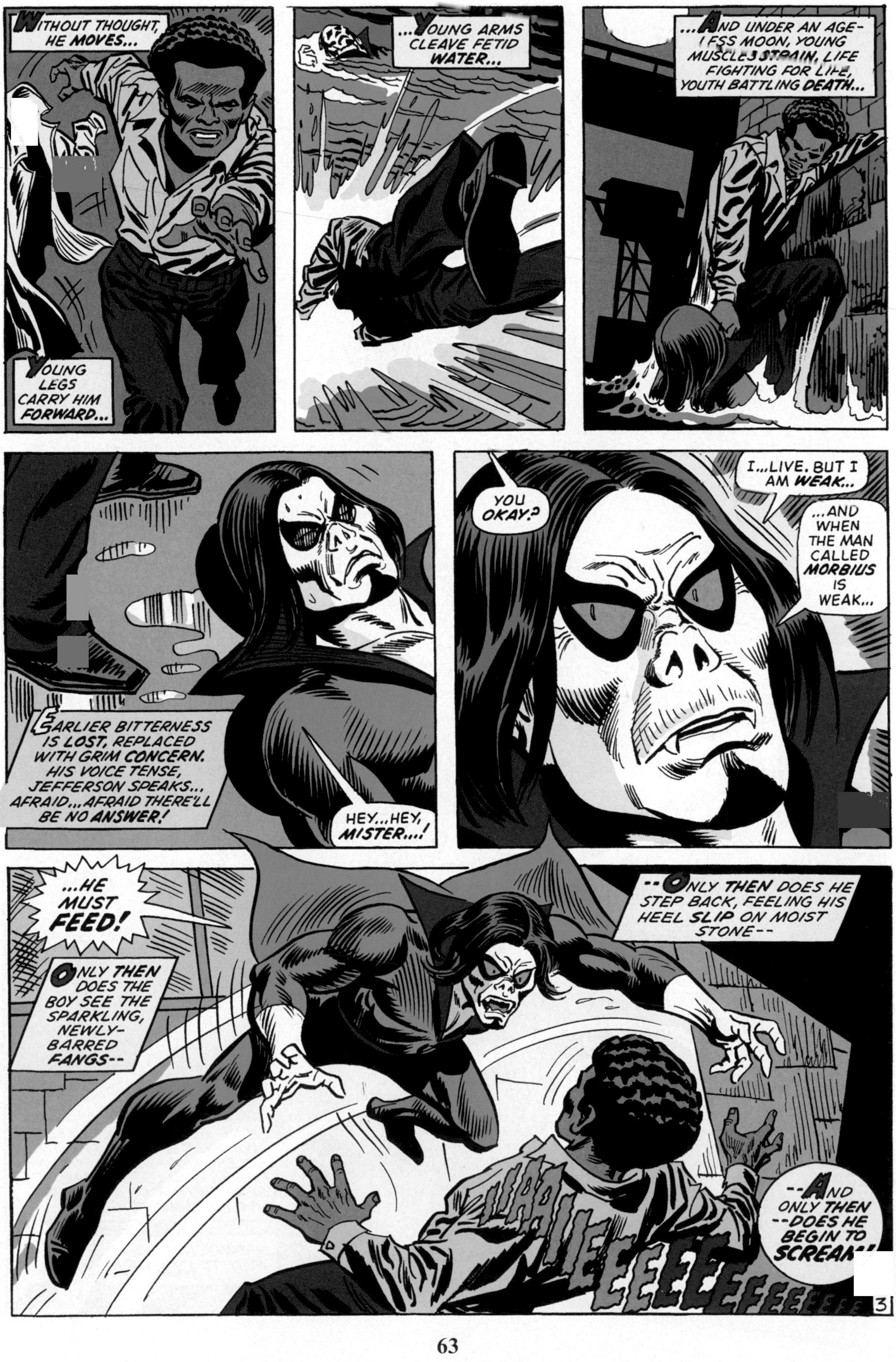
WITHOUT THOUGHT, HE MOVES...
YOUNG LEGS CARRY HIM FORWARD...
...YOUNG ARMS CLEAVE FETID WATER...
...AND UNDER AN AGELESS MOON, YOUNG MUSCLES STRAIN, LIFE FIGHTING FOR LIFE, YOUTH BATTLING DEATH...
EARLIER BITTERNESS IS LOST, REPLACED WITH GRIM CONCERN. HIS VOICE TENSE, JEFFERSON SPEAKS... AFRAID...AFRAID THERE'LL BE NO ANSWER!
HEY...HEY, MISTER...!
YOU OKAY?
I...LIVE. BUT I AM WEAK...
...AND WHEN THE MAN CALLED MORBIUS IS WEAK...
...HE MUST FEED!
ONLY THEN DOES THE BOY SEE THE SPARKLING, NEWLY-BARRED FANGS--
--ONLY THEN DOES HE STEP BACK, FEELING HIS HEEL SLIP ON MOIST STONE--
--AND ONLY THEN --DOES HE BEGIN TO SCREAM!
3

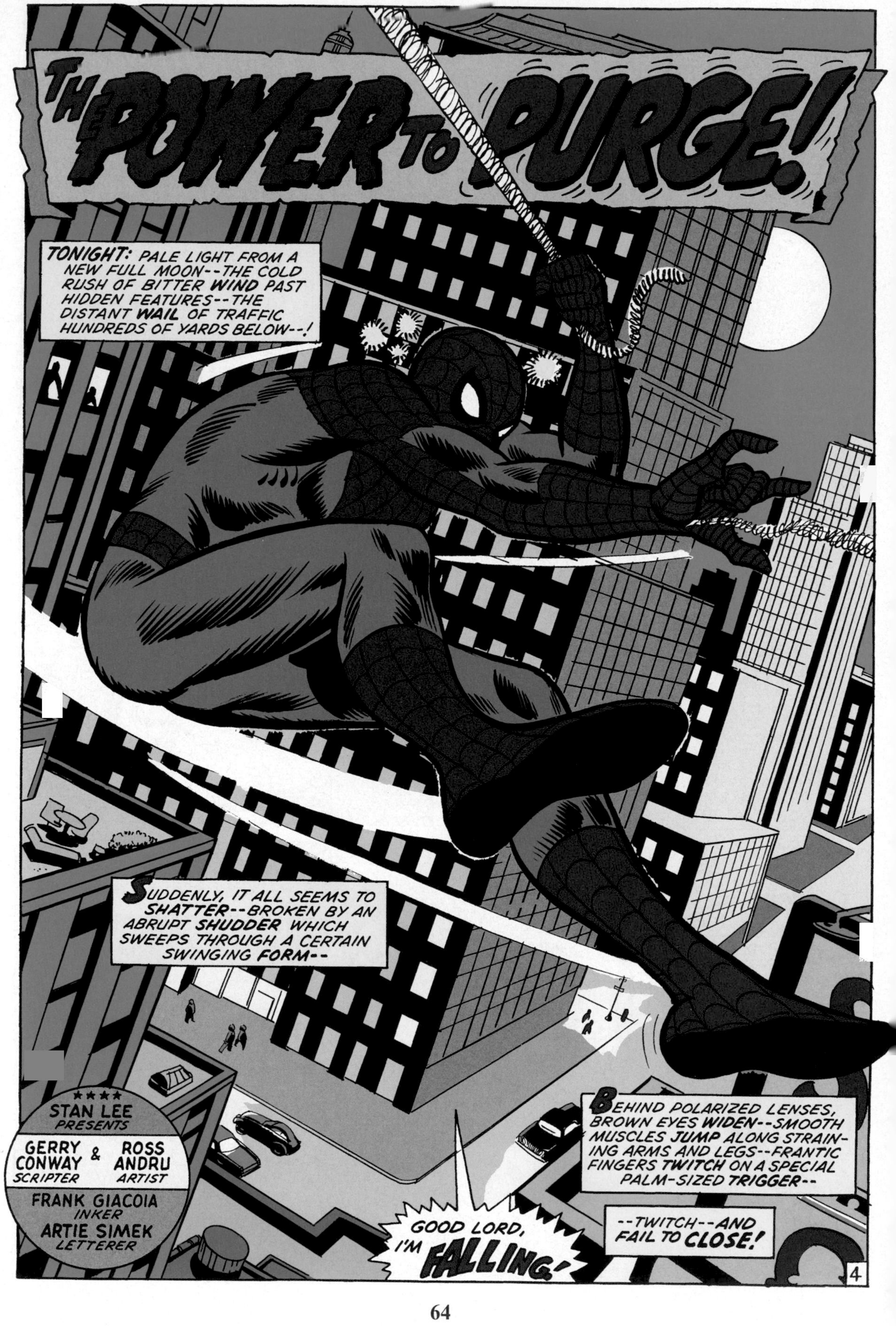
THE POWER TO PURGE!
TONIGHT: PALE LIGHT FROM A NEW FULL MOON--THE COLD RUSH OF BITTER WIND PAST HIDDEN FEATURES--THE DISTANT WAIL OF TRAFFIC HUNDREDS OF YARDS BELOW--!
SUDDENLY, IT ALL SEEMS TO SHATTER--BROKEN BY AN ABRUPT SHUDDER WHICH SWEEPS THROUGH A CERTAIN SWINGING FORM--
BEHIND POLARIZED LENSES, BROWN EYES WIDEN--SMOOTH MUSCLES JUMP ALONG STRAINING ARMS AND LEGS--FRANTIC FINGERS TWITCH ON A SPECIAL PALM-SIZED TRIGGER--
--TWITCH--AND FAIL TO CLOSE!
GOOD LORD, I'M FALLING!
★★★★ STAN LEE PRESENTS
GERRY CONWAY SCRIPTER & ROSS ANDRU ARTIST
FRANK GIACOIA INKER
ARTIE SIMEK LETTERER
4

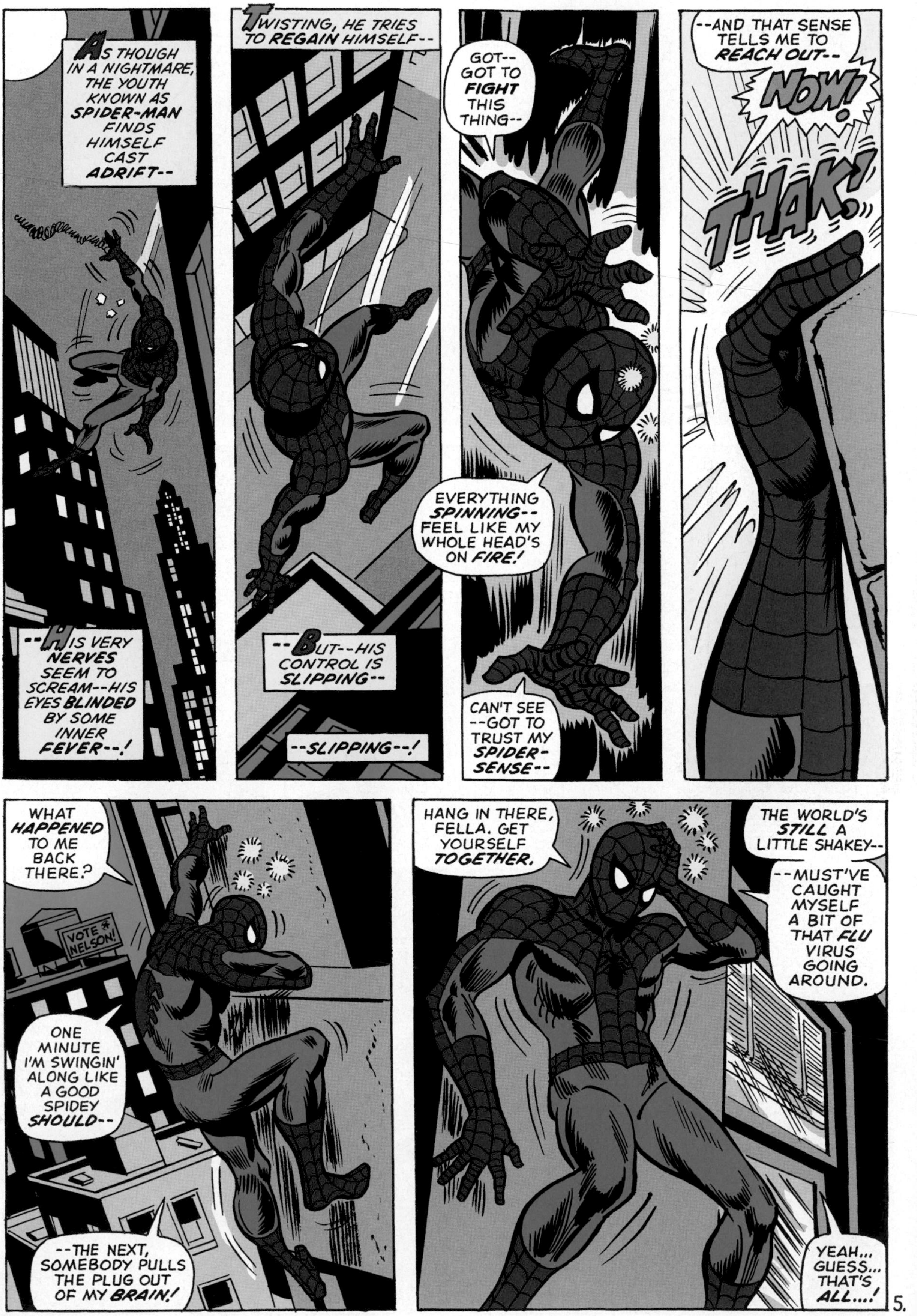
AS THOUGH IN A NIGHTMARE, THE YOUTH KNOWN AS SPIDER-MAN FINDS HIMSELF CAST ADRIFT--
--HIS VERY NERVES SEEM TO SCREAM--HIS EYES BLINDED BY SOME INNER FEVER--!
TWISTING, HE TRIES TO REGAIN HIMSELF--
--BUT--HIS CONTROL IS SLIPPING--
--SLIPPING--!
GOT-- GOT TO FIGHT THIS THING--
EVERYTHING SPINNING-- FEEL LIKE MY WHOLE HEAD'S ON FIRE!
CAN'T SEE --GOT TO TRUST MY SPIDER-SENSE--
--AND THAT SENSE TELLS ME TO REACH OUT--
NOW!
THAK!
WHAT HAPPENED TO ME BACK THERE?
VOTE NELSON!
ONE MINUTE I'M SWINGIN' ALONG LIKE A GOOD SPIDEY SHOULD--
--THE NEXT, SOMEBODY PULLS THE PLUG OUT OF MY BRAIN!
HANG IN THERE, FELLA. GET YOURSELF TOGETHER.
THE WORLD'S STILL A LITTLE SHAKEY--
--MUST'VE CAUGHT MYSELF A BIT OF THAT FLU VIRUS GOING AROUND.
YEAH... GUESS... THAT'S ALL...!
5.

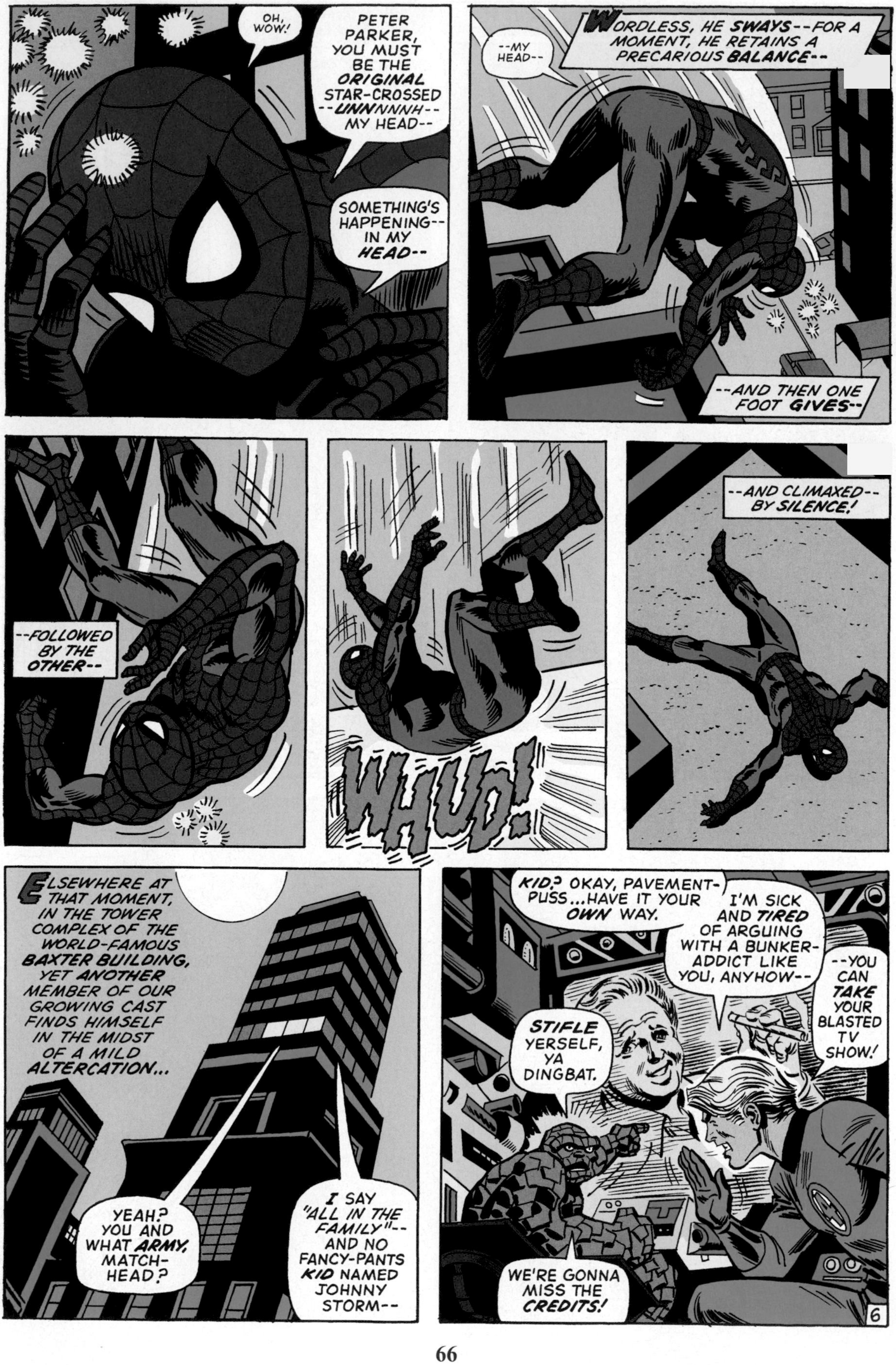
OH, WOW!
PETER PARKER, YOU MUST BE THE ORIGINAL STAR-CROSSED --UNNNNNH-- MY HEAD--
SOMETHING'S HAPPENING-- IN MY HEAD--
--MY HEAD--
WORDLESS, HE SWAYS--FOR A MOMENT, HE RETAINS A PRECARIOUS BALANCE--
--AND THEN ONE FOOT GIVES--
--FOLLOWED BY THE OTHER--
WHUD!
--AND CLIMAXED-- BY SILENCE!
ELSEWHERE AT THAT MOMENT, IN THE TOWER COMPLEX OF THE WORLD-FAMOUS BAXTER BUILDING, YET ANOTHER MEMBER OF OUR GROWING CAST FINDS HIMSELF IN THE MIDST OF A MILD ALTERCATION...
YEAH? YOU AND WHAT ARMY, MATCH-HEAD?
I SAY "ALL IN THE FAMILY"-- AND NO FANCY-PANTS KID NAMED JOHNNY STORM--
KID? OKAY, PAVEMENT-PUSS...HAVE IT YOUR OWN WAY.
I'M SICK AND TIRED OF ARGUING WITH A BUNKER-ADDICT LIKE YOU, ANYHOW--
--YOU CAN TAKE YOUR BLASTED TV SHOW!
STIFLE YERSELF, YA DINGBAT.
WE'RE GONNA MISS THE CREDITS!
6

HAH! LOOKS LIKE YOU'LL HAVE TO MISS THE OPENING AFTER ALL, BENJY!

YOU CAN SEE WHO'S CALLING UP FROM THE LOBBY--

--ME, I'M CUTTING OUT!

HAVE YOURSELF A REAL GOOD LAUGH, TORCH.

RRRNNNG

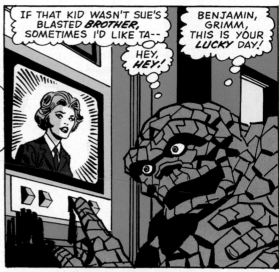

IF THAT KID WASN'T SUE'S BLASTED BROTHER, SOMETIMES I'D LIKE TA--

HEY, HEY!

BENJAMIN, GRIMM, THIS IS YOUR LUCKY DAY!

MOMENTS LATER, AS THE PNUEMATIC DOORS OF THE FANTASTIC FOUR'S PRIVATE ELEVATOR SLID SILENTLY OPEN...

HEY-- WOTTSA' MATTER?

I DON'T KNOW WHO YOU ARE, LADY--BUT YOU LOOK LIKE YOU'VE JUST LOST YOUR BEST FRIEND.

UH-OH. HEY, REED-- HEY, SUE!

PLEASE, MR. GRIMM...I'LL BE ALL RIGHT.

IT'S JUST... BEEN SO HARD...!

YEAH, YEAH. LOOK, I'VE HAD PEOPLE FAINT ON ME, BEFORE, LADY.

YOU GET USED TO IT WITH A MUG LIKE MINE.

THING... WHAT IS IT? WHAT'S WRONG?

YA GOT ME, STRETCHO.

LADY WUZ ASKIN' FOR YOU--

BENJAMIN GRIMM. YOU SHOULD BE ASHAMED OF YOURSELF.

CAN'T YOU SEE THE POOR WOMAN'S UPSET? HONESTLY, YOU MEN--!

BUT, HONEY--

AH, WHAT'S THE USE, REED?

WE MIGHT AS WELL WAIT OUTSIDE.

THE MINUTES PASS SLOWLY, AND WITH EACH, THERE COMES A NEW QUESTION, UNTIL FINALLY...

--YOU THINK YA RECOGNIZE HER?

BLAST IT, THEN WHY DON'T YA TELL ME WHO--?

TELL YOU WHAT, BLUE EYES?

WHAT'S GOING ON, REED--HAVE I MISSED SOMETHING?

WE'LL KNOW IN A MOMENT, JOHNNY.

7

67

REED, BEN--YOU CAN COME *IN* NOW.

TELL *THEM* WHAT YOU'VE TOLD ME, MARTINE.

YOU CAN *TRUST* US.

TRUST? HOW MAY I TRUST *ANYONE*-- AFTER WHAT'S *HAPPENED?*

ONCE, I TRUSTED MY FIANCE-- I WOULD HAVE GIVEN HIM MY *LIFE.*

"IT STARTED ON THE *YACHT* HE RENTED, WHEN I DISCOVERED HIS ASSISTANT--MY *FRIEND*--

"--*DEAD*, HIS SKIN *WHITER* THAN COULD EVER BE *NORMAL* FOR ONE AS STRONG AS *NIKOS* HAD BEEN.'

YET--HOW MAY I TRUST THE *HORROR* HE'S *BECOME?*

"SEARCHING HIS CABIN, DISCOVERING MY BELOVED MICHAEL GONE-- I FOUND CERTAIN NOTES--

"NOTES WHICH *EXPLAINED* THE REASON FOR OUR SUDDEN CRUISE--

"...BUT WHOSE UNFORESEEN *SIDE-EFFECTS* MIGHT MAKE OF HIM...

"MICHAEL WAS *DYING*, VICTIM OF SOME INCURABLE BLOOD DISEASE...

"IN A DESPERATE *GAMBLE*, HE'D DEVELOPED AN *ENZYME* WHICH WOULD STRENGTHEN HIS BLOOD COUNT...

"...A *VAMPIRE!*"

SOUNDS LIKE SOMETHING OUT OF AN OLD *KARLOFF* FLICK.

NOT THAT I THINK IT'S *TRUE*--BUT WHY COME TO *US?*

TELL THEM, MARTINE.

YOU SEE... MY FIANCE'S NAME WAS MICHAEL *MORBIUS!*

MORBIUS--? *GOOD LORD!* THE NOBEL PRIZE WINNER!

HE AND I CORRES-PONDED, ONCE!

YES, I FOUND YOUR *LETTERS*--

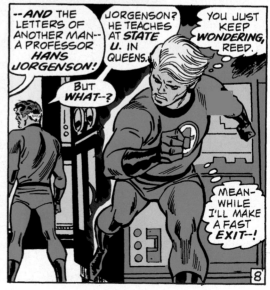

--AND THE LETTERS OF ANOTHER MAN-- A PROFESSOR *HANS JORGENSON!*

JORGENSON? HE TEACHES AT *STATE U.* IN QUEENS...

BUT *WHAT*--?

YOU JUST KEEP *WONDERING*, REED.

MEANWHILE I'LL MAKE A FAST *EXIT*--!

8

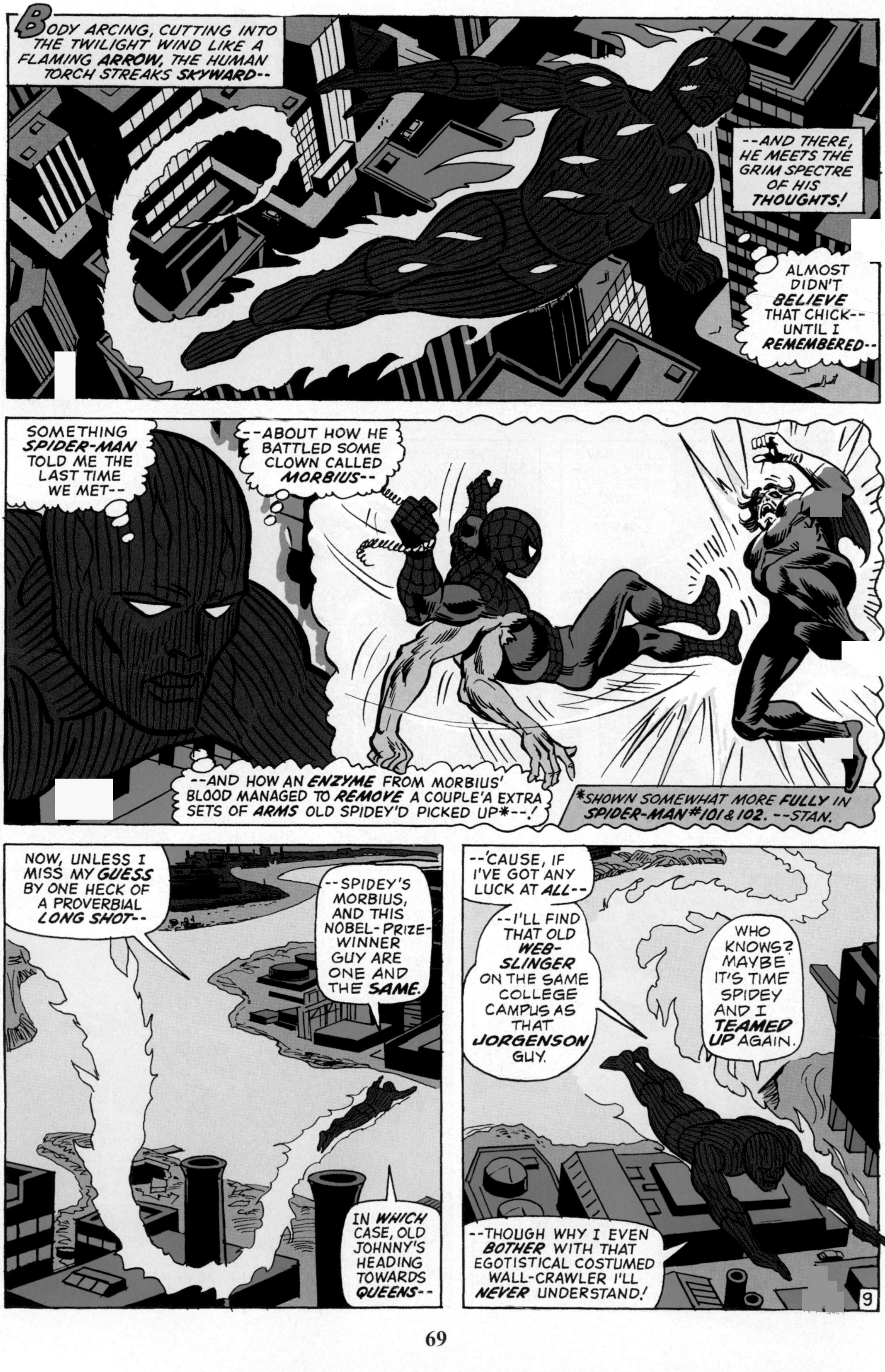

BODY ARCING, CUTTING INTO THE TWILIGHT WIND LIKE A FLAMING ARROW, THE HUMAN TORCH STREAKS SKYWARD--
--AND THERE, HE MEETS THE GRIM SPECTRE OF HIS THOUGHTS!
ALMOST DIDN'T BELIEVE THAT CHICK-- UNTIL I REMEMBERED--
SOMETHING SPIDER-MAN TOLD ME THE LAST TIME WE MET--
--ABOUT HOW HE BATTLED SOME CLOWN CALLED MORBIUS--
--AND HOW AN ENZYME FROM MORBIUS' BLOOD MANAGED TO REMOVE A COUPLE'A EXTRA SETS OF ARMS OLD SPIDEY'D PICKED UP*--!
*SHOWN SOMEWHAT MORE FULLY IN SPIDER-MAN #101 & 102. --STAN.
NOW, UNLESS I MISS MY GUESS BY ONE HECK OF A PROVERBIAL LONG SHOT--
--SPIDEY'S MORBIUS, AND THIS NOBEL-PRIZE-WINNER GUY ARE ONE AND THE SAME.
IN WHICH CASE, OLD JOHNNY'S HEADING TOWARDS QUEENS--
--'CAUSE, IF I'VE GOT ANY LUCK AT ALL--
--I'LL FIND THAT OLD WEB-SLINGER ON THE SAME COLLEGE CAMPUS AS THAT JORGENSON GUY.
WHO KNOWS? MAYBE IT'S TIME SPIDEY AND I TEAMED UP AGAIN.
--THOUGH WHY I EVEN BOTHER WITH THAT EGOTISTICAL COSTUMED WALL-CRAWLER I'LL NEVER UNDERSTAND!
9

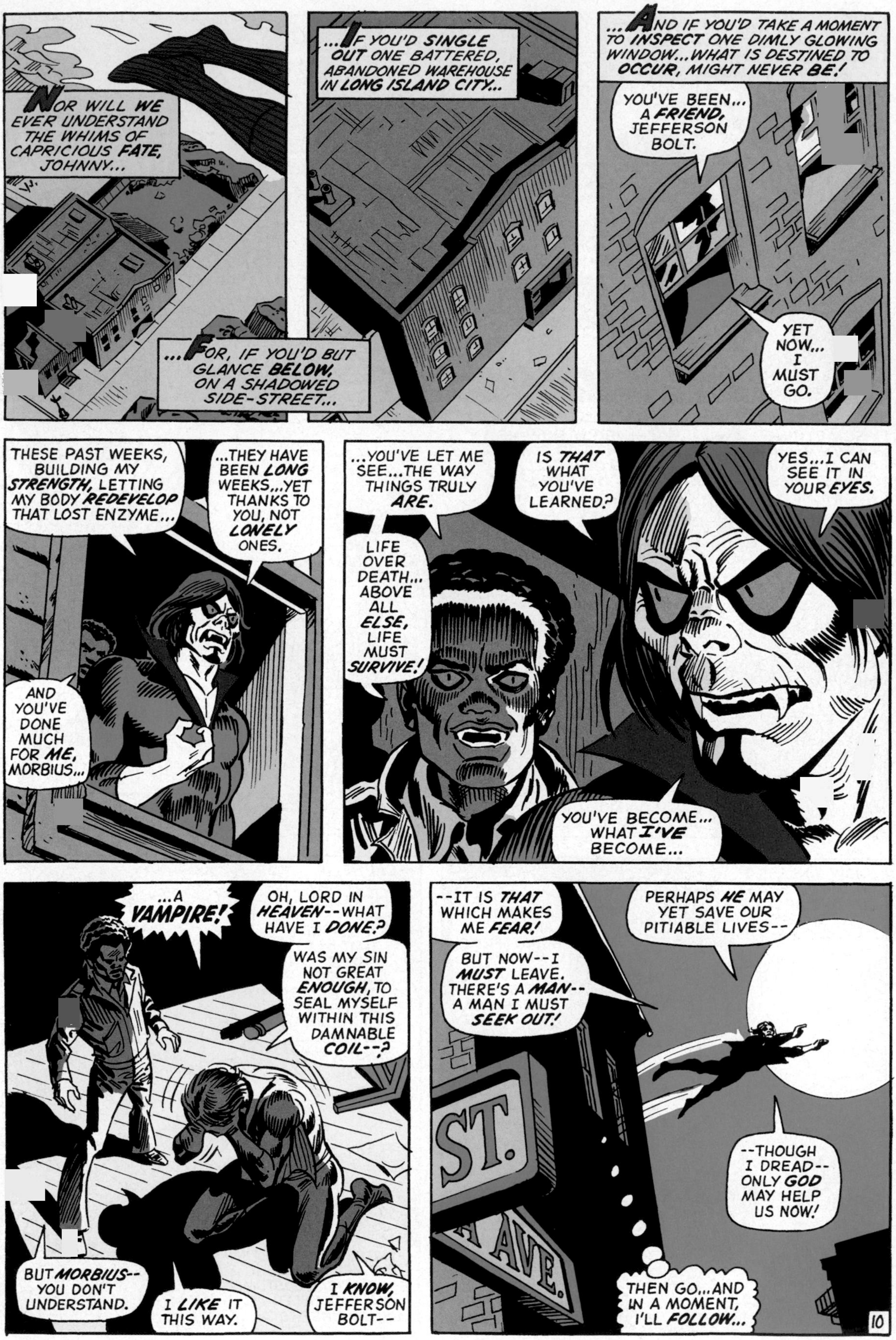
NOR WILL WE EVER UNDERSTAND THE WHIMS OF CAPRICIOUS FATE, JOHNNY...
...FOR, IF YOU'D BUT GLANCE BELOW, ON A SHADOWED SIDE-STREET...
...IF YOU'D SINGLE OUT ONE BATTERED, ABANDONED WAREHOUSE IN LONG ISLAND CITY...
...AND IF YOU'D TAKE A MOMENT TO INSPECT ONE DIMLY GLOWING WINDOW...WHAT IS DESTINED TO OCCUR, MIGHT NEVER BE!
YOU'VE BEEN... A FRIEND, JEFFERSON BOLT.
YET NOW... I MUST GO.
THESE PAST WEEKS, BUILDING MY STRENGTH, LETTING MY BODY REDEVELOP THAT LOST ENZYME...
...THEY HAVE BEEN LONG WEEKS...YET THANKS TO YOU, NOT LONELY ONES.
AND YOU'VE DONE MUCH FOR ME, MORBIUS...
...YOU'VE LET ME SEE...THE WAY THINGS TRULY ARE.
IS THAT WHAT YOU'VE LEARNED?
YES...I CAN SEE IT IN YOUR EYES.
LIFE OVER DEATH... ABOVE ALL ELSE, LIFE MUST SURVIVE!
YOU'VE BECOME... WHAT I'VE BECOME...
...A VAMPIRE!
OH, LORD IN HEAVEN--WHAT HAVE I DONE?
WAS MY SIN NOT GREAT ENOUGH, TO SEAL MYSELF WITHIN THIS DAMNABLE COIL--?
BUT MORBIUS-- YOU DON'T UNDERSTAND.
I LIKE IT THIS WAY.
I KNOW, JEFFERSON BOLT--
--IT IS THAT WHICH MAKES ME FEAR!
BUT NOW--I MUST LEAVE. THERE'S A MAN-- A MAN I MUST SEEK OUT!
PERHAPS HE MAY YET SAVE OUR PITIABLE LIVES--
--THOUGH I DREAD-- ONLY GOD MAY HELP US NOW!
THEN GO...AND IN A MOMENT, I'LL FOLLOW...
ST.
AVE.
10

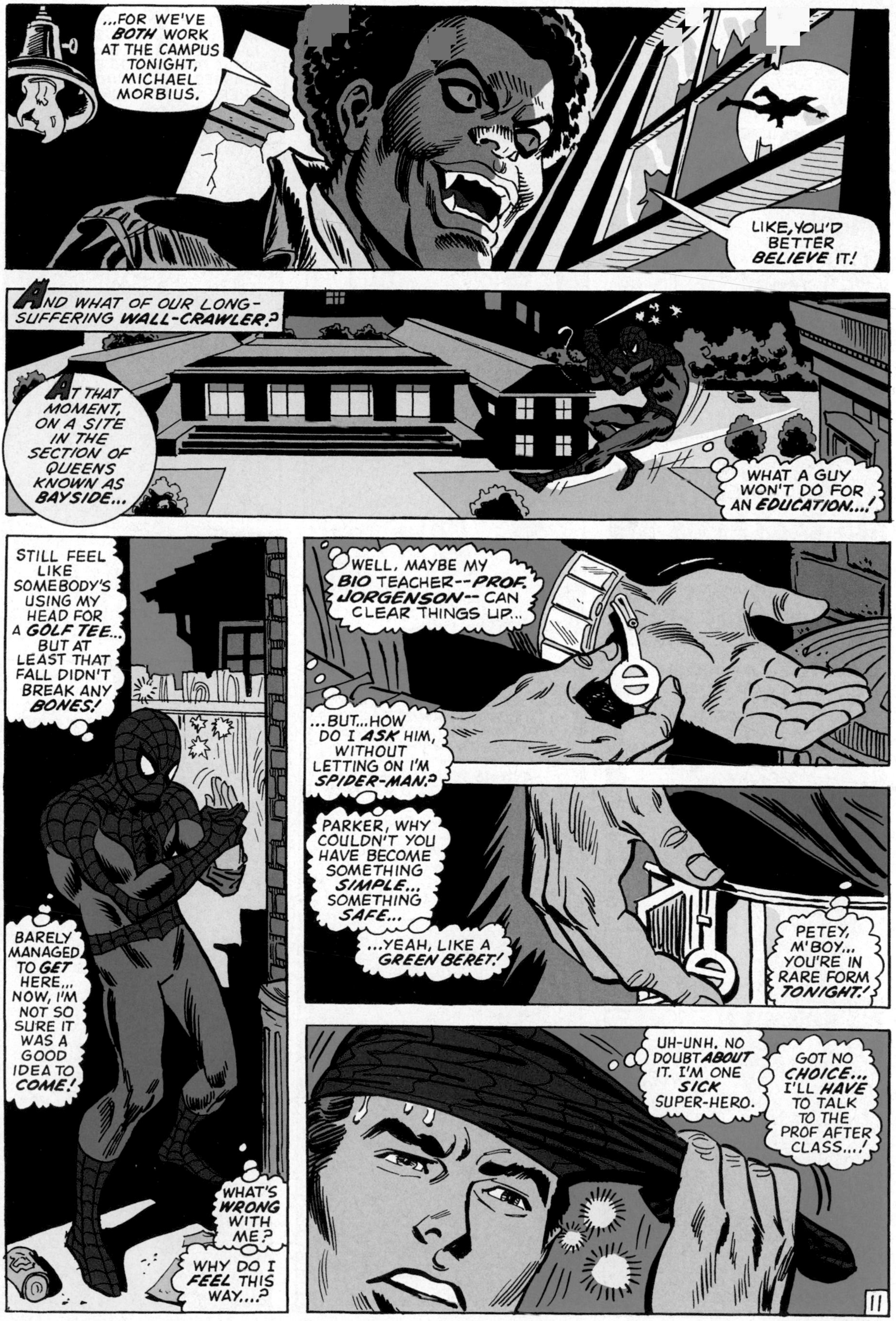
...FOR WE'VE BOTH WORK AT THE CAMPUS TONIGHT, MICHAEL MORBIUS.
LIKE, YOU'D BETTER BELIEVE IT!
AND WHAT OF OUR LONG-SUFFERING WALL-CRAWLER?
AT THAT MOMENT, ON A SITE IN THE SECTION OF QUEENS KNOWN AS BAYSIDE...
WHAT A GUY WON'T DO FOR AN EDUCATION...!
STILL FEEL LIKE SOMEBODY'S USING MY HEAD FOR A GOLF TEE... BUT AT LEAST THAT FALL DIDN'T BREAK ANY BONES!
BARELY MANAGED TO GET HERE... NOW, I'M NOT SO SURE IT WAS A GOOD IDEA TO COME!
WHAT'S WRONG WITH ME?
WHY DO I FEEL THIS WAY...?
WELL, MAYBE MY BIO TEACHER--PROF. JORGENSON--CAN CLEAR THINGS UP...
...BUT...HOW DO I ASK HIM, WITHOUT LETTING ON I'M SPIDER-MAN?
PARKER, WHY COULDN'T YOU HAVE BECOME SOMETHING SIMPLE... SOMETHING SAFE...
...YEAH, LIKE A GREEN BERET!
PETEY, M'BOY... YOU'RE IN RARE FORM TONIGHT!
UH-UNH. NO DOUBT ABOUT IT. I'M ONE SICK SUPER-HERO.
GOT NO CHOICE... I'LL HAVE TO TALK TO THE PROF AFTER CLASS...!
11

THAT IS...IF I *MAKE* IT TILL AFTER CLASS!

I'VE BEEN SICK *BEFORE*--BUT NEVER--*NEVER* LIKE THIS.

FEELS LIKE THE BOTTOM'S DROPPING OUT OF MY *GUT*--THESE CHILLS--*FEVER*--!

*S*TEELING HIMSELF, DRAWING HIS SHOULDERS *STRAIGHT* UNDER HIS *FRAYED* WINDBREAKER, PETER PARKER STEPS INTO THE GLOW OF A NEARBY *ARC LAMP*...

...*A*ND GLANCING *SKYWARD* AT A SUDDEN, FAMILIAR *SOUND*, LETS OUT A WEARY *GROAN*...

TERRIFIC.

I *KNEW* I SHOULDN'T HAVE TOLD STORM I TAKE CLASSES HERE.

IT *FIGURES* HE'D SHOW UP-- PROBABLY WANTS TO TELL ME ABOUT SOME STUPID *BATTLE* HE'S WON.

OKAY, SPIDEY-- LOOKS LIKE YOU'RE *ON* AGAIN.

--*IF* YOU CAN MAKE IT!

*T*HROUGHOUT HISTORY, MEN HAVE *WONDERED* AT THOSE SOMETIMES-CRUCIAL *COINCI-DENCES*--THOSE TWISTS OF *DESTINY* WHICH BRING MEN TOGETHER AGAINST ALL *REASON*--!

SUCH A COINCIDENCE BRINGS US *HERE*, TO A MAN CALLED *HANS JORGENSON*--

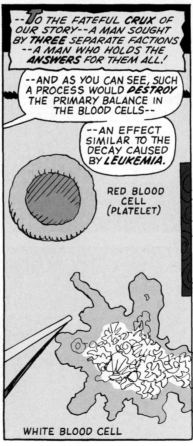

--*T*O THE FATEFUL *CRUX* OF OUR STORY--A MAN SOUGHT BY *THREE* SEPARATE FACTIONS --A MAN WHO HOLDS THE *ANSWERS* FOR THEM ALL!

--AND AS YOU CAN SEE, SUCH A PROCESS WOULD *DESTROY* THE PRIMARY BALANCE IN THE BLOOD CELLS--

--AN EFFECT SIMILAR TO THE DECAY CAUSED BY *LEUKEMIA.*

RED BLOOD CELL (PLATELET)

WHITE BLOOD CELL

RECENT STUDIES BY A COLLEAGUE OF MINE SEEM TO HAVE PROVEN QUITE THE *OPPOSITE*, HOWEVER.

THAT MAN, THE NOTED VASCULAR THEORIST *MICHAEL MORBIUS*, POSTULATES A *SECONDARY* BALANCE--

--ONE ESTAB-LISHED BY A SPLIT-PROTEIN *ENZYME* YET TO BE--

ONE *SECOND*, PROFESSOR--

12

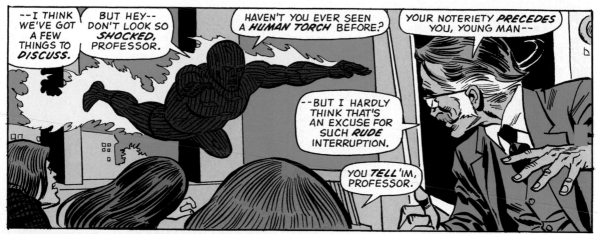

--I THINK WE'VE GOT A FEW THINGS TO *DISCUSS.*

BUT HEY-- DON'T LOOK SO *SHOCKED,* PROFESSOR.

HAVEN'T YOU EVER SEEN A *HUMAN TORCH* BEFORE?

YOUR *NOTERIETY PRECEDES* YOU, YOUNG MAN--

--BUT I HARDLY THINK THAT'S AN EXCUSE FOR SUCH *RUDE* INTERRUPTION.

YOU *TELL* 'IM, PROFESSOR.

TAKE IT *EASY,* SIR. SORRY I RILED YOU.

BUT YOU SEE-- THIS THING'S KINDA *IMPORTANT*--

IMPORTANT? AND MAY I ASK-- IN WHAT *WAY?*

IT'S ABOUT A GUY CALLED *MORBIUS.*

MICHAEL MORBIUS.

--AND I'LL BET YOU KNOW ALL *ABOUT* HIM, DON'TCHA, *TORCHY?*

SPIDER-MAN!

I MUST *PROTEST*--THIS IS JUST *TOO MUCH.*

FUNNY YOU SHOULD *SAY* THAT, PROF--

--I WAS JUST GONNA MENTION THE SAME THING *MYSELF.*

WHAT'S *UP,* STORM? IF YOU'RE TRYING SOME SORT OF *GAME*--

COOL IT, SPIDEY.

WE'RE THE *GOOD GUYS,* REMEMBER?

GENTLEMEN, *PLEASE.* I ASSUME THERE'S A *POINT* TO ALL THIS--

--IN WHICH CASE, WE'LL *DISCOVER* THAT POINT OVER A CUP OF *TEA*--

--BUT *AFTER* THE LECTURE, IF YOU PLEASE?

13

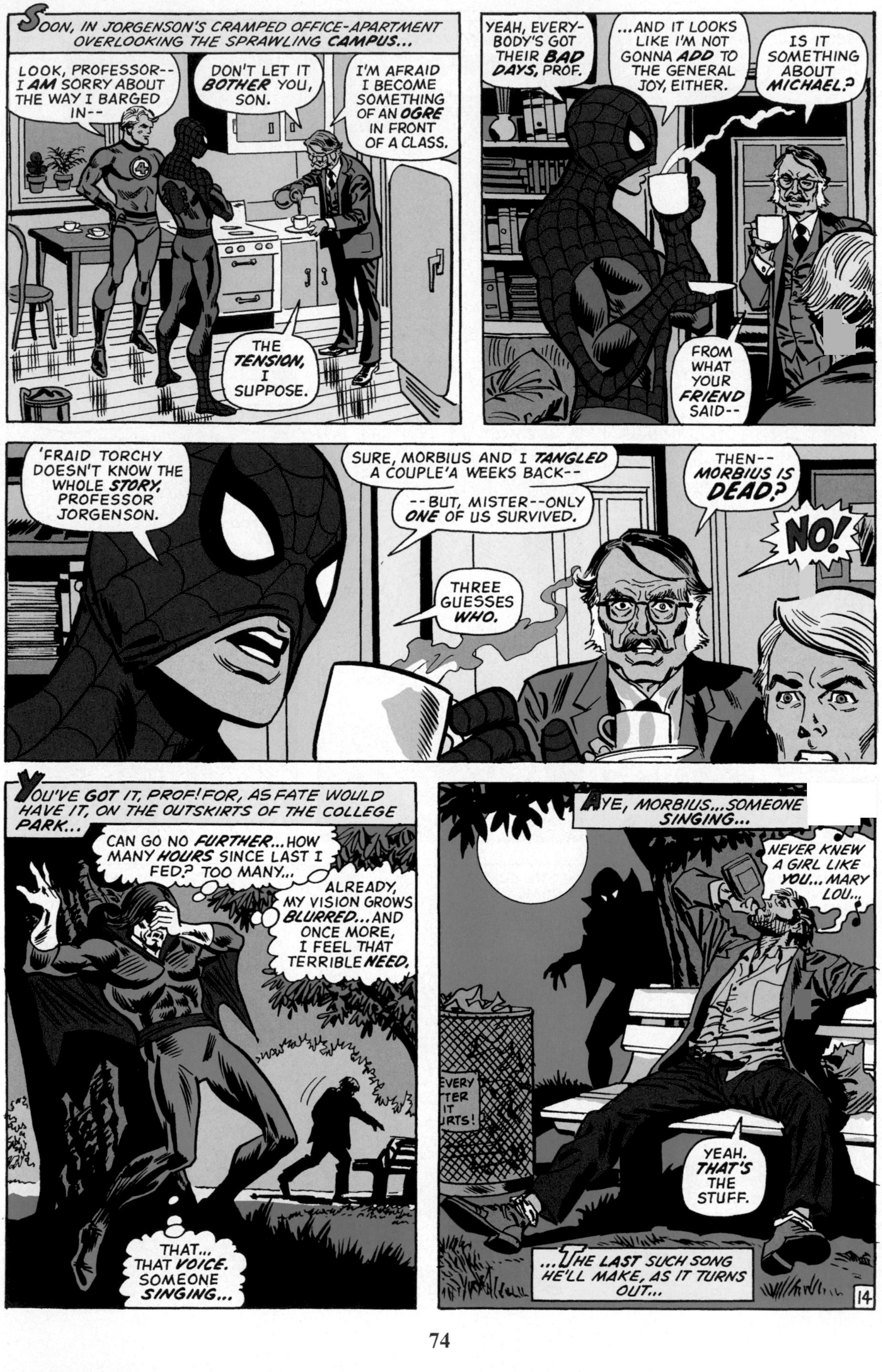
SOON, IN JORGENSON'S CRAMPED OFFICE-APARTMENT OVERLOOKING THE SPRAWLING CAMPUS...
LOOK, PROFESSOR-- I AM SORRY ABOUT THE WAY I BARGED IN--
DON'T LET IT BOTHER YOU, SON.
I'M AFRAID I BECOME SOMETHING OF AN OGRE IN FRONT OF A CLASS.
THE TENSION, I SUPPOSE.
YEAH, EVERYBODY'S GOT THEIR BAD DAYS, PROF.
...AND IT LOOKS LIKE I'M NOT GONNA ADD TO THE GENERAL JOY, EITHER.
IS IT SOMETHING ABOUT MICHAEL?
FROM WHAT YOUR FRIEND SAID--
'FRAID TORCHY DOESN'T KNOW THE WHOLE STORY, PROFESSOR JORGENSON.
SURE, MORBIUS AND I TANGLED A COUPLE'A WEEKS BACK--
--BUT, MISTER--ONLY ONE OF US SURVIVED.
THEN-- MORBIUS IS DEAD?
NO!
THREE GUESSES WHO.
YOU'VE GOT IT, PROF! FOR, AS FATE WOULD HAVE IT, ON THE OUTSKIRTS OF THE COLLEGE PARK...
CAN GO NO FURTHER... HOW MANY HOURS SINCE LAST I FED? TOO MANY...
ALREADY, MY VISION GROWS BLURRED... AND ONCE MORE, I FEEL THAT TERRIBLE NEED.
THAT... THAT VOICE. SOMEONE SINGING...
AYE, MORBIUS... SOMEONE SINGING...
NEVER KNEW A GIRL LIKE YOU... MARY LOU...
YEAH. THAT'S THE STUFF.
...THE LAST SUCH SONG HE'LL MAKE, AS IT TURNS OUT...
14

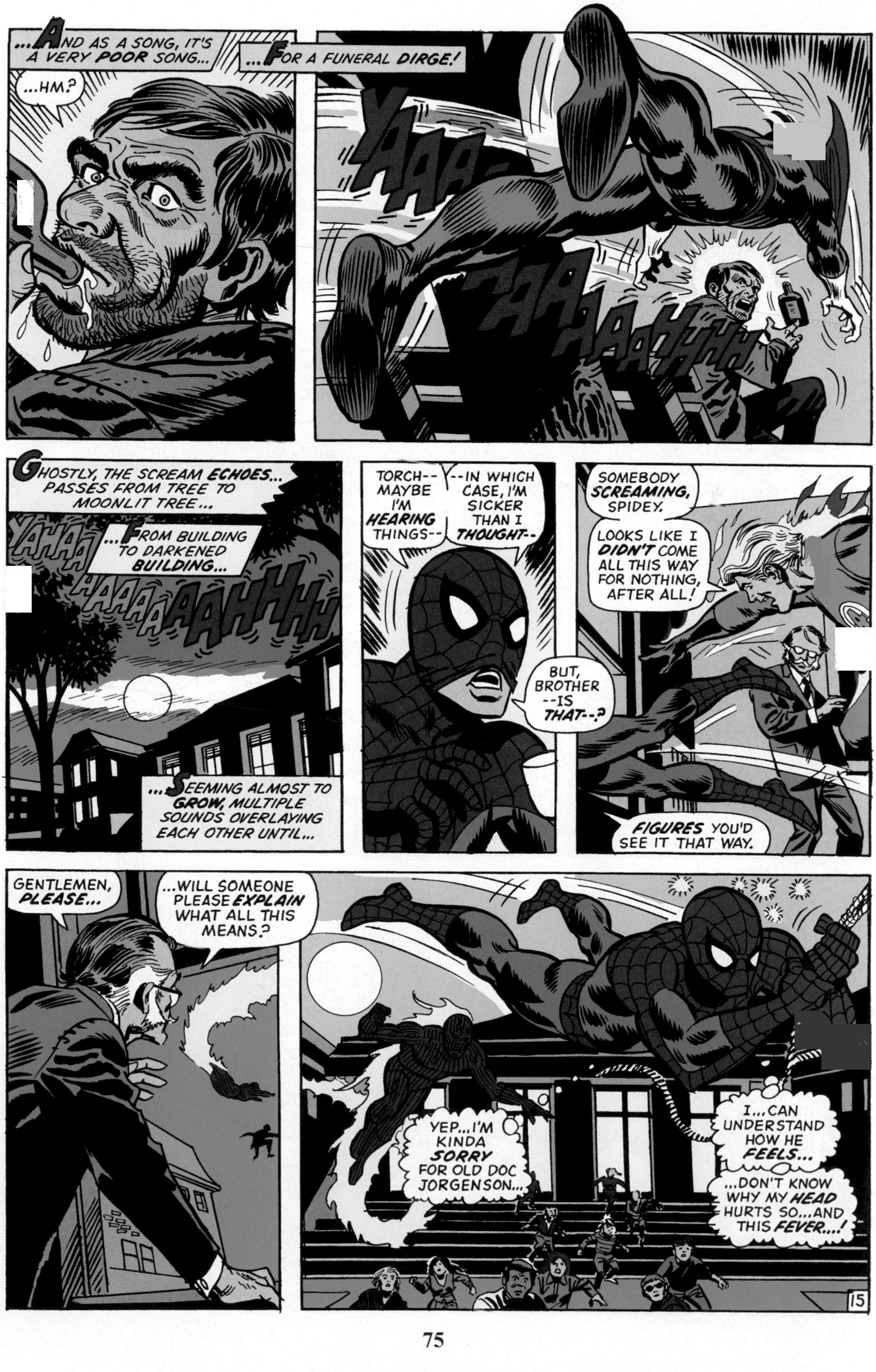
...AND AS A SONG, IT'S A VERY POOR SONG...
...HM?
...FOR A FUNERAL DIRGE!
YAAAA-
AAAAAHHHHH
GHOSTLY, THE SCREAM ECHOES... PASSES FROM TREE TO MOONLIT TREE...
...FROM BUILDING TO DARKENED BUILDING...
YAHAAAAAAAAHHHHH
...SEEMING ALMOST TO GROW, MULTIPLE SOUNDS OVERLAYING EACH OTHER UNTIL...
TORCH-- MAYBE I'M HEARING THINGS--
--IN WHICH CASE, I'M SICKER THAN I THOUGHT--
BUT, BROTHER --IS THAT--?
SOMEBODY SCREAMING, SPIDEY.
LOOKS LIKE I DIDN'T COME ALL THIS WAY FOR NOTHING, AFTER ALL!
FIGURES YOU'D SEE IT THAT WAY.
GENTLEMEN, PLEASE...
...WILL SOMEONE PLEASE EXPLAIN WHAT ALL THIS MEANS?
YEP...I'M KINDA SORRY FOR OLD DOC JORGENSON...
I...CAN UNDERSTAND HOW HE FEELS...
...DON'T KNOW WHY MY HEAD HURTS SO...AND THIS FEVER...!
15

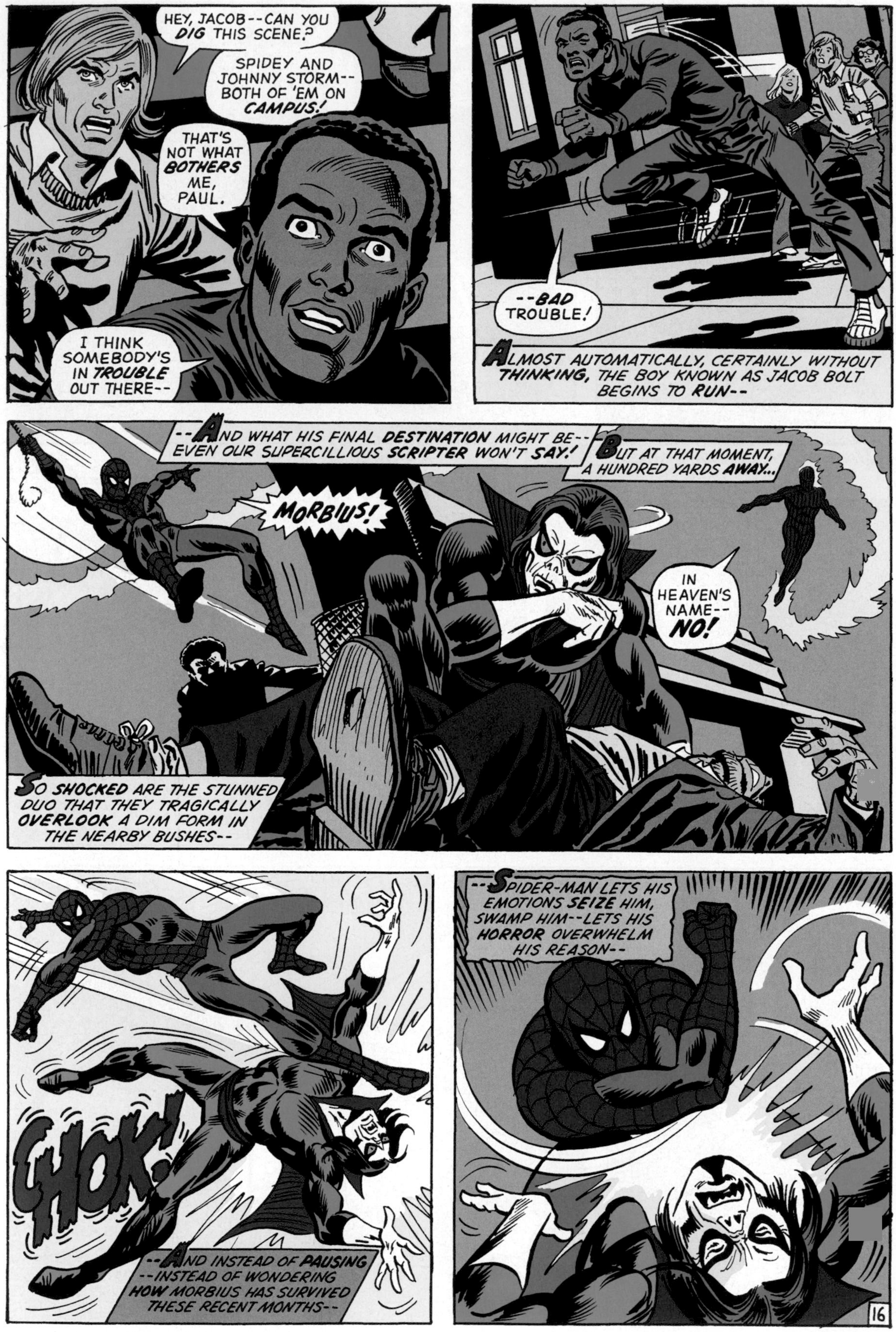
HEY, JACOB--CAN YOU DIG THIS SCENE?
SPIDEY AND JOHNNY STORM--BOTH OF 'EM ON CAMPUS!
THAT'S NOT WHAT BOTHERS ME, PAUL.
I THINK SOMEBODY'S IN TROUBLE OUT THERE--
--BAD TROUBLE!
ALMOST AUTOMATICALLY, CERTAINLY WITHOUT THINKING, THE BOY KNOWN AS JACOB BOLT BEGINS TO RUN--
--AND WHAT HIS FINAL DESTINATION MIGHT BE--EVEN OUR SUPERCILLIOUS SCRIPTER WON'T SAY!
BUT AT THAT MOMENT, A HUNDRED YARDS AWAY...
MORBIUS!
IN HEAVEN'S NAME--NO!
SO SHOCKED ARE THE STUNNED DUO THAT THEY TRAGICALLY OVERLOOK A DIM FORM IN THE NEARBY BUSHES--
CHOK!
--AND INSTEAD OF PAUSING--INSTEAD OF WONDERING HOW MORBIUS HAS SURVIVED THESE RECENT MONTHS--
--SPIDER-MAN LETS HIS EMOTIONS SEIZE HIM, SWAMP HIM--LETS HIS HORROR OVERWHELM HIS REASON--
16

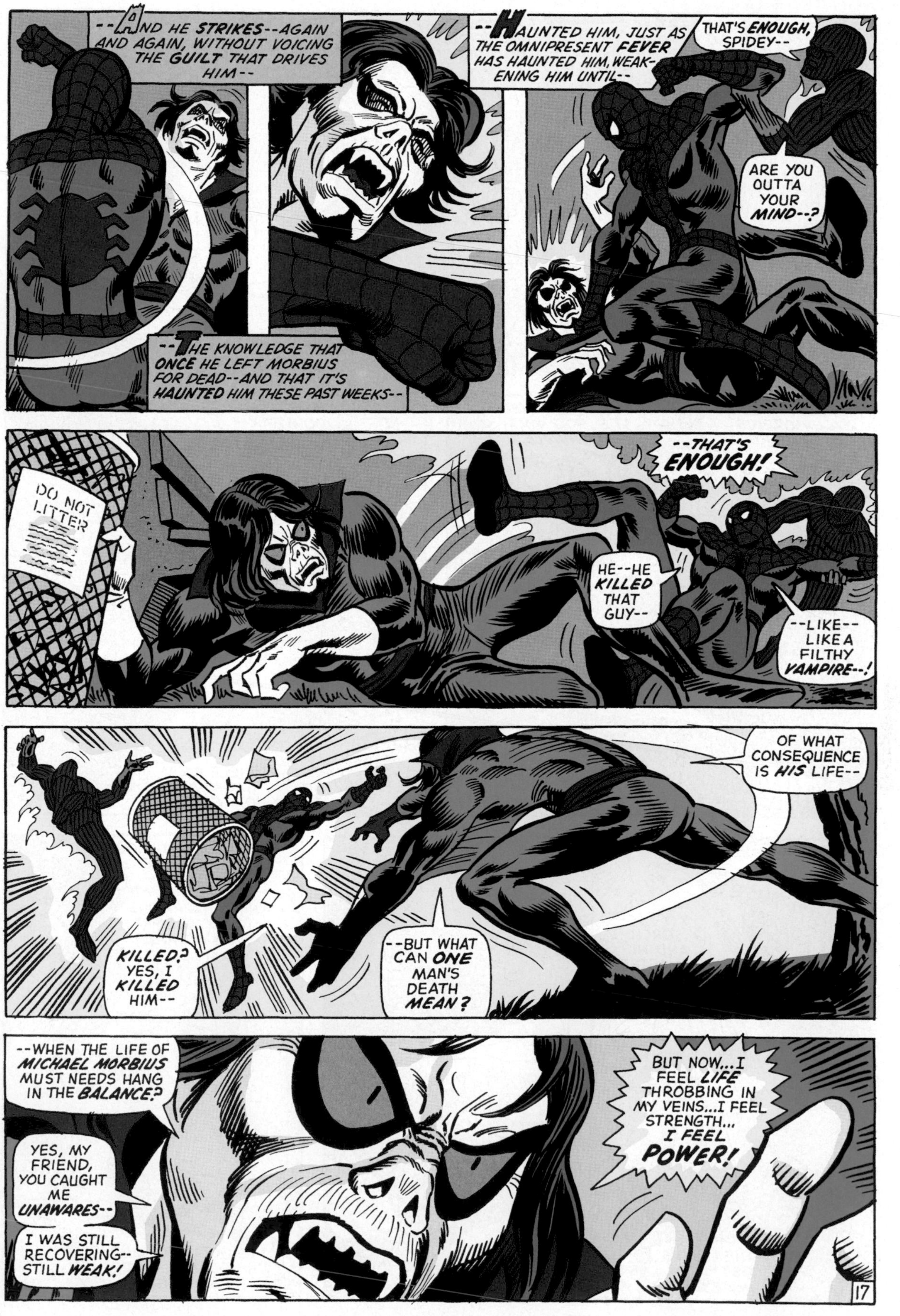
--AND HE STRIKES--AGAIN AND AGAIN, WITHOUT VOICING THE GUILT THAT DRIVES HIM--
--THE KNOWLEDGE THAT ONCE HE LEFT MORBIUS FOR DEAD--AND THAT IT'S HAUNTED HIM THESE PAST WEEKS--
--HAUNTED HIM, JUST AS THE OMNIPRESENT FEVER HAS HAUNTED HIM, WEAKENING HIM UNTIL--
THAT'S ENOUGH, SPIDEY--
ARE YOU OUTTA YOUR MIND--?
DO NOT LITTER
--THAT'S ENOUGH!
HE--HE KILLED THAT GUY--
--LIKE--LIKE A FILTHY VAMPIRE--!
OF WHAT CONSEQUENCE IS HIS LIFE--
KILLED? YES, I KILLED HIM--
--BUT WHAT CAN ONE MAN'S DEATH MEAN?
--WHEN THE LIFE OF MICHAEL MORBIUS MUST NEEDS HANG IN THE BALANCE?
YES, MY FRIEND, YOU CAUGHT ME UNAWARES--
I WAS STILL RECOVERING--STILL WEAK!
BUT NOW...I FEEL LIFE THROBBING IN MY VEINS...I FEEL STRENGTH... I FEEL POWER!
17

DON'T LET IT GO TO YOUR HEAD, MORB!
'CAUSE FROM WHAT SPIDEY WAS TELLING JORGENSON AND ME EARLIER--
MY EYES... THE LIGHT, TOO BRIGHT...!
--THIS SUN-BURST OUGHT TO PUT YOU IN YOUR PLACE!
BLAST IT, WHAT'S WRONG WITH ME--?
ALMOST...TRIED TO KILL MORBIUS BACK THERE...!
IT'S THIS FEVER. IT'S...TOO MUCH TO HANDLE...
GOTTA CALL THIS GAME SHORT...
...FIND OUT... WHY MORBIUS IS STILL ALIVE!
TIK
UNNNH! NO GOOD--
I'M GETTING TOO WEAK-- TO DIRECT MY WEBBING!
WHOLE BODY SHAKING... HOT...COLD...!
TORCH AND HIS BLASTED FIRE-BALLS--
--THE LIGHT'S GETTIN' IN MY EYES--
--AND EVERY TIME I TRY TO HIT MORBIUS--
--THE WHOLE--THING --SEEMS TO COME APART ON ME--
--WHAT'S HAPPENING --TO MY HEAD--? GETTIN' BLURRED--
I'VE GOTTA DO SOME-THING FAST-- 'FORE HE GETS AWAY--
18

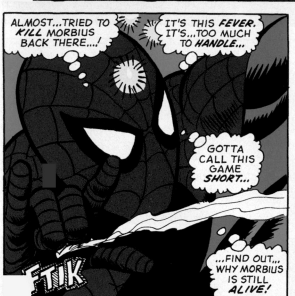

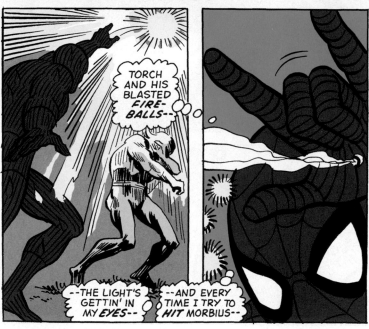

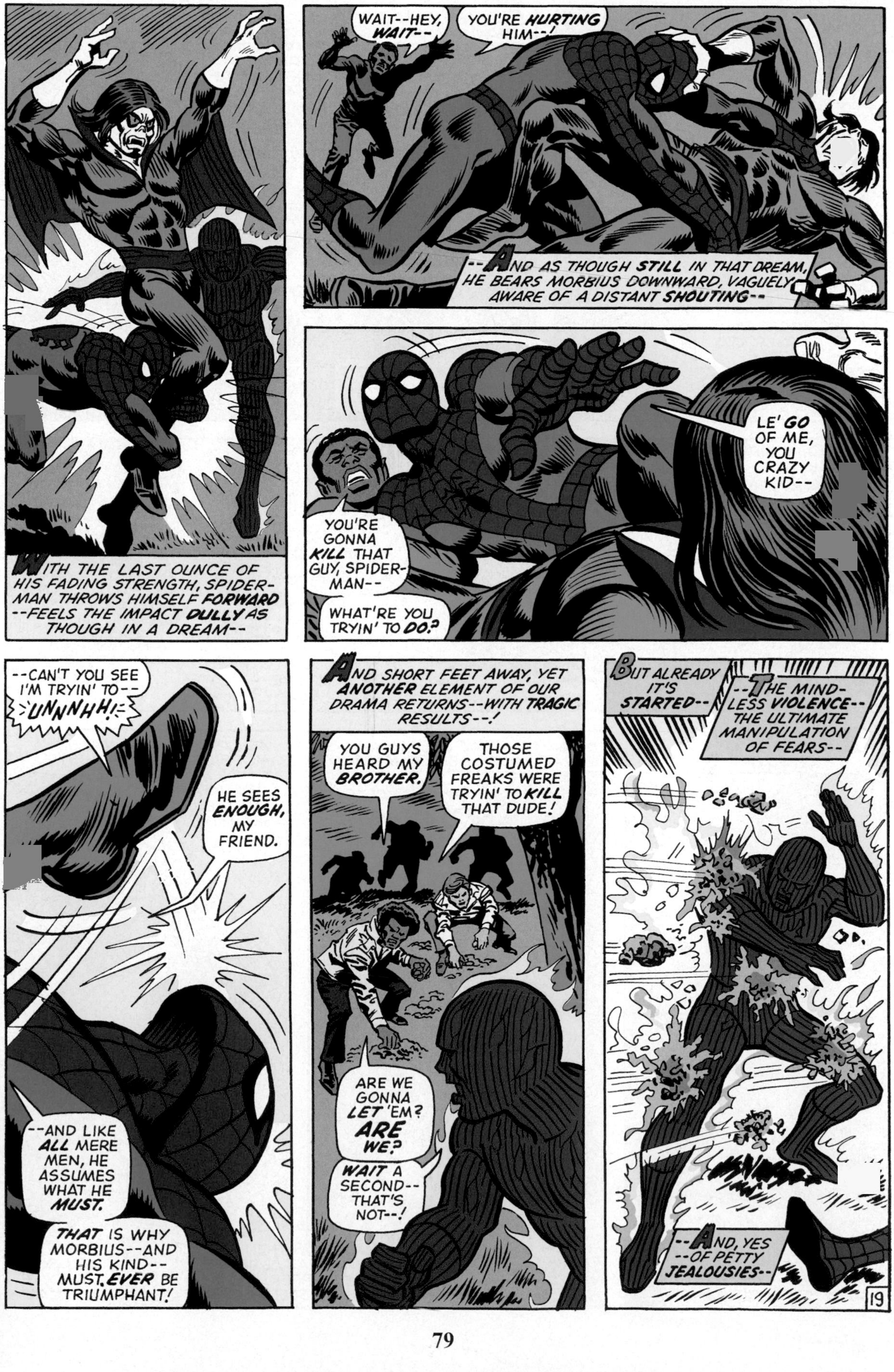
WITH THE LAST OUNCE OF HIS FADING STRENGTH, SPIDER-MAN THROWS HIMSELF FORWARD --FEELS THE IMPACT DULLY AS THOUGH IN A DREAM--
WAIT--HEY, WAIT--
YOU'RE HURTING HIM--!
--AND AS THOUGH STILL IN THAT DREAM, HE BEARS MORBIUS DOWNWARD, VAGUELY AWARE OF A DISTANT SHOUTING--
YOU'RE GONNA KILL THAT GUY, SPIDER-MAN--
WHAT'RE YOU TRYIN' TO DO?
LE' GO OF ME, YOU CRAZY KID--
--CAN'T YOU SEE I'M TRYIN' TO--
UNNNHH!
HE SEES ENOUGH, MY FRIEND.
--AND LIKE ALL MERE MEN, HE ASSUMES WHAT HE MUST.
THAT IS WHY MORBIUS--AND HIS KIND--MUST, EVER BE TRIUMPHANT!
AND SHORT FEET AWAY, YET ANOTHER ELEMENT OF OUR DRAMA RETURNS--WITH TRAGIC RESULTS--!
YOU GUYS HEARD MY BROTHER.
THOSE COSTUMED FREAKS WERE TRYIN' TO KILL THAT DUDE!
ARE WE GONNA LET 'EM? ARE WE?
WAIT A SECOND--THAT'S NOT--!
BUT ALREADY IT'S STARTED--
--THE MINDLESS VIOLENCE--THE ULTIMATE MANIPULATION OF FEARS--
--AND, YES --OF PETTY JEALOUSIES--
19

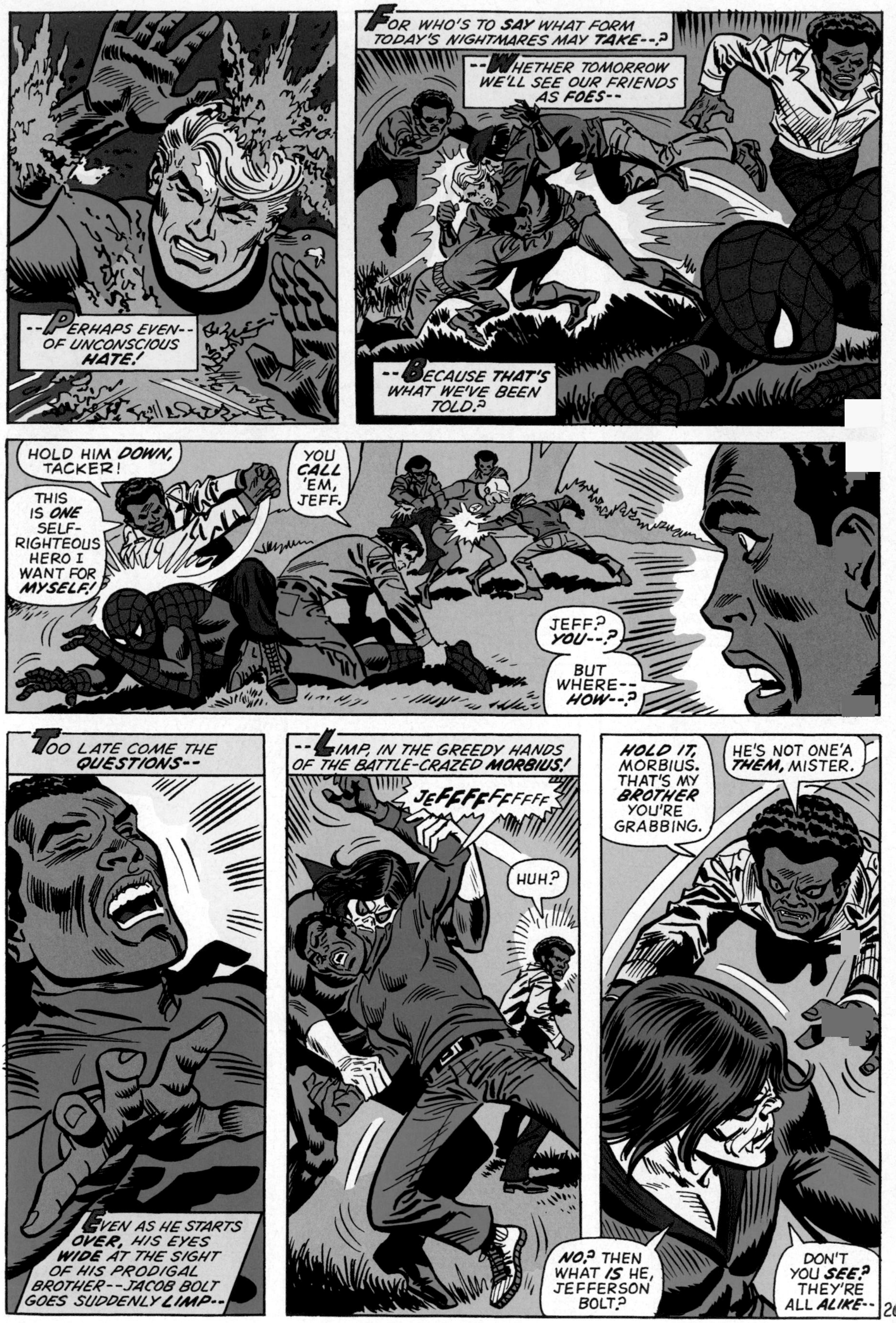
--PERHAPS EVEN--OF UNCONSCIOUS HATE!
FOR WHO'S TO SAY WHAT FORM TODAY'S NIGHTMARES MAY TAKE--?
--WHETHER TOMORROW WE'LL SEE OUR FRIENDS AS FOES--
--BECAUSE THAT'S WHAT WE'VE BEEN TOLD?
HOLD HIM DOWN, TACKER!
THIS IS ONE SELF-RIGHTEOUS HERO I WANT FOR MYSELF!
YOU CALL 'EM, JEFF.
JEFF? YOU--?
BUT WHERE--HOW--?
TOO LATE COME THE QUESTIONS--
EVEN AS HE STARTS OVER, HIS EYES WIDE AT THE SIGHT OF HIS PRODIGAL BROTHER--JACOB BOLT GOES SUDDENLY LIMP--
--LIMP, IN THE GREEDY HANDS OF THE BATTLE-CRAZED MORBIUS!
JEFFFFFFFFFF
HUH?
HOLD IT, MORBIUS. THAT'S MY BROTHER YOU'RE GRABBING.
HE'S NOT ONE'A THEM, MISTER.
NO? THEN WHAT IS HE, JEFFERSON BOLT?
DON'T YOU SEE? THEY'RE ALL ALIKE--

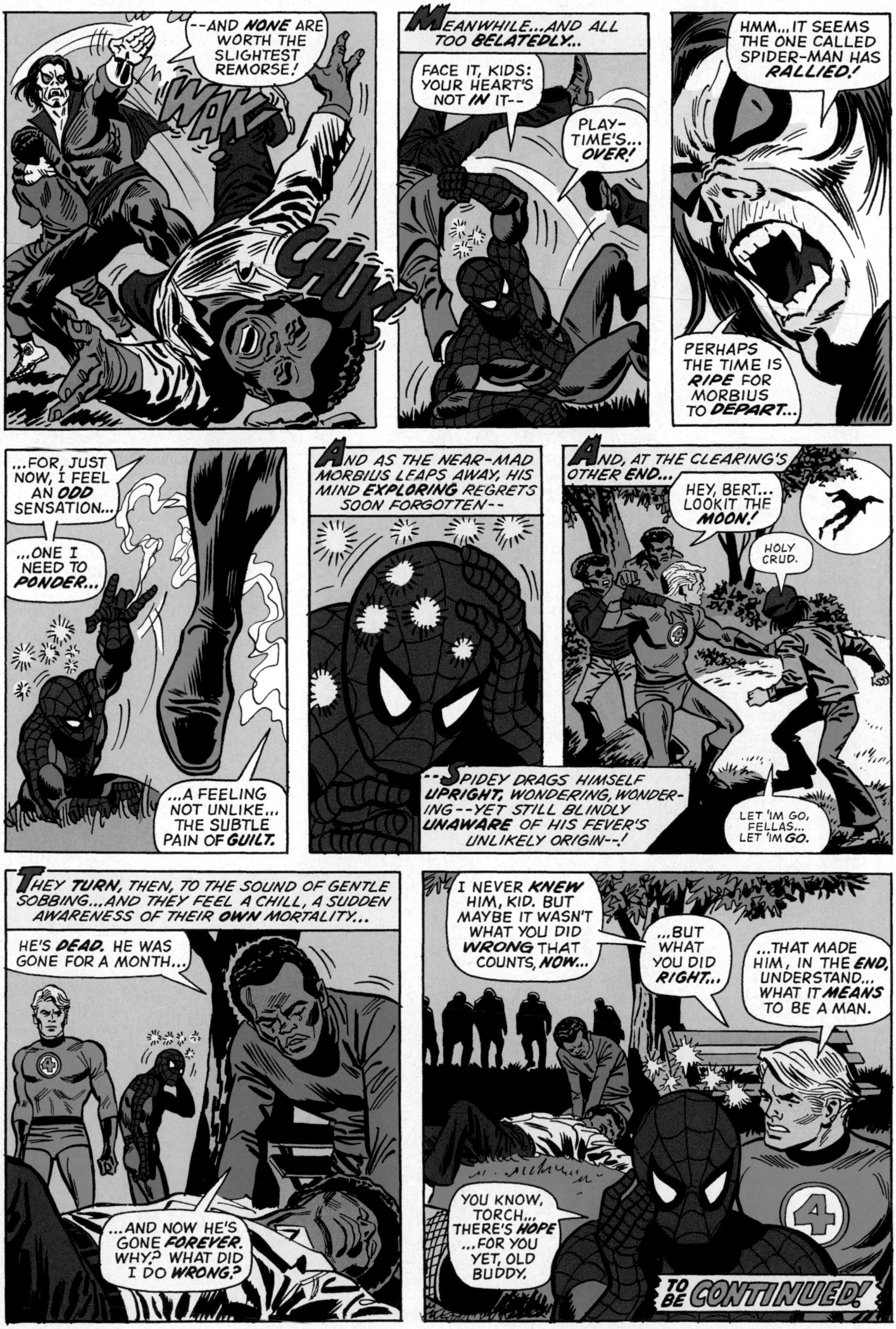
--AND NONE ARE WORTH THE SLIGHTEST REMORSE!
WAK!
CHUK!
MEANWHILE...AND ALL TOO BELATEDLY...
FACE IT, KIDS: YOUR HEART'S NOT IN IT--
PLAY-TIME'S... OVER!
HMM...IT SEEMS THE ONE CALLED SPIDER-MAN HAS RALLIED!
PERHAPS THE TIME IS RIPE FOR MORBIUS TO DEPART...
...FOR, JUST NOW, I FEEL AN ODD SENSATION...
...ONE I NEED TO PONDER...
...A FEELING NOT UNLIKE... THE SUBTLE PAIN OF GUILT.
AND AS THE NEAR-MAD MORBIUS LEAPS AWAY, HIS MIND EXPLORING REGRETS SOON FORGOTTEN--
--SPIDEY DRAGS HIMSELF UPRIGHT, WONDERING, WONDERING--YET STILL BLINDLY UNAWARE OF HIS FEVER'S UNLIKELY ORIGIN--!
AND, AT THE CLEARING'S OTHER END...
HEY, BERT... LOOKIT THE MOON!
HOLY CRUD.
LET 'IM GO, FELLAS... LET 'IM GO.
THEY TURN, THEN, TO THE SOUND OF GENTLE SOBBING...AND THEY FEEL A CHILL, A SUDDEN AWARENESS OF THEIR OWN MORTALITY...
HE'S DEAD. HE WAS GONE FOR A MONTH...
...AND NOW HE'S GONE FOREVER. WHY? WHAT DID I DO WRONG?
I NEVER KNEW HIM, KID. BUT MAYBE IT WASN'T WHAT YOU DID WRONG THAT COUNTS, NOW...
...BUT WHAT YOU DID RIGHT...
...THAT MADE HIM, IN THE END, UNDERSTAND... WHAT IT MEANS TO BE A MAN.
YOU KNOW, TORCH... THERE'S HOPE ...FOR YOU YET, OLD BUDDY.
TO BE CONTINUED!

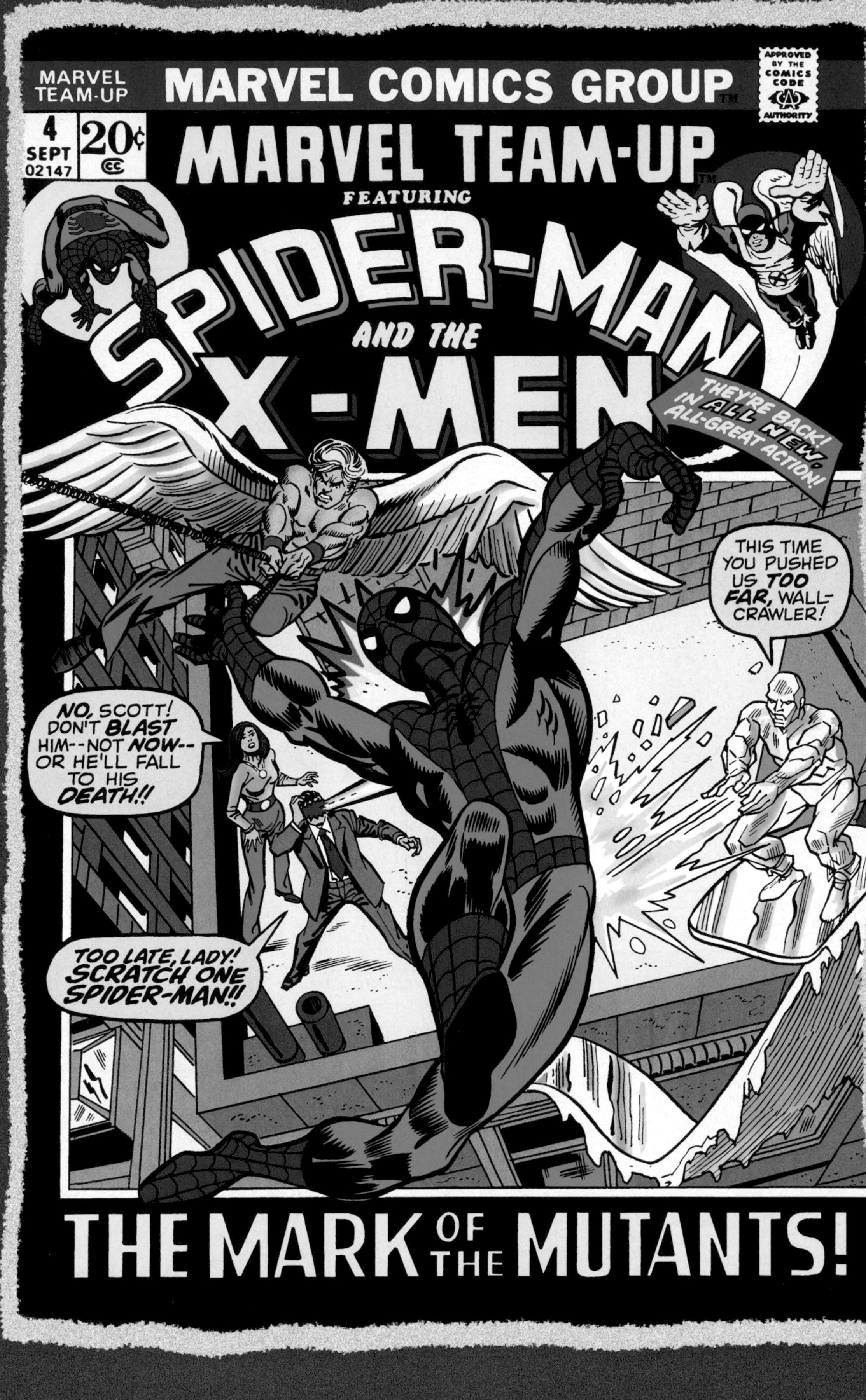
MARVEL TEAM-UP
MARVEL COMICS GROUP
APPROVED BY THE COMICS CODE AUTHORITY
4 SEPT 02147
20¢
MARVEL TEAM-UP
FEATURING
SPIDER-MAN
AND THE
X-MEN
THEY'RE BACK! IN ALL NEW, ALL-GREAT ACTION!
THIS TIME YOU PUSHED US TOO FAR, WALL-CRAWLER!
NO, SCOTT! DON'T BLAST HIM--NOT NOW--OR HE'LL FALL TO HIS DEATH!!
TOO LATE, LADY! SCRATCH ONE SPIDER-MAN!!
THE MARK OF THE MUTANTS!

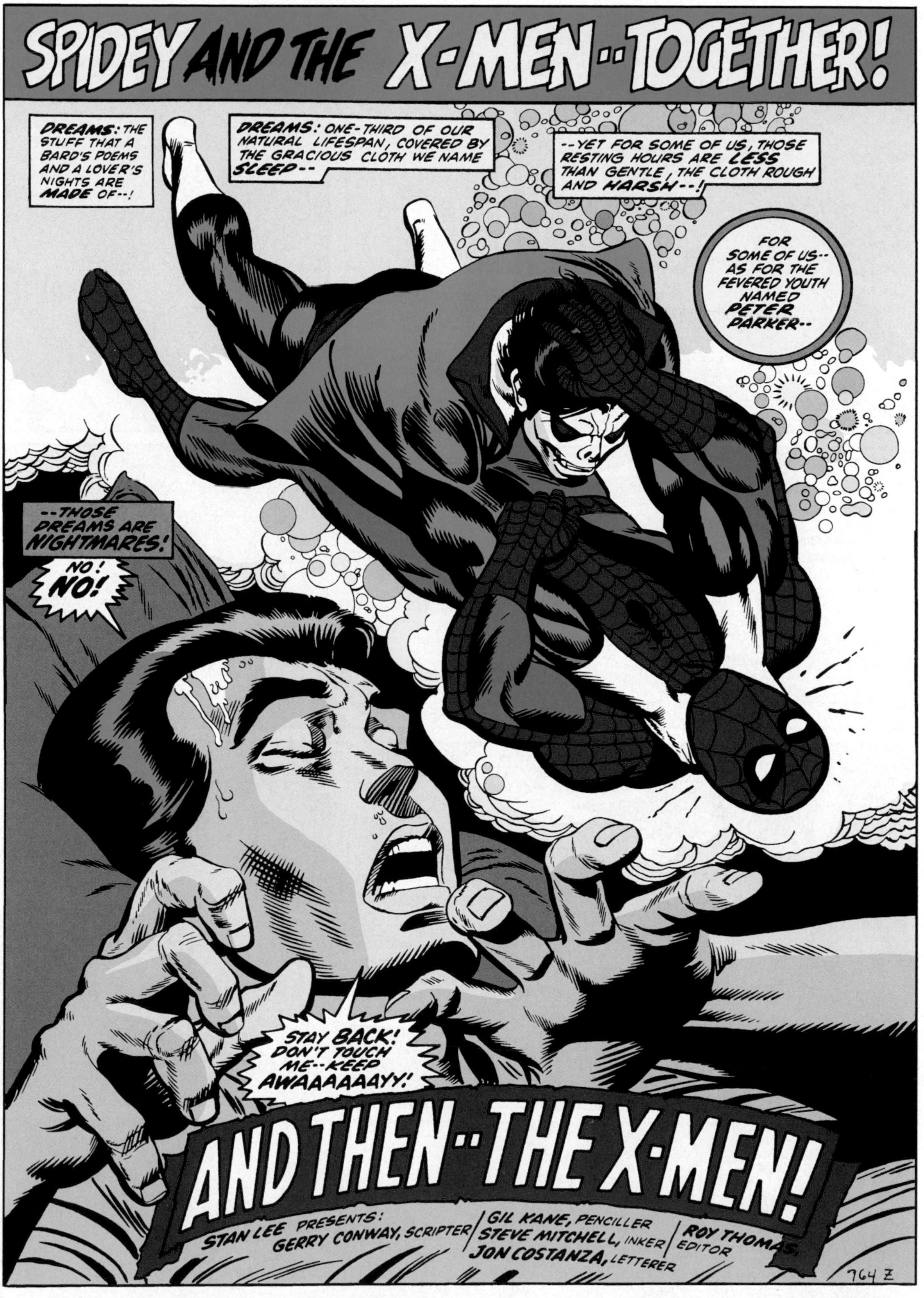

SPIDEY AND THE X-MEN..TOGETHER!
DREAMS: THE STUFF THAT A BARD'S POEMS AND A LOVER'S NIGHTS ARE MADE OF--!
DREAMS: ONE-THIRD OF OUR NATURAL LIFESPAN, COVERED BY THE GRACIOUS CLOTH WE NAME SLEEP--
--YET FOR SOME OF US, THOSE RESTING HOURS ARE LESS THAN GENTLE, THE CLOTH ROUGH AND HARSH--!
FOR SOME OF US-- AS FOR THE FEVERED YOUTH NAMED PETER PARKER--
--THOSE DREAMS ARE NIGHTMARES!
NO! NO!
STAY BACK! DON'T TOUCH ME--KEEP AWAAAAAAYY!
AND THEN..THE X-MEN!
STAN LEE PRESENTS: GERRY CONWAY, SCRIPTER
GIL KANE, PENCILLER STEVE MITCHELL, INKER JON COSTANZA, LETTERER
ROY THOMAS, EDITOR
764 Z

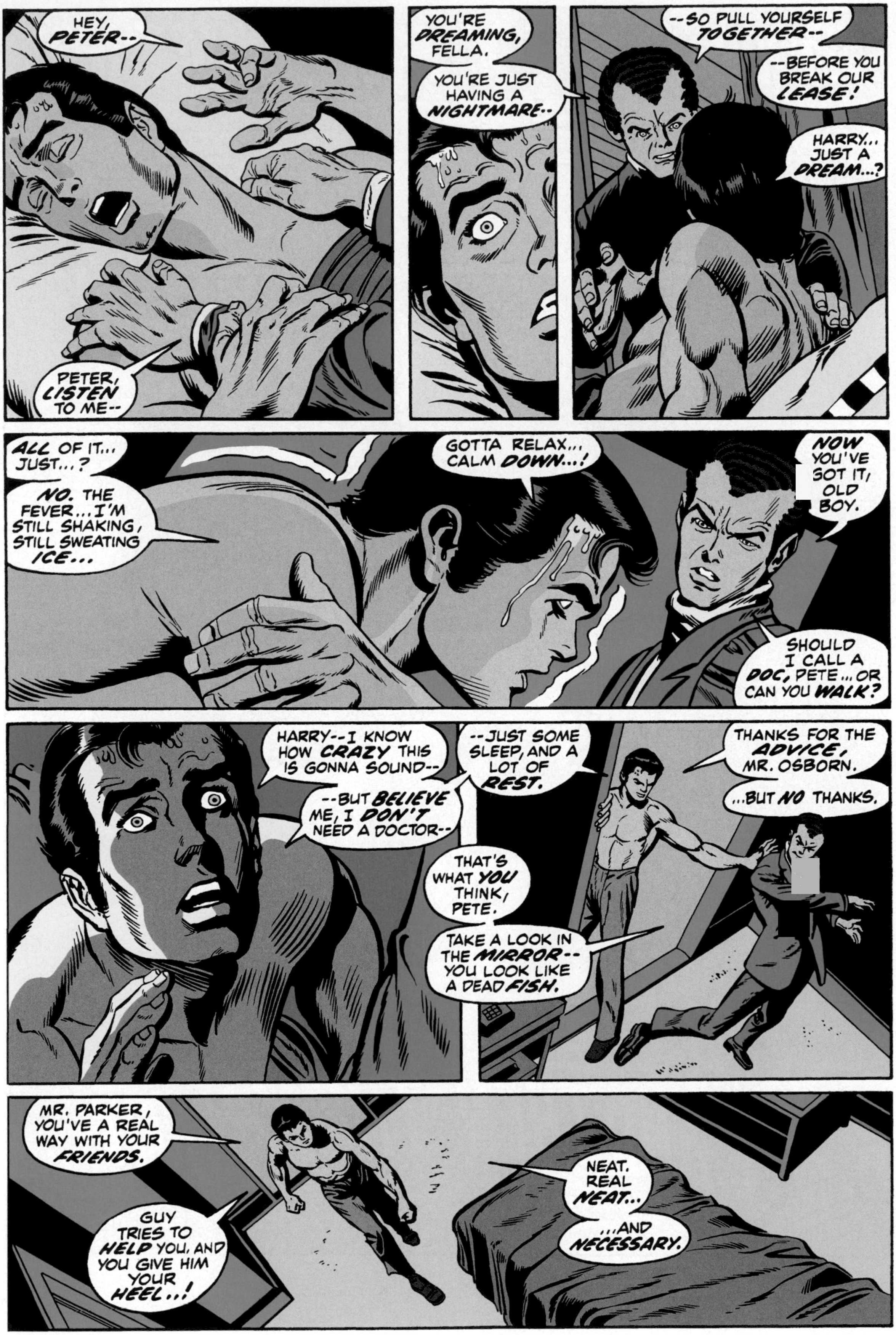
HEY, PETER--
PETER, LISTEN TO ME--
YOU'RE DREAMING, FELLA.
YOU'RE JUST HAVING A NIGHTMARE..
--SO PULL YOURSELF TOGETHER--
--BEFORE YOU BREAK OUR LEASE!
HARRY... JUST A DREAM...?
ALL OF IT... JUST...?
NO. THE FEVER... I'M STILL SHAKING, STILL SWEATING ICE...
GOTTA RELAX... CALM DOWN...!
NOW YOU'VE GOT IT, OLD BOY.
SHOULD I CALL A DOC, PETE... OR CAN YOU WALK?
HARRY--I KNOW HOW CRAZY THIS IS GONNA SOUND--
--BUT BELIEVE ME, I DON'T NEED A DOCTOR--
--JUST SOME SLEEP, AND A LOT OF REST.
THAT'S WHAT YOU THINK, PETE.
TAKE A LOOK IN THE MIRROR--YOU LOOK LIKE A DEAD FISH.
THANKS FOR THE ADVICE, MR. OSBORN.
...BUT NO THANKS.
MR. PARKER, YOU'VE A REAL WAY WITH YOUR FRIENDS.
GUY TRIES TO HELP YOU, AND YOU GIVE HIM YOUR HEEL..!
NEAT. REAL NEAT...
...AND NECESSARY.

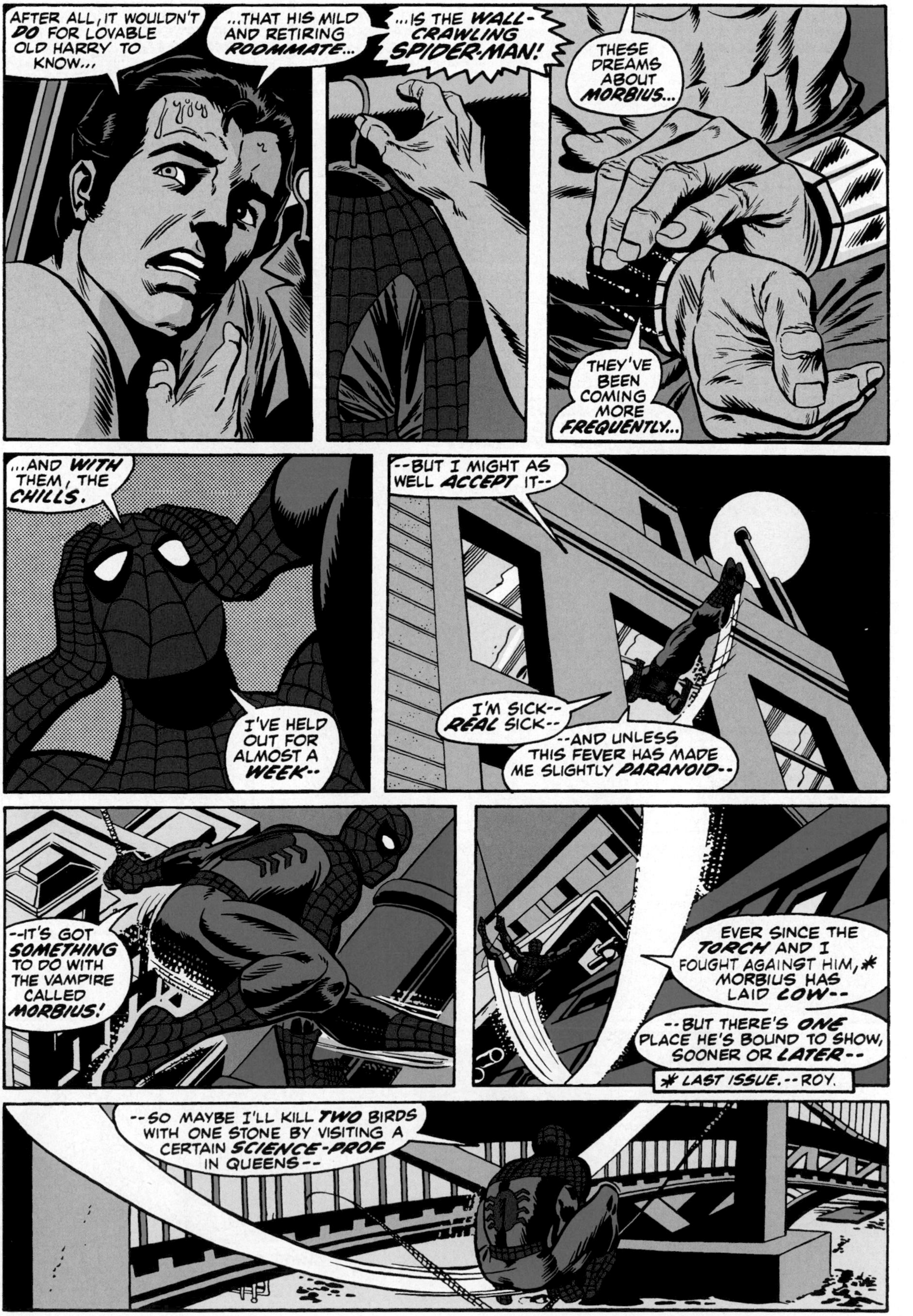
AFTER ALL, IT WOULDN'T DO FOR LOVABLE OLD HARRY TO KNOW...
...THAT HIS MILD AND RETIRING ROOMMATE...
...IS THE WALL-CRAWLING SPIDER-MAN!
THESE DREAMS ABOUT MORBIUS...
THEY'VE BEEN COMING MORE FREQUENTLY...
...AND WITH THEM, THE CHILLS.
I'VE HELD OUT FOR ALMOST A WEEK--
--BUT I MIGHT AS WELL ACCEPT IT--
I'M SICK-- REAL SICK--
--AND UNLESS THIS FEVER HAS MADE ME SLIGHTLY PARANOID--
--IT'S GOT SOMETHING TO DO WITH THE VAMPIRE CALLED MORBIUS!
EVER SINCE THE TORCH AND I FOUGHT AGAINST HIM,* MORBIUS HAS LAID LOW--
--BUT THERE'S ONE PLACE HE'S BOUND TO SHOW, SOONER OR LATER--
* LAST ISSUE.--ROY.
--SO MAYBE I'LL KILL TWO BIRDS WITH ONE STONE BY VISITING A CERTAIN SCIENCE-PROF IN QUEENS--

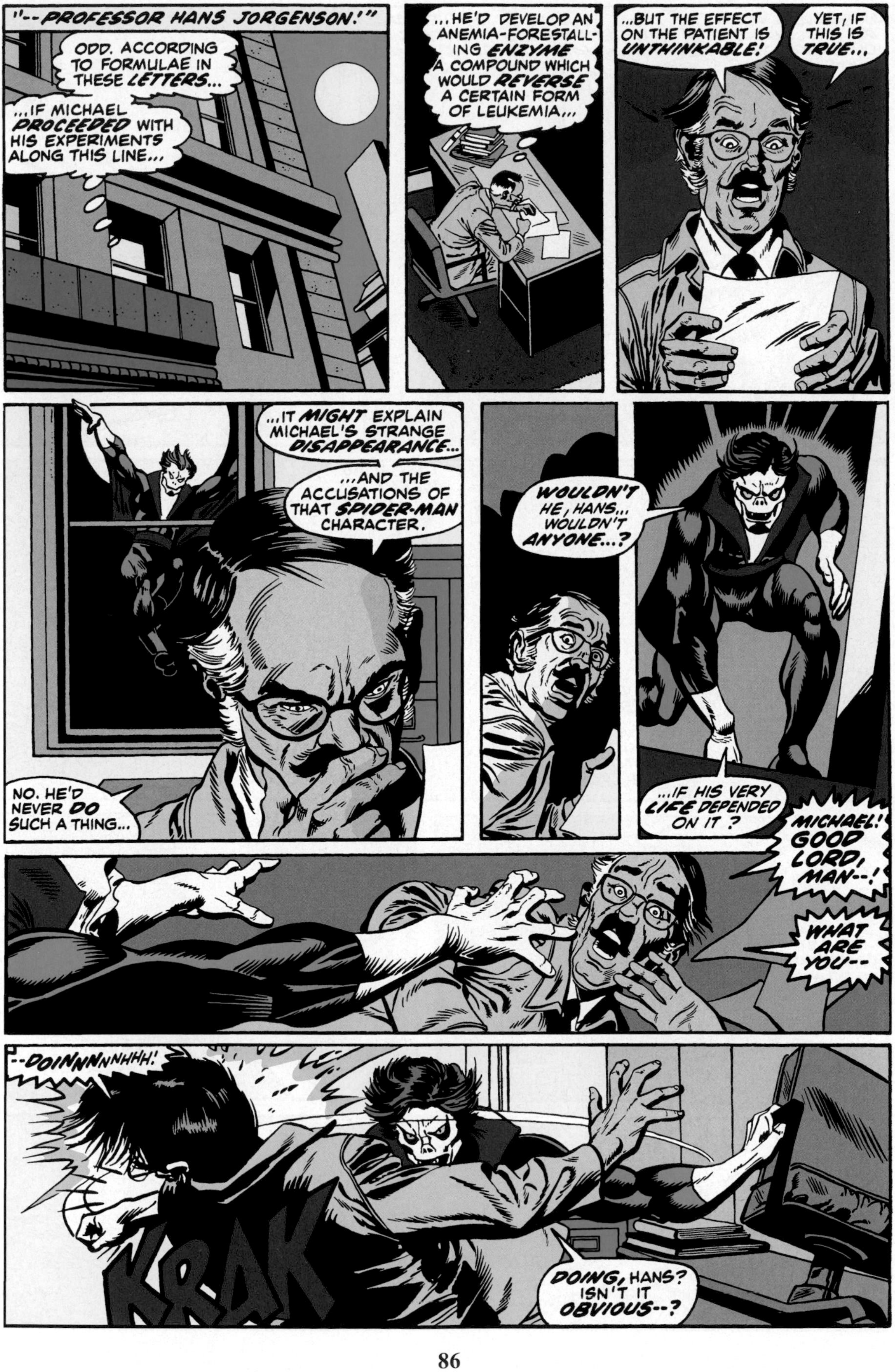
"--PROFESSOR HANS JORGENSON!"
ODD. ACCORDING TO FORMULAE IN THESE LETTERS...
...IF MICHAEL PROCEEDED WITH HIS EXPERIMENTS ALONG THIS LINE...
...HE'D DEVELOP AN ANEMIA-FORESTALLING ENZYME A COMPOUND WHICH WOULD REVERSE A CERTAIN FORM OF LEUKEMIA...
...BUT THE EFFECT ON THE PATIENT IS UNTHINKABLE!
YET, IF THIS IS TRUE...
...IT MIGHT EXPLAIN MICHAEL'S STRANGE DISAPPEARANCE...
...AND THE ACCUSATIONS OF THAT SPIDER-MAN CHARACTER.
NO. HE'D NEVER DO SUCH A THING...
WOULDN'T HE, HANS... WOULDN'T ANYONE...?
...IF HIS VERY LIFE DEPENDED ON IT?
MICHAEL! GOOD LORD, MAN--!
WHAT ARE YOU--
--DOINNNNNHHH!
KRAK
DOING, HANS? ISN'T IT OBVIOUS--?

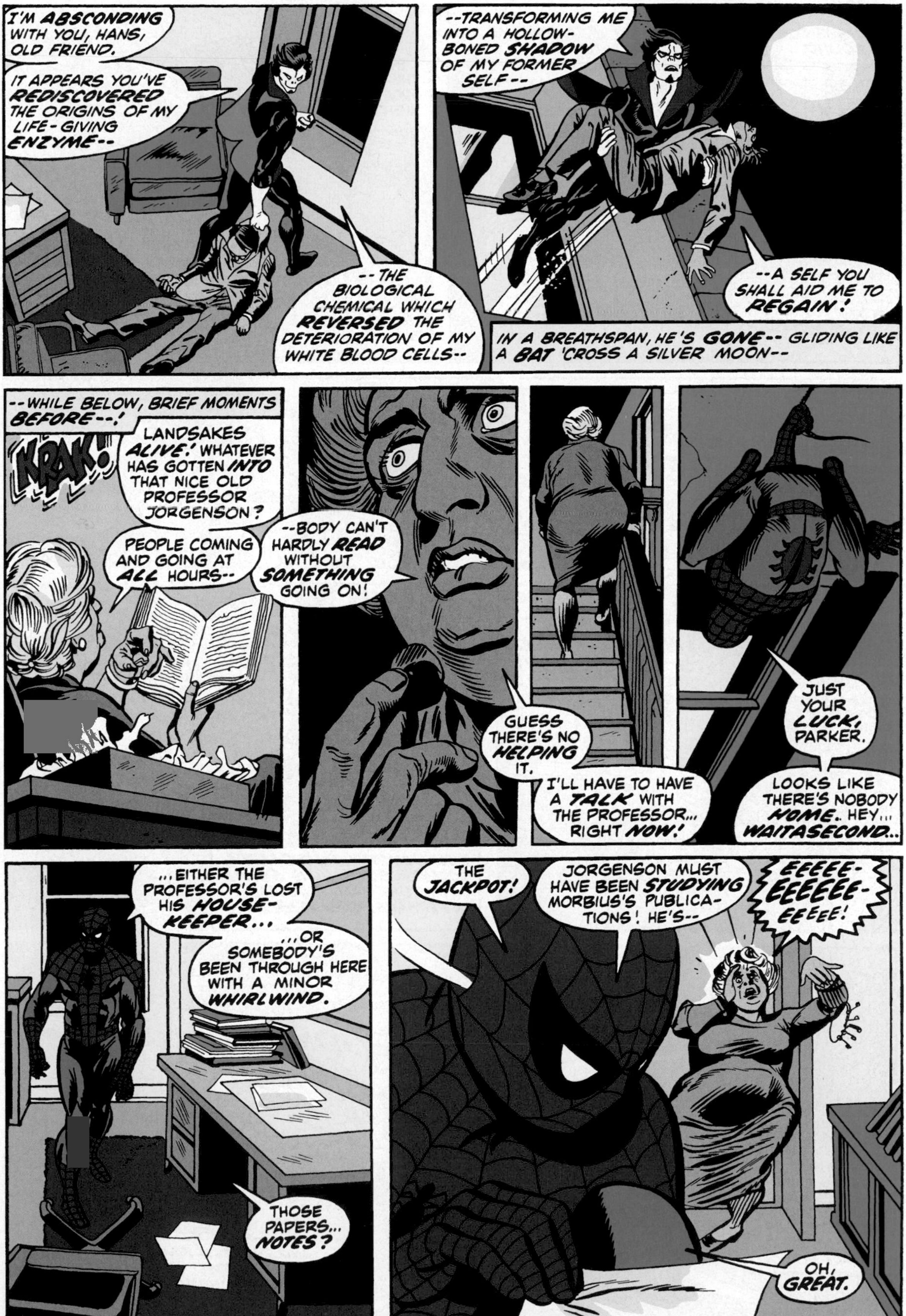
I'M ABSCONDING WITH YOU, HANS, OLD FRIEND.
IT APPEARS YOU'VE REDISCOVERED THE ORIGINS OF MY LIFE-GIVING ENZYME--
--THE BIOLOGICAL CHEMICAL WHICH REVERSED THE DETERIORATION OF MY WHITE BLOOD CELLS--
--TRANSFORMING ME INTO A HOLLOW-BONED SHADOW OF MY FORMER SELF--
--A SELF YOU SHALL AID ME TO REGAIN!
IN A BREATHSPAN, HE'S GONE-- GLIDING LIKE A BAT 'CROSS A SILVER MOON--
--WHILE BELOW, BRIEF MOMENTS BEFORE--!
KRAK!
LANDSAKES ALIVE! WHATEVER HAS GOTTEN INTO THAT NICE OLD PROFESSOR JORGENSON?
PEOPLE COMING AND GOING AT ALL HOURS--
--BODY CAN'T HARDLY READ WITHOUT SOMETHING GOING ON!
GUESS THERE'S NO HELPING IT.
I'LL HAVE TO HAVE A TALK WITH THE PROFESSOR... RIGHT NOW!
JUST YOUR LUCK, PARKER.
LOOKS LIKE THERE'S NOBODY HOME.. HEY... WAITASECOND...
...EITHER THE PROFESSOR'S LOST HIS HOUSE-KEEPER...
...OR SOMEBODY'S BEEN THROUGH HERE WITH A MINOR WHIRLWIND.
THOSE PAPERS... NOTES?
THE JACKPOT!
JORGENSON MUST HAVE BEEN STUDYING MORBIUS'S PUBLICA-TIONS! HE'S--
EEEEE-EEEEEE-EEEEE!
OH, GREAT.

MAYBE IF I *WAIT* TILL SHE COMES AROUND...

UH-UH, SHE'D NEVER *BELIEVE* ME...AND NEITHER WOULD THE *POLICE.*

BESIDES... THE WAY MY *HEAD* FEELS RIGHT NOW...

...WHEN *SHE* WAKES... I MIGHT BE *OUT*...

...AND *THAT* WOULD BE EXACTLY WHAT I *NEED!*

THE NEXT MORNING, IN WEST-CHESTER...

SPIDER-MAN KIDNAPS NOTED SCIENTIST

THE SPIDER-MAN MENACE
BY J. JONAH JAMESON
PUBLISHER OF THE BUGLE

JORGENSON ABDUCTED FROM SUITE!

WELL-KNOWN CARTOONIST

HANS... *KIDNAPPED?*

IT SEEMS *ABSURD*... AND *YET*...

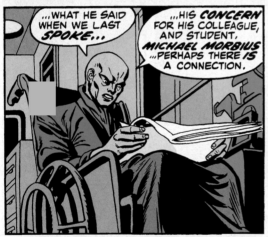

...WHAT HE SAID WHEN WE LAST *SPOKE*...

...HIS *CONCERN* FOR HIS COLLEAGUE, AND STUDENT, *MICHAEL MORBIUS*...PERHAPS THERE *IS* A CONNECTION.

...AND IF THERE *IS*, CHARLES XAVIER *CANNOT* AVERT HIS *EYES*...

...OR HIS *BRAIN!*

THEN, SOMETHING *UNCANNY* OCCURS: SOMETHING *SOME* MEN MIGHT CALL SURREAL, OR PERHAPS *IMPOSSIBLE*--

--THE MIND OF CHARLES XAVIER REACHES *OUT*, TO A DISTANT ROOM OF THIS MANY-LEVELED PRIVATE SCHOOL--

--AND THERE, IT FINDS TWO *MORE* MINDS, OF TWO UTTERLY *FANTASTIC* HUMAN BEINGS-- ONE KNOWN AS *THE ANGEL*, THE OTHER SIMPLY AS *ICEMAN*--!

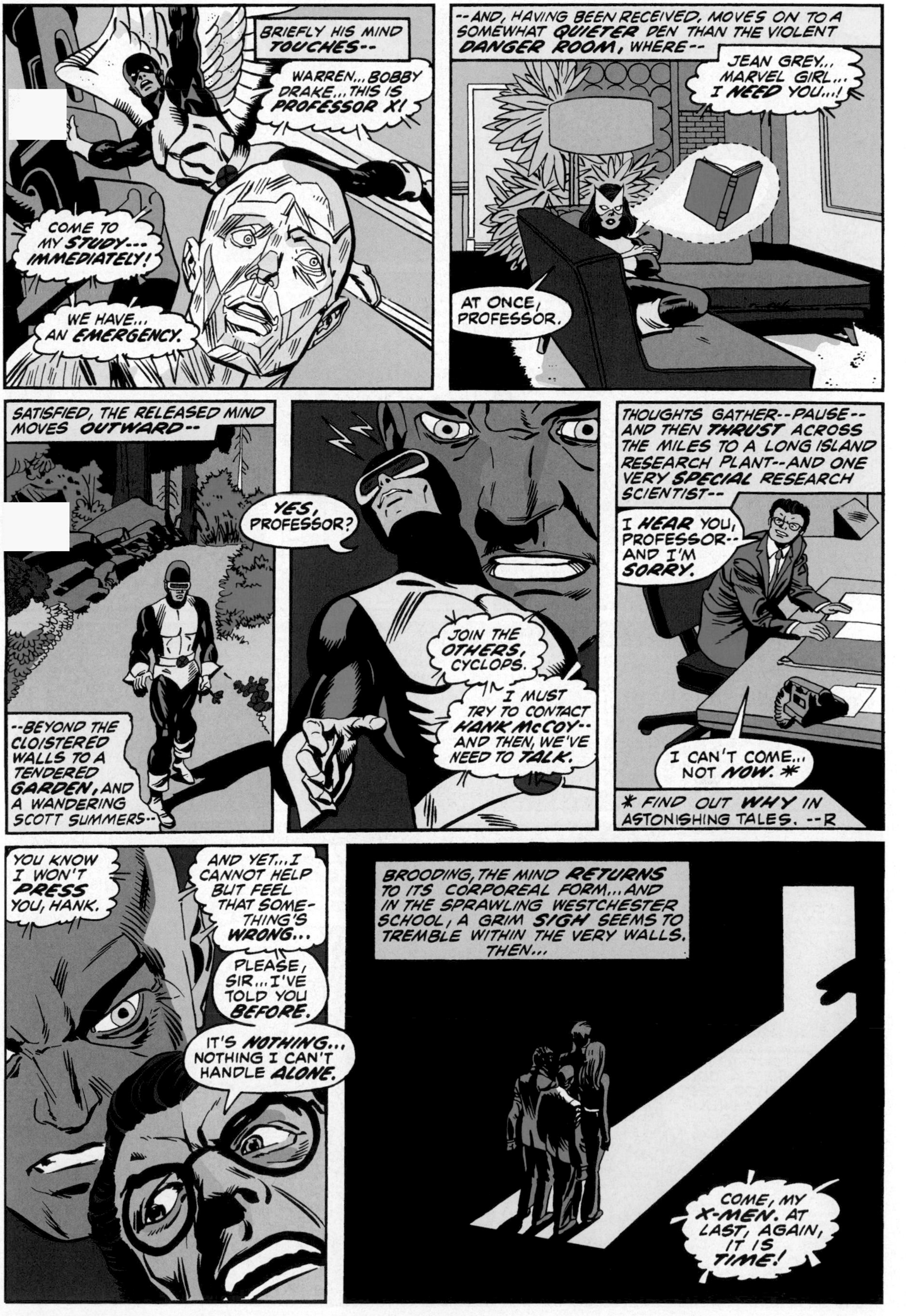
BRIEFLY HIS MIND TOUCHES--
WARREN... BOBBY DRAKE... THIS IS PROFESSOR X!
COME TO MY STUDY--- IMMEDIATELY!
WE HAVE... AN EMERGENCY.
--AND, HAVING BEEN RECEIVED, MOVES ON TO A SOMEWHAT QUIETER DEN THAN THE VIOLENT DANGER ROOM, WHERE--
JEAN GREY... MARVEL GIRL... I NEED YOU...!
AT ONCE, PROFESSOR.
SATISFIED, THE RELEASED MIND MOVES OUTWARD--
--BEYOND THE CLOISTERED WALLS TO A TENDERED GARDEN, AND A WANDERING SCOTT SUMMERS--
YES, PROFESSOR?
JOIN THE OTHERS, CYCLOPS.
I MUST TRY TO CONTACT HANK McCOY-- AND THEN, WE'VE NEED TO TALK.
THOUGHTS GATHER--PAUSE-- AND THEN THRUST ACROSS THE MILES TO A LONG ISLAND RESEARCH PLANT--AND ONE VERY SPECIAL RESEARCH SCIENTIST--
I HEAR YOU, PROFESSOR-- AND I'M SORRY.
I CAN'T COME... NOT NOW. *
* FIND OUT WHY IN ASTONISHING TALES. --R
YOU KNOW I WON'T PRESS YOU, HANK.
AND YET... I CANNOT HELP BUT FEEL THAT SOME-THING'S WRONG...
PLEASE, SIR... I'VE TOLD YOU BEFORE.
IT'S NOTHING... NOTHING I CAN'T HANDLE ALONE.
BROODING, THE MIND RETURNS TO ITS CORPOREAL FORM... AND IN THE SPRAWLING WESTCHESTER SCHOOL, A GRIM SIGH SEEMS TO TREMBLE WITHIN THE VERY WALLS. THEN...
COME, MY X-MEN. AT LAST, AGAIN, IT IS TIME!

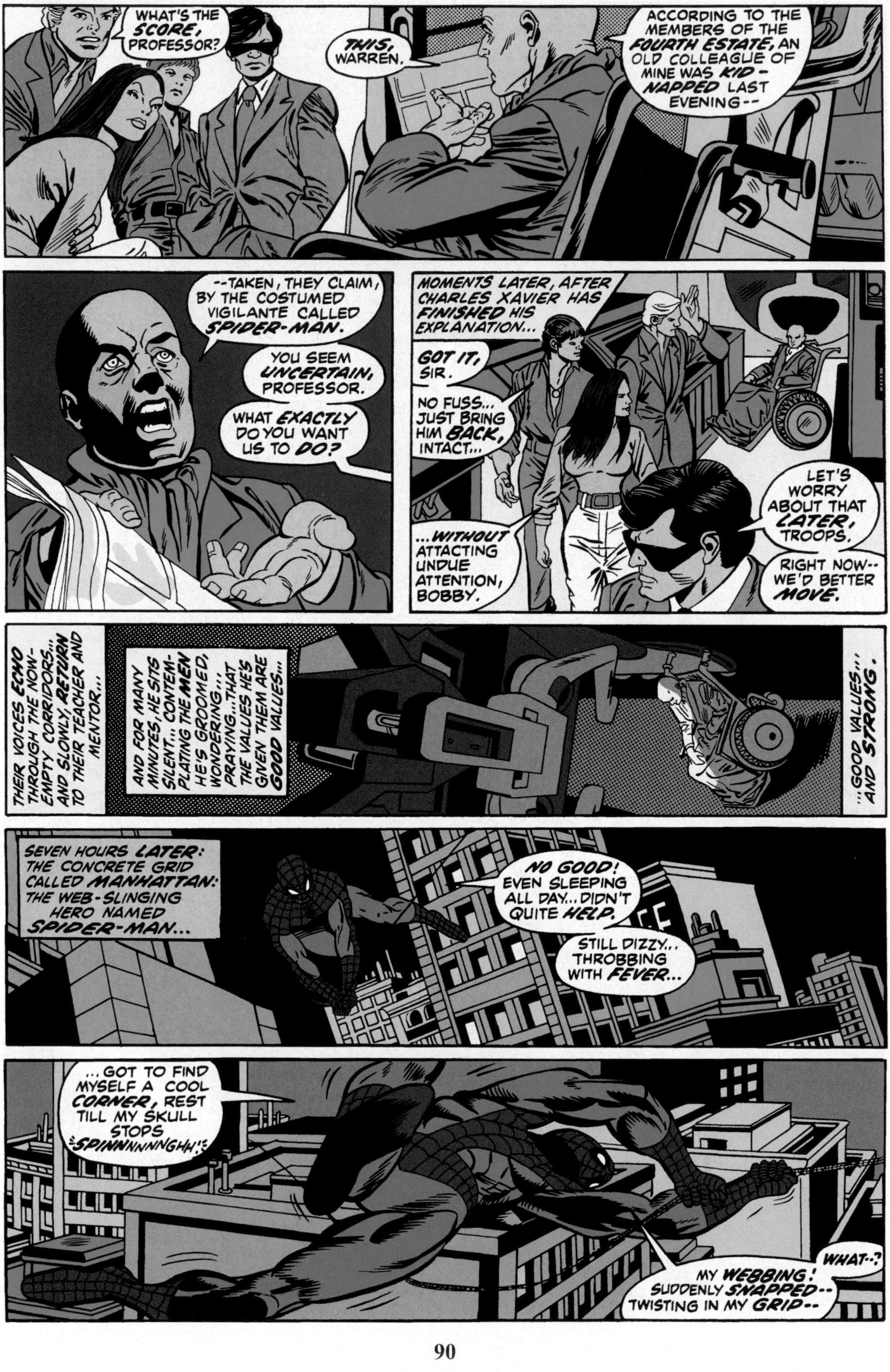
WHAT'S THE SCORE, PROFESSOR?
THIS, WARREN.
ACCORDING TO THE MEMBERS OF THE FOURTH ESTATE, AN OLD COLLEAGUE OF MINE WAS KID-NAPPED LAST EVENING--
--TAKEN, THEY CLAIM, BY THE COSTUMED VIGILANTE CALLED SPIDER-MAN.
YOU SEEM UNCERTAIN, PROFESSOR.
WHAT EXACTLY DO YOU WANT US TO DO?
MOMENTS LATER, AFTER CHARLES XAVIER HAS FINISHED HIS EXPLANATION...
GOT IT, SIR.
NO FUSS... JUST BRING HIM BACK, INTACT...
...WITHOUT ATTACTING UNDUE ATTENTION, BOBBY.
LET'S WORRY ABOUT THAT LATER, TROOPS.
RIGHT NOW-- WE'D BETTER MOVE.
THEIR VOICES ECHO THROUGH THE NOW-EMPTY CORRIDORS... AND SLOWLY, CWLY, RETURN TO THEIR TEACHER AND MENTOR...
AND FOR MANY MINUTES, HE SITS SILENT... CONTEM-PLATING THE MEN HE'S GROOMED, WONDERING... PRAYING... THAT THE VALUES HE'S GIVEN THEM ARE GOOD VALUES...
...GOOD VALUES... AND STRONG.
SEVEN HOURS LATER: THE CONCRETE GRID CALLED MANHATTAN: THE WEB-SLINGING HERO NAMED SPIDER-MAN...
NO GOOD! EVEN SLEEPING ALL DAY... DIDN'T QUITE HELP.
STILL DIZZY... THROBBING WITH FEVER...
...GOT TO FIND MYSELF A COOL CORNER, REST TILL MY SKULL STOPS SPINNNNNNGHH!
WHAT--?
MY WEBBING! SUDDENLY SNAPPED-- TWISTING IN MY GRIP--

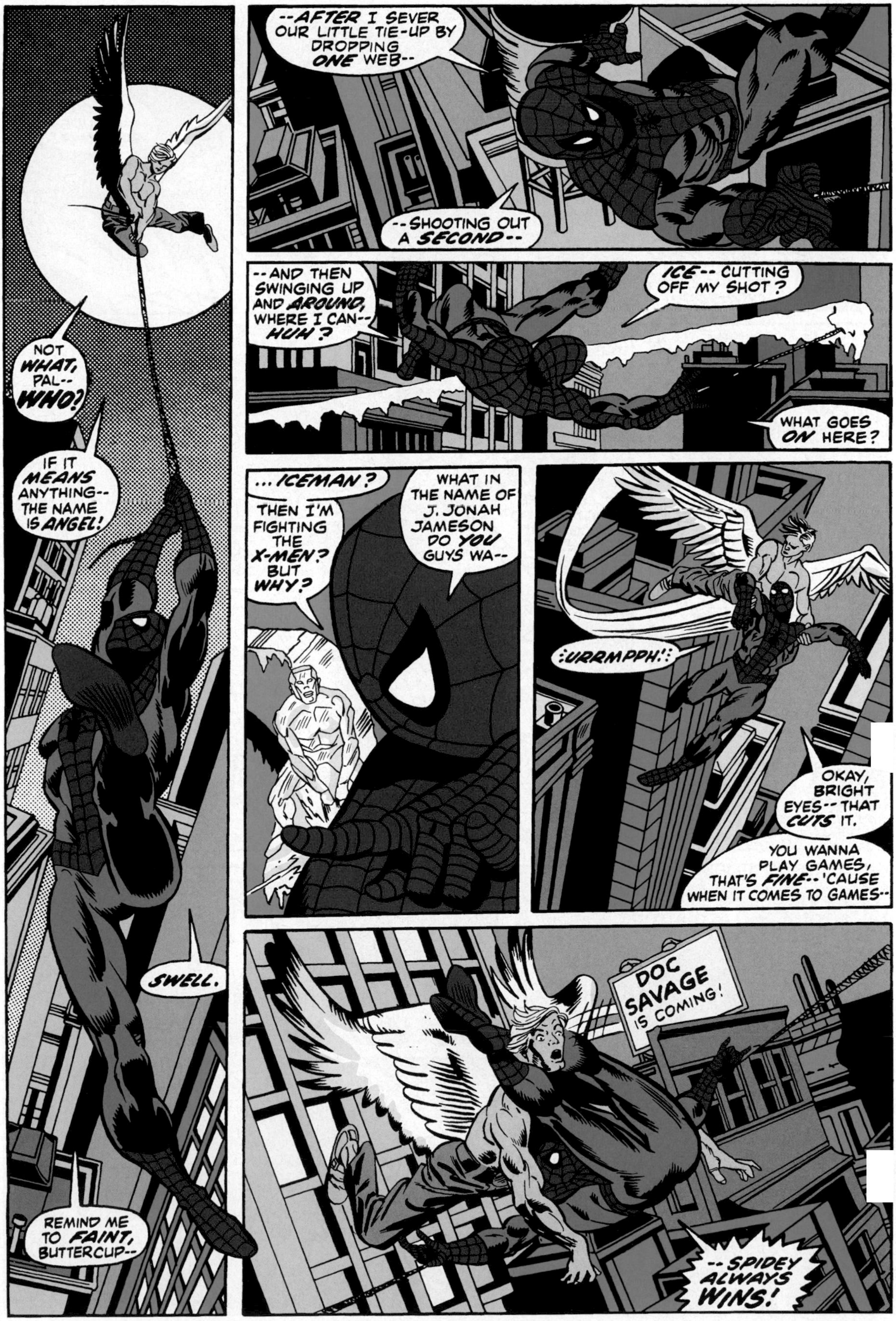
--AFTER I SEVER OUR LITTLE TIE-UP BY DROPPING ONE WEB--
--SHOOTING OUT A SECOND--
--AND THEN SWINGING UP AND AROUND, WHERE I CAN-- HUH?
ICE-- CUTTING OFF MY SHOT?
WHAT GOES ON HERE?
NOT WHAT, PAL-- WHO?
IF IT MEANS ANYTHING-- THE NAME IS ANGEL!
...ICEMAN? THEN I'M FIGHTING THE X-MEN? BUT WHY?
WHAT IN THE NAME OF J. JONAH JAMESON DO YOU GUYS WA--
:URRMPPH!:
OKAY, BRIGHT EYES-- THAT CUTS IT.
YOU WANNA PLAY GAMES, THAT'S FINE--'CAUSE WHEN IT COMES TO GAMES--
SWELL.
REMIND ME TO FAINT, BUTTERCUP--
DOC SAVAGE IS COMING!
--SPIDEY ALWAYS WINS!

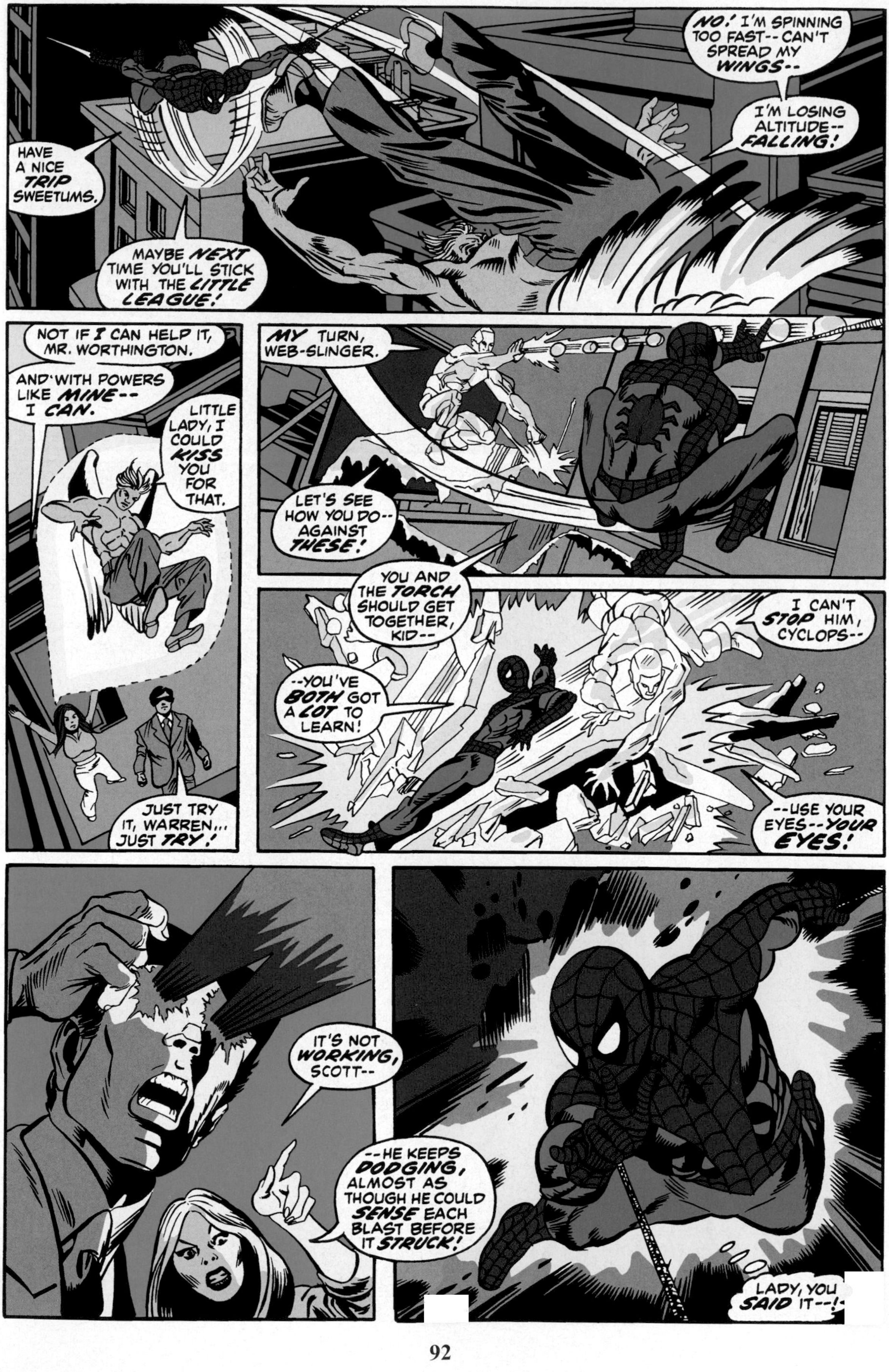
NO! I'M SPINNING TOO FAST-- CAN'T SPREAD MY WINGS--
I'M LOSING ALTITUDE-- FALLING!
HAVE A NICE TRIP SWEETUMS.
MAYBE NEXT TIME YOU'LL STICK WITH THE LITTLE LEAGUE!
NOT IF I CAN HELP IT, MR. WORTHINGTON.
AND WITH POWERS LIKE MINE-- I CAN.
LITTLE LADY, I COULD KISS YOU FOR THAT.
JUST TRY IT, WARREN... JUST TRY!
MY TURN, WEB-SLINGER.
LET'S SEE HOW YOU DO-- AGAINST THESE!
YOU AND THE TORCH SHOULD GET TOGETHER, KID--
--YOU'VE BOTH GOT A LOT TO LEARN!
I CAN'T STOP HIM, CYCLOPS--
--USE YOUR EYES--YOUR EYES!
IT'S NOT WORKING, SCOTT--
--HE KEEPS DODGING, ALMOST AS THOUGH HE COULD SENSE EACH BLAST BEFORE IT STRUCK!
LADY, YOU SAID IT--!

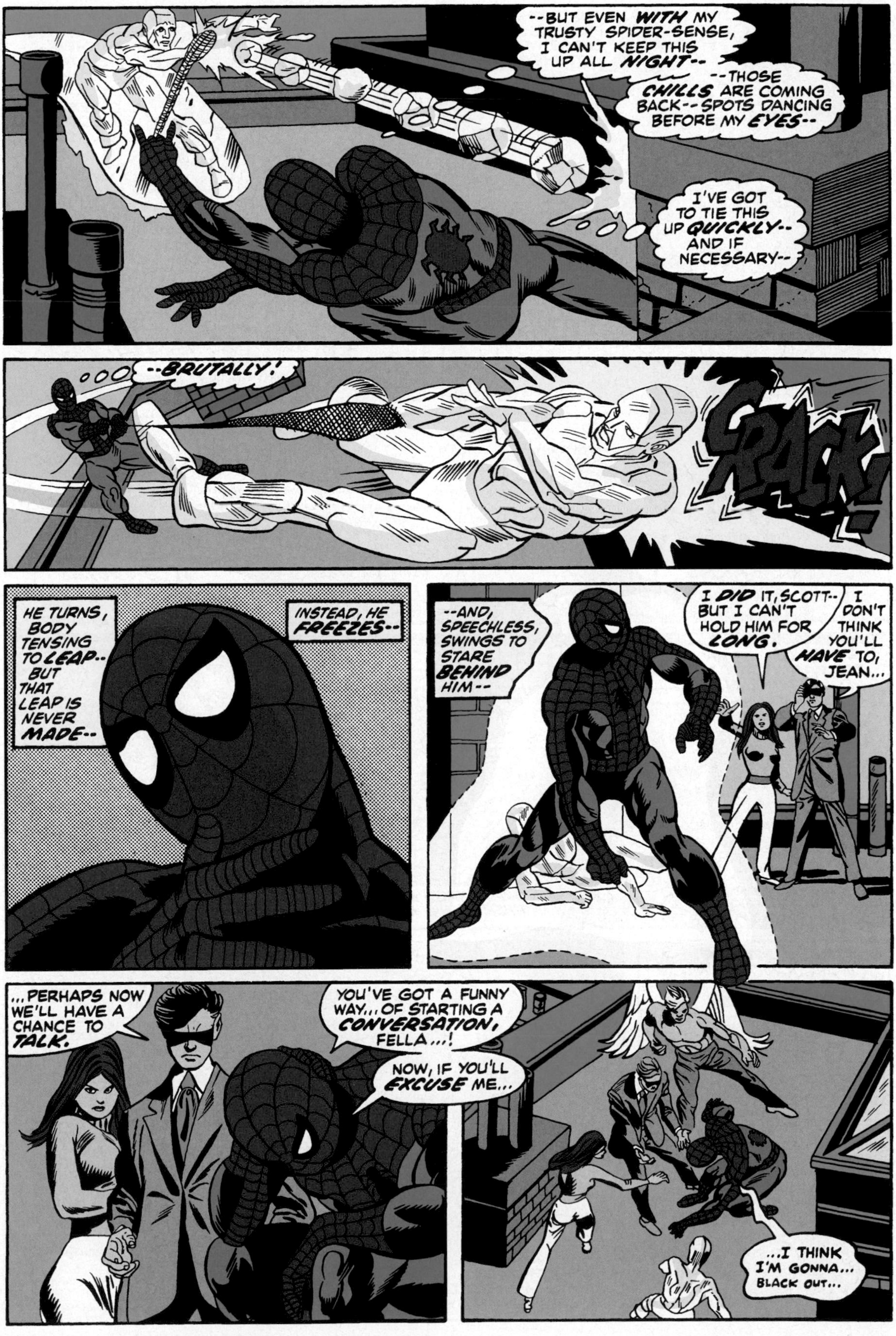
--BUT EVEN WITH MY TRUSTY SPIDER-SENSE, I CAN'T KEEP THIS UP ALL NIGHT--
--THOSE CHILLS ARE COMING BACK--SPOTS DANCING BEFORE MY EYES--
I'VE GOT TO TIE THIS UP QUICKLY--AND IF NECESSARY--
--BRUTALLY!
CRACK!
HE TURNS, BODY TENSING TO LEAP--BUT THAT LEAP IS NEVER MADE--
INSTEAD, HE FREEZES--
--AND, SPEECHLESS, SWINGS TO STARE BEHIND HIM--
I DID IT, SCOTT--BUT I CAN'T HOLD HIM FOR LONG.
I DON'T THINK YOU'LL HAVE TO, JEAN...
...PERHAPS NOW WE'LL HAVE A CHANCE TO TALK.
YOU'VE GOT A FUNNY WAY...OF STARTING A CONVERSATION, FELLA...!
NOW, IF YOU'LL EXCUSE ME...
...I THINK I'M GONNA... BLACK OUT...

DON'T *THINK* IT, PROFESSOR. I GUESS WE'VE *ALL* GOT THE SAME IDEA. WE'LL GET HIM BACK TO YOU... *PRONTO.*

SOON..., THEN THE NOTES *ARE* AUTHENTIC, SIR?

BUT IF PROFESSOR JORGENSON *DID* WRITE THEM... THEN THAT MEANS...

...*SPIDER-MAN* HAS LESS THAN FOUR HOURS TO *LIVE!*

PRECISELY, JEAN.

...NOW BE SILENT, *ALL* OF YOU. IF WE'RE TO *SAVE* OUR YOUNG FRIEND...

...I NEED *TOTAL* CONCENTRATION...TO EXPLORE THE VERY *DEPTHS* OF HIS UNCONSCIOUS MIND!

SILENCE: LAYER BY LAYER, THE MAN KNOWN AS *PROFESSOR X* DELVES THROUGH THE DARKNESS OF A HUMAN MIND...

IN THAT DARKNESS, HE FINDS *VISIONS* --

-- GRIM SNATCHES OF ANOTHER MAN'S *MEMORY* --

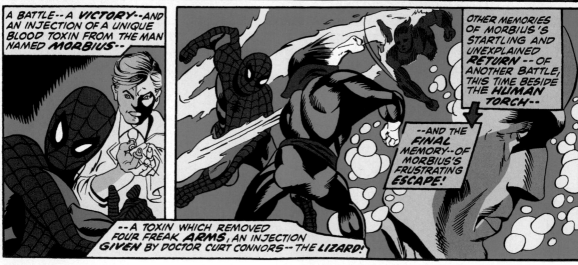

A BATTLE -- A *VICTORY* -- AND AN INJECTION OF A UNIQUE BLOOD TOXIN FROM THE MAN NAMED *MORBIUS* --

OTHER MEMORIES OF MORBIUS'S STARTLING AND UNEXPLAINED *RETURN* -- OF ANOTHER BATTLE, THIS TIME BESIDE THE *HUMAN TORCH* --

-- AND THE *FINAL* MEMORY -- OF MORBIUS'S FRUSTRATING *ESCAPE!*

-- A TOXIN WHICH REMOVED FOUR FREAK *ARMS,* AN INJECTION *GIVEN* BY DOCTOR CURT CONNORS -- THE *LIZARD!*

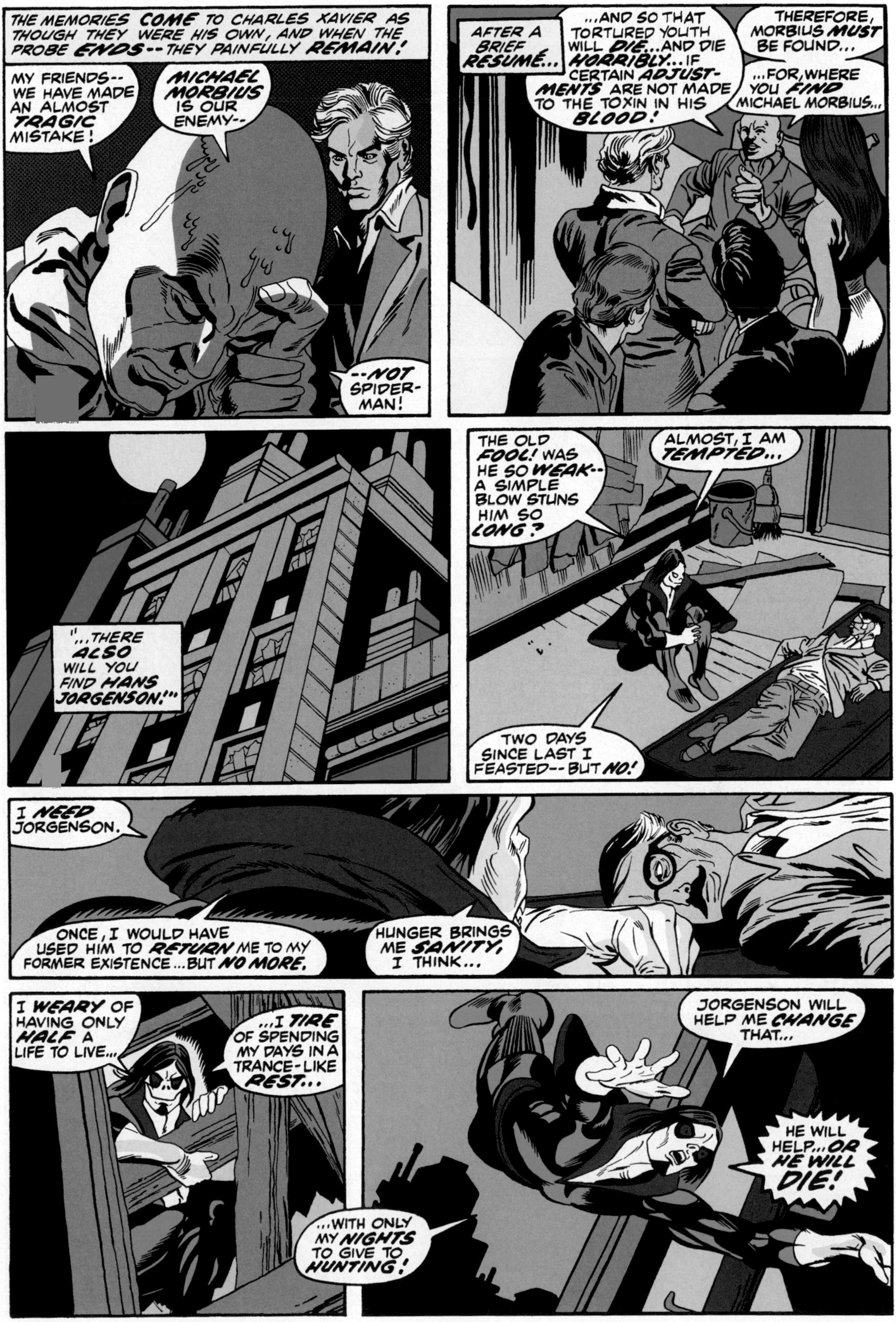
THE MEMORIES COME TO CHARLES XAVIER AS THOUGH THEY WERE HIS OWN, AND WHEN THE PROBE ENDS--THEY PAINFULLY REMAIN!
MY FRIENDS--WE HAVE MADE AN ALMOST TRAGIC MISTAKE!
MICHAEL MORBIUS IS OUR ENEMY--
--NOT SPIDER-MAN!
AFTER A BRIEF RESUMÉ...
...AND SO THAT TORTURED YOUTH WILL DIE...AND DIE HORRIBLY...IF CERTAIN ADJUSTMENTS ARE NOT MADE TO THE TOXIN IN HIS BLOOD!
THEREFORE, MORBIUS MUST BE FOUND...
...FOR, WHERE YOU FIND MICHAEL MORBIUS...
"...THERE ALSO WILL YOU FIND HANS JORGENSON!"
THE OLD FOOL! WAS HE SO WEAK--A SIMPLE BLOW STUNS HIM SO LONG?
ALMOST, I AM TEMPTED...
TWO DAYS SINCE LAST I FEASTED--BUT NO!
I NEED JORGENSON.
ONCE, I WOULD HAVE USED HIM TO RETURN ME TO MY FORMER EXISTENCE...BUT NO MORE.
HUNGER BRINGS ME SANITY, I THINK...
I WEARY OF HAVING ONLY HALF A LIFE TO LIVE...
...I TIRE OF SPENDING MY DAYS IN A TRANCE-LIKE REST...
...WITH ONLY MY NIGHTS TO GIVE TO HUNTING!
JORGENSON WILL HELP ME CHANGE THAT...
HE WILL HELP...OR HE WILL DIE!

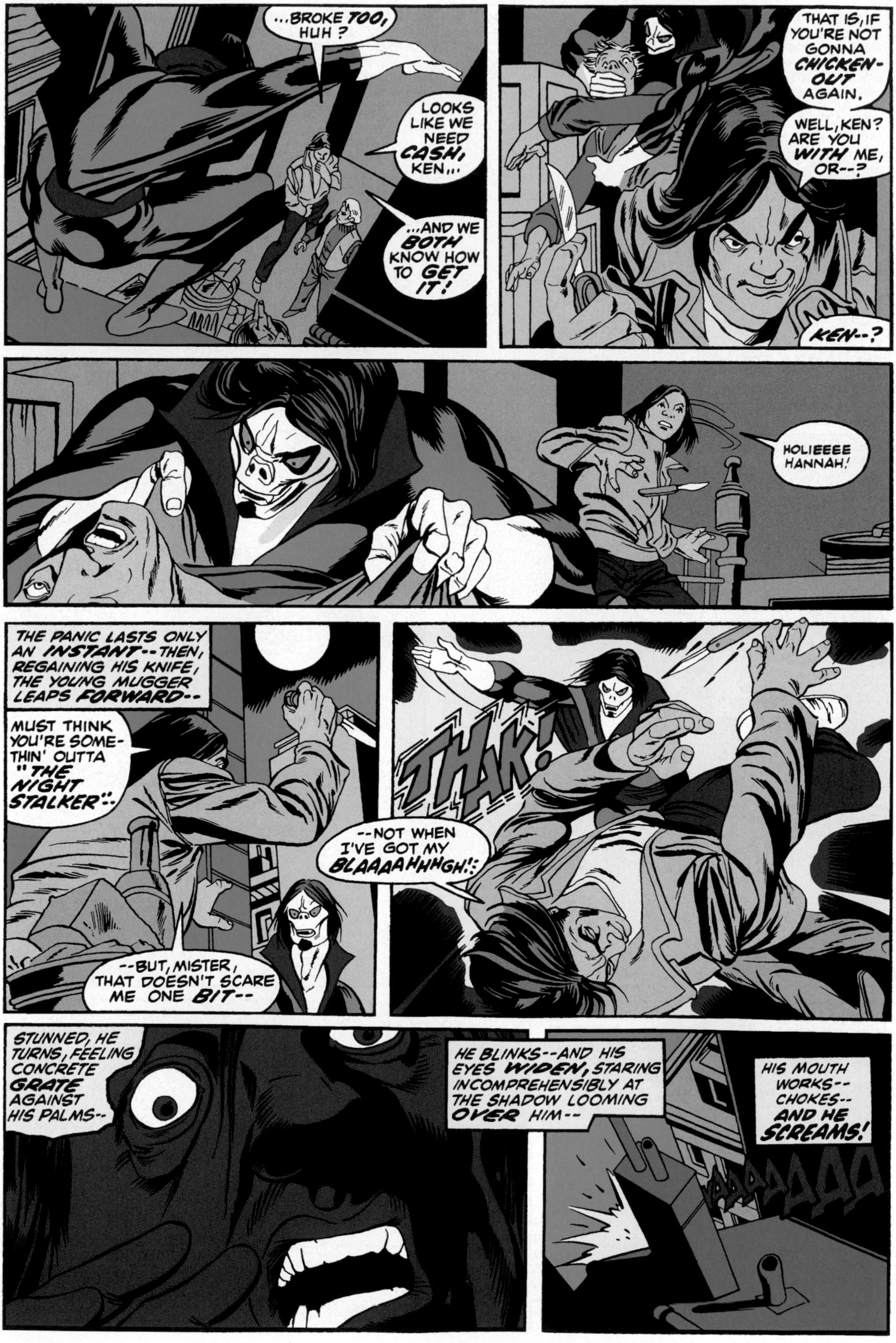
...BROKE TOO, HUH ?
LOOKS LIKE WE NEED CASH, KEN...
...AND WE BOTH KNOW HOW TO GET IT!
THAT IS, IF YOU'RE NOT GONNA CHICKEN-OUT AGAIN.
WELL, KEN? ARE YOU WITH ME, OR--?
KEN--?
HOLIEEEE HANNAH!
THE PANIC LASTS ONLY AN INSTANT--THEN, REGAINING HIS KNIFE, THE YOUNG MUGGER LEAPS FORWARD--
MUST THINK YOU'RE SOME-THIN' OUTTA "THE NIGHT STALKER"..
--BUT, MISTER, THAT DOESN'T SCARE ME ONE BIT--
--NOT WHEN I'VE GOT MY BLAAAAHHHGH!!
THAK!
STUNNED, HE TURNS, FEELING CONCRETE GRATE AGAINST HIS PALMS--
HE BLINKS--AND HIS EYES WIDEN, STARING INCOMPREHENSIBLY AT THE SHADOW LOOMING OVER HIM--
HIS MOUTH WORKS--CHOKES--AND HE SCREAMS!
AAAAAAAA

LIKE A CLOUD ACROSS THE MOON, THE MUTANT **ANGEL** BOWS AND SHIFTS--

HE GLANCES BACK-- DOWN INTO THE ALLEY **BELOW.** HIS EYES **HARDEN--**

--AND HE SWINGS **AWAY!**

FELLAS, BACK TOWARD **SECOND AVENUE--**

I THINK I'VE FOUND MORBIUS -- BUT YOU'RE NOT GONNA **BELIEVE** WHAT YOU SEE--

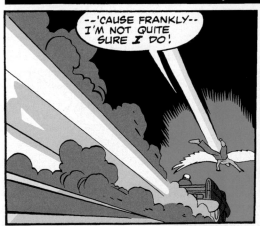

--'CAUSE FRANKLY-- I'M NOT QUITE SURE **I** DO!

SATIATED, HIS PULSE **POUNDING** WITH FRESHLY-GAINED BLOOD, MORBIUS BEGINS TO RISE--

--AND **STOPS** AT A SOUND FROM THE STREET BEHIND HIM!

SOMETHING IN HIS PINK-STAINED EYES **HALTS** THE APPROACHING X-MEN--

SOMETHING IN THE **SNARL** WITH WHICH HE GREETS THEM SENDS A SUDDEN **CHILL** THROUGH THEIR SPINES --

HE'S MAD...HOPELESSLY, IRREVOC-ABLY **INSANE!** THE PRESSURE-- THE INHUMAN **STRAIN** HAS TAKEN ITS **TOLL**...AND SO, BEFORE THE STARTLED MUTANTS CAN **GATHER** THEMSELVES--

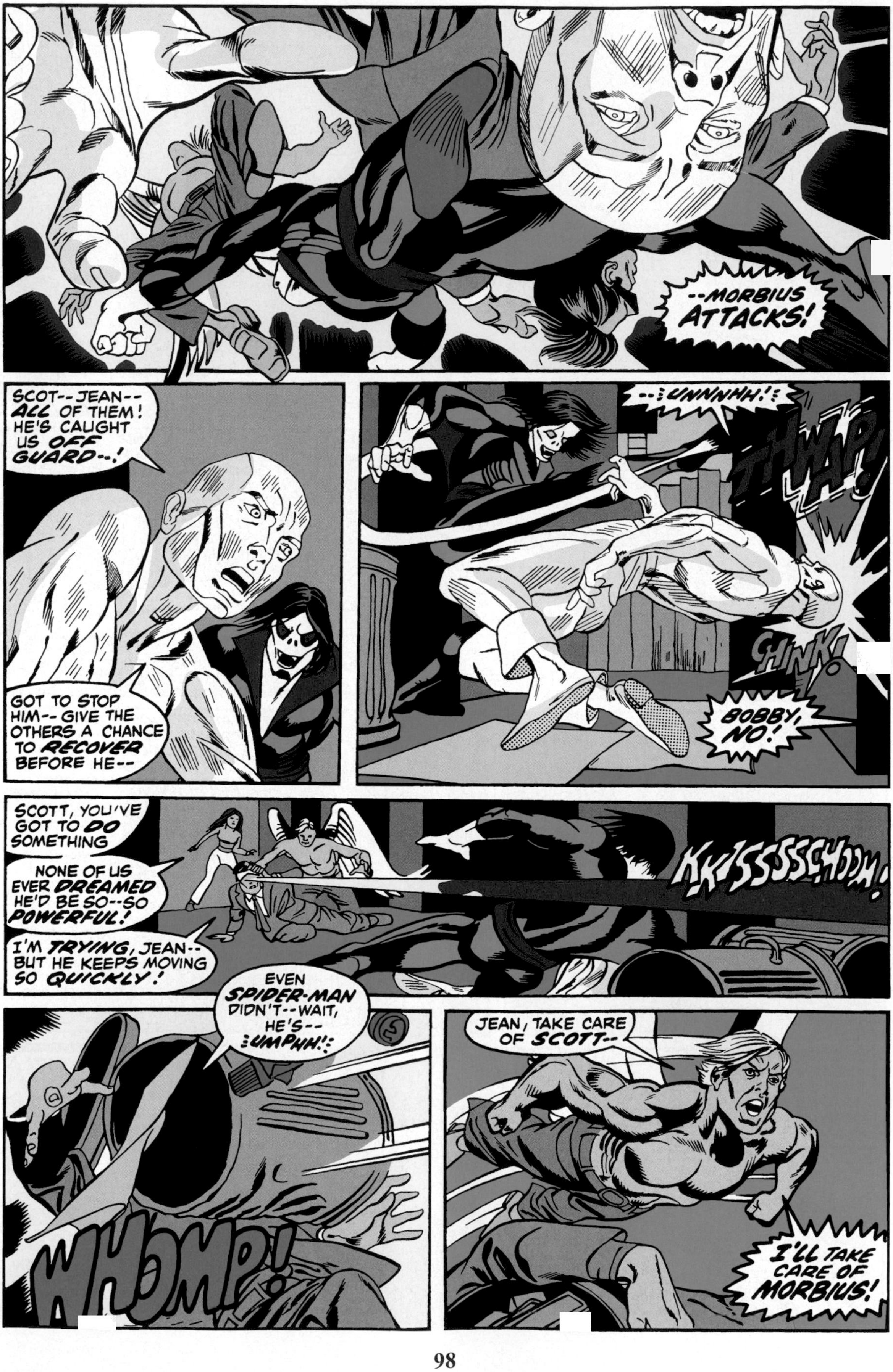
--MORBIUS ATTACKS!
SCOT--JEAN--ALL OF THEM! HE'S CAUGHT US OFF GUARD--!
GOT TO STOP HIM--GIVE THE OTHERS A CHANCE TO RECOVER BEFORE HE--
--UNNNHH!--
THWAP!
CHINK!
BOBBY, NO!
SCOTT, YOU'VE GOT TO DO SOMETHING
NONE OF US EVER DREAMED HE'D BE SO--SO POWERFUL!
I'M TRYING, JEAN--BUT HE KEEPS MOVING SO QUICKLY!
KKRISSSSSCHOOM!
EVEN SPIDER-MAN DIDN'T--WAIT, HE'S--UMPHH!
WHOMP!
JEAN, TAKE CARE OF SCOTT--
I'LL TAKE CARE OF MORBIUS!

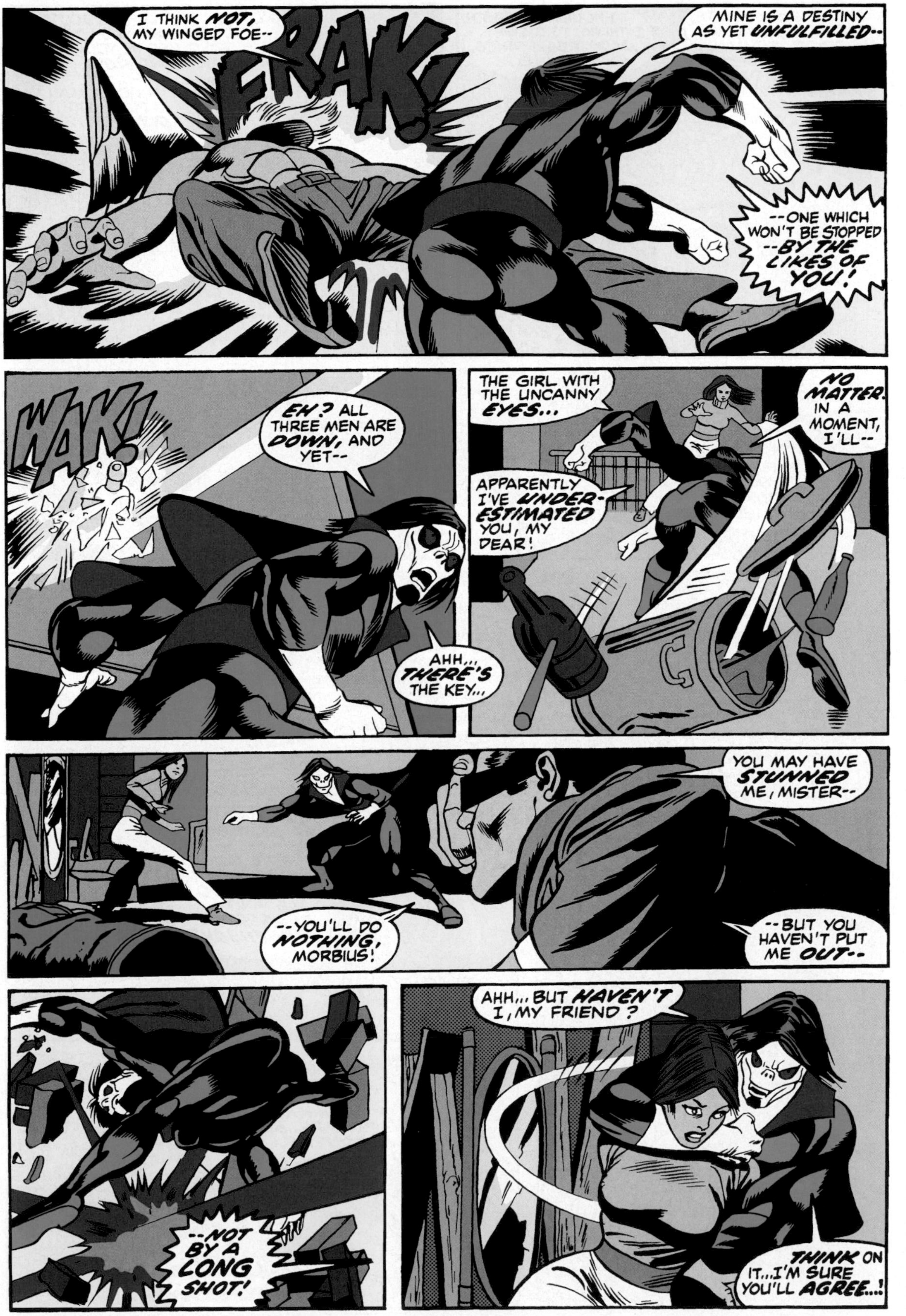
I THINK NOT, MY WINGED FOE--
FRAK!
MINE IS A DESTINY AS YET UNFULFILLED--
--ONE WHICH WON'T BE STOPPED --BY THE LIKES OF YOU!
WAK!
EH? ALL THREE MEN ARE DOWN, AND YET--
AHH... THERE'S THE KEY...
THE GIRL WITH THE UNCANNY EYES...
APPARENTLY I'VE UNDERESTIMATED YOU, MY DEAR!
NO MATTER. IN A MOMENT, I'LL--
--YOU'LL DO NOTHING, MORBIUS!
YOU MAY HAVE STUNNED ME, MISTER--
--BUT YOU HAVEN'T PUT ME OUT--
--NOT BY A LONG SHOT!
AHH... BUT HAVEN'T I, MY FRIEND?
THINK ON IT... I'M SURE YOU'LL AGREE...!

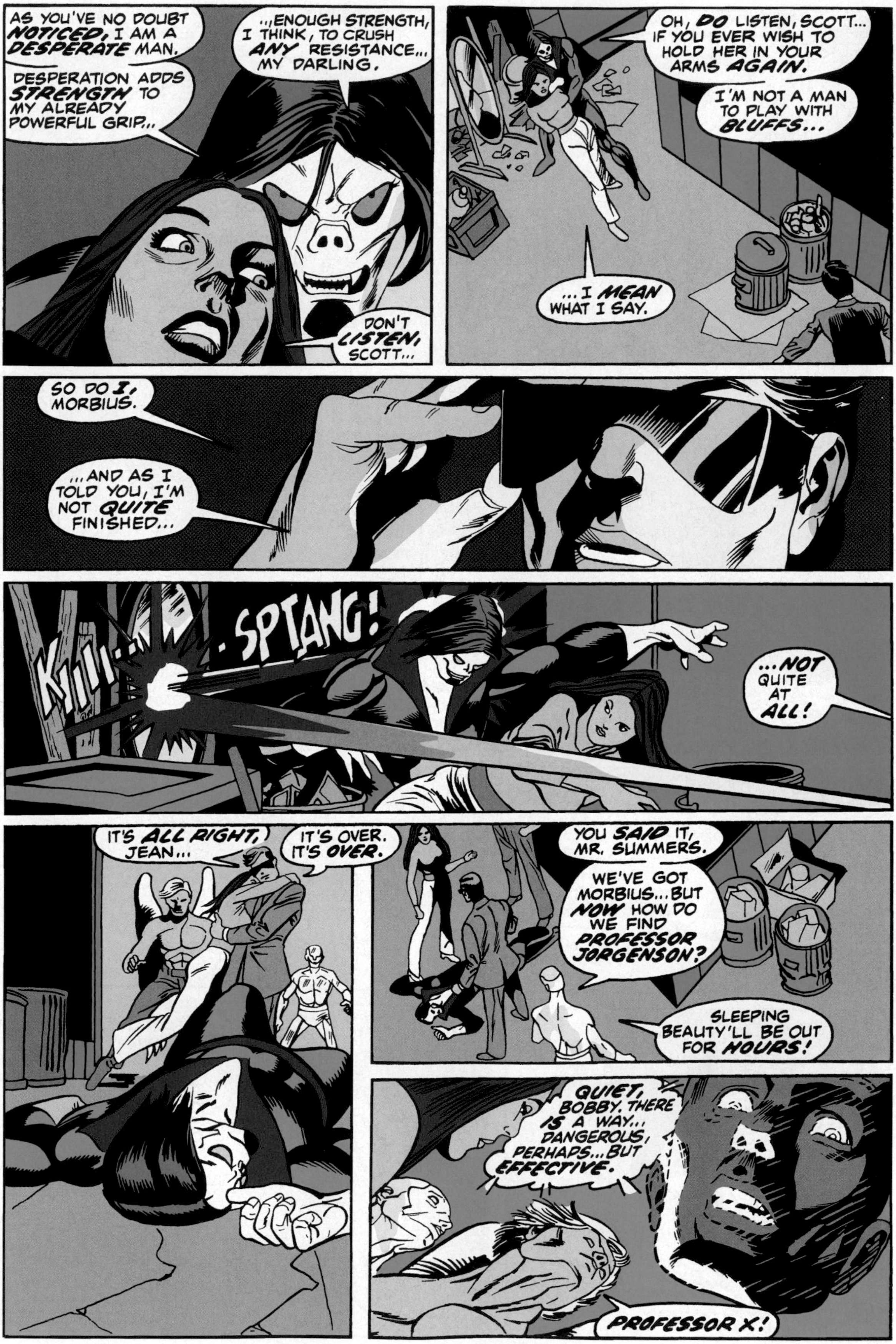
AS YOU'VE NO DOUBT NOTICED, I AM A DESPERATE MAN.
DESPERATION ADDS STRENGTH TO MY ALREADY POWERFUL GRIP...
...ENOUGH STRENGTH, I THINK, TO CRUSH ANY RESISTANCE... MY DARLING.
DON'T LISTEN, SCOTT...
OH, DO LISTEN, SCOTT... IF YOU EVER WISH TO HOLD HER IN YOUR ARMS AGAIN.
I'M NOT A MAN TO PLAY WITH BLUFFS...
...I MEAN WHAT I SAY.
SO DO I, MORBIUS.
...AND AS I TOLD YOU, I'M NOT QUITE FINISHED...
KHHH...
SPTANG!
...NOT QUITE AT ALL!
IT'S ALL RIGHT, JEAN...
IT'S OVER. IT'S OVER.
YOU SAID IT, MR. SUMMERS.
WE'VE GOT MORBIUS... BUT NOW HOW DO WE FIND PROFESSOR JORGENSON?
SLEEPING BEAUTY'LL BE OUT FOR HOURS!
QUIET, BOBBY. THERE IS A WAY... DANGEROUS, PERHAPS... BUT EFFECTIVE.
PROFESSOR X!

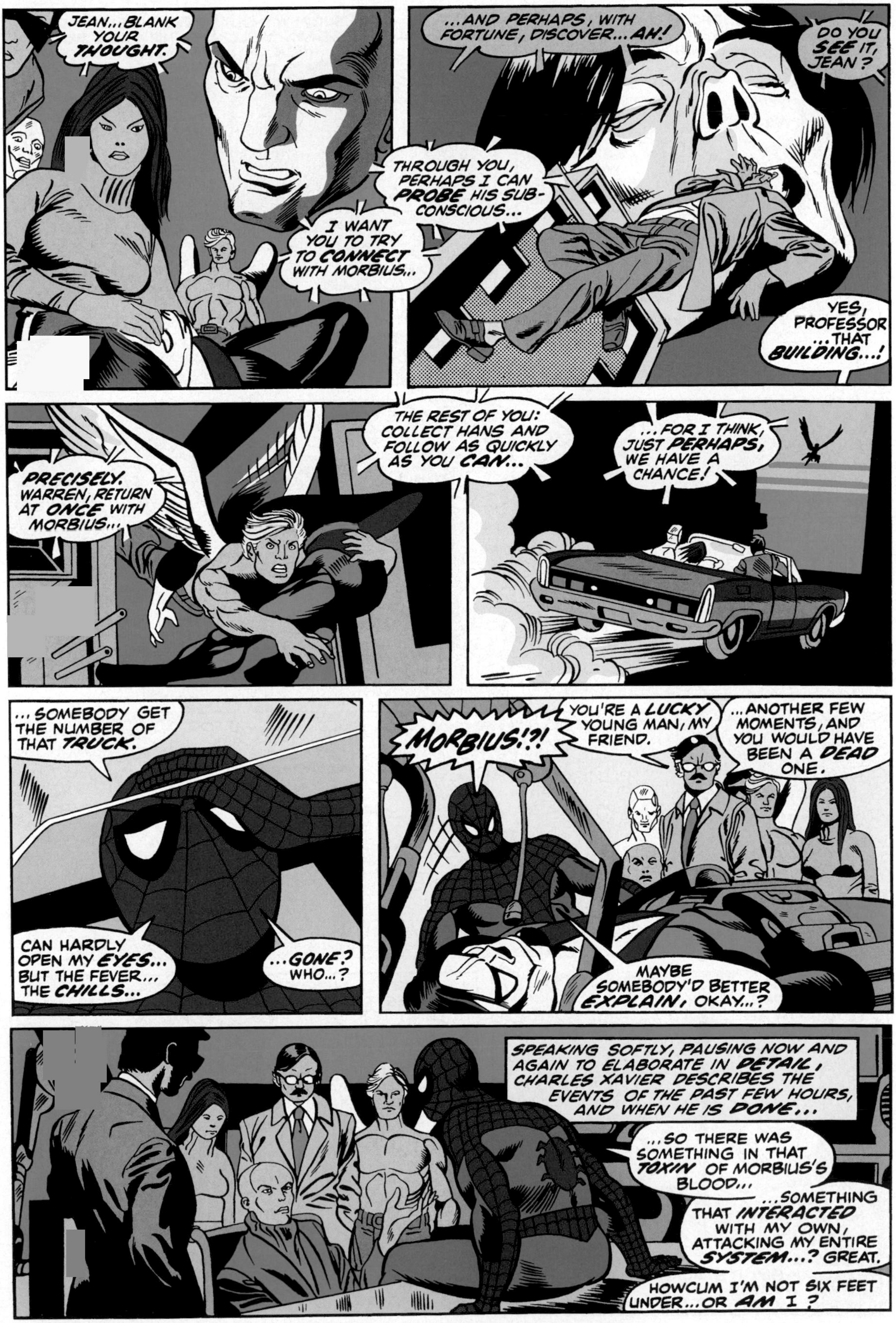

JEAN...BLANK YOUR THOUGHT.
I WANT YOU TO TRY TO CONNECT WITH MORBIUS...
THROUGH YOU, PERHAPS I CAN PROBE HIS SUB-CONSCIOUS...
...AND PERHAPS, WITH FORTUNE, DISCOVER...AH!
DO YOU SEE IT, JEAN?
YES, PROFESSOR ...THAT BUILDING...!
PRECISELY. WARREN, RETURN AT ONCE WITH MORBIUS...
THE REST OF YOU: COLLECT HANS AND FOLLOW AS QUICKLY AS YOU CAN...
...FOR I THINK, JUST PERHAPS, WE HAVE A CHANCE!
...SOMEBODY GET THE NUMBER OF THAT TRUCK.
CAN HARDLY OPEN MY EYES... BUT THE FEVER... THE CHILLS...
...GONE? WHO...?
MORBIUS!?!
YOU'RE A LUCKY YOUNG MAN, MY FRIEND.
...ANOTHER FEW MOMENTS, AND YOU WOULD HAVE BEEN A DEAD ONE.
MAYBE SOMEBODY'D BETTER EXPLAIN, OKAY...?
SPEAKING SOFTLY, PAUSING NOW AND AGAIN TO ELABORATE IN DETAIL, CHARLES XAVIER DESCRIBES THE EVENTS OF THE PAST FEW HOURS, AND WHEN HE IS DONE...
...SO THERE WAS SOMETHING IN THAT TOXIN OF MORBIUS'S BLOOD...
...SOMETHING THAT INTERACTED WITH MY OWN, ATTACKING MY ENTIRE SYSTEM...? GREAT.
HOWCUM I'M NOT SIX FEET UNDER...OR AM I?

THIS IS *HARDLY* PARADISE, MY FRIEND. ...THOUGH YOU WOULD HAVE *FOUND* IT, I THINK, IF CHARLES HADN'T LENT ME THE USE OF HIS *EQUIPMENT.*

WE *INNOC-ULATED* YOU WITH AN EXTRACT OF THE ORIGINAL ENZYME...A DIFFICULT PROCEDURE, BUT LUCKILY, *QUITE* EFFICIENT.

LOOKS LIKE I OWE YOU MY *LIFE,* PROFESSOR.

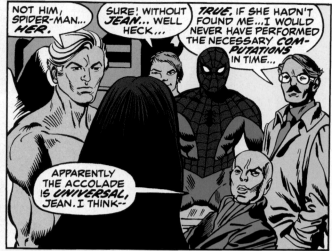

NOT HIM, SPIDER-MAN... *HER.*

SURE! WITHOUT *JEAN*...WELL HECK...

TRUE, IF SHE HADN'T *FOUND* ME...I WOULD NEVER HAVE PERFORMED THE NECESSARY *COM-PUTATIONS* IN TIME...

APPARENTLY THE ACCOLADE IS *UNIVERSAL,* JEAN. I THINK--

DON'T, PROFESSOR!

AFTER ALL, I CAN'T *REALLY* THANK ANY OF *YOU* GUYS--

--BUT AS FOR THE LADY *JEAN*--

--I CAN THANK HER!

AND NOW THAT *THAT'S* DONE, I'VE GOTTA BE SAYING *G'BYE--*

CRACH!

--'CAUSE NOT ONLY AM I SLIGHTLY *ANTI-SOCIAL--*

--BUT IT'S ALREADY *HOURS* PAST MY *BEDTIME!*

WELL, SIR...I...SUPPOSE THAT TIES IT *UP,* DOESN'T IT?

I WONDER, JEAN...I TRULY *WONDER.*

NEXT: THE EYE OF THE BASILISK!

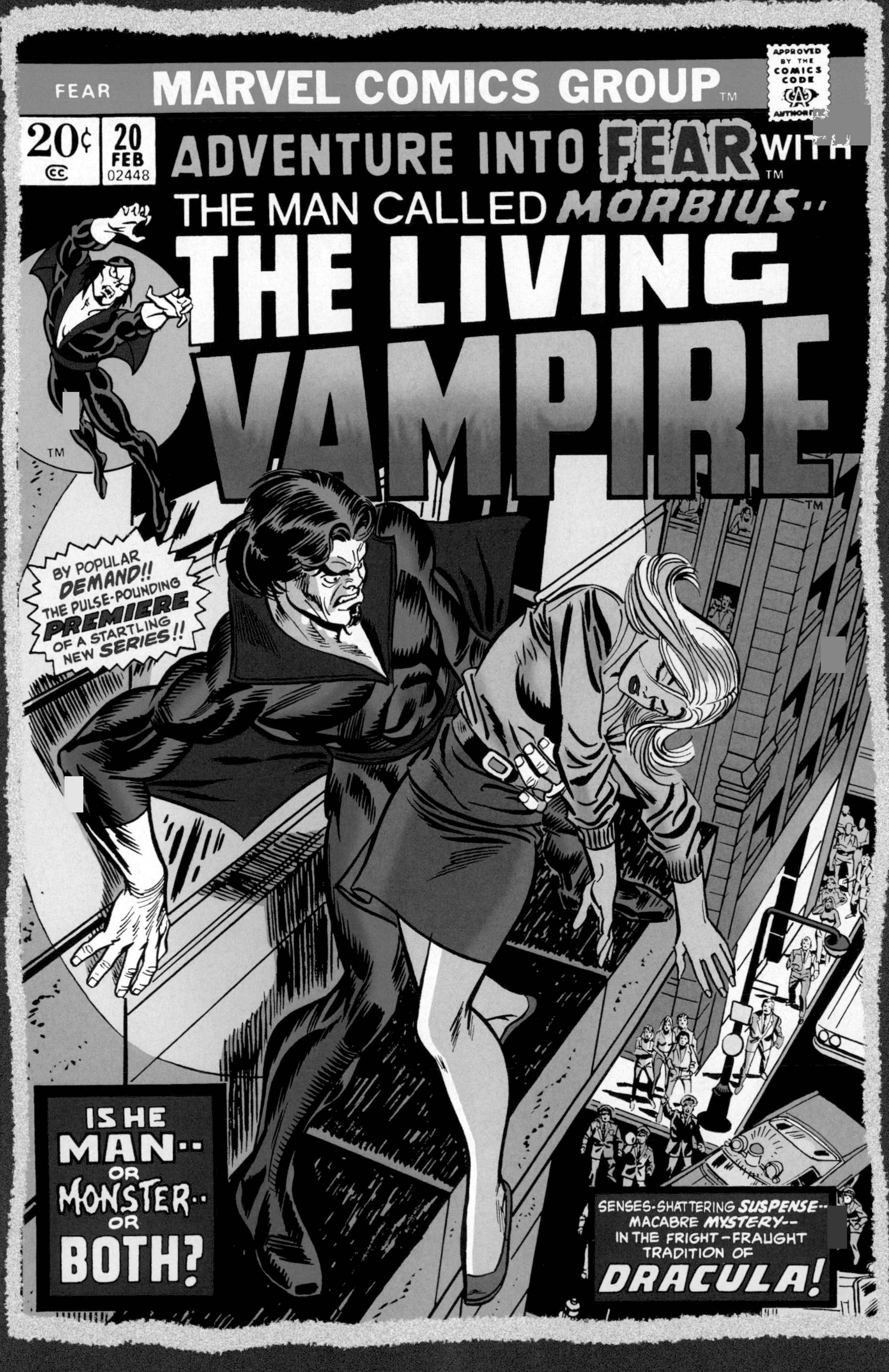
FEAR
MARVEL COMICS GROUP™
APPROVED BY THE COMICS CODE AUTHORITY
20¢
20 FEB 02448
ADVENTURE INTO FEAR WITH™
THE MAN CALLED MORBIUS..
THE LIVING VAMPIRE™
BY POPULAR DEMAND!! THE PULSE-POUNDING PREMIERE OF A STARTLING NEW SERIES!!
IS HE MAN.. OR MONSTER.. OR BOTH?
SENSES-SHATTERING SUSPENSE-- MACABRE MYSTERY-- IN THE FRIGHT-FRAUGHT TRADITION OF DRACULA!

MIKE FRIEDRICH	PAUL GULACY	J. ABEL	TOM ORZECHOWSKI	GEORGE ROUSSOS	ROY THOMAS
WRITER	ARTIST	INKER	LETTERER	COLORIST	EDITOR

AND NOW IT BEGINS, THE **STARTLING SAGA** OF

MORBIUS™

THE LIVING VAMPIRE!

THE CAVEMEN HAD THEIR **OMENS**, WHICH WARNED WHEN NOT TO DARE **VENTURE** FROM THEIR ROCK-BOUND **SHELTERS**, FOR FEAR OF THE **DEMONS** ROAMING JUST BEYOND THEIR FLICKERING **CAMPFIRES**...

TONIGHT, THE UNCOMMONLY HOT AUTUMN **WIND** IS AN OMEN TO THOSE OF **LOS ANGELES** THAT THEY, **TOO**, OUGHT REMAIN SAFELY **INSIDE THEIR** SHELTERS...

...FOR TONIGHT, THERE STALKS

...A **VAMPIRE!**

BECAUSE YOU SHOUTED FOR IT,

Stan Lee PRESENTS:

A NEW SERIES-- A NEW **ADVENTURE INTO FEAR!**

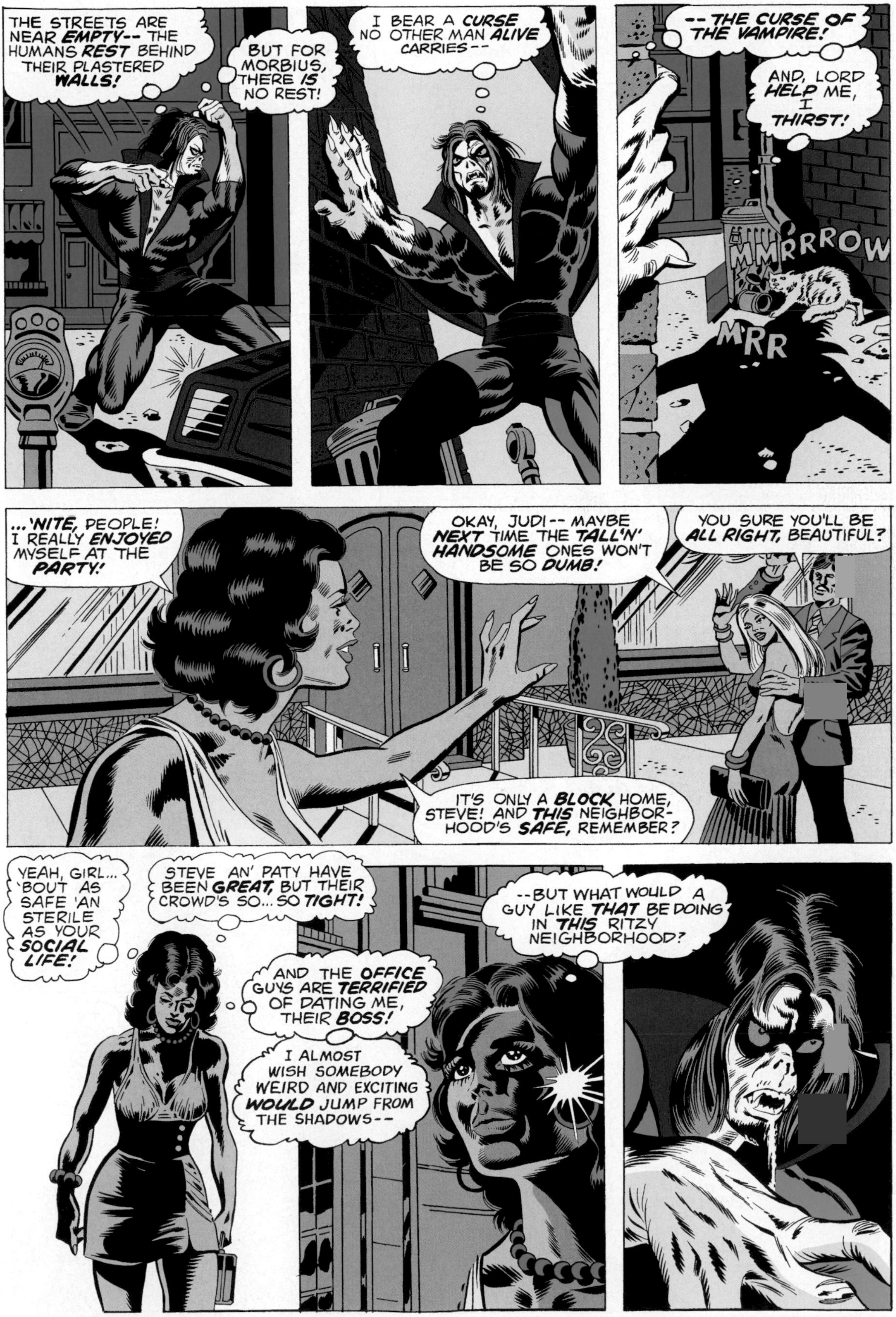
THE STREETS ARE NEAR EMPTY-- THE HUMANS REST BEHIND THEIR PLASTERED WALLS!
BUT FOR MORBIUS, THERE IS NO REST!
I BEAR A CURSE NO OTHER MAN ALIVE CARRIES--
--THE CURSE OF THE VAMPIRE!
AND, LORD HELP ME, I THIRST!
MMRRROW
MRR
...'NITE, PEOPLE! I REALLY ENJOYED MYSELF AT THE PARTY!
OKAY, JUDI-- MAYBE NEXT TIME THE TALL'N' HANDSOME ONES WON'T BE SO DUMB!
YOU SURE YOU'LL BE ALL RIGHT, BEAUTIFUL?
IT'S ONLY A BLOCK HOME, STEVE! AND THIS NEIGHBOR-HOOD'S SAFE, REMEMBER?
YEAH, GIRL... 'BOUT AS SAFE 'AN STERILE AS YOUR SOCIAL LIFE!
STEVE AN' PATY HAVE BEEN GREAT, BUT THEIR CROWD'S SO... SO TIGHT!
AND THE OFFICE GUYS ARE TERRIFIED OF DATING ME, THEIR BOSS!
I ALMOST WISH SOMEBODY WEIRD AND EXCITING WOULD JUMP FROM THE SHADOWS--
--BUT WHAT WOULD A GUY LIKE THAT BE DOING IN THIS RITZY NEIGHBORHOOD?

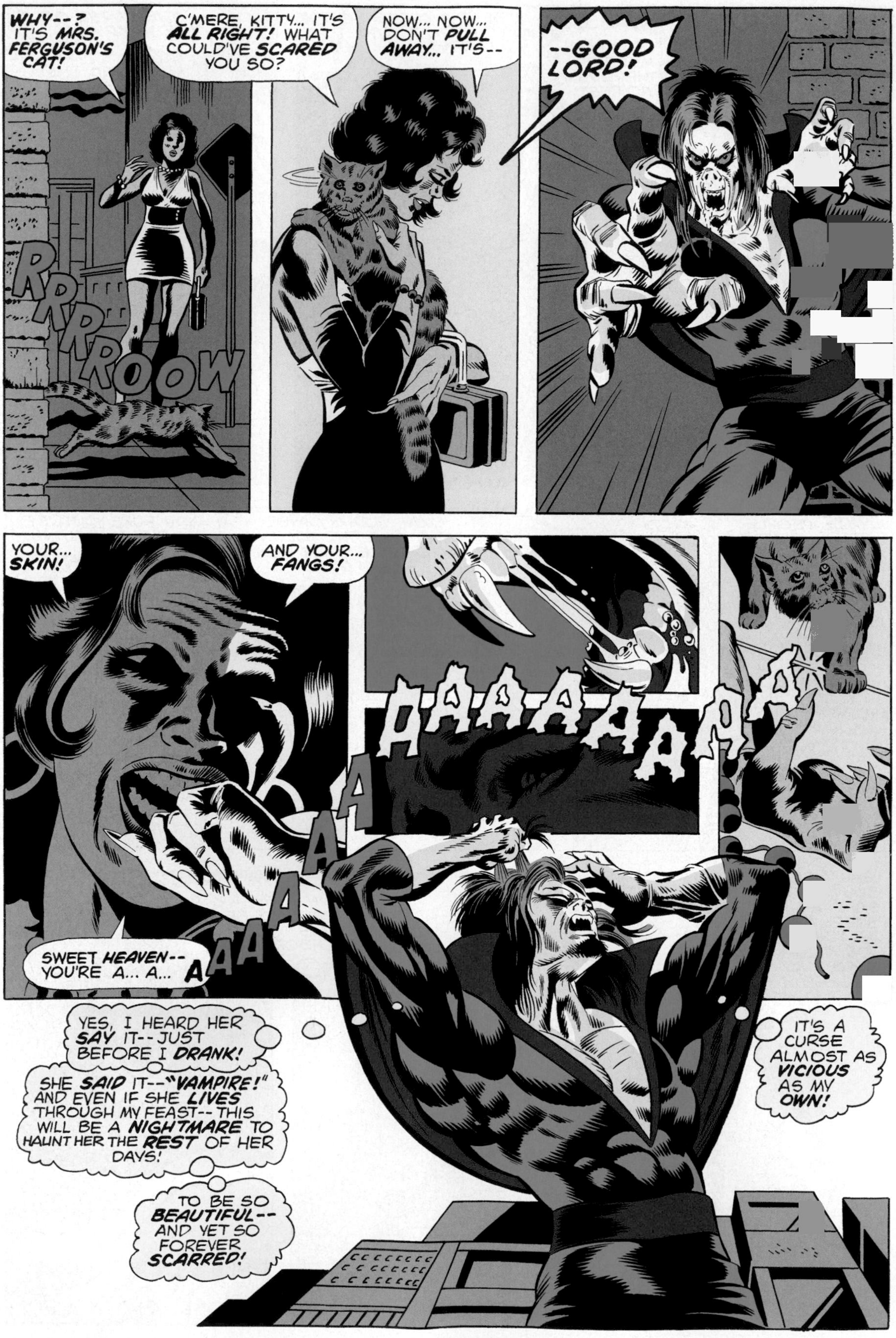
WHY--? IT'S MRS. FERGUSON'S CAT!
RRRRROOW
C'MERE, KITTY... IT'S ALL RIGHT! WHAT COULD'VE SCARED YOU SO?
NOW... NOW... DON'T PULL AWAY... IT'S--
--GOOD LORD!
YOUR... SKIN!
AND YOUR... FANGS!
SWEET HEAVEN-- YOU'RE A... A...
AAAAAAAAAAAAAAAA
YES, I HEARD HER SAY IT-- JUST BEFORE I DRANK!
SHE SAID IT--"VAMPIRE!" AND EVEN IF SHE LIVES THROUGH MY FEAST-- THIS WILL BE A NIGHTMARE TO HAUNT HER THE REST OF HER DAYS!
TO BE SO BEAUTIFUL-- AND YET SO FOREVER SCARRED!
IT'S A CURSE ALMOST AS VICIOUS AS MY OWN!

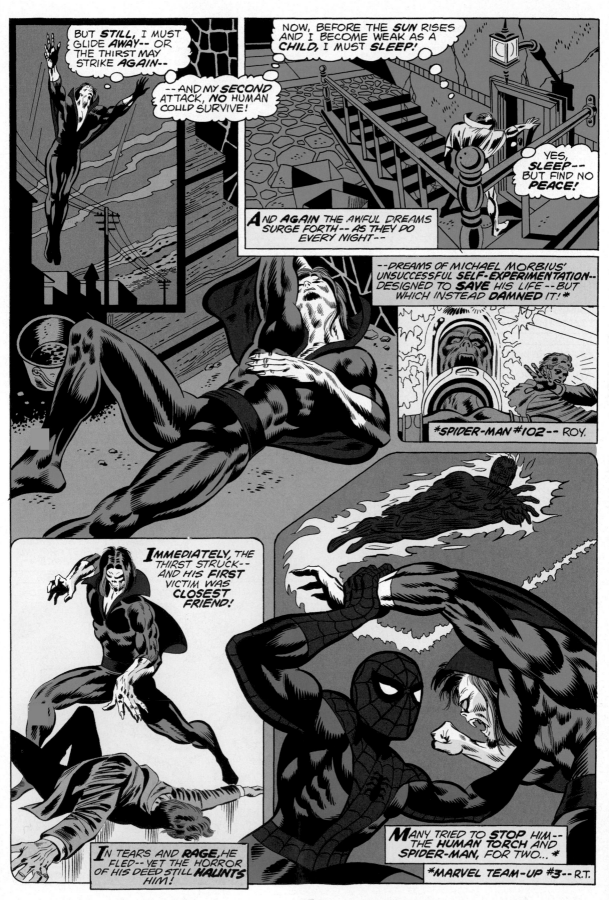

BUT *STILL*, I MUST GLIDE *AWAY*-- OR THE THIRST MAY STRIKE *AGAIN*--

--AND MY *SECOND* ATTACK, *NO* HUMAN COULD SURVIVE!

NOW, BEFORE THE *SUN* RISES AND I BECOME WEAK AS A *CHILD*, I MUST *SLEEP!*

YES, SLEEP-- BUT FIND NO *PEACE!*

*A*ND *AGAIN* THE AWFUL DREAMS SURGE FORTH-- AS THEY DO EVERY NIGHT--

--DREAMS OF MICHAEL MORBIUS' UNSUCCESSFUL *SELF-EXPERIMENTATION*-- DESIGNED TO *SAVE* HIS LIFE-- BUT WHICH INSTEAD *DAMNED* IT! *

*SPIDER-MAN #102-- ROY.

*I*MMEDIATELY, THE THIRST STRUCK-- AND HIS *FIRST* VICTIM WAS *CLOSEST FRIEND!*

*I*N TEARS AND *RAGE*, HE FLED-- YET THE HORROR OF HIS DEED STILL *HAUNTS* HIM!

*M*ANY TRIED TO *STOP* HIM-- THE *HUMAN TORCH* AND *SPIDER-MAN*, FOR TWO... *

*MARVEL TEAM-UP #3-- R.T.

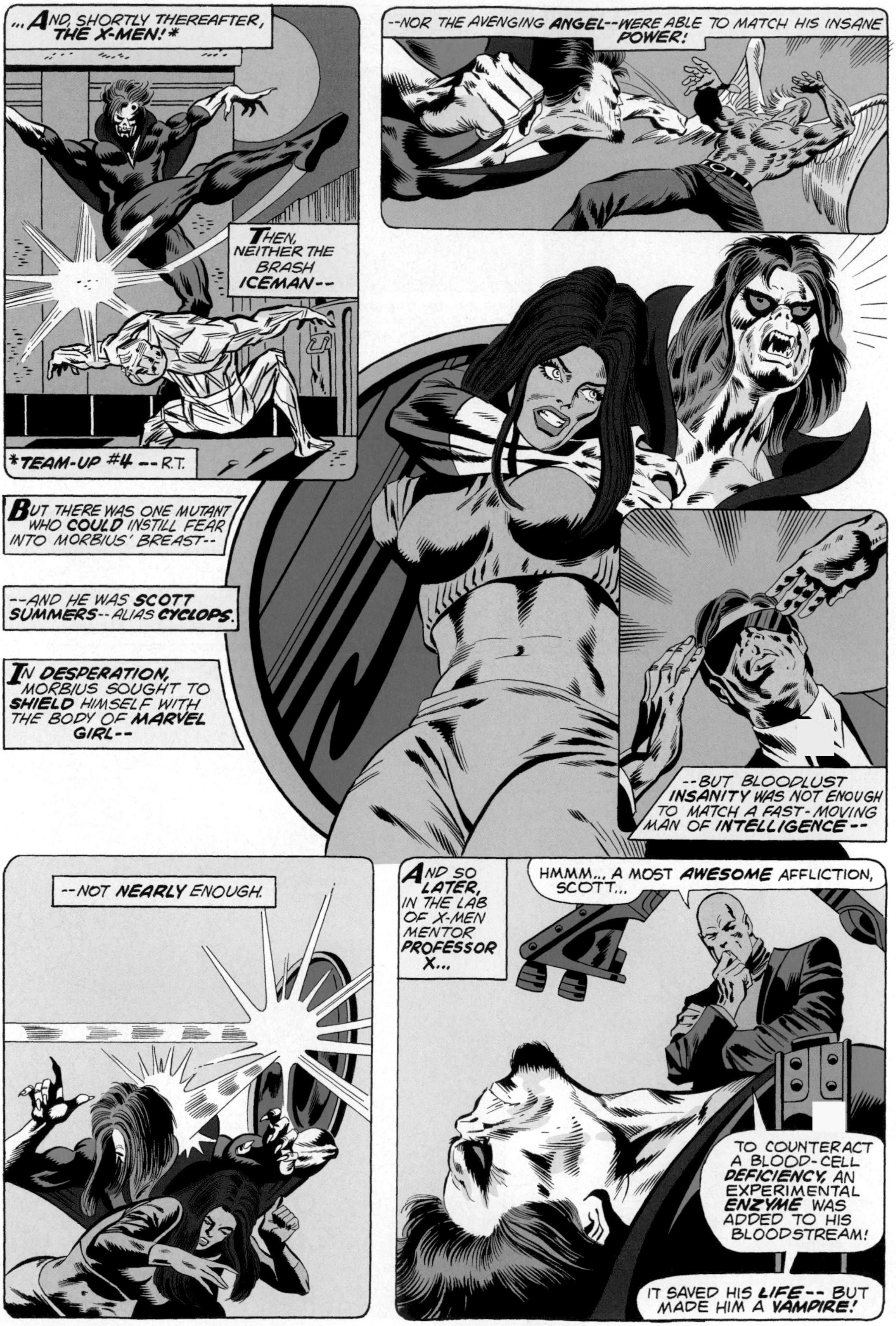
...AND, SHORTLY THEREAFTER, THE X-MEN!*
THEN, NEITHER THE BRASH ICEMAN--
*TEAM-UP #4 -- R.T.
--NOR THE AVENGING ANGEL--WERE ABLE TO MATCH HIS INSANE POWER!
BUT THERE WAS ONE MUTANT WHO COULD INSTILL FEAR INTO MORBIUS' BREAST--
--AND HE WAS SCOTT SUMMERS-- ALIAS CYCLOPS.
IN DESPERATION, MORBIUS SOUGHT TO SHIELD HIMSELF WITH THE BODY OF MARVEL GIRL--
--BUT BLOODLUST INSANITY WAS NOT ENOUGH TO MATCH A FAST-MOVING MAN OF INTELLIGENCE--
--NOT NEARLY ENOUGH.
AND SO LATER, IN THE LAB OF X-MEN MENTOR PROFESSOR X...
HMMM... A MOST AWESOME AFFLICTION, SCOTT...
TO COUNTERACT A BLOOD-CELL DEFICIENCY, AN EXPERIMENTAL ENZYME WAS ADDED TO HIS BLOODSTREAM!
IT SAVED HIS LIFE-- BUT MADE HIM A VAMPIRE!

IS THERE **HOPE** FOR HIM, SIR?

I-- I-- DON'T **KNOW,** SCOTT! I HAVE RUN THE MOST **THOROUGH** OF TESTS--AND FEEL ON THE **VERGE** OF AN ANSWER--!

BUT THERE'S SOMETHING **MISSING**-- SOMETHING I CANNOT **PIN DOWN!**

AND THERE IS **JUST** NOT ENOUGH--**TIME!**

UNKNOWN **ENEMIES** THREATEN US, AND--

SNAP!

KRASH!

FREE! I MUST BE **FREE!**

SNAP!

I'LL **STOP** HIM, SIR!

ZZAP!

BLAST! HE'S **GLIDED** AWAY FROM MY **POWER BEAM!**

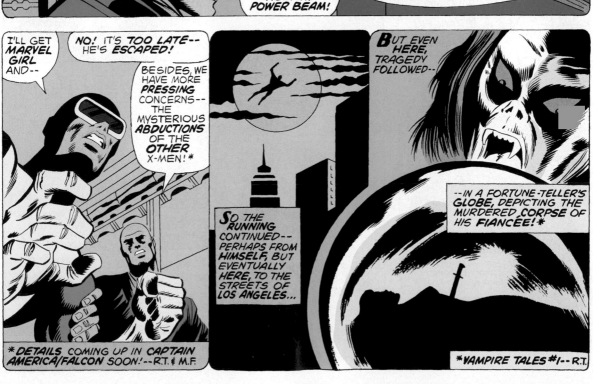

I'LL GET **MARVEL GIRL** AND--

NO! IT'S **TOO LATE**-- HE'S **ESCAPED!**

BESIDES, WE HAVE MORE **PRESSING** CONCERNS-- THE MYSTERIOUS **ABDUCTIONS** OF THE **OTHER** X-MEN! *

SO THE **RUNNING** CONTINUED-- PERHAPS FROM **HIMSELF,** BUT EVENTUALLY **HERE,** TO THE STREETS OF **LOS ANGELES...**

BUT EVEN **HERE,** TRAGEDY FOLLOWED--

--IN A FORTUNE-TELLER'S **GLOBE,** DEPICTING THE **MURDERED CORPSE** OF HIS **FIANCÉE!** *

DETAILS COMING UP IN *CAPTAIN AMERICA/FALCON* SOON!--R.T. & M.F.

*VAMPIRE TALES #1-- R.T.

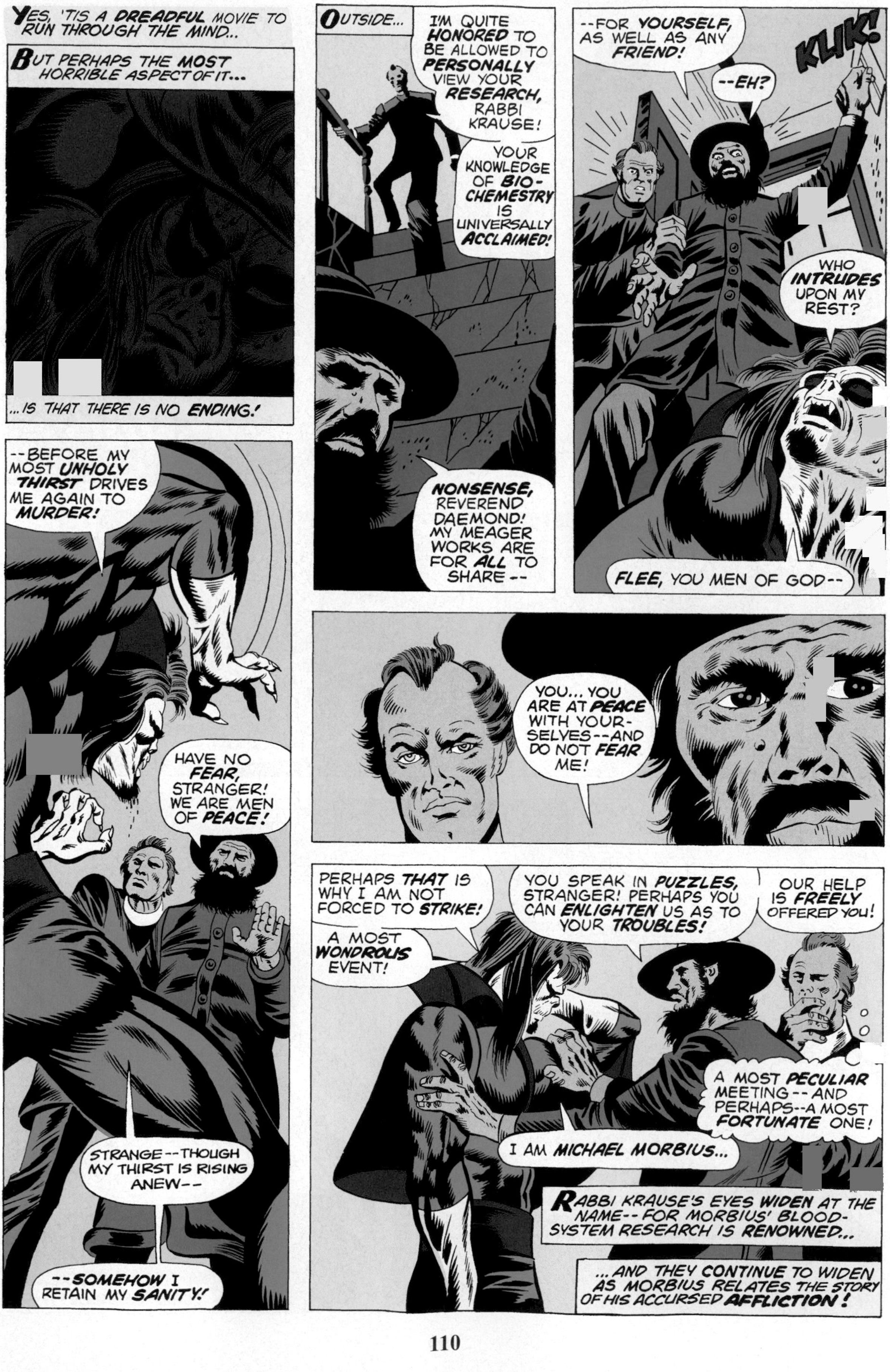

YES, 'TIS A DREADFUL MOVIE TO RUN THROUGH THE MIND...
BUT PERHAPS THE MOST HORRIBLE ASPECT OF IT...
...IS THAT THERE IS NO ENDING!
OUTSIDE...
I'M QUITE HONORED TO BE ALLOWED TO PERSONALLY VIEW YOUR RESEARCH, RABBI KRAUSE!
YOUR KNOWLEDGE OF BIO-CHEMESTRY IS UNIVERSALLY ACCLAIMED!
NONSENSE, REVEREND DAEMOND! MY MEAGER WORKS ARE FOR ALL TO SHARE--
--FOR YOURSELF, AS WELL AS ANY FRIEND!
KLIK!
--EH?
WHO INTRUDES UPON MY REST?
FLEE, YOU MEN OF GOD--
--BEFORE MY MOST UNHOLY THIRST DRIVES ME AGAIN TO MURDER!
HAVE NO FEAR, STRANGER! WE ARE MEN OF PEACE!
STRANGE--THOUGH MY THIRST IS RISING ANEW--
--SOMEHOW I RETAIN MY SANITY!
YOU... YOU ARE AT PEACE WITH YOURSELVES--AND DO NOT FEAR ME!
PERHAPS THAT IS WHY I AM NOT FORCED TO STRIKE!
A MOST WONDROUS EVENT!
YOU SPEAK IN PUZZLES, STRANGER! PERHAPS YOU CAN ENLIGHTEN US AS TO YOUR TROUBLES!
OUR HELP IS FREELY OFFERED YOU!
A MOST PECULIAR MEETING--AND PERHAPS--A MOST FORTUNATE ONE!
I AM MICHAEL MORBIUS...
RABBI KRAUSE'S EYES WIDEN AT THE NAME--FOR MORBIUS' BLOOD-SYSTEM RESEARCH IS RENOWNED...
...AND THEY CONTINUE TO WIDEN AS MORBIUS RELATES THE STORY OF HIS ACCURSED AFFLICTION!

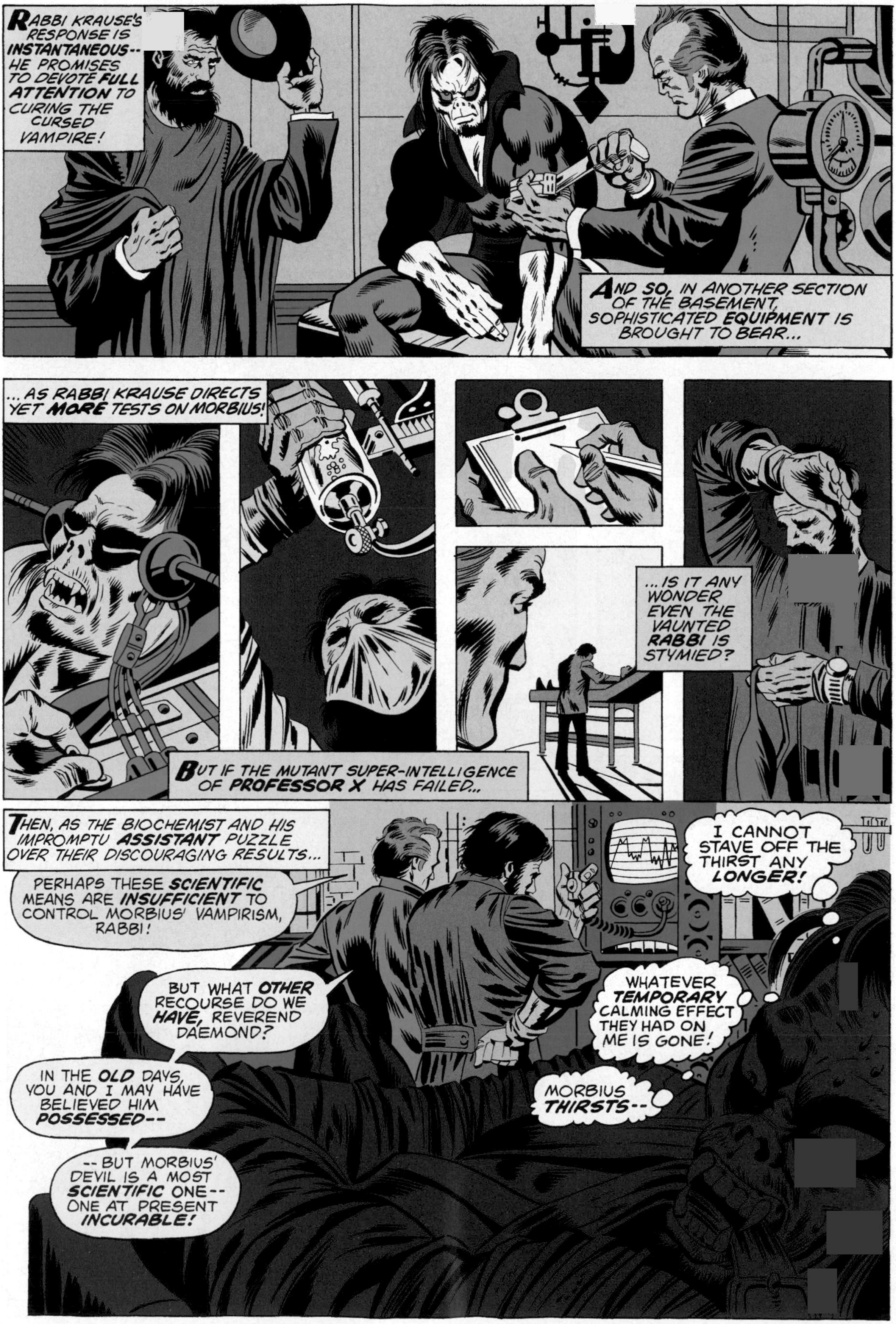
RABBI KRAUSE'S RESPONSE IS INSTANTANEOUS-- HE PROMISES TO DEVOTE FULL ATTENTION TO CURING THE CURSED VAMPIRE!
AND SO, IN ANOTHER SECTION OF THE BASEMENT, SOPHISTICATED EQUIPMENT IS BROUGHT TO BEAR...
...AS RABBI KRAUSE DIRECTS YET MORE TESTS ON MORBIUS!
...IS IT ANY WONDER EVEN THE VAUNTED RABBI IS STYMIED?
BUT IF THE MUTANT SUPER-INTELLIGENCE OF PROFESSOR X HAS FAILED...
THEN, AS THE BIOCHEMIST AND HIS IMPROMPTU ASSISTANT PUZZLE OVER THEIR DISCOURAGING RESULTS...
PERHAPS THESE SCIENTIFIC MEANS ARE INSUFFICIENT TO CONTROL MORBIUS' VAMPIRISM, RABBI!
BUT WHAT OTHER RECOURSE DO WE HAVE, REVEREND DAEMOND?
IN THE OLD DAYS, YOU AND I MAY HAVE BELIEVED HIM POSSESSED--
--BUT MORBIUS' DEVIL IS A MOST SCIENTIFIC ONE-- ONE AT PRESENT INCURABLE!
I CANNOT STAVE OFF THE THIRST ANY LONGER!
WHATEVER TEMPORARY CALMING EFFECT THEY HAD ON ME IS GONE!
MORBIUS THIRSTS--

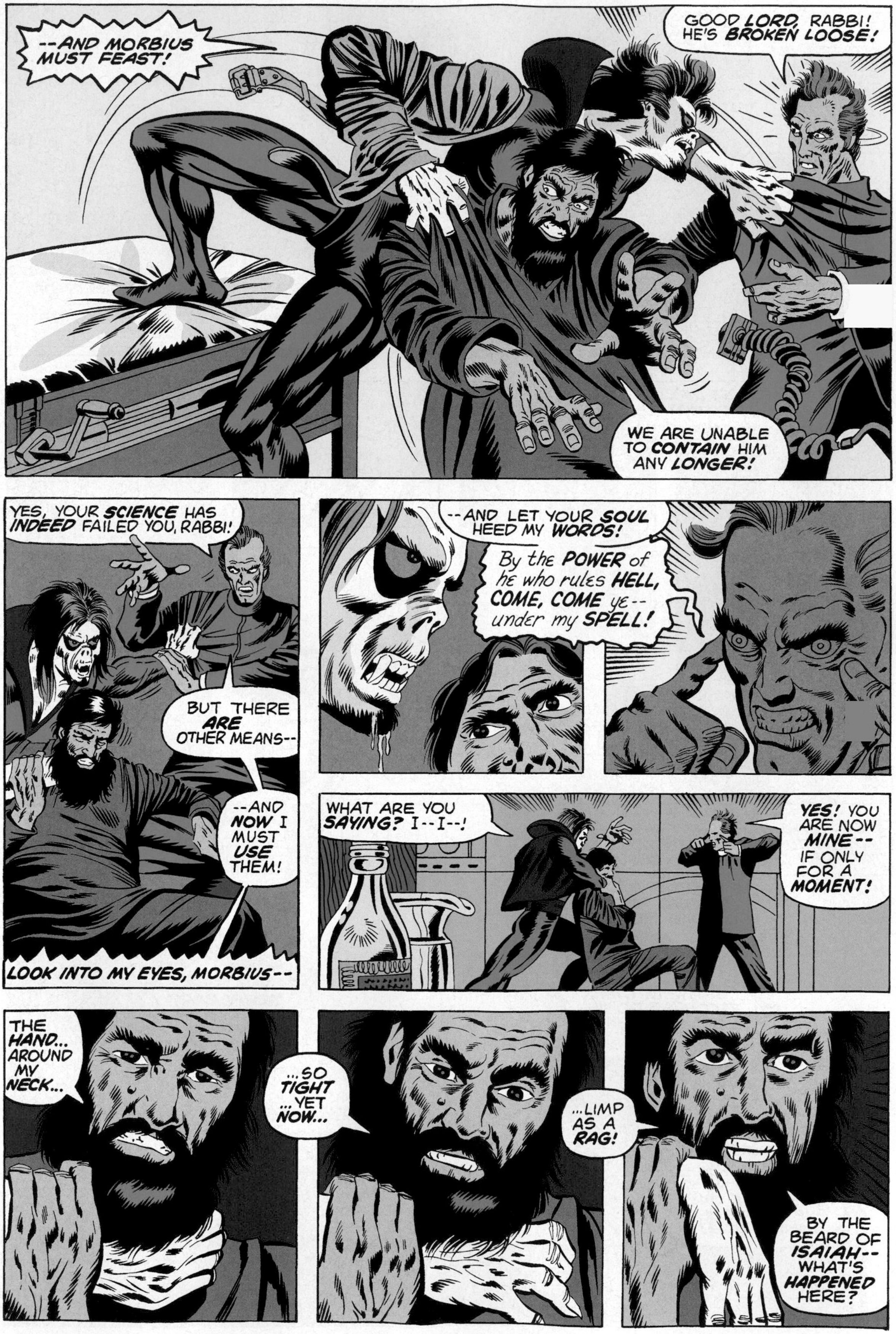
--AND MORBIUS MUST FEAST!
GOOD LORD, RABBI! HE'S BROKEN LOOSE!
WE ARE UNABLE TO CONTAIN HIM ANY LONGER!
YES, YOUR SCIENCE HAS INDEED FAILED YOU, RABBI!
BUT THERE ARE OTHER MEANS--
--AND NOW I MUST USE THEM!
LOOK INTO MY EYES, MORBIUS--
--AND LET YOUR SOUL HEED MY WORDS!
By the POWER of he who rules HELL, COME, COME ye-- under my SPELL!
WHAT ARE YOU SAYING? I--I--!
YES! YOU ARE NOW MINE-- IF ONLY FOR A MOMENT!
THE HAND... AROUND MY NECK...
...SO TIGHT ...YET NOW...
...LIMP AS A RAG!
BY THE BEARD OF ISAIAH-- WHAT'S HAPPENED HERE?

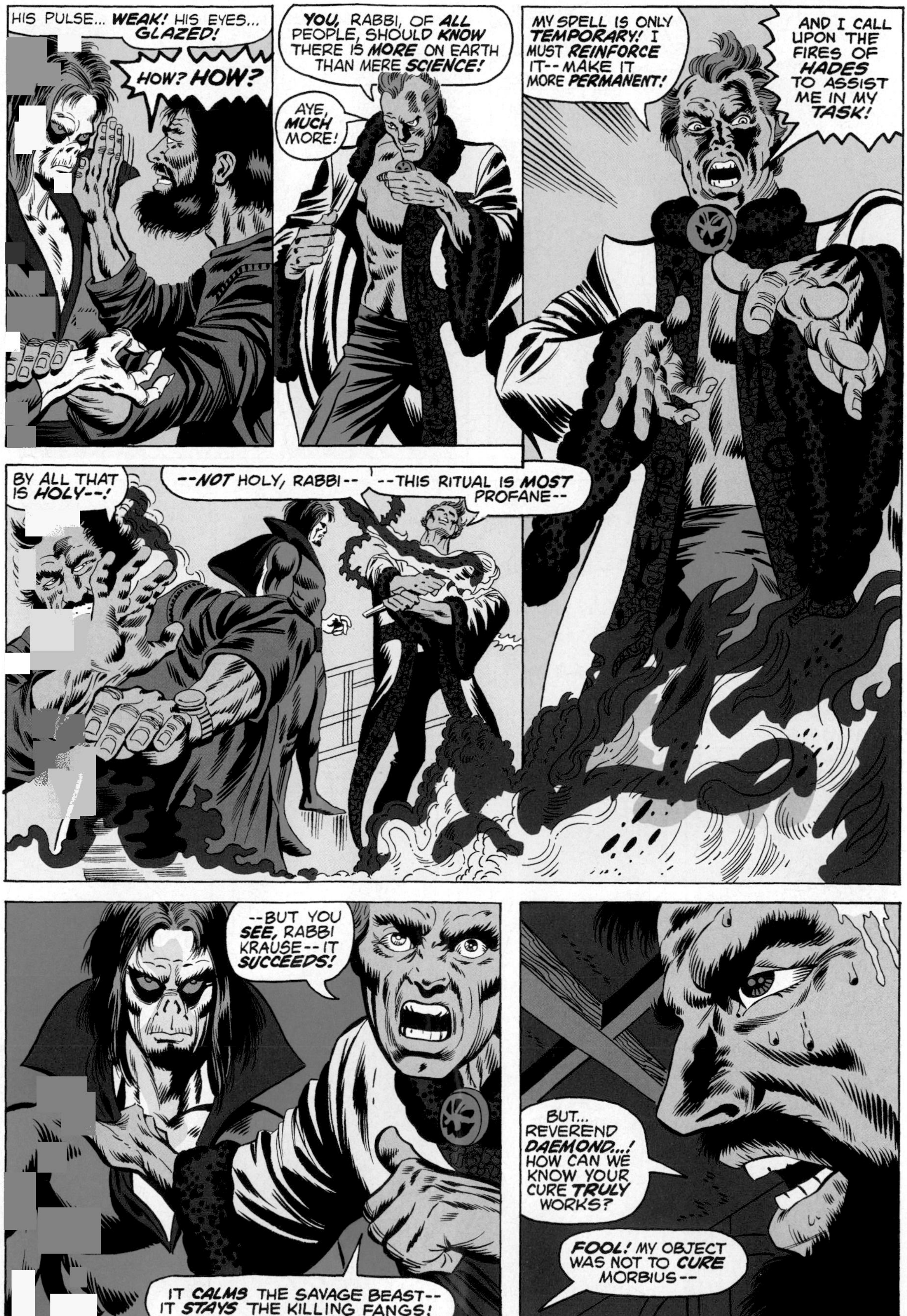
HIS PULSE... WEAK! HIS EYES... GLAZED!
HOW? HOW?
YOU, RABBI, OF ALL PEOPLE, SHOULD KNOW THERE IS MORE ON EARTH THAN MERE SCIENCE!
AYE, MUCH MORE!
MY SPELL IS ONLY TEMPORARY! I MUST REINFORCE IT-- MAKE IT MORE PERMANENT!
AND I CALL UPON THE FIRES OF HADES TO ASSIST ME IN MY TASK!
BY ALL THAT IS HOLY--!
--NOT HOLY, RABBI--
--THIS RITUAL IS MOST PROFANE--
--BUT YOU SEE, RABBI KRAUSE-- IT SUCCEEDS!
IT CALMS THE SAVAGE BEAST-- IT STAYS THE KILLING FANGS!
BUT... REVEREND DAEMOND...! HOW CAN WE KNOW YOUR CURE TRULY WORKS?
FOOL! MY OBJECT WAS NOT TO CURE MORBIUS--

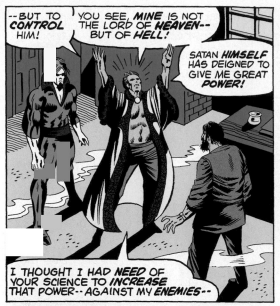

--BUT TO **CONTROL** HIM!

YOU SEE, MINE IS NOT THE LORD OF **HEAVEN**-- BUT OF **HELL!**

SATAN **HIMSELF** HAS DEIGNED TO GIVE ME GREAT **POWER!**

I THOUGHT I HAD **NEED** OF YOUR SCIENCE TO **INCREASE** THAT POWER--AGAINST MY **ENEMIES**--

--BUT WITH **MORBIUS'** FORTUNATE APPEARANCE, YOU BECOME **SUPERFLUOUS!**

ATTACK, MORBIUS-- AS I **COMMAND!**

KILL HIM!

STRANGE ARE THE THOUGHTS AT DEATH'S DOOR... **HEAR** THEM:

Michael... A **HEBREW** NAME...

"WHO IS LIKE GOD" ...TO BE **EXACT!**...

HOW... HOW... IRONIC... THAT SUCH A NAME... IS THAT OF...

...A VAMPIRE...

ENOUGH, MORBIUS-- HE IS **DEAD!**

ENOUGH, I SAID!

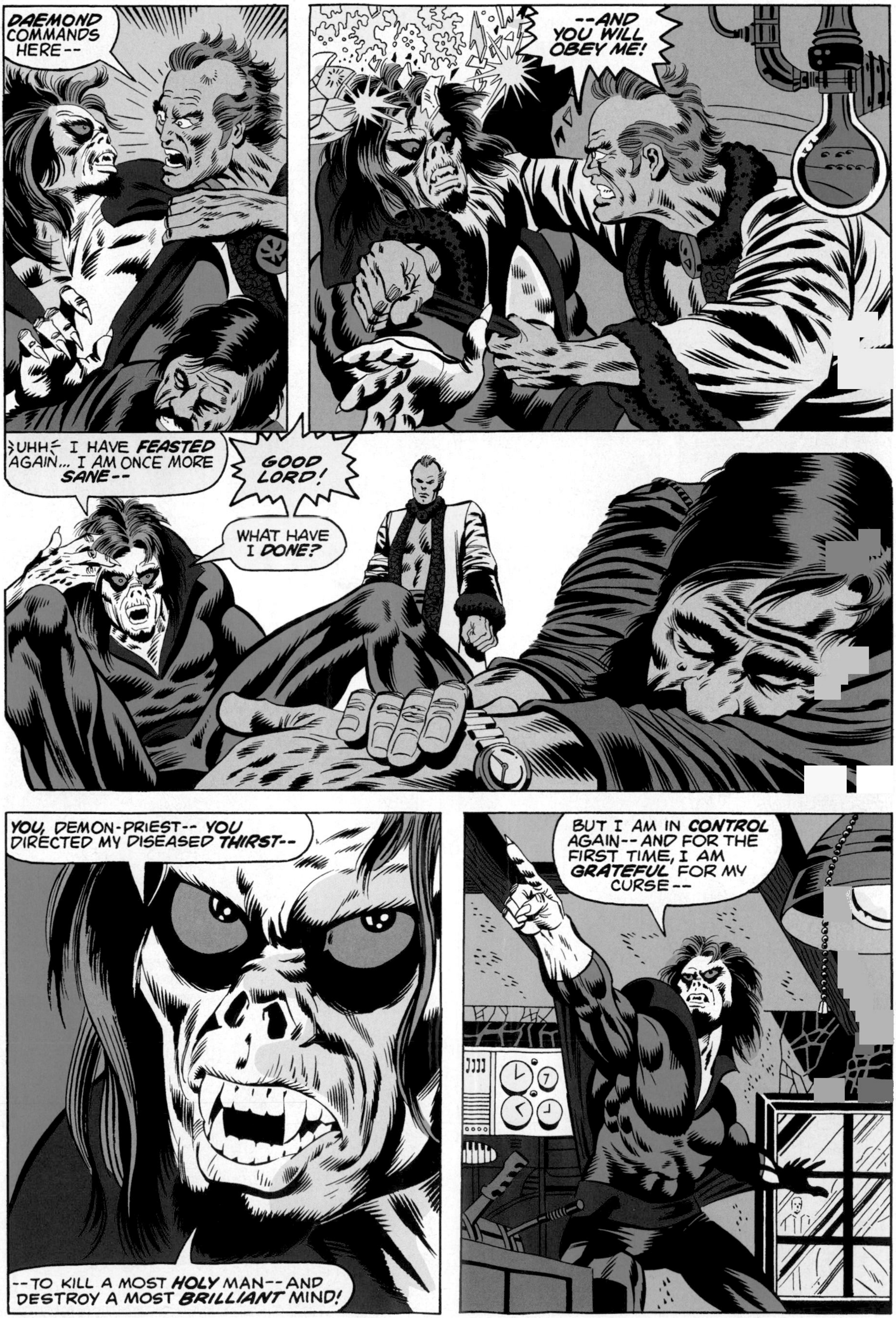
DAEMOND COMMANDS HERE--
--AND YOU WILL OBEY ME!
UHH... I HAVE FEASTED AGAIN... I AM ONCE MORE SANE--
WHAT HAVE I DONE?
GOOD LORD!
YOU, DEMON-PRIEST-- YOU DIRECTED MY DISEASED THIRST--
--TO KILL A MOST HOLY MAN--AND DESTROY A MOST BRILLIANT MIND!
BUT I AM IN CONTROL AGAIN-- AND FOR THE FIRST TIME, I AM GRATEFUL FOR MY CURSE--

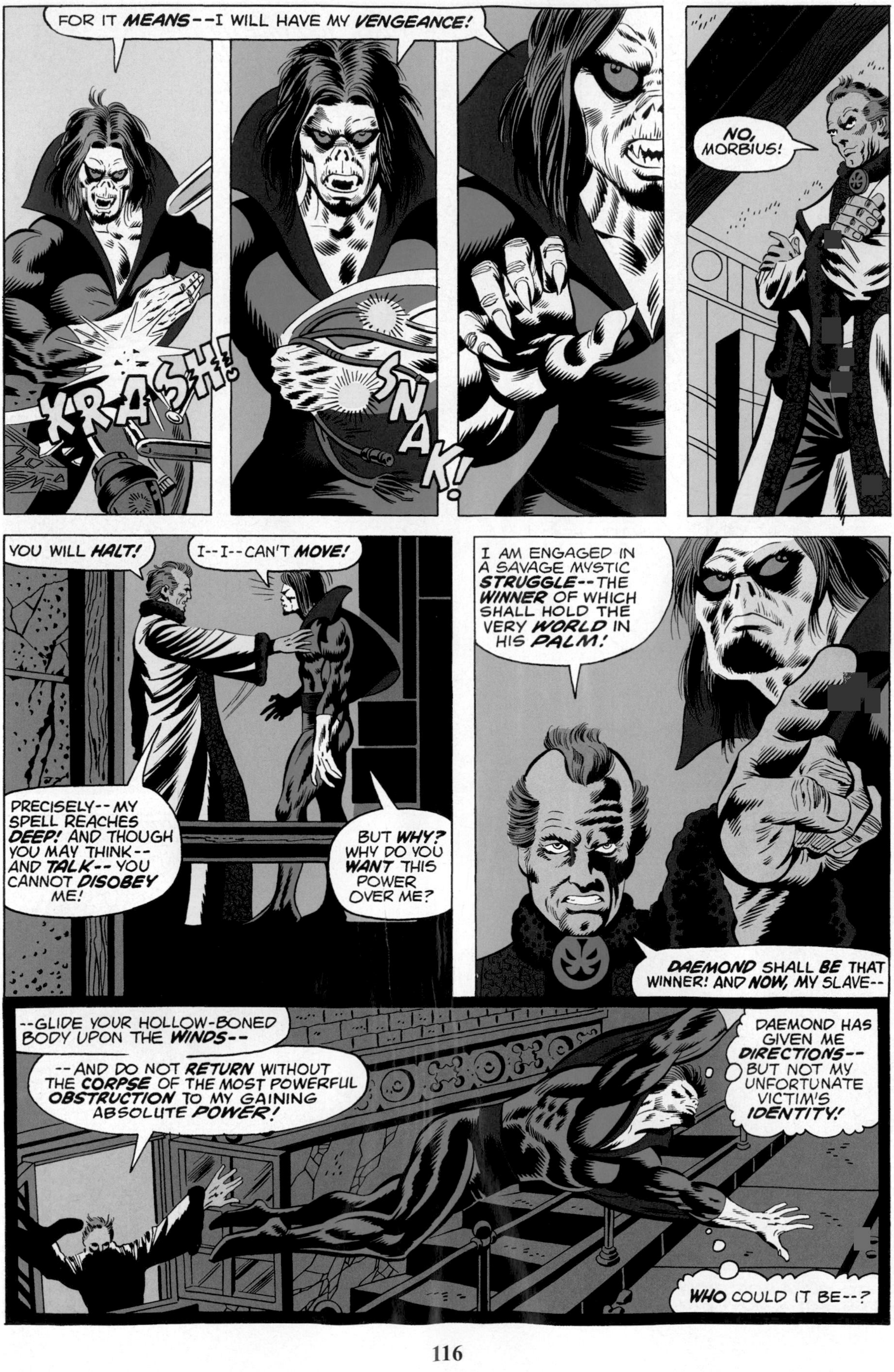
FOR IT MEANS--I WILL HAVE MY VENGEANCE!
KRASH!
SNAK!
NO, MORBIUS!
YOU WILL HALT!
I--I--CAN'T MOVE!
PRECISELY--MY SPELL REACHES DEEP! AND THOUGH YOU MAY THINK--AND TALK--YOU CANNOT DISOBEY ME!
BUT WHY? WHY DO YOU WANT THIS POWER OVER ME?
I AM ENGAGED IN A SAVAGE MYSTIC STRUGGLE--THE WINNER OF WHICH SHALL HOLD THE VERY WORLD IN HIS PALM!
DAEMOND SHALL BE THAT WINNER! AND NOW, MY SLAVE--
--GLIDE YOUR HOLLOW-BONED BODY UPON THE WINDS--
--AND DO NOT RETURN WITHOUT THE CORPSE OF THE MOST POWERFUL OBSTRUCTION TO MY GAINING ABSOLUTE POWER!
DAEMOND HAS GIVEN ME DIRECTIONS--BUT NOT MY UNFORTUNATE VICTIM'S IDENTITY!
WHO COULD IT BE--?

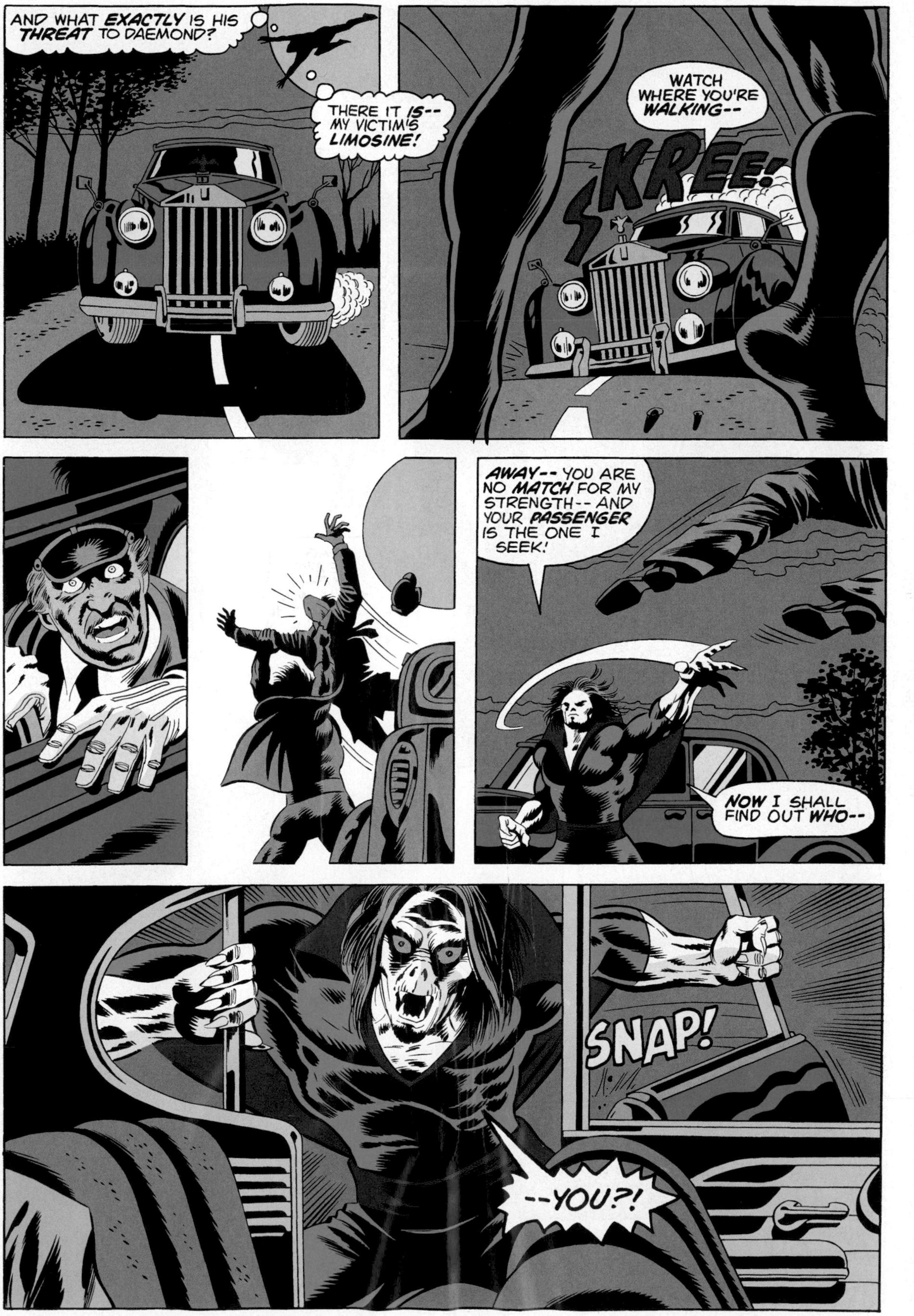
AND WHAT EXACTLY IS HIS THREAT TO DAEMOND?
THERE IT IS-- MY VICTIM'S LIMOSINE!
WATCH WHERE YOU'RE WALKING--
SKREE!
AWAY-- YOU ARE NO MATCH FOR MY STRENGTH-- AND YOUR PASSENGER IS THE ONE I SEEK!
NOW I SHALL FIND OUT WHO--
SNAP!
--YOU?!

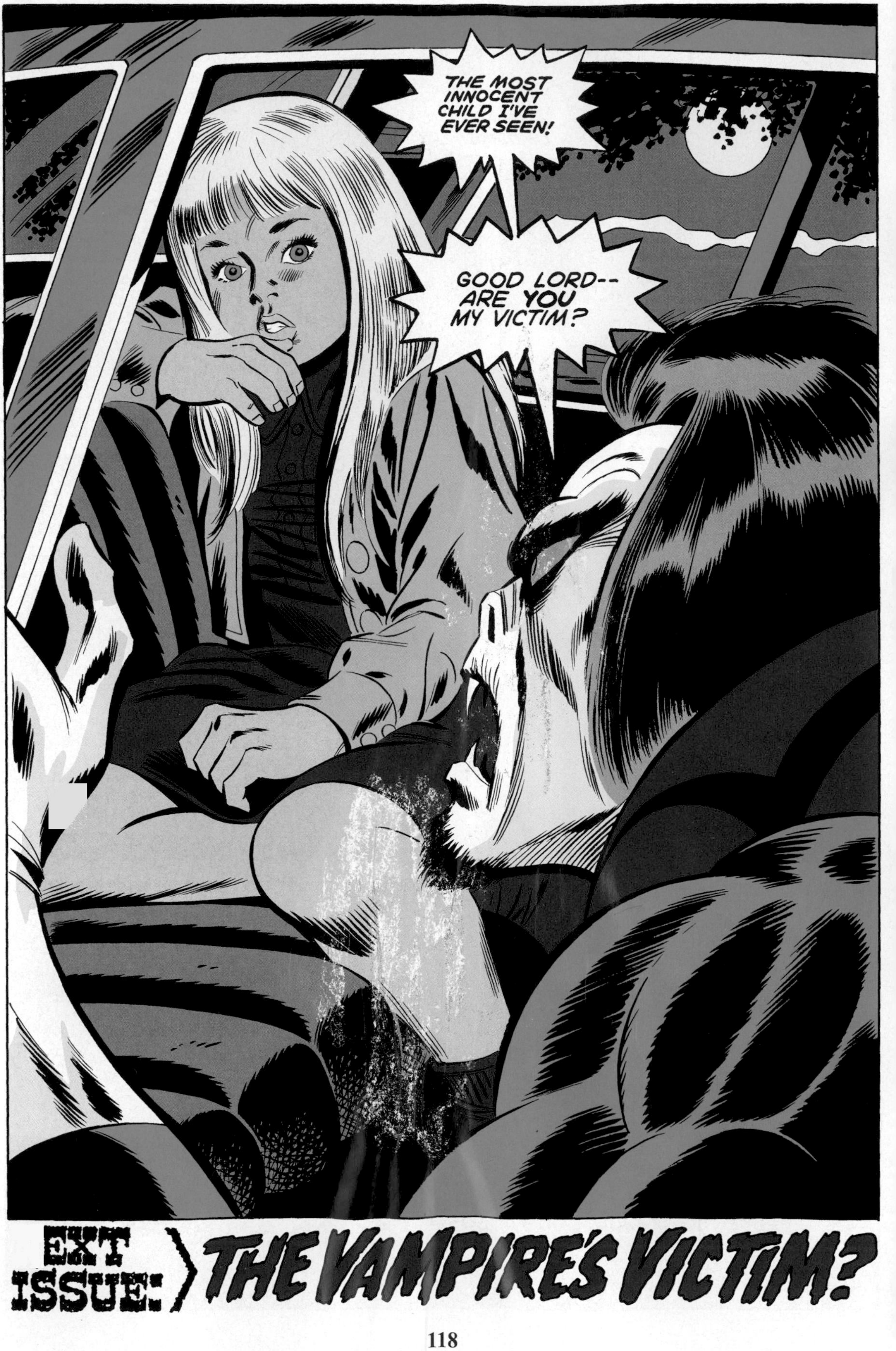
THE MOST INNOCENT CHILD I'VE EVER SEEN!
GOOD LORD-- ARE YOU MY VICTIM?

EXT ISSUE: THE VAMPIRE'S VICTIM?

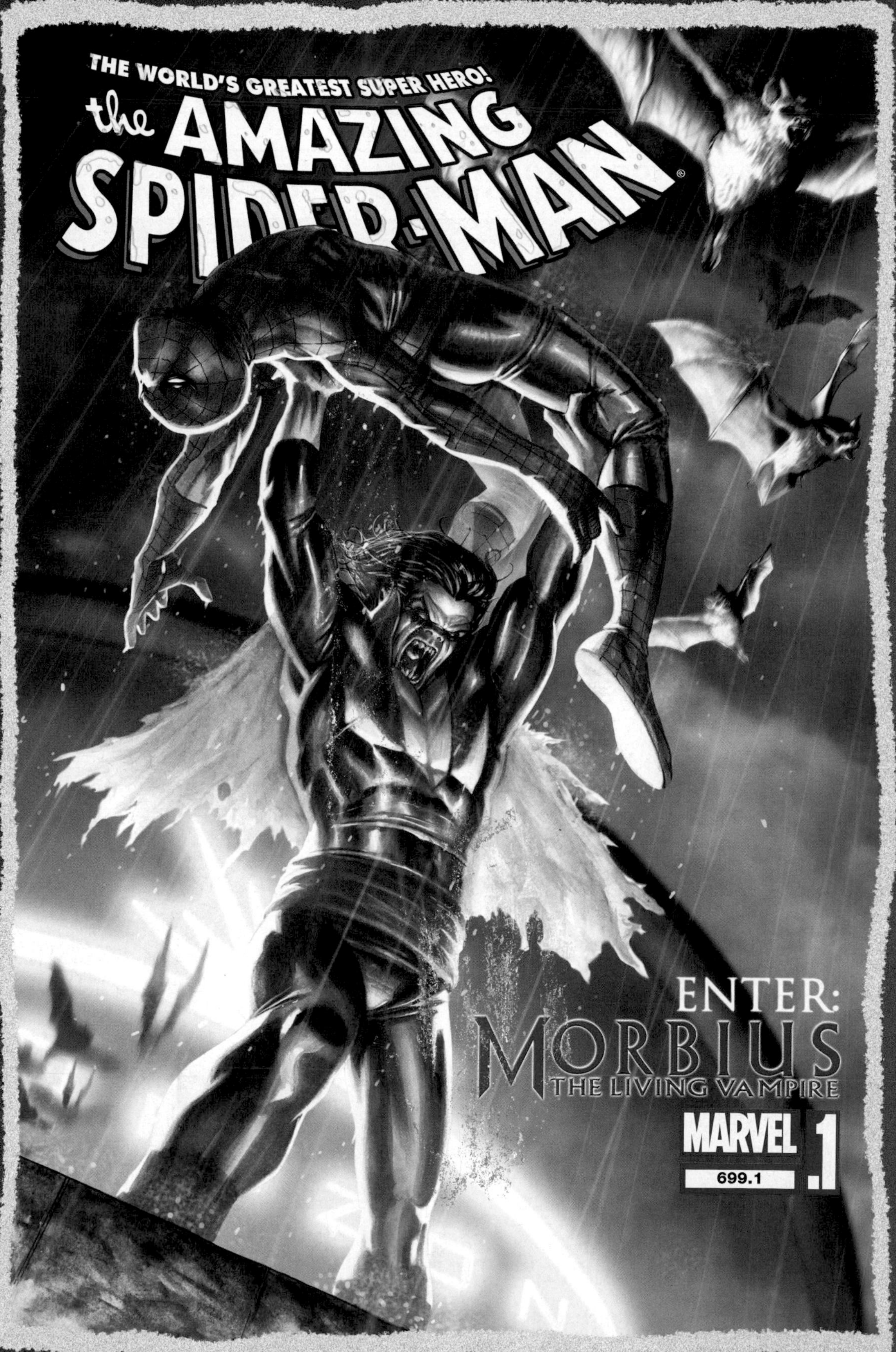
THE WORLD'S GREATEST SUPER HERO!
the AMAZING SPIDER-MAN
ENTER: MORBIUS THE LIVING VAMPIRE
MARVEL
699.1
.1

FINAL ☆☆☆☆

DAILY BUGLE®

NEW YORK'S FINEST DAILY NEWSPAPER

SINCE 1897 ☆☆☆☆☆ $1.00 (in NYC) $1.50 (outside city)

INSIDE: STARK STOCK DROPS; CAROL DANVERS CHASING SHIPS; ALLEGED CRIME LORDS CONVERGE ON MADRIPOOR.

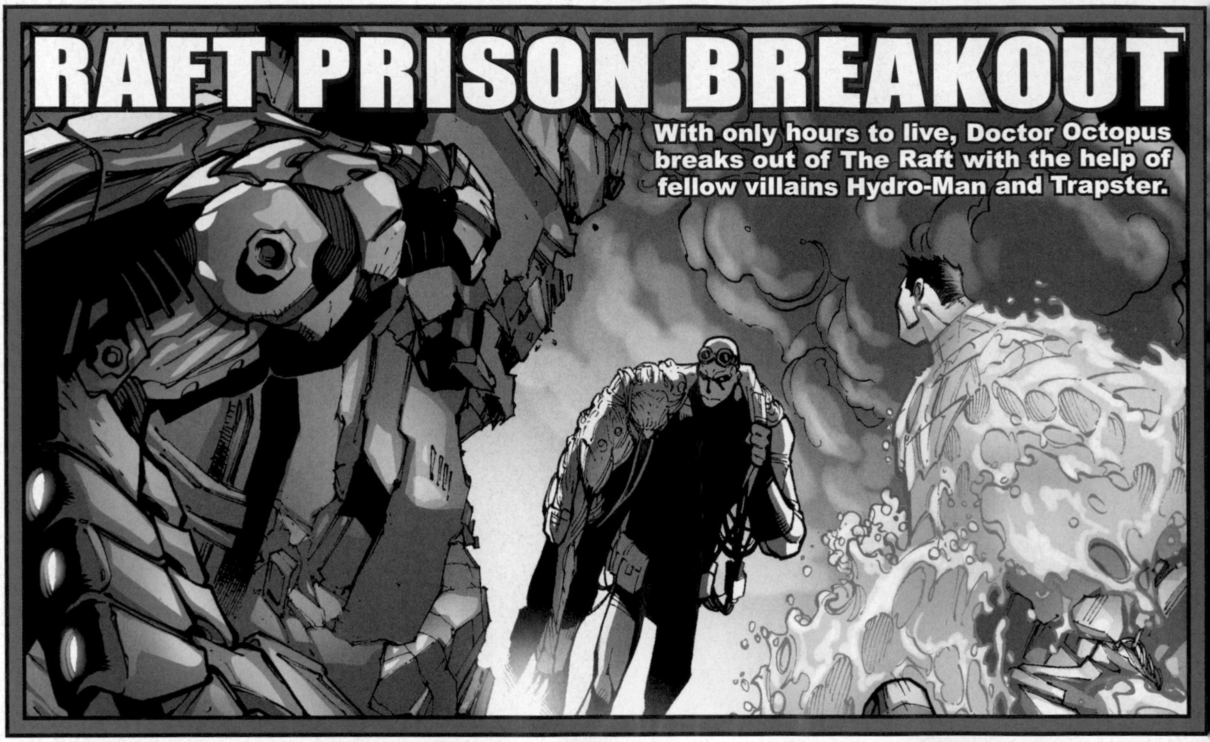

RAFT PRISON BREAKOUT

With only hours to live, Doctor Octopus breaks out of The Raft with the help of fellow villains Hydro-Man and Trapster.

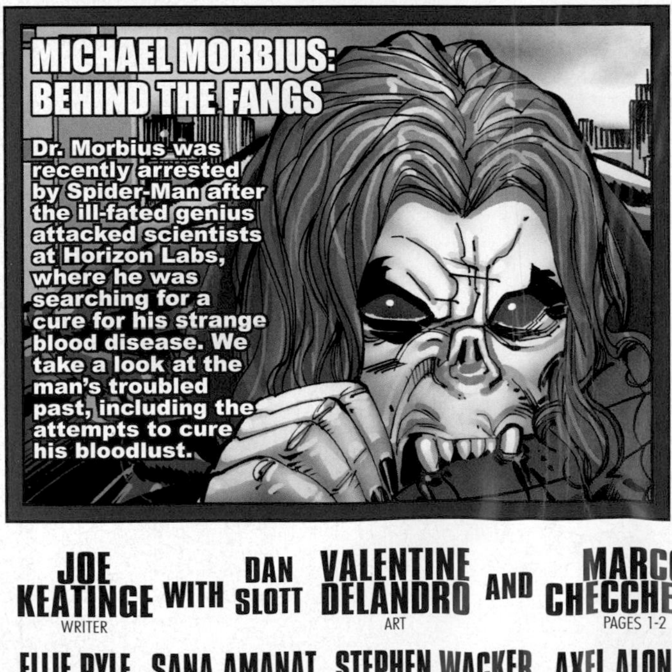

MICHAEL MORBIUS: BEHIND THE FANGS

Dr. Morbius was recently arrested by Spider-Man after the ill-fated genius attacked scientists at Horizon Labs, where he was searching for a cure for his strange blood disease. We take a look at the man's troubled past, including the attempts to cure his bloodlust.

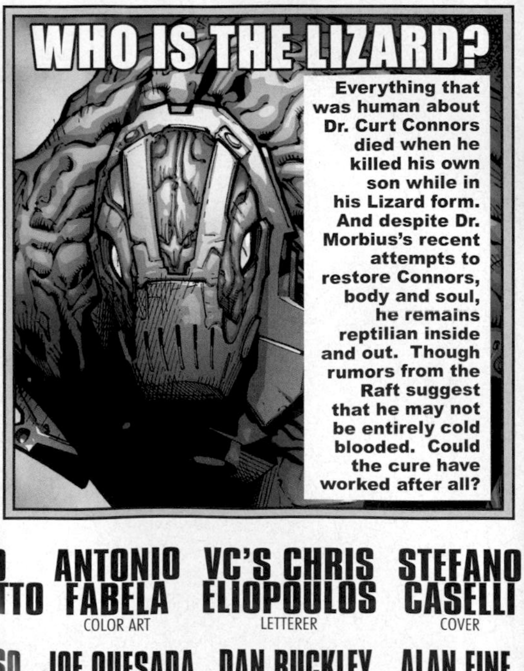

WHO IS THE LIZARD?

Everything that was human about Dr. Curt Connors died when he killed his own son while in his Lizard form. And despite Dr. Morbius's recent attempts to restore Connors, body and soul, he remains reptilian inside and out. Though rumors from the Raft suggest that he may not be entirely cold blooded. Could the cure have worked after all?

JOE KEATINGE WRITER WITH DAN SLOTT | VALENTINE DELANDRO ART AND MARCO CHECCHETTO PAGES 1-2 | ANTONIO FABELA COLOR ART | VC'S CHRIS ELIOPOULOS LETTERER | STEFANO CASELLI COVER

ELLIE PYLE ASSISTANT EDITOR | SANA AMANAT ASSOCIATE EDITOR | STEPHEN WACKER EDITOR | AXEL ALONSO EDITOR IN CHIEF | JOE QUESADA CHIEF CREATIVE OFFICER | DAN BUCKLEY PUBLISHER | ALAN FINE EXEC. PRODUCER

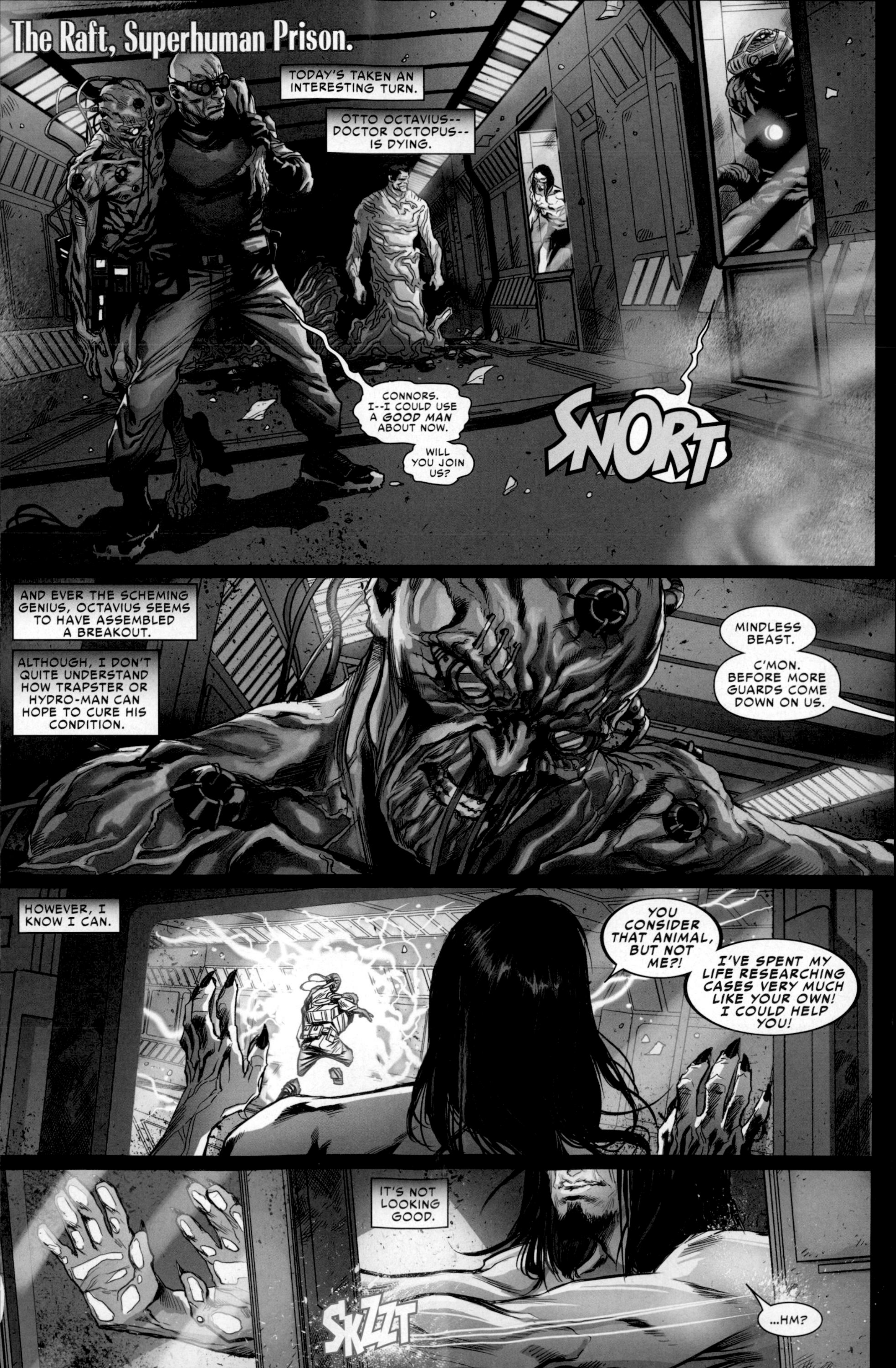
The Raft, Superhuman Prison.
TODAY'S TAKEN AN INTERESTING TURN.
OTTO OCTAVIUS-- DOCTOR OCTOPUS-- IS DYING.
CONNORS. I--I COULD USE A GOOD MAN ABOUT NOW.
WILL YOU JOIN US?
SNORT
AND EVER THE SCHEMING GENIUS, OCTAVIUS SEEMS TO HAVE ASSEMBLED A BREAKOUT.
ALTHOUGH, I DON'T QUITE UNDERSTAND HOW TRAPSTER OR HYDRO-MAN CAN HOPE TO CURE HIS CONDITION.
MINDLESS BEAST.
C'MON. BEFORE MORE GUARDS COME DOWN ON US.
HOWEVER, I KNOW I CAN.
YOU CONSIDER THAT ANIMAL, BUT NOT ME?!
I'VE SPENT MY LIFE RESEARCHING CASES VERY MUCH LIKE YOUR OWN! I COULD HELP YOU!
IT'S NOT LOOKING GOOD.
SKZZZT
...HM?

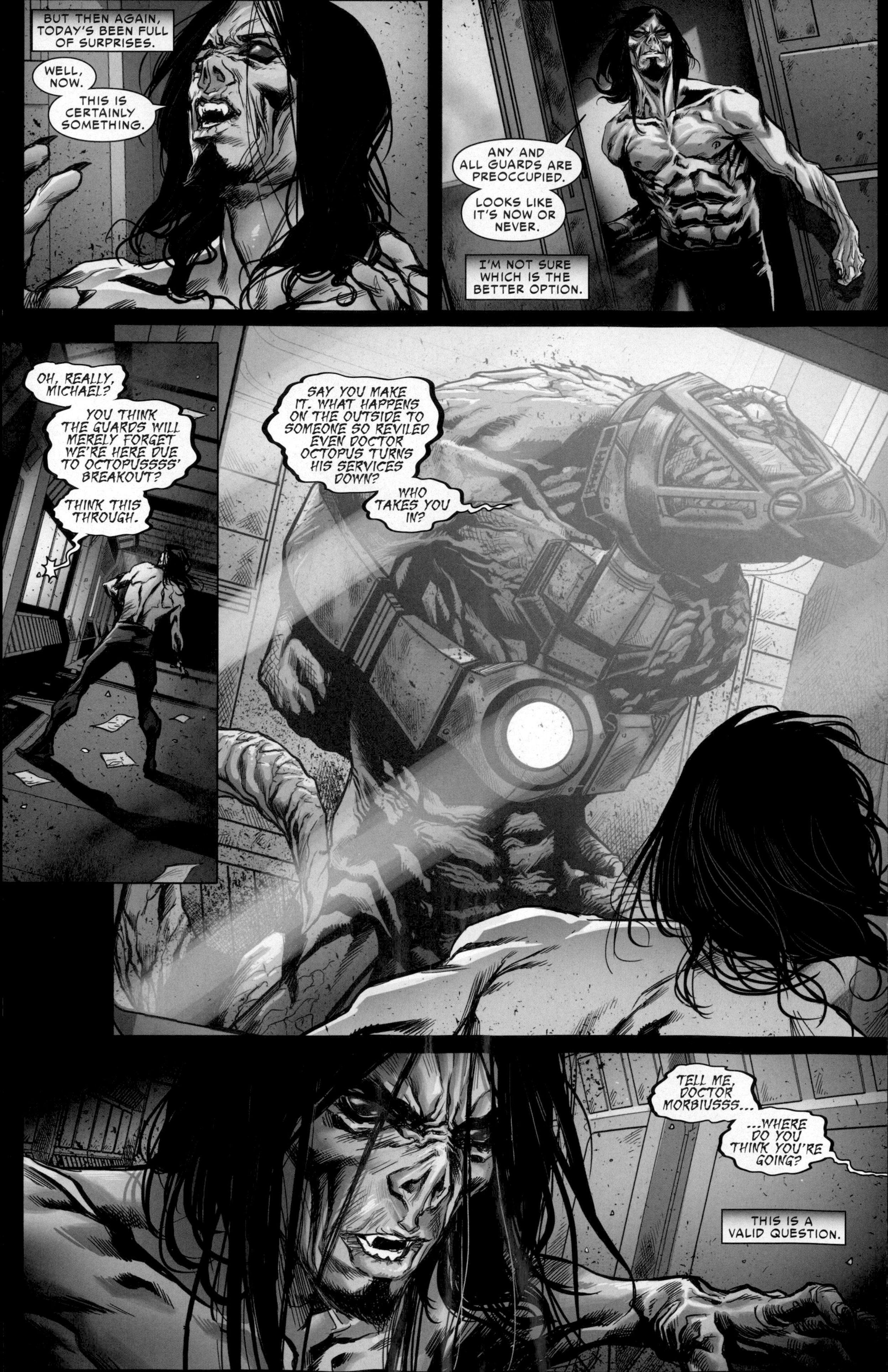
BUT THEN AGAIN, TODAY'S BEEN FULL OF SURPRISES.
WELL, NOW.
THIS IS CERTAINLY SOMETHING.
ANY AND ALL GUARDS ARE PREOCCUPIED.
LOOKS LIKE IT'S NOW OR NEVER.
I'M NOT SURE WHICH IS THE BETTER OPTION.
OH, REALLY, MICHAEL?
YOU THINK THE GUARDS WILL MERELY FORGET WE'RE HERE DUE TO OCTOPUSSSS' BREAKOUT?
THINK THIS THROUGH.
SAY YOU MAKE IT. WHAT HAPPENS ON THE OUTSIDE TO SOMEONE SO REVILED EVEN DOCTOR OCTOPUS TURNS HIS SERVICES DOWN?
WHO TAKES YOU IN?
TELL ME, DOCTOR MORBIUSSS...
...WHERE DO YOU THINK YOU'RE GOING?
THIS IS A VALID QUESTION.

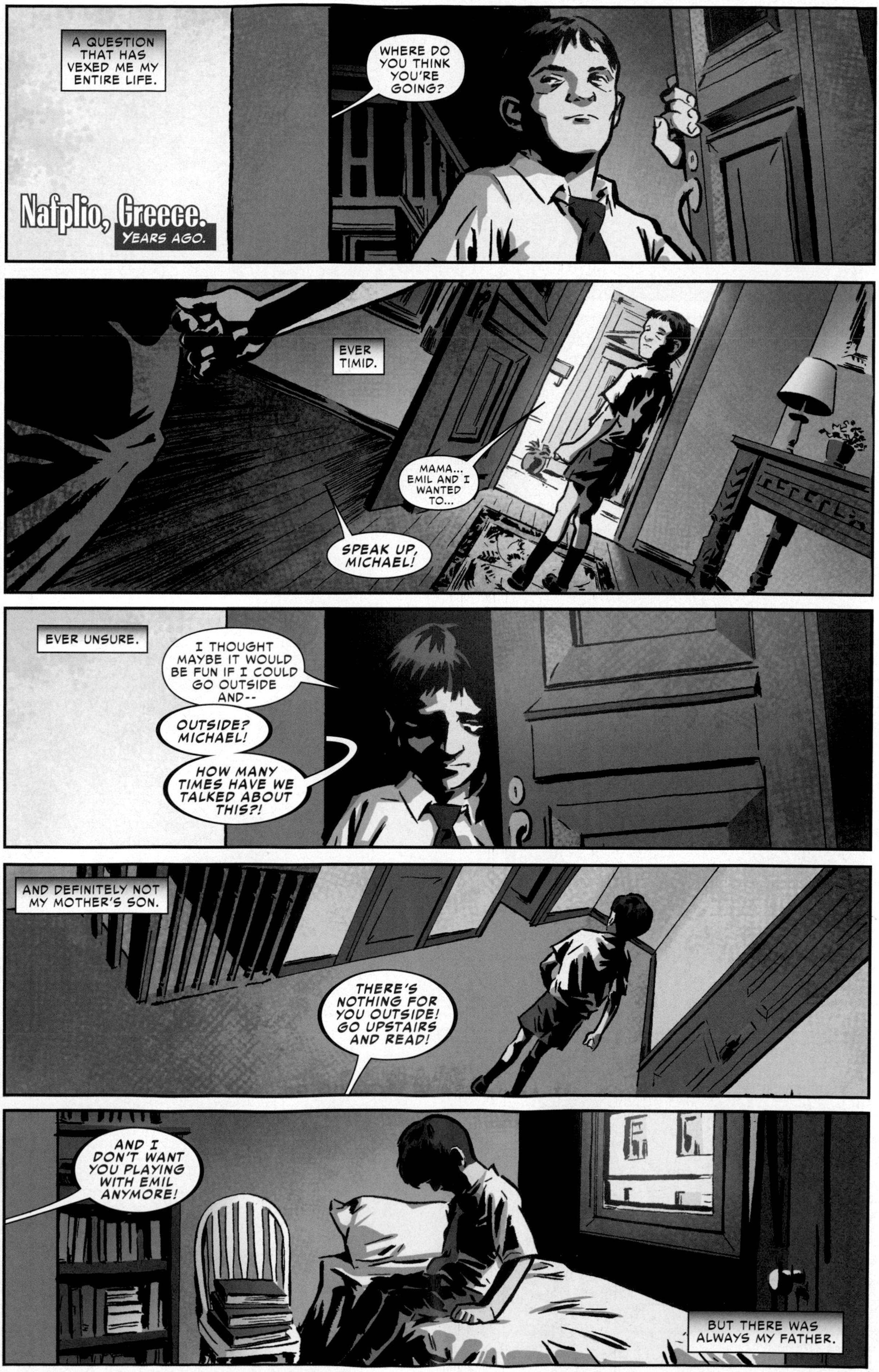
A QUESTION THAT HAS VEXED ME MY ENTIRE LIFE.
WHERE DO YOU THINK YOU'RE GOING?
Nafplio, Greece.
YEARS AGO.
EVER TIMID.
MAMA... EMIL AND I WANTED TO...
SPEAK UP, MICHAEL!
EVER UNSURE.
I THOUGHT MAYBE IT WOULD BE FUN IF I COULD GO OUTSIDE AND--
OUTSIDE? MICHAEL!
HOW MANY TIMES HAVE WE TALKED ABOUT THIS?!
AND DEFINITELY NOT MY MOTHER'S SON.
THERE'S NOTHING FOR YOU OUTSIDE! GO UPSTAIRS AND READ!
AND I DON'T WANT YOU PLAYING WITH EMIL ANYMORE!
BUT THERE WAS ALWAYS MY FATHER.

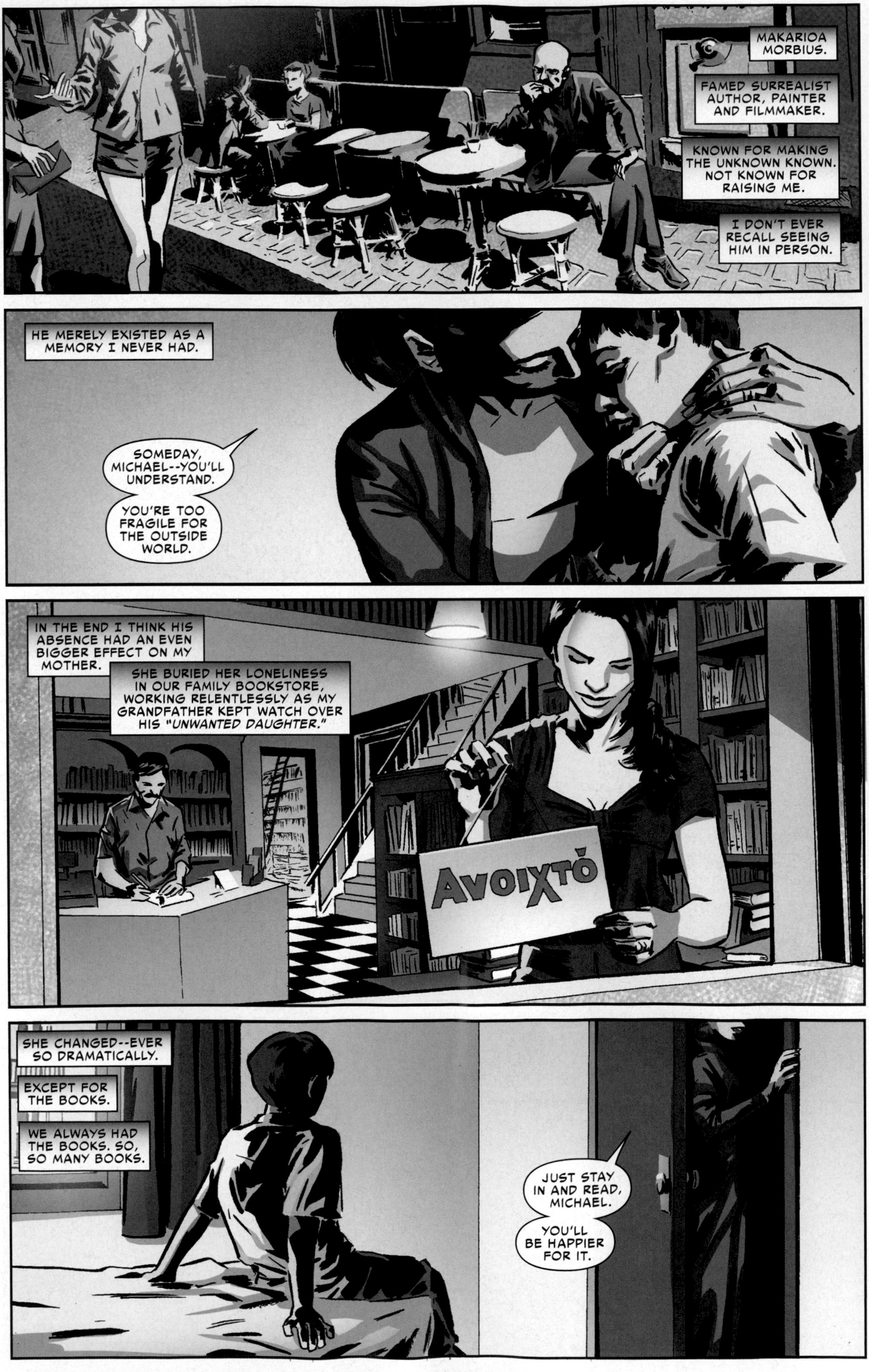
MAKARIOA MORBIUS.
FAMED SURREALIST AUTHOR, PAINTER AND FILMMAKER.
KNOWN FOR MAKING THE UNKNOWN KNOWN. NOT KNOWN FOR RAISING ME.
I DON'T EVER RECALL SEEING HIM IN PERSON.
HE MERELY EXISTED AS A MEMORY I NEVER HAD.
SOMEDAY, MICHAEL--YOU'LL UNDERSTAND.
YOU'RE TOO FRAGILE FOR THE OUTSIDE WORLD.
IN THE END I THINK HIS ABSENCE HAD AN EVEN BIGGER EFFECT ON MY MOTHER.
SHE BURIED HER LONELINESS IN OUR FAMILY BOOKSTORE, WORKING RELENTLESSLY AS MY GRANDFATHER KEPT WATCH OVER HIS *"UNWANTED DAUGHTER."*
ΑΝΟΙΧΤΌ
SHE CHANGED--EVER SO DRAMATICALLY.
EXCEPT FOR THE BOOKS.
WE ALWAYS HAD THE BOOKS. SO, SO MANY BOOKS.
JUST STAY IN AND READ, MICHAEL.
YOU'LL BE HAPPIER FOR IT.

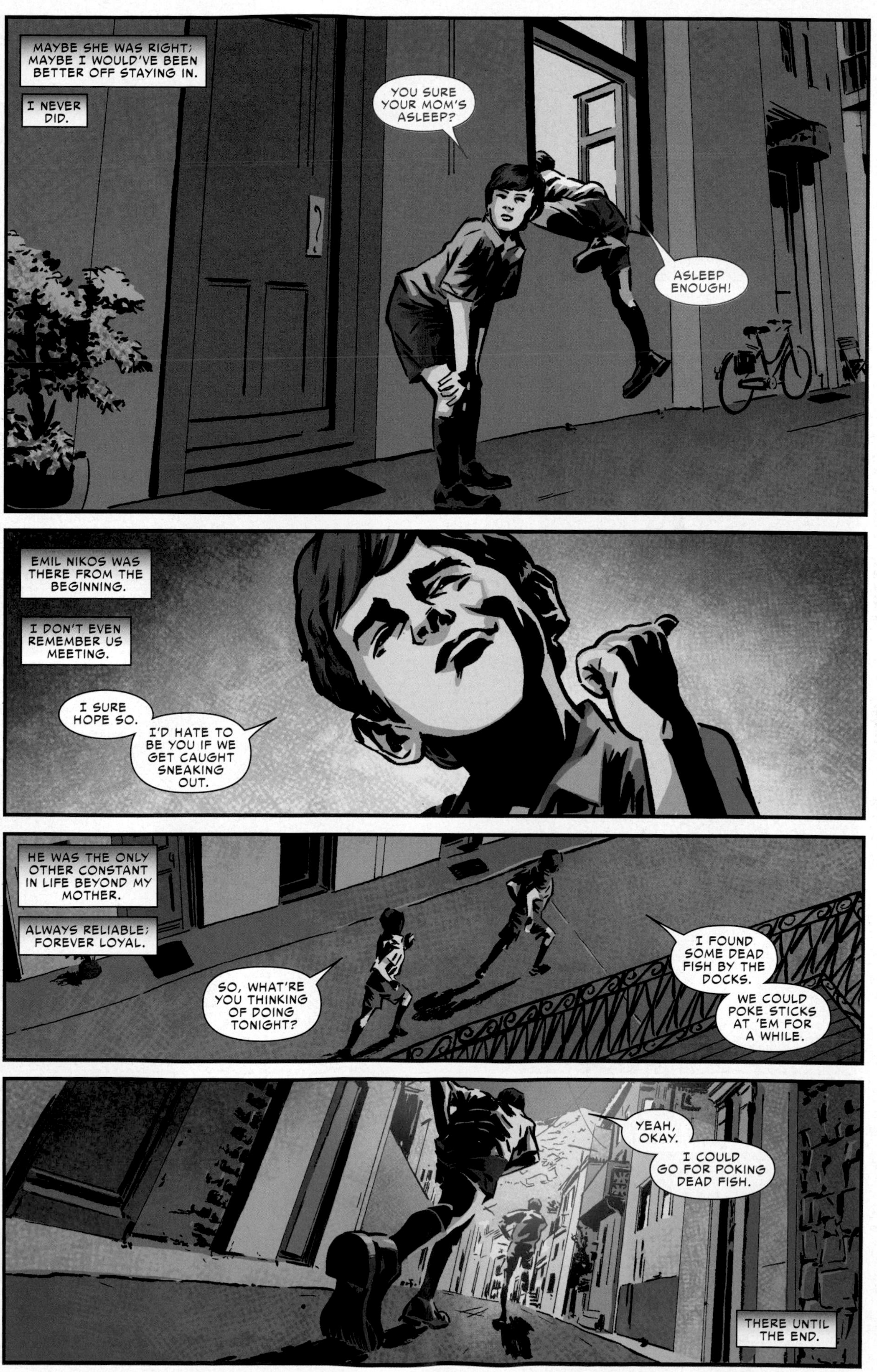
MAYBE SHE WAS RIGHT; MAYBE I WOULD'VE BEEN BETTER OFF STAYING IN.
I NEVER DID.
YOU SURE YOUR MOM'S ASLEEP?
ASLEEP ENOUGH!
EMIL NIKOS WAS THERE FROM THE BEGINNING.
I DON'T EVEN REMEMBER US MEETING.
I SURE HOPE SO.
I'D HATE TO BE YOU IF WE GET CAUGHT SNEAKING OUT.
HE WAS THE ONLY OTHER CONSTANT IN LIFE BEYOND MY MOTHER.
ALWAYS RELIABLE; FOREVER LOYAL.
SO, WHAT'RE YOU THINKING OF DOING TONIGHT?
I FOUND SOME DEAD FISH BY THE DOCKS.
WE COULD POKE STICKS AT 'EM FOR A WHILE.
YEAH, OKAY.
I COULD GO FOR POKING DEAD FISH.
THERE UNTIL THE END.

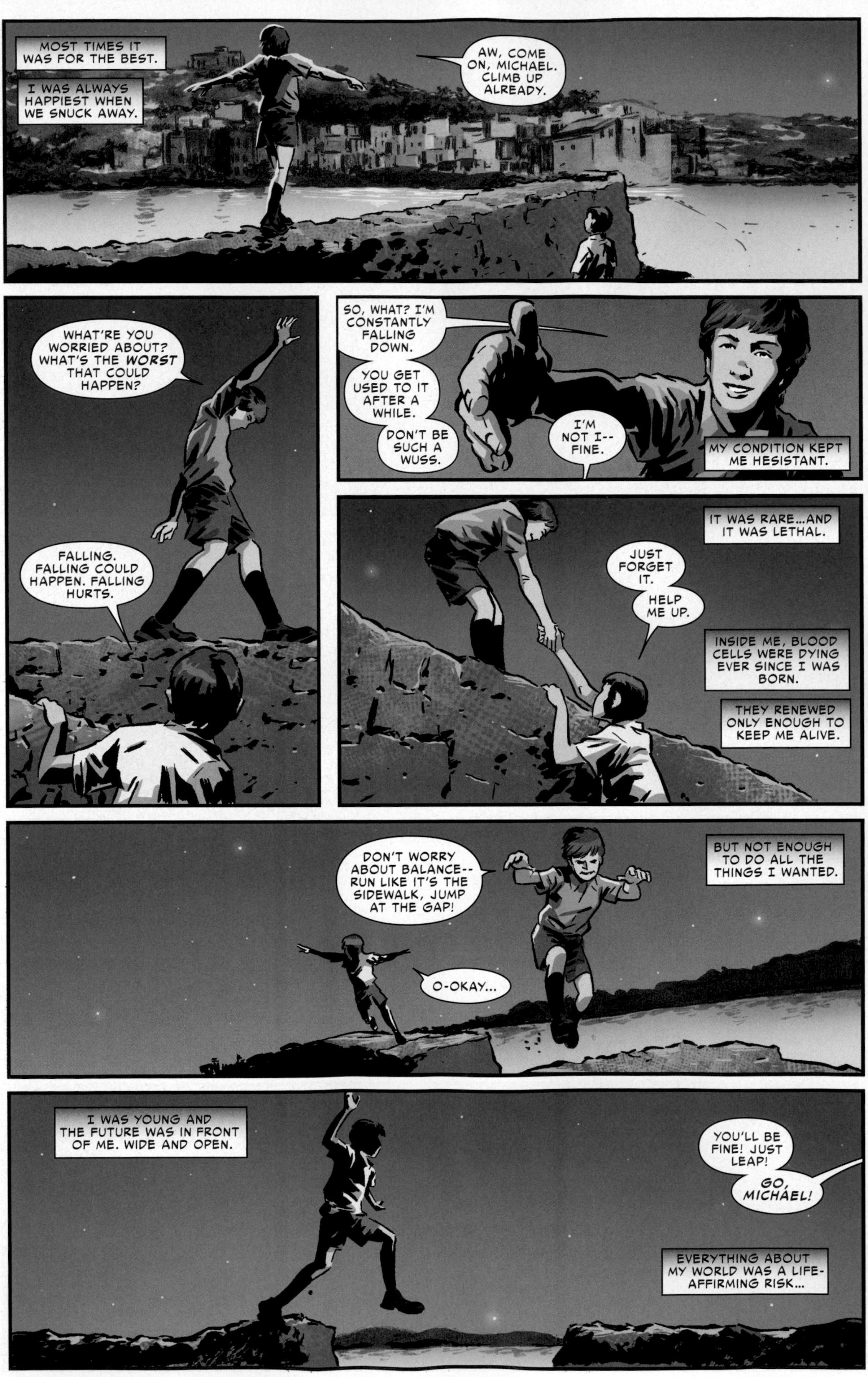
MOST TIMES IT WAS FOR THE BEST.
I WAS ALWAYS HAPPIEST WHEN WE SNUCK AWAY.
AW, COME ON, MICHAEL. CLIMB UP ALREADY.
WHAT'RE YOU WORRIED ABOUT? WHAT'S THE *WORST* THAT COULD HAPPEN?
FALLING. FALLING COULD HAPPEN. FALLING HURTS.
SO, WHAT? I'M CONSTANTLY FALLING DOWN.
YOU GET USED TO IT AFTER A WHILE.
DON'T BE SUCH A WUSS.
I'M NOT I-- FINE.
MY CONDITION KEPT ME HESISTANT.
IT WAS RARE...AND IT WAS LETHAL.
JUST FORGET IT.
HELP ME UP.
INSIDE ME, BLOOD CELLS WERE DYING EVER SINCE I WAS BORN.
THEY RENEWED ONLY ENOUGH TO KEEP ME ALIVE.
BUT NOT ENOUGH TO DO ALL THE THINGS I WANTED.
DON'T WORRY ABOUT BALANCE-- RUN LIKE IT'S THE SIDEWALK, JUMP AT THE GAP!
O-OKAY...
I WAS YOUNG AND THE FUTURE WAS IN FRONT OF ME. WIDE AND OPEN.
YOU'LL BE FINE! JUST LEAP!
GO, MICHAEL!
EVERYTHING ABOUT MY WORLD WAS A LIFE-AFFIRMING RISK...

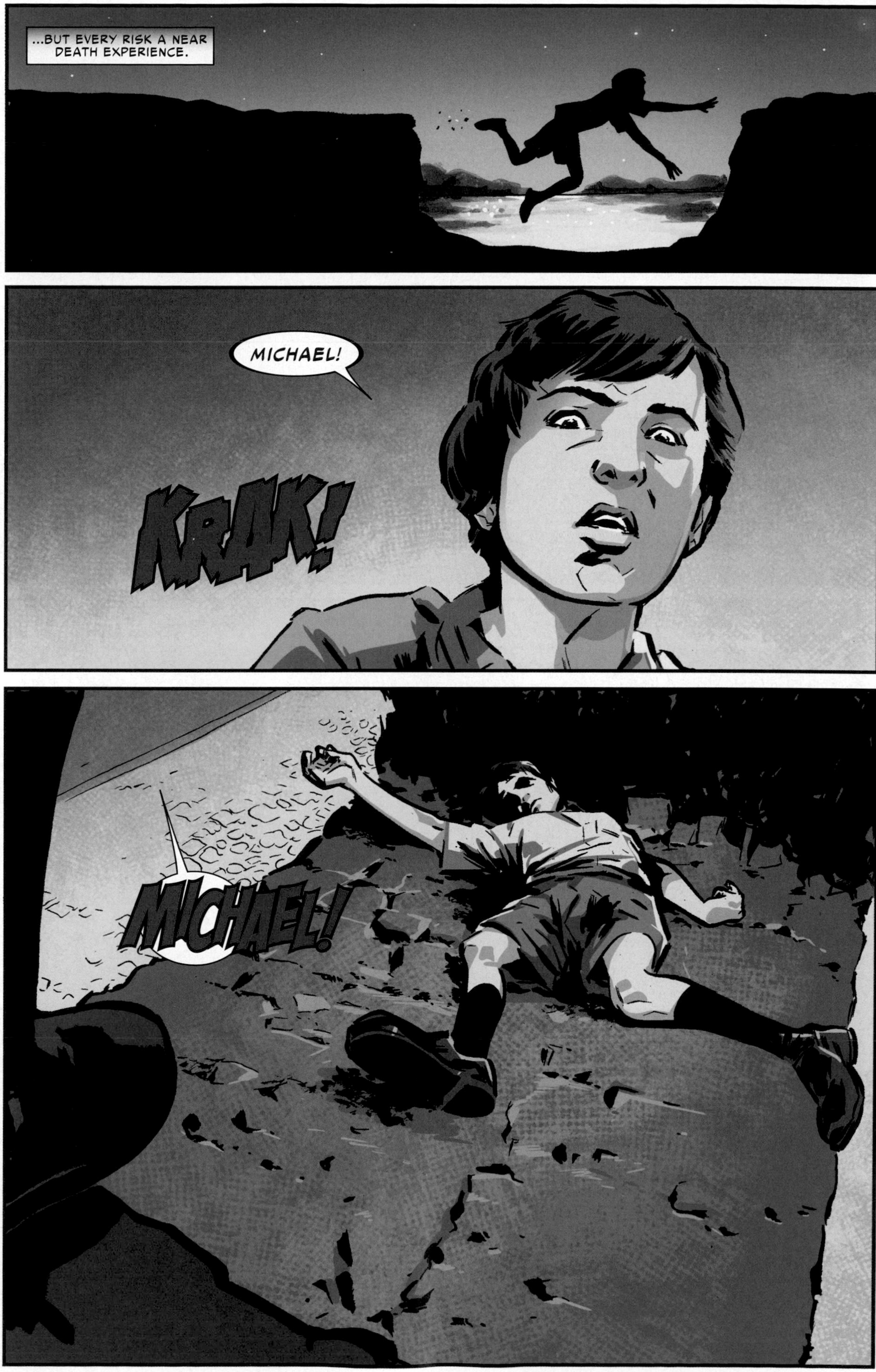
...BUT EVERY RISK A NEAR DEATH EXPERIENCE.
MICHAEL!
KRAK!
MICHAEL!

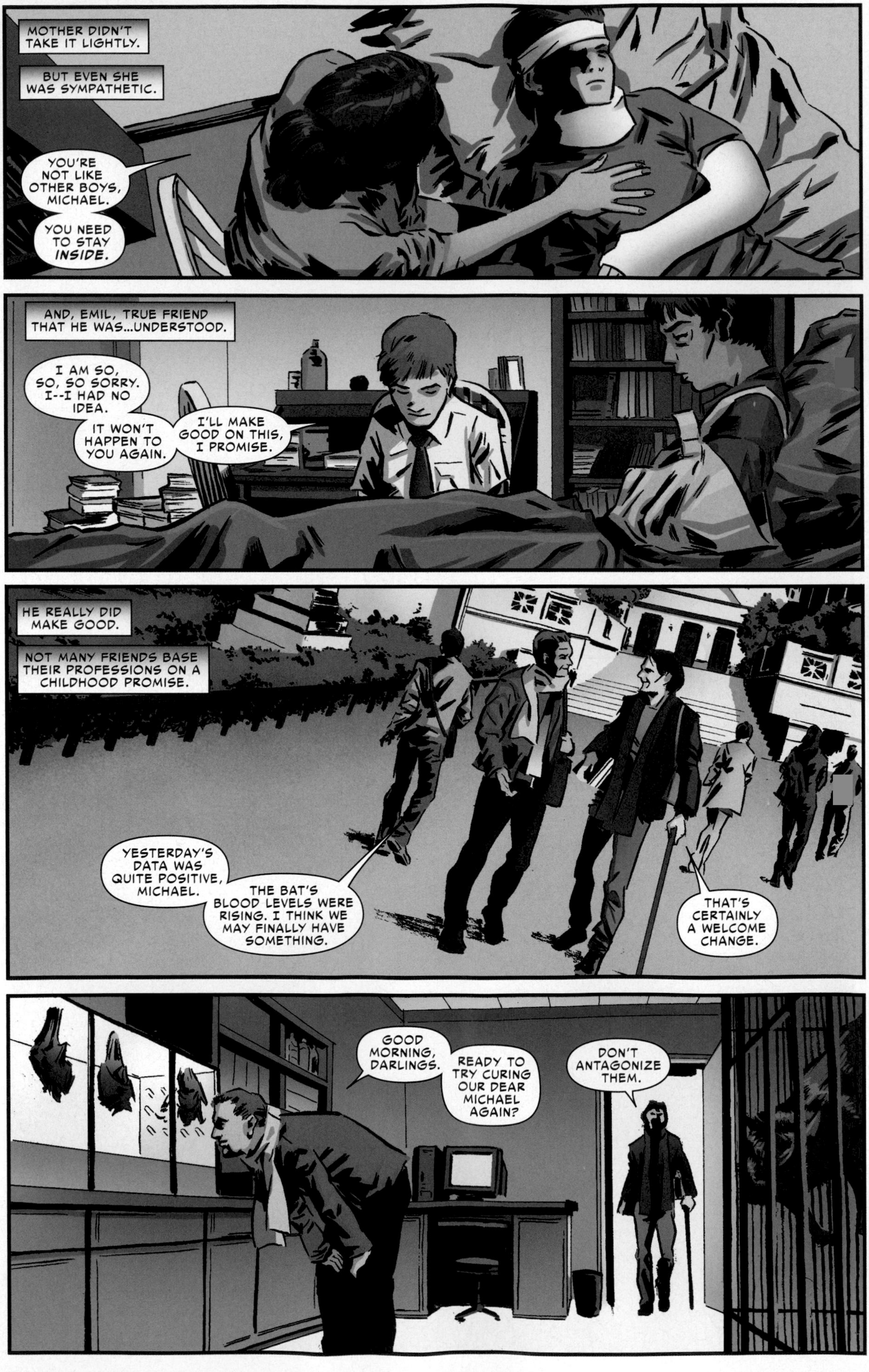
MOTHER DIDN'T TAKE IT LIGHTLY.
BUT EVEN SHE WAS SYMPATHETIC.
YOU'RE NOT LIKE OTHER BOYS, MICHAEL.
YOU NEED TO STAY *INSIDE*.
AND, EMIL, TRUE FRIEND THAT HE WAS...UNDERSTOOD.
I AM SO, SO, SO SORRY. I--I HAD NO IDEA.
IT WON'T HAPPEN TO YOU AGAIN.
I'LL MAKE GOOD ON THIS, I PROMISE.
HE REALLY DID MAKE GOOD.
NOT MANY FRIENDS BASE THEIR PROFESSIONS ON A CHILDHOOD PROMISE.
YESTERDAY'S DATA WAS QUITE POSITIVE, MICHAEL.
THE BAT'S BLOOD LEVELS WERE RISING. I THINK WE MAY FINALLY HAVE SOMETHING.
THAT'S CERTAINLY A WELCOME CHANGE.
GOOD MORNING, DARLINGS.
READY TO TRY CURING OUR DEAR MICHAEL AGAIN?
DON'T ANTAGONIZE THEM.

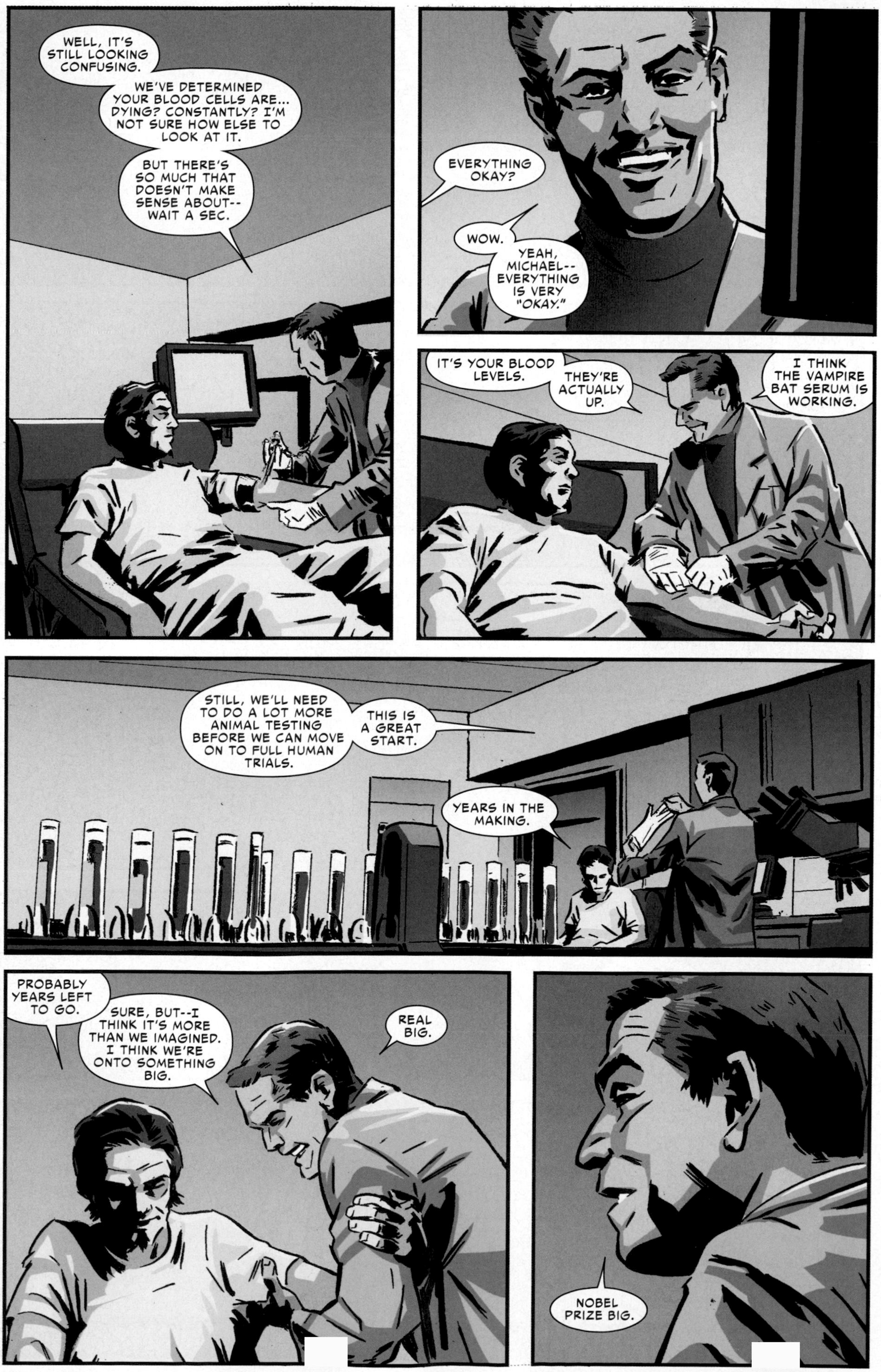
WELL, IT'S STILL LOOKING CONFUSING.
WE'VE DETERMINED YOUR BLOOD CELLS ARE... DYING? CONSTANTLY? I'M NOT SURE HOW ELSE TO LOOK AT IT.
BUT THERE'S SO MUCH THAT DOESN'T MAKE SENSE ABOUT-- WAIT A SEC.
EVERYTHING OKAY?
WOW.
YEAH, MICHAEL-- EVERYTHING IS VERY "OKAY."
IT'S YOUR BLOOD LEVELS.
THEY'RE ACTUALLY UP.
I THINK THE VAMPIRE BAT SERUM IS WORKING.
STILL, WE'LL NEED TO DO A LOT MORE ANIMAL TESTING BEFORE WE CAN MOVE ON TO FULL HUMAN TRIALS.
THIS IS A GREAT START.
YEARS IN THE MAKING.
PROBABLY YEARS LEFT TO GO.
SURE, BUT--I THINK IT'S MORE THAN WE IMAGINED. I THINK WE'RE ONTO SOMETHING BIG.
REAL BIG.
NOBEL PRIZE BIG.

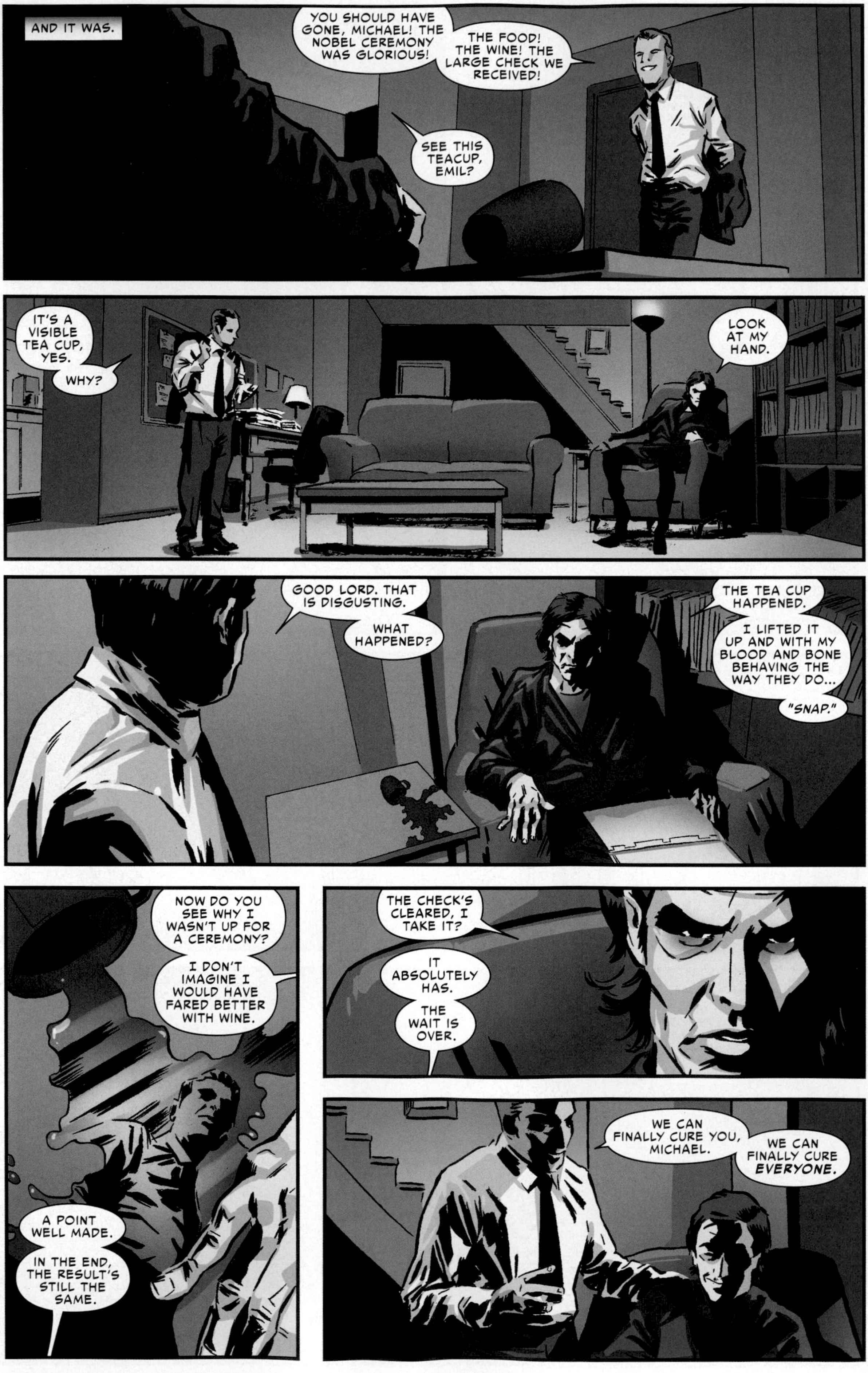
AND IT WAS.
YOU SHOULD HAVE GONE, MICHAEL! THE NOBEL CEREMONY WAS GLORIOUS!
THE FOOD! THE WINE! THE LARGE CHECK WE RECEIVED!
SEE THIS TEACUP, EMIL?
IT'S A VISIBLE TEA CUP, YES.
WHY?
LOOK AT MY HAND.
GOOD LORD. THAT IS DISGUSTING.
WHAT HAPPENED?
THE TEA CUP HAPPENED.
I LIFTED IT UP AND WITH MY BLOOD AND BONE BEHAVING THE WAY THEY DO...
"SNAP."
NOW DO YOU SEE WHY I WASN'T UP FOR A CEREMONY?
I DON'T IMAGINE I WOULD HAVE FARED BETTER WITH WINE.
A POINT WELL MADE.
IN THE END, THE RESULT'S STILL THE SAME.
THE CHECK'S CLEARED, I TAKE IT?
IT ABSOLUTELY HAS.
THE WAIT IS OVER.
WE CAN FINALLY CURE YOU, MICHAEL.
WE CAN FINALLY CURE *EVERYONE*.

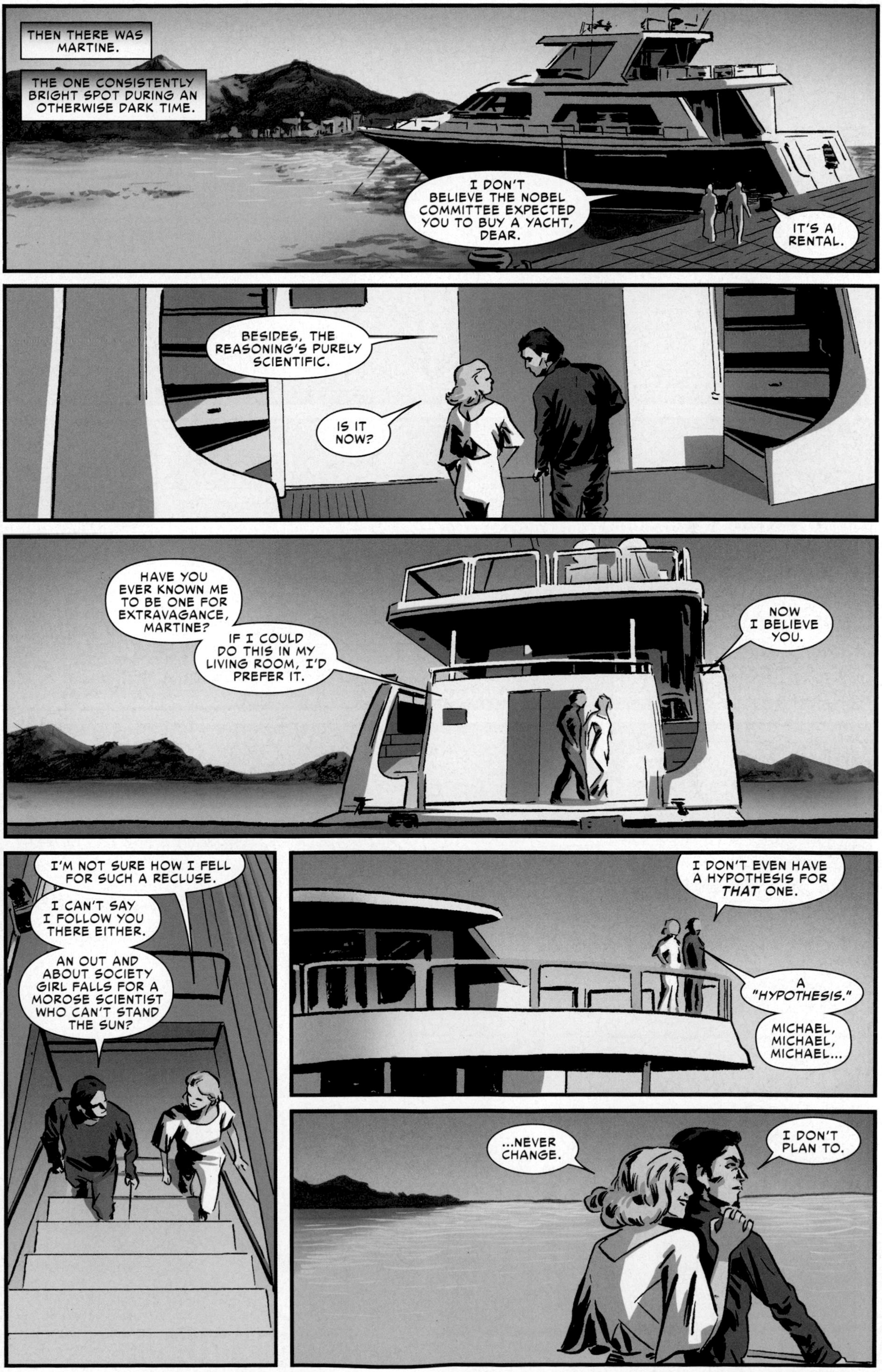
THEN THERE WAS MARTINE.
THE ONE CONSISTENTLY BRIGHT SPOT DURING AN OTHERWISE DARK TIME.
I DON'T BELIEVE THE NOBEL COMMITTEE EXPECTED YOU TO BUY A YACHT, DEAR.
IT'S A RENTAL.
BESIDES, THE REASONING'S PURELY SCIENTIFIC.
IS IT NOW?
HAVE YOU EVER KNOWN ME TO BE ONE FOR EXTRAVAGANCE, MARTINE?
IF I COULD DO THIS IN MY LIVING ROOM, I'D PREFER IT.
NOW I BELIEVE YOU.
I'M NOT SURE HOW I FELL FOR SUCH A RECLUSE.
I CAN'T SAY I FOLLOW YOU THERE EITHER.
AN OUT AND ABOUT SOCIETY GIRL FALLS FOR A MOROSE SCIENTIST WHO CAN'T STAND THE SUN?
I DON'T EVEN HAVE A HYPOTHESIS FOR *THAT* ONE.
A "*HYPOTHESIS.*"
MICHAEL, MICHAEL, MICHAEL...
...NEVER CHANGE.
I DON'T PLAN TO.

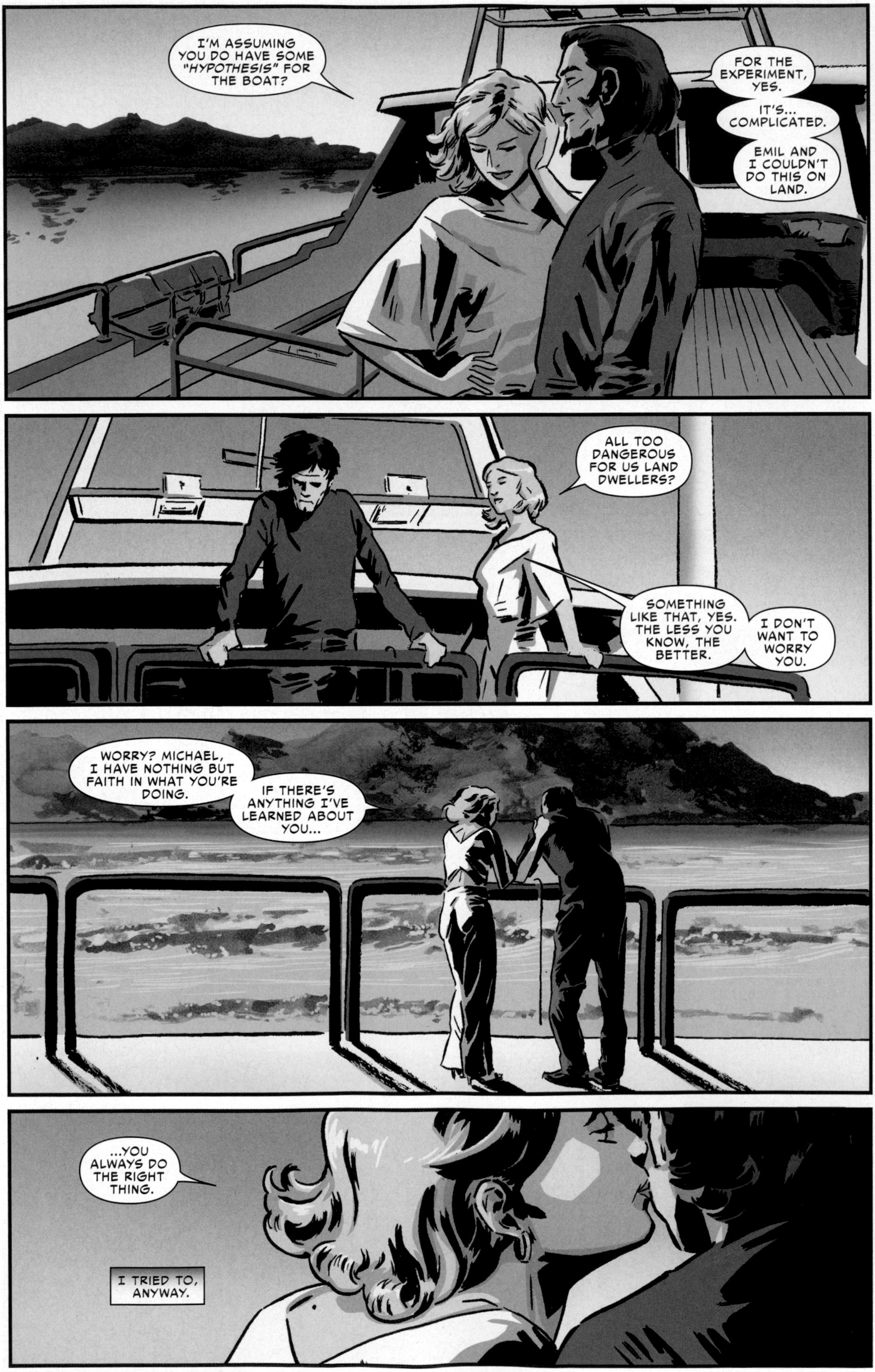
I'M ASSUMING YOU DO HAVE SOME "HYPOTHESIS" FOR THE BOAT?
FOR THE EXPERIMENT, YES.
IT'S... COMPLICATED.
EMIL AND I COULDN'T DO THIS ON LAND.
ALL TOO DANGEROUS FOR US LAND DWELLERS?
SOMETHING LIKE THAT, YES. THE LESS YOU KNOW, THE BETTER.
I DON'T WANT TO WORRY YOU.
WORRY? MICHAEL, I HAVE NOTHING BUT FAITH IN WHAT YOU'RE DOING.
IF THERE'S ANYTHING I'VE LEARNED ABOUT YOU...
...YOU ALWAYS DO THE RIGHT THING.
I TRIED TO, ANYWAY.

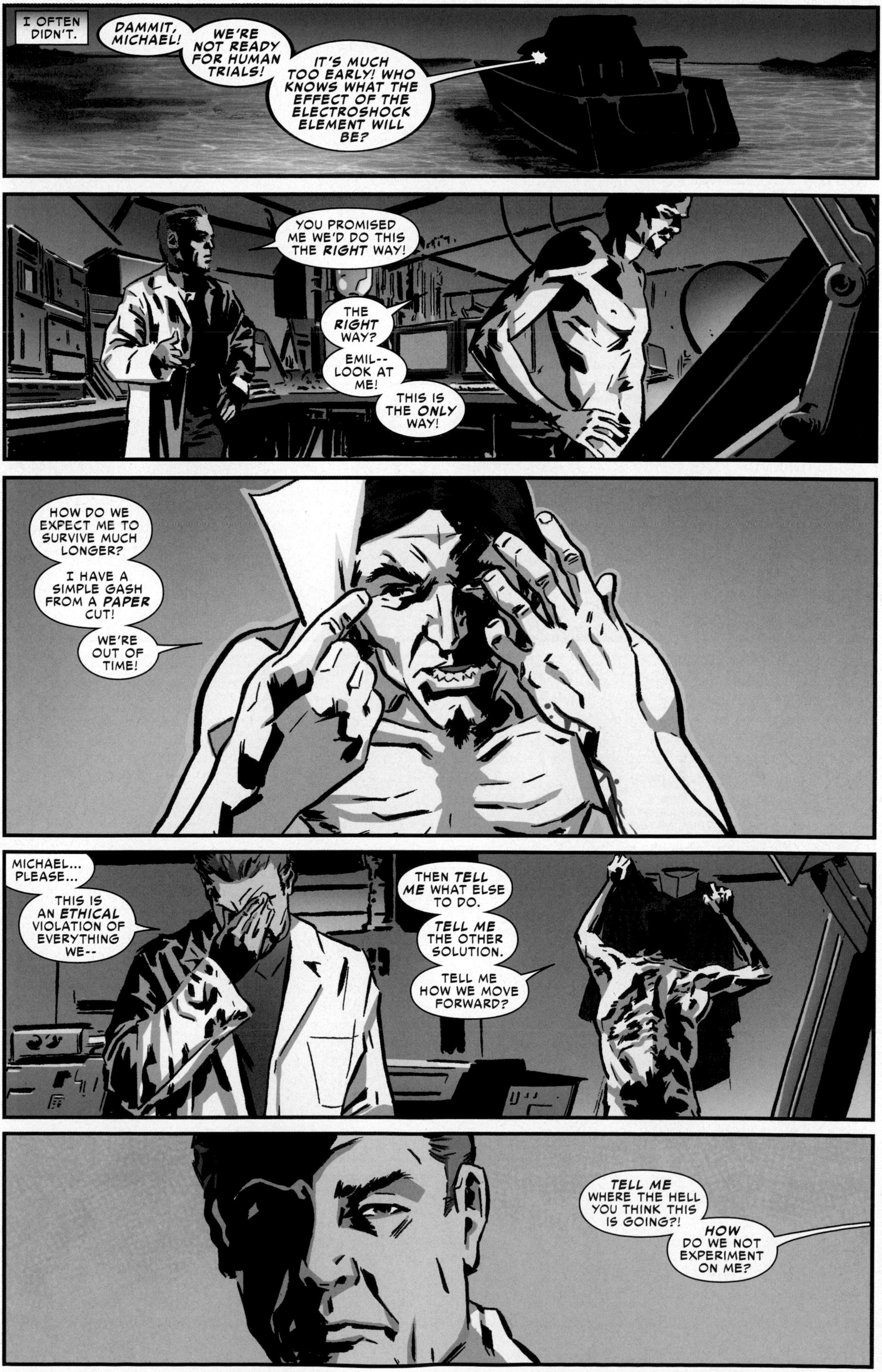
I OFTEN DIDN'T.
DAMMIT, MICHAEL!
WE'RE NOT READY FOR HUMAN TRIALS!
IT'S MUCH TOO EARLY! WHO KNOWS WHAT THE EFFECT OF THE ELECTROSHOCK ELEMENT WILL BE?
YOU PROMISED ME WE'D DO THIS THE RIGHT WAY!
THE RIGHT WAY?
EMIL-- LOOK AT ME!
THIS IS THE ONLY WAY!
HOW DO WE EXPECT ME TO SURVIVE MUCH LONGER?
I HAVE A SIMPLE GASH FROM A PAPER CUT!
WE'RE OUT OF TIME!
MICHAEL... PLEASE...
THIS IS AN ETHICAL VIOLATION OF EVERYTHING WE--
THEN TELL ME WHAT ELSE TO DO.
TELL ME THE OTHER SOLUTION.
TELL ME HOW WE MOVE FORWARD?
TELL ME WHERE THE HELL YOU THINK THIS IS GOING?!
HOW DO WE NOT EXPERIMENT ON ME?

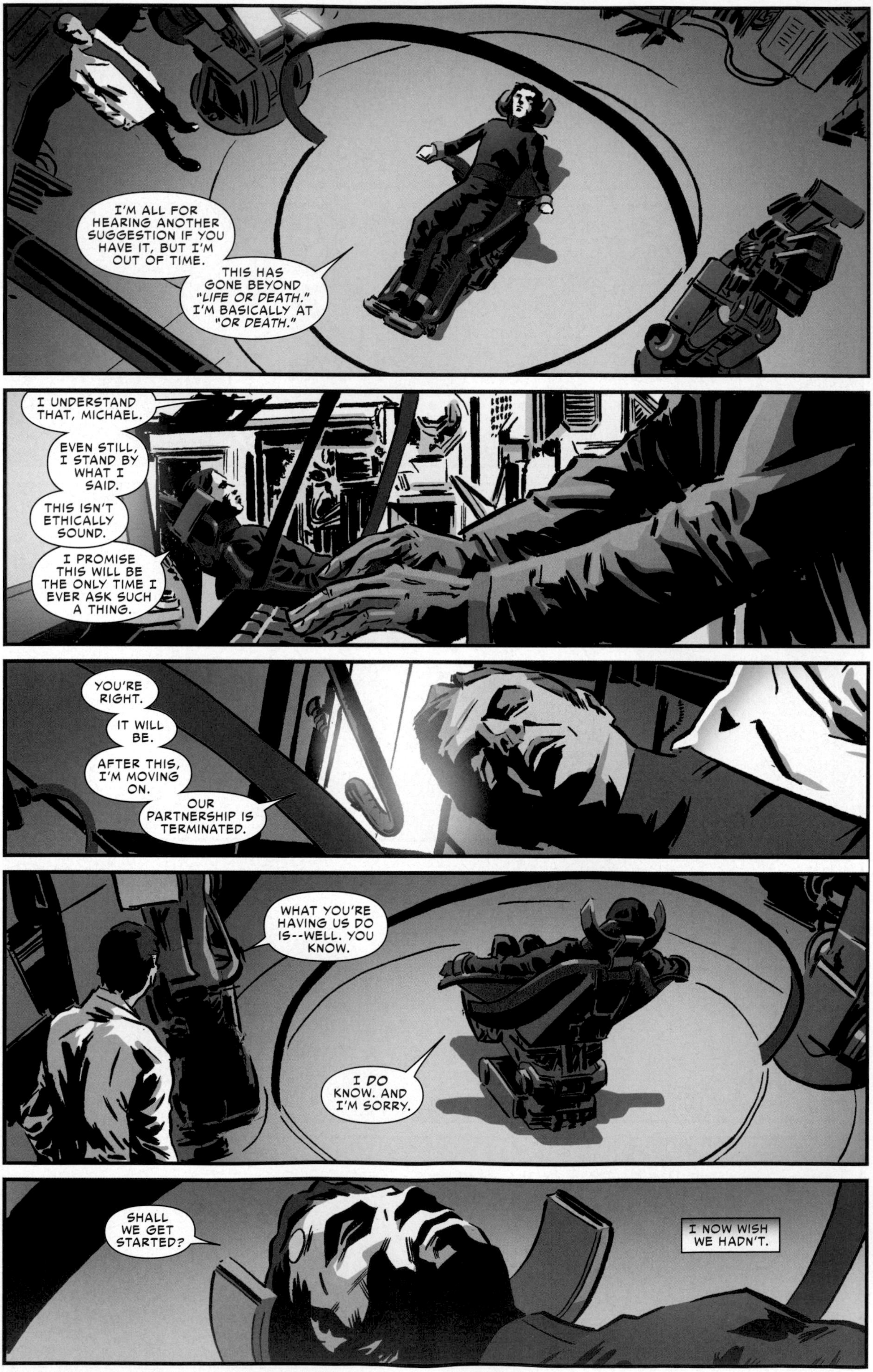
I'M ALL FOR HEARING ANOTHER SUGGESTION IF YOU HAVE IT, BUT I'M OUT OF TIME.
THIS HAS GONE BEYOND "LIFE OR DEATH." I'M BASICALLY AT "OR DEATH."
I UNDERSTAND THAT, MICHAEL.
EVEN STILL, I STAND BY WHAT I SAID.
THIS ISN'T ETHICALLY SOUND.
I PROMISE THIS WILL BE THE ONLY TIME I EVER ASK SUCH A THING.
YOU'RE RIGHT.
IT WILL BE.
AFTER THIS, I'M MOVING ON.
OUR PARTNERSHIP IS TERMINATED.
WHAT YOU'RE HAVING US DO IS--WELL. YOU KNOW.
I DO KNOW. AND I'M SORRY.
SHALL WE GET STARTED?
I NOW WISH WE HADN'T.

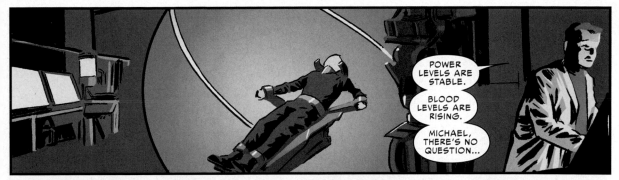

POWER LEVELS ARE STABLE.

BLOOD LEVELS ARE RISING.

MICHAEL, THERE'S NO QUESTION...

...WE'VE ACTUALLY DONE IT.

EVERYTHING WE'VE WORKED FOR, FOUGHT FOR. WE'VE MADE IT A REALITY.

I WISH I COULD CELEBRATE. AS IT IS--

WAIT A SECOND. SOMETHING'S NOT RIGHT.

I'M GETTING AN ODD READING! WE HAVE TO SHUT THIS DOWN!

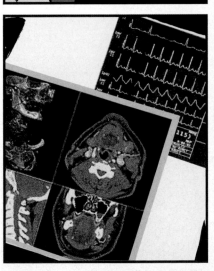

DAMN IT! I TOLD YOU--IT WASN'T READY!

IF I DIDN'T SHUT IT OFF IN TIME--

SZZT!

...MICHAEL?

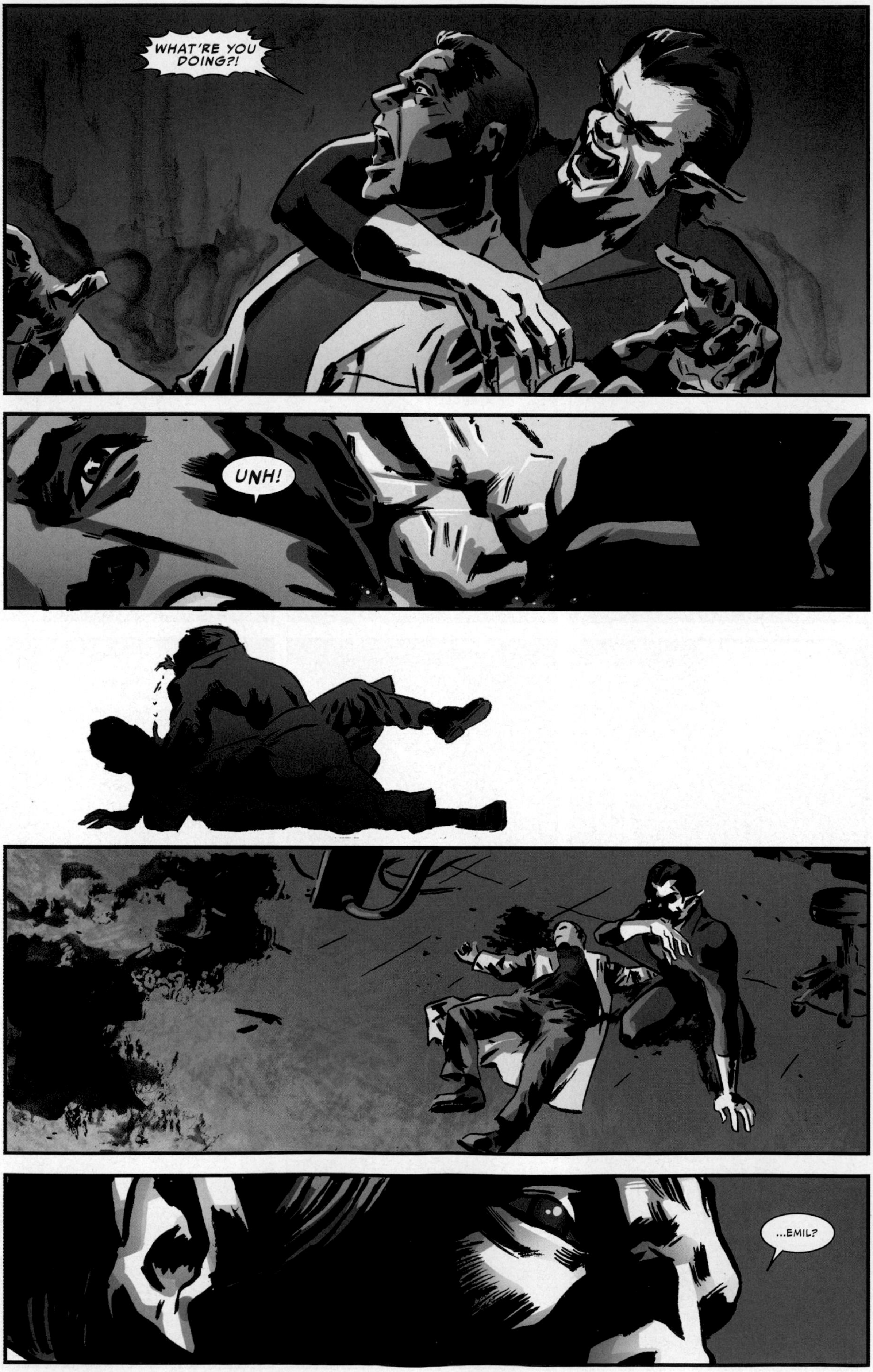
WHAT'RE YOU DOING?!
UNH!
...EMIL?

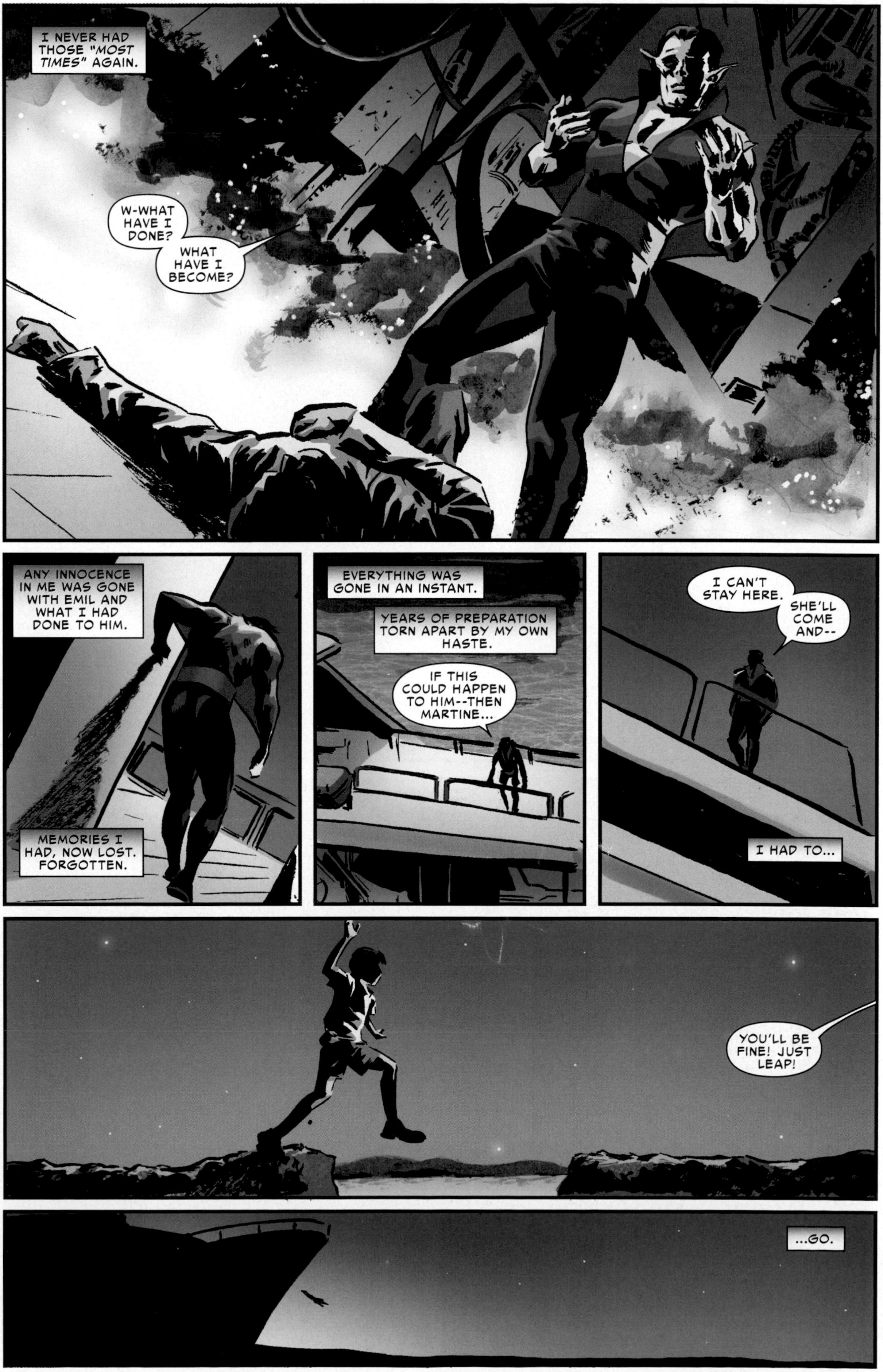

I NEVER HAD THOSE "MOST TIMES" AGAIN.
W-WHAT HAVE I DONE?
WHAT HAVE I BECOME?
ANY INNOCENCE IN ME WAS GONE WITH EMIL AND WHAT I HAD DONE TO HIM.
MEMORIES I HAD, NOW LOST. FORGOTTEN.
EVERYTHING WAS GONE IN AN INSTANT.
YEARS OF PREPARATION TORN APART BY MY OWN HASTE.
IF THIS COULD HAPPEN TO HIM--THEN MARTINE...
I CAN'T STAY HERE.
SHE'LL COME AND--
I HAD TO...
YOU'LL BE FINE! JUST LEAP!
...GO.

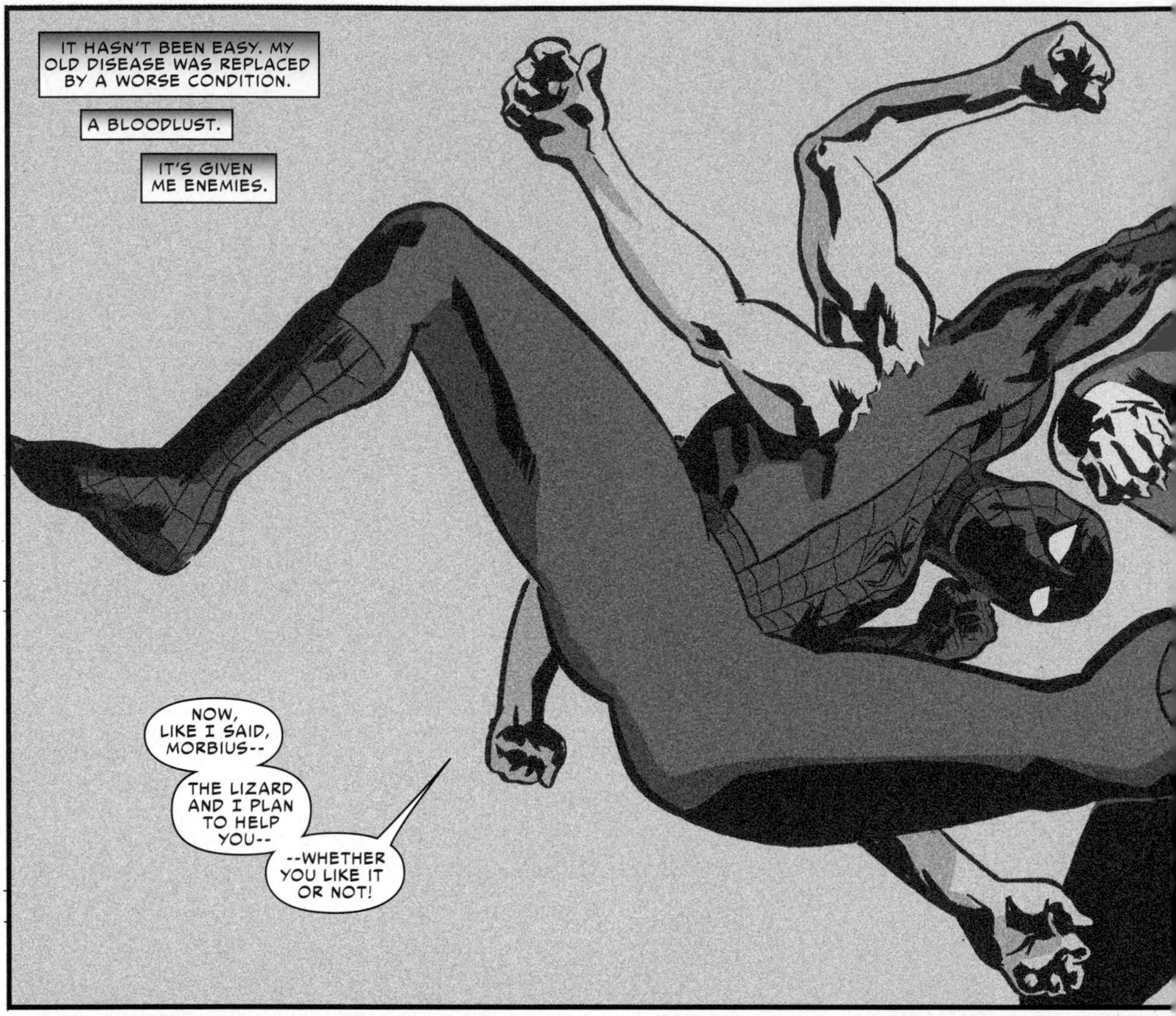
IT HASN'T BEEN EASY. MY OLD DISEASE WAS REPLACED BY A WORSE CONDITION.
A BLOODLUST.
IT'S GIVEN ME ENEMIES.
NOW, LIKE I SAID, MORBIUS--
THE LIZARD AND I PLAN TO HELP YOU--
--WHETHER YOU LIKE IT OR NOT!
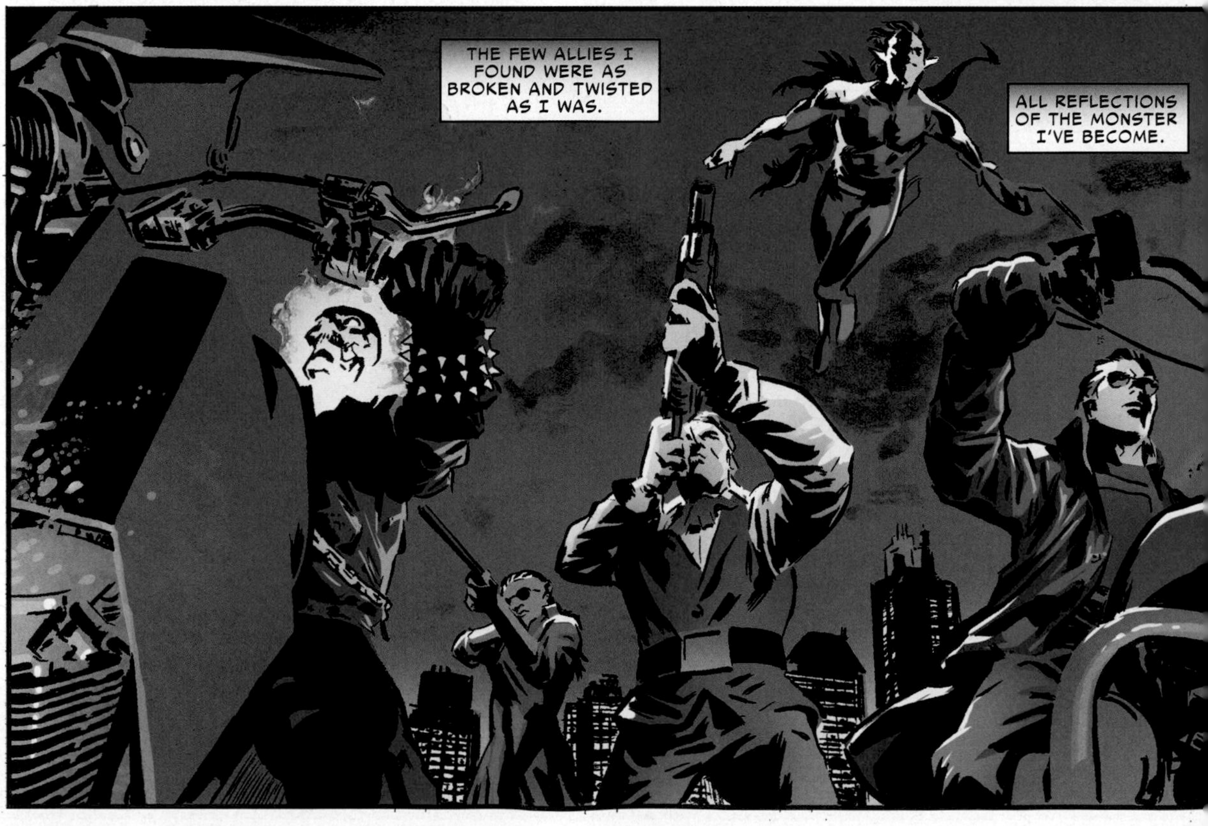
THE FEW ALLIES I FOUND WERE AS BROKEN AND TWISTED AS I WAS.
ALL REFLECTIONS OF THE MONSTER I'VE BECOME.

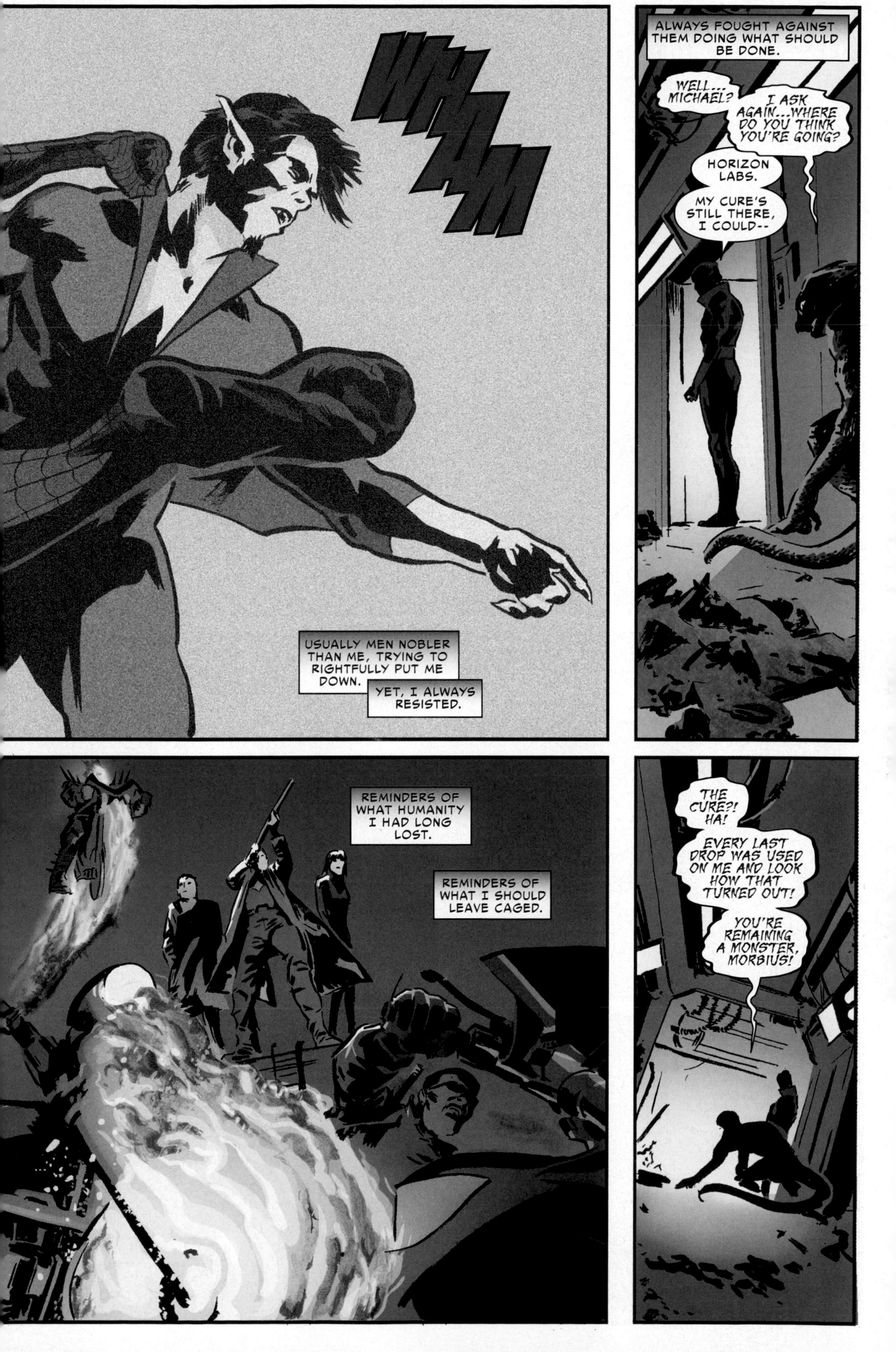
WHAM
USUALLY MEN NOBLER THAN ME, TRYING TO RIGHTFULLY PUT ME DOWN.
YET, I ALWAYS RESISTED.
ALWAYS FOUGHT AGAINST THEM DOING WHAT SHOULD BE DONE.
WELL... MICHAEL?
I ASK AGAIN...WHERE DO YOU THINK YOU'RE GOING?
HORIZON LABS.
MY CURE'S STILL THERE, I COULD--
REMINDERS OF WHAT HUMANITY I HAD LONG LOST.
REMINDERS OF WHAT I SHOULD LEAVE CAGED.
THE CURE?! HA!
EVERY LAST DROP WAS USED ON ME AND LOOK HOW THAT TURNED OUT!
YOU'RE REMAINING A MONSTER, MORBIUS!

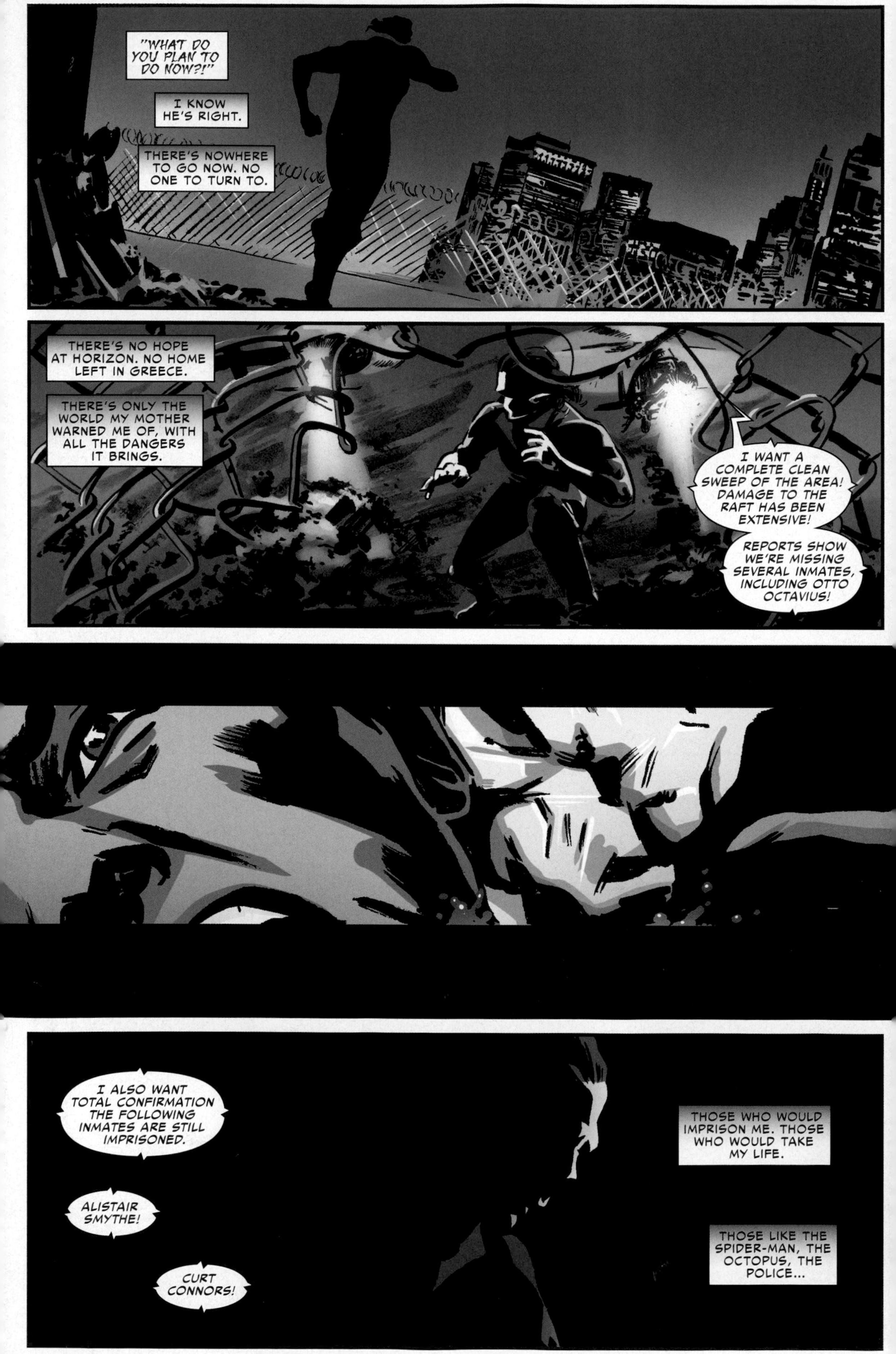
"WHAT DO YOU PLAN TO DO NOW?!"
I KNOW HE'S RIGHT.
THERE'S NOWHERE TO GO NOW. NO ONE TO TURN TO.
THERE'S NO HOPE AT HORIZON. NO HOME LEFT IN GREECE.
THERE'S ONLY THE WORLD MY MOTHER WARNED ME OF, WITH ALL THE DANGERS IT BRINGS.
I WANT A COMPLETE CLEAN SWEEP OF THE AREA! DAMAGE TO THE RAFT HAS BEEN EXTENSIVE!
REPORTS SHOW WE'RE MISSING SEVERAL INMATES, INCLUDING OTTO OCTAVIUS!
I ALSO WANT TOTAL CONFIRMATION THE FOLLOWING INMATES ARE STILL IMPRISONED.
ALISTAIR SMYTHE!
CURT CONNORS!
THOSE WHO WOULD IMPRISON ME. THOSE WHO WOULD TAKE MY LIFE.
THOSE LIKE THE SPIDER-MAN, THE OCTOPUS, THE POLICE...

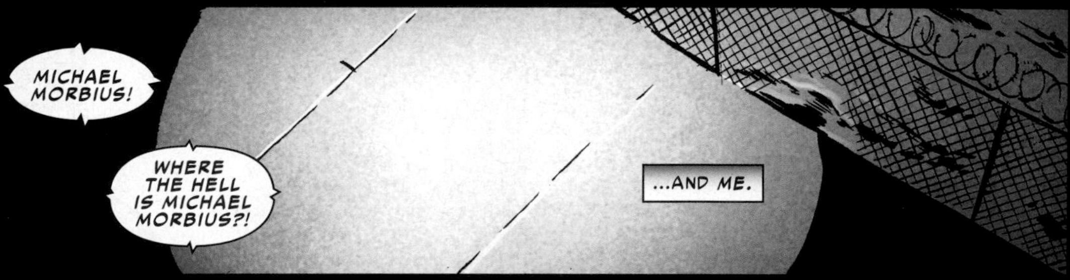
MICHAEL MORBIUS!
WHERE THE HELL IS MICHAEL MORBIUS?!
...AND ME.

MORBIUS

HISTORY: Nobel Prize-winning biochemist Dr. Michael Morbius discovered he was dying of a rare disorder dissolving his blood cells. Not wanting to distress his fiancée Martine Bancroft, Morbius began secretly working on a cure. Aided by his partner Emil Nikos, Morbius tried using distilled fluids from bats to stay his disease. While experimenting with such serums on board his yacht, Morbius had Nikos run an electrical shock through his system. The combination profoundly changed Michael's body, transforming him into something resembling a vampire. Now driven by a blinding hunger for blood, Morbius slew Nikos, but stopped short of draining his friend's body. Fearful that he would strike at Martine next, Michael tried ending his life by jumping into the sea, but self-preservation led him to escape the water's embrace. Found adrift by a fishing vessel, he made its helpful crewmen his first victims. He left the ship and swam ashore when nobody was left to satiate his bloodthirst.

On shore in Southampton he found shelter in the seemingly empty beach house of Dr. Curt Connors, but Morbius' bloodthirst soon drew him into conflict with Spider-Man (Peter Parker, then possessing six arms) and Connors, who transformed into the Lizard. Morbius bit the Lizard and fled the scene. Affected by the bite, Connors regained his intelligence in Lizard form, but couldn't fully revert back to human form. Connors and Spider-Man soon realized that Morbius' blood could cure them both of their current mutations, so they pursued Morbius and took a blood sample to create a serum for themselves. Fleeing Spider-Man, Morbius seemingly drowned, but he was pulled from the river by young gang member Jefferson Bolt, whom Morbius bit, turning Bolt into a pseudo-vampire like himself. Meanwhile, Martine visited Morbius' correspondent Reed Richards of the Fantastic Four for help finding her missing fiancé. The FF's Human Torch (Johnny Storm) and Spider-Man met with another correspondent, ESU biologist Professor Hans Jorgensen, coincidentally as Morbius also sought him out. Stopping to ease his hunger, the heroes discovered Morbius standing over another victim in a nearby park, but Jefferson's gang attacked them. When Morbius bit Jefferson's brother, Jacob, Jefferson turned on him, and Morbius accidentally slew him. A week later, Morbius kidnapped Jorgensen hoping he might find a cure for Morbius' condition, but was captured by the X-Men before his unconscious abductee awoke.

Morbius soon escaped and traveled the country, foiling the plots of the Demon-Fire coven and its master, Apocalypse (Kazarian). In Los Angeles, Morbius met the Children of Satan, fought the demon Nilrac and was drawn into a war between the otherworldly Caretakers and their renegade member, the sorcerer Daemond, who turned Martine into one of his pawns. The Caretakers approached Morbius after he caught their creation Tara, and he sided with them. He fought Daemond, who summoned the demonic Cat People's Balkatar (Grigar) to attack Morbius. Instead the Balkatar took Morbius on a journey to other worlds and dimensions, including the Land Within, home of the Cat People, and the planet Arcturus IV, where Morbius encountered the Caretakers' vastly mutated descendants. Their leader Lord I asked Morbius to kill the Caretakers to save Earth from suffering Arcturus IV's fate. Morbius traveled back to Earth alongside Lord I, upon whom he fed to survive the journey. He fought the vampire-hunter Blade (Eric Brooks) before he again faced Daemond and the Caretakers, whose base was destroyed in an explosion after Morbius slew the treacherous Tara.

Still seeking her fiancé, Martine convinced him to return to her after he encountered the Werewolf (Jack Russell). Using the last of Michael's Nobel Prize monies, Martine purchased the reputedly haunted Mason House just outside Boston, feeling it would afford them privacy while Morbius sought a cure. CIA agent Simon Stroud, seeking a killer vampire in Boston, came to view Morbius as the prime suspect. While Morbius discovered that he had a psychological need to drink blood from living victims, Stroud arrested Martine. As the police questioned his fiancée, Morbius discovered his new home was a portal to a world ruled by the

REAL NAME: Dr. Michael Morbius
ALIASES: The Living Vampire; formerly Morgan Michaels, Nikos Michaels
IDENTITY: Publicly known
OCCUPATION: Licensed super hero; former vigilante, biochemist, hematologist
CITIZENSHIP: Citizen of unrevealed European country; criminal record in the USA
PLACE OF BIRTH: Unrevealed
KNOWN RELATIVES: None
GROUP AFFILIATION: ARMOR (Alternate Reality Monitoring and Operational Response), Initiative, Midnight Sons; formerly Nine, "Legion of Monsters"
EDUCATION: Ph.D. in biochemistry
FIRST APPEARANCE: Amazing Spider-Man #101 (1971)

demonic entity Helleyes. Stroud, still pursuing Morbius, worked with him to escape Helleyes, discovering the demon's weakness and fleeing Mason House.

Art by Paul Gulacy with Ron Wagner (inset)

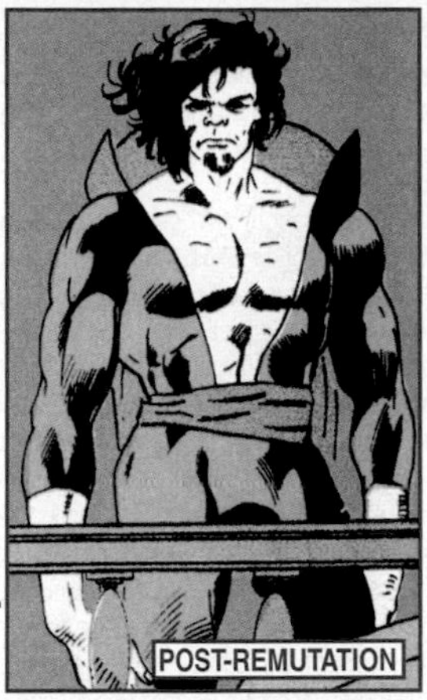
POST-REMUTATION
Art by Jackson Guice

During their time away, Martine was attacked by the killer vampire and transformed into a pseudo-vampire like Morbius. She was eventually cured of her condition when Morbius created an antidote derived from his own blood. Frustrated at both his inability to cure himself and the perpetual danger to Martine, Morbius ended their relationship. Once more alone, the Living Vampire continued his search for a cure. He sought help from hematologist Harold Ward and used the Godstone to turn Man-Wolf (John Jameson) into his thrall to distract Spider-Man, but the hero foiled his plan. Morbius left the USA and sought hematologist Samuel Harkins' aid, but instead destroyed the vampire Harkins and his Brotherhood of Judas vampire cult, who had sought to take over England by vampirizing people of influence. Morbius next turned to his old Scottish colleague Ronson Slade, but also slew him after finding he had turned himself into a monster. Returning to the USA, Morbius had a short-lived alliance with the Ghost Rider (John Blaze), Man-Thing and Werewolf. This "Legion of Monsters" unwittingly slew the benevolent Starseed before going their separate ways. Morbius later helped Thing (Ben Grimm) stop the alien Living Eraser and then used the villain's Dimensionizer palm bands to flee Earth entirely, hoping to avoid feeding on more innocents. Instead Morbius became the unwilling host to the extradimensional Empathoid, who possessed him and forced him back to Earth and into further conflict with Spider-Man. After being freed from the alien's control, Morbius resumed his search for a cure.

Eventually, Morbius clashed with Spider-Man atop a Long Island mansion. He was struck by a bolt of lightning while draining Spider-Man's blood, catalyzing its radioactive elements and reversing much of his vampiric condition. Though he no longer required blood to survive, he retained a physiological need to drink it. Fleeing to Los Angeles, Morbius found work in a neuroradiology lab at the University of California. While working on a cure for his blood craving, Morbius was attacked by Thomas LeClerc, father of one of his victims. Morbius later met Jennifer Walters, the She-Hulk and gave her his serum, curing her of a degenerative disease and allowing her to control her transformations into She-Hulk. Walters later served as Morbius' defense attorney during his trial for the murder she committed as a pseudo-vampire. The jury, convinced that Morbius had been unable to control his urges, convicted him only of involuntary manslaughter and sentenced him to five years in prison, to be served after completing his cure. Angered by the verdict the LeClercs hired former android Zodiac member Gemini to kill Morbius, but Gemini determined the verdict was fair and saved Morbius' life when he tried to commit suicide. The LeClercs then realized that Morbius wasn't a monster and let him go. After succeeding to cure himself, Morbius went to prison willingly and was soon paroled for good behavior. He was later one of the scientists who tried to help Mr. Fantastic save his wife and her unborn second child when her pregnancy encountered complications. Moving back to Los Angeles, Morbius aided Jack Russell in his attempts to control his Werewolf transformations. He also assisted the Avengers, who consulted him regarding the Cat People.

Eventually, however, Morbius was re-mutated by Marie Laveau, who needed a new source of vampire blood since the Montesi Formula had destroyed all true vampires. Before he escaped her clutches, Morbius saw the arrival of vampire Victor Strange, who was protected from destruction by a Vishanti spell cast by his brother Dr. Stephen Strange. Morbius helped Dr. Strange free Victor from Laveau's influence, but couldn't stop the vampire lord Varnae's resurrection. Failing to get the help he desired from Dr. Strange, Morbius allowed himself to fall in with the Subhumans, a group of homeless people living in the Morlock Tunnels. These people brought him victims, which led to another confrontation with Spider-Man. Sickened to discover that the victims upon whom he had fed were innocents, Morbius once more fled into the night. By this time, the new Ghost Rider (Dan Ketch) and John Blaze had begun pursuing Morbius, in preparation for the coming war with the demon queen Lilith and her children. Morbius was reunited with Martine, who had also decided to help Michael once more. She had contacted Dr. David Langford, who had created a new serum from Morbius' notes. Unbeknownst to Martine, Langford planned to kill Morbius and sell his manuscripts to Dr. Paine. One of Lilith's children, Fang, added his own blood to the serum, transformed it, and it altered Morbius on the cellular level. Blinded by pain, Morbius sought out an old friend, Dr. Jacob Weisenthal, for help. When Martine was slain by Langford after discovering his plans, Morbius went berserk and slew Langford in turn. Realizing that he felt no guilt for this murder, Morbius swore to Ghost Rider that he would only drink the blood of the guilty in the future.

Simon Stroud returned to the US upon learning Morbius was active again. After fighting off Stroud and Dr. Paine's agents, Morbius obtained a blood sample from Spider-Man. With Weisenthal's help, Morbius used it to refine his serum, combining it with dialysis treatments and periods spent in a hyperbaric chamber. Now able to regain a normal appearance, Morbius adopted the identity of Dr. Morgan Michaels and worked in the hematology department of St. Jude's. He also began a relationship with co-worker Mandy Tyler. While some aspects of his life seemed to be stabilizing at last, Morbius found himself battling the Basilisk (Wayne Gifford), Simon Stroud again, the fear-lord Nightmare, Bloodbath (Mordecai Kovax) and his own vampiric "son," Vic Slaughter. Blaming himself for Slaughter's transformation from mercenary to undead killer, Morbius fought him alone and alongside the Nightstalkers, who ran into trouble with Slaughter when he worked with the demonic alchemist Stonecold (Johann Bessler). After Slaughter and Stonecold were defeated, Morbius asked Frank Drake to use his necrotech-powered Exorcist gun on him, but it couldn't cure his condition. Morbius was slain by a temporarily Darkhold-empowered Blade, but was soon resurrected by Darkhold Redeemer Louise Hastings. Allied with several other heroes, Morbius helped fight serial killer Carnage and his "family" and later the Darkhold-transformed Spider-X.

Bolstered by the return of his friend Jack Russell to his life, Morbius continued seeking a cure. Dr. Strange informed him that he was a soulless being after his resurrection, which brought about further depression. Using a page of the Darkhold, Morbius revived Martine, but found she was now the host for a Lilin named Parasite. The dark part of his soul tainted by Fang's blood began to emerge as well, calling itself Bloodthirst and trying to alter Morbius in both body and mind. The Werewolf and the Ghost Rider (Ketch) both sought to capture him when he lost control over his own body to Bloodthirst. In Werewolf's case the fear-lord D'Spayre helped, desiring to feed off the Living Vampire's torment. Under Bloodthirst's control, Morbius joined

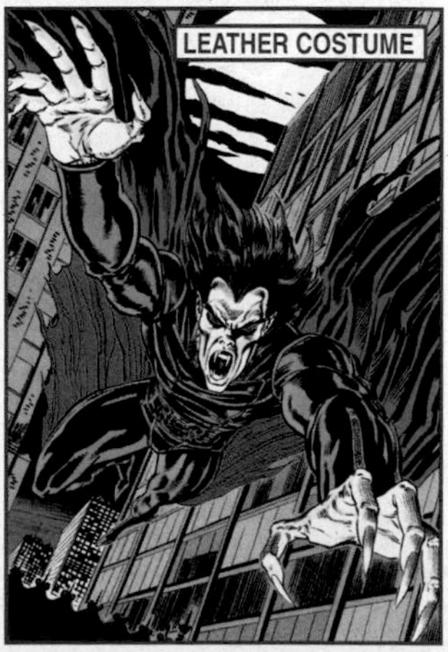
LEATHER COSTUME
Art by Ron Wagner

the Midnight Sons in their ongoing battle against Lilith and her children and betrayed them along with Parasite (in Martine's body). After he had killed Louise Hastings and helped the Lilin invade the Sanctum Sanctorum, Morbius regained control over his body with Dr. Strange's aid. Now a part of the Midnight Sons again, Morbius helped them drive Lilith and the Lilin off Earth only to encounter a new threat in the form of the demon Zarathos and the immortals called the Fallen. Morbius slew Martine when he had to protect the immortal Raydar from her demonic side. After the Lilin Parasite had left Martine's body, Raydar's daughter Embyrre resurrected her spirit. Morbius continued to aid the Midnight Sons until they defeated Zarathos and the Fallen. Morbius and Martine were denied happiness as Martine was now emotionless, and increasingly frustrated with the fact that Morbius would not allow her the peace of death.

After briefly seeking the About Face virus for its transforming properties, Morbius joined Daredevil (Matt Murdock) against the Snakeroot cult to prevent their obtaining the virus. Unwillingly teleported to San Francisco by goblins, Morbius fought and destroyed them along with Venom (Eddie Brock) and Demogoblin. Following further battles with Deathlok (Michael Collins), the Wraith (Brian DeWolff), Salomé, Bloodthirst (now in his own body after being filtered out of Morbius' bloodstream), Nate Mare, the vampire-wannabes System and the returning Basilisk and Vic Slaughter, Morbius met the young Lena Ivana. Rescuing her from a life of forced prostitution, he joined her in a tumultuous romance. Though Morbius continued to aid friends like Blade against such threats as the demon Nezaral and a Deacon Frost clone, he was still distraught over his failed relationship with Martine and his ongoing existence as a living vampire. Morbius killed himself, only to be revived by Weisenthal, who had created a serum to reanimate his friend. Lena left Morbius when a jealous Martine told her that Dr. Michaels was Morbius. Enraged, Morbius killed his first innocent man in a very long time.

Art by Isaac Cordova

BLOODTHIRST MUTATED

Morbius then began a period of wandering, leaving behind his life as Morgan Michaels. While trying to help Martine's relatives with their drug-addicted daughter, he encountered Blade in New Orleans as an unwilling pawn in Ulysses Sojourner's plot to unite the East Coast vampires under his rule. He returned to New York City and fought X-Man (Nate Grey) and Spider-Man. A few weeks later, Morbius sought Dr. Andrea Janson's help in finding a cure, only to discover that she was in league with subversive group Hydra and the villain Crown. Morbius seemingly sacrificed himself to destroy Crown, but was actually taken prisoner and experimented upon. After Crown's transformation into the vampiric Hunger, Morbius was rescued by Blade and Spider-Man, who fought the Kingpin and his men to free Morbius. Nearly mindless with bloodlust, Morbius bit Blade and then passed out. Months later, Morbius tried to feed on a paralyzed young man named Joey Beal, but was foiled by Spider-Man. Baron Blood (John Falsworth) and his vampire coven soon hunted down Morbius to punish him for the creation of pseudo-vampires. Morbius was confronted by Emil Nikos, who had been vampirized by Falsworth to kill Morbius, but Nikos showed mercy. Morbius followed less selfish goals when he learned that his mentor Dr. Hammond was dying of amyotrophic lateral sclerosis. He stole Dr. Strange's mystic powers with the Vaal Talisman to help Hammond, accidentally enabling Set-Dagon and his people (products of the union between the Elder God Set and the god Dagon)

to invade Earth. Spider-Man destroyed the Vaal Talisman to return the mystic powers to Dr. Strange in time to banish the serpents back to their dimension. Dr. Strange then offered to use his medical contacts to get Dr. Hammond the proper help.

After the federal Superhuman Registration Act passed, Morbius registered and even helped SHIELD capture Blade in Long Beach, California. Still depressed by his life, he quit drinking blood again and went to San Francisco where he lived among drug addicts. One night the addict Roxy died of an overdose and Morbius turned her into a pseudo-vampire on her boyfriend's plea. Thus empowered, she killed most of her friends before Morbius broke her neck. Morbius returned to his costumed life and was approached by Spider-Man, who asked him to save the dying May Parker, but Morbius couldn't help. Morbius began working for ARMOR to combat threats from alternate realities, but was captured and replaced by his zombie Earth-2149 counterpart as part of a plot to open a portal to the zombie's Earth. A week later Morbius helped foil the zombie plot, and he killed his zombie counterpart, but some zombies escaped to Greenland using ARMOR's teleporter. Morbius volunteered to lead a team to hunt them down and was authorized to form a new incarnation of the Midnight Sons.

HEIGHT: 5'10"   EYES: Blue
WEIGHT: 170 lbs.   HAIR: Black

ABILITIES/ACCESSORIES: Morbius' unique form of pseudo-vampirism gives him enhanced strength (lifting up to 1500 lbs.), durability, self-regeneration, minor hypnotic powers, the ability to float on air currents, and limited control over his body's physical properties. Like true vampire, Morbius needs to drink blood to survive. In his case the blood is needed to replenish the blood cells dissolved by his disease. Though he currently has the hunger under control, he has often lost control over it in the past, and is likely to do so in the future.

Though he is not invulnerable, Morbius can regenerate injured tissue within a brief time though it becomes harder to regenerate if he has not consumed sufficient blood. His hypnotic powers enable him to control even strong-willed persons like Spider-Man for a short time. Under certain, unspecified circumstances his bite can transform others into pseudo-vampires like himself through an enzyme deposited in their bloodstream. Such victims usually do not truly die, and they act purely on bloodlust like true vampires. They possess none of Morbius' regenerative powers and died or even disintegrated upon being mortally wounded. Morbius is not affected by true vampires' weaknesses like garlic, religious symbols or sunlight, though he has a natural aversion to the latter. During a time when Morbius was infected with Lilin blood, he was temporarily granted eternal life and the ability to liquefy his body. His regenerative powers were also tripled during this period.

Morbius is one of the world's foremost experts on biochemistry and blood-related diseases. His expertise enabled him to create an antidote for his victims, curing them of their pseudo-vampirism, though the cure didn't work on himself. Morbius sometimes wears protective leather bodysuits.

POWER GRID	1	2	3	4	5	6	7
INTELLIGENCE							
STRENGTH							
SPEED							
DURABILITY							
ENERGY PROJECTION							
FIGHTING SKILLS							

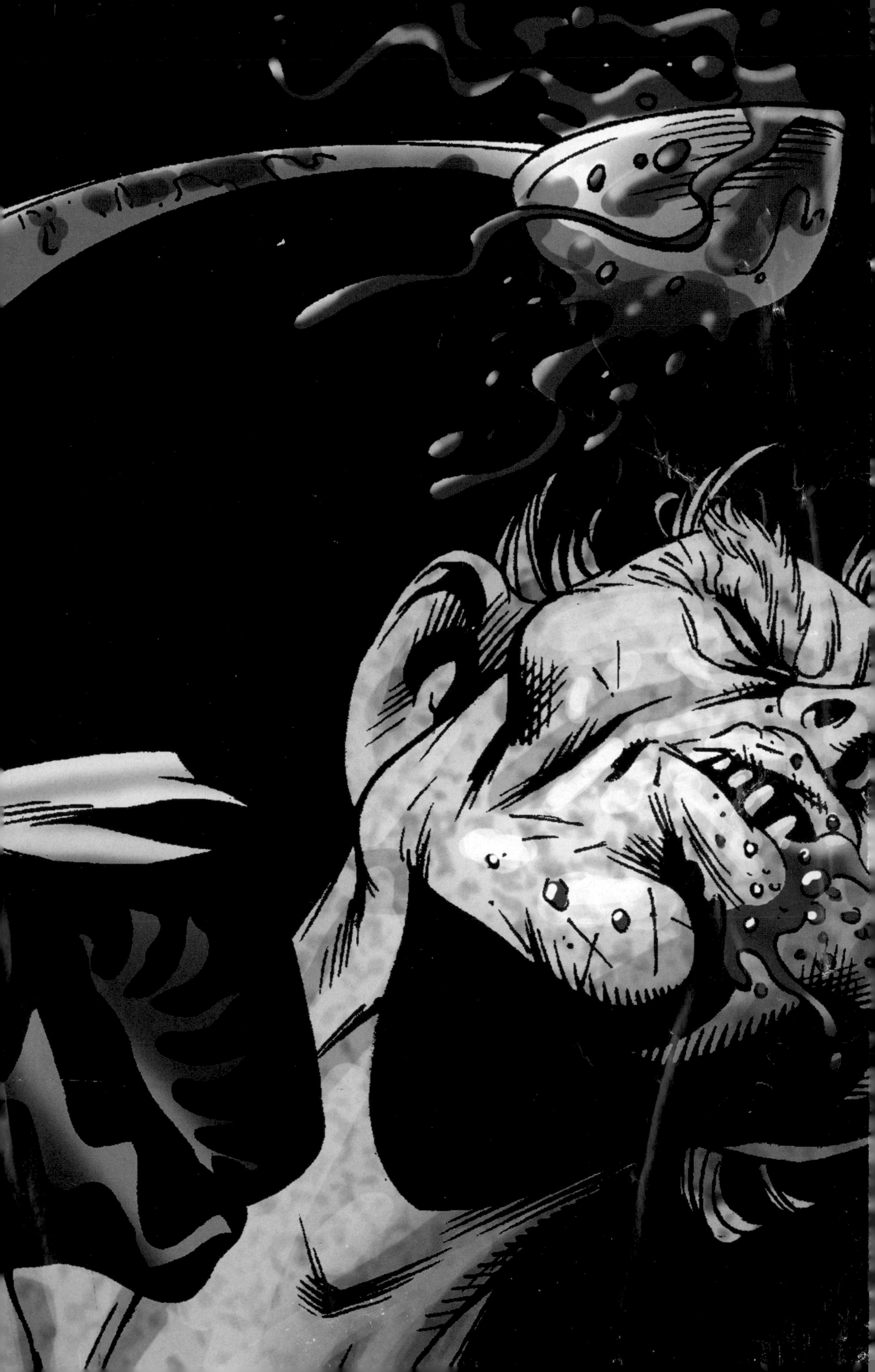

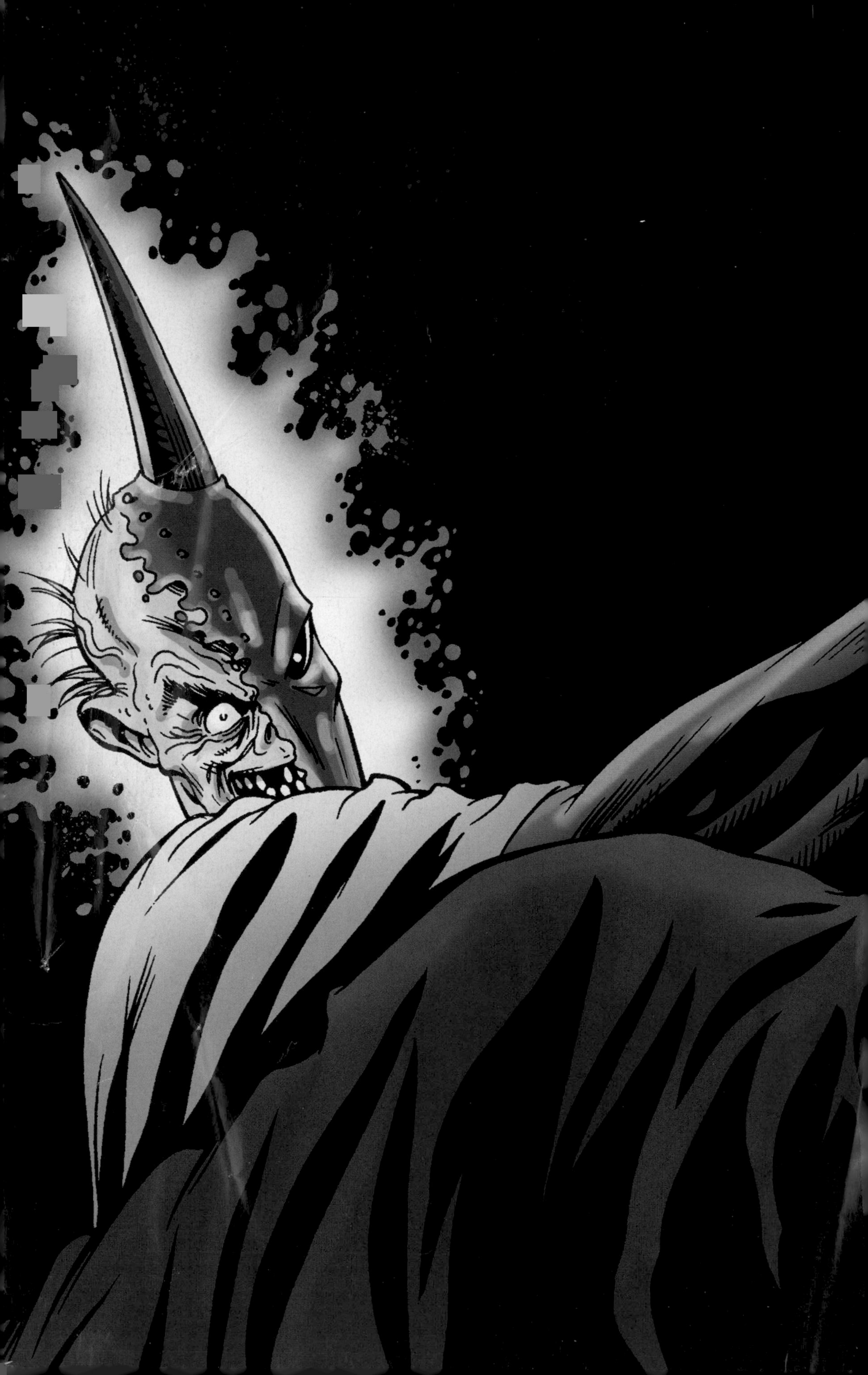

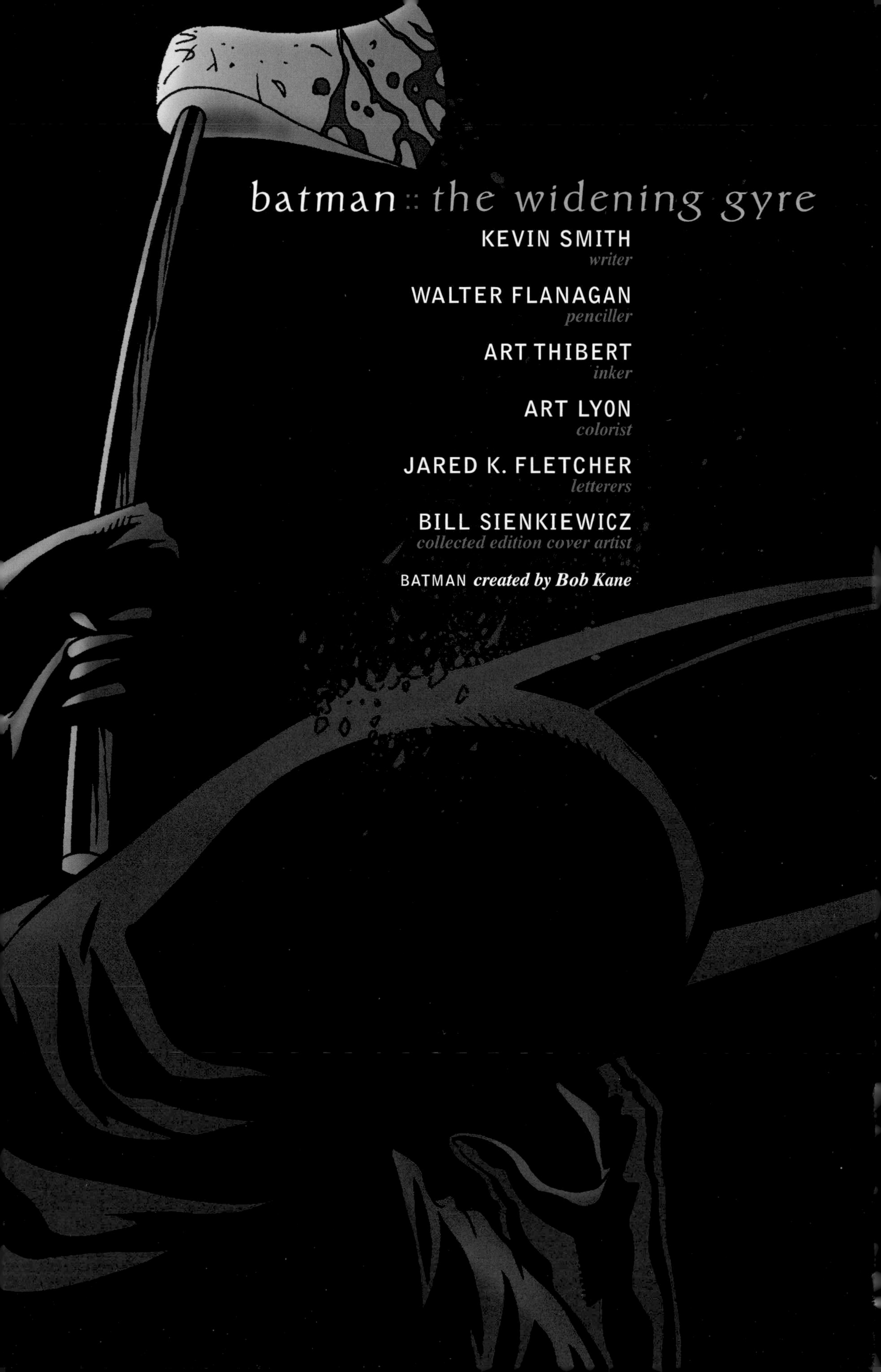

batman :: the widening gyre

KEVIN SMITH
writer

WALTER FLANAGAN
penciller

ART THIBERT
inker

ART LYON
colorist

JARED K. FLETCHER
letterers

BILL SIENKIEWICZ
collected edition cover artist

BATMAN ***created by Bob Kane***

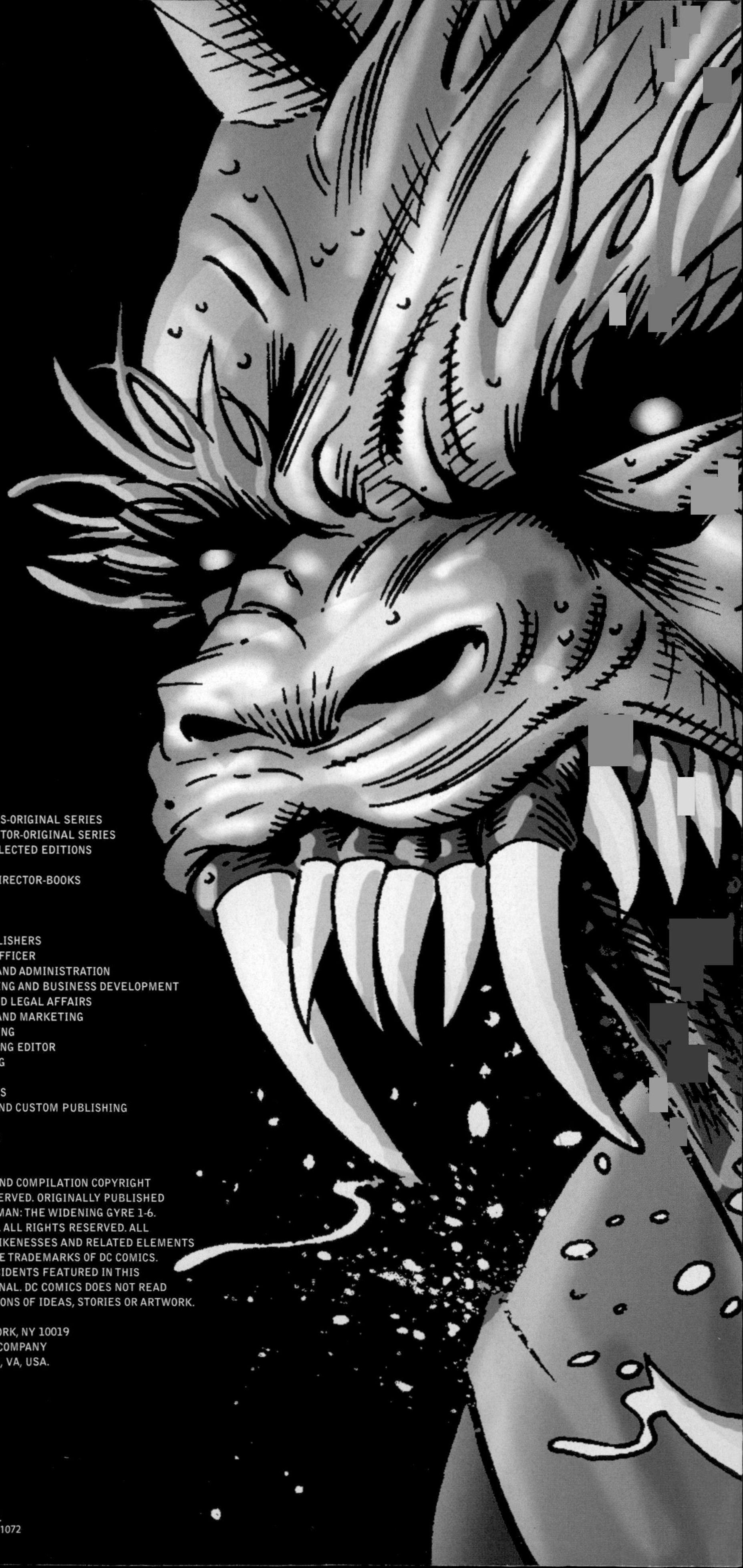

MIKE MARTS DAN DIDIO :: EDITORS-ORIGINAL SERIES
JANELLE SIEGEL :: ASSISTANT EDITOR-ORIGINAL SERIES
BOB HARRAS :: GROUP EDITOR-COLLECTED EDITIONS
BOB JOY :: EDITOR
ROBBIN BROSTERMAN :: DESIGN DIRECTOR-BOOKS

DC COMICS
DIANE NELSON :: PRESIDENT
DAN DIDIO AND JIM LEE :: CO-PUBLISHERS
GEOFF JOHNS :: CHIEF CREATIVE OFFICER
PATRICK CALDON :: EVP-FINANCE AND ADMINISTRATION
JOHN ROOD :: EVP-SALES, MARKETING AND BUSINESS DEVELOPMENT
AMY GENKINS :: SVP-BUSINESS AND LEGAL AFFAIRS
STEVE ROTTERDAM :: SVP-SALES AND MARKETING
JOHN CUNNINGHAM :: VP-MARKETING
TERRI CUNNINGHAM :: VP-MANAGING EDITOR
ALISON GILL :: VP-MANUFACTURING
DAVID HYDE :: VP-PUBLICITY
SUE POHJA :: VP-BOOK TRADE SALES
ALYSSE SOLL :: VP-ADVERTISING AND CUSTOM PUBLISHING
BOB WAYNE :: VP-SALES
MARK CHIARELLO :: ART DIRECTOR

DC COMICS, 1700 BROADWAY, NEW YORK, NY 10019
A WARNER BROS. ENTERTAINMENT COMPANY
PRINTED BY RR DONNELLEY, SALEM, VA, USA.
8/26/11. FIRST PRINTING.
ISBN: 978-1-4012-2876-7

SUSTAINABLE FORESTRY INITIATIVE
Certified Chain of Custody
Promoting Sustainable Forest Management
www.sfiprogram.org

Fiber used in this product line meets the
sourcing requirements of the SFI program.
www.sfiprogram.org SGS-SFI/COC-US10/81072

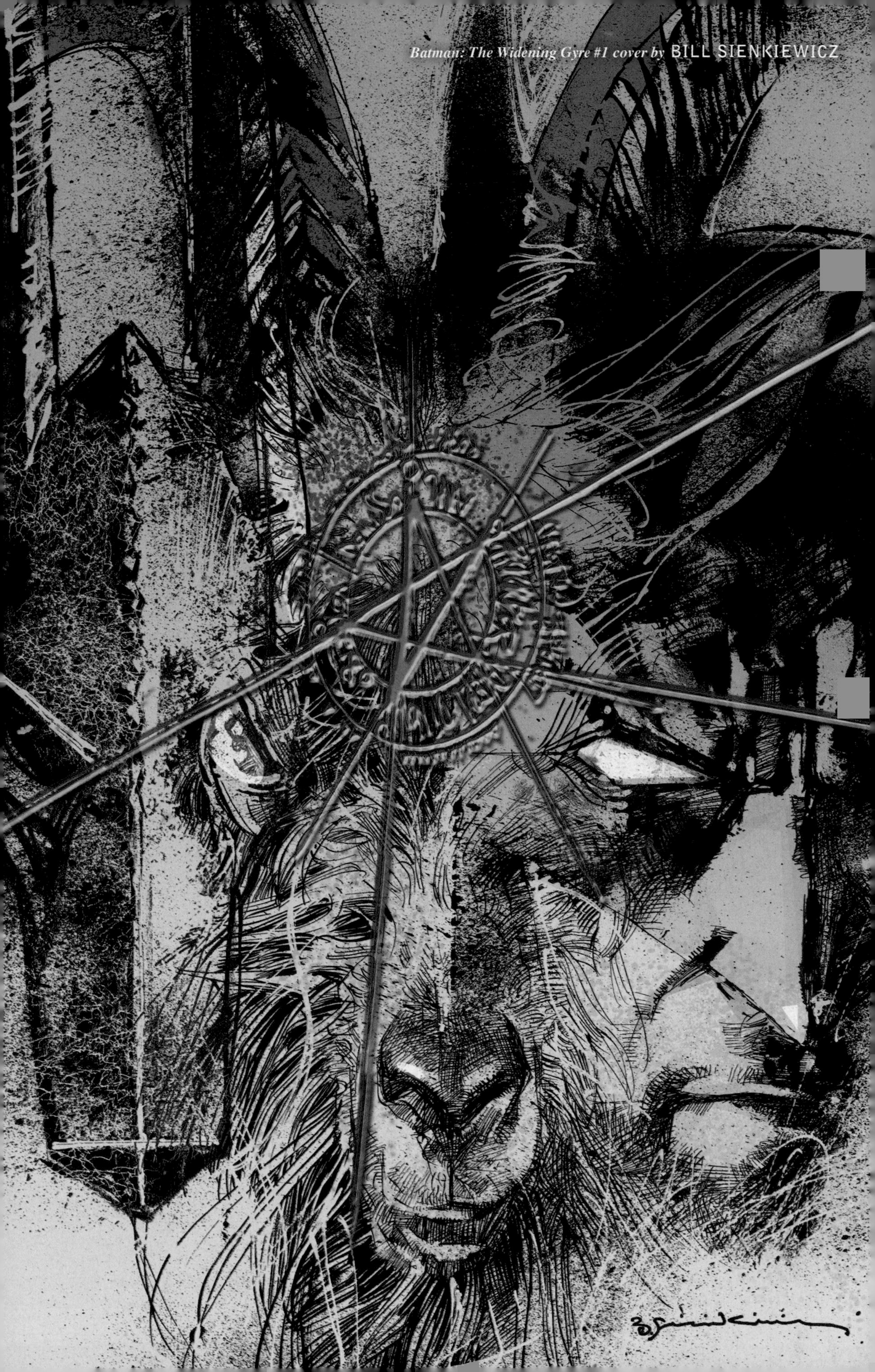

Batman: The Widening Gyre #1 cover by BILL SIENKIEWICZ

Batman: The Widening Gyre #1 alternate cover art by GENE HA

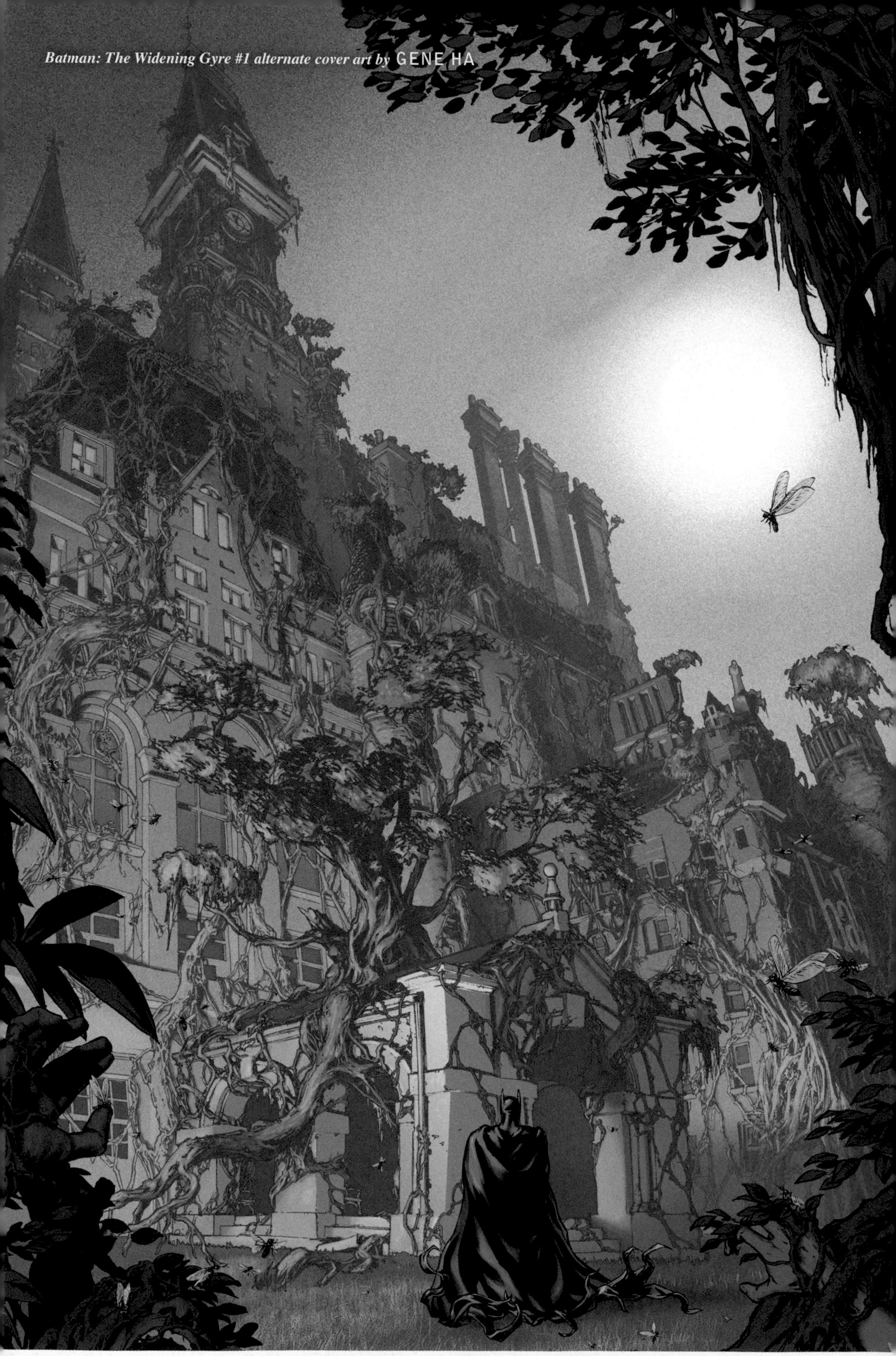

part one TURNING AND TURNING

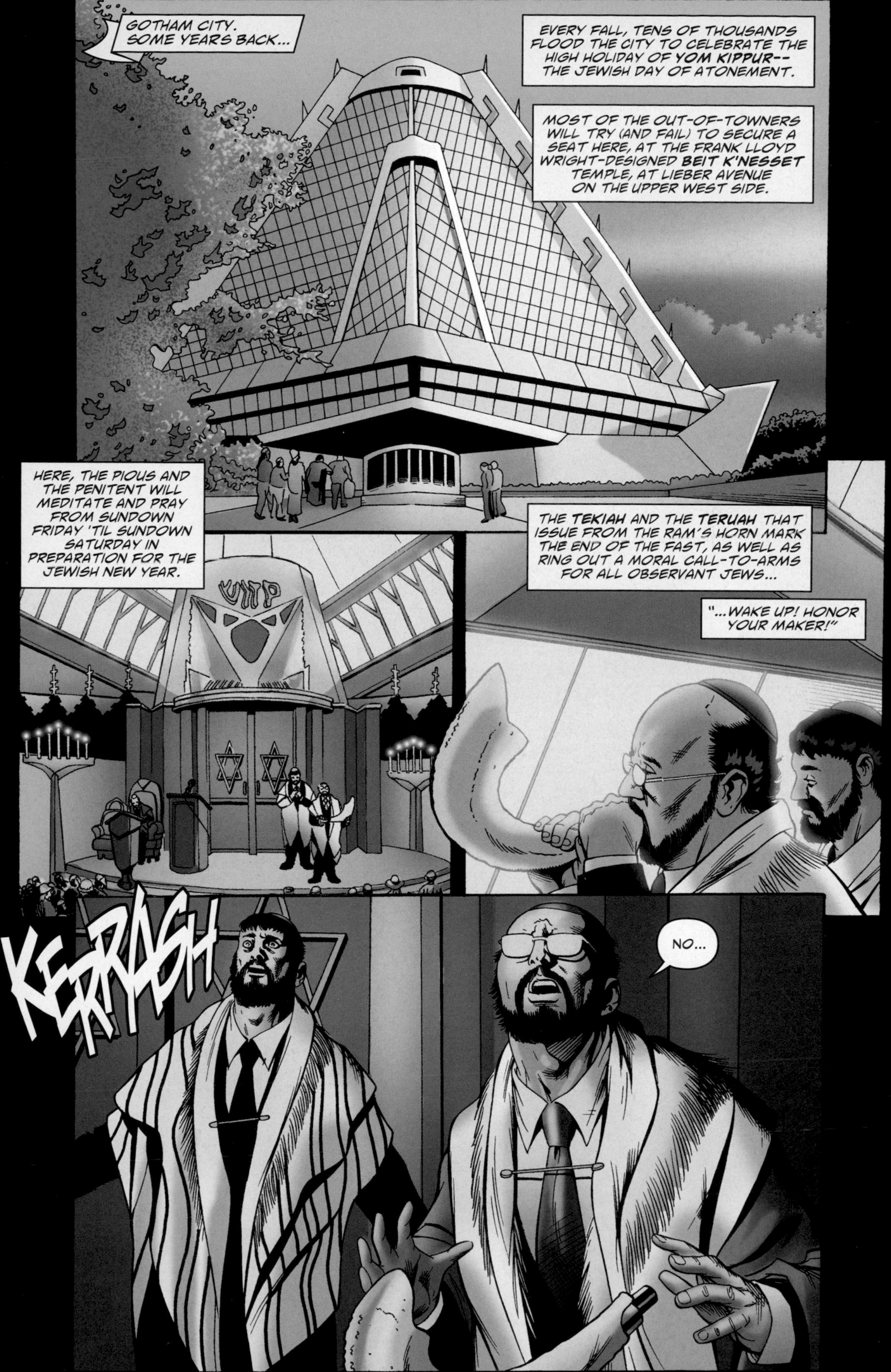

GOTHAM CITY. SOME YEARS BACK...
EVERY FALL, TENS OF THOUSANDS FLOOD THE CITY TO CELEBRATE THE HIGH HOLIDAY OF YOM KIPPUR-- THE JEWISH DAY OF ATONEMENT.
MOST OF THE OUT-OF-TOWNERS WILL TRY (AND FAIL) TO SECURE A SEAT HERE, AT THE FRANK LLOYD WRIGHT-DESIGNED BEIT K'NESSET TEMPLE, AT LIEBER AVENUE ON THE UPPER WEST SIDE.
HERE, THE PIOUS AND THE PENITENT WILL MEDITATE AND PRAY FROM SUNDOWN FRIDAY 'TIL SUNDOWN SATURDAY IN PREPARATION FOR THE JEWISH NEW YEAR.
THE TEKIAH AND THE TERUAH THAT ISSUE FROM THE RAM'S HORN MARK THE END OF THE FAST, AS WELL AS RING OUT A MORAL CALL-TO-ARMS FOR ALL OBSERVANT JEWS...
"...WAKE UP! HONOR YOUR MAKER!"
KERRASH
NO...

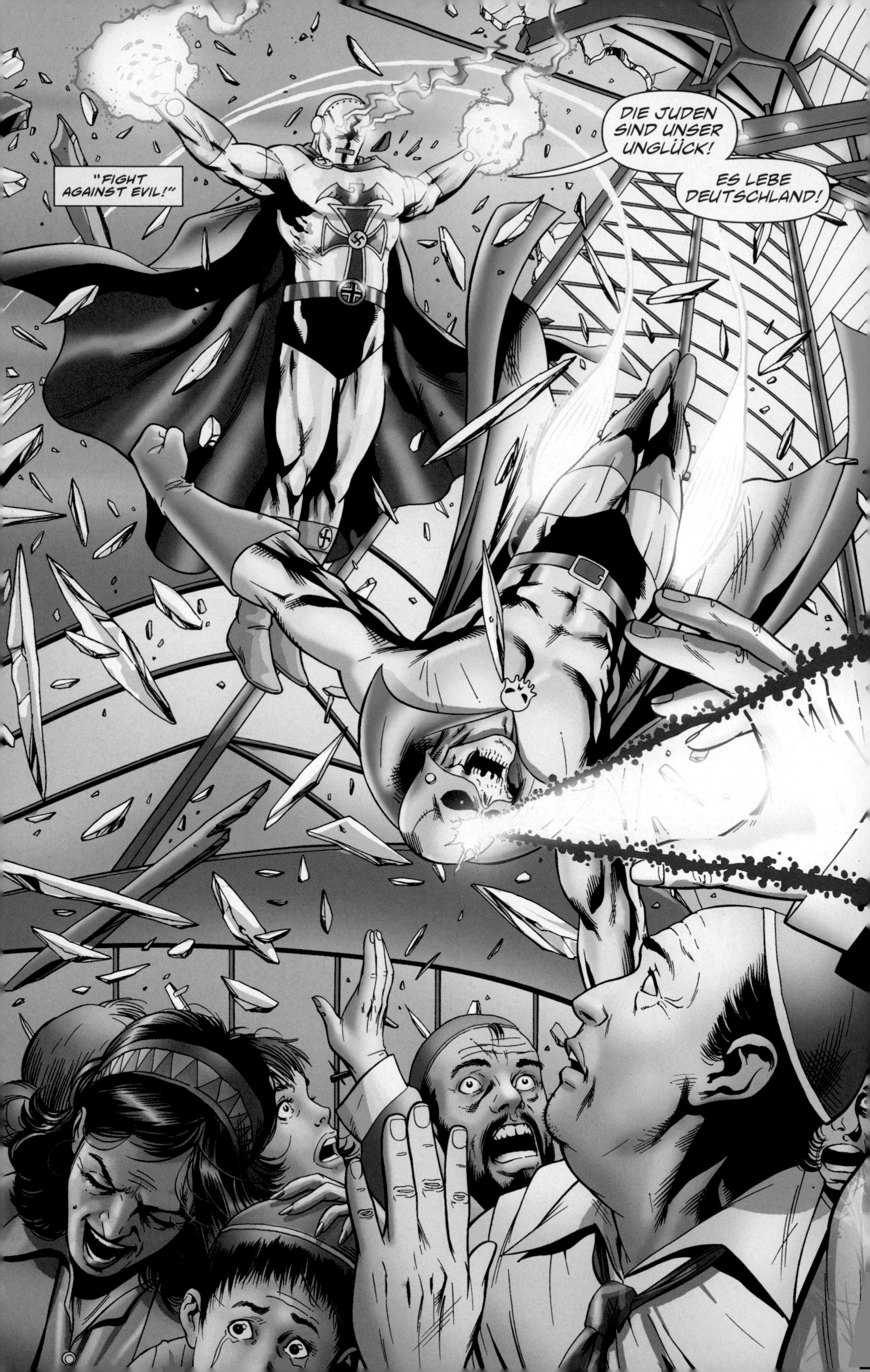
"FIGHT AGAINST EVIL!"
DIE JUDEN SIND UNSER UNGLÜCK!
ES LEBE DEUTSCHLAND!

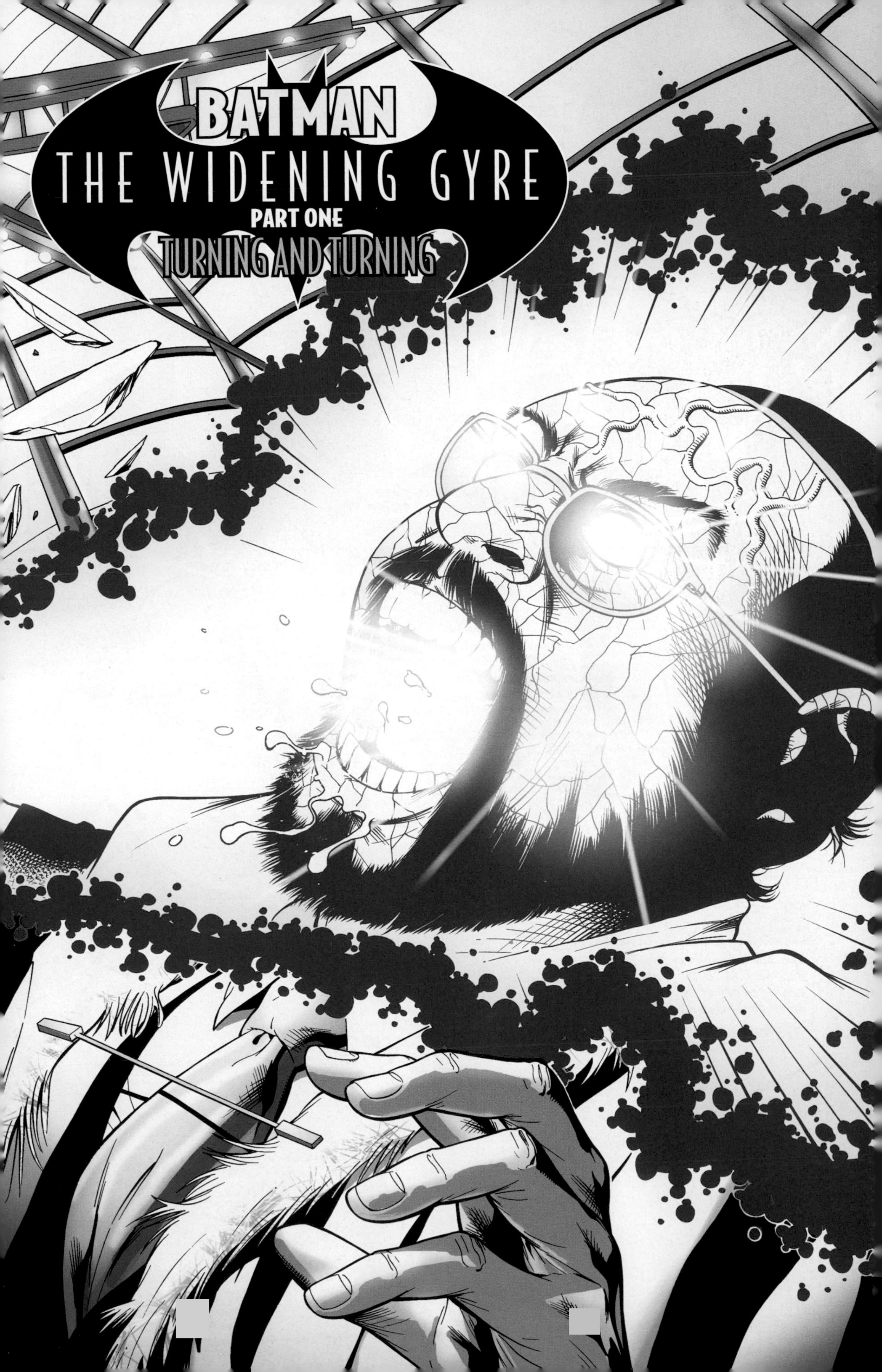
BATMAN
THE WIDENING GYRE
PART ONE
TURNING AND TURNING

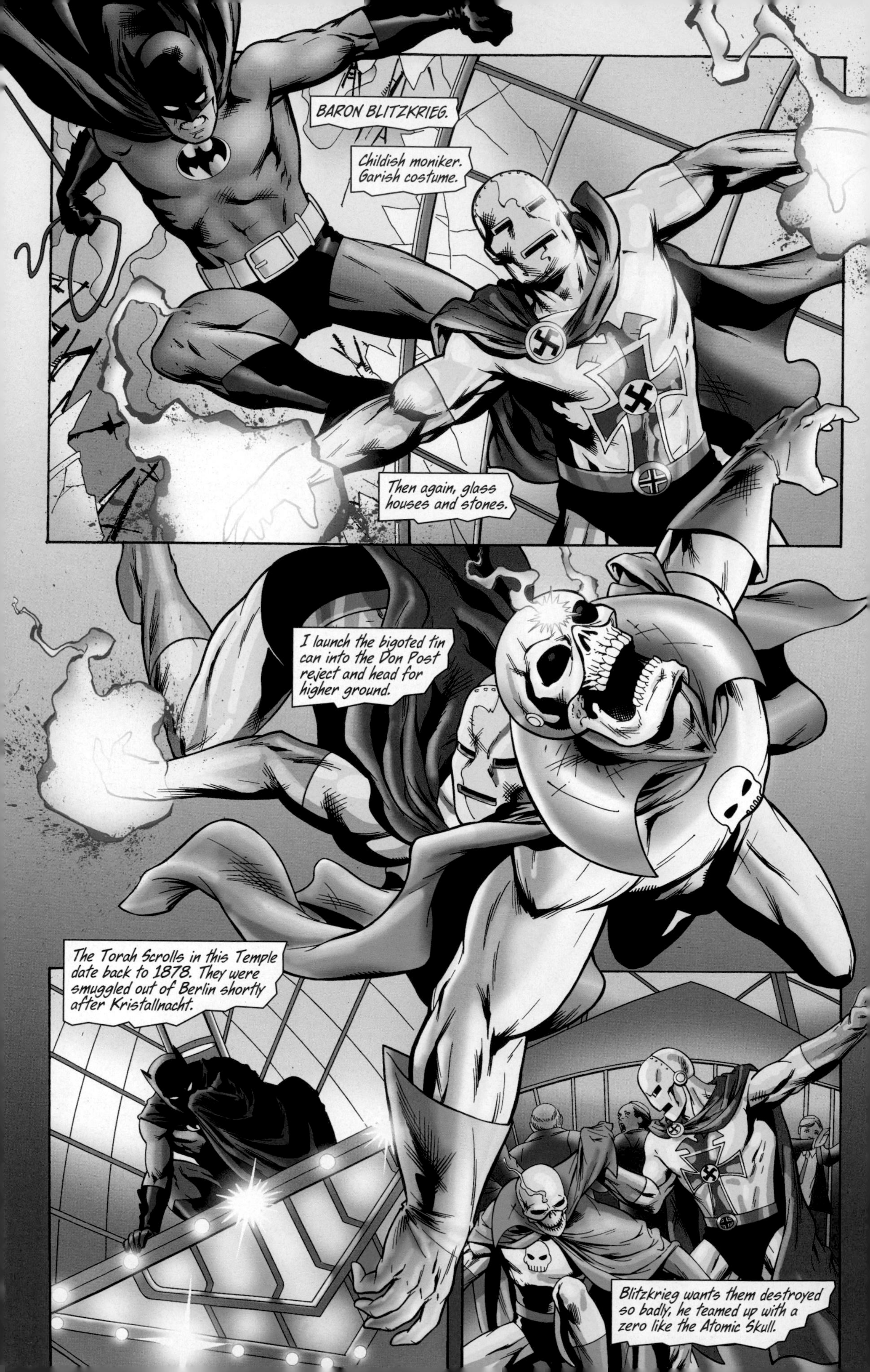
BARON BLITZKRIEG.
Childish moniker. Garish costume.
Then again, glass houses and stones.
I launch the bigoted tin can into the Don Post reject and head for higher ground.
The Torah Scrolls in this Temple date back to 1878. They were smuggled out of Berlin shortly after Kristallnacht.
Blitzkrieg wants them destroyed so badly, he teamed up with a zero like the Atomic Skull.

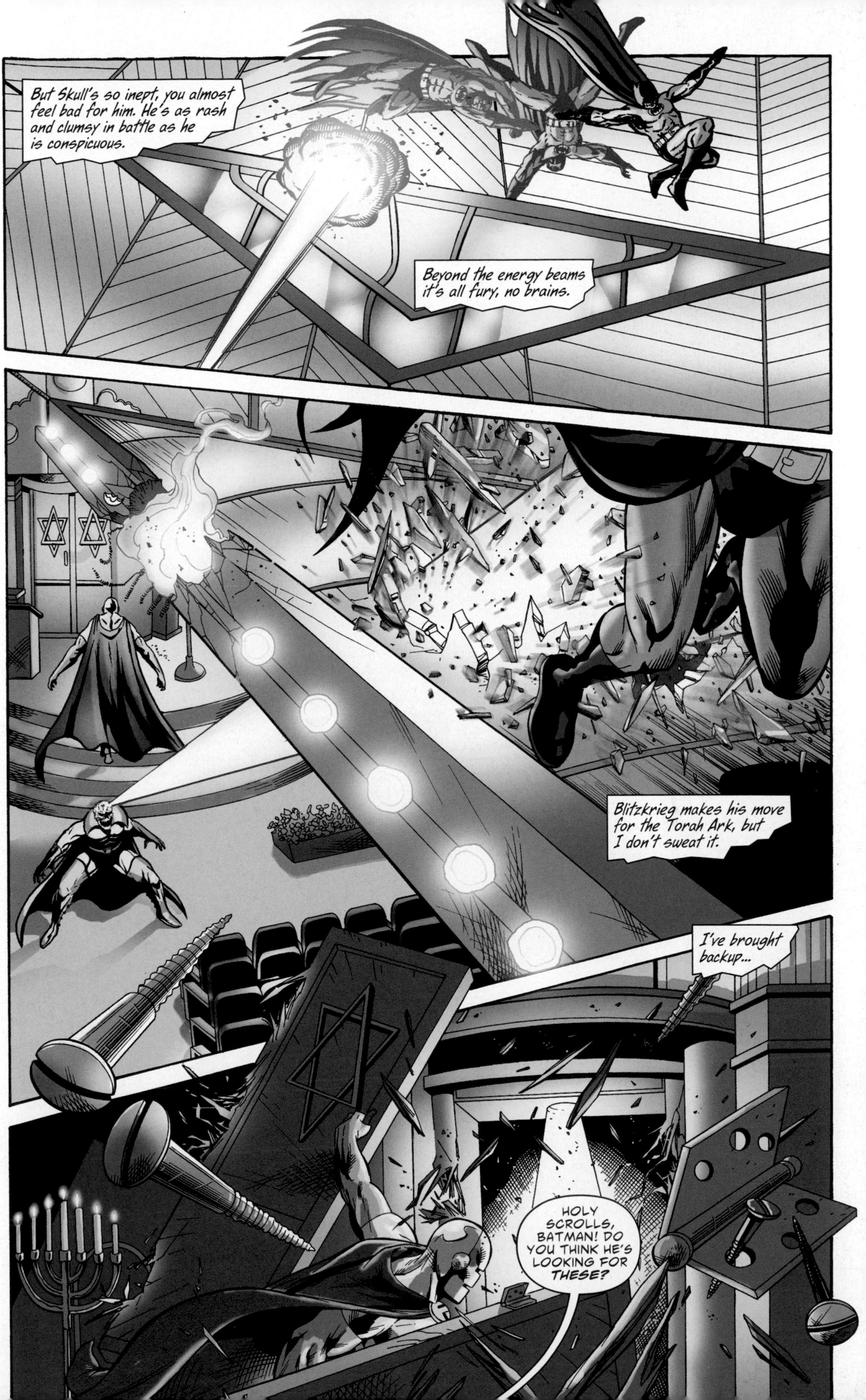
But Skull's so inept, you almost feel bad for him. He's as rash and clumsy in battle as he is conspicuous.
Beyond the energy beams it's all fury, no brains.
Blitzkrieg makes his move for the Torah Ark, but I don't sweat it.
I've brought backup...
HOLY SCROLLS, BATMAN! DO YOU THINK HE'S LOOKING FOR THESE?

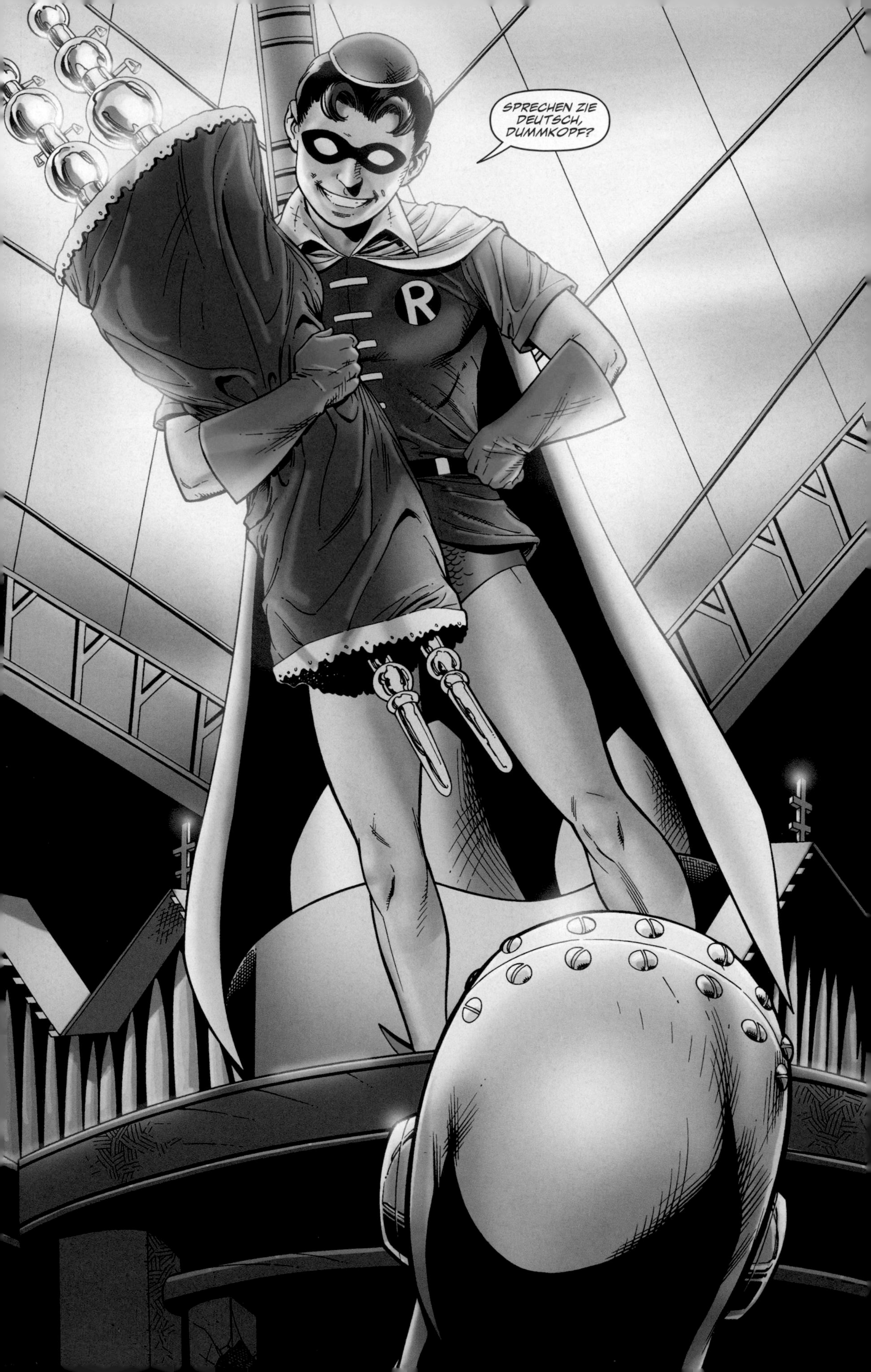
SPRECHEN ZIE DEUTSCH, DUMMKOPF?

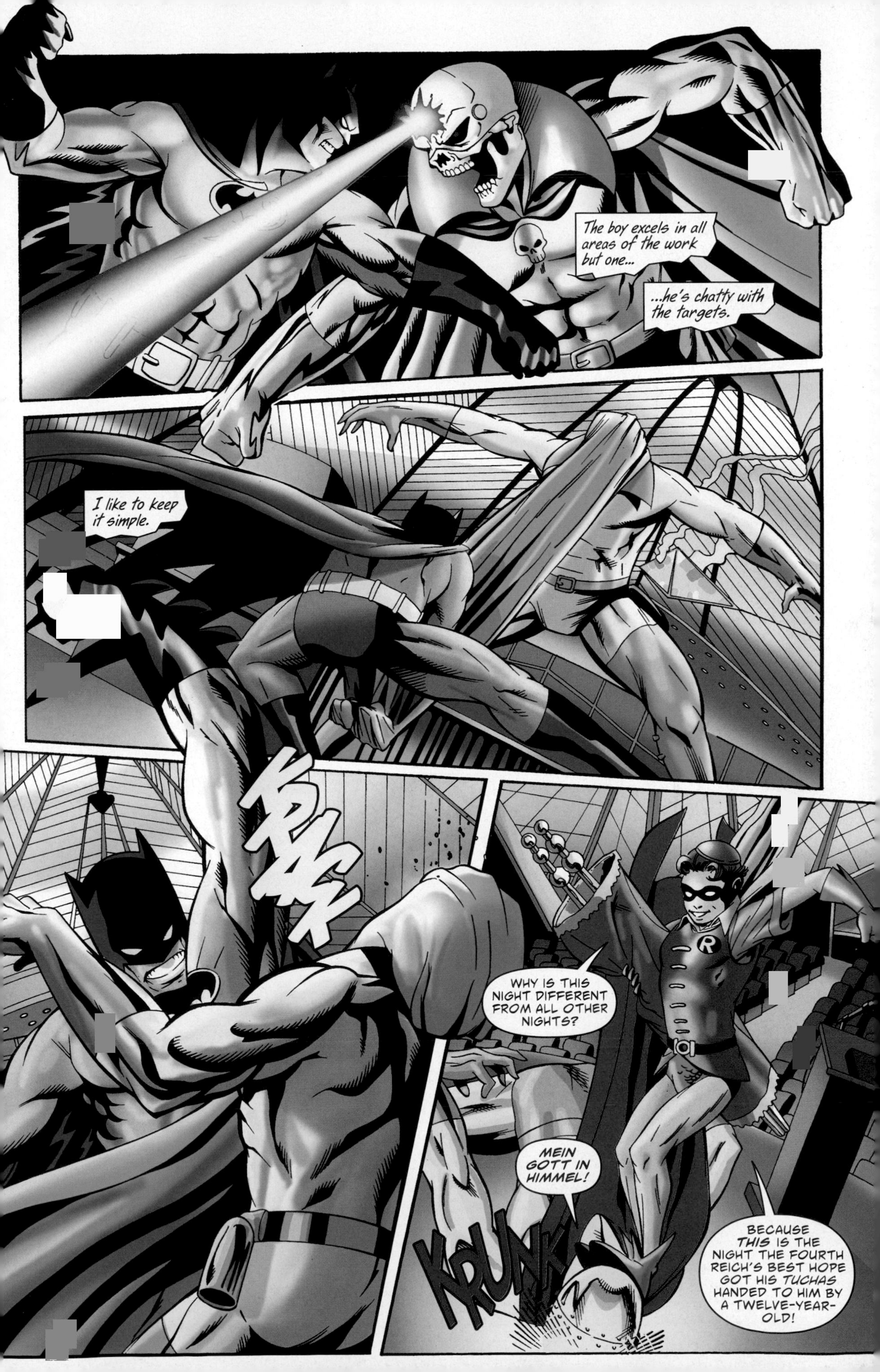
The boy excels in all areas of the work but one...
...he's chatty with the targets.
I like to keep it simple.
KRAACK
WHY IS THIS NIGHT DIFFERENT FROM ALL OTHER NIGHTS?
MEIN GOTT IN HIMMEL!
KRUNK!
BECAUSE *THIS* IS THE NIGHT THE FOURTH REICH'S BEST HOPE GOT HIS *TUCHAS* HANDED TO HIM BY A TWELVE-YEAR-OLD!

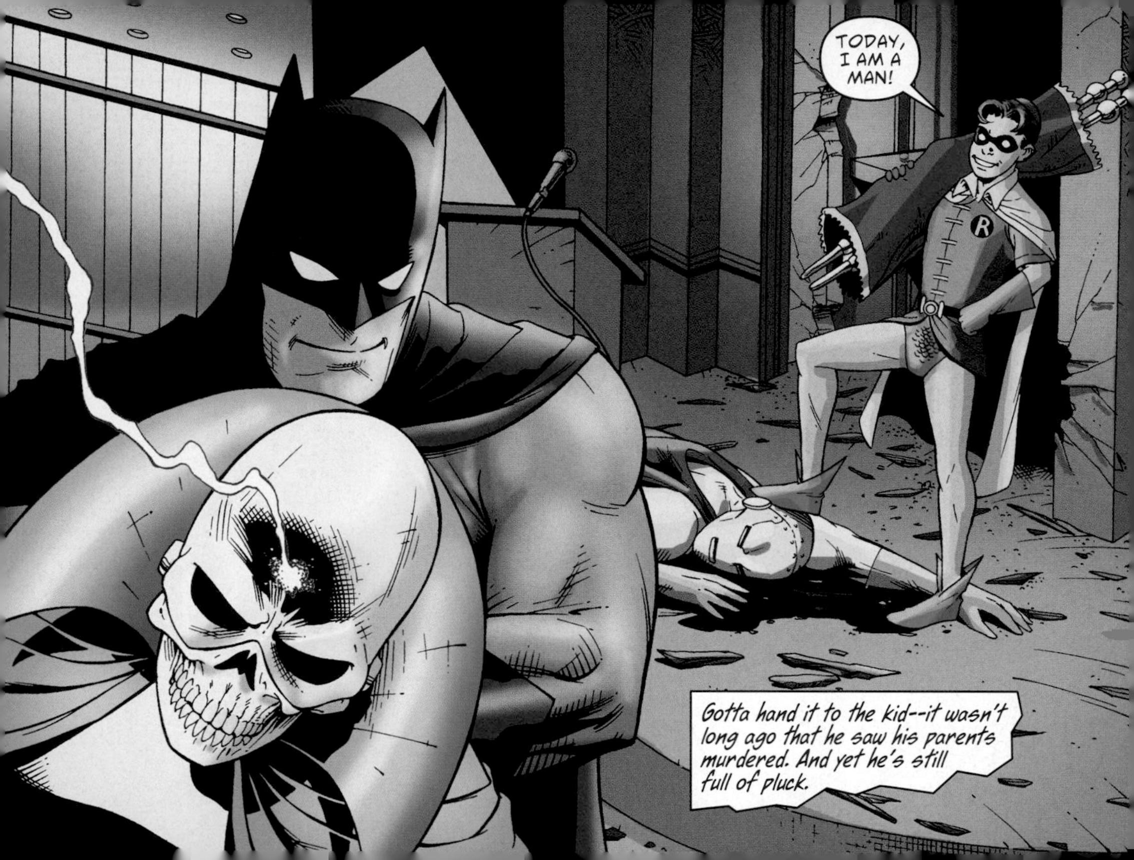
TODAY, I AM A MAN!
Gotta hand it to the kid--it wasn't long ago that he saw his parents murdered. And yet he's still full of pluck.

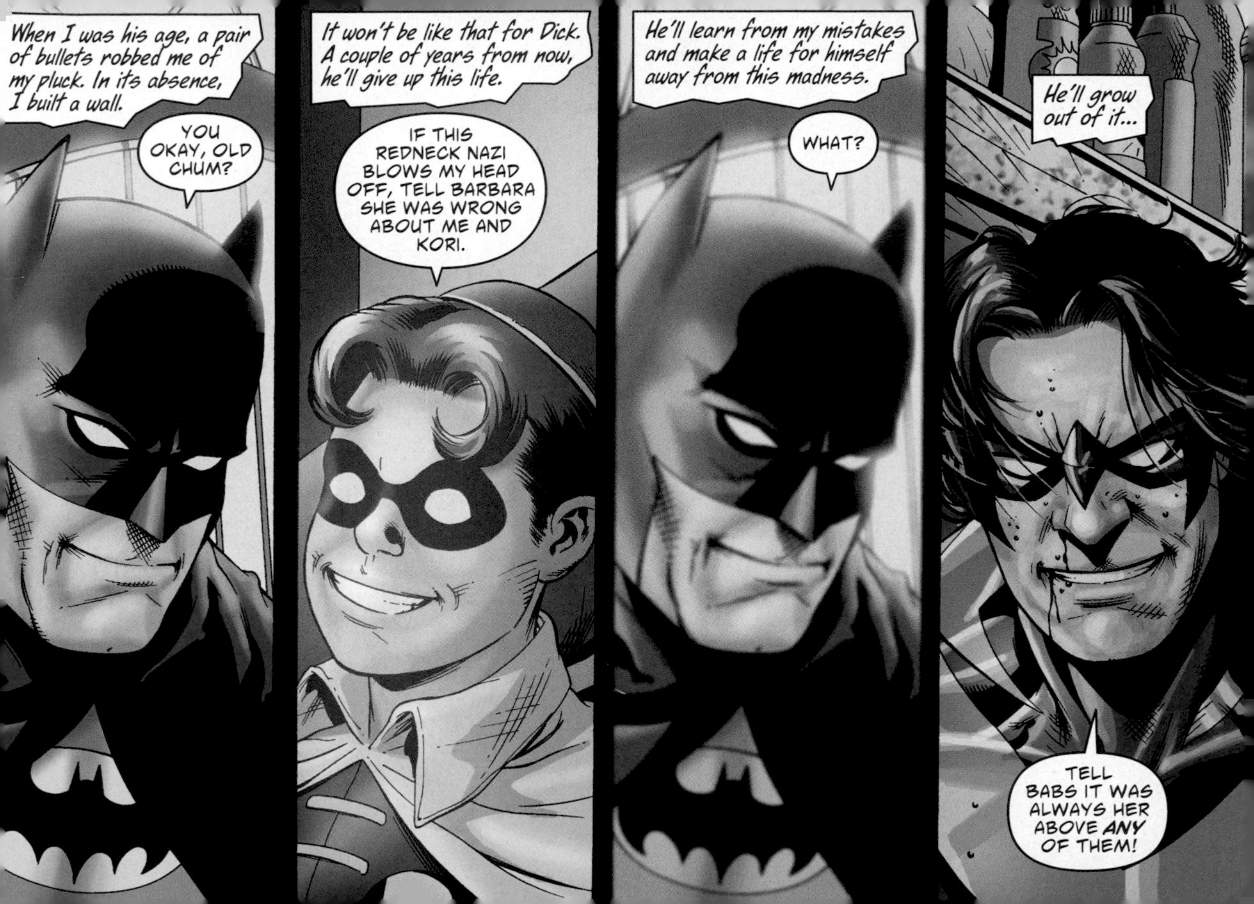
When I was his age, a pair of bullets robbed me of my pluck. In its absence, I built a wall.
YOU OKAY, OLD CHUM?
It won't be like that for Dick. A couple of years from now, he'll give up this life.
IF THIS REDNECK NAZI BLOWS MY HEAD OFF, TELL BARBARA SHE WAS WRONG ABOUT ME AND KORI.
He'll learn from my mistakes and make a life for himself away from this madness.
WHAT?
He'll grow out of it...
TELL BABS IT WAS ALWAYS HER ABOVE *ANY* OF THEM!

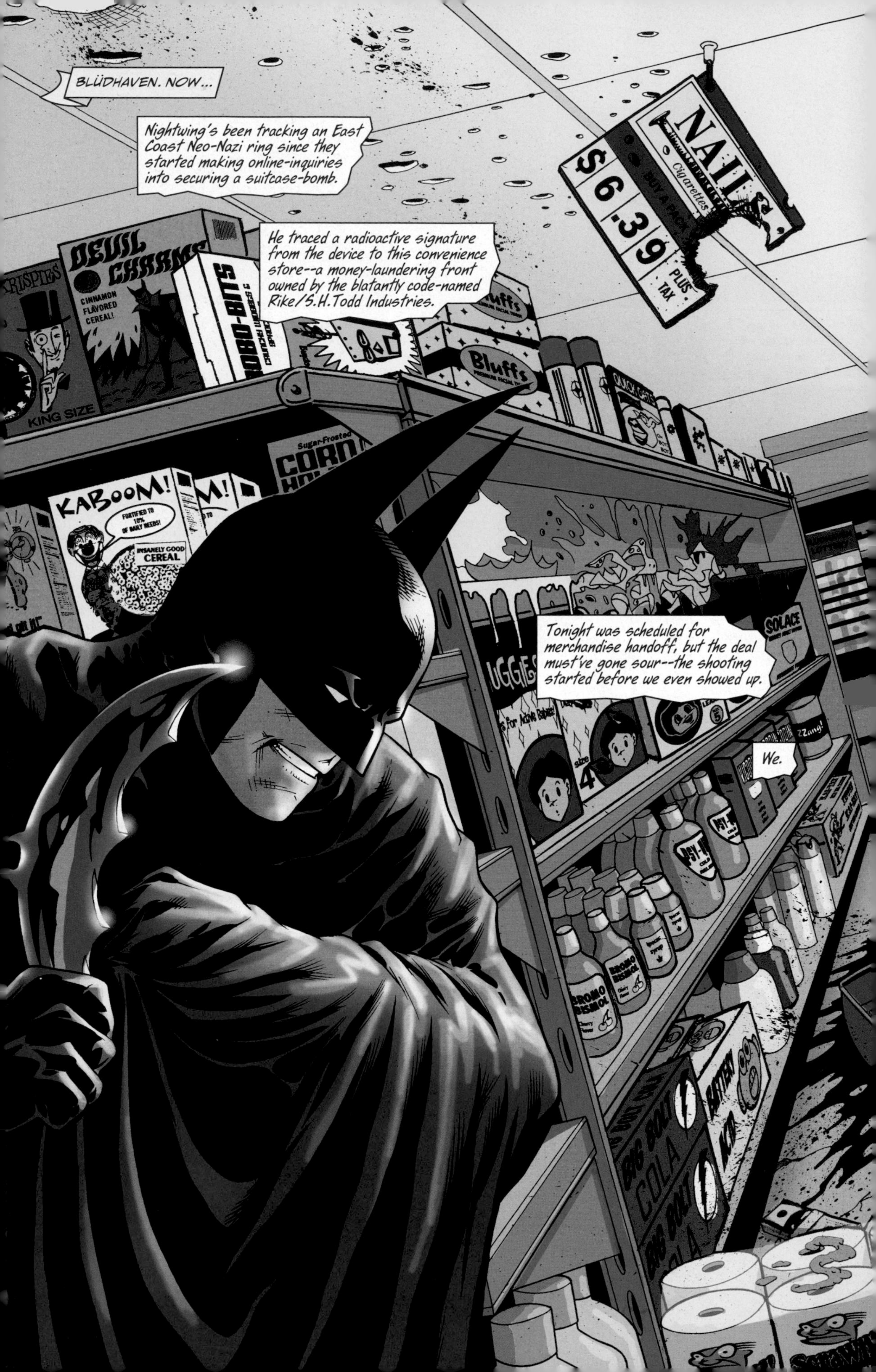

BLÜDHAVEN. NOW...
Nightwing's been tracking an East Coast Neo-Nazi ring since they started making online-inquiries into securing a suitcase-bomb.
He traced a radioactive signature from the device to this convenience store--a money-laundering front owned by the blatantly code-named Rike/S.H.Todd Industries.
Tonight was scheduled for merchandise handoff, but the deal must've gone sour--the shooting started before we even showed up.
We.
NAIL Cigarettes
$6.39 PLUS TAX
DEVIL CHARMS
CINNAMON FLAVORED CEREAL!
KING SIZE
KABOOM!
INSANELY GOOD CEREAL
Bluffs
SOLACE
BROMO BISMOL
BIG BOLT COLA

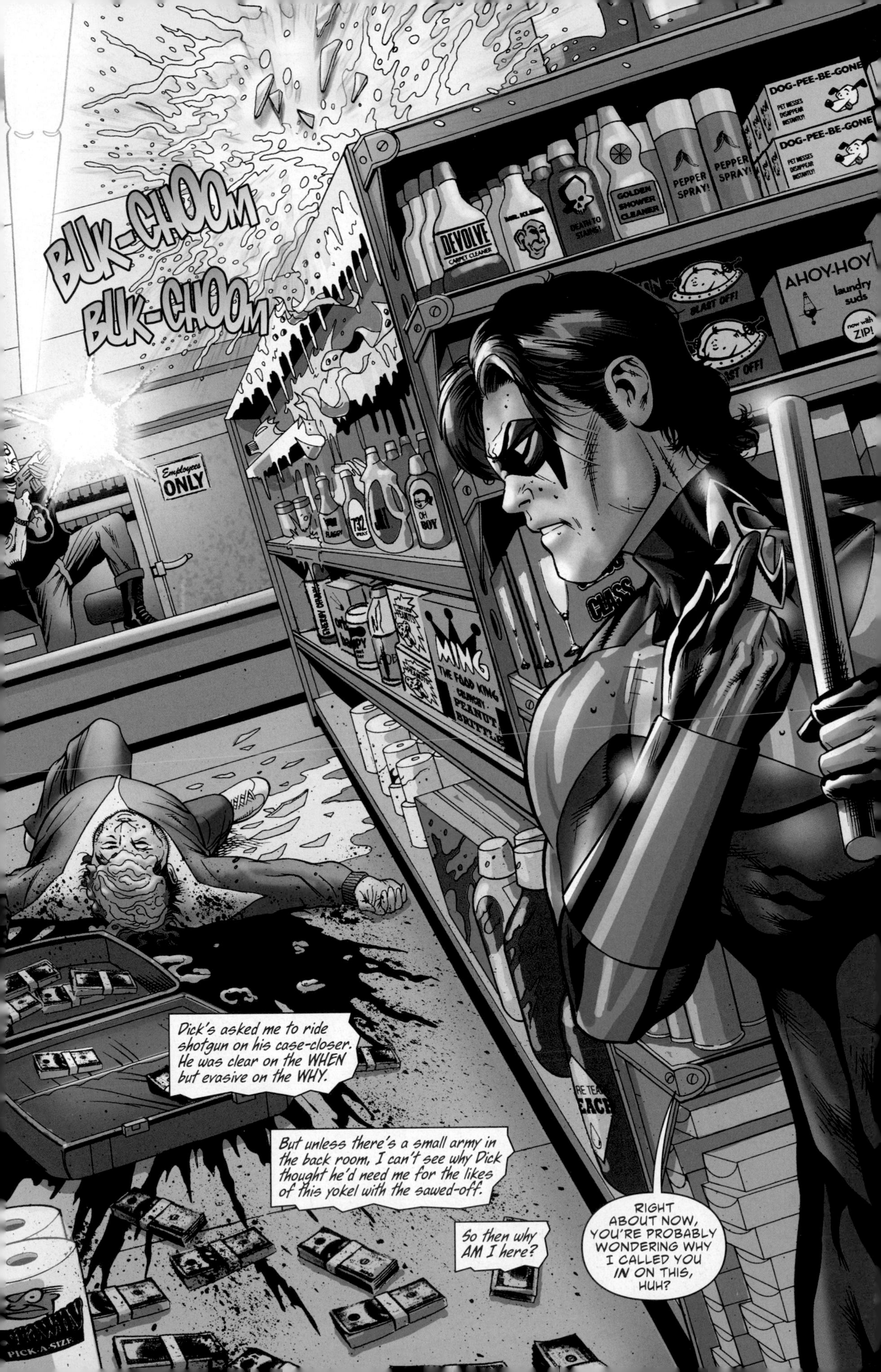
BUK-CHOOM
BUK-CHOOM
Employees ONLY
Dick's asked me to ride shotgun on his case-closer. He was clear on the WHEN but evasive on the WHY.
But unless there's a small army in the back room, I can't see why Dick thought he'd need me for the likes of this yokel with the sawed-off.
So then why AM I here?
RIGHT ABOUT NOW, YOU'RE PROBABLY WONDERING WHY I CALLED YOU IN ON THIS, HUH?

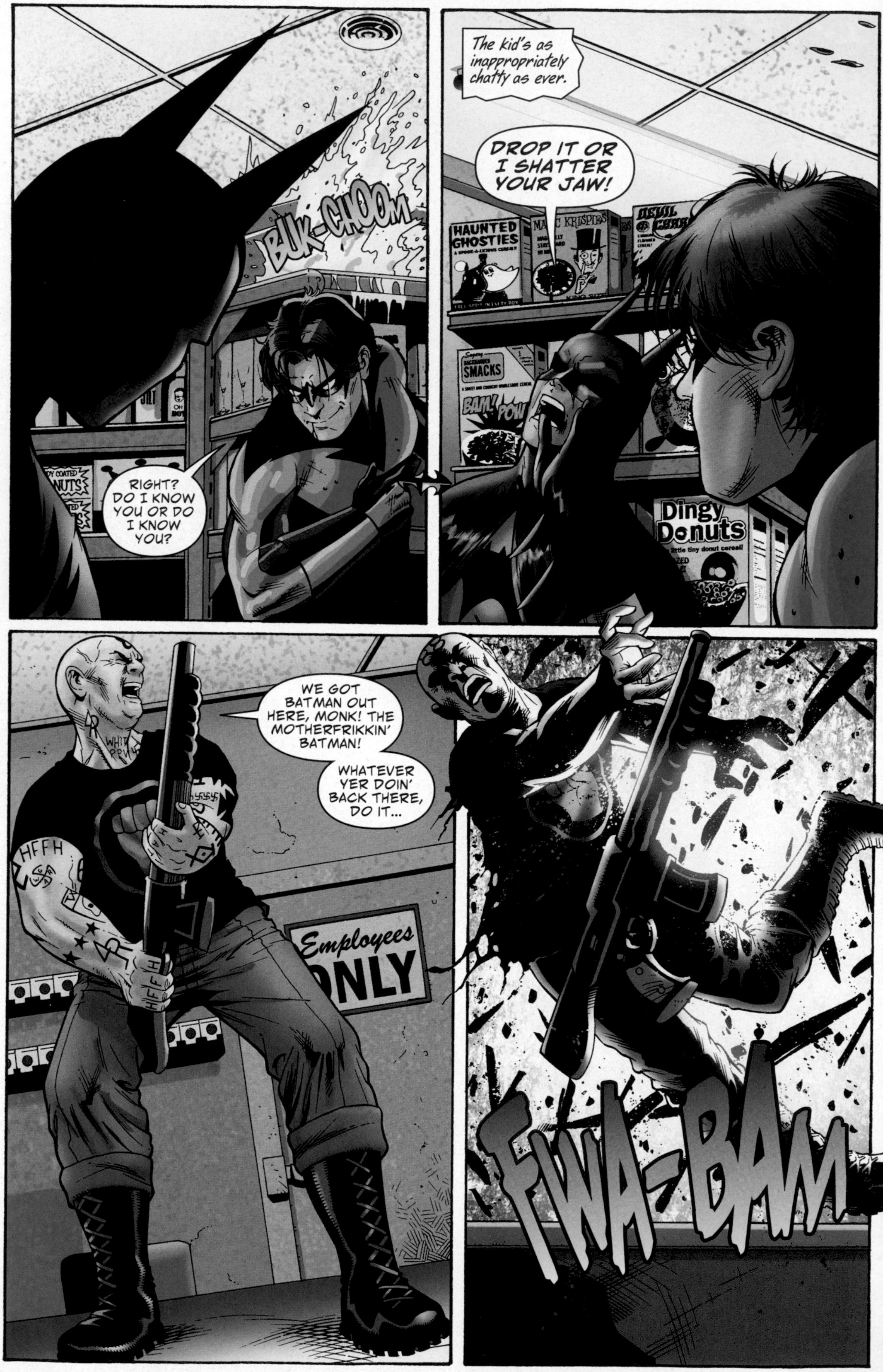
BUK-CHOOM
RIGHT? DO I KNOW YOU OR DO I KNOW YOU?
The kid's as inappropriately chatty as ever.
DROP IT OR I SHATTER YOUR JAW!
HAUNTED GHOSTIES
SMACKS
Dingy Donuts
WE GOT BATMAN OUT HERE, MONK! THE MOTHERFRIKKIN' BATMAN!
WHATEVER YER DOIN' BACK THERE, DO IT...
Employees ONLY
FWA-BAM

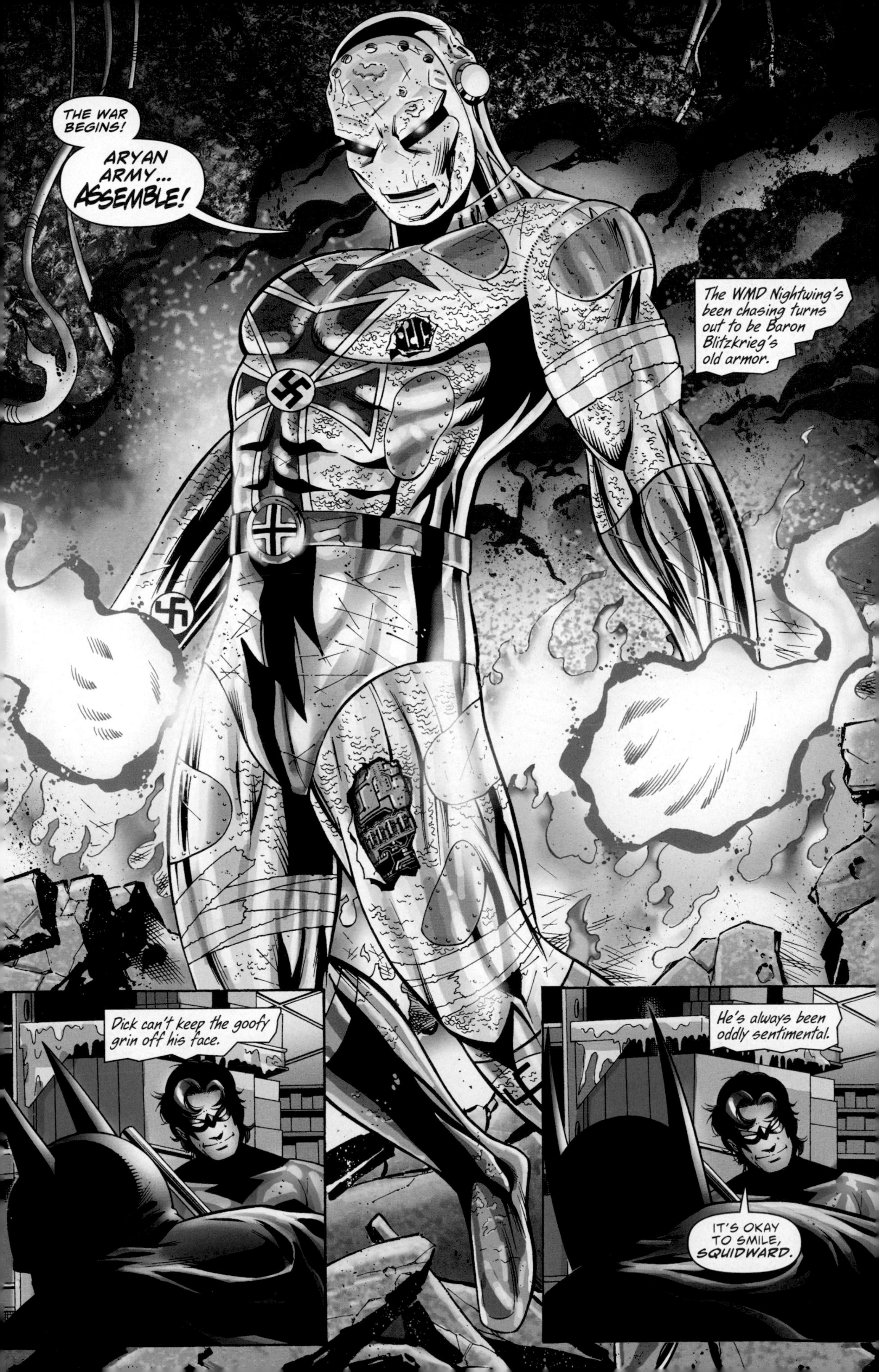
THE WAR BEGINS!
ARYAN ARMY... ASSEMBLE!
The WMD Nightwing's been chasing turns out to be Baron Blitzkrieg's old armor.
Dick can't keep the goofy grin off his face.
He's always been oddly sentimental.
IT'S OKAY TO SMILE, SQUIDWARD.

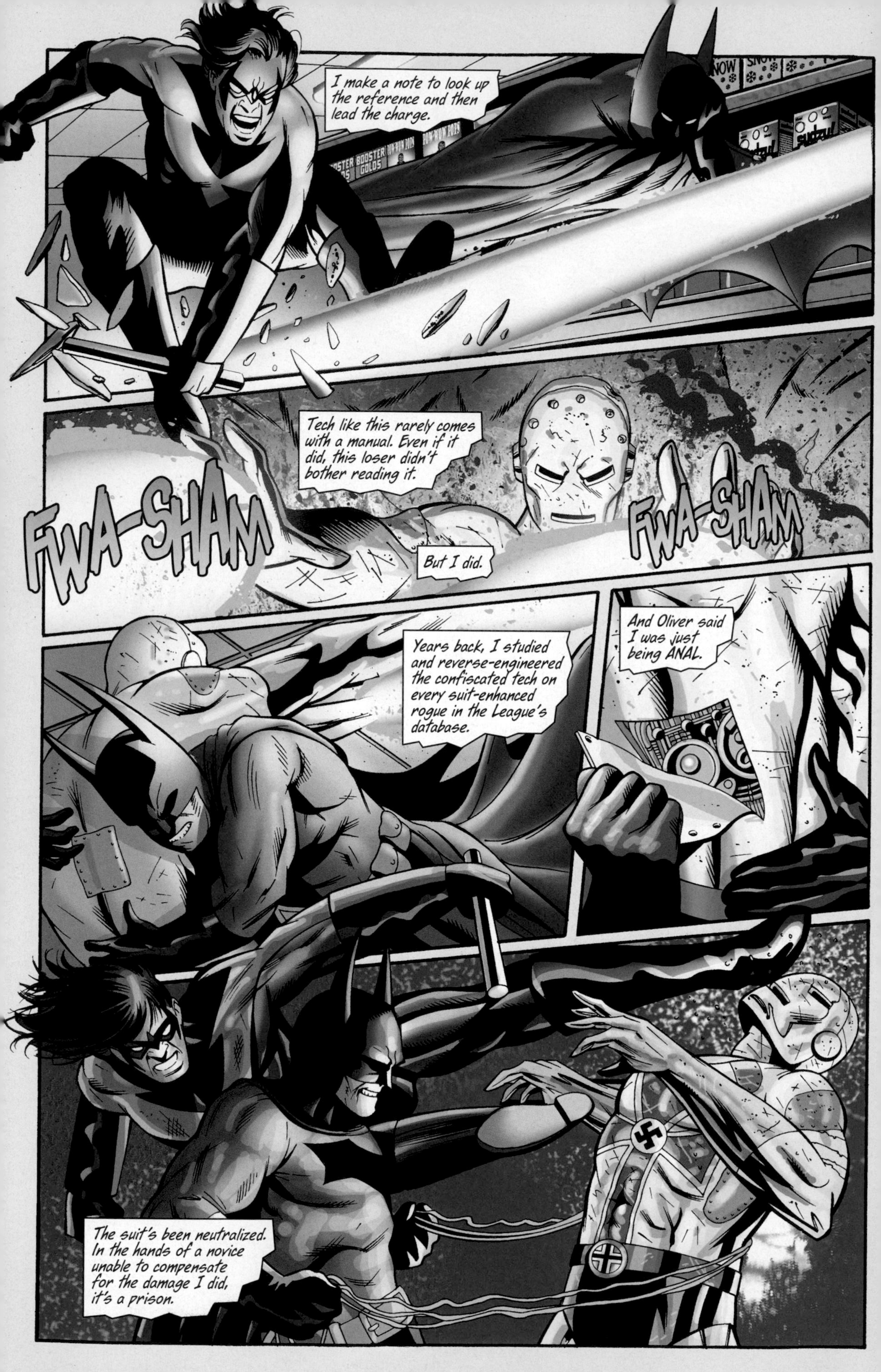
I make a note to look up the reference and then lead the charge.
Tech like this rarely comes with a manual. Even if it did, this loser didn't bother reading it.
FWA-SHAM
FWA-SHAM
But I did.
Years back, I studied and reverse-engineered the confiscated tech on every suit-enhanced rogue in the League's database.
And Oliver said I was just being ANAL.
The suit's been neutralized. In the hands of a novice unable to compensate for the damage I did, it's a prison.

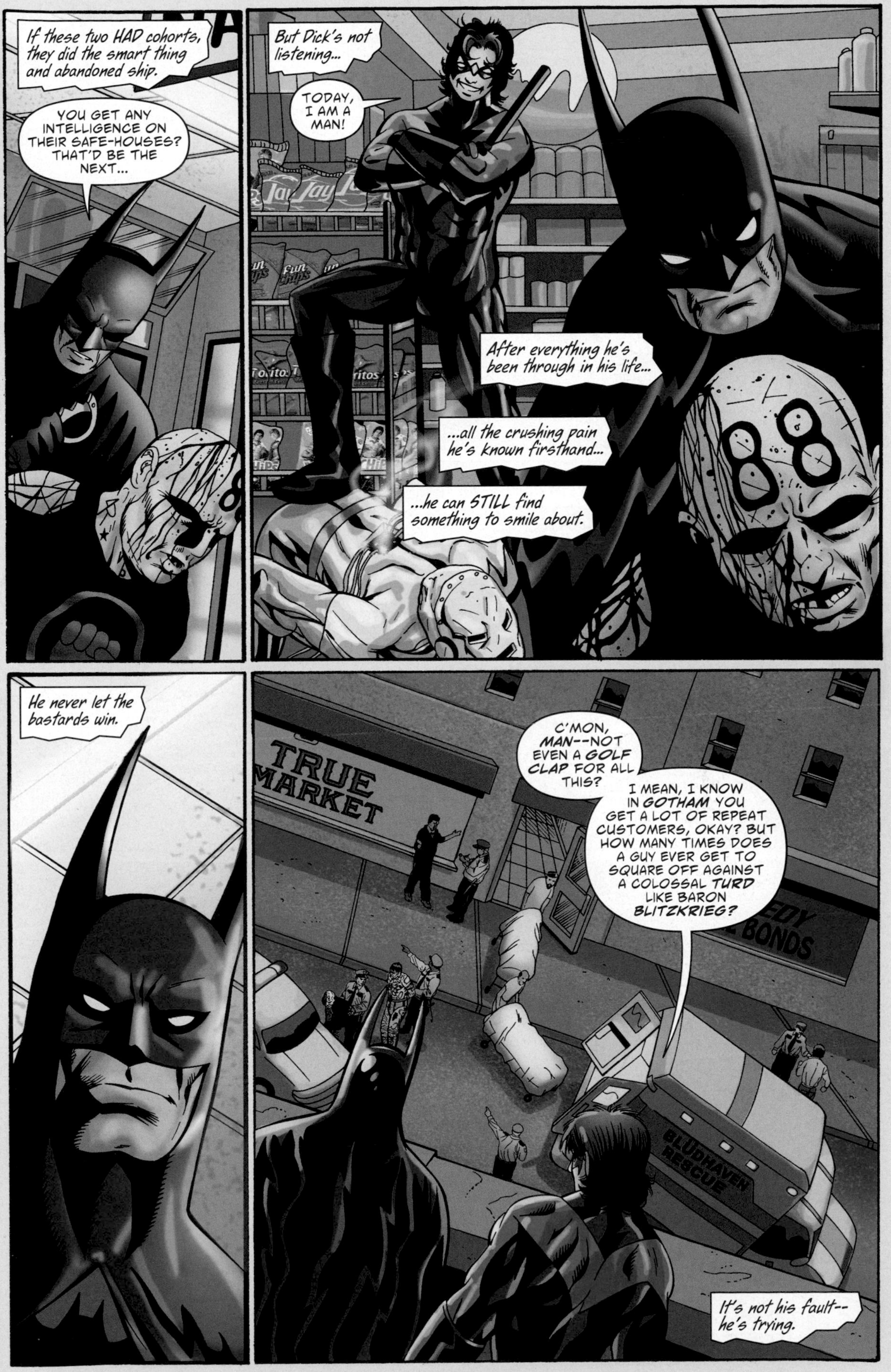
If these two HAD cohorts, they did the smart thing and abandoned ship.
YOU GET ANY INTELLIGENCE ON THEIR SAFE-HOUSES? THAT'D BE THE NEXT...
But Dick's not listening...
TODAY, I AM A MAN!
After everything he's been through in his life...
...all the crushing pain he's known firsthand...
...he can STILL find something to smile about.
He never let the bastards win.
TRUE MARKET
C'MON, MAN--NOT EVEN A GOLF CLAP FOR ALL THIS?
I MEAN, I KNOW IN GOTHAM YOU GET A LOT OF REPEAT CUSTOMERS, OKAY? BUT HOW MANY TIMES DOES A GUY EVER GET TO SQUARE OFF AGAINST A COLOSSAL TURD LIKE BARON BLITZKRIEG?
BLÜDHAVEN RESCUE
It's not his fault--he's trying.

PLUS, Y'KNOW-- HE **WAS** ONE OF THE FIRST COSTUMES I EVER TOOK DOWN ALL BY **MYSELF.**

I just have a hard time relating to anyone about anything outside of the work.

IF THERE'S NOTHING ELSE, I SHOULD GET BACK TO THE CITY...

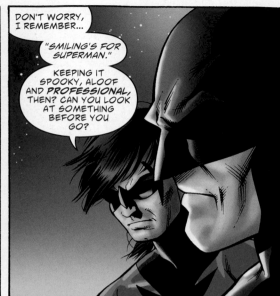

DON'T WORRY, I REMEMBER...

"SMILING'S FOR SUPERMAN."

KEEPING IT SPOOKY, ALOOF AND **PROFESSIONAL,** THEN? CAN YOU LOOK AT SOMETHING BEFORE YOU GO?

THE BLÜDHAVEN CITY MORGUE...

SOME KIDS HAVING A KEGGER FOUND HIM IN THE RUSHES OVER AT SNAKE LAKE. WHEN I HEARD ABOUT HIM, I THOUGHT OF YOU IMMEDIATELY.

VIC'S NAME IS GAVIN ADAM.

HE WAS A PSYCH MAJOR AT BLÜDHAVEN MED.

I CALLED AND THEY SAID SHE'S BEEN IN LOCK-DOWN FOR THE LAST YEAR. SAID IT'S ANOTHER SIX MONTHS BEFORE SHE EVEN GETS IN FRONT OF THE RELEASE REVIEW COMMITTEE.

BUT IF ISLEY'S IN ARKHAM...

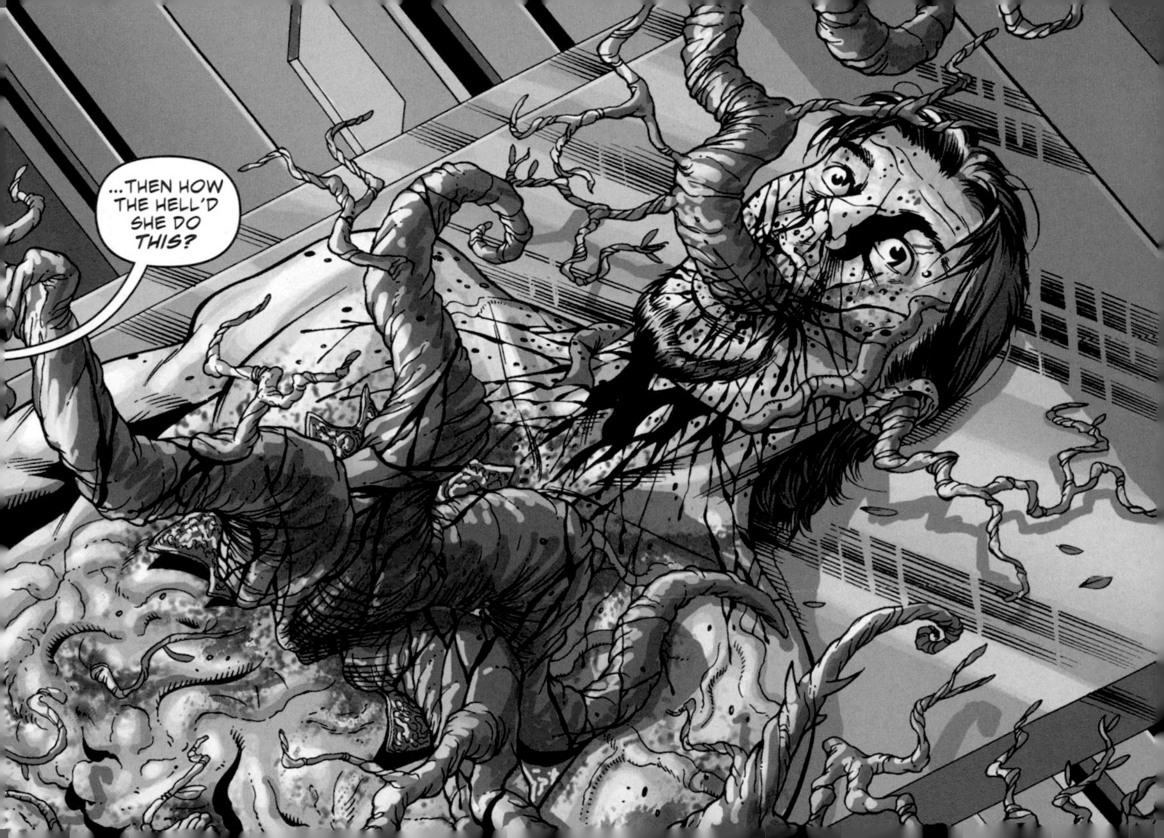
...THEN HOW THE HELL'D SHE DO *THIS?*

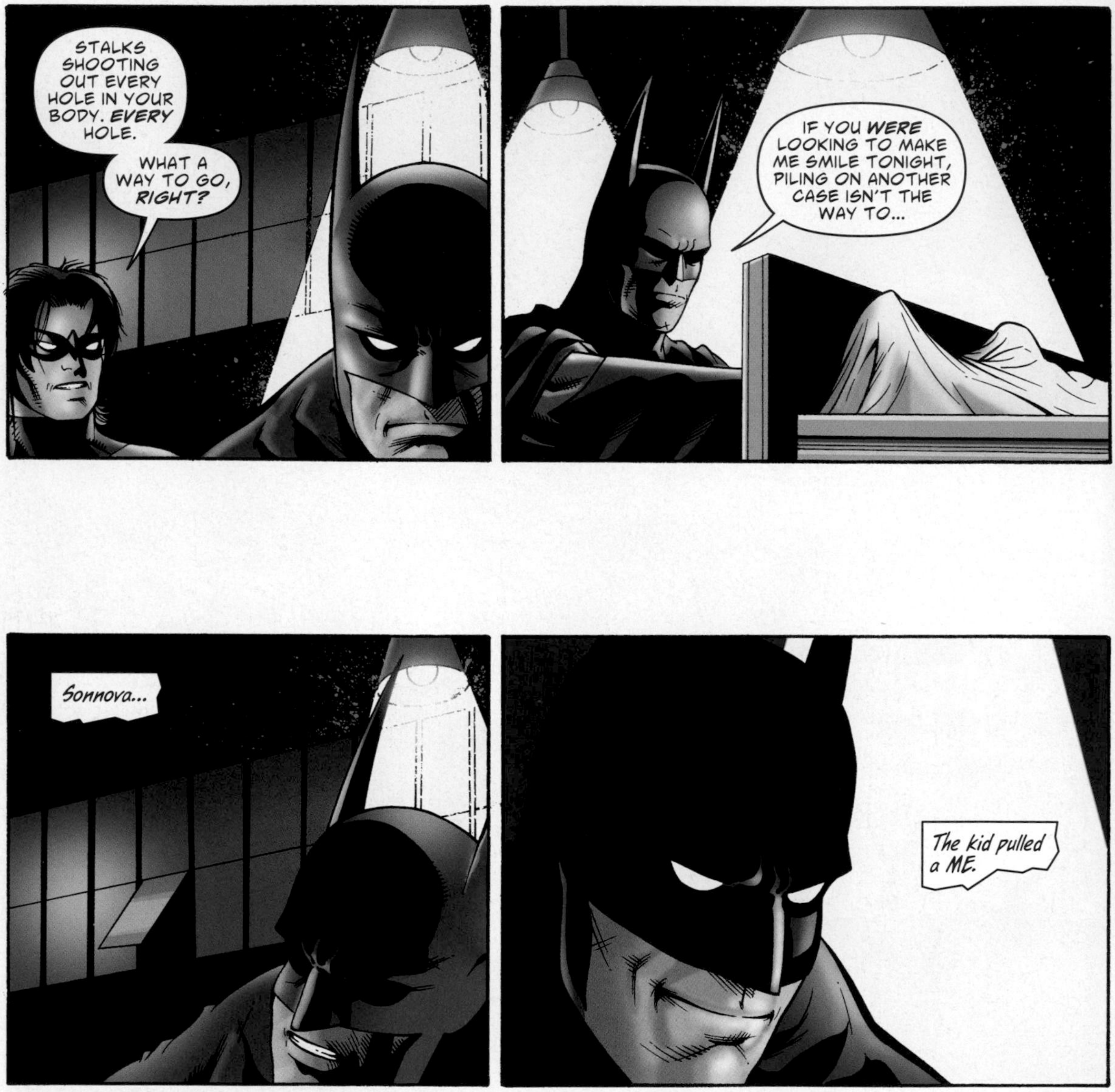
STALKS SHOOTING OUT EVERY HOLE IN YOUR BODY. *EVERY* HOLE.
WHAT A WAY TO GO, *RIGHT?*
IF YOU *WERE* LOOKING TO MAKE ME SMILE TONIGHT, PILING ON ANOTHER CASE ISN'T THE WAY TO...
Sonnova...
The kid pulled a ME.

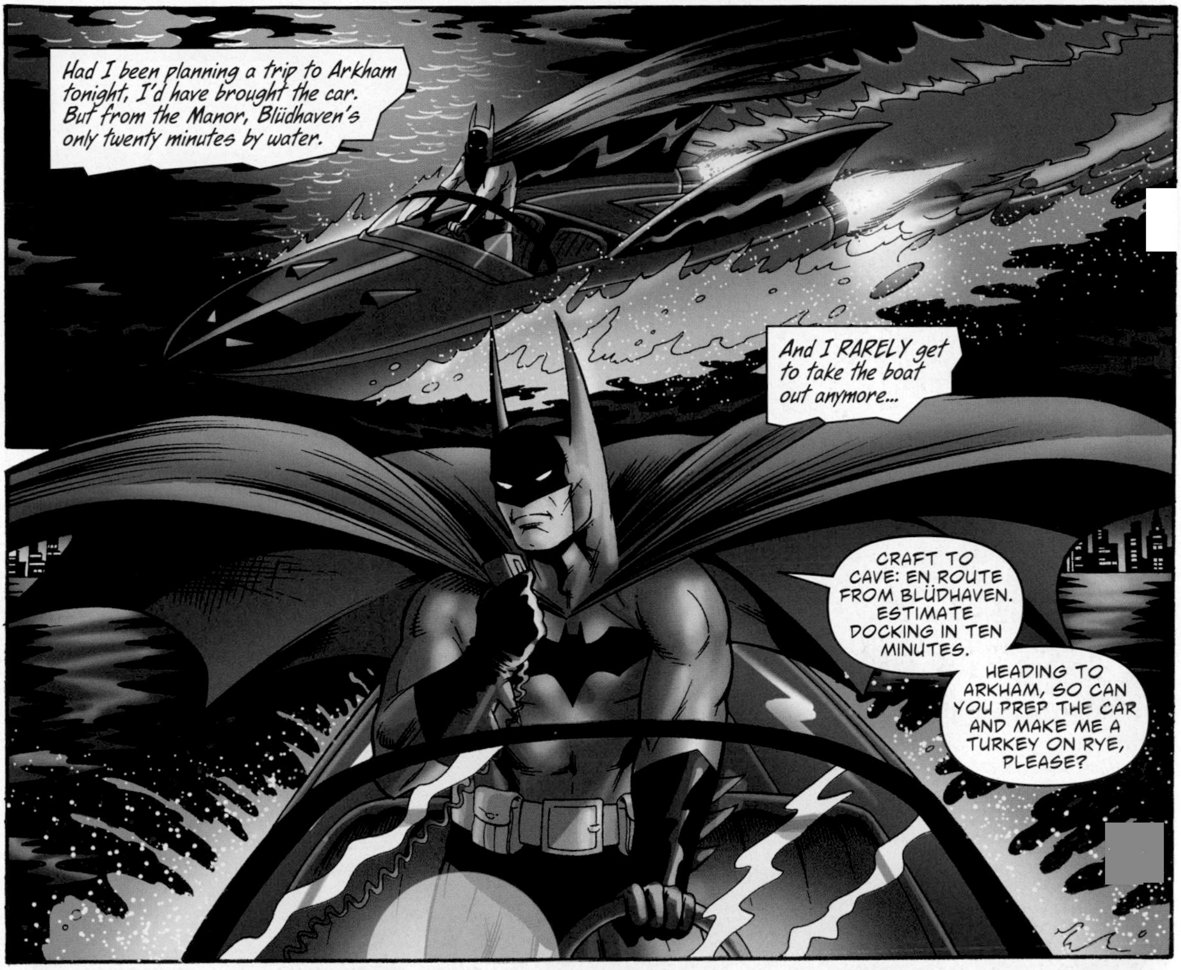
Had I been planning a trip to Arkham tonight, I'd have brought the car. But from the Manor, Blüdhaven's only twenty minutes by water.
And I RARELY get to take the boat out anymore...
CRAFT TO CAVE: EN ROUTE FROM BLÜDHAVEN. ESTIMATE DOCKING IN TEN MINUTES.
HEADING TO ARKHAM, SO CAN YOU PREP THE CAR AND MAKE ME A TURKEY ON RYE, PLEASE?

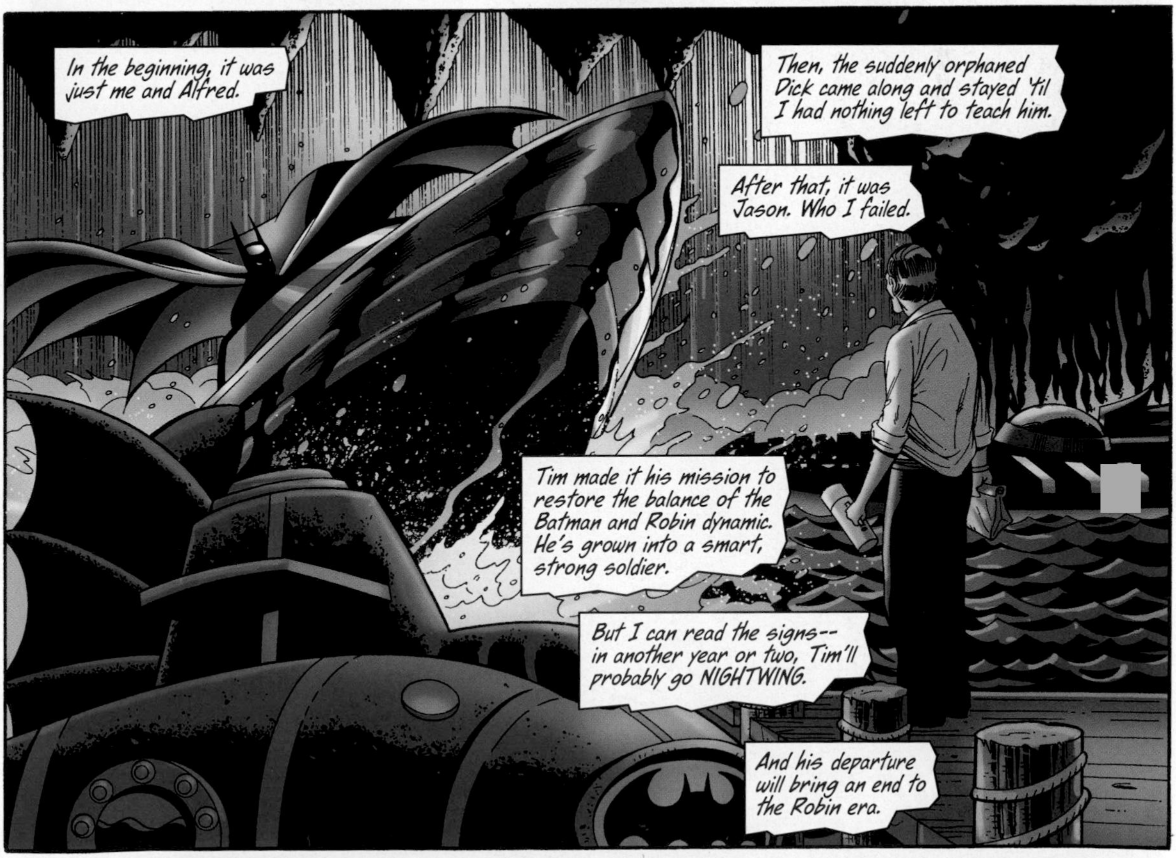
In the beginning, it was just me and Alfred.
Then, the suddenly orphaned Dick came along and stayed 'til I had nothing left to teach him.
After that, it was Jason. Who I failed.
Tim made it his mission to restore the balance of the Batman and Robin dynamic. He's grown into a smart, strong soldier.
But I can read the signs-- in another year or two, Tim'll probably go NIGHTWING.
And his departure will bring an end to the Robin era.

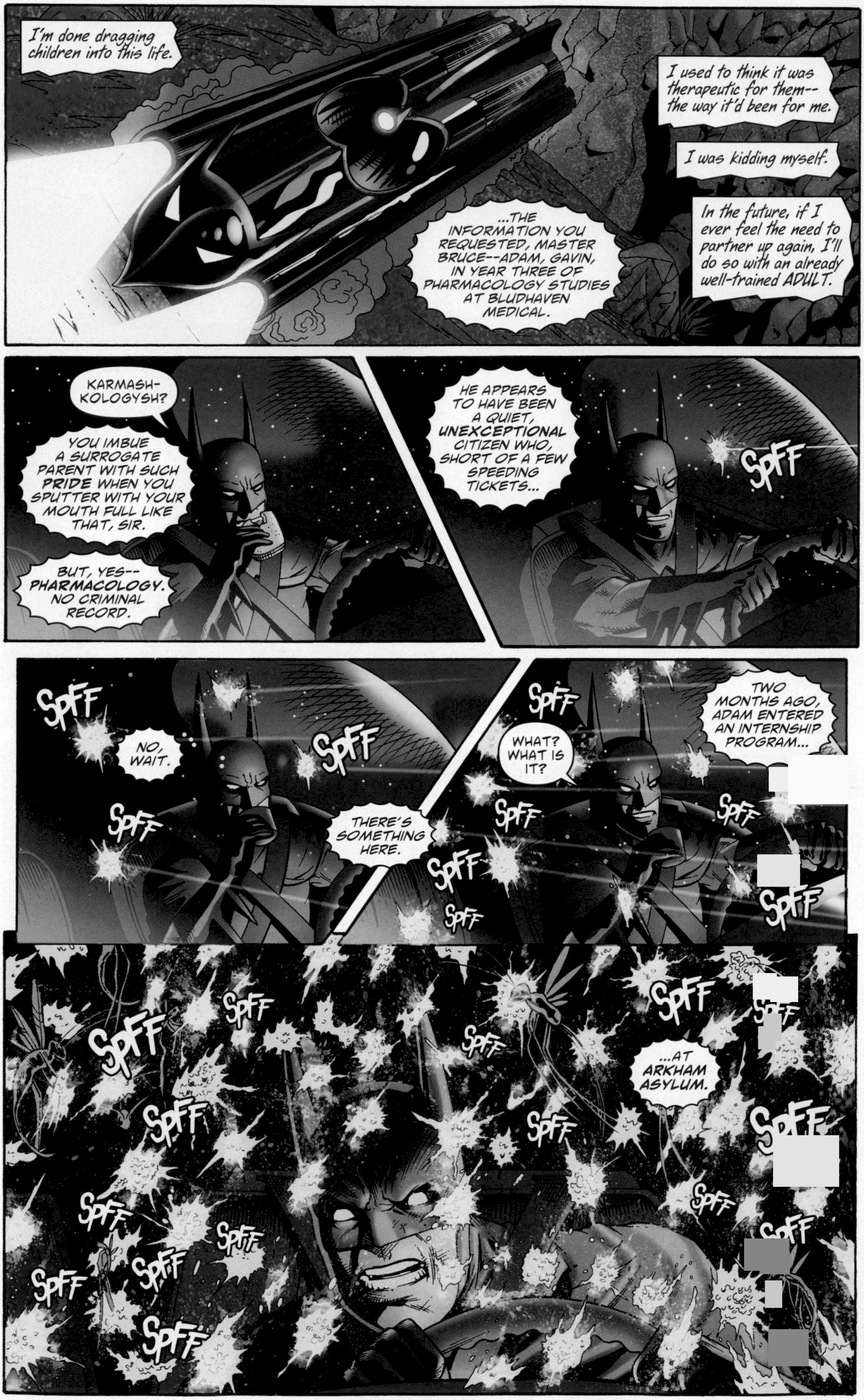

I'm done dragging children into this life.
I used to think it was therapeutic for them--the way it'd been for me.
I was kidding myself.
In the future, if I ever feel the need to partner up again, I'll do so with an already well-trained ADULT.
...THE INFORMATION YOU REQUESTED, MASTER BRUCE--ADAM, GAVIN, IN YEAR THREE OF PHARMACOLOGY STUDIES AT BLUDHAVEN MEDICAL.
KARMASH-KOLOGYSH?
YOU IMBUE A SURROGATE PARENT WITH SUCH PRIDE WHEN YOU SPUTTER WITH YOUR MOUTH FULL LIKE THAT, SIR.
BUT, YES--PHARMACOLOGY. NO CRIMINAL RECORD.
HE APPEARS TO HAVE BEEN A QUIET, UNEXCEPTIONAL CITIZEN WHO, SHORT OF A FEW SPEEDING TICKETS...
SPFF
SPFF
NO, WAIT.
SPFF
SPFF
THERE'S SOMETHING HERE.
SPFF
WHAT? WHAT IS IT?
TWO MONTHS AGO, ADAM ENTERED AN INTERNSHIP PROGRAM...
SPFF
SPFF
SPFF
SPFF
...AT ARKHAM ASYLUM.
SPFF
SPFF
SPFF
SPFF
SPFF
SPFF

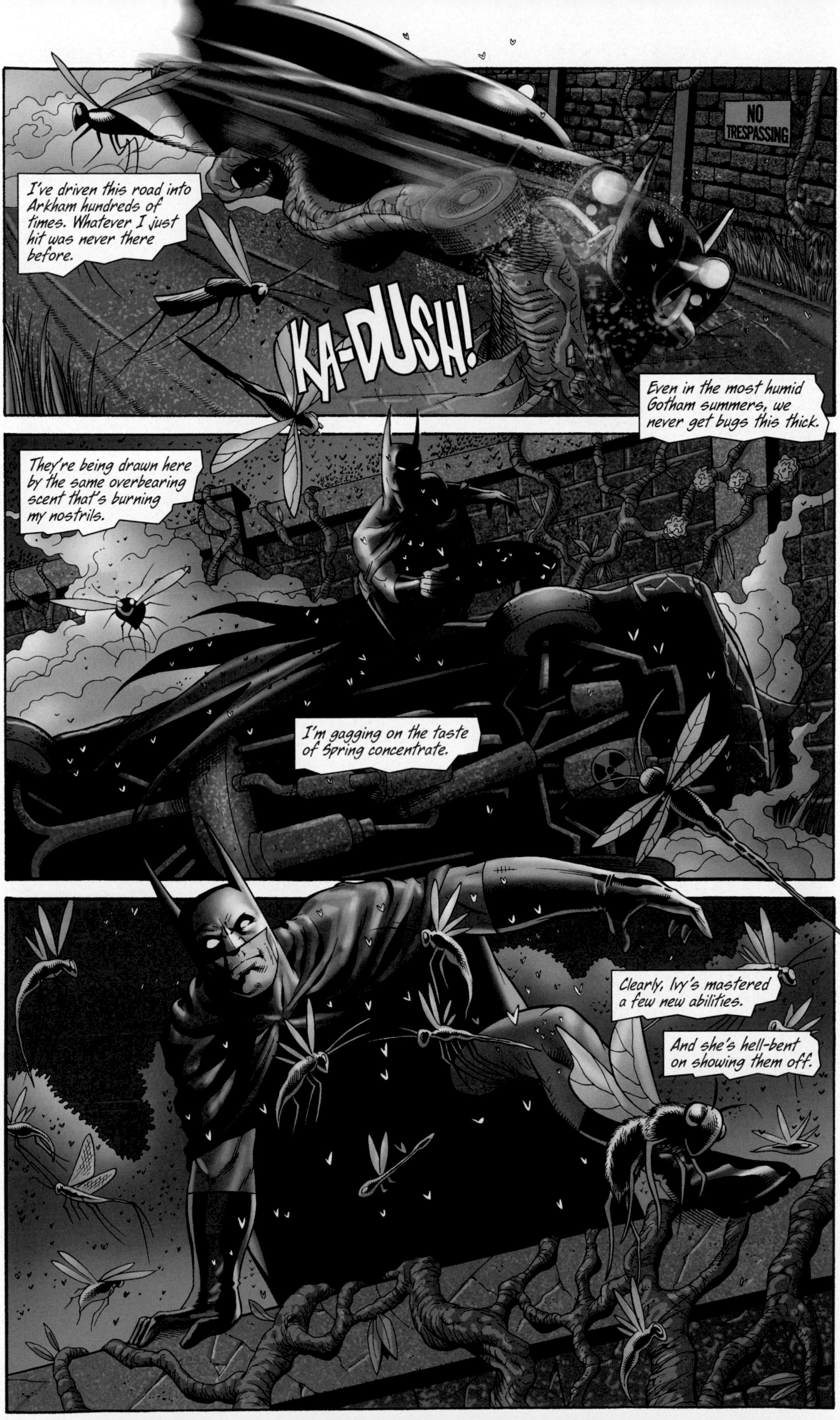
NO TRESPASSING
I've driven this road into Arkham hundreds of times. Whatever I just hit was never there before.
KA-DUSH!
Even in the most humid Gotham summers, we never get bugs this thick.
They're being drawn here by the same overbearing scent that's burning my nostrils.
I'm gagging on the taste of Spring concentrate.
Clearly, Ivy's mastered a few new abilities.
And she's hell-bent on showing them off.

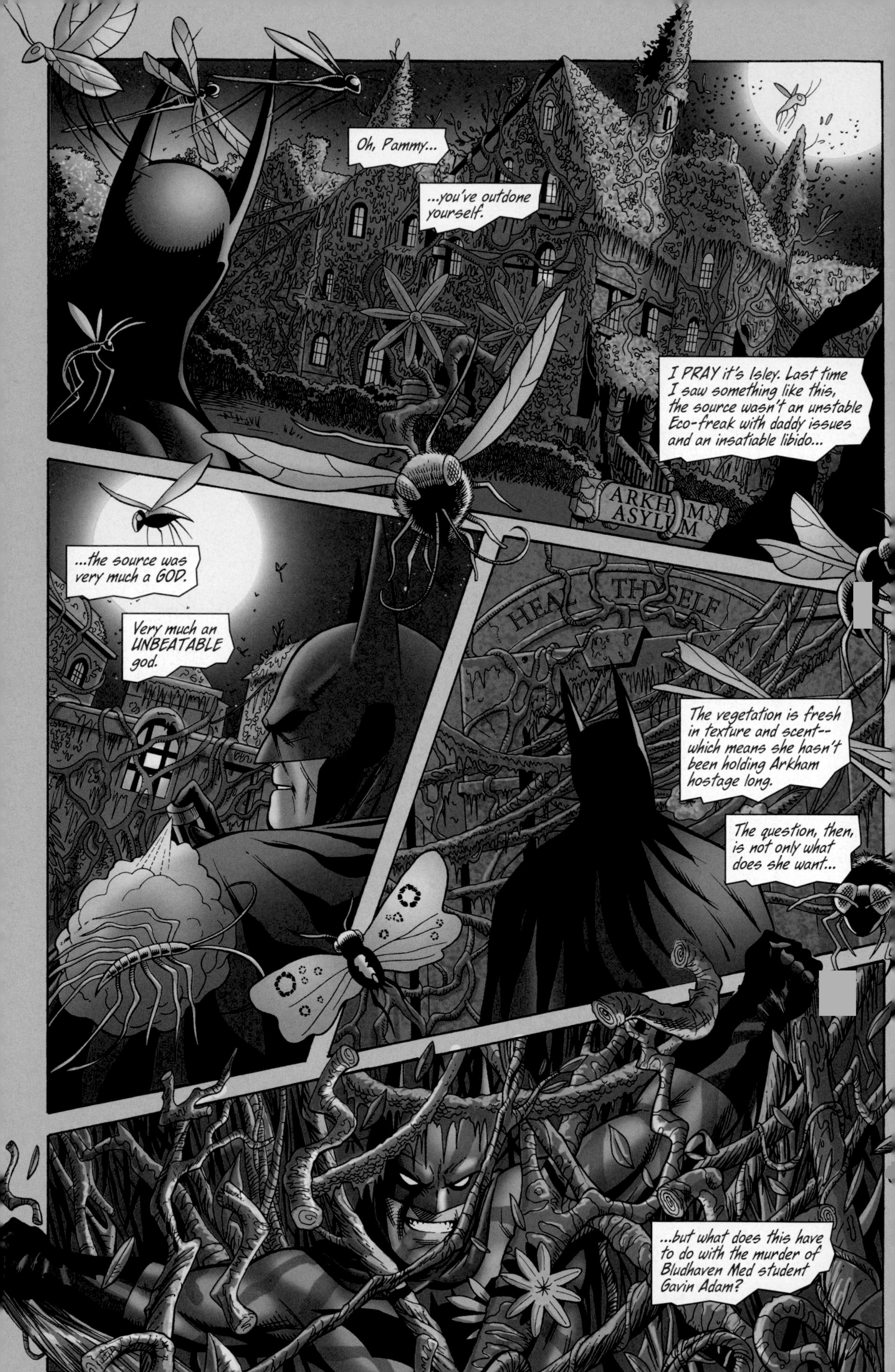
Oh, Pammy...
...you've outdone yourself.
I PRAY it's Isley. Last time I saw something like this, the source wasn't an unstable Eco-freak with daddy issues and an insatiable libido...
ARKHAM ASYLUM
...the source was very much a GOD.
Very much an UNBEATABLE god.
HEAL THYSELF
The vegetation is fresh in texture and scent--which means she hasn't been holding Arkham hostage long.
The question, then, is not only what does she want...
...but what does this have to do with the murder of Bludhaven Med student Gavin Adam?

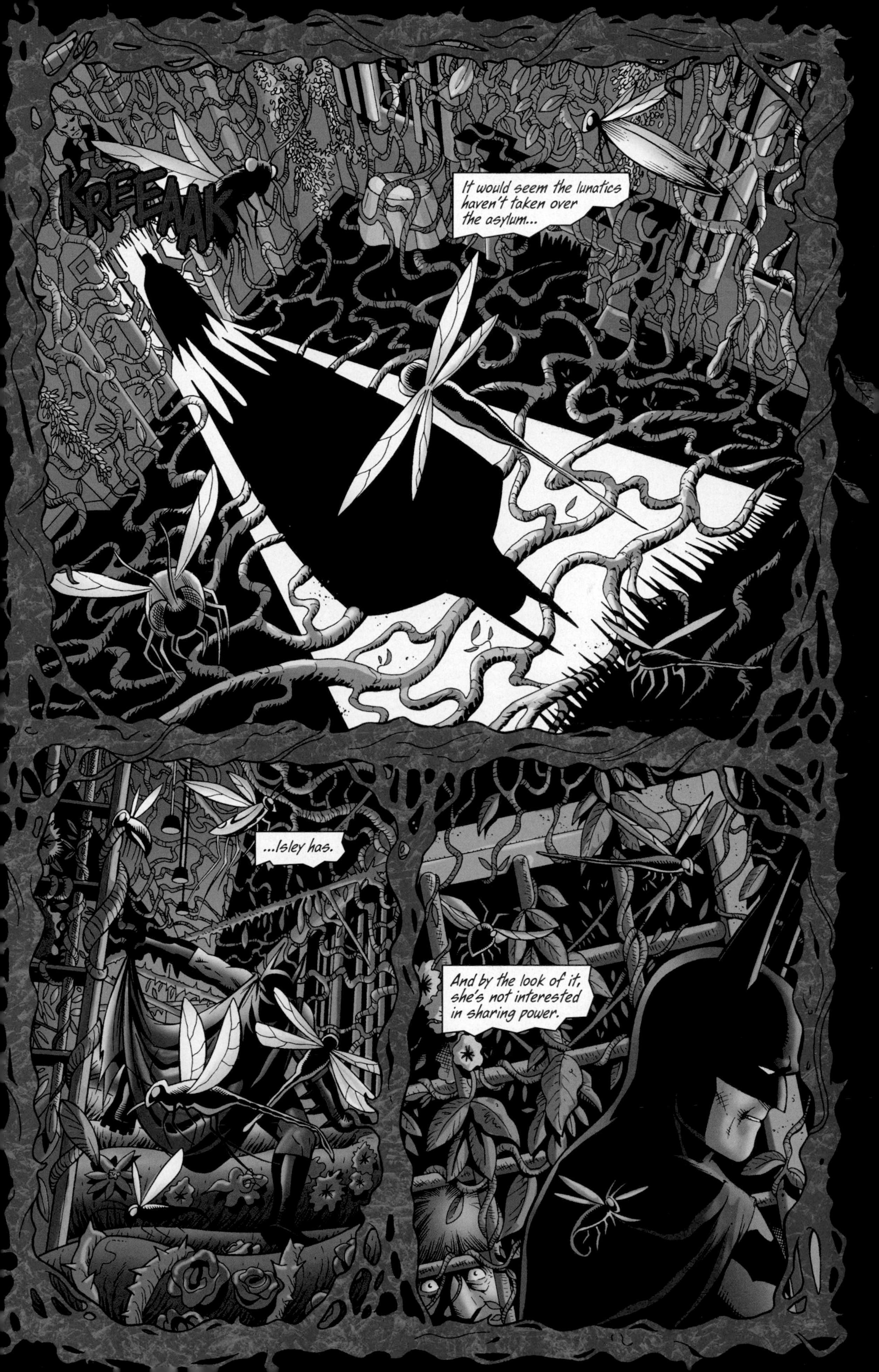
KREEAAK
It would seem the lunatics haven't taken over the asylum...
...Isley has.
And by the look of it, she's not interested in sharing power.

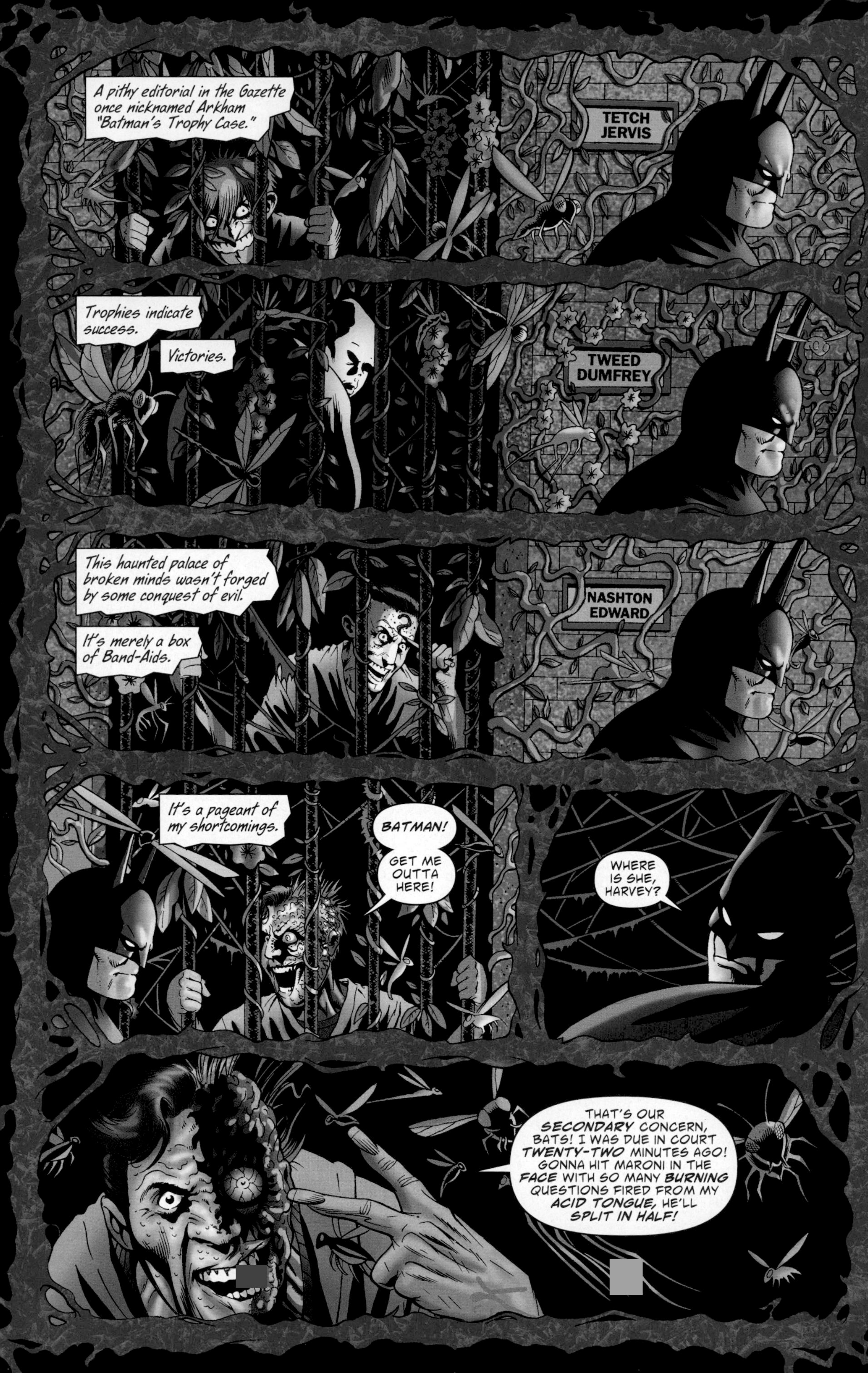
A pithy editorial in the Gazette once nicknamed Arkham "Batman's Trophy Case."
TETCH JERVIS
Trophies indicate success.
Victories.
TWEED DUMFREY
This haunted palace of broken minds wasn't forged by some conquest of evil.
It's merely a box of Band-Aids.
NASHTON EDWARD
It's a pageant of my shortcomings.
BATMAN!
GET ME OUTTA HERE!
WHERE IS SHE, HARVEY?
THAT'S OUR SECONDARY CONCERN, BATS! I WAS DUE IN COURT TWENTY-TWO MINUTES AGO! GONNA HIT MARONI IN THE FACE WITH SO MANY BURNING QUESTIONS FIRED FROM MY ACID TONGUE, HE'LL SPLIT IN HALF!

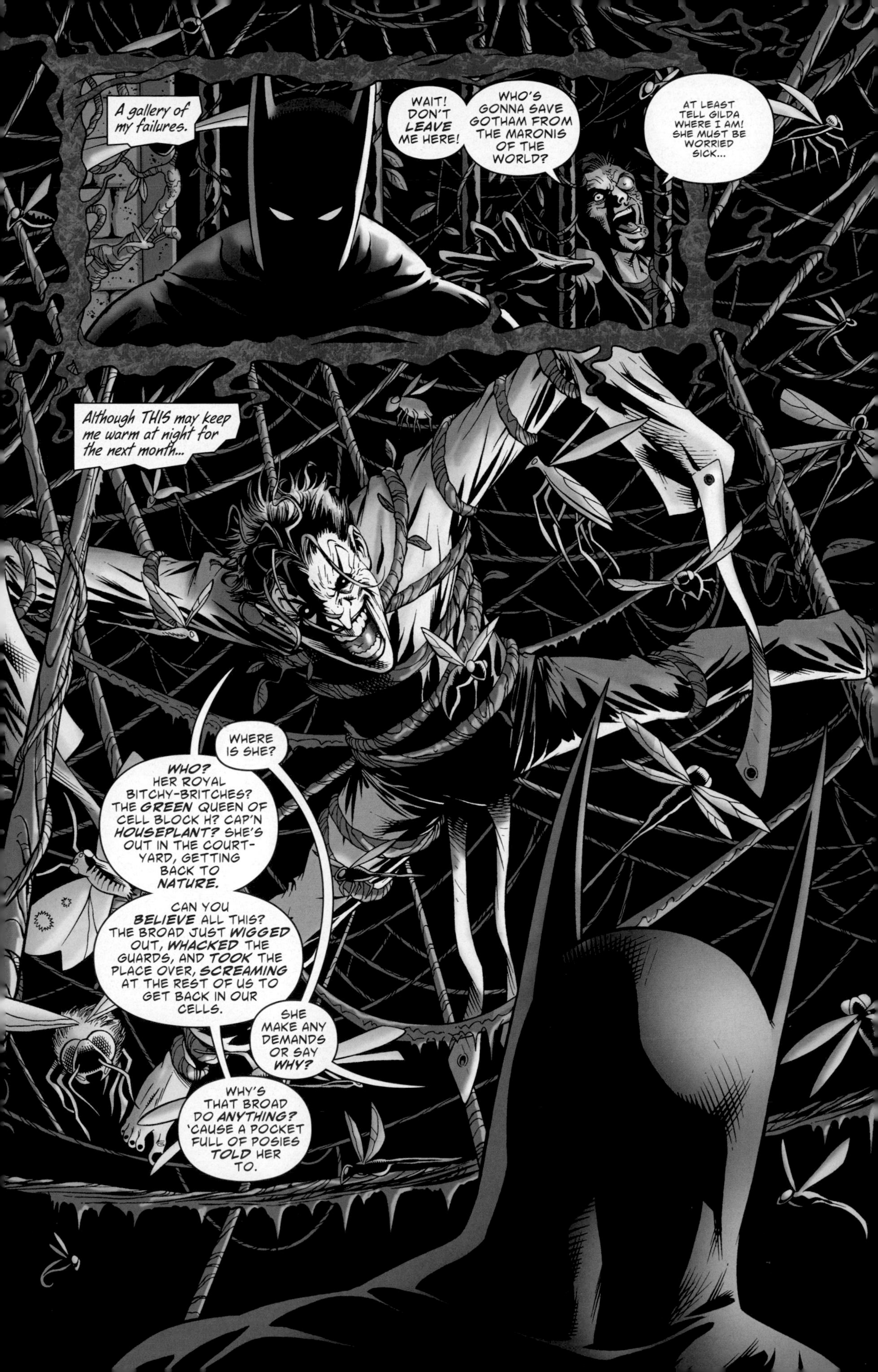
A gallery of my failures.
WAIT! DON'T LEAVE ME HERE!
WHO'S GONNA SAVE GOTHAM FROM THE MARONIS OF THE WORLD?
AT LEAST TELL GILDA WHERE I AM! SHE MUST BE WORRIED SICK...
Although THIS may keep me warm at night for the next month...
WHERE IS SHE?
WHO? HER ROYAL BITCHY-BRITCHES? THE GREEN QUEEN OF CELL BLOCK H? CAP'N HOUSEPLANT? SHE'S OUT IN THE COURTYARD, GETTING BACK TO NATURE.
CAN YOU BELIEVE ALL THIS? THE BROAD JUST WIGGED OUT, WHACKED THE GUARDS, AND TOOK THE PLACE OVER, SCREAMING AT THE REST OF US TO GET BACK IN OUR CELLS.
SHE MAKE ANY DEMANDS OR SAY WHY?
WHY'S THAT BROAD DO ANYTHING? 'CAUSE A POCKET FULL OF POSIES TOLD HER TO.

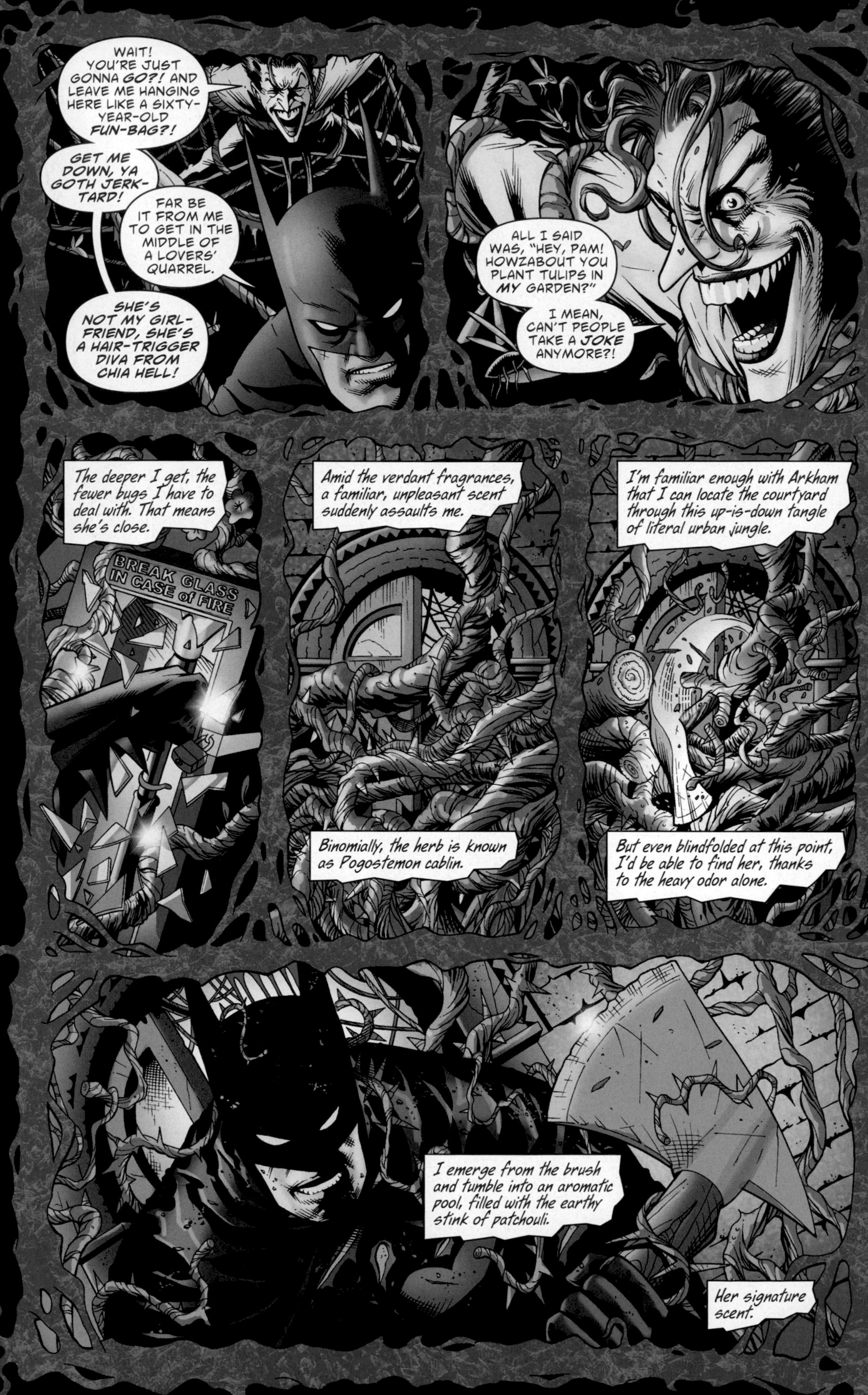
WAIT! YOU'RE JUST GONNA GO?! AND LEAVE ME HANGING HERE LIKE A SIXTY-YEAR-OLD FUN-BAG?!
GET ME DOWN, YA GOTH JERK-TARD!
FAR BE IT FROM ME TO GET IN THE MIDDLE OF A LOVERS' QUARREL.
SHE'S NOT MY GIRLFRIEND, SHE'S A HAIR-TRIGGER DIVA FROM CHIA HELL!
ALL I SAID WAS, "HEY, PAM! HOWZABOUT YOU PLANT TULIPS IN MY GARDEN?"
I MEAN, CAN'T PEOPLE TAKE A JOKE ANYMORE?!
The deeper I get, the fewer bugs I have to deal with. That means she's close.
BREAK GLASS IN CASE of FIRE
Amid the verdant fragrances, a familiar, unpleasant scent suddenly assaults me.
Binomially, the herb is known as Pogostemon cablin.
I'm familiar enough with Arkham that I can locate the courtyard through this up-is-down tangle of literal urban jungle.
But even blindfolded at this point, I'd be able to find her, thanks to the heavy odor alone.
I emerge from the brush and tumble into an aromatic pool, filled with the earthy stink of patchouli.
Her signature scent.

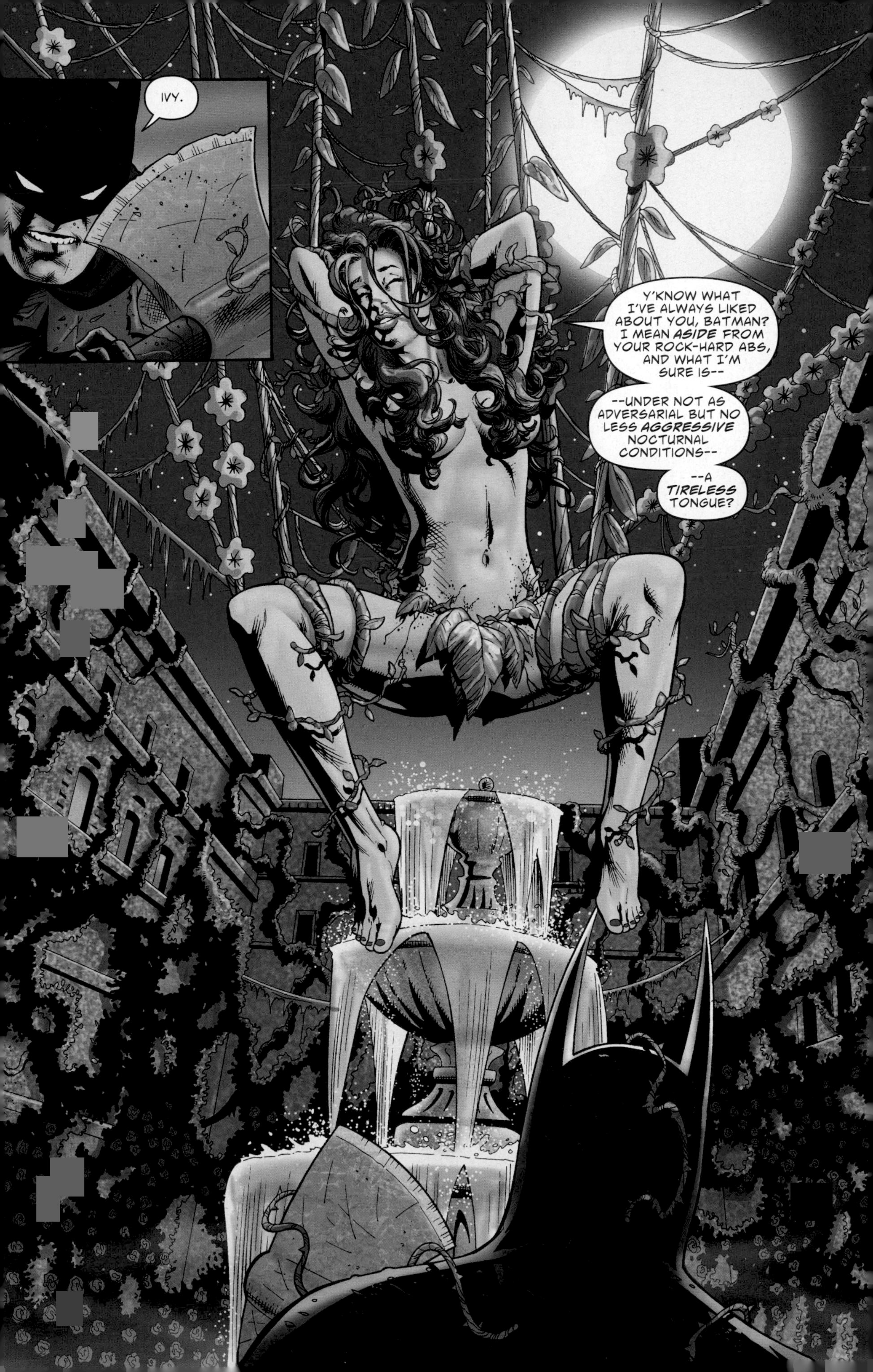
IVY.
Y'KNOW WHAT I'VE ALWAYS LIKED ABOUT YOU, BATMAN? I MEAN *ASIDE* FROM YOUR ROCK-HARD ABS, AND WHAT I'M SURE IS--
--UNDER NOT AS ADVERSARIAL BUT NO LESS *AGGRESSIVE* NOCTURNAL CONDITIONS--
--A *TIRELESS* TONGUE?

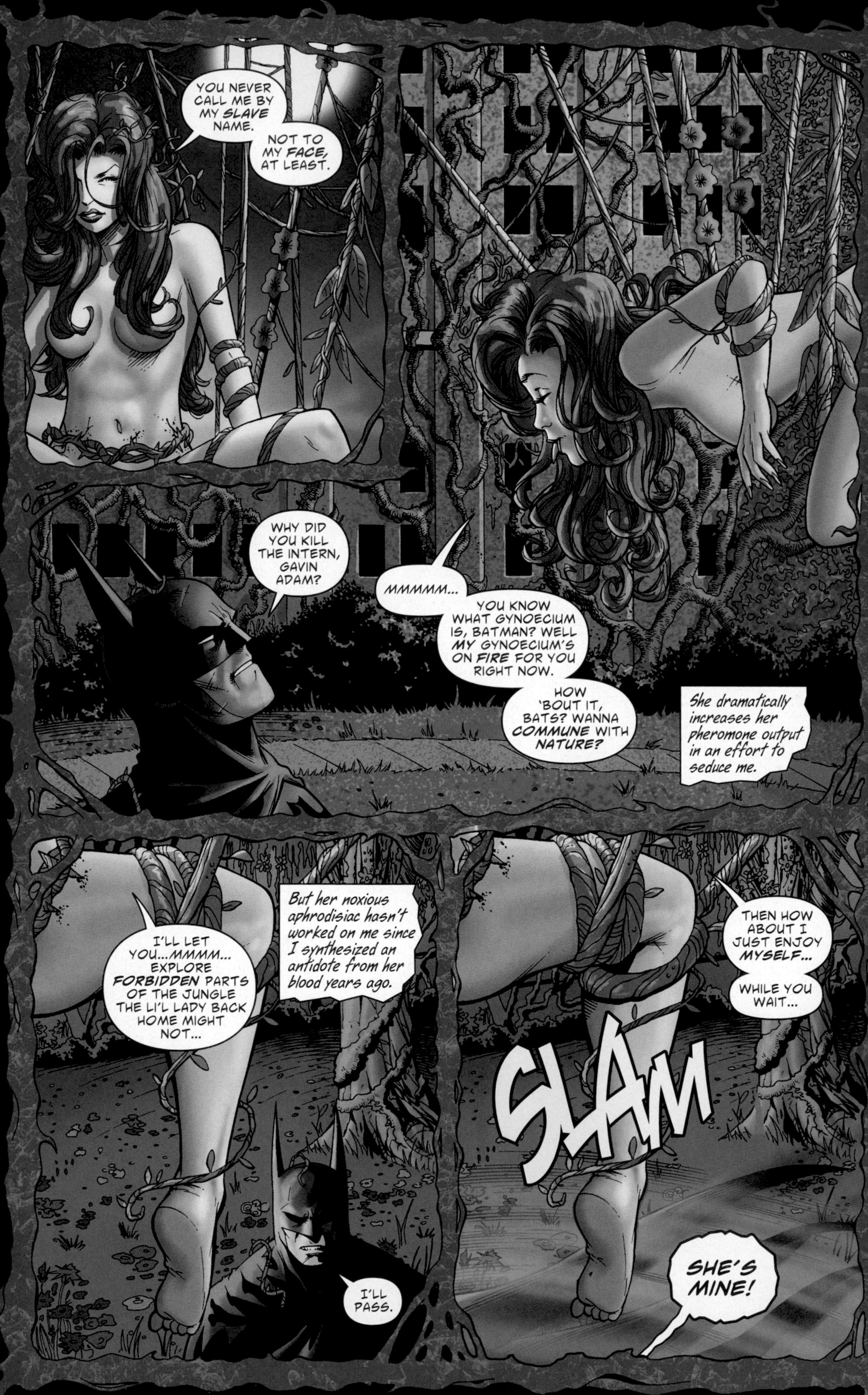

YOU NEVER CALL ME BY MY SLAVE NAME.
NOT TO MY FACE, AT LEAST.
WHY DID YOU KILL THE INTERN, GAVIN ADAM?
MMMMM...
YOU KNOW WHAT GYNOECIUM IS, BATMAN? WELL MY GYNOECIUM'S ON FIRE FOR YOU RIGHT NOW.
HOW 'BOUT IT, BATS? WANNA COMMUNE WITH NATURE?
She dramatically increases her pheromone output in an effort to seduce me.
I'LL LET YOU...MMMM... EXPLORE FORBIDDEN PARTS OF THE JUNGLE THE LI'L LADY BACK HOME MIGHT NOT...
But her noxious aphrodisiac hasn't worked on me since I synthesized an antidote from her blood years ago.
I'LL PASS.
THEN HOW ABOUT I JUST ENJOY MYSELF...
WHILE YOU WAIT...
SLAM
SHE'S MINE!

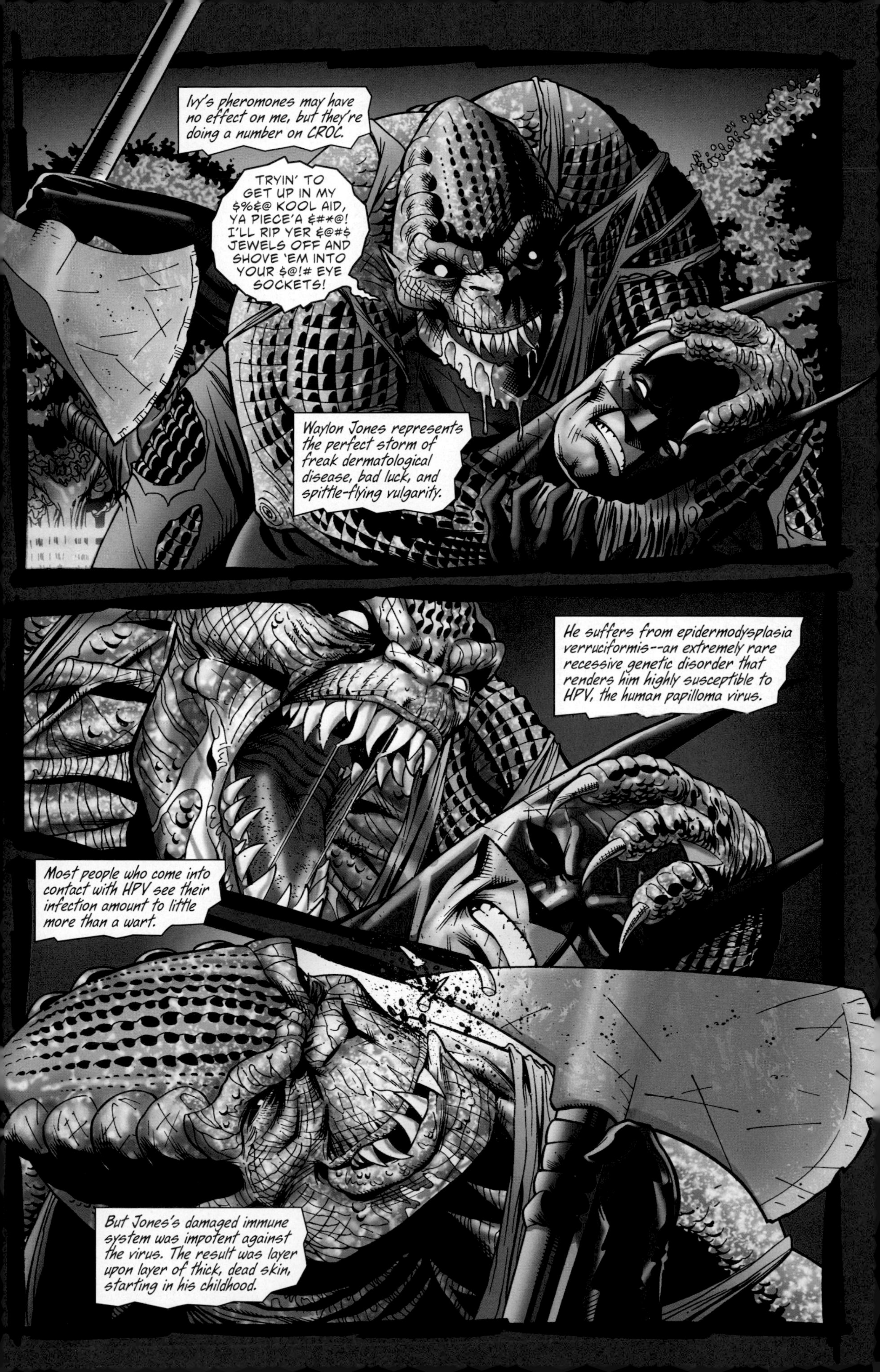
Ivy's pheromones may have no effect on me, but they're doing a number on CROC.
TRYIN' TO GET UP IN MY $%&@ KOOL AID, YA PIECE'A &#*@! I'LL RIP YER &@#$ JEWELS OFF AND SHOVE 'EM INTO YOUR $@!# EYE SOCKETS!
Waylon Jones represents the perfect storm of freak dermatological disease, bad luck, and spittle-flying vulgarity.
He suffers from epidermodysplasia verruciformis--an extremely rare recessive genetic disorder that renders him highly susceptible to HPV, the human papilloma virus.
Most people who come into contact with HPV see their infection amount to little more than a wart.
But Jones's damaged immune system was impotent against the virus. The result was layer upon layer of thick, dead skin, starting in his childhood.

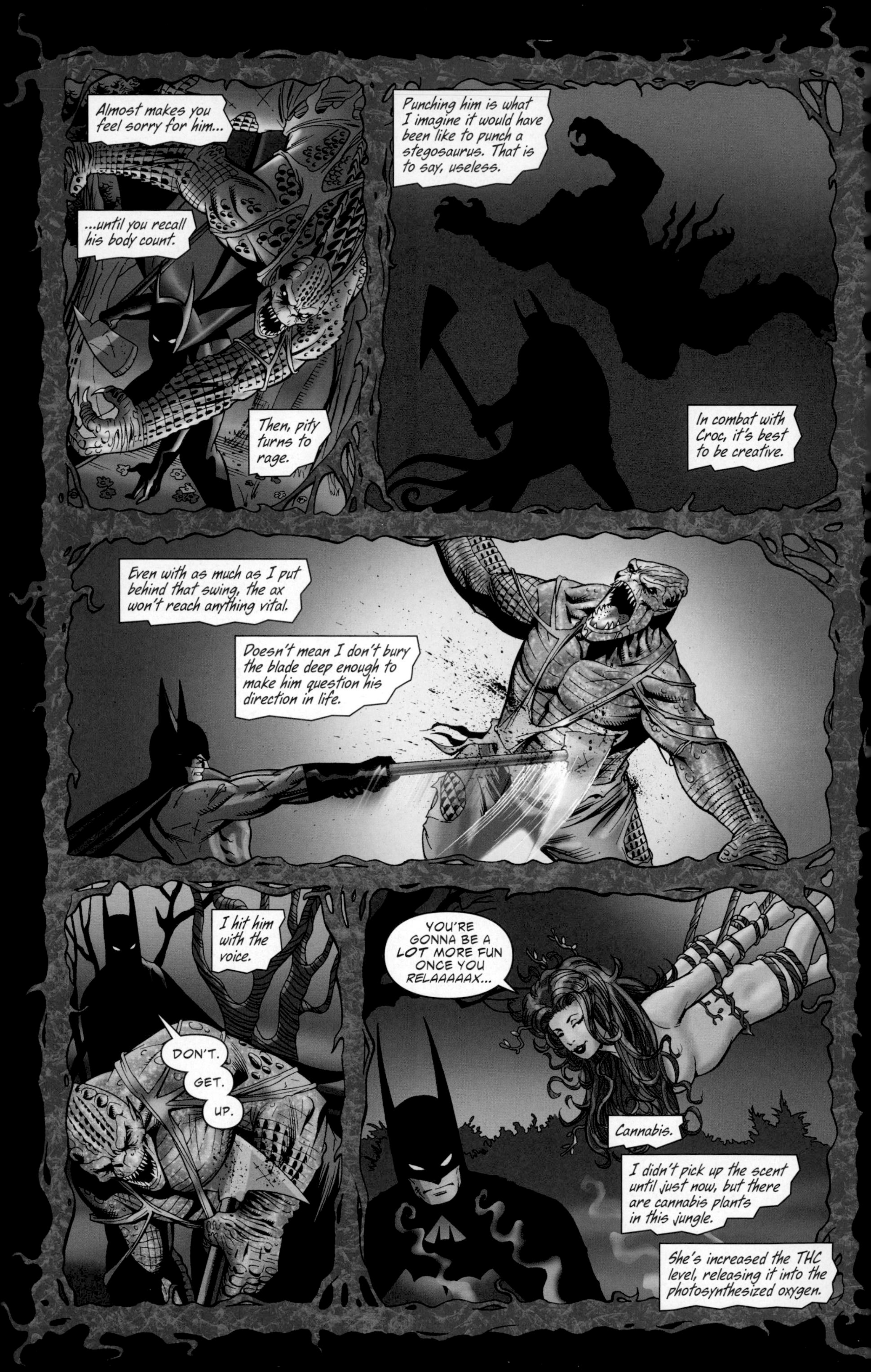

Almost makes you feel sorry for him...
...until you recall his body count.
Then, pity turns to rage.
Punching him is what I imagine it would have been like to punch a stegosaurus. That is to say, useless.
In combat with Croc, it's best to be creative.
Even with as much as I put behind that swing, the ax won't reach anything vital.
Doesn't mean I don't bury the blade deep enough to make him question his direction in life.
I hit him with the voice.
DON'T.
GET.
UP.
YOU'RE GONNA BE A LOT MORE FUN ONCE YOU RELAAAAAAX...
Cannabis.
I didn't pick up the scent until just now, but there are cannabis plants in this jungle.
She's increased the THC level, releasing it into the photosynthesized oxygen.

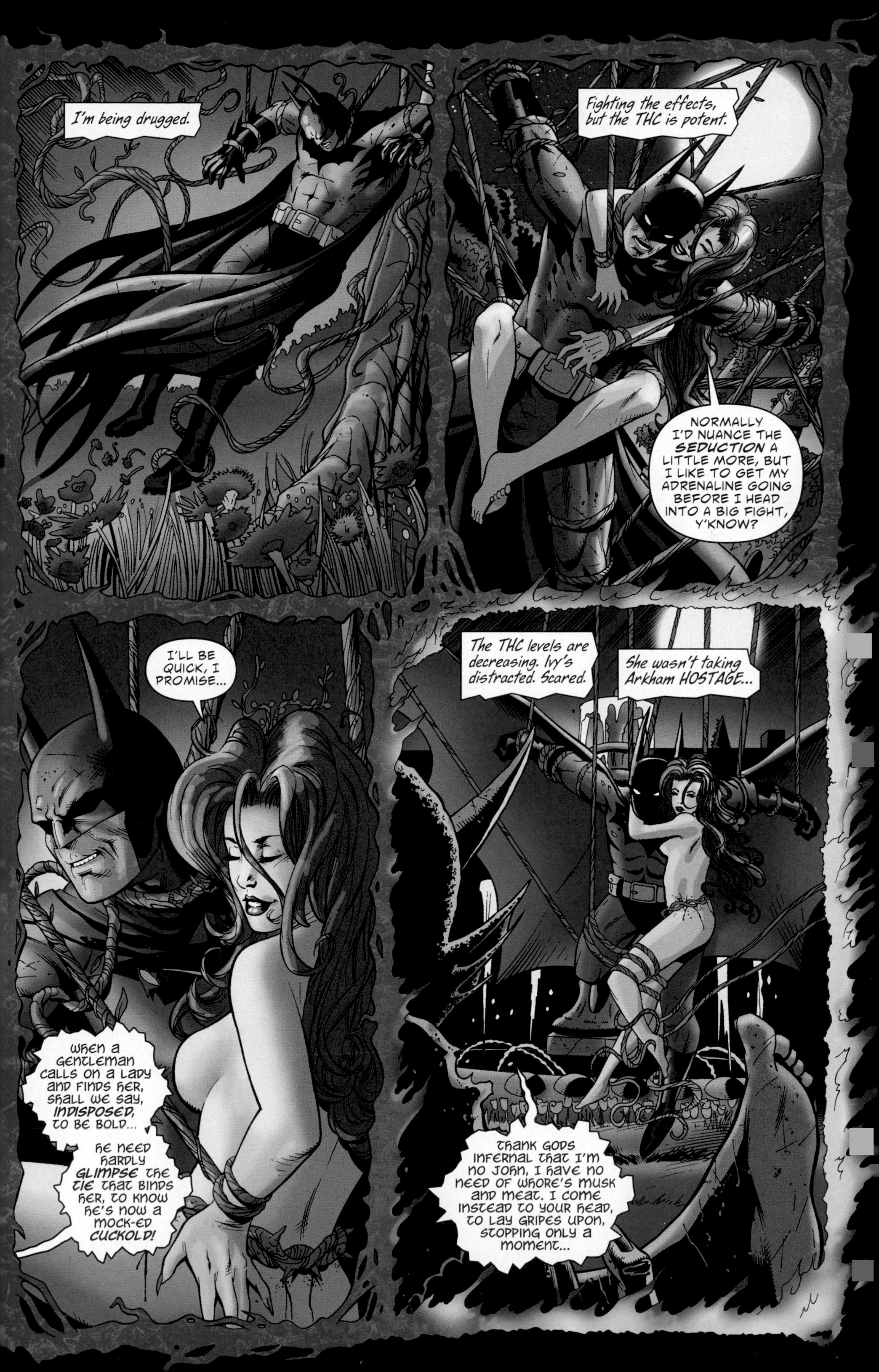
I'm being drugged.
Fighting the effects, but the THC is potent.
NORMALLY I'D NUANCE THE SEDUCTION A LITTLE MORE, BUT I LIKE TO GET MY ADRENALINE GOING BEFORE I HEAD INTO A BIG FIGHT, Y'KNOW?
I'LL BE QUICK, I PROMISE...
WHEN A GENTLEMAN CALLS ON A LADY AND FINDS HER, SHALL WE SAY, INDISPOSED, TO BE BOLD...
HE NEED HARDLY GLIMPSE THE TIE THAT BINDS HER, TO KNOW HE'S NOW A MOCK-ED CUCKOLD!
The THC levels are decreasing. Ivy's distracted. Scared.
She wasn't taking Arkham HOSTAGE...
THANK GODS INFERNAL THAT I'M NO JOHN, I HAVE NO NEED OF WHORE'S MUSK AND MEAT. I COME INSTEAD TO YOUR HEAD, TO LAY GRIPES UPON, STOPPING ONLY A MOMENT...

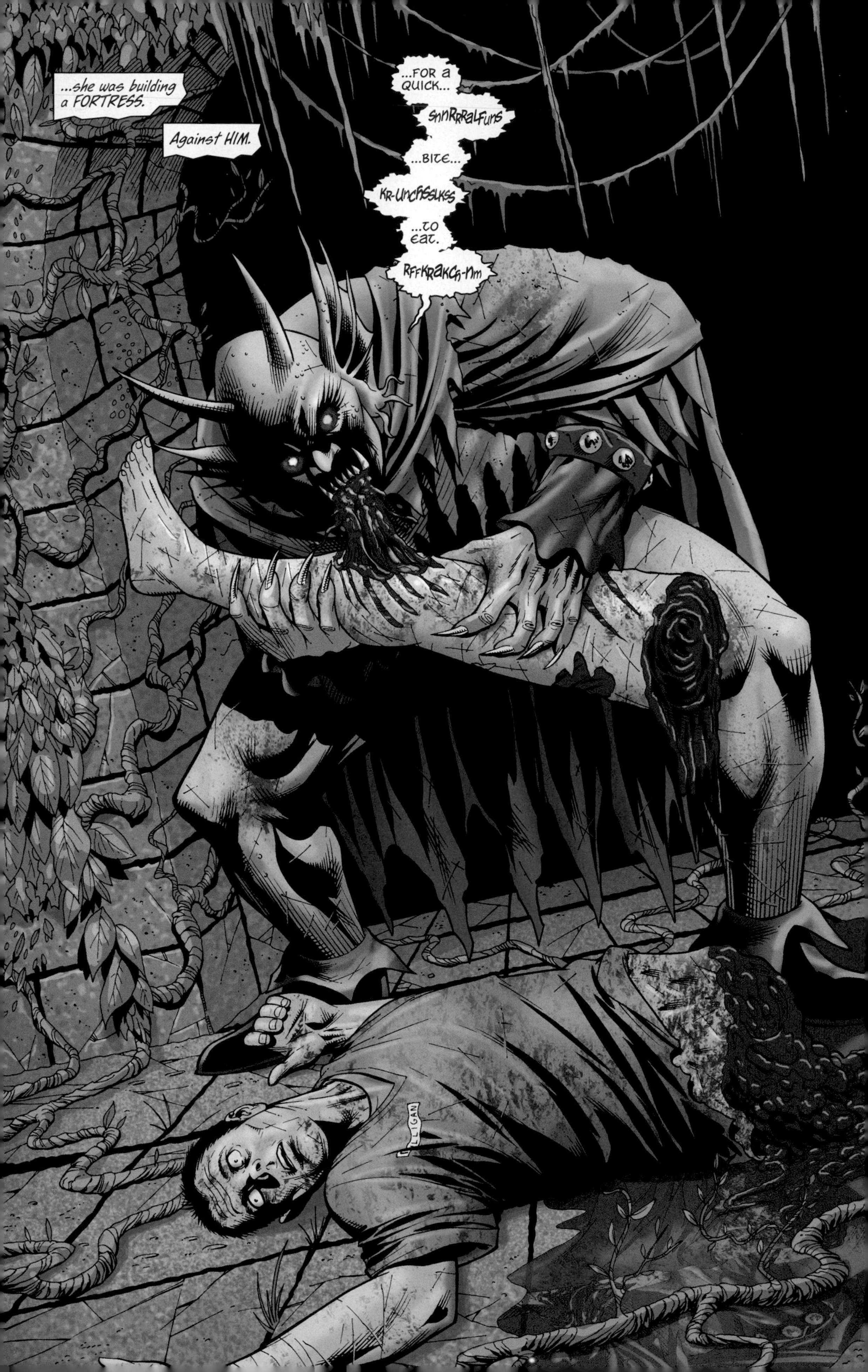
...she was building a FORTRESS.
Against HIM.
...FOR a QUICK...
SNNRRRALFUNS
...BITE...
KR-UNCHSSLKSS
...TO EAT.
RFFKRAKCH-NM

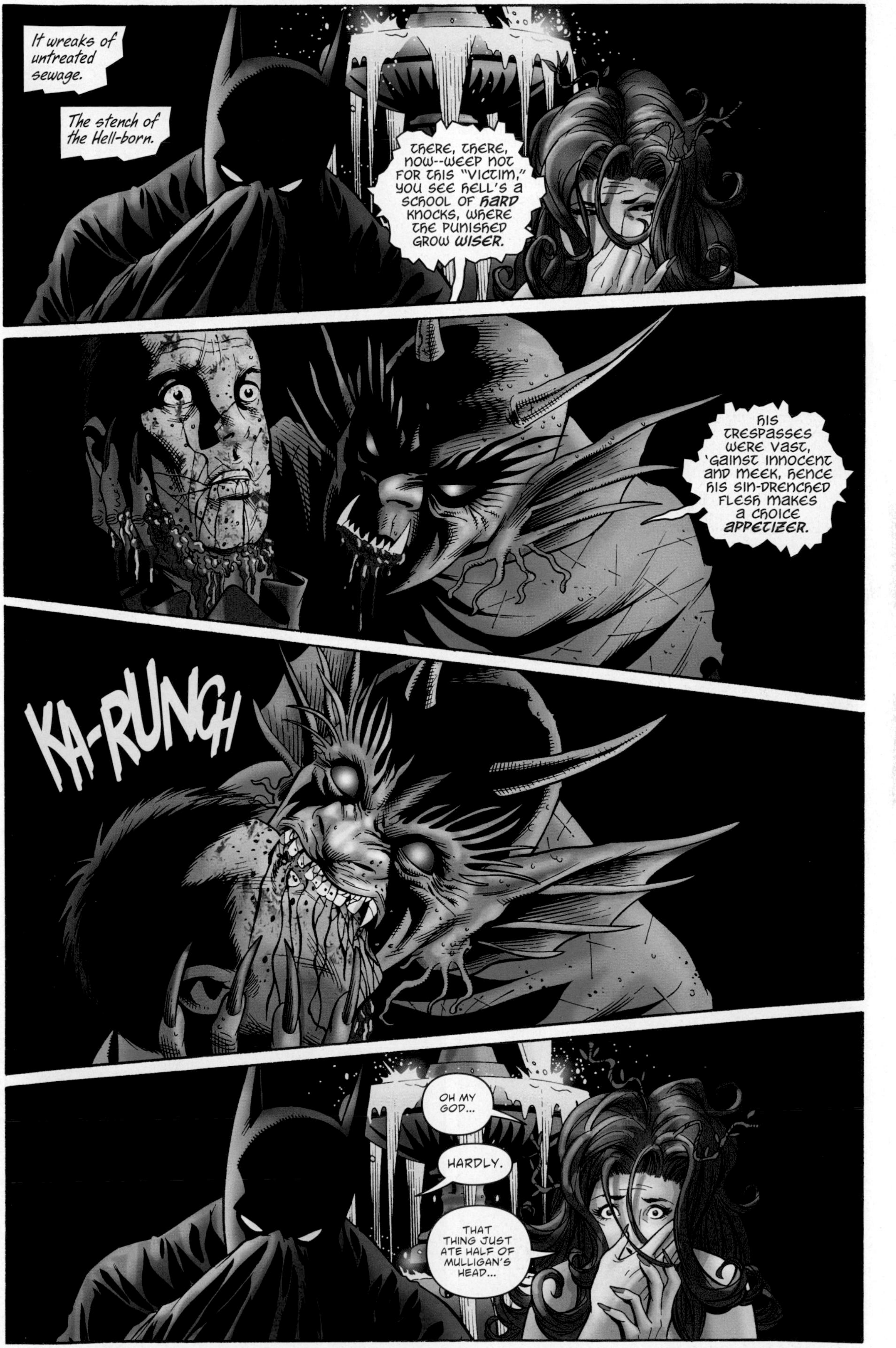
It wreaks of untreated sewage.
The stench of the Hell-born.
THERE, THERE, NOW--WEEP NOT FOR THIS "VICTIM," YOU SEE HELL'S A SCHOOL OF HARD KNOCKS, WHERE THE PUNISHED GROW WISER.
HIS TRESPASSES WERE VAST, 'GAINST INNOCENT AND MEEK, HENCE HIS SIN-DRENCHED FLESH MAKES A CHOICE APPETIZER.
KA-RUNCH
OH MY GOD...
HARDLY.
THAT THING JUST ATE HALF OF MULLIGAN'S HEAD...

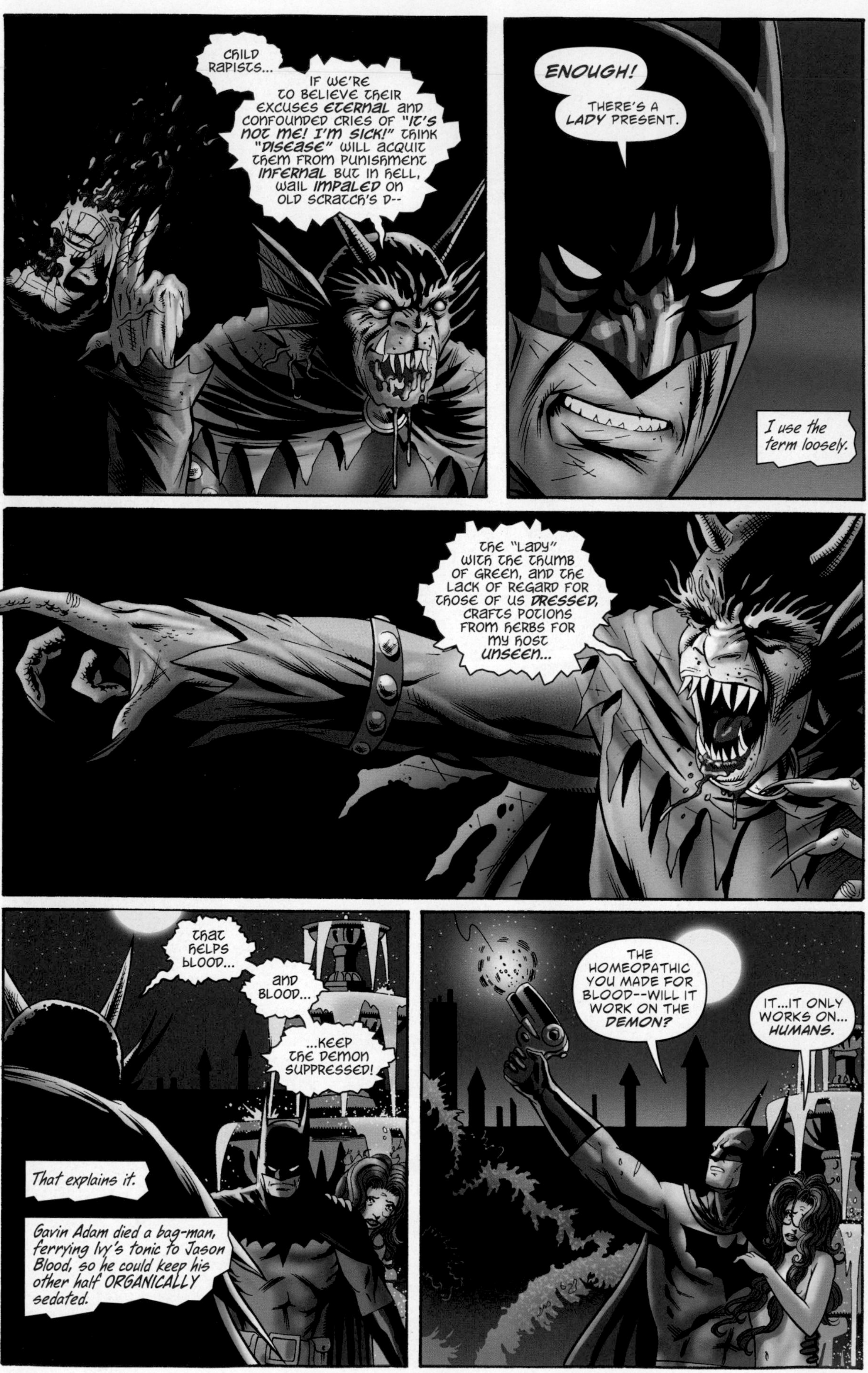
CHILD RAPISTS...
IF WE'RE TO BELIEVE THEIR EXCUSES ETERNAL AND CONFOUNDED CRIES OF "IT'S NOT ME! I'M SICK!" THINK "DISEASE" WILL ACQUIT THEM FROM PUNISHMENT INFERNAL BUT IN HELL, WAIL IMPALED ON OLD SCRATCH'S D--
ENOUGH!
THERE'S A LADY PRESENT.
I use the term loosely.
THE "LADY" WITH THE THUMB OF GREEN, AND THE LACK OF REGARD FOR THOSE OF US DRESSED, CRAFTS POTIONS FROM HERBS FOR MY HOST UNSEEN...
THAT HELPS BLOOD...
AND BLOOD...
...KEEP THE DEMON SUPPRESSED!
That explains it.
Gavin Adam died a bag-man, ferrying Ivy's tonic to Jason Blood, so he could keep his other half ORGANICALLY sedated.
THE HOMEOPATHIC YOU MADE FOR BLOOD--WILL IT WORK ON THE DEMON?
IT...IT ONLY WORKS ON... HUMANS.

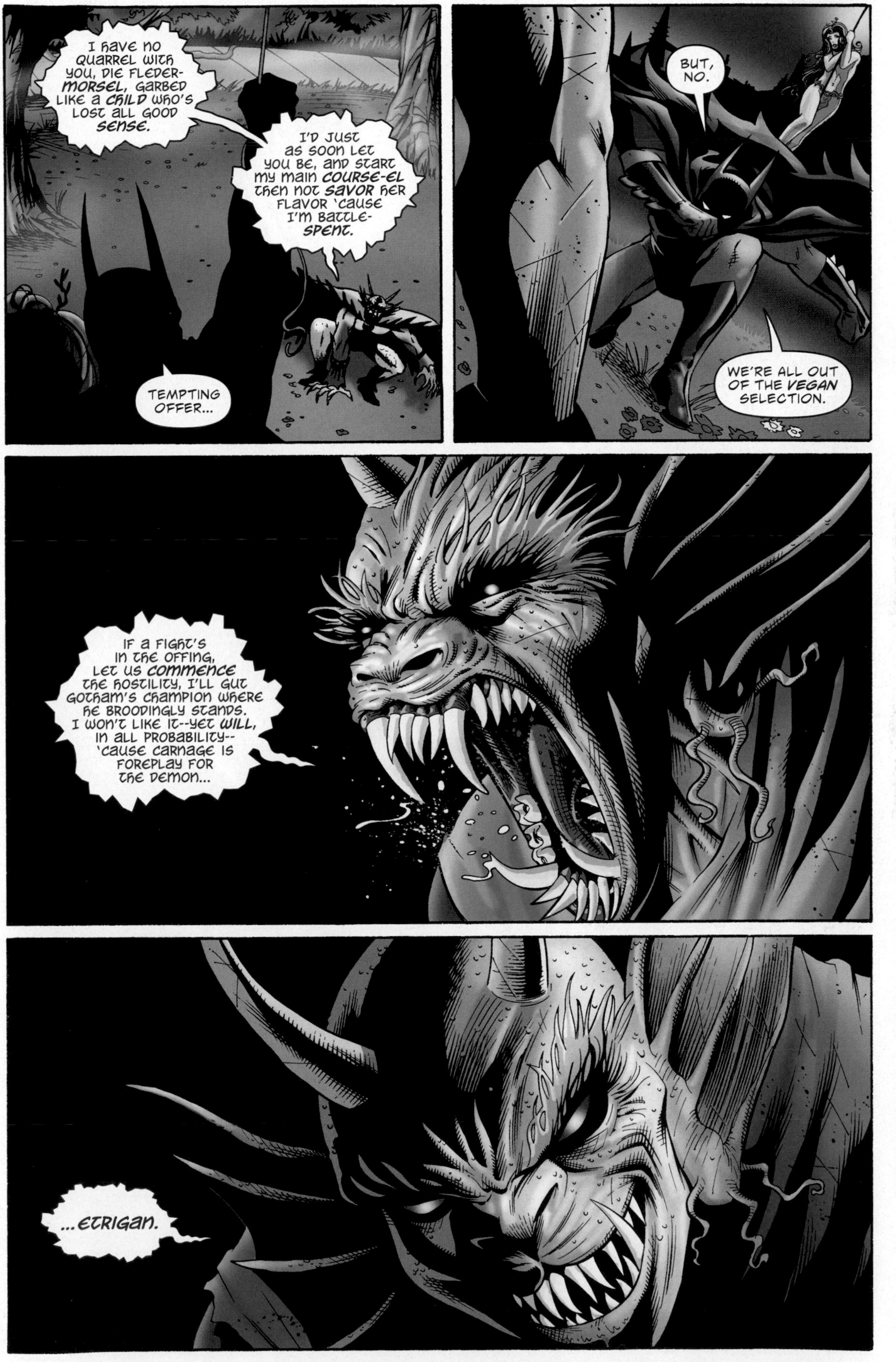
I have no quarrel with you, Die Fleder-morsel, garbed like a child who's lost all good sense.
I'd just as soon let you be, and start my main course-el then not savor her flavor 'cause I'm battle-spent.
TEMPTING OFFER...
BUT, NO.
WE'RE ALL OUT OF THE VEGAN SELECTION.
If a fight's in the offing, let us commence the hostility, I'll gut Gotham's champion where he broodingly stands. I won't like it--yet will, in all probability-- 'cause carnage is foreplay for the demon...
...Etrigan.

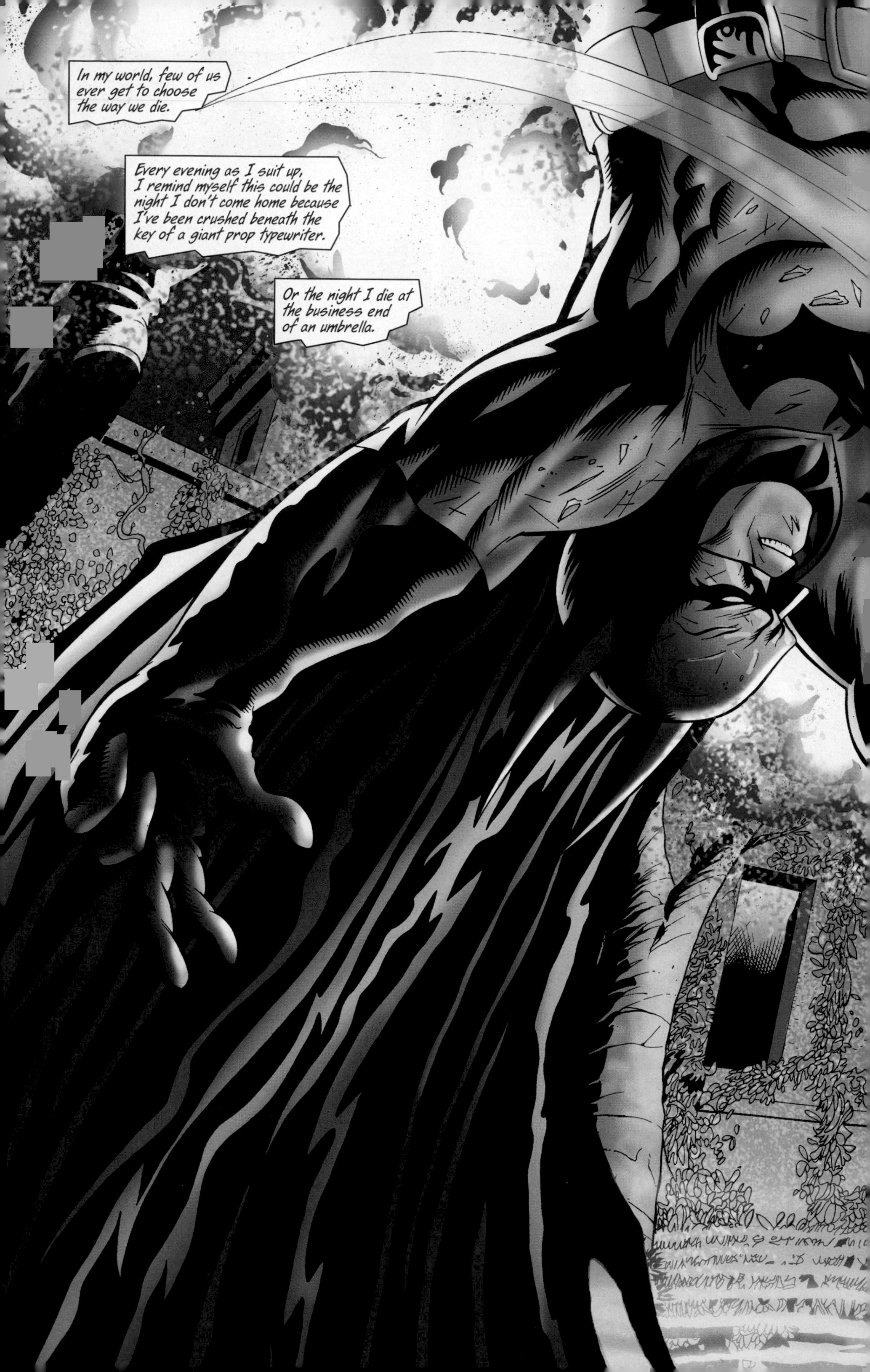

In my world, few of us ever get to choose the way we die.
Every evening as I suit up, I remind myself this could be the night I don't come home because I've been crushed beneath the key of a giant prop typewriter.
Or the night I die at the business end of an umbrella.

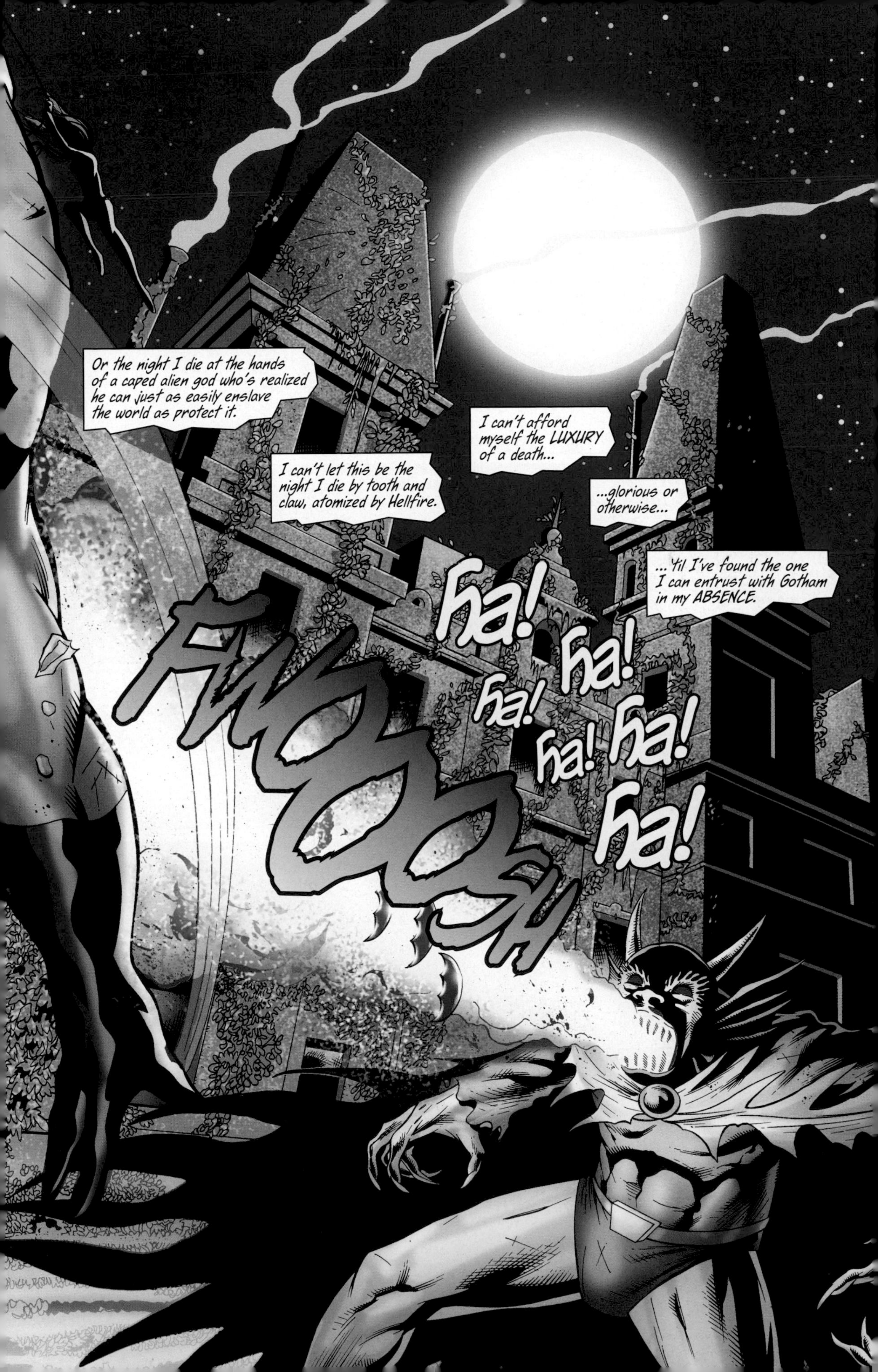
Or the night I die at the hands of a caped alien god who's realized he can just as easily enslave the world as protect it.
I can't let this be the night I die by tooth and claw, atomized by Hellfire.
I can't afford myself the LUXURY of a death...
...glorious or otherwise...
...'til I've found the one I can entrust with Gotham in my ABSENCE.
FWOOOSH
Ha! Ha! Ha! Ha! Ha! Ha!

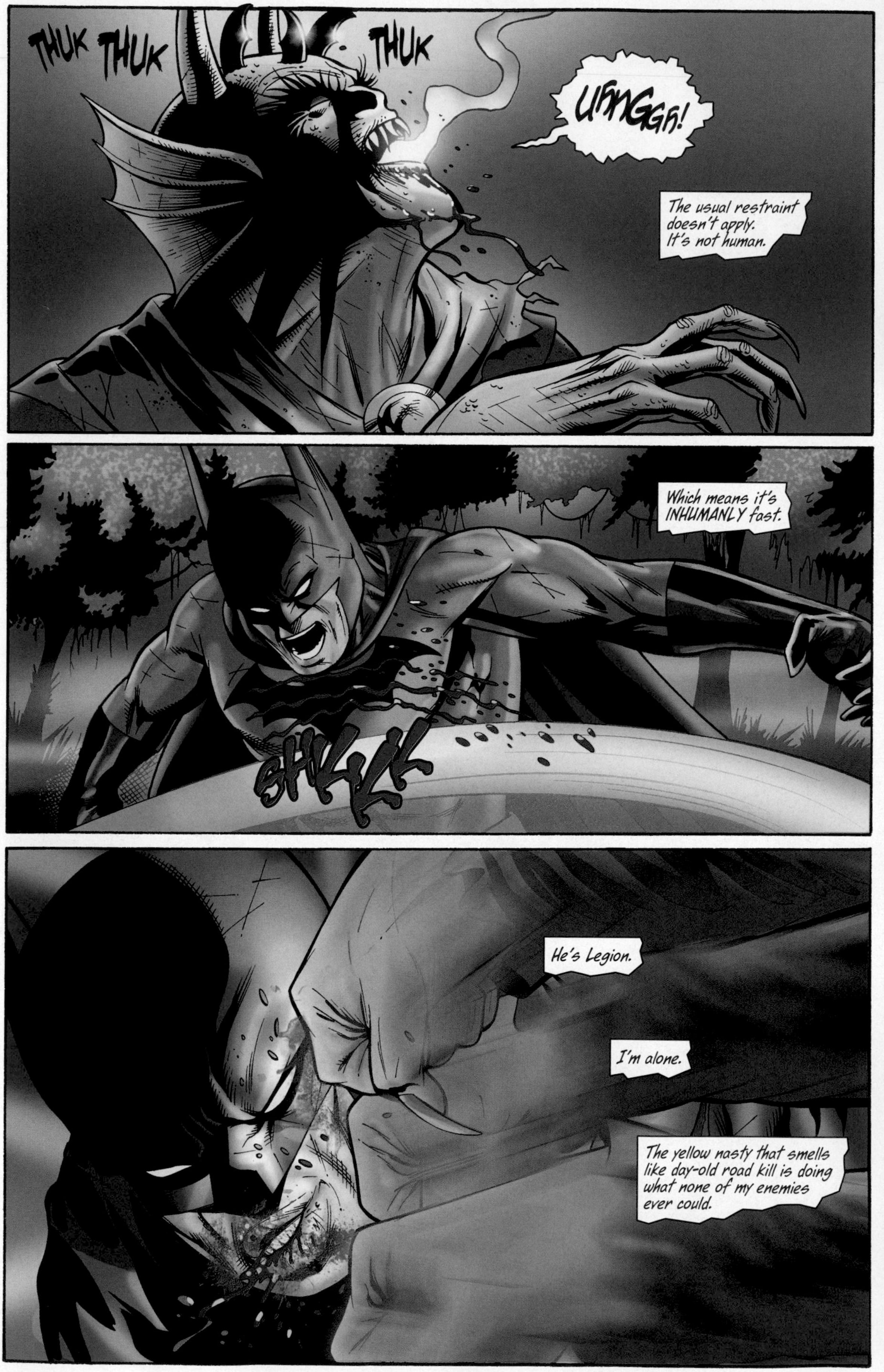
THUK THUK
THUK
UFNGGH!
The usual restraint doesn't apply. It's not human.
Which means it's INHUMANLY fast.
He's Legion.
I'm alone.
The yellow nasty that smells like day-old road kill is doing what none of my enemies ever could.

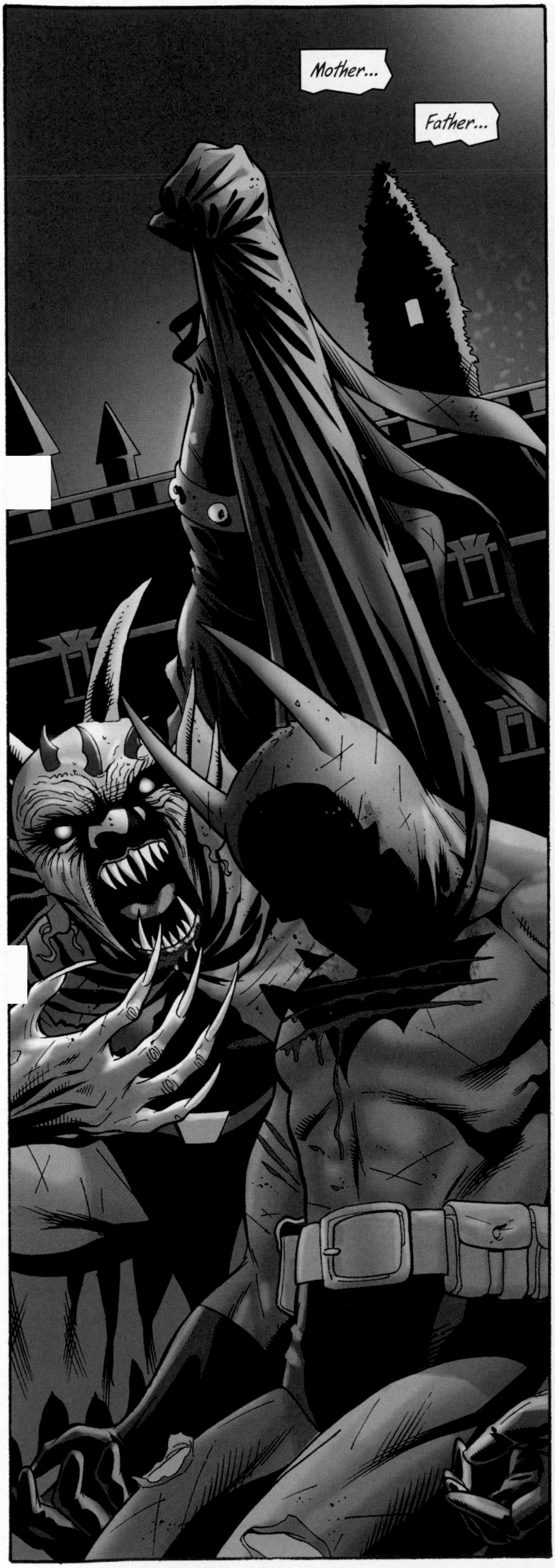
Mother...
Father...

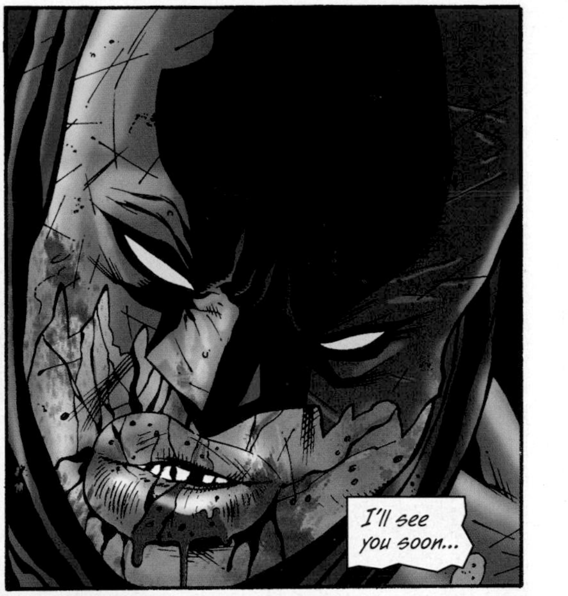
I'll see you soon...

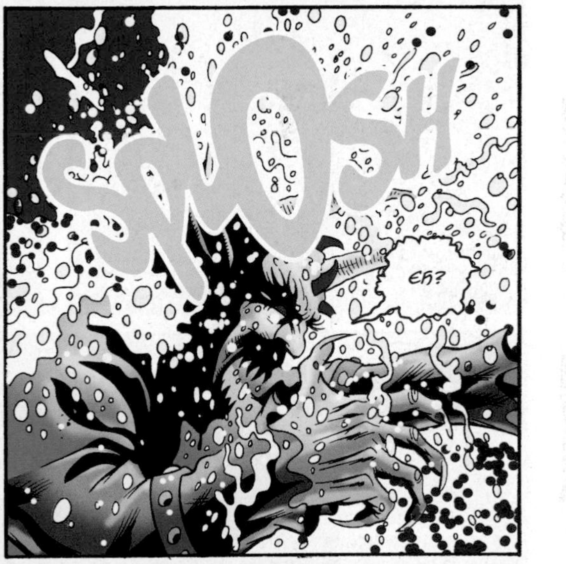
SPLOOSH
EH?

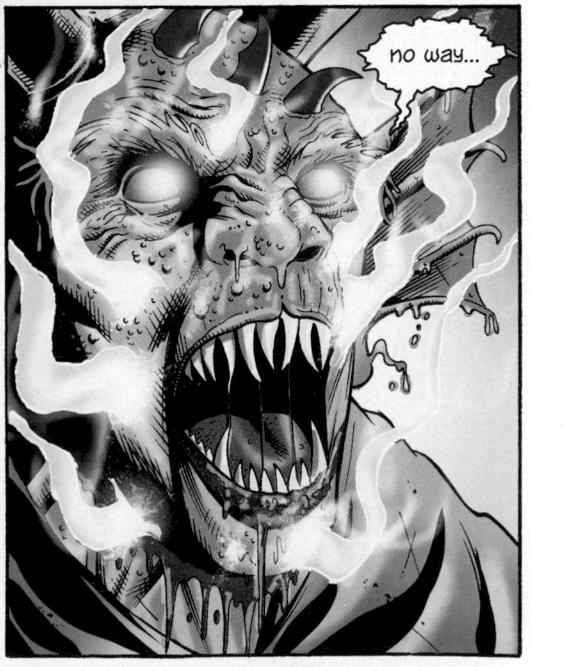
no way...

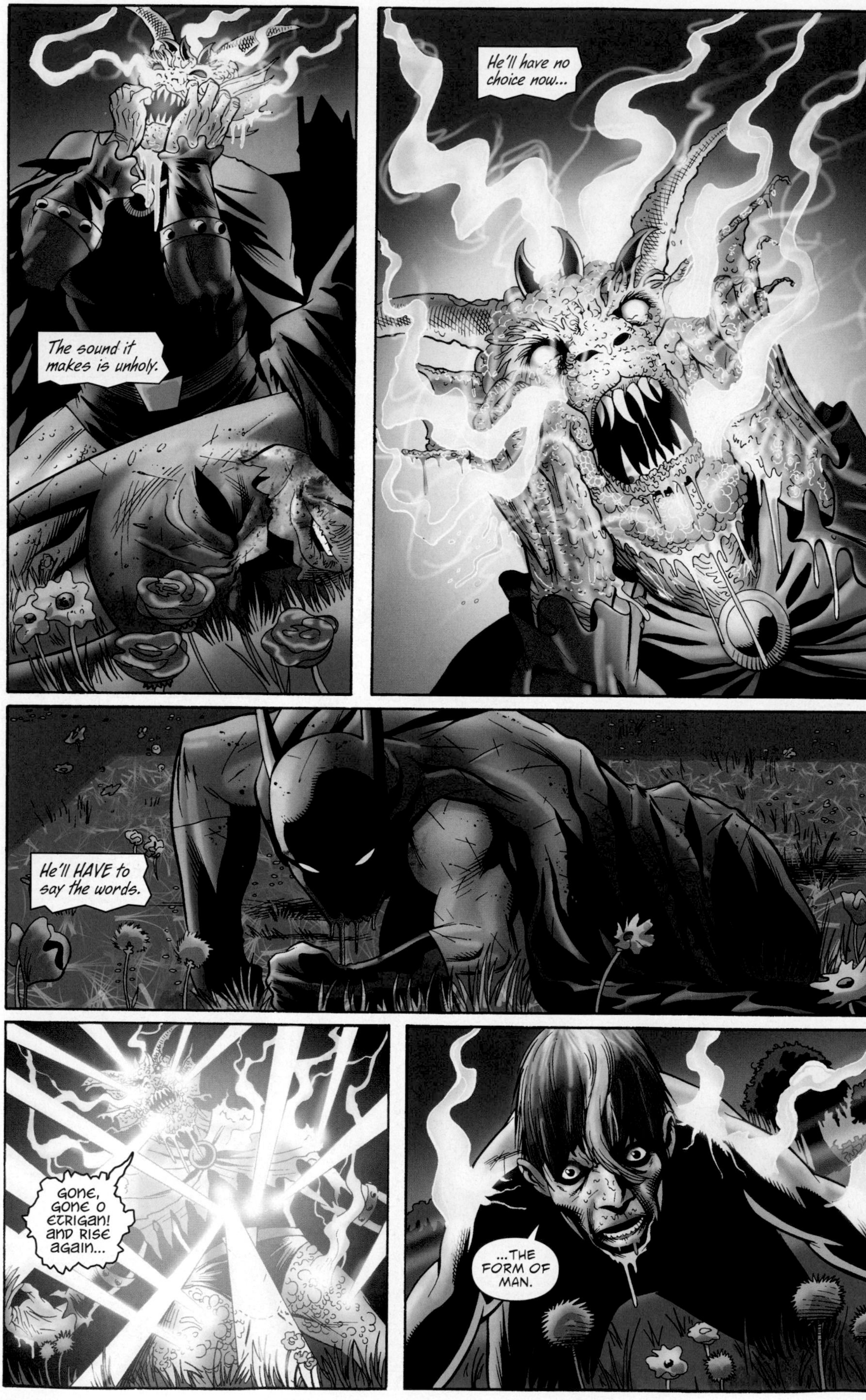
The sound it makes is unholy.
He'll have no choice now...
He'll HAVE to say the words.
GONE, GONE O ETRIGAN! AND RISE AGAIN...
...THE FORM OF MAN.

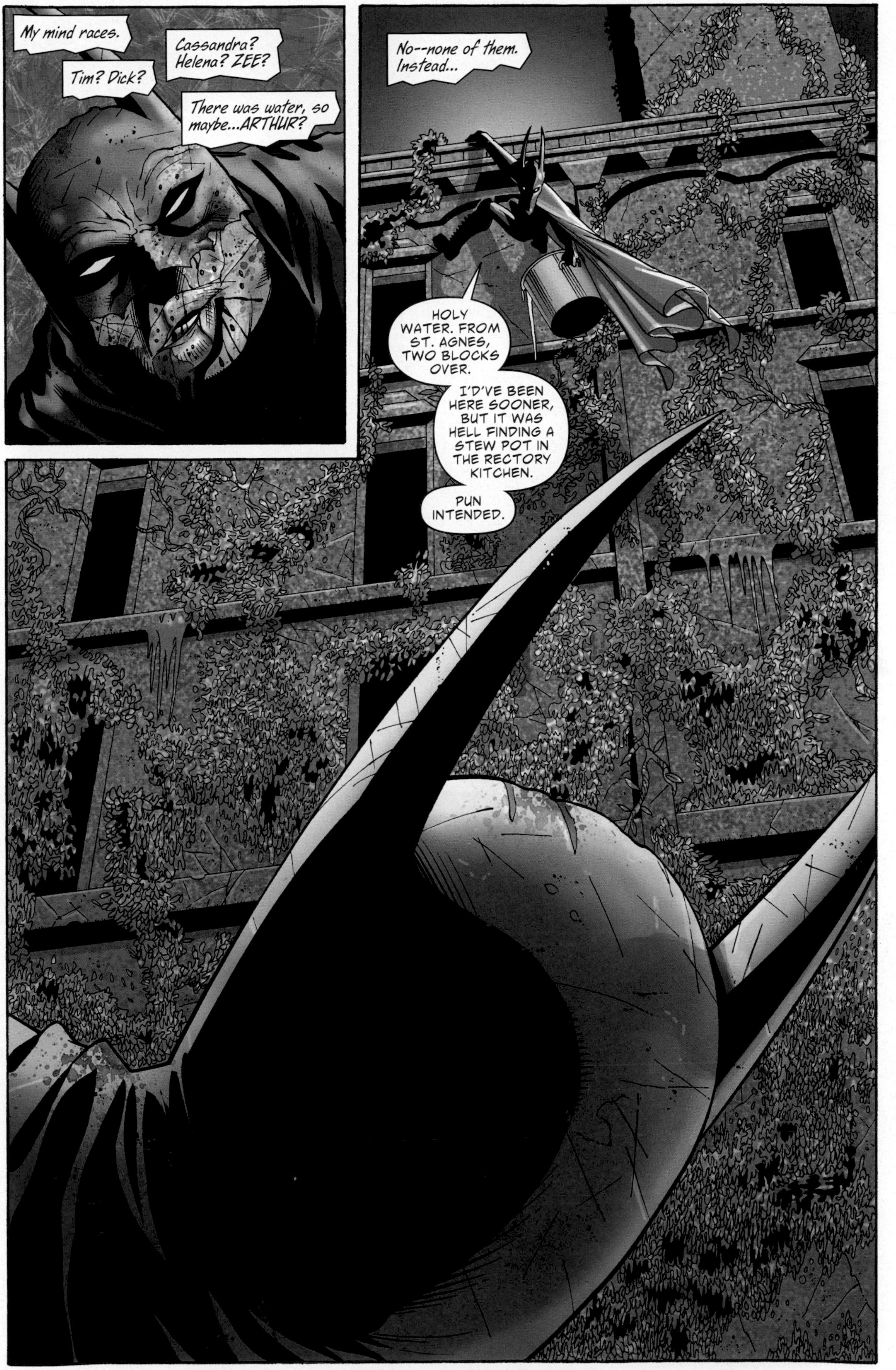
My mind races.
Tim? Dick?
Cassandra? Helena? ZEE?
There was water, so maybe...ARTHUR?
No--none of them. Instead...
HOLY WATER. FROM ST. AGNES, TWO BLOCKS OVER.
I'D'VE BEEN HERE SOONER, BUT IT WAS HELL FINDING A STEW POT IN THE RECTORY KITCHEN.
PUN INTENDED.

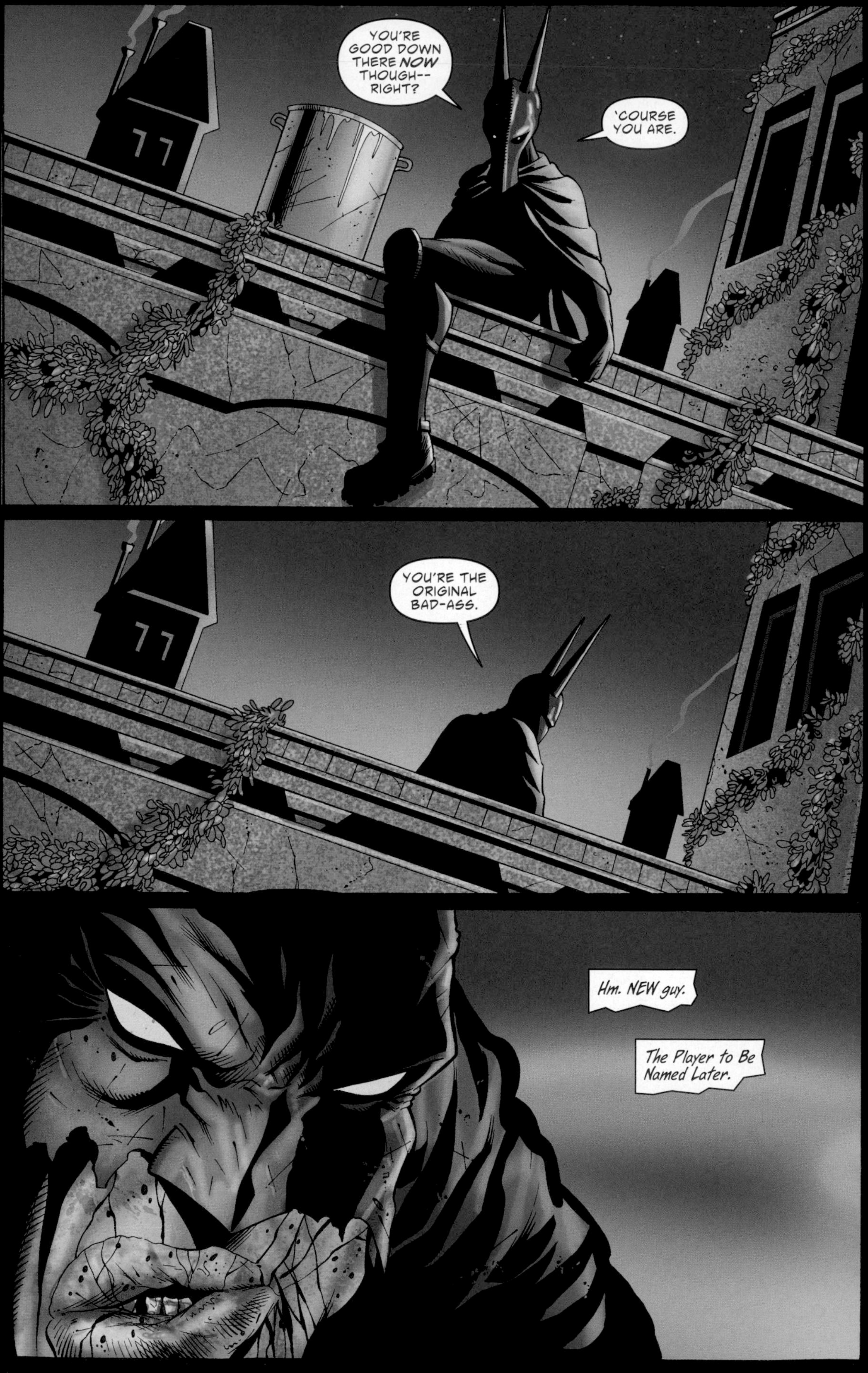
YOU'RE GOOD DOWN THERE *NOW* THOUGH-- RIGHT?
'COURSE YOU ARE.
YOU'RE THE ORIGINAL BAD-ASS.
Hm. NEW guy.
The Player to Be Named Later.

Batman: The Widening Gyre #2 cover by BILL SIENKIEWICZ

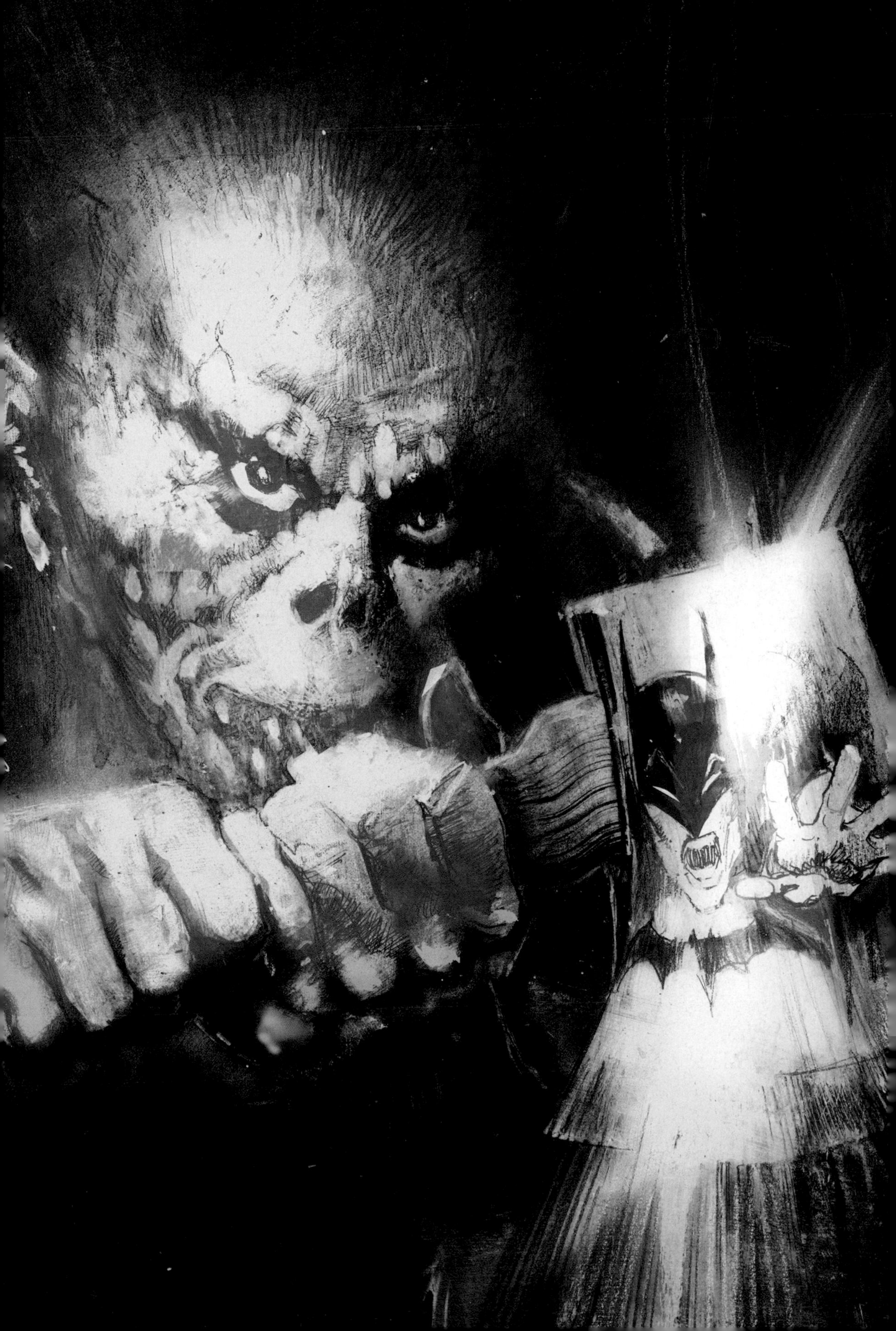

Batman: The Widening Gyre #2 alternate cover art by GENE HA

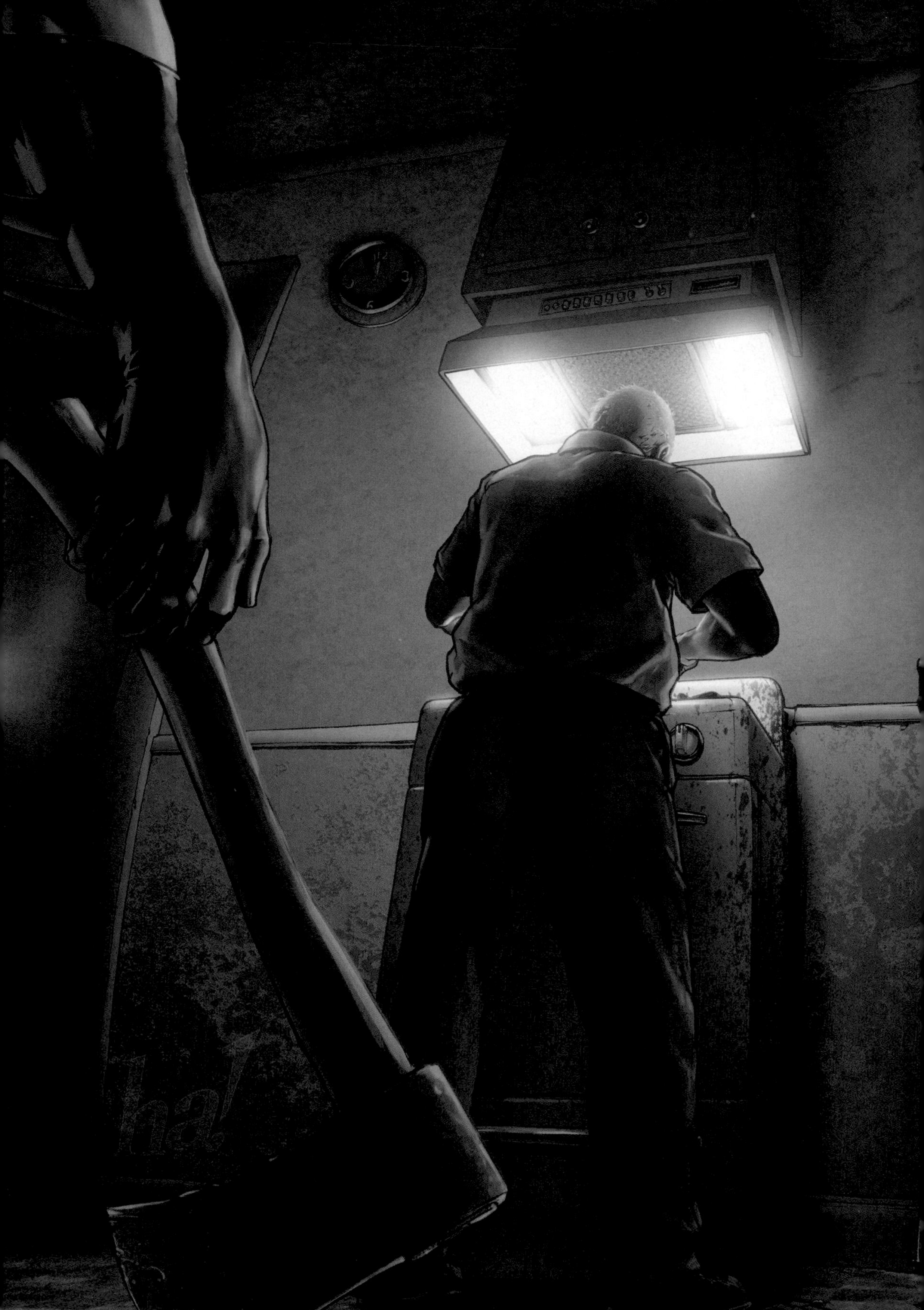

part two THE FALCONER

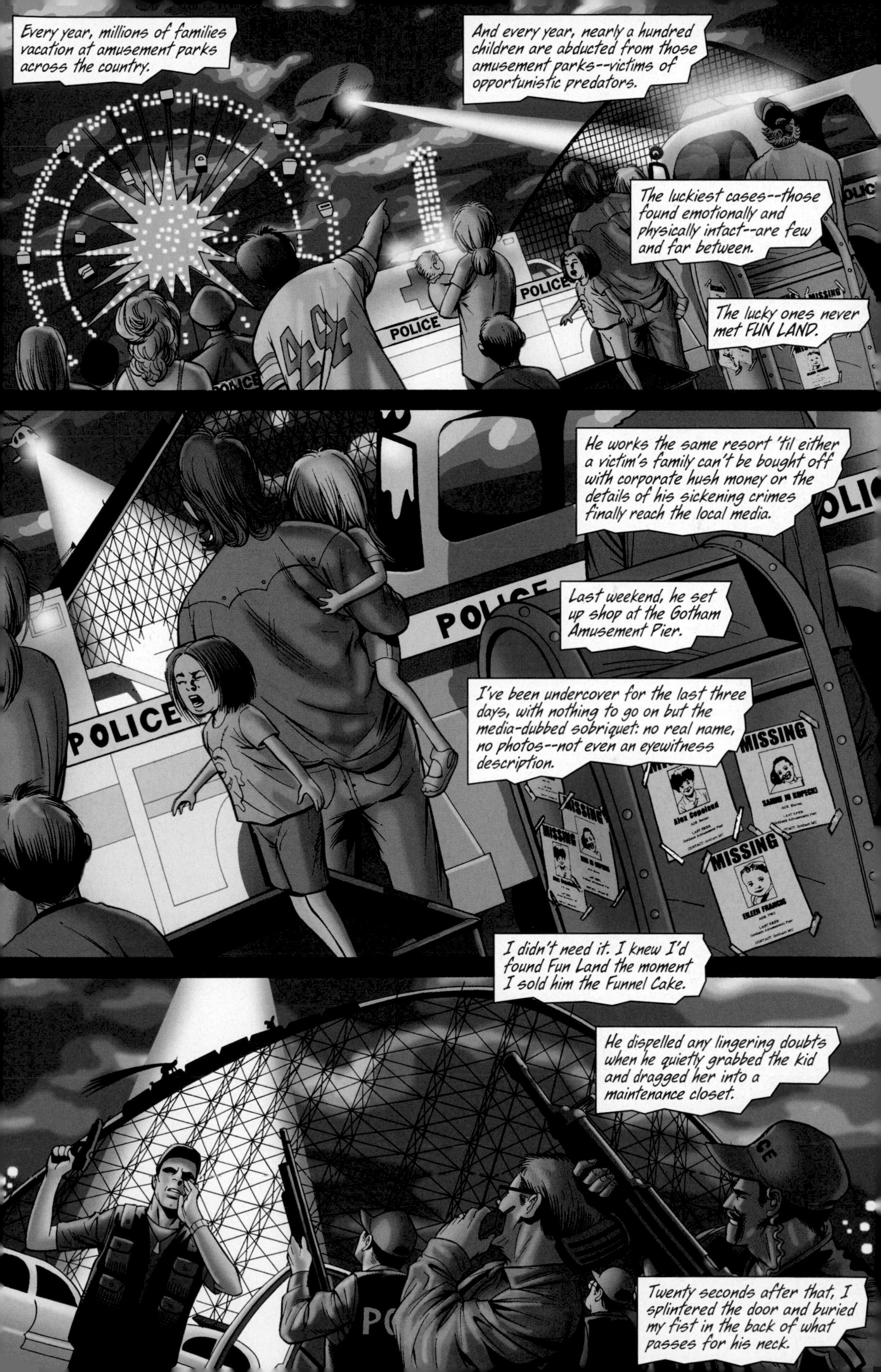
Every year, millions of families vacation at amusement parks across the country.
And every year, nearly a hundred children are abducted from those amusement parks--victims of opportunistic predators.
The luckiest cases--those found emotionally and physically intact--are few and far between.
The lucky ones never met FUN LAND.
POLICE
He works the same resort 'til either a victim's family can't be bought off with corporate hush money or the details of his sickening crimes finally reach the local media.
Last weekend, he set up shop at the Gotham Amusement Pier.
I've been undercover for the last three days, with nothing to go on but the media-dubbed sobriquet: no real name, no photos--not even an eyewitness description.
MISSING
MISSING
I didn't need it. I knew I'd found Fun Land the moment I sold him the Funnel Cake.
He dispelled any lingering doubts when he quietly grabbed the kid and dragged her into a maintenance closet.
Twenty seconds after that, I splintered the door and buried my fist in the back of what passes for his neck.

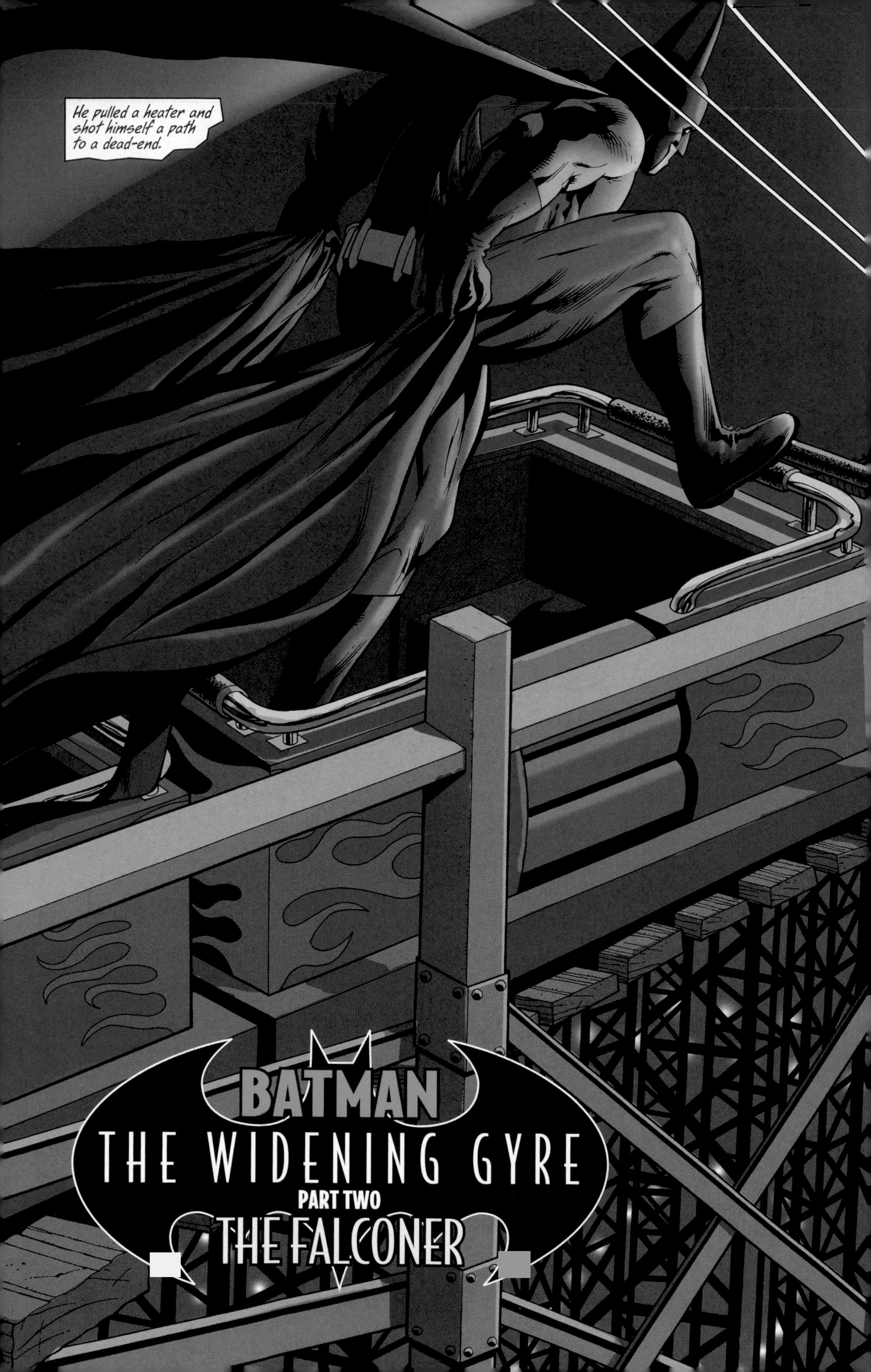

He pulled a heater and shot himself a path to a dead-end.
BATMAN
THE WIDENING GYRE
PART TWO
THE FALCONER

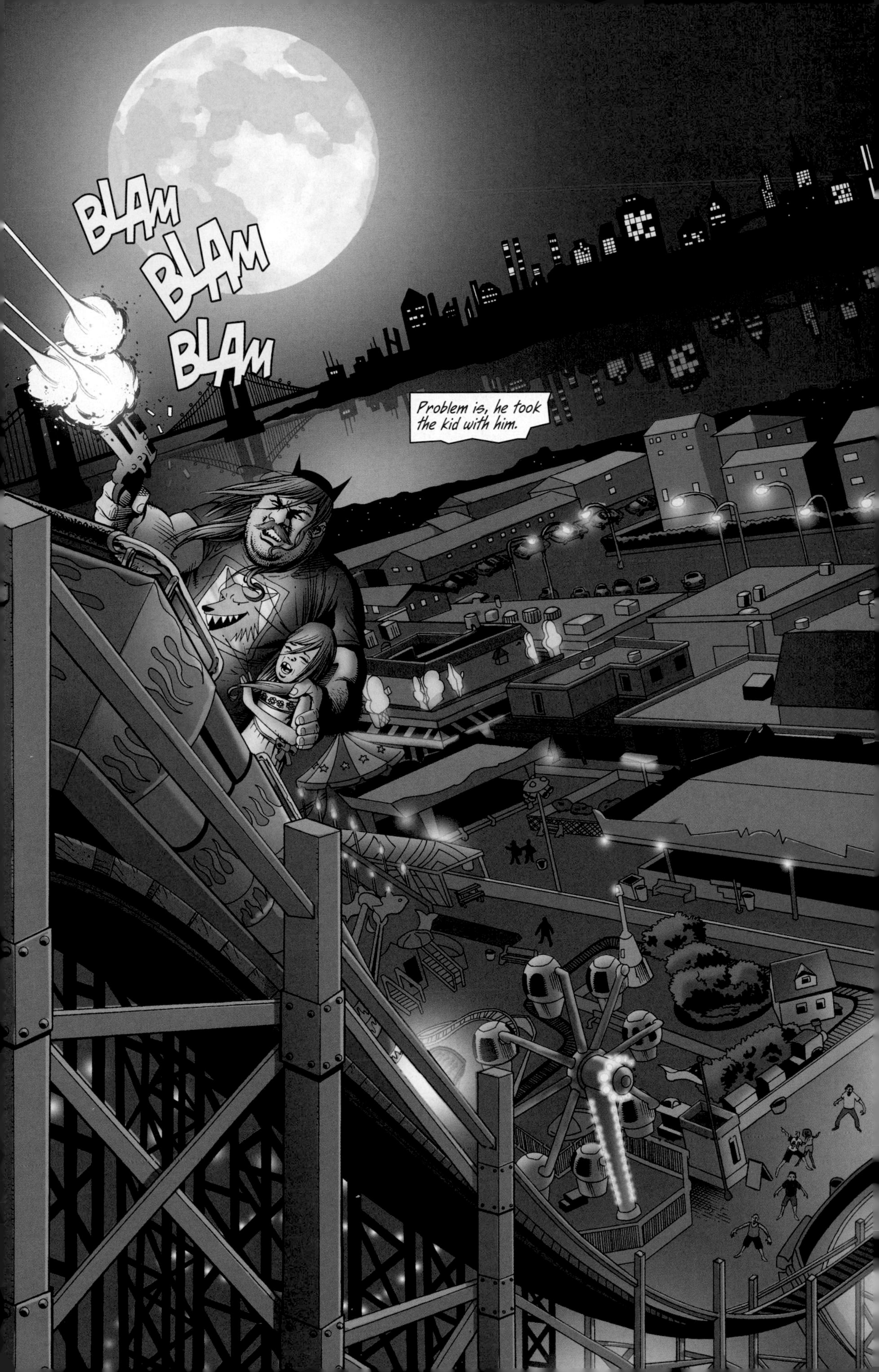
BLAM
BLAM
BLAM
Problem is, he took the kid with him.

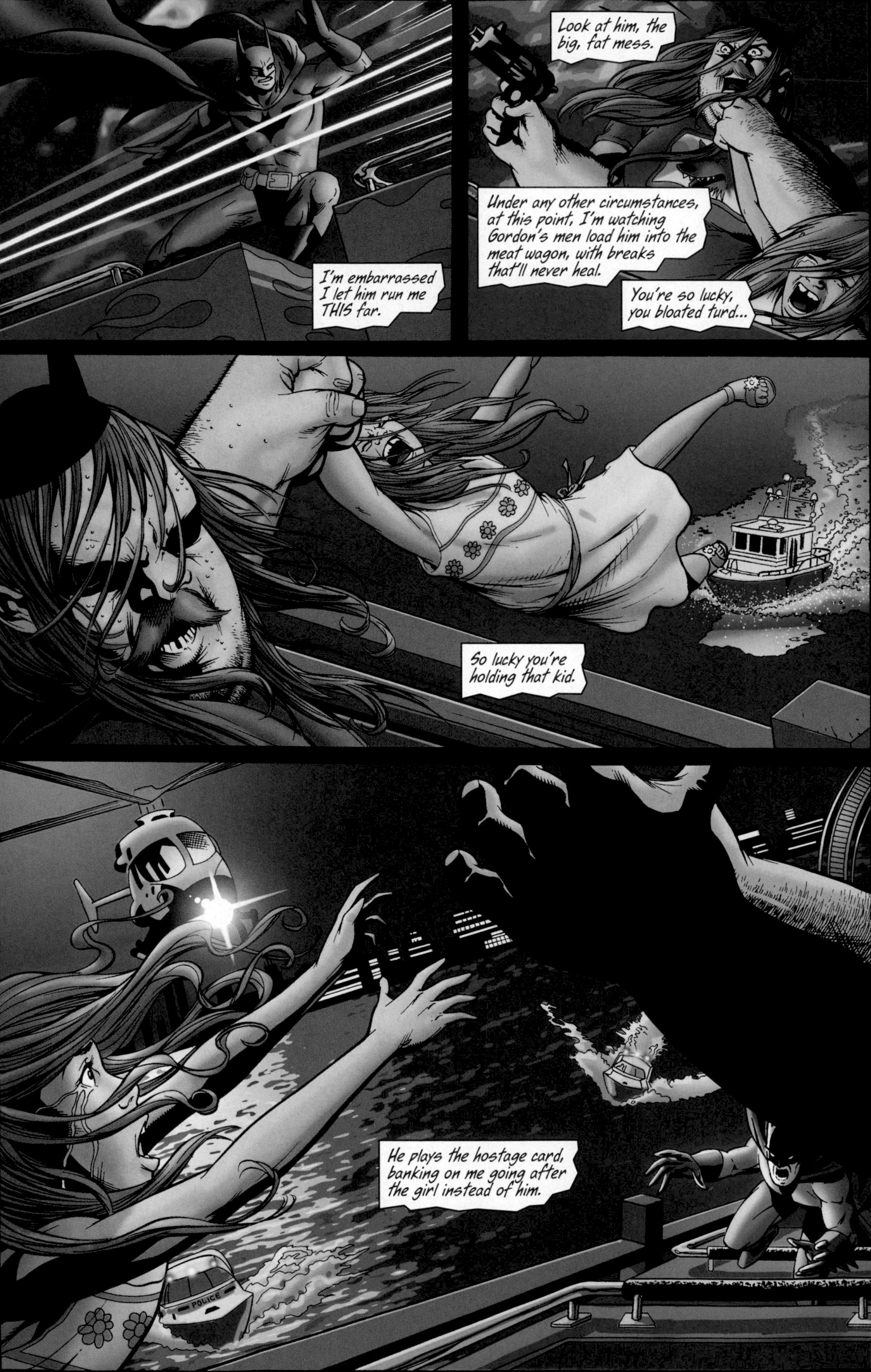
I'm embarrassed I let him run me THIS far.
Look at him, the big, fat mess.
Under any other circumstances, at this point, I'm watching Gordon's men load him into the meat wagon, with breaks that'll never heal.
You're so lucky, you bloated turd...
So lucky you're holding that kid.
He plays the hostage card, banking on me going after the girl instead of him.
POLICE

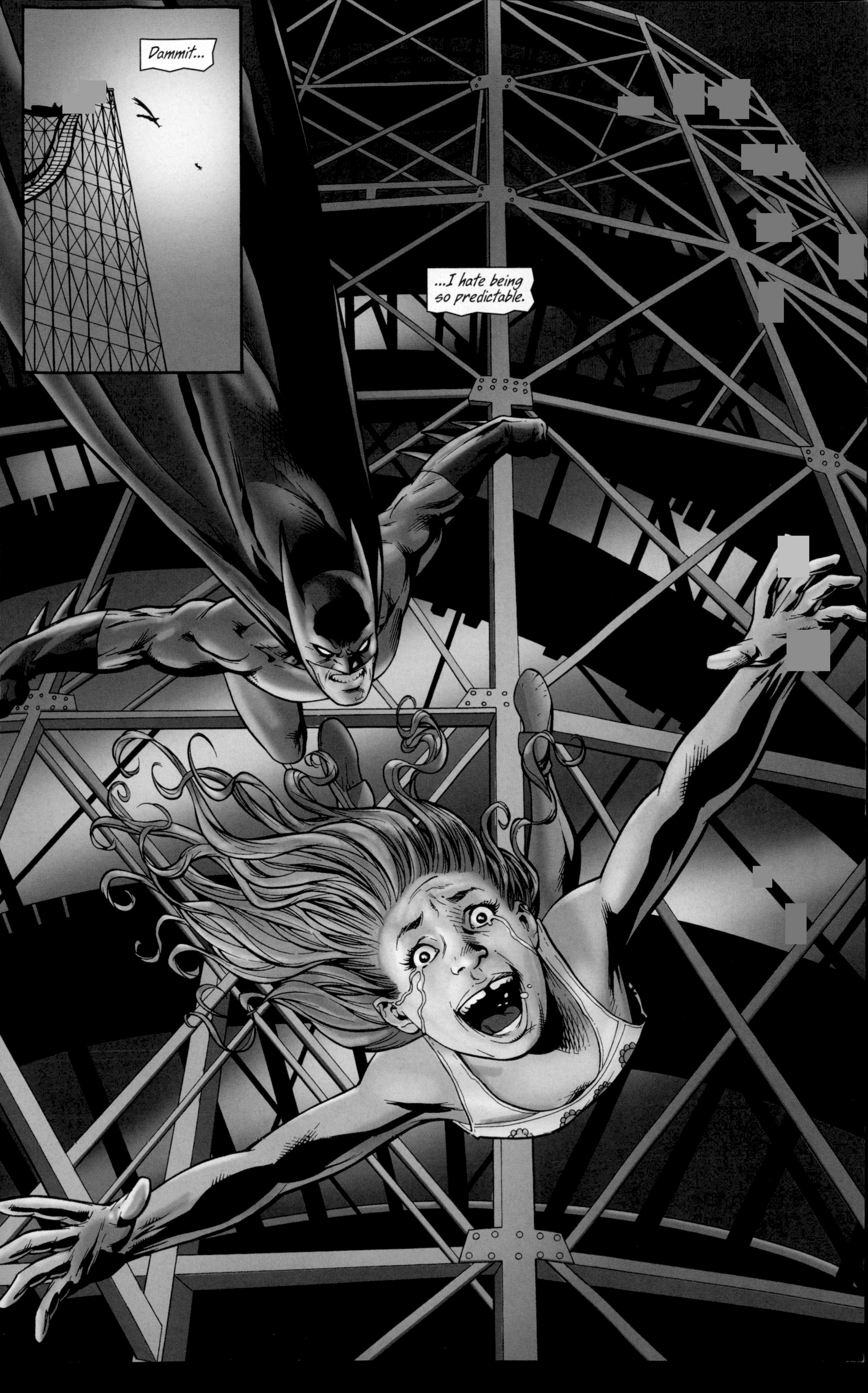
Dammit...
...I hate being so predictable.

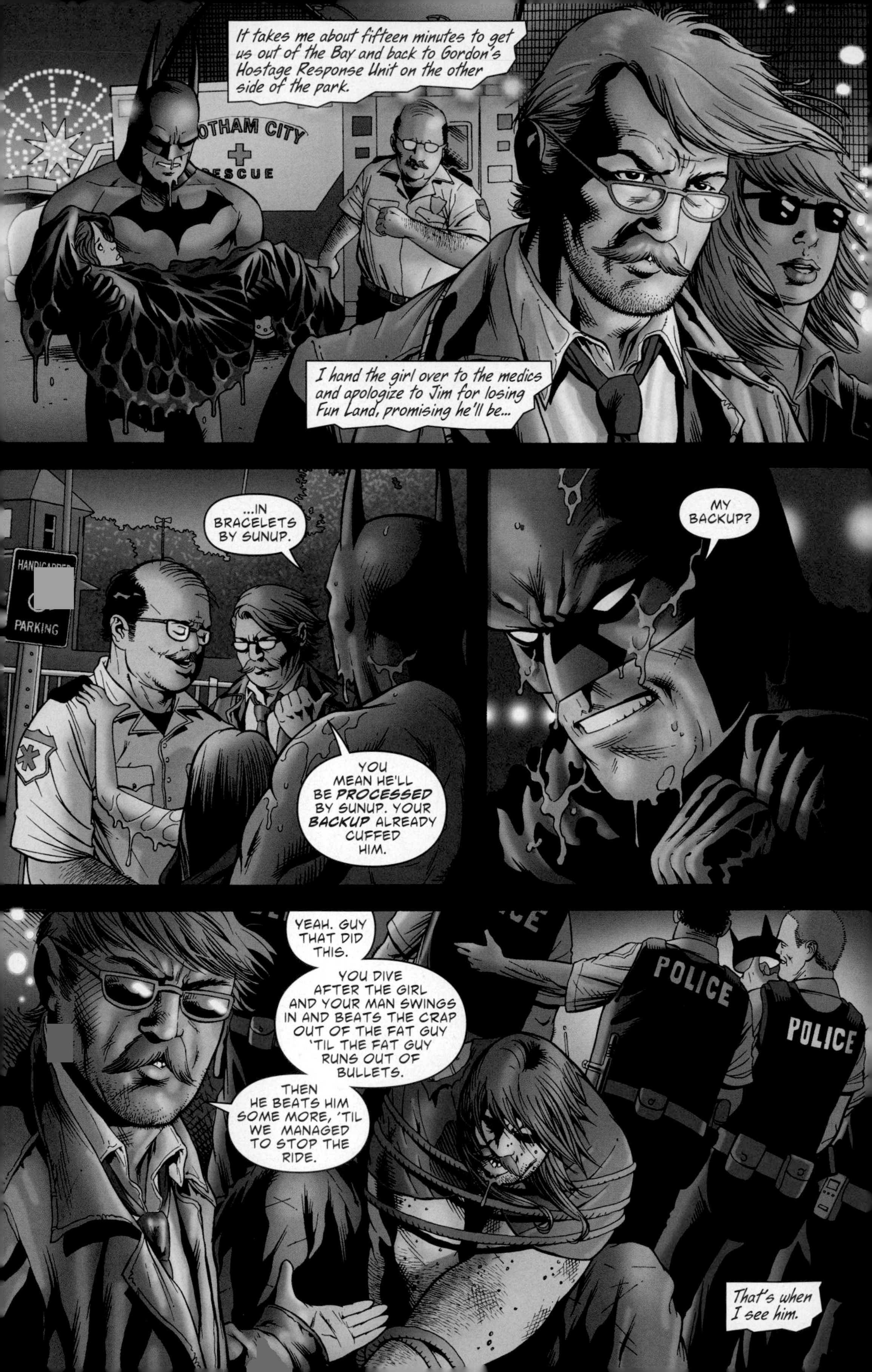

It takes me about fifteen minutes to get us out of the Bay and back to Gordon's Hostage Response Unit on the other side of the park.
OTHAM CITY
ESCUE
I hand the girl over to the medics and apologize to Jim for losing Fun Land, promising he'll be...
...IN BRACELETS BY SUNUP.
PARKING
YOU MEAN HE'LL BE **PROCESSED** BY SUNUP. YOUR **BACKUP** ALREADY CUFFED HIM.
MY BACKUP?
YEAH. GUY THAT DID THIS.
YOU DIVE AFTER THE GIRL AND YOUR MAN SWINGS IN AND BEATS THE CRAP OUT OF THE FAT GUY 'TIL THE FAT GUY RUNS OUT OF BULLETS.
THEN HE BEATS HIM SOME MORE, 'TIL WE MANAGED TO STOP THE RIDE.
POLICE
POLICE
That's when I see him.

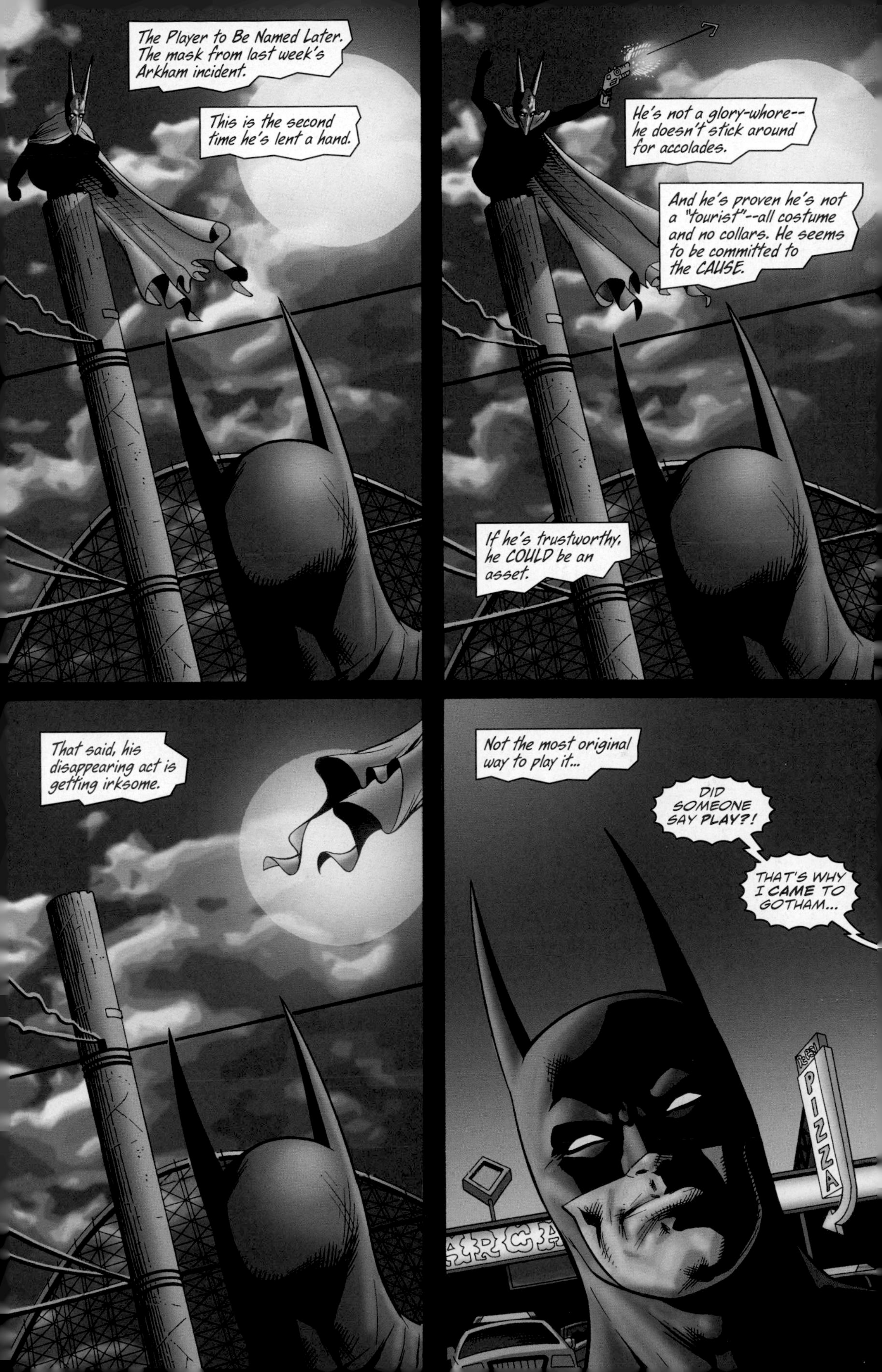
The Player to Be Named Later. The mask from last week's Arkham incident.
This is the second time he's lent a hand.
He's not a glory-whore--he doesn't stick around for accolades.
And he's proven he's not a "tourist"--all costume and no collars. He seems to be committed to the CAUSE.
If he's trustworthy, he COULD be an asset.
That said, his disappearing act is getting irksome.
Not the most original way to play it...
DID SOMEONE SAY PLAY?!
THAT'S WHY I CAME TO GOTHAM...
PIZZA
ARCA

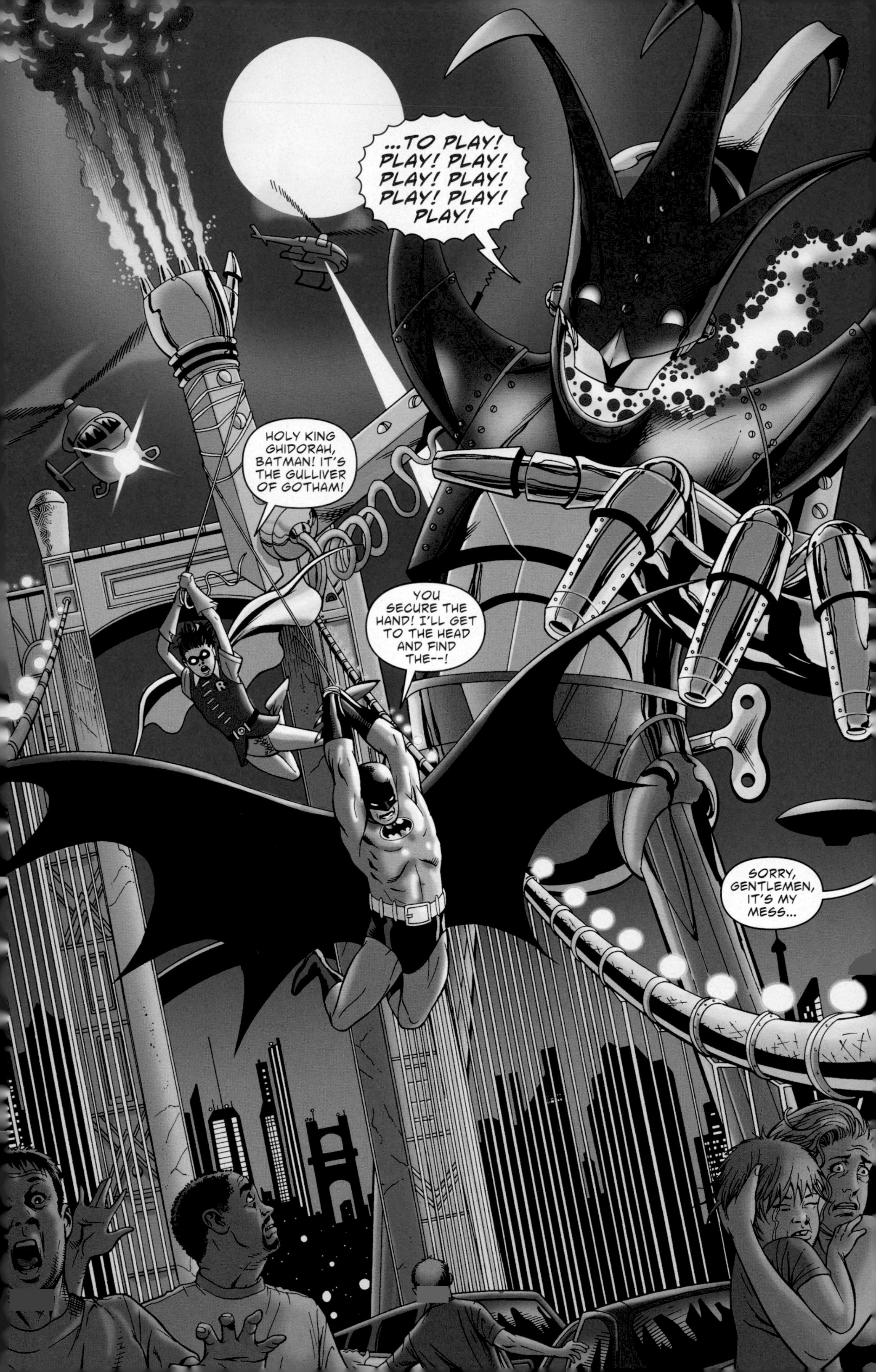
...TO PLAY! PLAY! PLAY! PLAY! PLAY! PLAY! PLAY! PLAY!
HOLY KING GHIDORAH, BATMAN! IT'S THE GULLIVER OF GOTHAM!
YOU SECURE THE HAND! I'LL GET TO THE HEAD AND FIND THE--!
SORRY, GENTLEMEN, IT'S MY MESS...

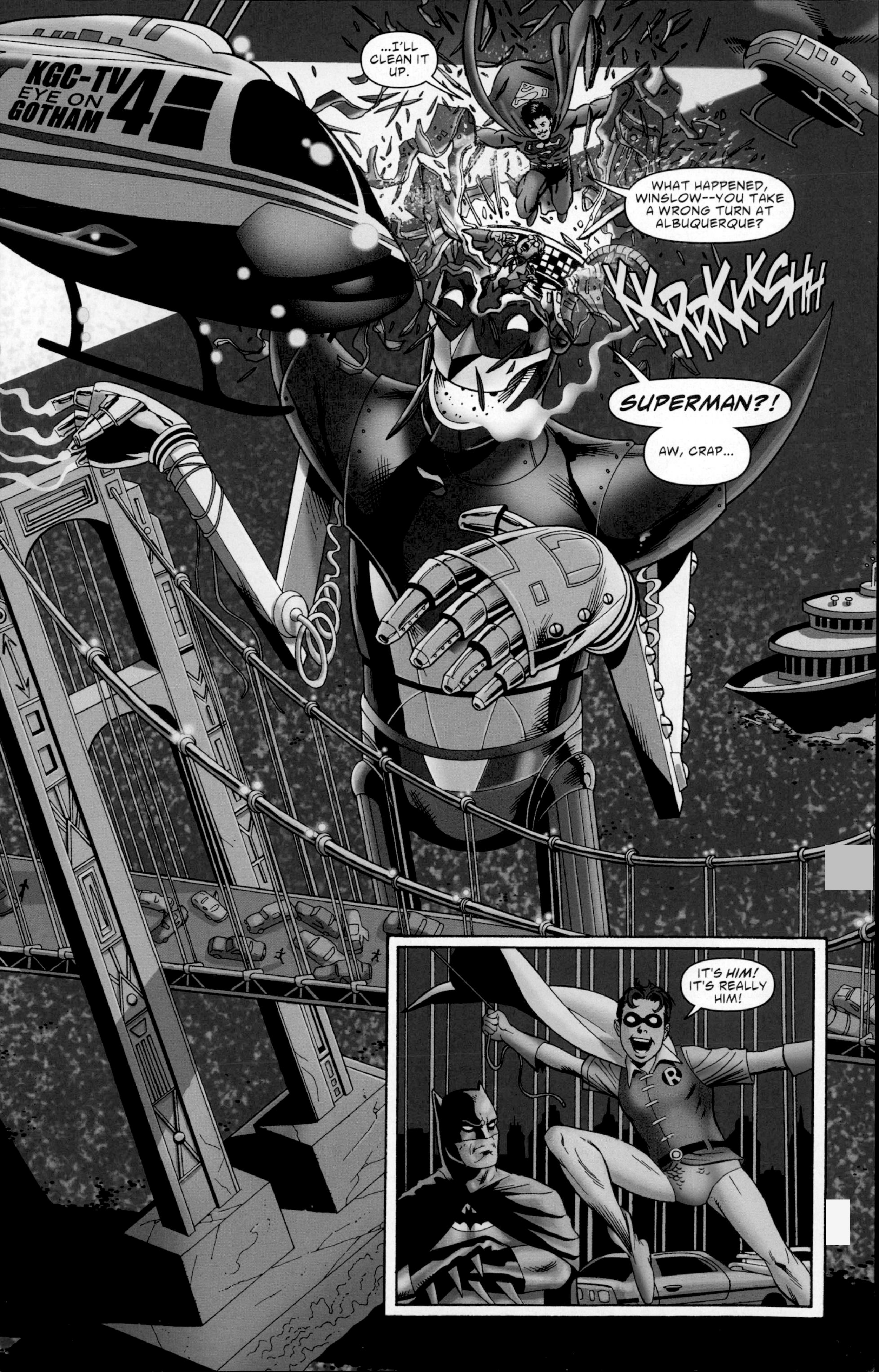

...I'LL CLEAN IT UP.
KGC-TV 4 EYE ON GOTHAM
WHAT HAPPENED, WINSLOW--YOU TAKE A WRONG TURN AT ALBUQUERQUE?
KKRRKKKSHH
SUPERMAN?!
AW, CRAP...
IT'S HIM! IT'S REALLY HIM!

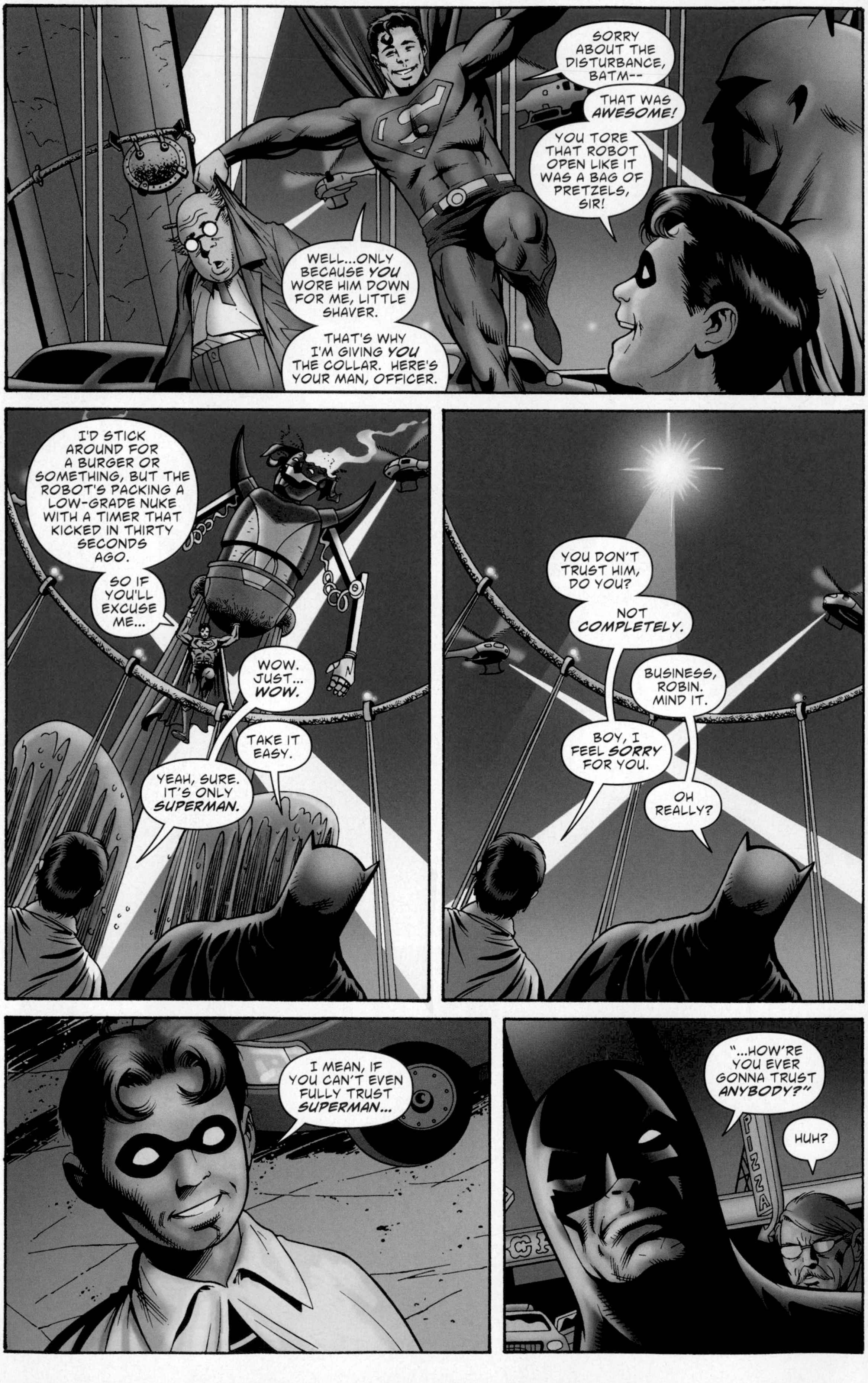
SORRY ABOUT THE DISTURBANCE, BATM--
THAT WAS AWESOME!
YOU TORE THAT ROBOT OPEN LIKE IT WAS A BAG OF PRETZELS, SIR!
WELL...ONLY BECAUSE YOU WORE HIM DOWN FOR ME, LITTLE SHAVER.
THAT'S WHY I'M GIVING YOU THE COLLAR. HERE'S YOUR MAN, OFFICER.
I'D STICK AROUND FOR A BURGER OR SOMETHING, BUT THE ROBOT'S PACKING A LOW-GRADE NUKE WITH A TIMER THAT KICKED IN THIRTY SECONDS AGO.
SO IF YOU'LL EXCUSE ME...
WOW. JUST... WOW.
TAKE IT EASY.
YEAH, SURE. IT'S ONLY SUPERMAN.
YOU DON'T TRUST HIM, DO YOU?
NOT COMPLETELY.
BUSINESS, ROBIN. MIND IT.
BOY, I FEEL SORRY FOR YOU.
OH REALLY?
I MEAN, IF YOU CAN'T EVEN FULLY TRUST SUPERMAN...
"...HOW'RE YOU EVER GONNA TRUST ANYBODY?"
HUH?
PIZZA

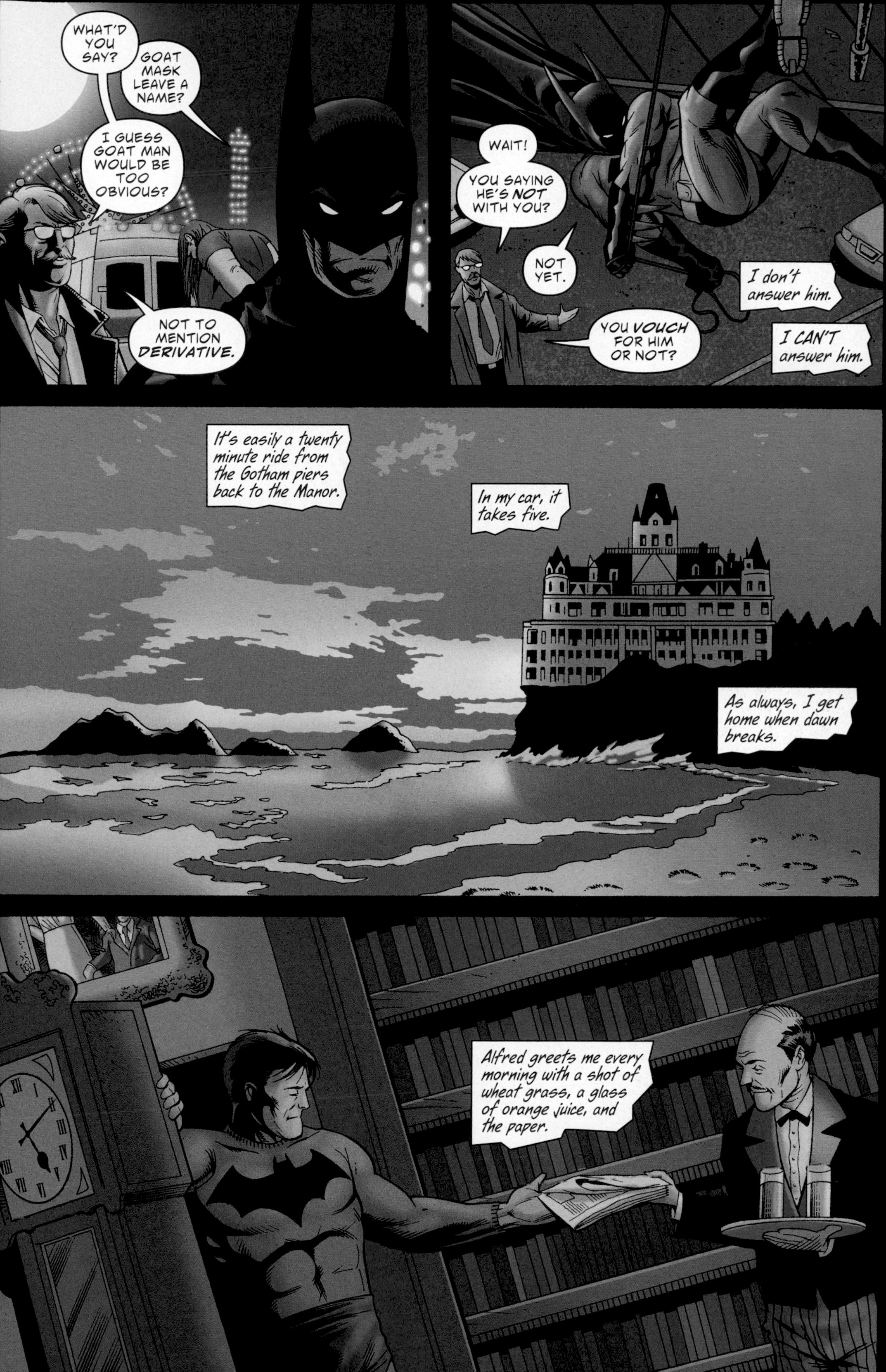
WHAT'D YOU SAY?
GOAT MASK LEAVE A NAME?
I GUESS GOAT MAN WOULD BE TOO OBVIOUS?
NOT TO MENTION *DERIVATIVE.*
WAIT!
YOU SAYING HE'S ***NOT*** WITH YOU?
NOT YET.
YOU ***VOUCH*** FOR HIM OR NOT?
I don't answer him.
I CAN'T answer him.
It's easily a twenty minute ride from the Gotham piers back to the Manor.
In my car, it takes five.
As always, I get home when dawn breaks.
Alfred greets me every morning with a shot of wheat grass, a glass of orange juice, and the paper.

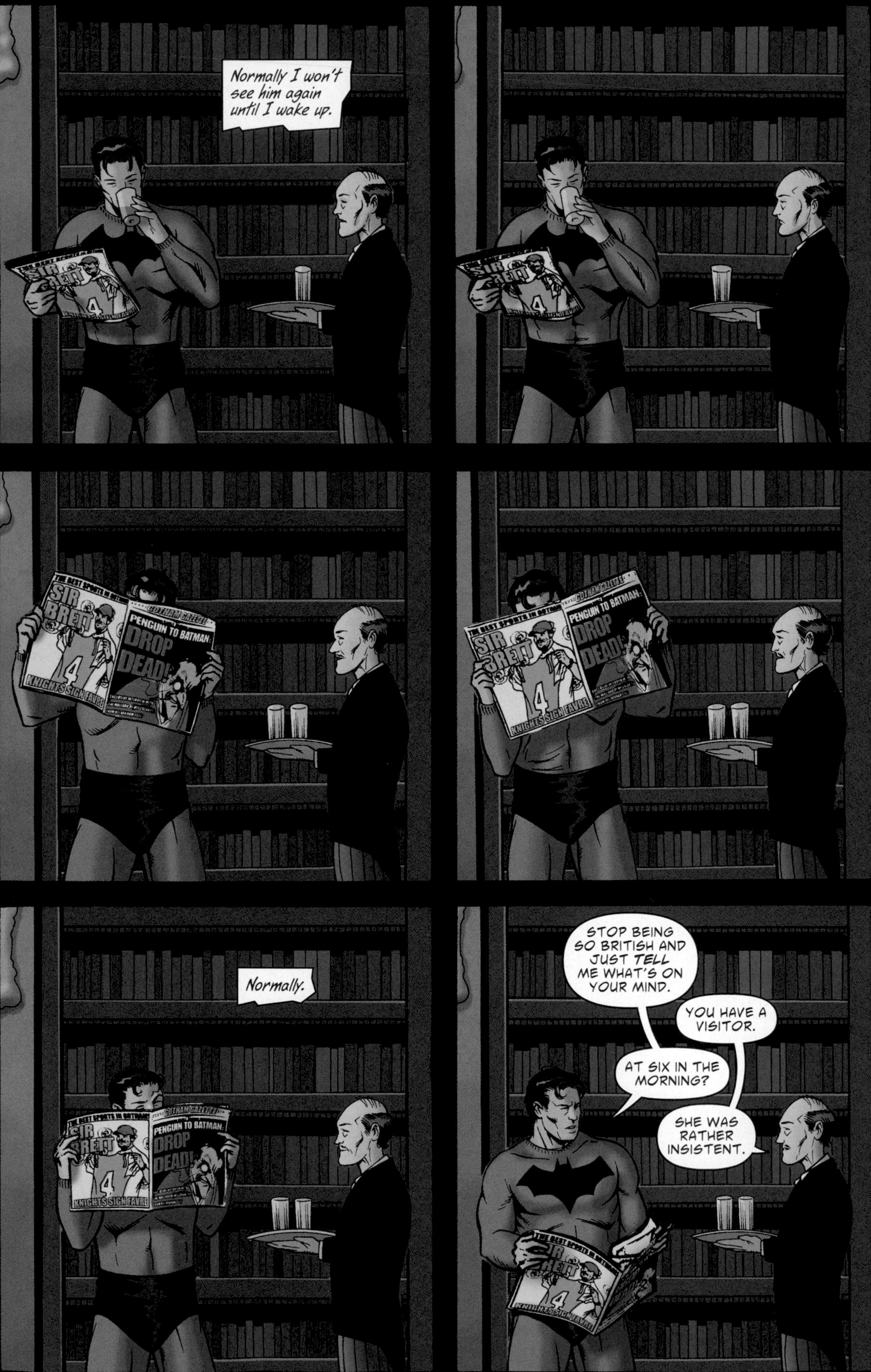
Normally I won't see him again until I wake up.
SIR BRETT
4
KNIGHTS SIGN FAVRE
GOTHAM GAZETTE
PENGUIN TO BATMAN:
DROP DEAD!
Normally.
STOP BEING SO BRITISH AND JUST TELL ME WHAT'S ON YOUR MIND.
YOU HAVE A VISITOR.
AT SIX IN THE MORNING?
SHE WAS RATHER INSISTENT.

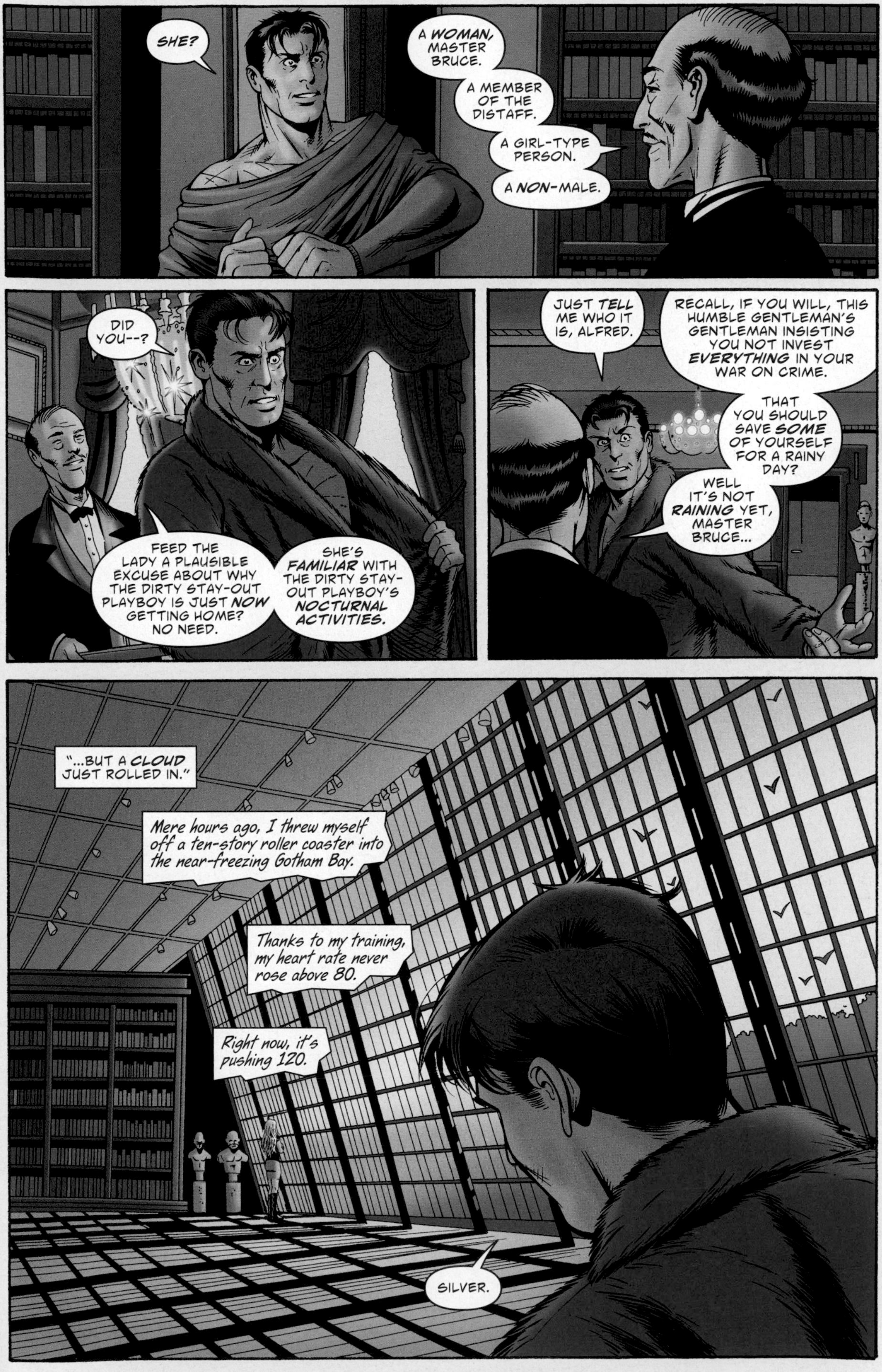
SHE?
A WOMAN, MASTER BRUCE.
A MEMBER OF THE DISTAFF.
A GIRL-TYPE PERSON.
A NON-MALE.
DID YOU--?
FEED THE LADY A PLAUSIBLE EXCUSE ABOUT WHY THE DIRTY STAY-OUT PLAYBOY IS JUST NOW GETTING HOME? NO NEED.
SHE'S FAMILIAR WITH THE DIRTY STAY-OUT PLAYBOY'S NOCTURNAL ACTIVITIES.
JUST TELL ME WHO IT IS, ALFRED.
RECALL, IF YOU WILL, THIS HUMBLE GENTLEMAN'S GENTLEMAN INSISTING YOU NOT INVEST EVERYTHING IN YOUR WAR ON CRIME.
THAT YOU SHOULD SAVE SOME OF YOURSELF FOR A RAINY DAY?
WELL IT'S NOT RAINING YET, MASTER BRUCE...
"...BUT A CLOUD JUST ROLLED IN."
Mere hours ago, I threw myself off a ten-story roller coaster into the near-freezing Gotham Bay.
Thanks to my training, my heart rate never rose above 80.
Right now, it's pushing 120.
SILVER.

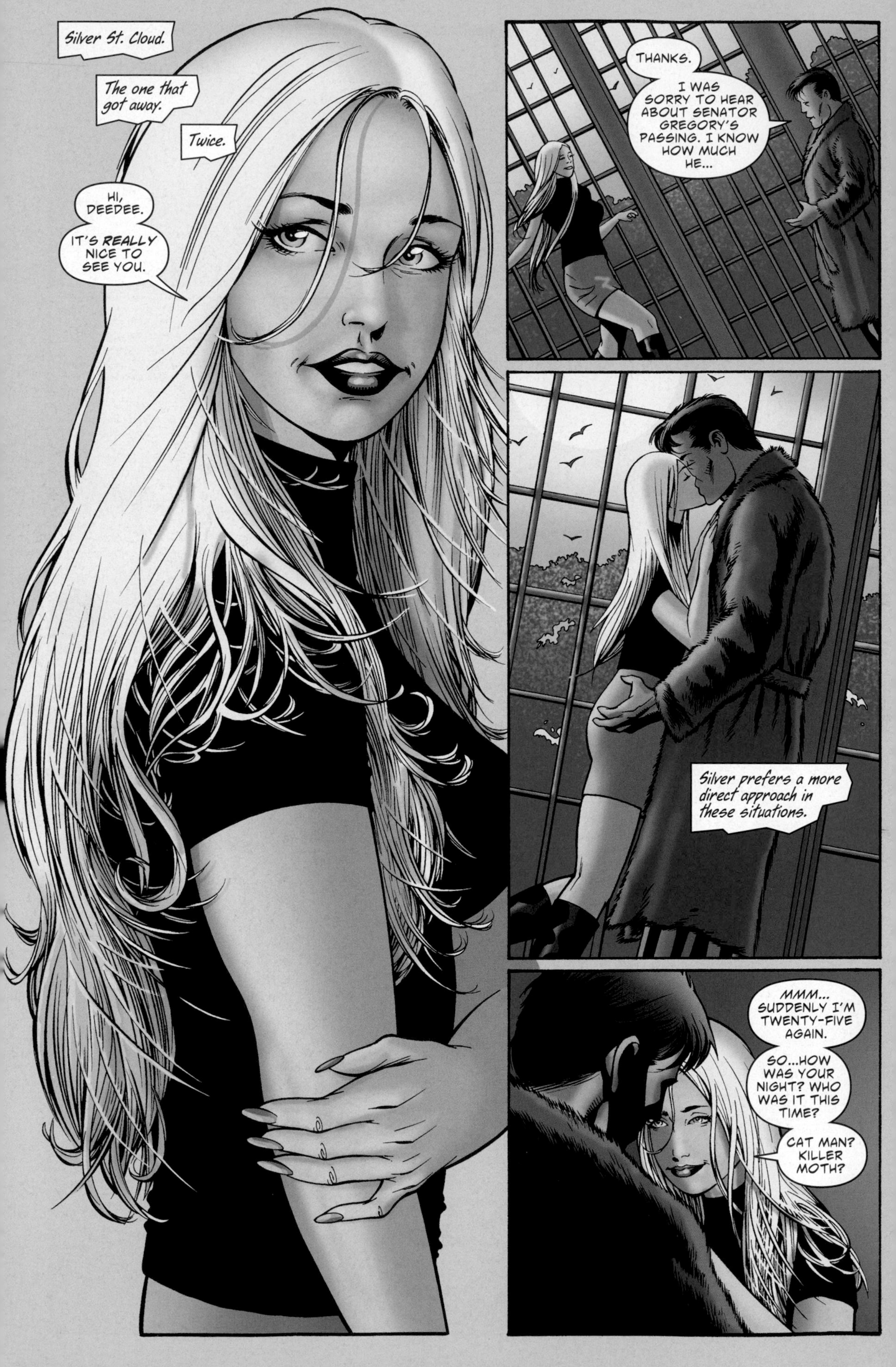
Silver St. Cloud.
The one that got away.
Twice.
HI, DEEDEE.
IT'S REALLY NICE TO SEE YOU.
THANKS.
I WAS SORRY TO HEAR ABOUT SENATOR GREGORY'S PASSING. I KNOW HOW MUCH HE...
Silver prefers a more direct approach in these situations.
MMM... SUDDENLY I'M TWENTY-FIVE AGAIN.
SO...HOW WAS YOUR NIGHT? WHO WAS IT THIS TIME?
CAT MAN? KILLER MOTH?

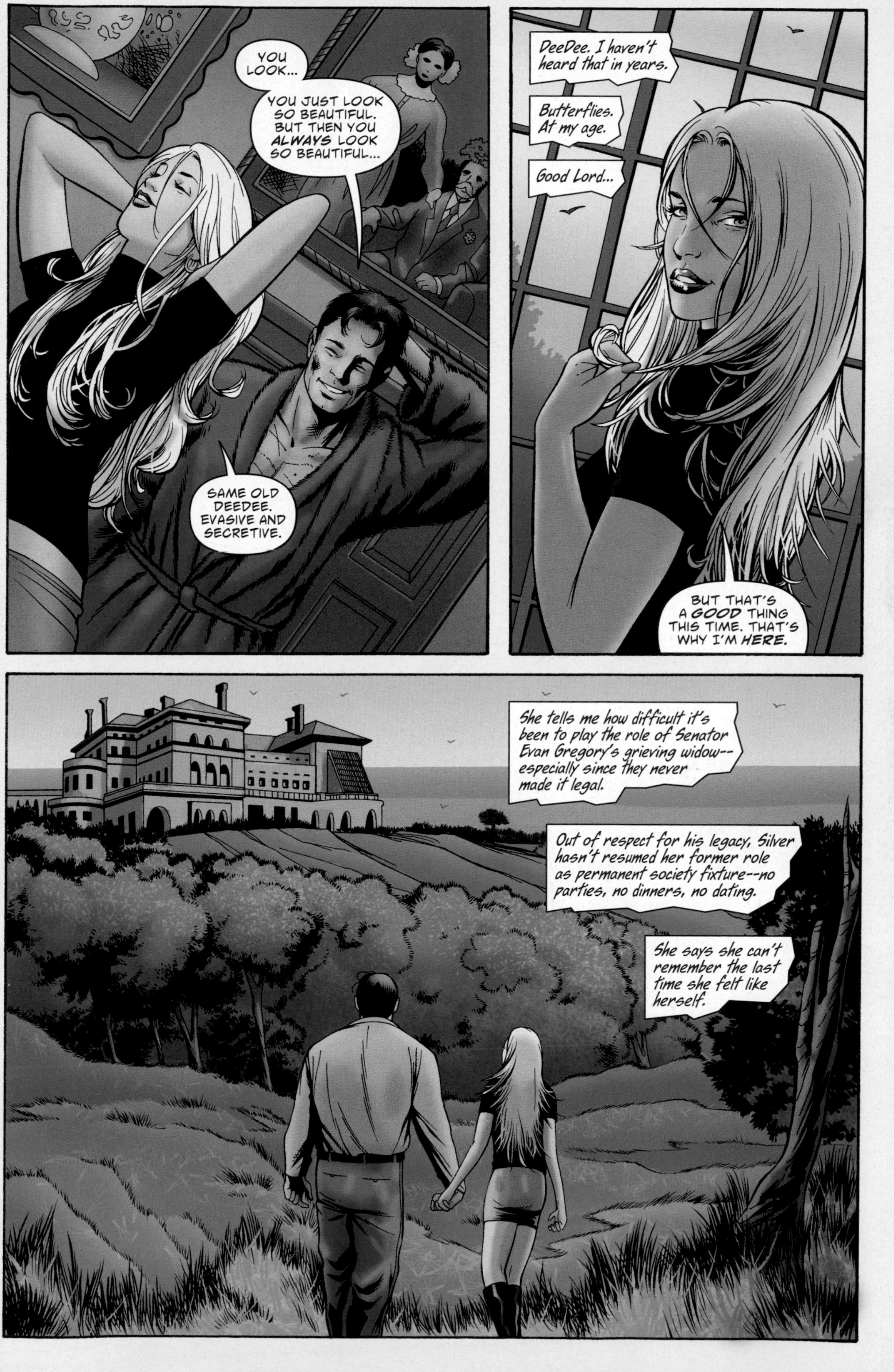
YOU LOOK...
YOU JUST LOOK SO BEAUTIFUL. BUT THEN YOU ALWAYS LOOK SO BEAUTIFUL...
SAME OLD DEEDEE. EVASIVE AND SECRETIVE.
DeeDee. I haven't heard that in years.
Butterflies. At my age.
Good Lord...
BUT THAT'S A GOOD THING THIS TIME. THAT'S WHY I'M HERE.
She tells me how difficult it's been to play the role of Senator Evan Gregory's grieving widow--especially since they never made it legal.
Out of respect for his legacy, Silver hasn't resumed her former role as permanent society fixture--no parties, no dinners, no dating.
She says she can't remember the last time she felt like herself.

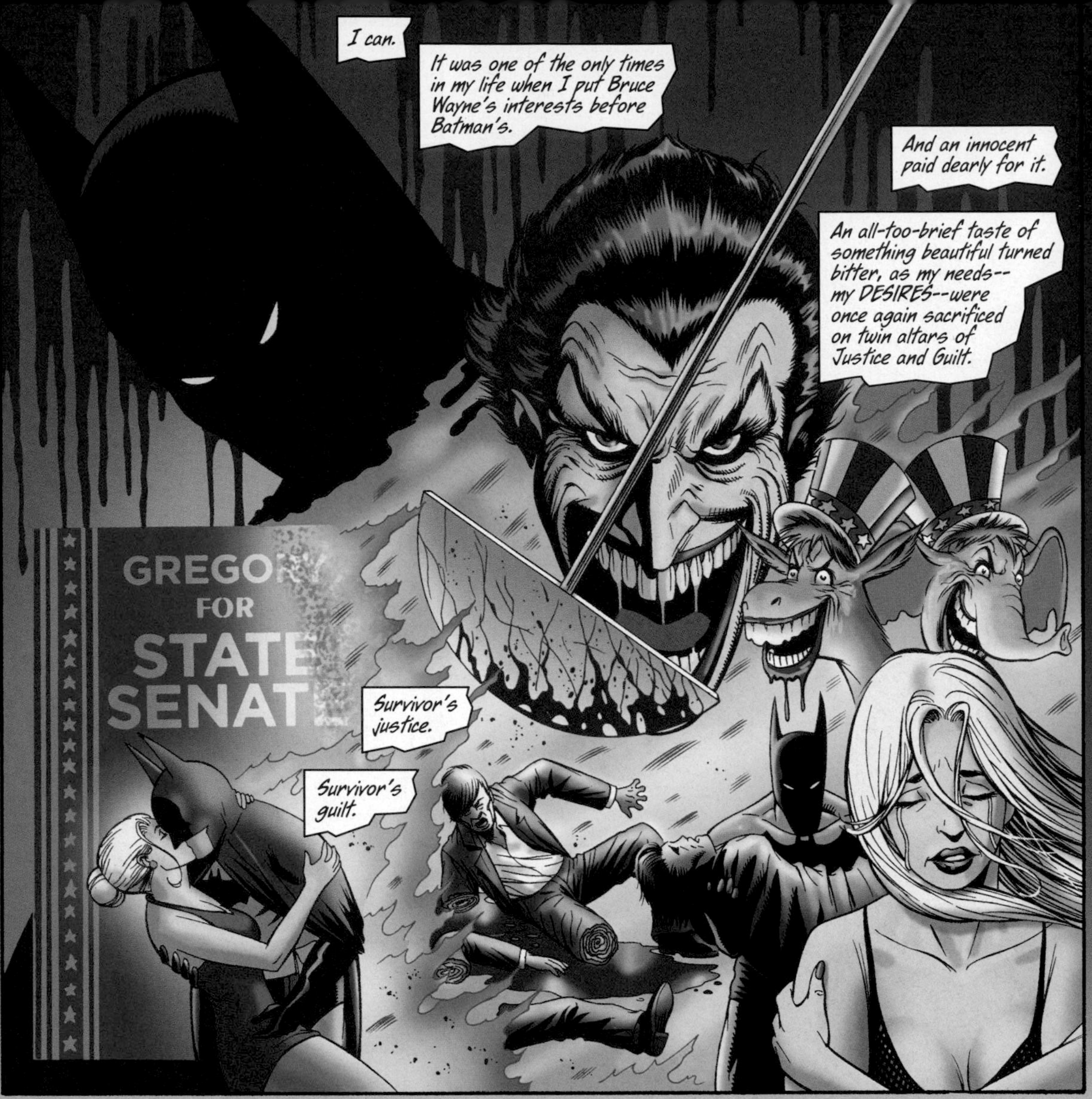
I can.
It was one of the only times in my life when I put Bruce Wayne's interests before Batman's.
And an innocent paid dearly for it.
An all-too-brief taste of something beautiful turned bitter, as my needs--my DESIRES--were once again sacrificed on twin altars of Justice and Guilt.
GREGO
FOR
STATE
SENAT
Survivor's justice.
Survivor's guilt.

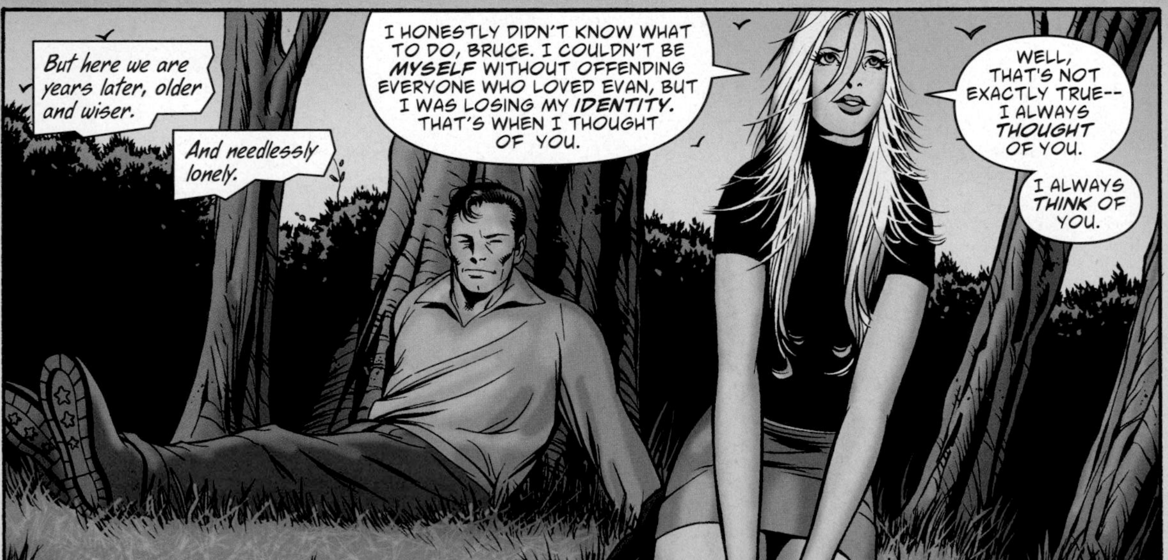
But here we are years later, older and wiser.
And needlessly lonely.
I HONESTLY DIDN'T KNOW WHAT TO DO, BRUCE. I COULDN'T BE *MYSELF* WITHOUT OFFENDING EVERYONE WHO LOVED EVAN, BUT I WAS LOSING MY *IDENTITY*. THAT'S WHEN I THOUGHT OF YOU.
WELL, THAT'S NOT EXACTLY TRUE--I ALWAYS *THOUGHT* OF YOU.
I ALWAYS *THINK* OF YOU.

I HOPE NOT *ALWAYS*--FOR GREGORY'S SAKE.

YOU'RE NOT FOLLOWING, DEEDEE.

WHEN HE DIED, I HADN'T BEEN WITH EVAN SINCE *BEFORE* THE ACCIDENT.

YOU'RE THE LAST MAN I WAS WITH.

SILVER, I...

I WASN'T *YOUR* LAST, I KNOW.

I CAN EITHER SULK ABOUT IT... OR TRY TO CATCH *UP*.

ONE SOUNDS A LOT MORE FUN, DOESN'T IT?

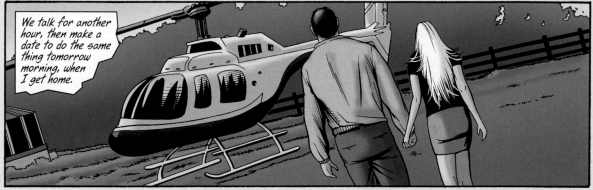

We talk for another hour, then make a date to do the same thing tomorrow morning, when I get home.

This is what the woman who just suddenly reappeared in my life after two years refers to as "taking it slow".

And I feel a slight wave of unfamiliar panic as I realize I'm straying from my area of expertise.

I'm getting into foreign territory.

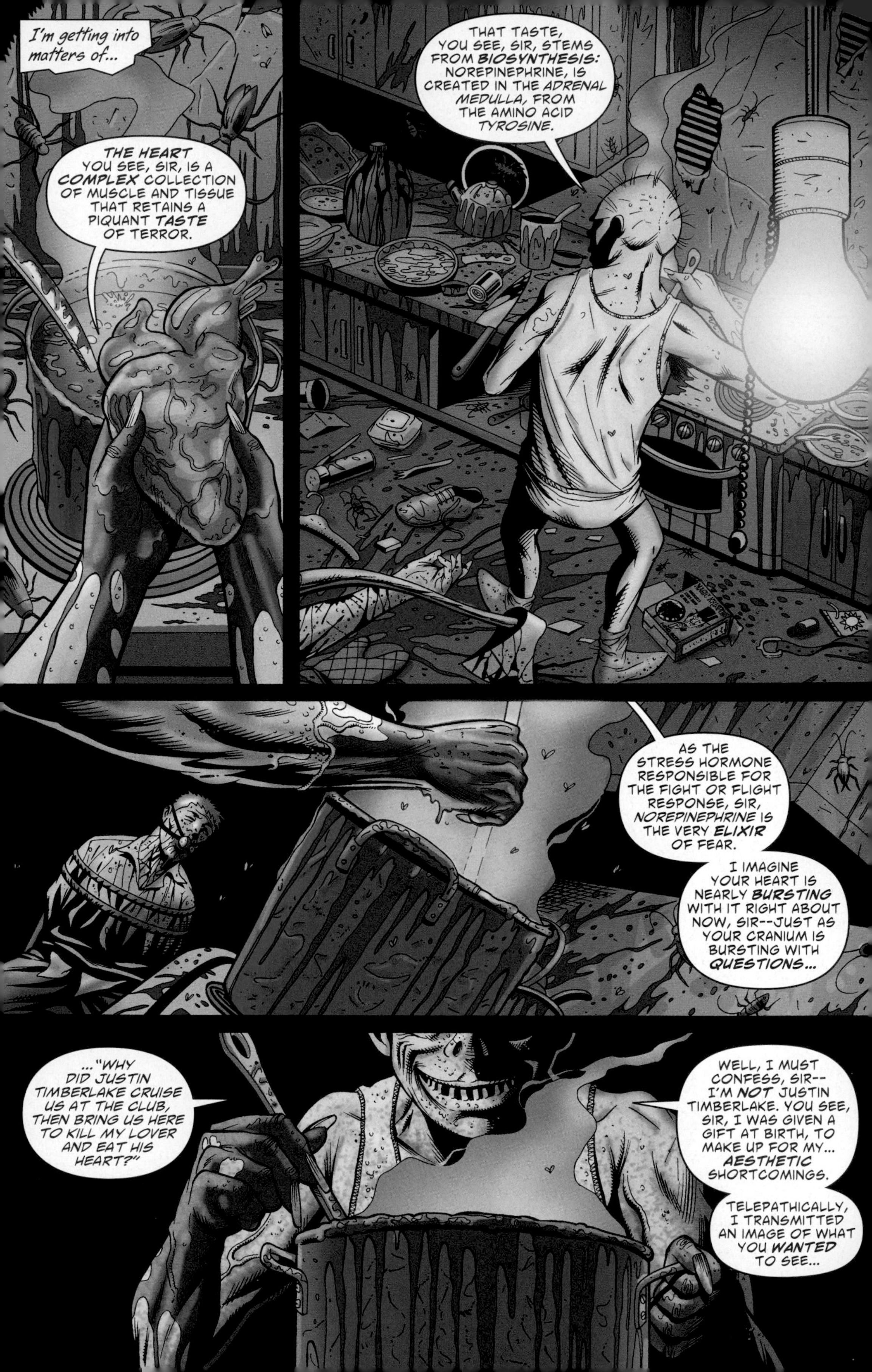
I'm getting into matters of...
THE HEART YOU SEE, SIR, IS A COMPLEX COLLECTION OF MUSCLE AND TISSUE THAT RETAINS A PIQUANT TASTE OF TERROR.
THAT TASTE, YOU SEE, SIR, STEMS FROM BIOSYNTHESIS: NOREPINEPHRINE, IS CREATED IN THE ADRENAL MEDULLA, FROM THE AMINO ACID TYROSINE.
AS THE STRESS HORMONE RESPONSIBLE FOR THE FIGHT OR FLIGHT RESPONSE, SIR, NOREPINEPHRINE IS THE VERY ELIXIR OF FEAR.
I IMAGINE YOUR HEART IS NEARLY BURSTING WITH IT RIGHT ABOUT NOW, SIR--JUST AS YOUR CRANIUM IS BURSTING WITH QUESTIONS...
..."WHY DID JUSTIN TIMBERLAKE CRUISE US AT THE CLUB, THEN BRING US HERE TO KILL MY LOVER AND EAT HIS HEART?"
WELL, I MUST CONFESS, SIR-- I'M NOT JUSTIN TIMBERLAKE. YOU SEE, SIR, I WAS GIVEN A GIFT AT BIRTH, TO MAKE UP FOR MY... AESTHETIC SHORTCOMINGS.
TELEPATHICALLY, I TRANSMITTED AN IMAGE OF WHAT YOU WANTED TO SEE...

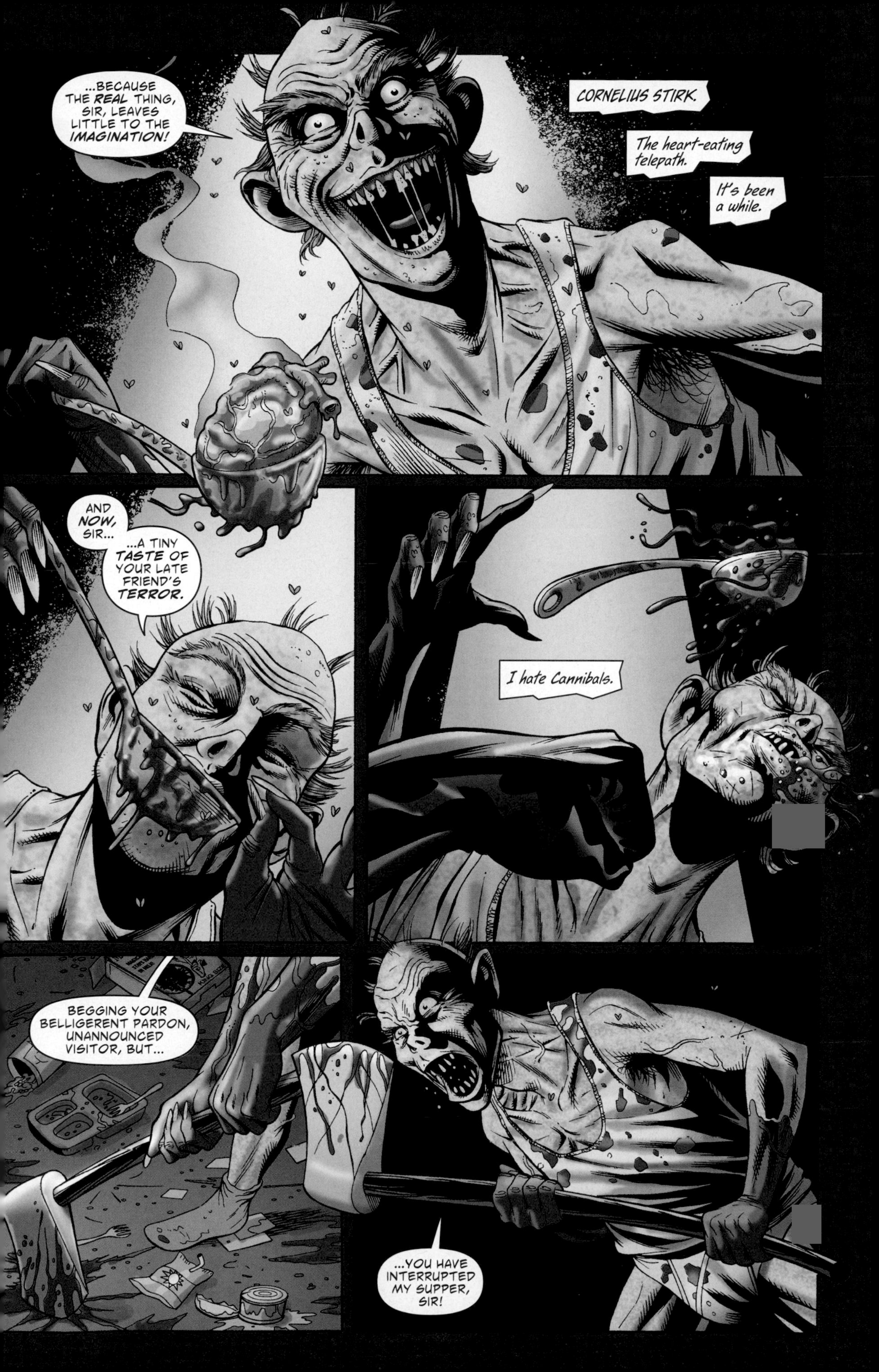
...BECAUSE THE REAL THING, SIR, LEAVES LITTLE TO THE IMAGINATION!
CORNELIUS STIRK.
The heart-eating telepath.
It's been a while.
AND NOW, SIR...
...A TINY TASTE OF YOUR LATE FRIEND'S TERROR.
I hate Cannibals.
BEGGING YOUR BELLIGERENT PARDON, UNANNOUNCED VISITOR, BUT...
...YOU HAVE INTERRUPTED MY SUPPER, SIR!

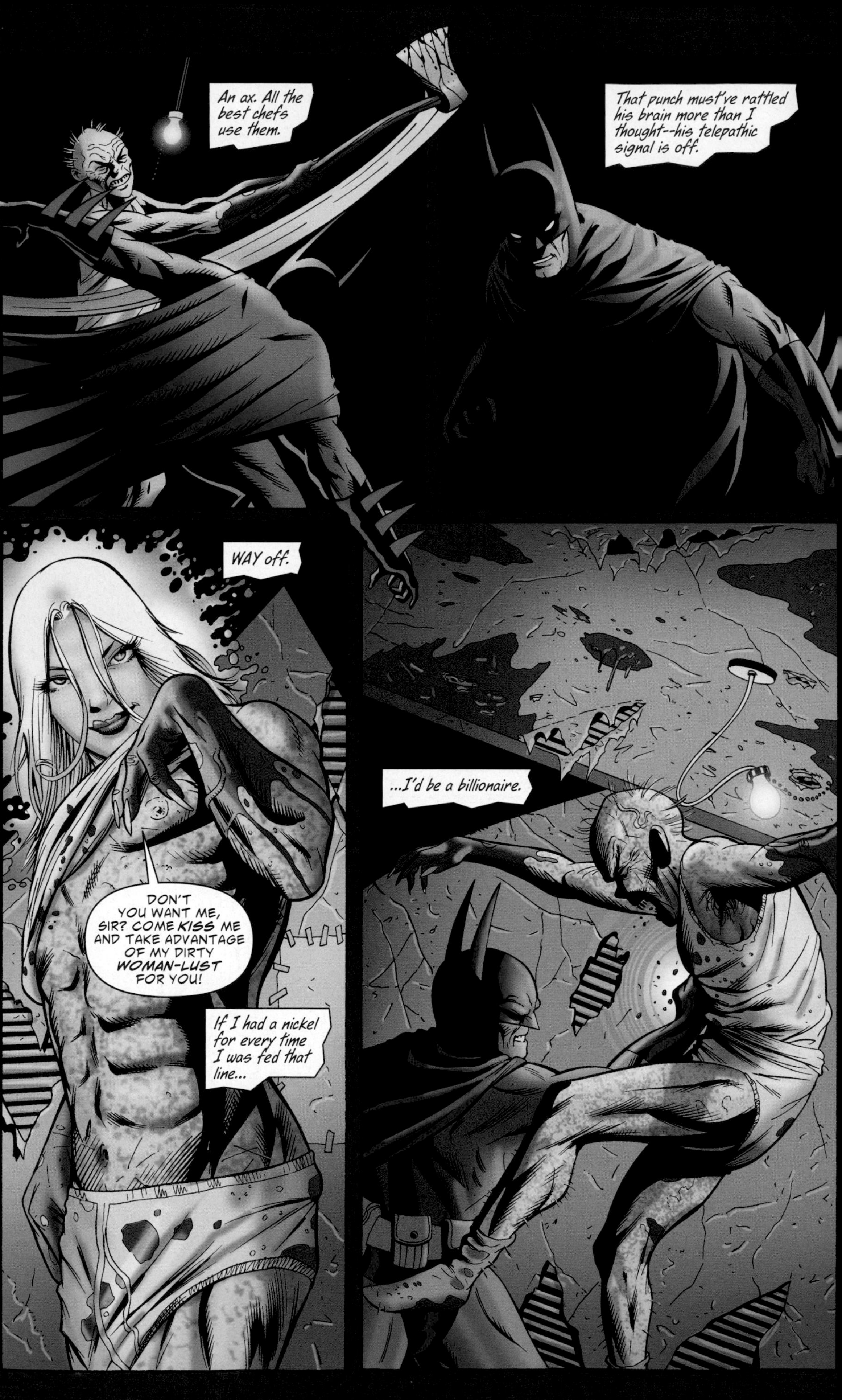

An ax. All the best chefs use them.
That punch must've rattled his brain more than I thought--his telepathic signal is off.
WAY off.
DON'T YOU WANT ME, SIR? COME KISS ME AND TAKE ADVANTAGE OF MY DIRTY WOMAN-LUST FOR YOU!
If I had a nickel for every time I was fed that line...
...I'd be a billionaire.

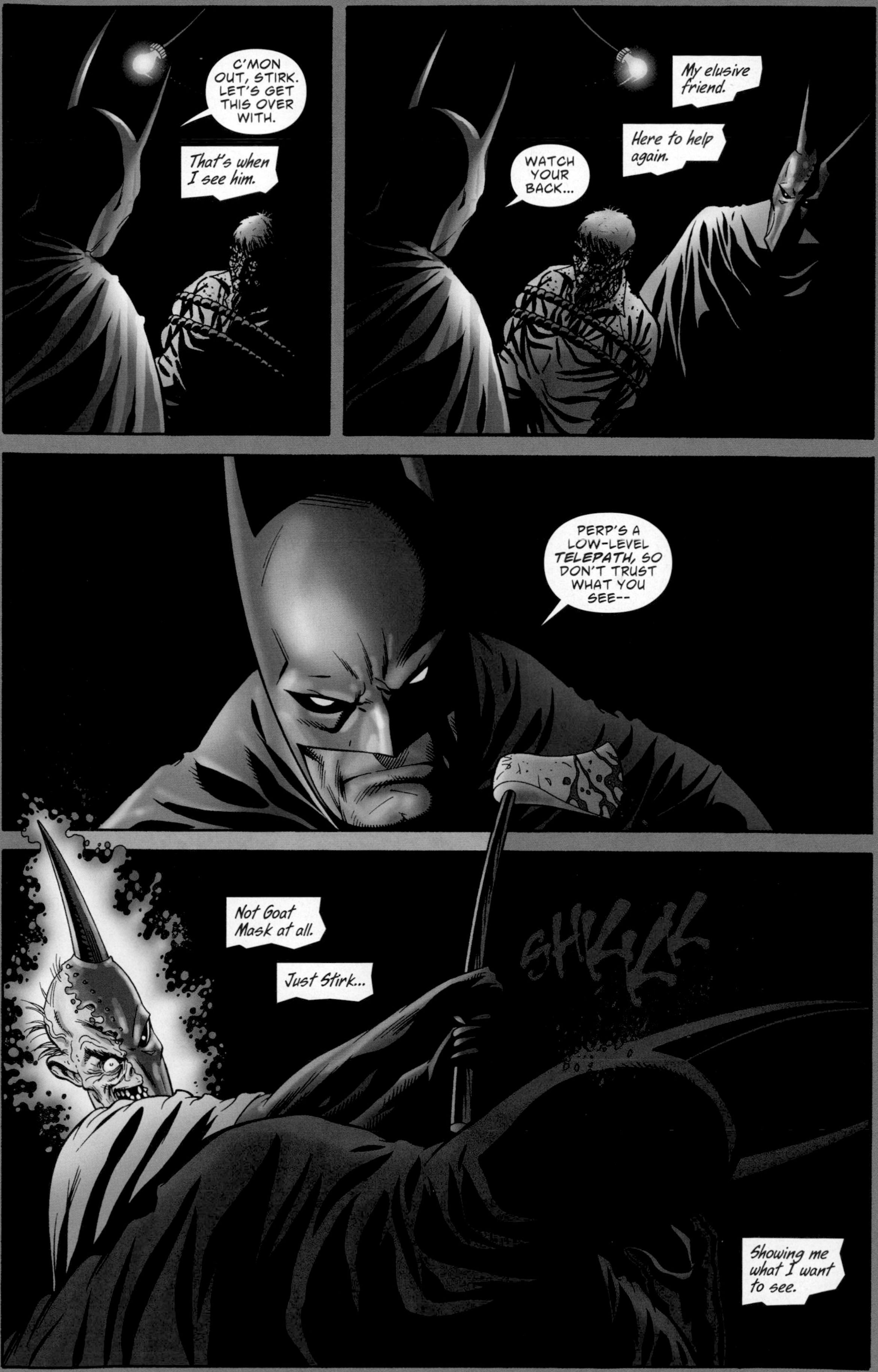

C'MON OUT, STIRK. LET'S GET THIS OVER WITH.
That's when I see him.
My elusive friend.
Here to help again.
WATCH YOUR BACK...
PERP'S A LOW-LEVEL TELEPATH, SO DON'T TRUST WHAT YOU SEE--
Not Goat Mask at all.
Just Stirk...
SHKLK
Showing me what I want to see.

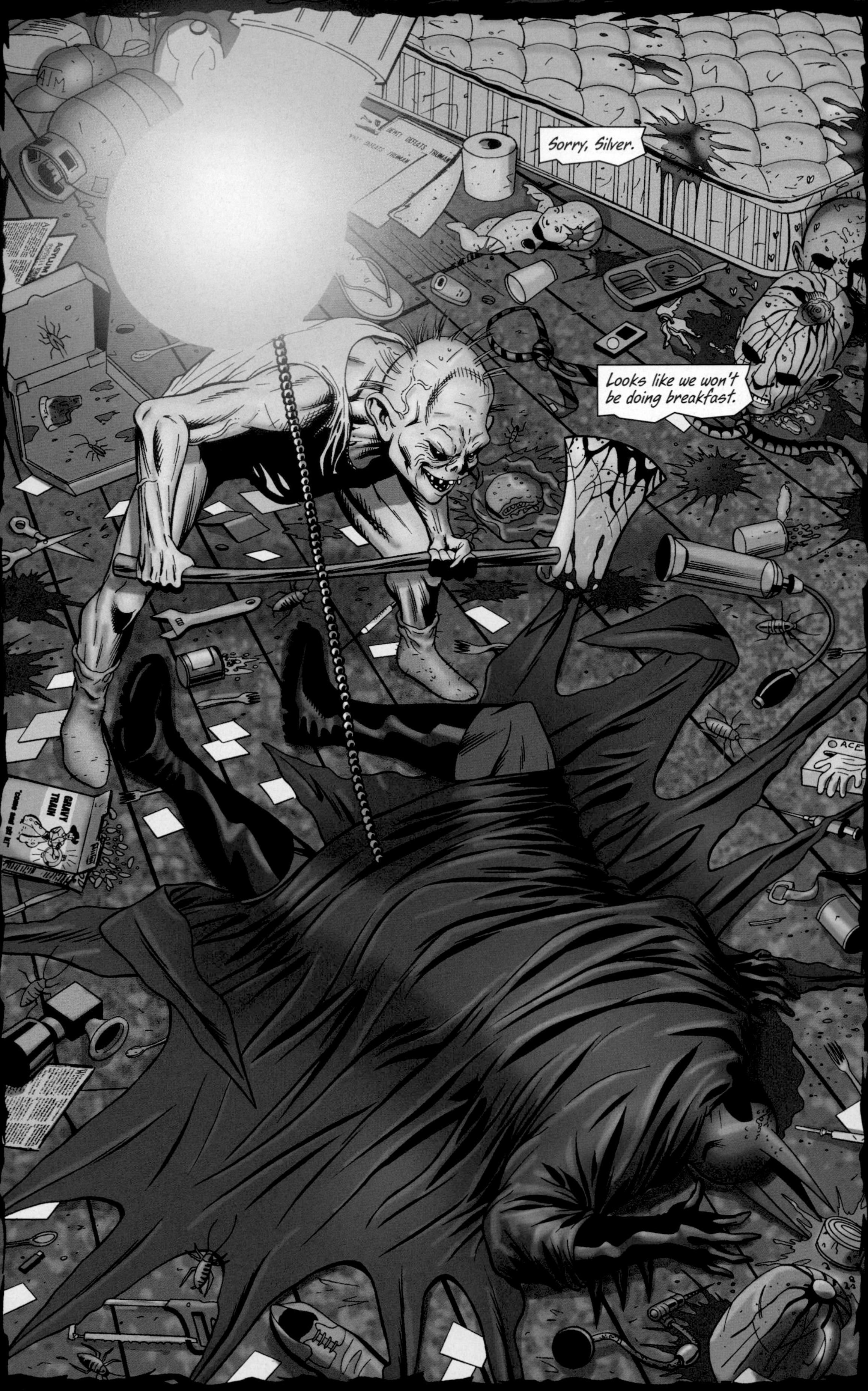
Sorry, Silver.
Looks like we won't be doing breakfast.

Batman: The Widening Gyre #3 cover by BILL SIENKIEWICZ

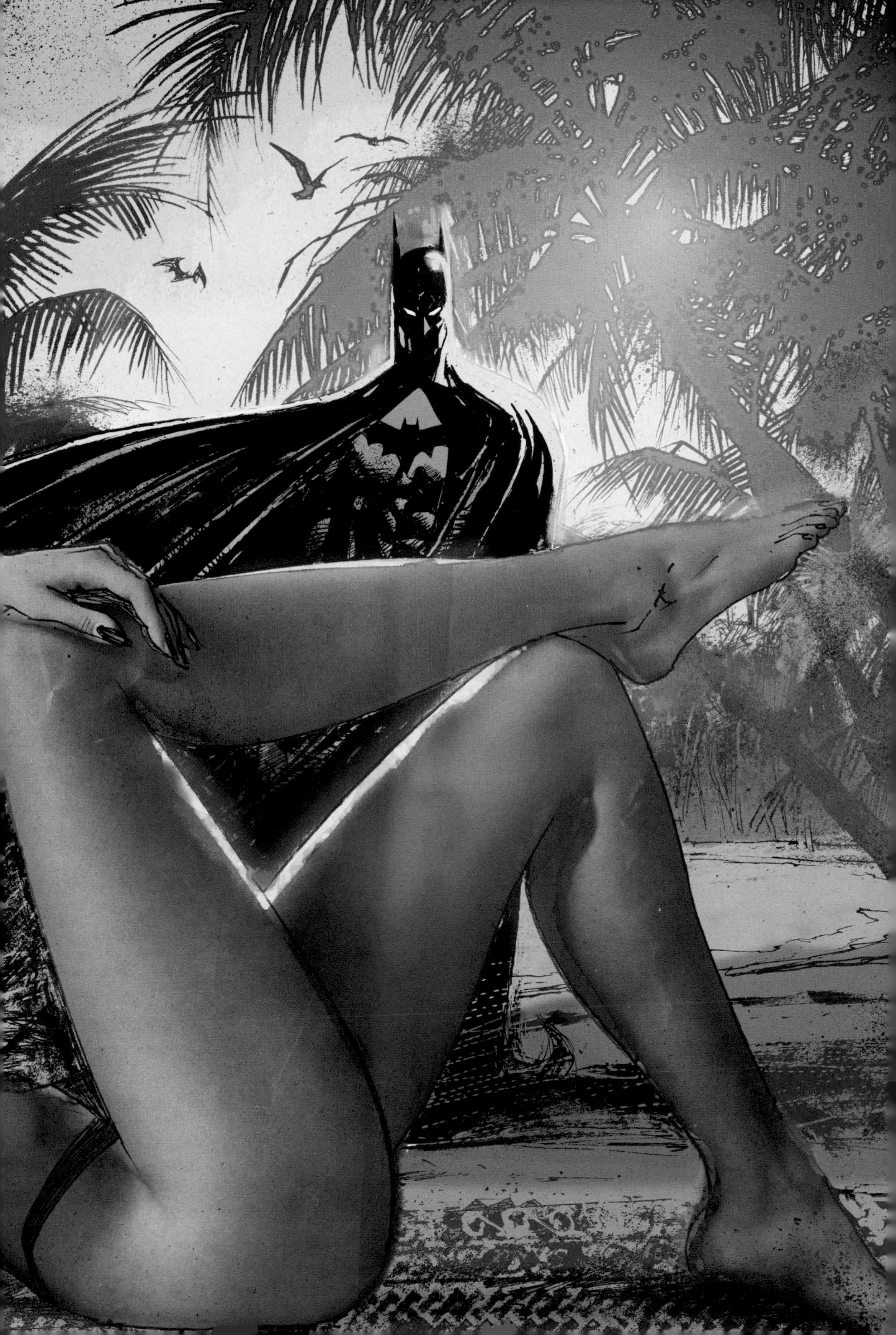

Batman: The Widening Gyre #3 alternate cover art by GENE HA

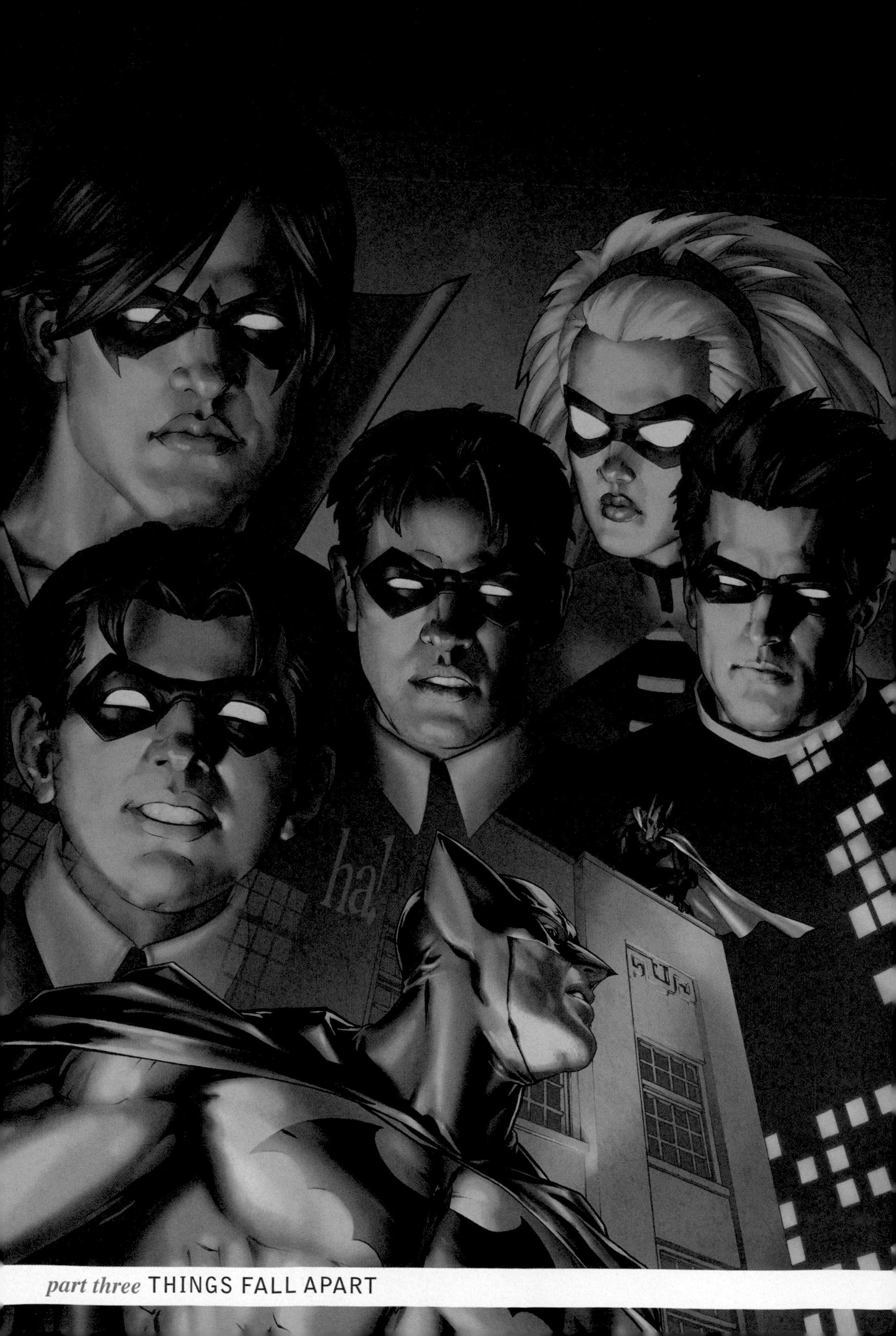

part three THINGS FALL APART

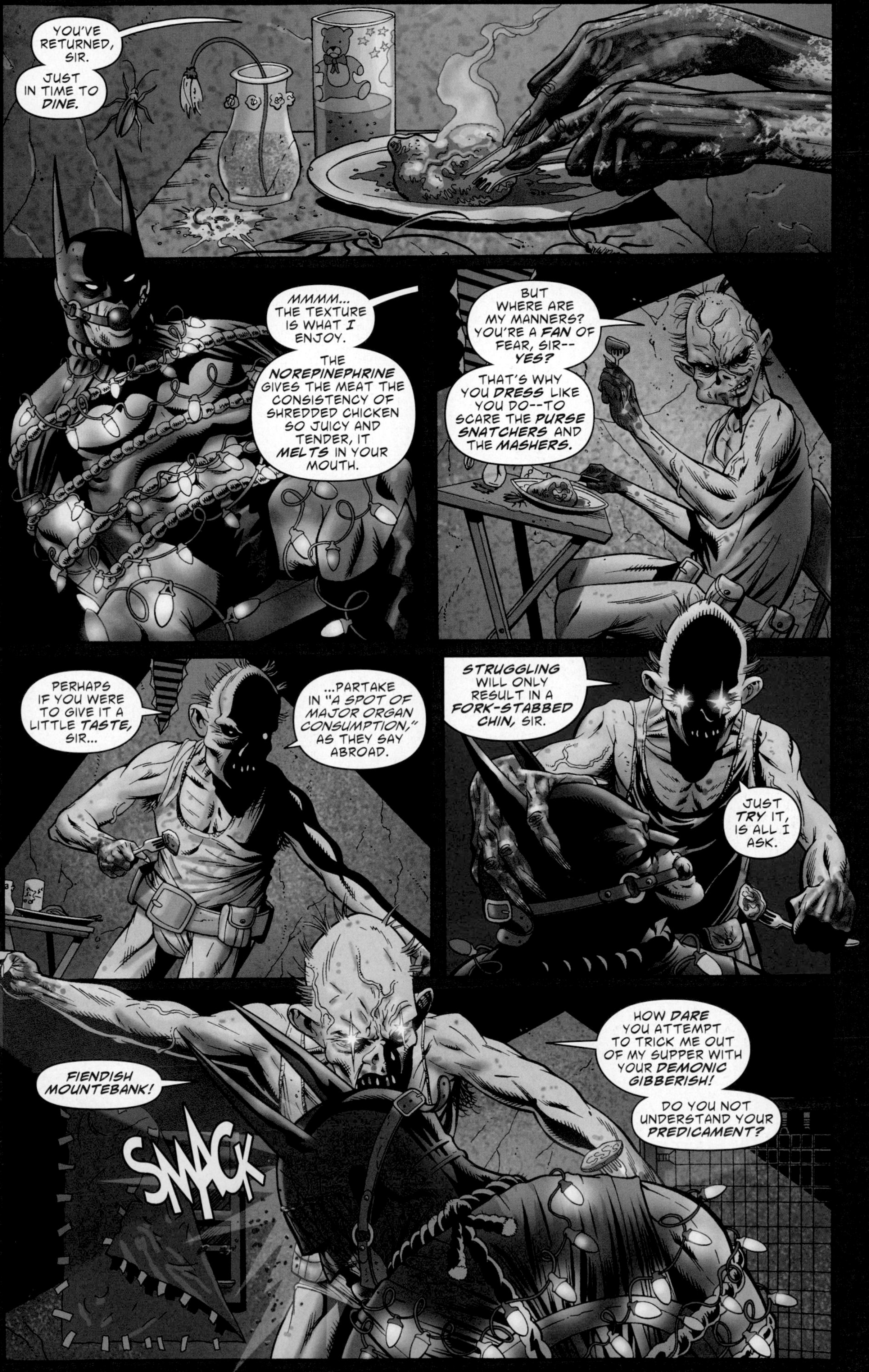
YOU'VE RETURNED, SIR.
JUST IN TIME TO DINE.
MMMM... THE TEXTURE IS WHAT I ENJOY.
THE NOREPINEPHRINE GIVES THE MEAT THE CONSISTENCY OF SHREDDED CHICKEN SO JUICY AND TENDER, IT MELTS IN YOUR MOUTH.
BUT WHERE ARE MY MANNERS? YOU'RE A FAN OF FEAR, SIR-- YES?
THAT'S WHY YOU DRESS LIKE YOU DO--TO SCARE THE PURSE SNATCHERS AND THE MASHERS.
PERHAPS IF YOU WERE TO GIVE IT A LITTLE TASTE, SIR...
...PARTAKE IN "A SPOT OF MAJOR ORGAN CONSUMPTION," AS THEY SAY ABROAD.
STRUGGLING WILL ONLY RESULT IN A FORK-STABBED CHIN, SIR.
JUST TRY IT, IS ALL I ASK.
FIENDISH MOUNTEBANK!
HOW DARE YOU ATTEMPT TO TRICK ME OUT OF MY SUPPER WITH YOUR DEMONIC GIBBERISH!
DO YOU NOT UNDERSTAND YOUR PREDICAMENT?
SMACK

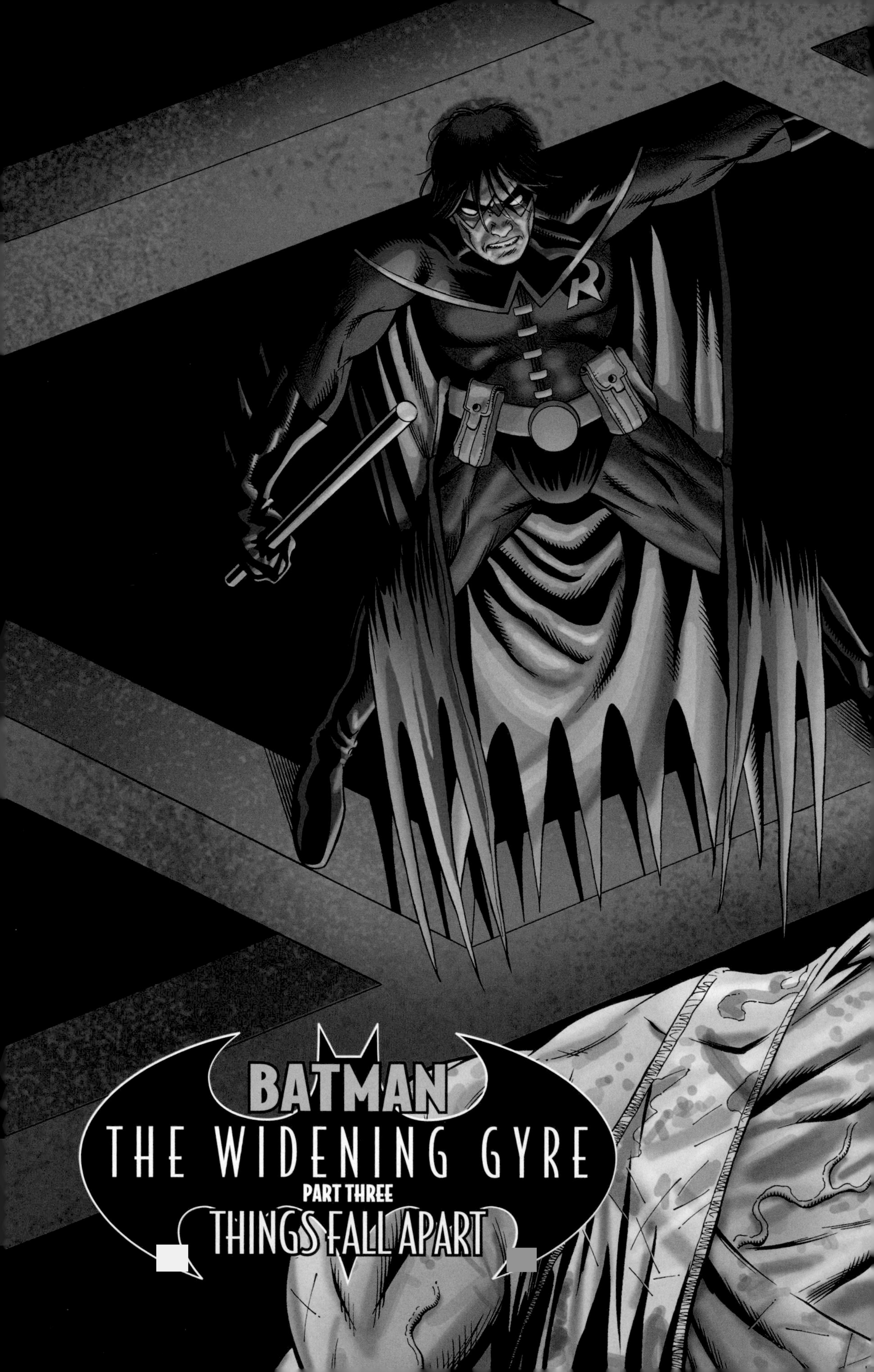
BATMAN
THE WIDENING GYRE
PART THREE
THINGS FALL APART

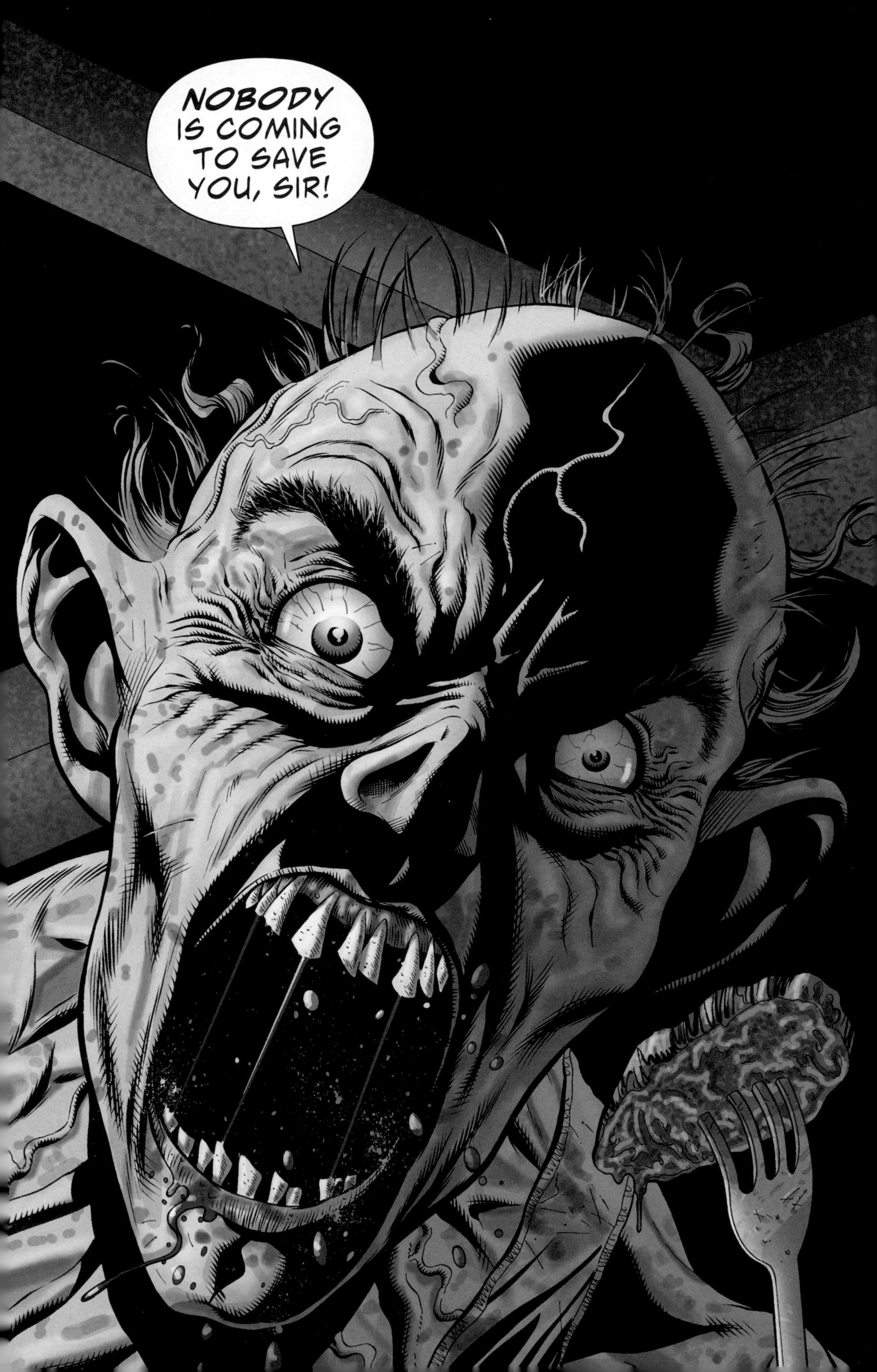
NOBODY IS COMING TO SAVE YOU, SIR!

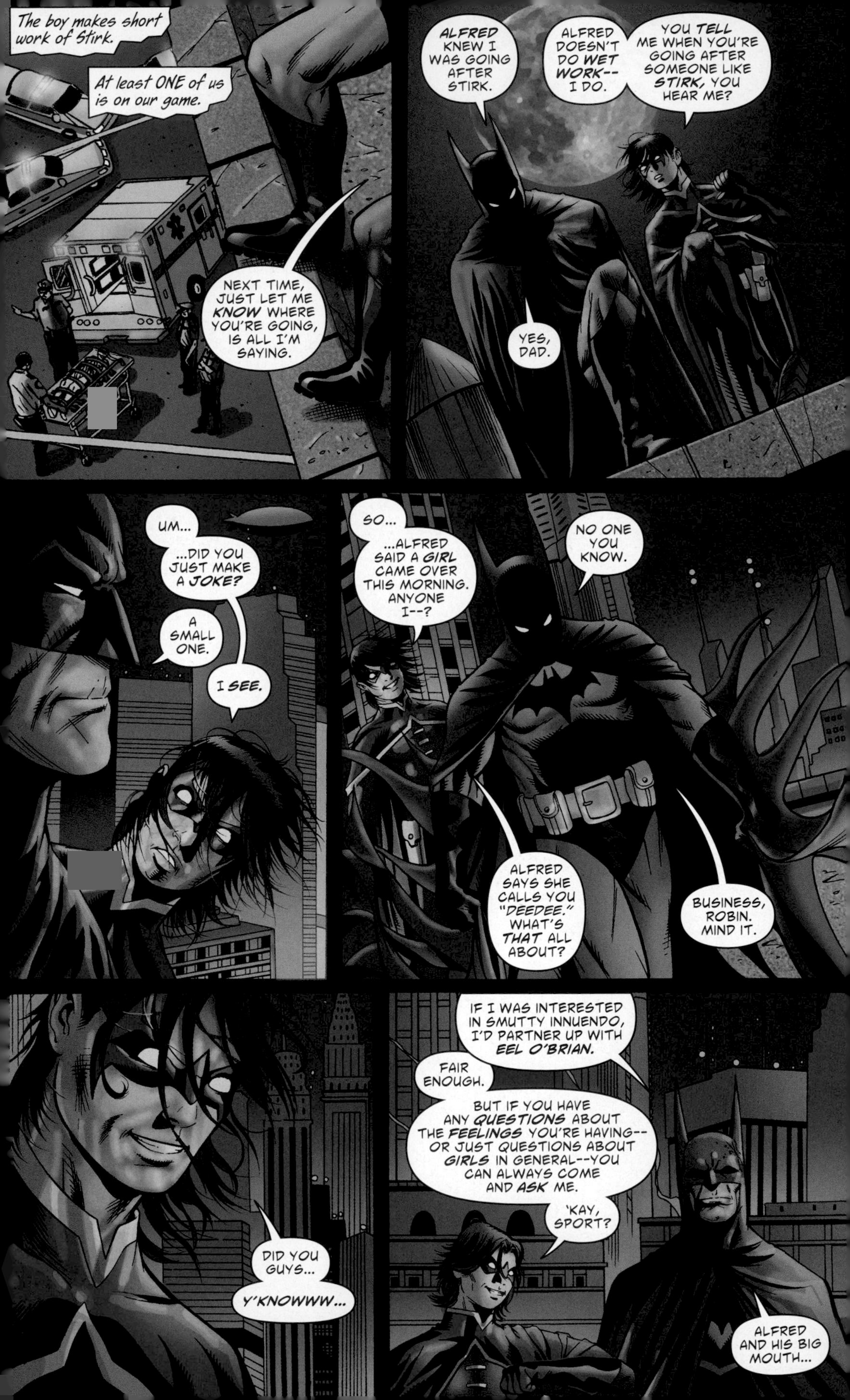

The boy makes short work of Stirk.
At least ONE of us is on our game.
NEXT TIME, JUST LET ME KNOW WHERE YOU'RE GOING, IS ALL I'M SAYING.
ALFRED KNEW I WAS GOING AFTER STIRK.
ALFRED DOESN'T DO WET WORK-- I DO.
YOU TELL ME WHEN YOU'RE GOING AFTER SOMEONE LIKE STIRK, YOU HEAR ME?
YES, DAD.
UM...
...DID YOU JUST MAKE A JOKE?
A SMALL ONE.
I SEE.
SO...
...ALFRED SAID A GIRL CAME OVER THIS MORNING. ANYONE I--?
NO ONE YOU KNOW.
ALFRED SAYS SHE CALLS YOU "DEEDEE." WHAT'S THAT ALL ABOUT?
BUSINESS, ROBIN. MIND IT.
DID YOU GUYS...
Y'KNOWWW...
IF I WAS INTERESTED IN SMUTTY INNUENDO, I'D PARTNER UP WITH EEL O'BRIAN.
FAIR ENOUGH.
BUT IF YOU HAVE ANY QUESTIONS ABOUT THE FEELINGS YOU'RE HAVING-- OR JUST QUESTIONS ABOUT GIRLS IN GENERAL--YOU CAN ALWAYS COME AND ASK ME.
'KAY, SPORT?
ALFRED AND HIS BIG MOUTH...

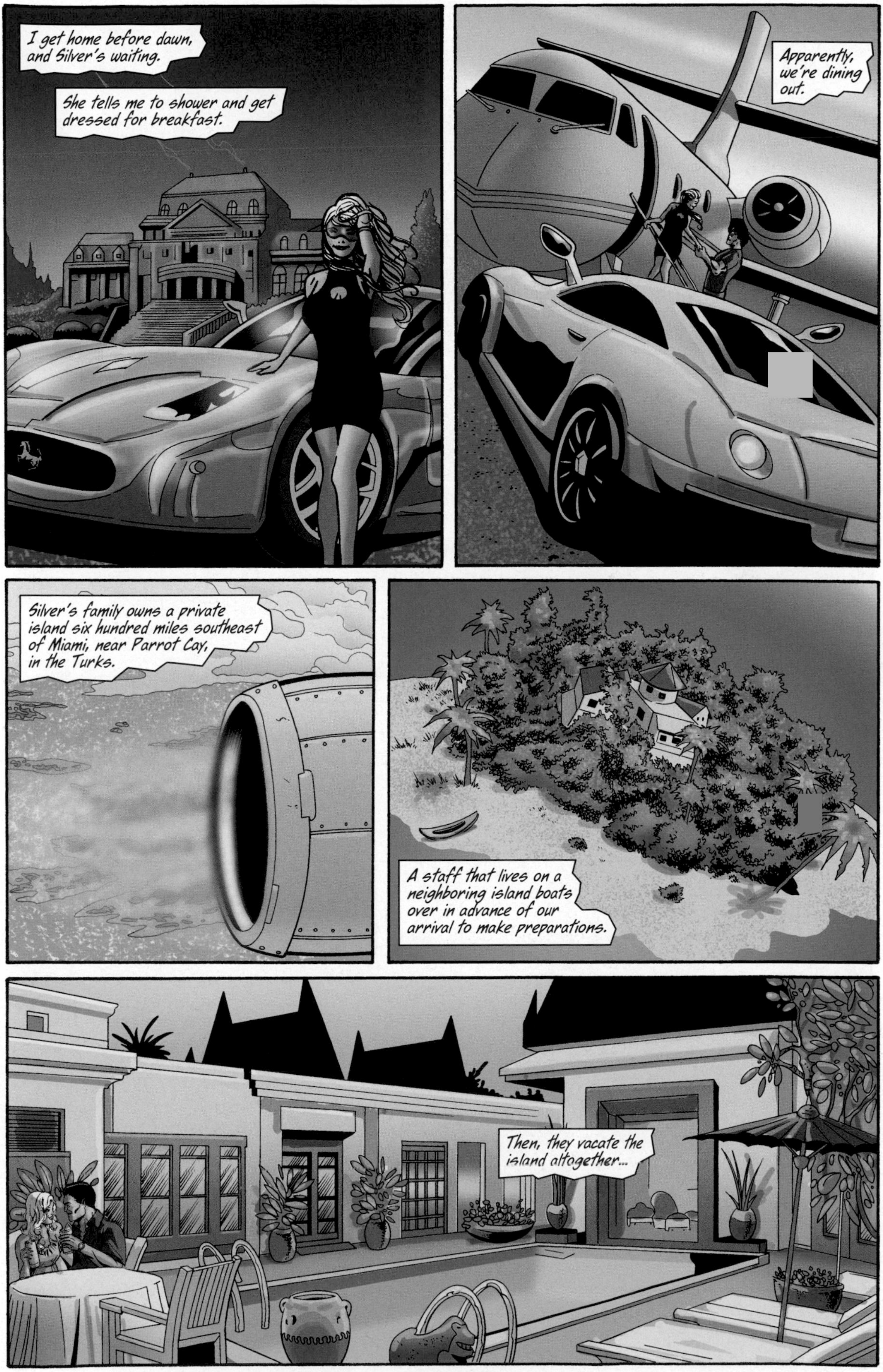
I get home before dawn, and Silver's waiting.
She tells me to shower and get dressed for breakfast.
Apparently, we're dining out.
Silver's family owns a private island six hundred miles southeast of Miami, near Parrot Cay, in the Turks.
A staff that lives on a neighboring island boats over in advance of our arrival to make preparations.
Then, they vacate the island altogether...

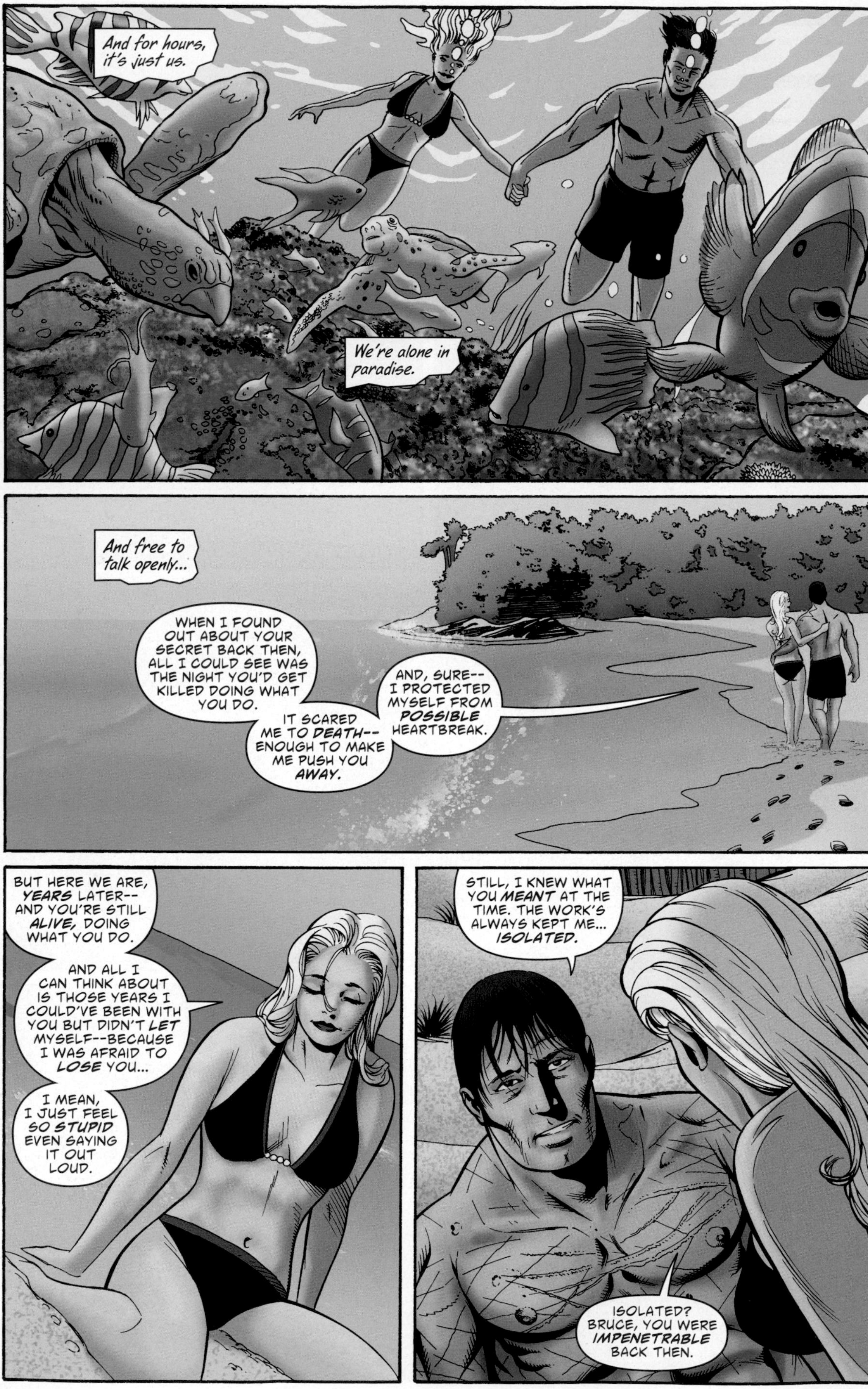
And for hours, it's just us.
We're alone in paradise.
And free to talk openly...
WHEN I FOUND OUT ABOUT YOUR SECRET BACK THEN, ALL I COULD SEE WAS THE NIGHT YOU'D GET KILLED DOING WHAT YOU DO.
IT SCARED ME TO DEATH-- ENOUGH TO MAKE ME PUSH YOU AWAY.
AND, SURE-- I PROTECTED MYSELF FROM POSSIBLE HEARTBREAK.
BUT HERE WE ARE, YEARS LATER-- AND YOU'RE STILL ALIVE, DOING WHAT YOU DO.
AND ALL I CAN THINK ABOUT IS THOSE YEARS I COULD'VE BEEN WITH YOU BUT DIDN'T LET MYSELF--BECAUSE I WAS AFRAID TO LOSE YOU...
I MEAN, I JUST FEEL SO STUPID EVEN SAYING IT OUT LOUD.
STILL, I KNEW WHAT YOU MEANT AT THE TIME. THE WORK'S ALWAYS KEPT ME... ISOLATED.
ISOLATED? BRUCE, YOU WERE IMPENETRABLE BACK THEN.

THAT HASN'T REALLY CHANGED MUCH, SILS.
BUT THAT DOESN'T MATTER ANYMORE, BECAUSE I'VE CHANGED. I'M NOT THE GIGGLY SOCIALITE CELEBUTANTE I WAS WHEN WE MET.
I'M A GROWN WOMAN--AND OVER THE YEARS, I'VE FIGURED OUT WHAT I WANT IN LIFE.
AND WHAT I WANT IS TO SPEND SOME ALONE TIME WITH YOU, DEEDEE--AWAY FROM PRYING EYES. AND SINCE YOU'RE BUSY AT NIGHTS...WELL, I GUESS WE'LL JUST HAVE TO DATE DURING THE DAY.
AND IF IT TURNS INTO SOMETHING? GREAT. BUT IF IT DOESN'T...
It will, Silver.
This time, I promise...
It will.
For a moment...the world melts away.
Nothing else matters.
NOTHING else...
...but her.

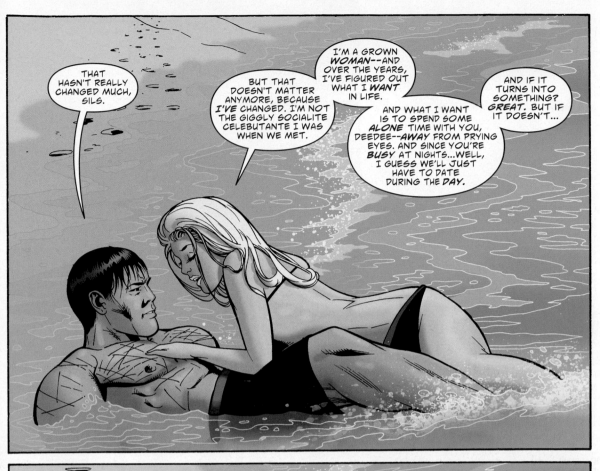

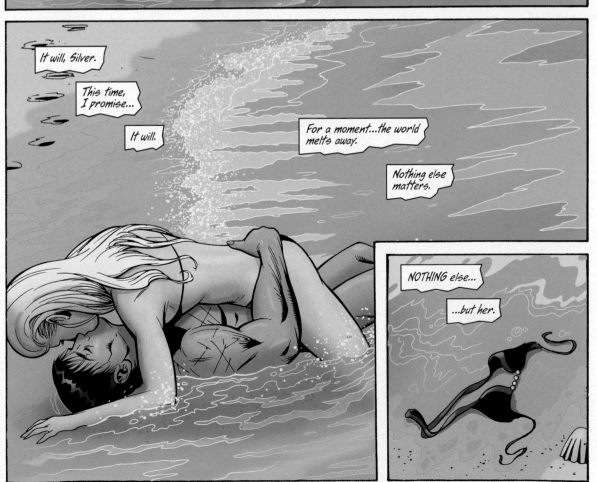

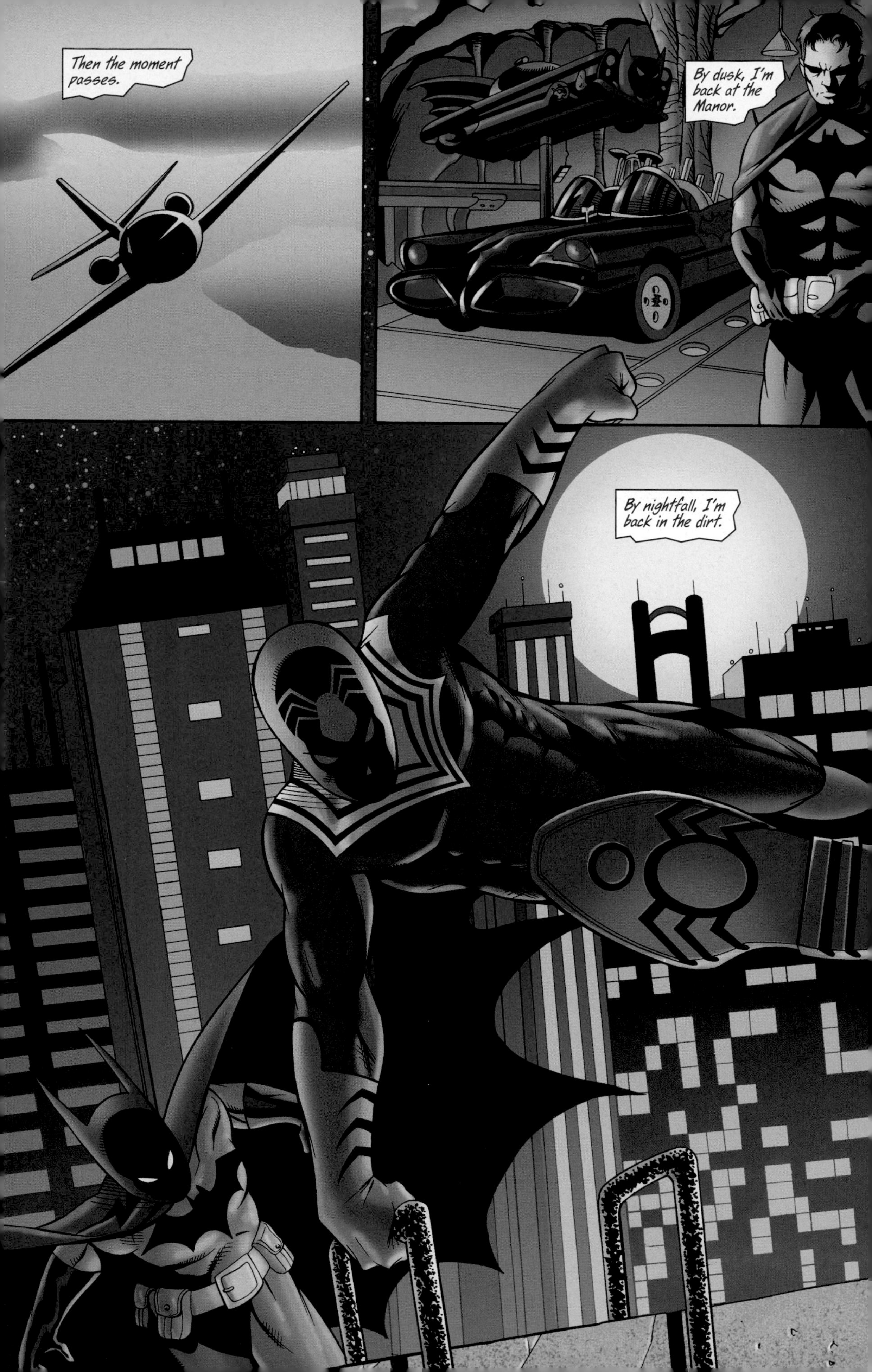
Then the moment passes.
By dusk, I'm back at the Manor.
By nightfall, I'm back in the dirt.

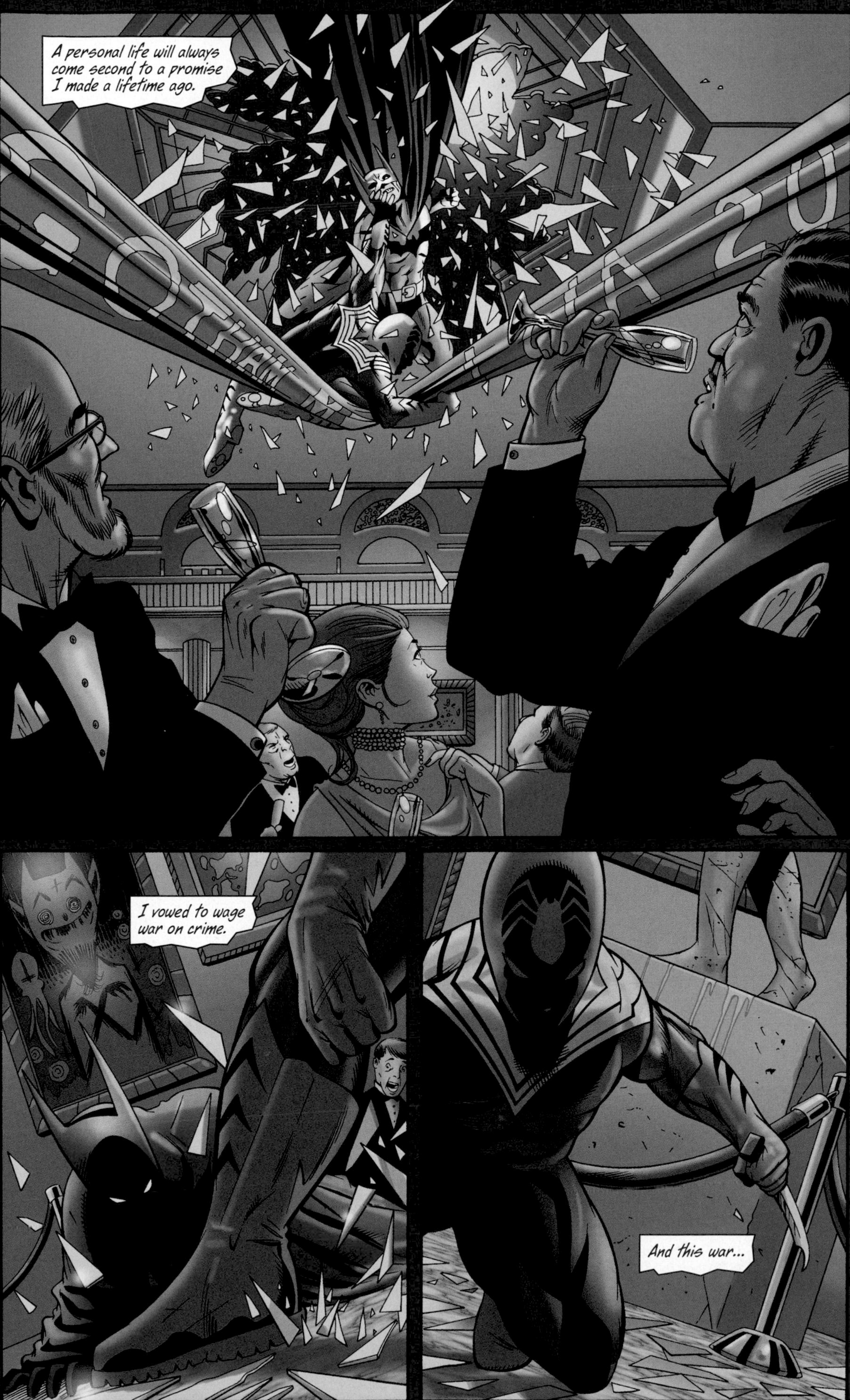
A personal life will always come second to a promise I made a lifetime ago.
I vowed to wage war on crime.
And this war...

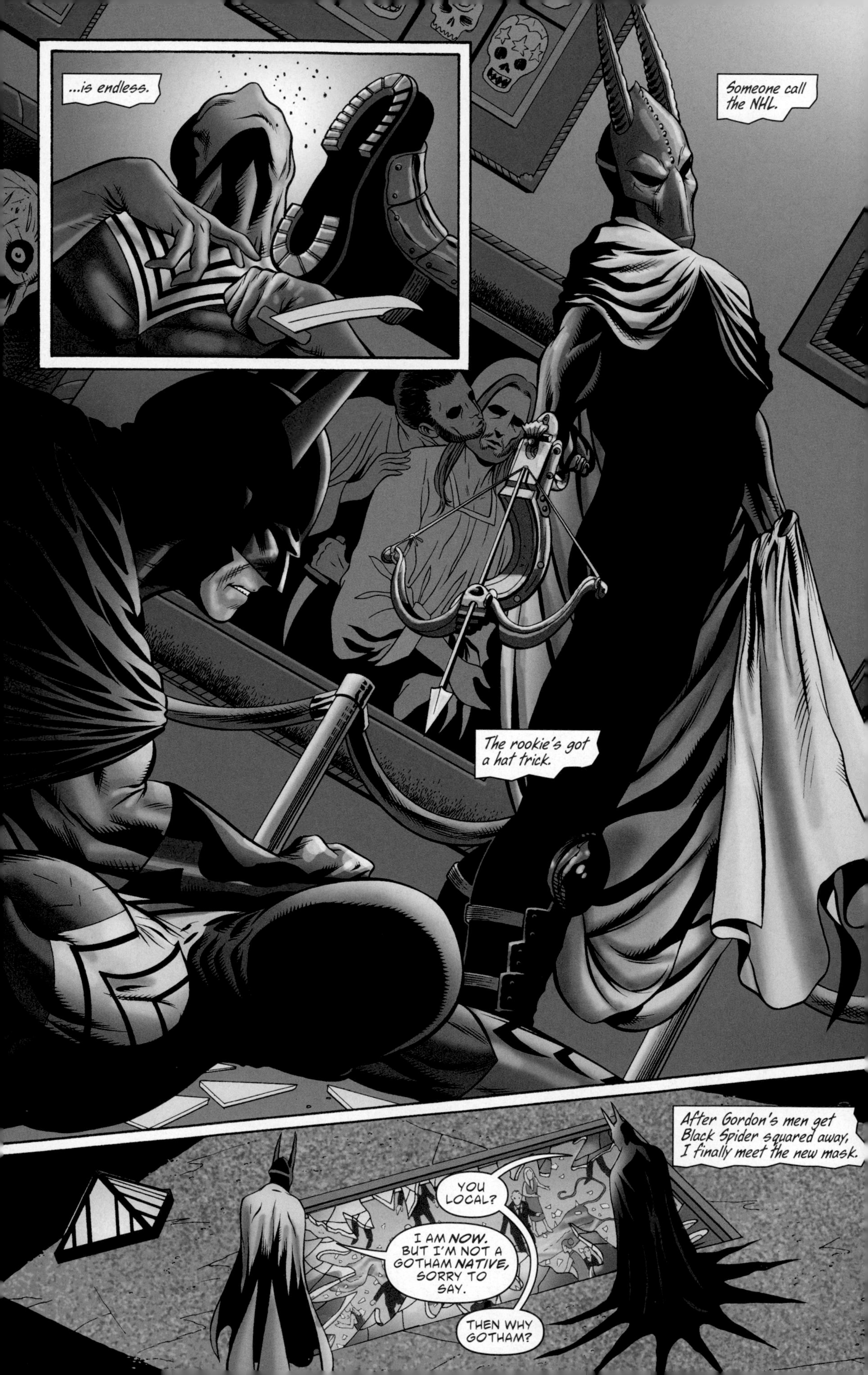

...is endless.
Someone call the NHL.
The rookie's got a hat trick.
After Gordon's men get Black Spider squared away, I finally meet the new mask.
YOU LOCAL?
I AM NOW. BUT I'M NOT A GOTHAM NATIVE, SORRY TO SAY.
THEN WHY GOTHAM?

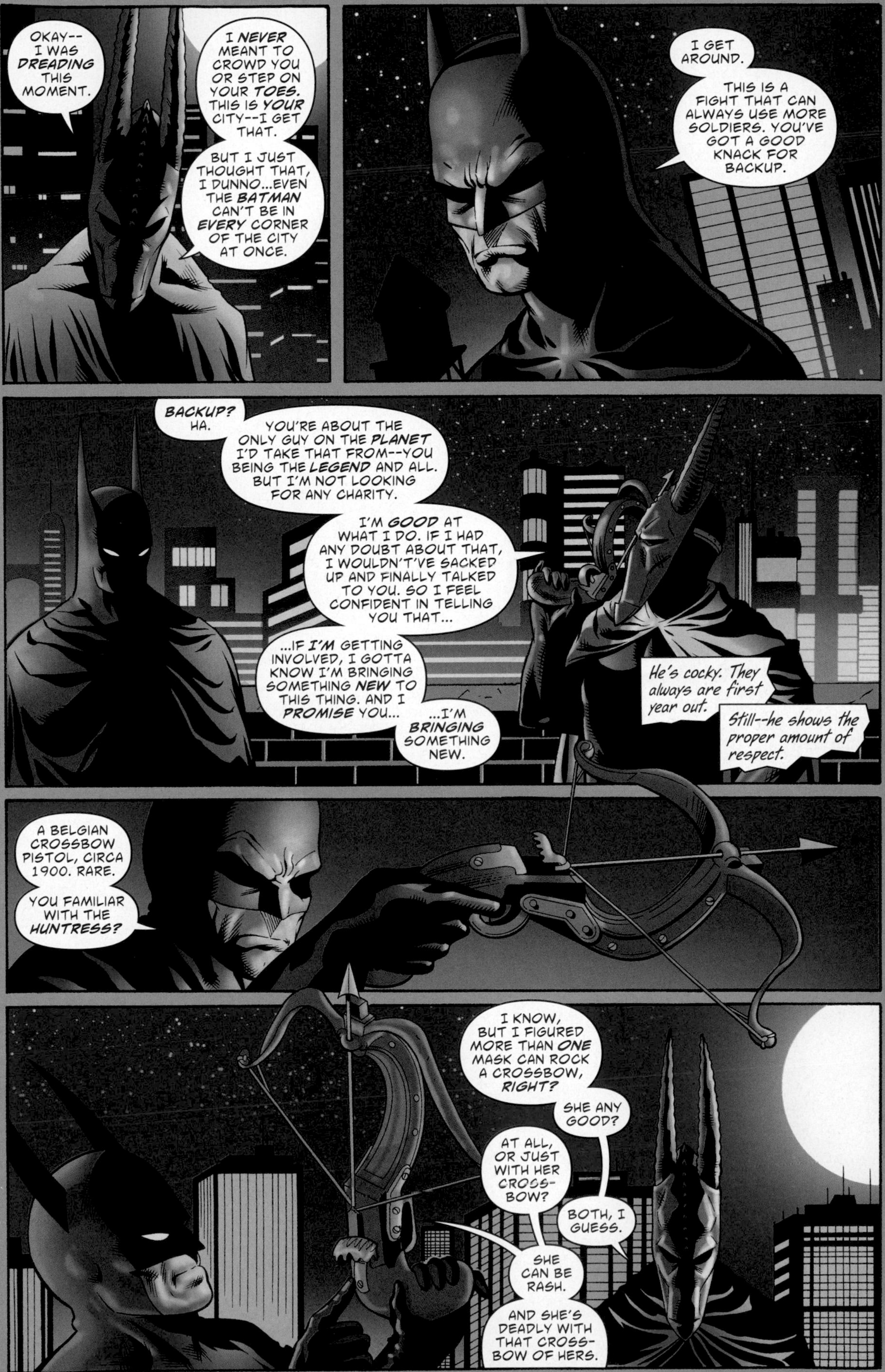
OKAY-- I WAS DREADING THIS MOMENT.
I NEVER MEANT TO CROWD YOU OR STEP ON YOUR TOES. THIS IS YOUR CITY--I GET THAT.
BUT I JUST THOUGHT THAT, I DUNNO...EVEN THE BATMAN CAN'T BE IN EVERY CORNER OF THE CITY AT ONCE.
I GET AROUND.
THIS IS A FIGHT THAT CAN ALWAYS USE MORE SOLDIERS. YOU'VE GOT A GOOD KNACK FOR BACKUP.
BACKUP? HA.
YOU'RE ABOUT THE ONLY GUY ON THE PLANET I'D TAKE THAT FROM--YOU BEING THE LEGEND AND ALL. BUT I'M NOT LOOKING FOR ANY CHARITY.
I'M GOOD AT WHAT I DO. IF I HAD ANY DOUBT ABOUT THAT, I WOULDN'T'VE SACKED UP AND FINALLY TALKED TO YOU. SO I FEEL CONFIDENT IN TELLING YOU THAT...
...IF I'M GETTING INVOLVED, I GOTTA KNOW I'M BRINGING SOMETHING NEW TO THIS THING. AND I PROMISE YOU...
...I'M BRINGING SOMETHING NEW.
He's cocky. They always are first year out.
Still--he shows the proper amount of respect.
A BELGIAN CROSSBOW PISTOL, CIRCA 1900. RARE.
YOU FAMILIAR WITH THE HUNTRESS?
I KNOW, BUT I FIGURED MORE THAN ONE MASK CAN ROCK A CROSSBOW, RIGHT?
SHE ANY GOOD?
AT ALL, OR JUST WITH HER CROSS-BOW?
BOTH, I GUESS.
SHE CAN BE RASH.
AND SHE'S DEADLY WITH THAT CROSS-BOW OF HERS.

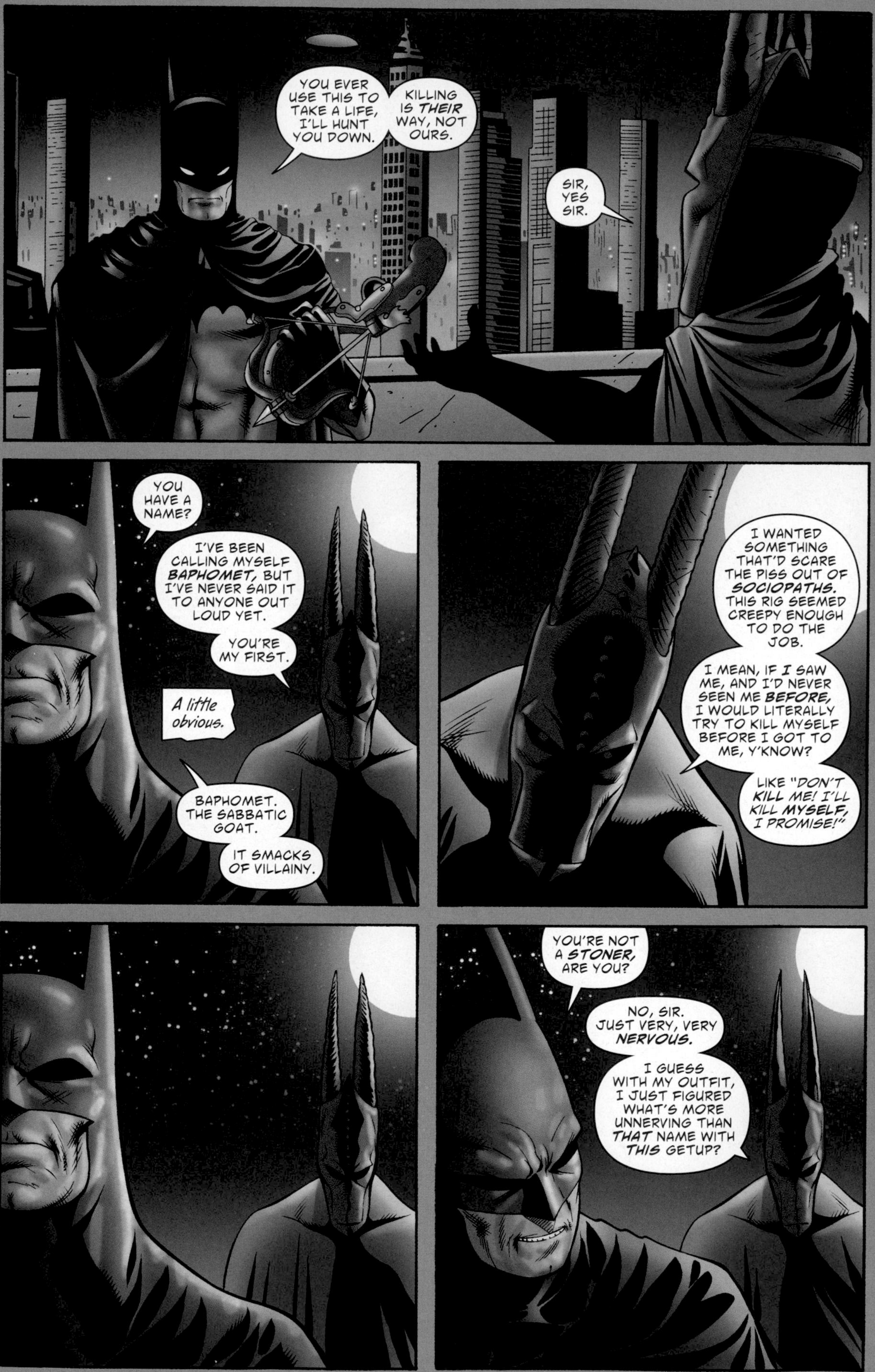

YOU EVER USE THIS TO TAKE A LIFE, I'LL HUNT YOU DOWN.
KILLING IS *THEIR* WAY, NOT OURS.
SIR, YES SIR.
YOU HAVE A NAME?
I'VE BEEN CALLING MYSELF *BAPHOMET,* BUT I'VE NEVER SAID IT TO ANYONE OUT LOUD YET.
YOU'RE MY FIRST.
A little obvious.
BAPHOMET. THE SABBATIC GOAT.
IT SMACKS OF VILLAINY.
I WANTED SOMETHING THAT'D SCARE THE PISS OUT OF *SOCIOPATHS.* THIS RIG SEEMED CREEPY ENOUGH TO DO THE JOB.
I MEAN, IF *I* SAW ME, AND I'D NEVER SEEN ME *BEFORE,* I WOULD LITERALLY TRY TO KILL MYSELF BEFORE I GOT TO ME, Y'KNOW?
LIKE "*DON'T KILL ME! I'LL KILL MYSELF, I PROMISE!*"
YOU'RE NOT A *STONER,* ARE YOU?
NO, SIR. JUST VERY, VERY *NERVOUS.*
I GUESS WITH MY OUTFIT, I JUST FIGURED WHAT'S MORE UNNERVING THAN *THAT* NAME WITH *THIS* GETUP?

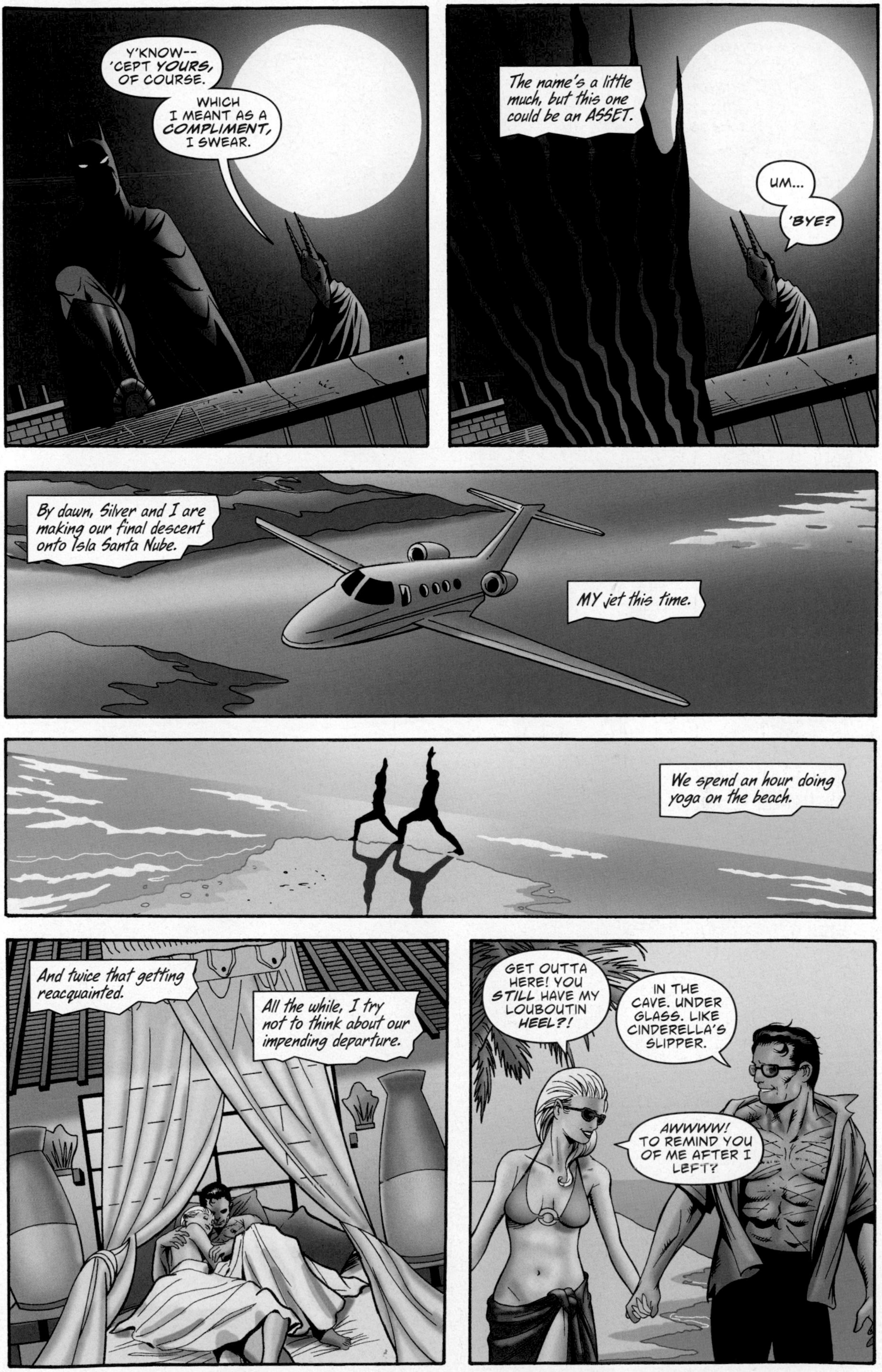
Y'KNOW-- 'CEPT YOURS, OF COURSE.
WHICH I MEANT AS A COMPLIMENT, I SWEAR.
The name's a little much, but this one could be an ASSET.
UM...
'BYE?
By dawn, Silver and I are making our final descent onto Isla Santa Nube.
MY jet this time.
We spend an hour doing yoga on the beach.
And twice that getting reacquainted.
All the while, I try not to think about our impending departure.
GET OUTTA HERE! YOU STILL HAVE MY LOUBOUTIN HEEL?!
IN THE CAVE. UNDER GLASS. LIKE CINDERELLA'S SLIPPER.
AWWWW! TO REMIND YOU OF ME AFTER I LEFT?

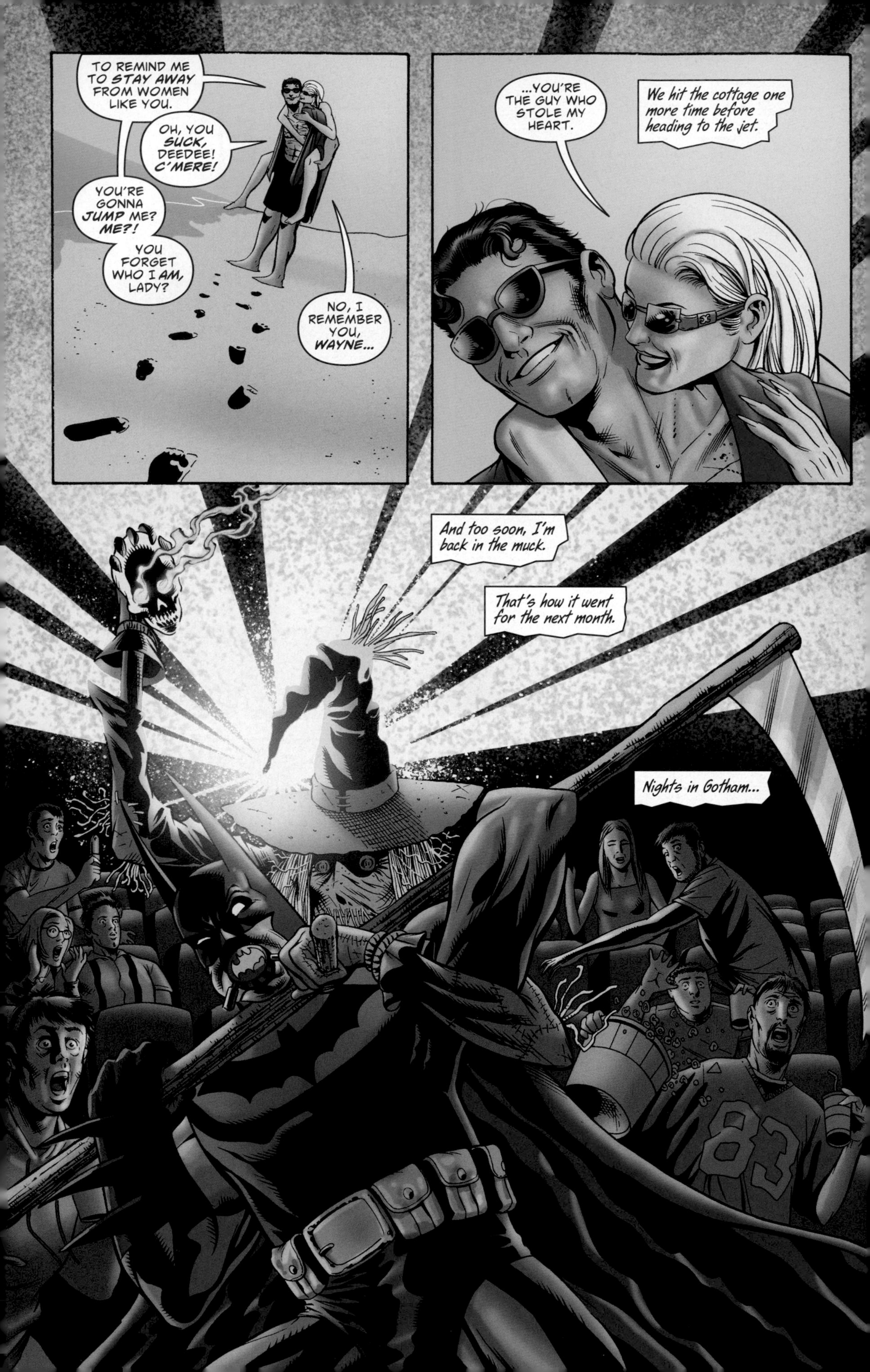
TO REMIND ME TO STAY AWAY FROM WOMEN LIKE YOU.
OH, YOU SUCK, DEEDEE! C'MERE!
YOU'RE GONNA JUMP ME? ME?!
YOU FORGET WHO I AM, LADY?
NO, I REMEMBER YOU, WAYNE...
...YOU'RE THE GUY WHO STOLE MY HEART.
We hit the cottage one more time before heading to the jet.
And too soon, I'm back in the muck.
That's how it went for the next month.
Nights in Gotham...

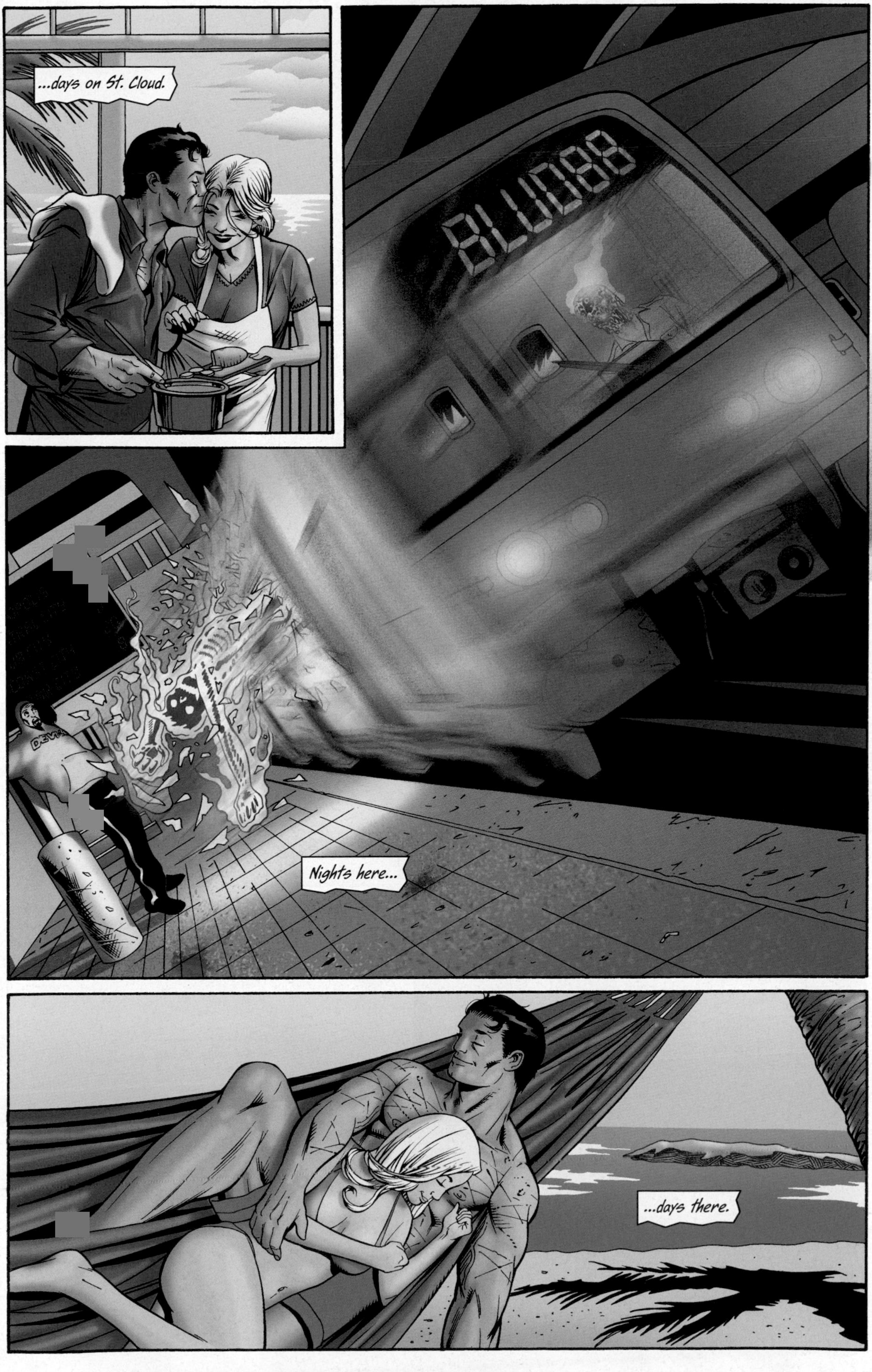
...days on St. Cloud.
Nights here...
...days there.

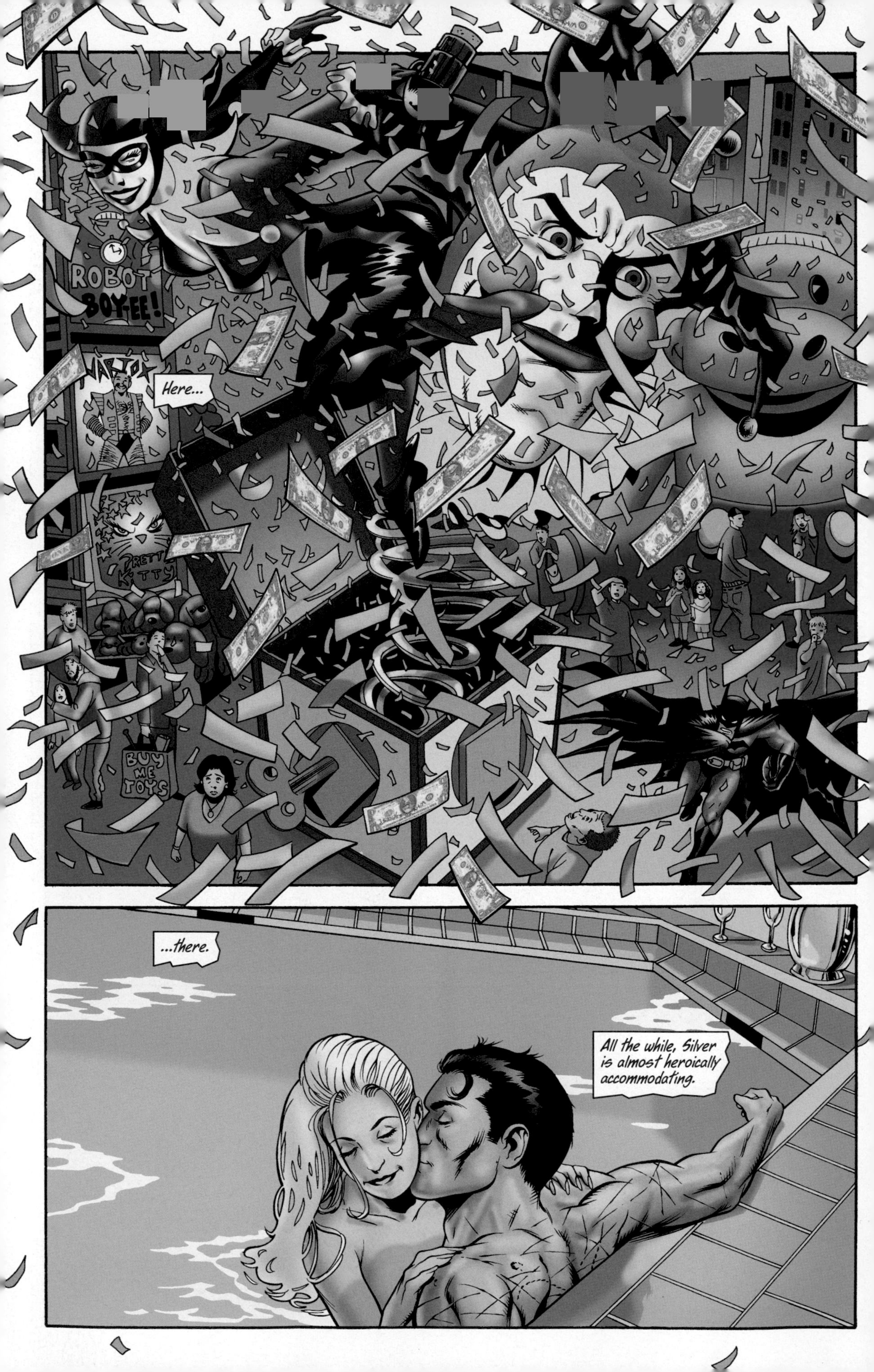
ROBOT BOY-EE!
Here...
PRETTY KITTY
BUY ME TOYS
...there.
All the while, Silver is almost heroically accommodating.

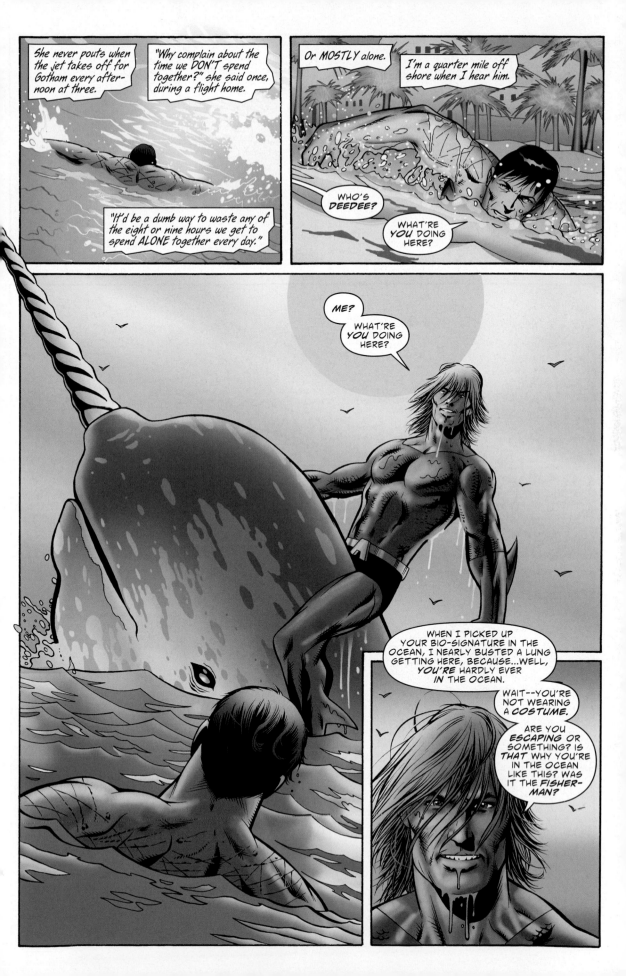

She never pouts when the jet takes off for Gotham every afternoon at three.

"Why complain about the time we DON'T spend together?" she said once, during a flight home.

"It'd be a dumb way to waste any of the eight or nine hours we get to spend ALONE together every day."

Or MOSTLY alone.

I'm a quarter mile off shore when I hear him.

WHO'S DEEDEE?

WHAT'RE *YOU* DOING HERE?

ME? WHAT'RE *YOU* DOING HERE?

WHEN I PICKED UP YOUR BIO-SIGNATURE IN THE OCEAN, I NEARLY BUSTED A LUNG GETTING HERE, BECAUSE...WELL, *YOU'RE* HARDLY EVER IN THE OCEAN.

WAIT--YOU'RE NOT WEARING A *COSTUME*.

ARE YOU *ESCAPING* OR SOMETHING? IS *THAT* WHY YOU'RE IN THE OCEAN LIKE THIS? WAS IT THE *FISHERMAN*?

I'M JUST *SWIMMING.*

WHAT, LIKE--FOR *FUN?*

SOMETHING I CAN *DO* FOR YOU, ARTHUR?

NO, I'M JUST GLAD YOU'RE *ALL RIGHT,* REALLY. THEY TOLD ME THERE'D BEEN YELLING AND SCREAMING, SO I WAS EXPECTING THE *WORST.*

WHO TOLD YOU THERE WAS YELLING AND SCREAMING?

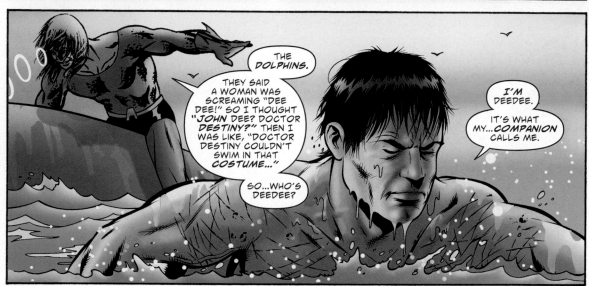

THE *DOLPHINS.*

THEY SAID A WOMAN WAS SCREAMING "DEE DEE!" SO I THOUGHT *"JOHN* DEE? DOCTOR *DESTINY?"* THEN I WAS LIKE, "DOCTOR DESTINY COULDN'T SWIM IN THAT *COSTUME..."*

SO...WHO'S DEEDEE?

I'M DEEDEE.

IT'S WHAT MY...*COMPANION* CALLS ME.

ROBIN CALLS YOU *DEEDEE?*

MY *GIRLFRIEND* CALLS ME DEEDEE-- ALL RIGHT, ARTHUR?!

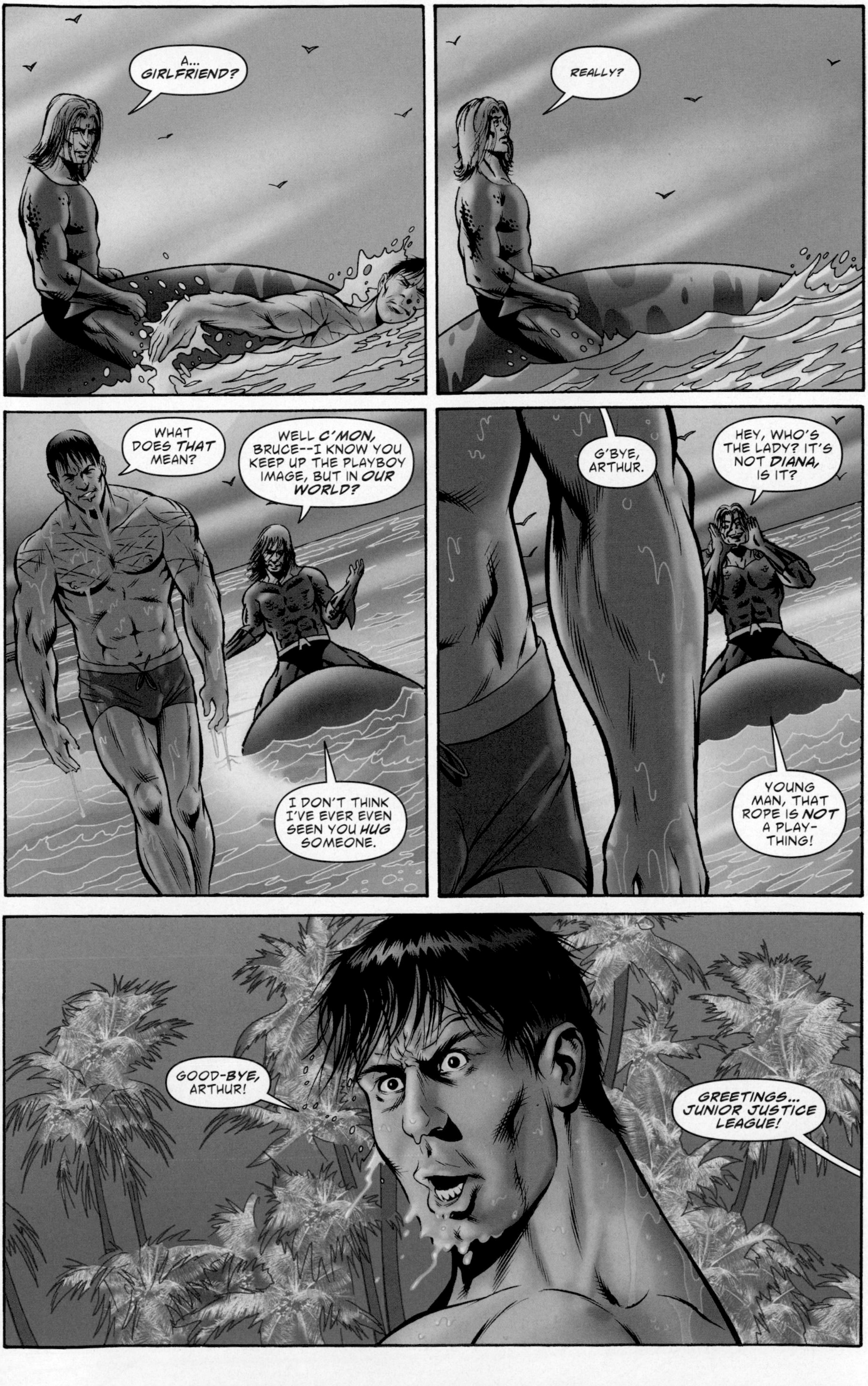
A... GIRLFRIEND?
REALLY?
WHAT DOES THAT MEAN?
WELL C'MON, BRUCE--I KNOW YOU KEEP UP THE PLAYBOY IMAGE, BUT IN OUR WORLD?
I DON'T THINK I'VE EVER EVEN SEEN YOU HUG SOMEONE.
G'BYE, ARTHUR.
HEY, WHO'S THE LADY? IT'S NOT DIANA, IS IT?
YOUNG MAN, THAT ROPE IS NOT A PLAY-THING!
GOOD-BYE, ARTHUR!
GREETINGS... JUNIOR JUSTICE LEAGUE!

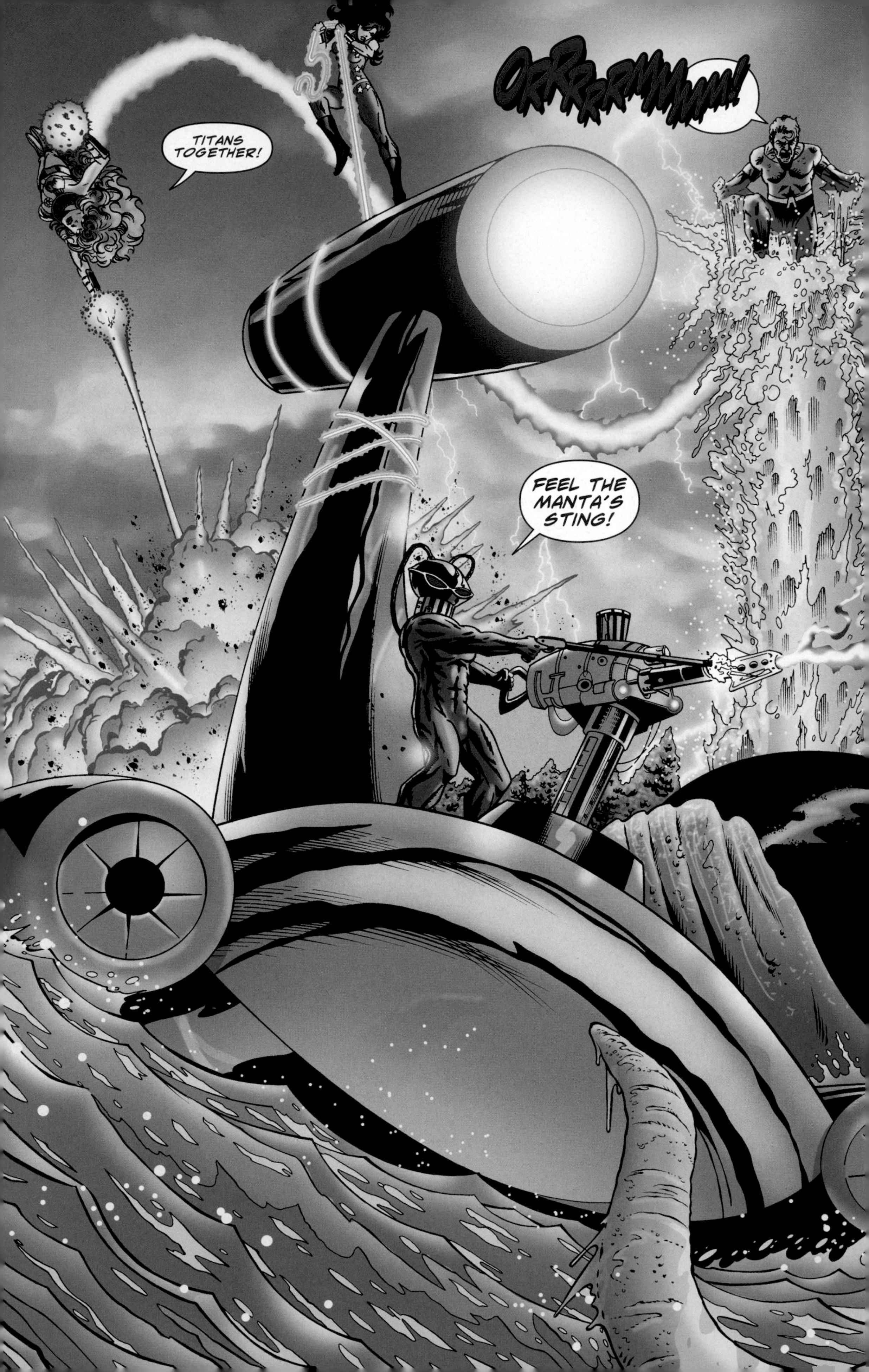
TITANS TOGETHER!
ORRRRRRMMMMM!
FEEL THE MANTA'S STING!

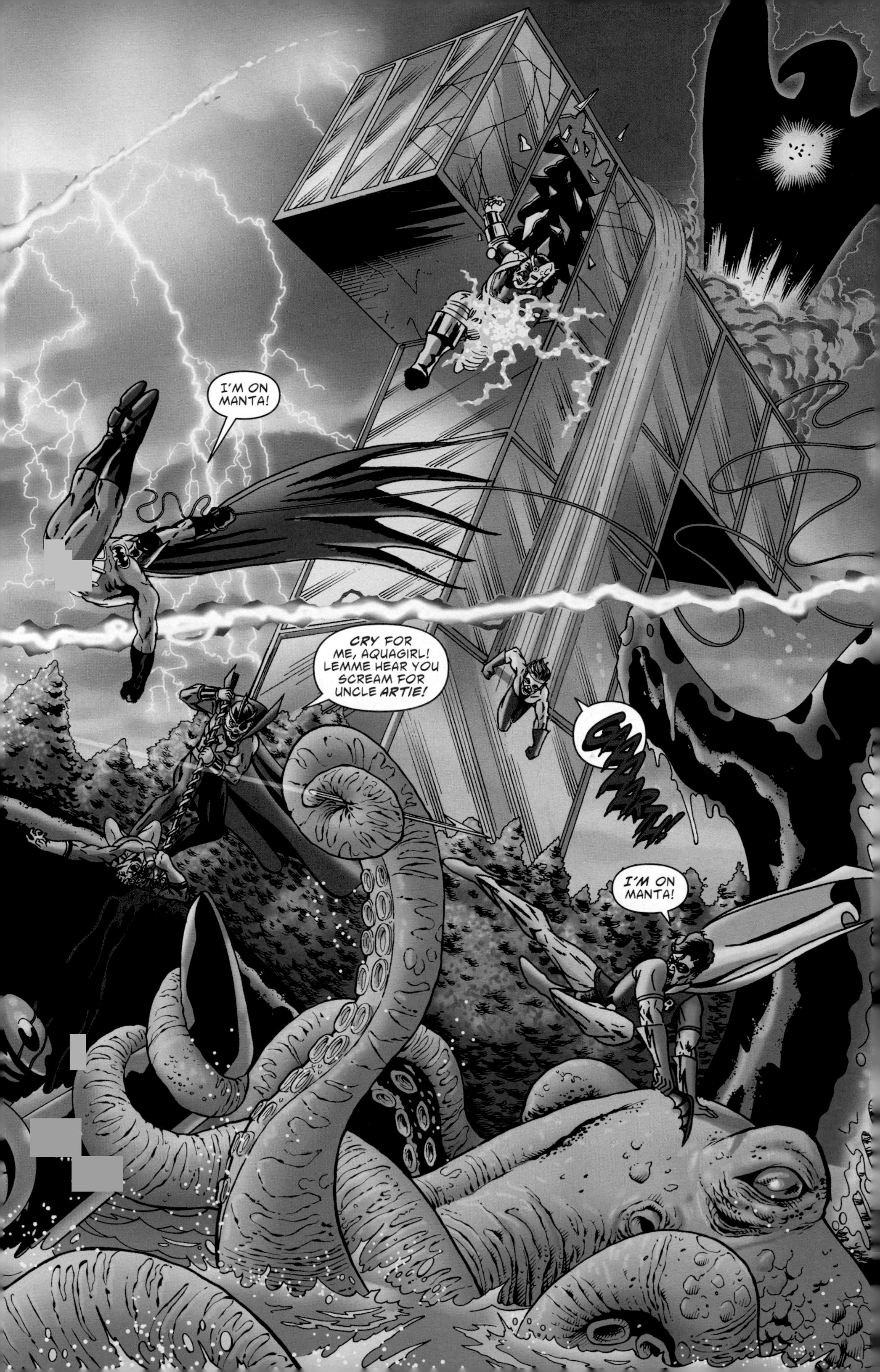
I'M ON MANTA!
CRY FOR ME, AQUAGIRL! LEMME HEAR YOU SCREAM FOR UNCLE ARTIE!
I'M ON MANTA!

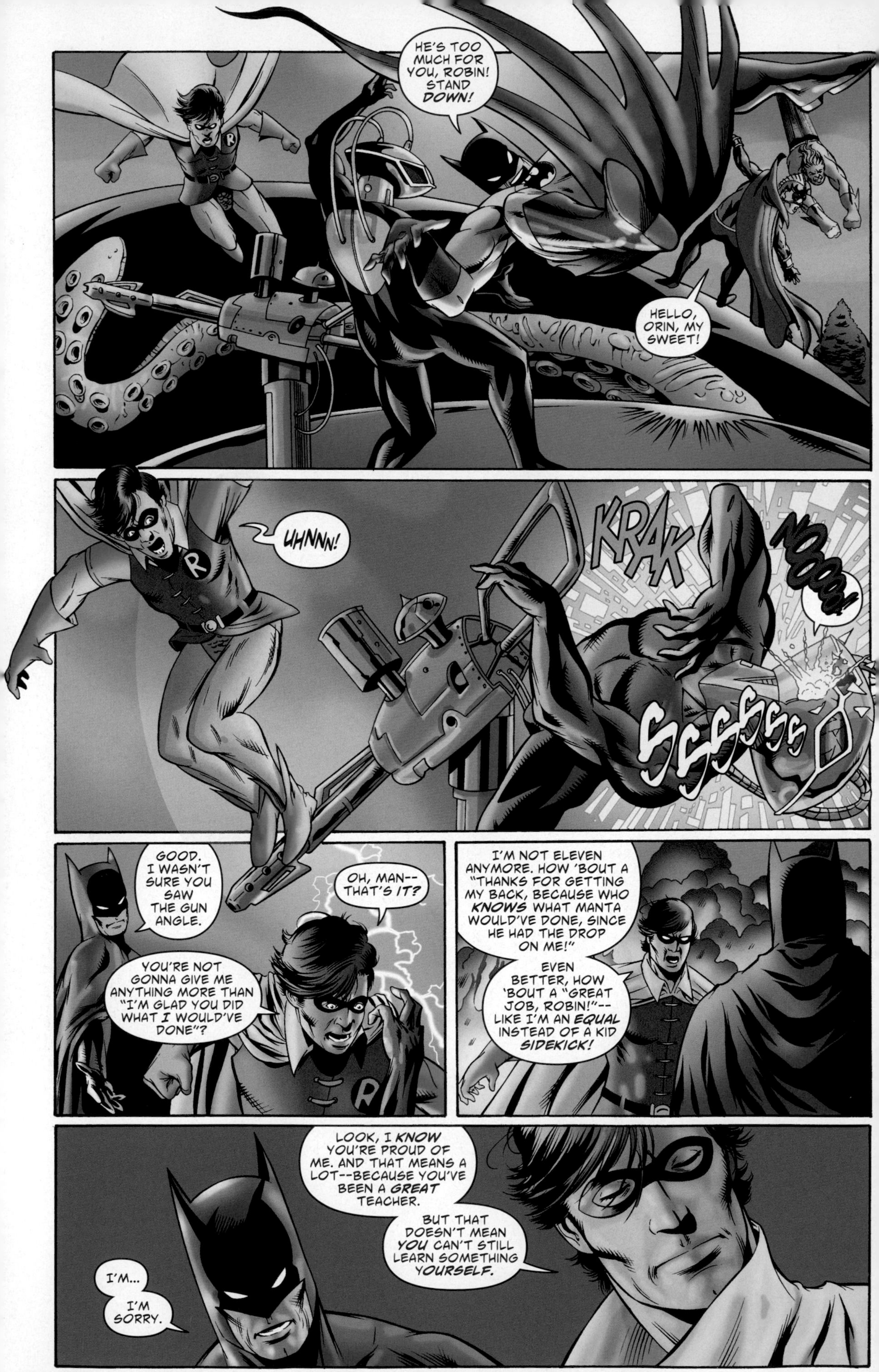
HE'S TOO MUCH FOR YOU, ROBIN! STAND DOWN!
HELLO, ORIN, MY SWEET!
UHNNN!
KRAK
NOOOOO!
SSSSSS
GOOD. I WASN'T SURE YOU SAW THE GUN ANGLE.
OH, MAN-- THAT'S IT?
YOU'RE NOT GONNA GIVE ME ANYTHING MORE THAN "I'M GLAD YOU DID WHAT I WOULD'VE DONE"?
I'M NOT ELEVEN ANYMORE. HOW 'BOUT A "THANKS FOR GETTING MY BACK, BECAUSE WHO KNOWS WHAT MANTA WOULD'VE DONE, SINCE HE HAD THE DROP ON ME!"
EVEN BETTER, HOW 'BOUT A "GREAT JOB, ROBIN!"-- LIKE I'M AN EQUAL INSTEAD OF A KID SIDEKICK!
LOOK, I KNOW YOU'RE PROUD OF ME. AND THAT MEANS A LOT--BECAUSE YOU'VE BEEN A GREAT TEACHER.
BUT THAT DOESN'T MEAN YOU CAN'T STILL LEARN SOMETHING YOURSELF.
I'M...
I'M SORRY.

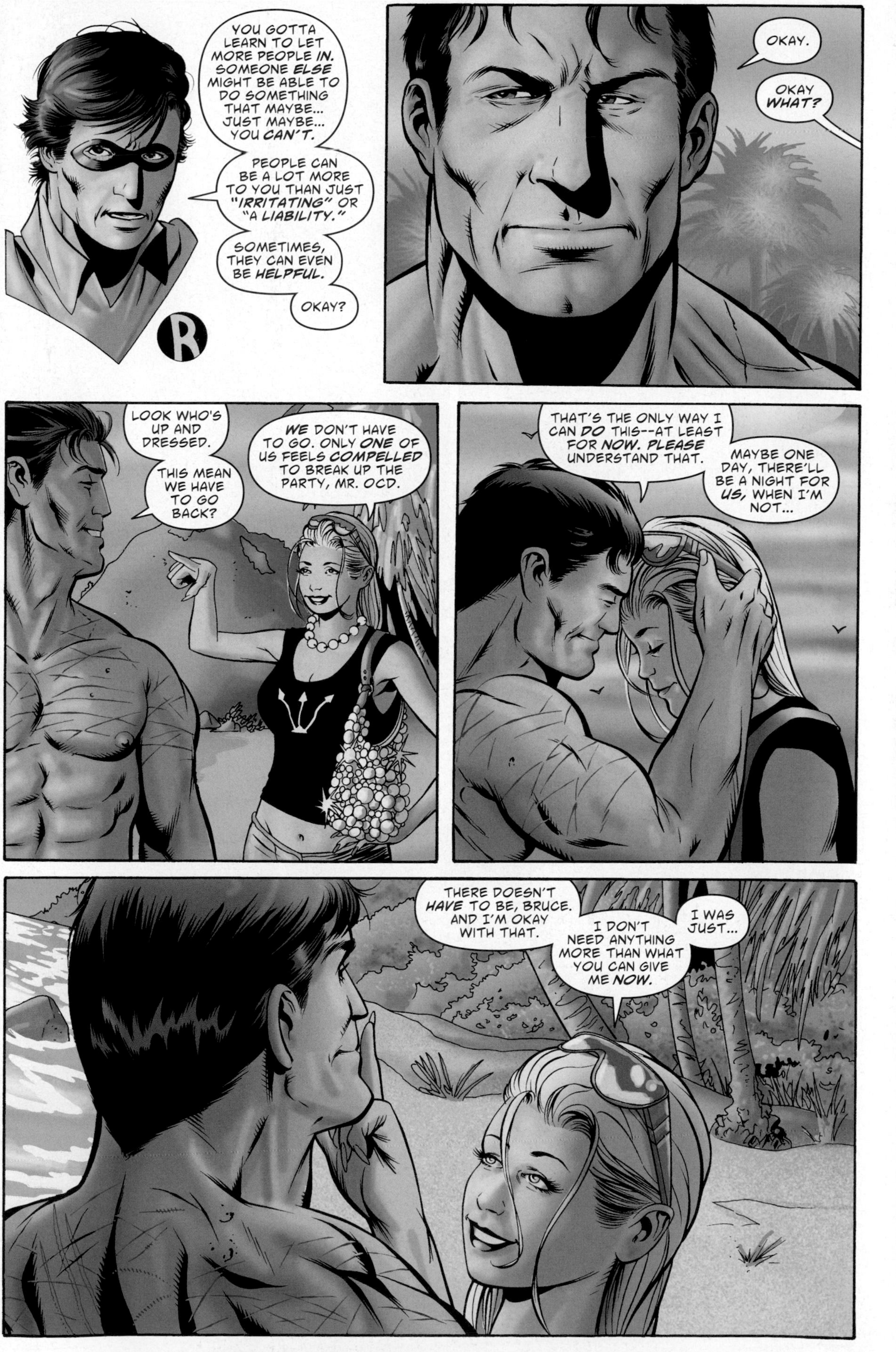

YOU GOTTA LEARN TO LET MORE PEOPLE IN. SOMEONE ELSE MIGHT BE ABLE TO DO SOMETHING THAT MAYBE... JUST MAYBE... YOU CAN'T.
PEOPLE CAN BE A LOT MORE TO YOU THAN JUST "IRRITATING" OR "A LIABILITY."
SOMETIMES, THEY CAN EVEN BE HELPFUL.
OKAY?
OKAY.
OKAY WHAT?
LOOK WHO'S UP AND DRESSED.
THIS MEAN WE HAVE TO GO BACK?
WE DON'T HAVE TO GO. ONLY ONE OF US FEELS COMPELLED TO BREAK UP THE PARTY, MR. OCD.
THAT'S THE ONLY WAY I CAN DO THIS--AT LEAST FOR NOW. PLEASE UNDERSTAND THAT.
MAYBE ONE DAY, THERE'LL BE A NIGHT FOR US, WHEN I'M NOT...
THERE DOESN'T HAVE TO BE, BRUCE. AND I'M OKAY WITH THAT.
I DON'T NEED ANYTHING MORE THAN WHAT YOU CAN GIVE ME NOW.
I WAS JUST...

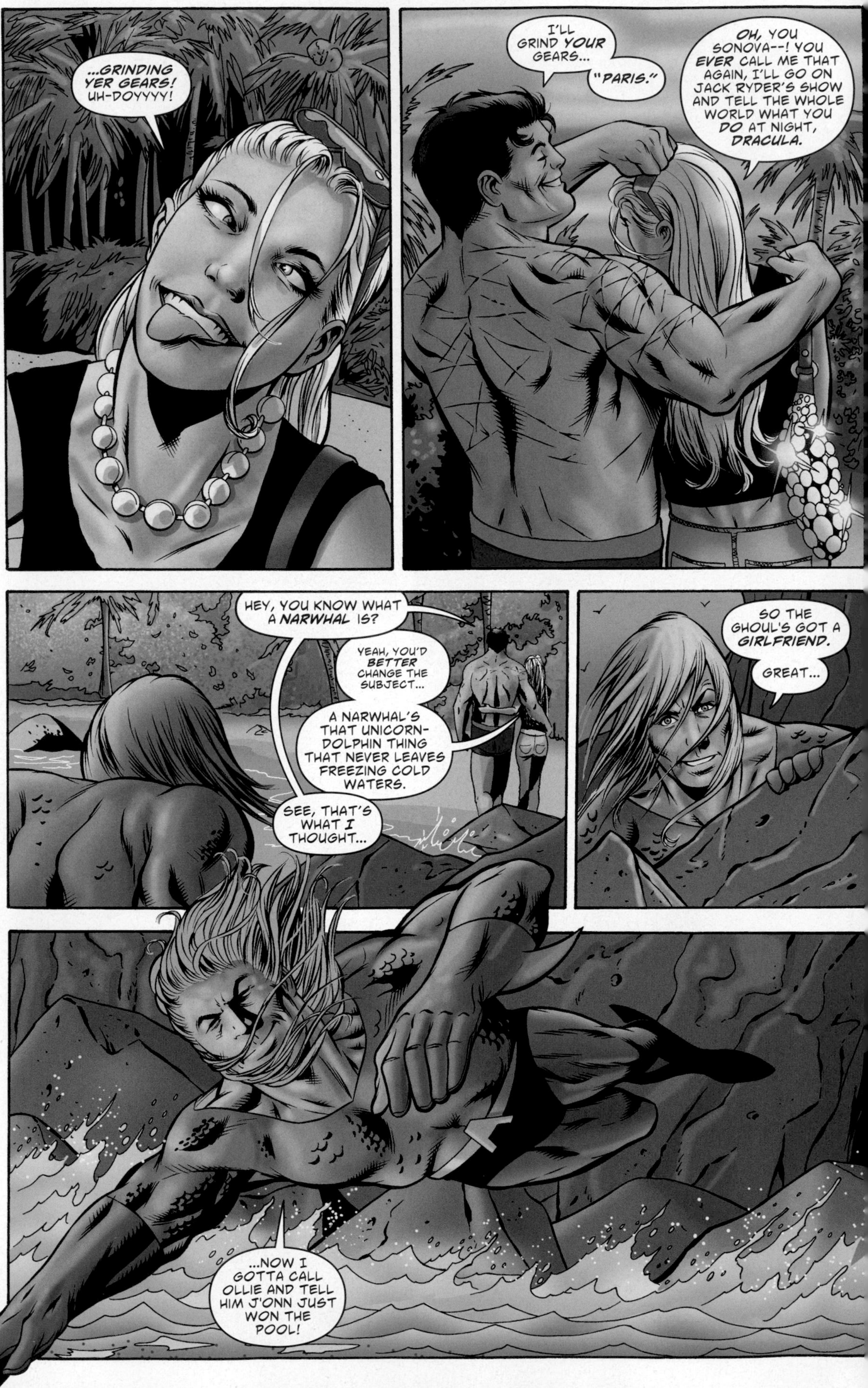
...GRINDING YER GEARS! UH-DOYYYY!
I'LL GRIND YOUR GEARS...
"PARIS."
OH, YOU SONOVA--! YOU EVER CALL ME THAT AGAIN, I'LL GO ON JACK RYDER'S SHOW AND TELL THE WHOLE WORLD WHAT YOU DO AT NIGHT, DRACULA.
HEY, YOU KNOW WHAT A NARWHAL IS?
YEAH, YOU'D BETTER CHANGE THE SUBJECT...
A NARWHAL'S THAT UNICORN-DOLPHIN THING THAT NEVER LEAVES FREEZING COLD WATERS.
SEE, THAT'S WHAT I THOUGHT...
SO THE GHOUL'S GOT A GIRLFRIEND.
GREAT...
...NOW I GOTTA CALL OLLIE AND TELL HIM J'ONN JUST WON THE POOL!

Batman: The Widening Gyre #4 cover by BILL SIENKIEWICZ

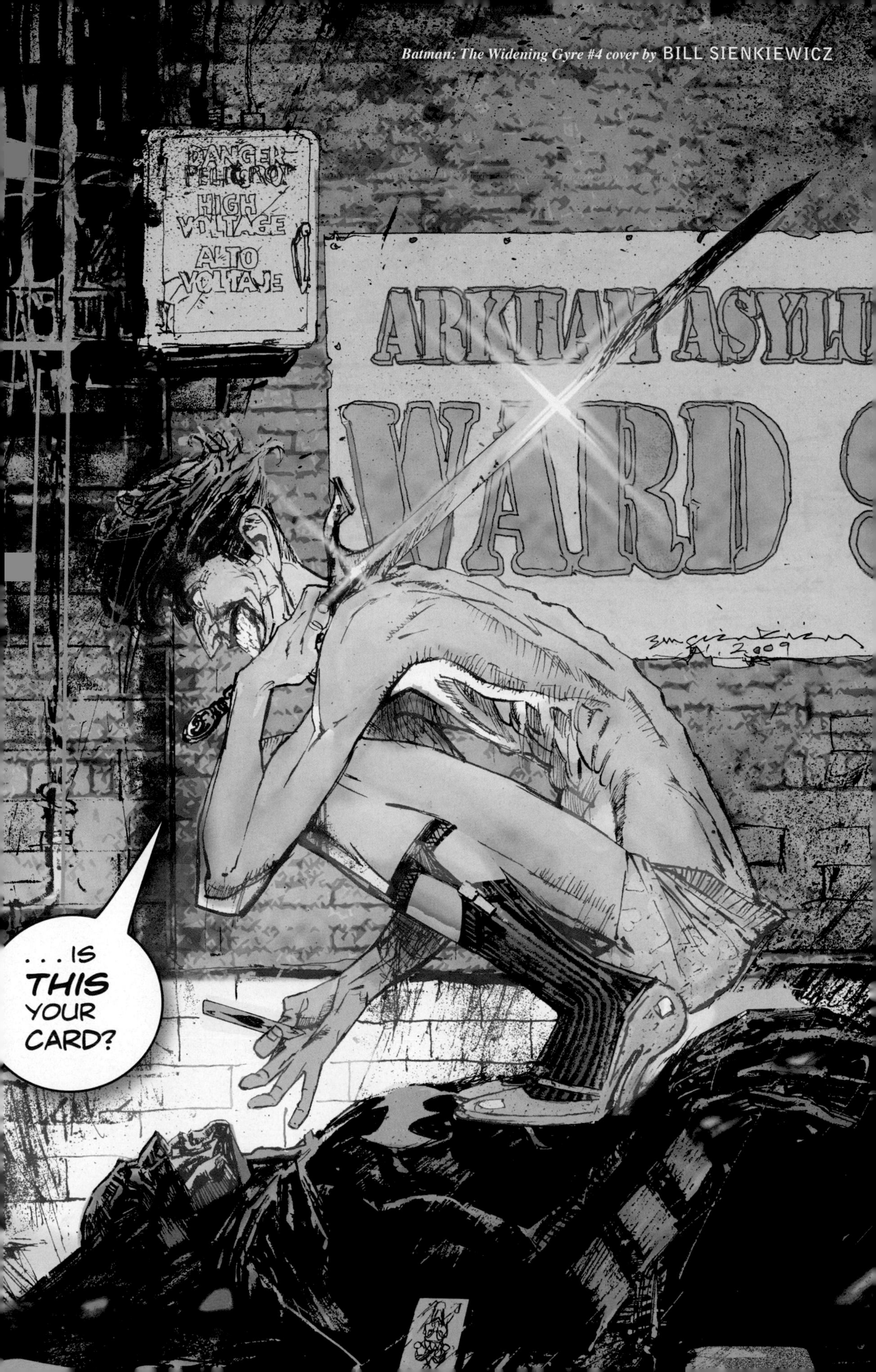
DANGER
PELIGRO
HIGH VOLTAGE
ALTO VOLTAJE
ARKHAM ASYLUM
WARD
. . . IS THIS YOUR CARD?

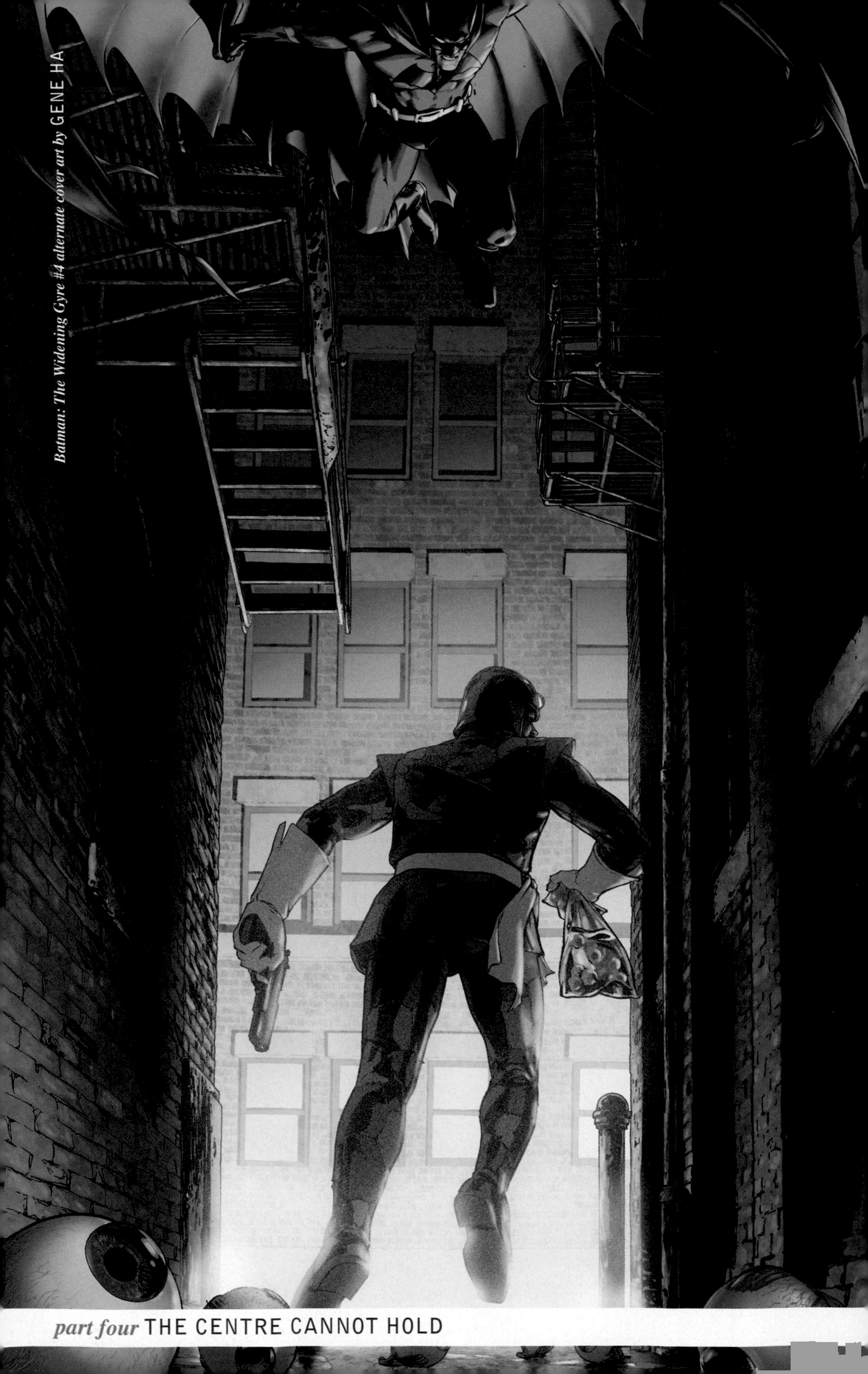

Batman: The Widening Gyre #4 alternate cover art by GENE HA

part four THE CENTRE CANNOT HOLD

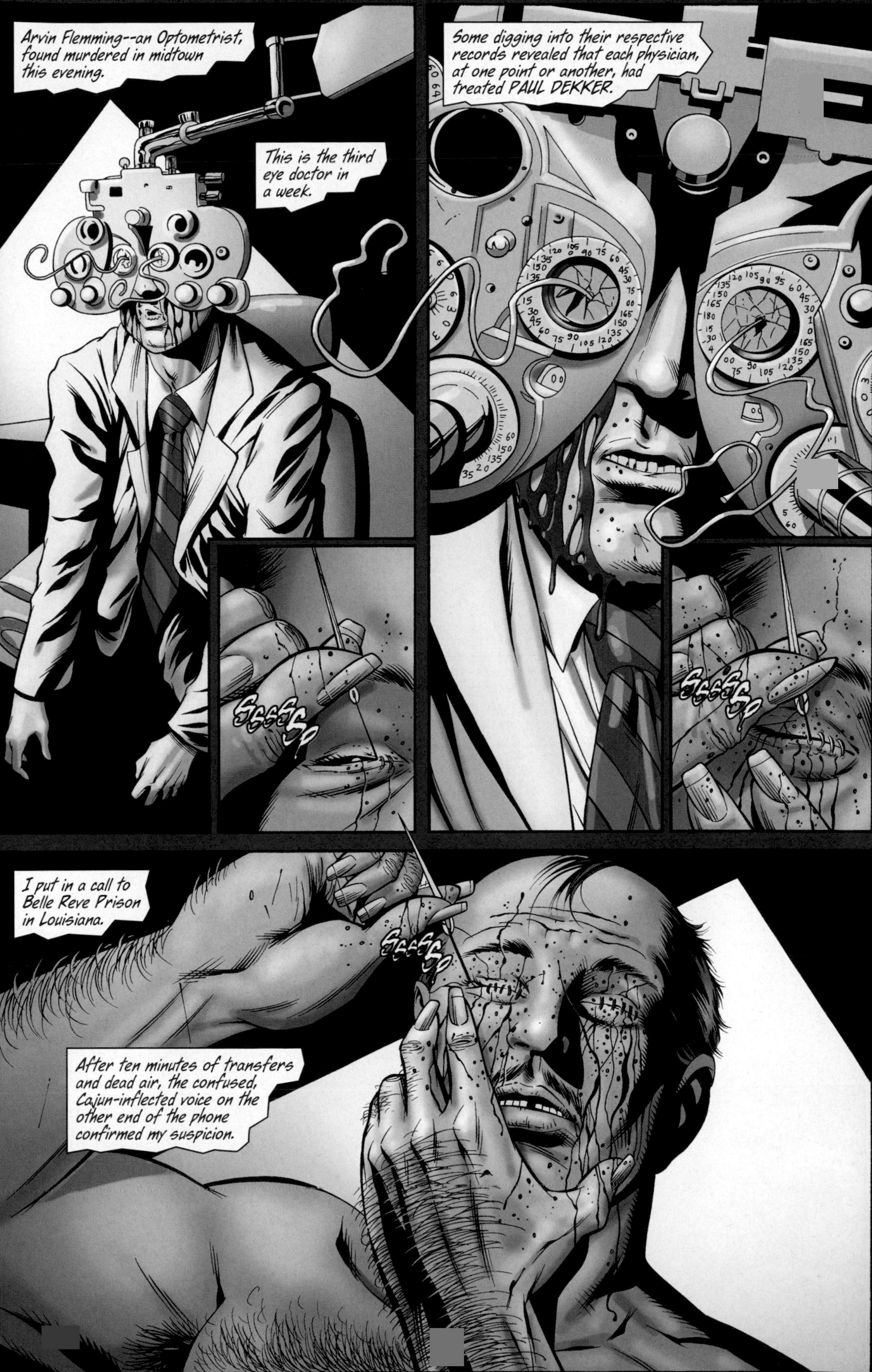
Arvin Flemming--an Optometrist, found murdered in midtown this evening.
This is the third eye doctor in a week.
Some digging into their respective records revealed that each physician, at one point or another, had treated PAUL DEKKER.
SSSSSP
SSSSSP
I put in a call to Belle Reve Prison in Louisiana.
SSSSSP
After ten minutes of transfers and dead air, the confused, Cajun-inflected voice on the other end of the phone confirmed my suspicion.

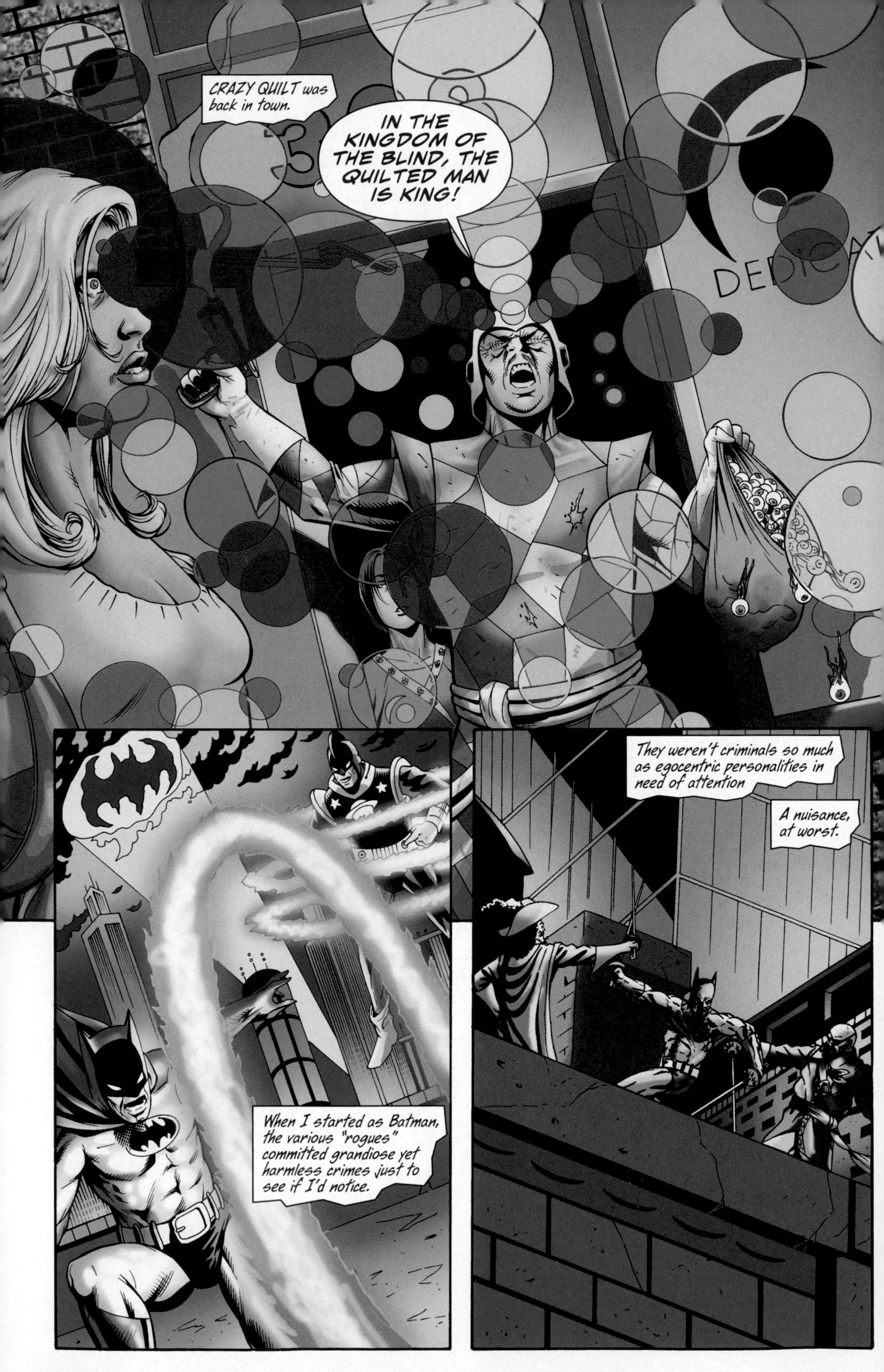
CRAZY QUILT was back in town.
IN THE KINGDOM OF THE BLIND, THE QUILTED MAN IS KING!
When I started as Batman, the various "rogues" committed grandiose yet harmless crimes just to see if I'd notice.
They weren't criminals so much as egocentric personalities in need of attention
A nuisance, at worst.

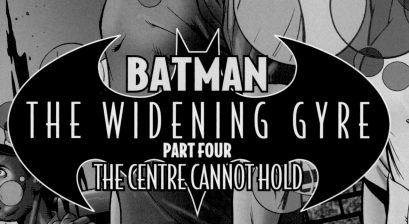

BATMAN
THE WIDENING GYRE
PART FOUR
THE CENTRE CANNOT HOLD

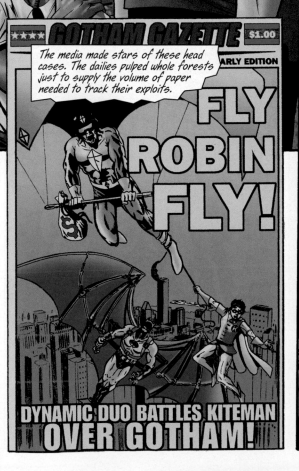

GOTHAM GAZETTE $1.00

EARLY EDITION

The media made stars of these head cases. The dailies pulped whole forests just to supply the volume of paper needed to track their exploits.

FLY ROBIN FLY!

DYNAMIC DUO BATTLES KITEMAN OVER GOTHAM!

They were painted as outsiders and dreamers who dared to be "fabulous" against the urban criminal landscape.

And everyone thought they were "a real hoot."

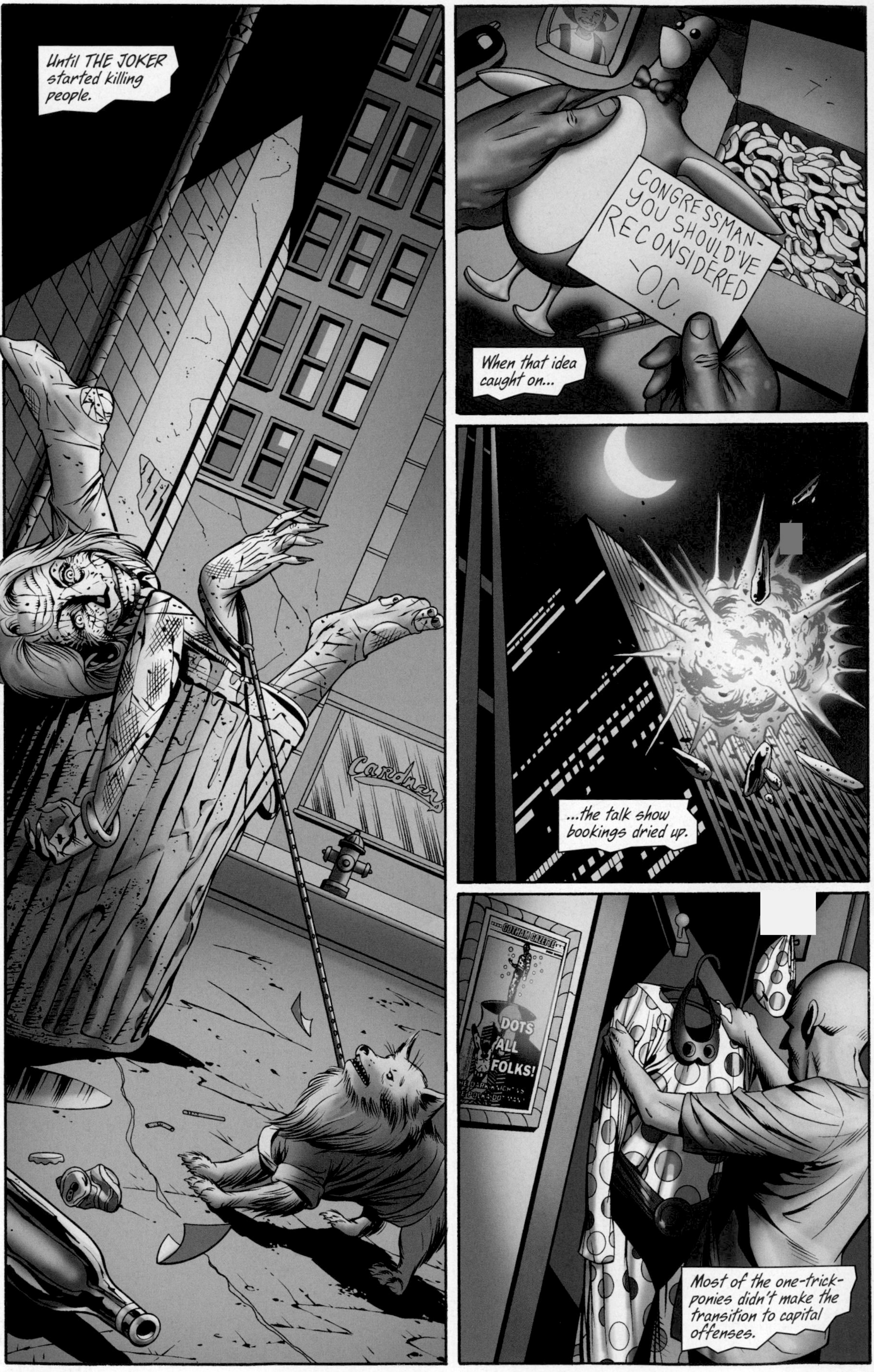
Until THE JOKER started killing people.
CONGRESSMAN-
YOU SHOULD'VE RECONSIDERED
-O.C.
When that idea caught on...
...the talk show bookings dried up.
GOTHAM GAZETTE
DOTS ALL FOLKS!
Most of the one-trick-ponies didn't make the transition to capital offenses.

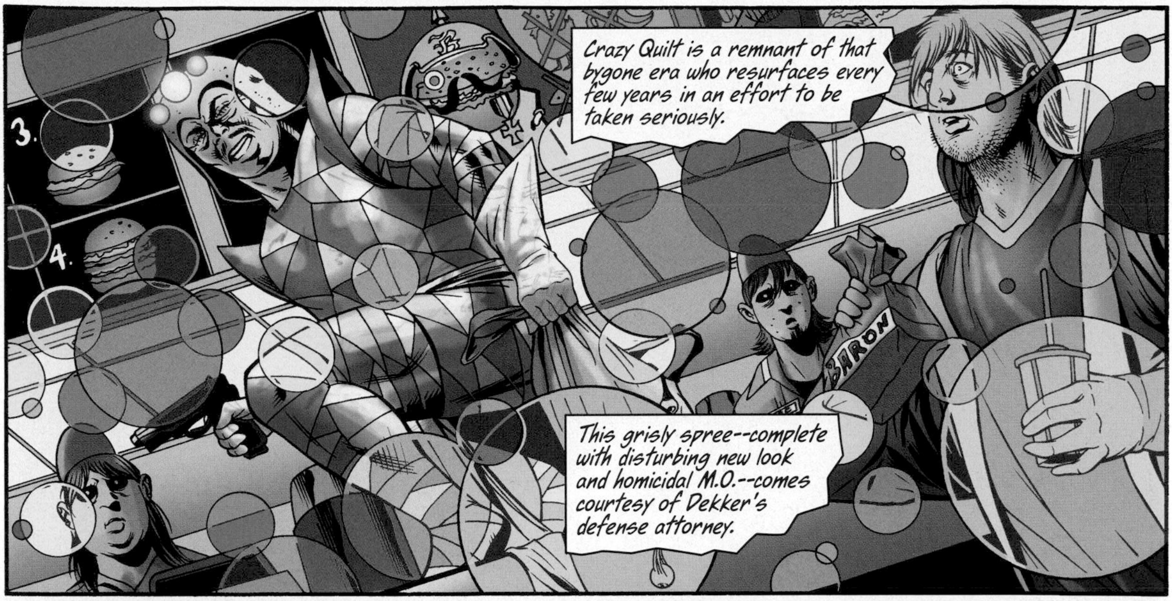
3.
4.
Crazy Quilt is a remnant of that bygone era who resurfaces every few years in an effort to be taken seriously.
BARON
This grisly spree--complete with disturbing new look and homicidal M.O.--comes courtesy of Dekker's defense attorney.

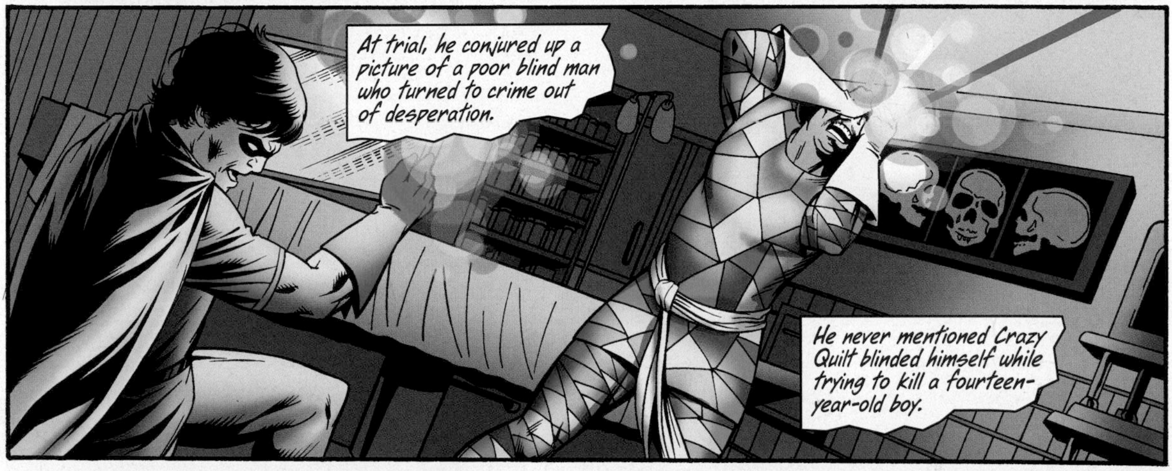
At trial, he conjured up a picture of a poor blind man who turned to crime out of desperation.
He never mentioned Crazy Quilt blinded himself while trying to kill a fourteen-year-old boy.

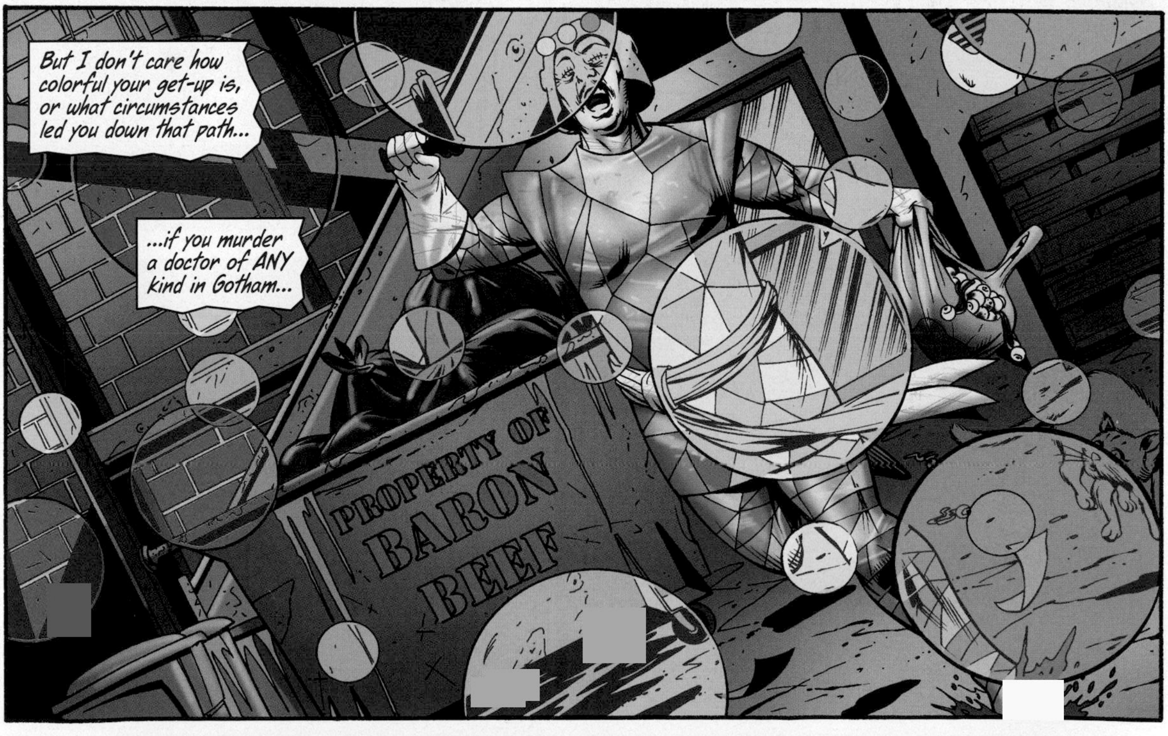
But I don't care how colorful your get-up is, or what circumstances led you down that path...
...if you murder a doctor of ANY kind in Gotham...
PROPERTY OF
BARON
BEEF

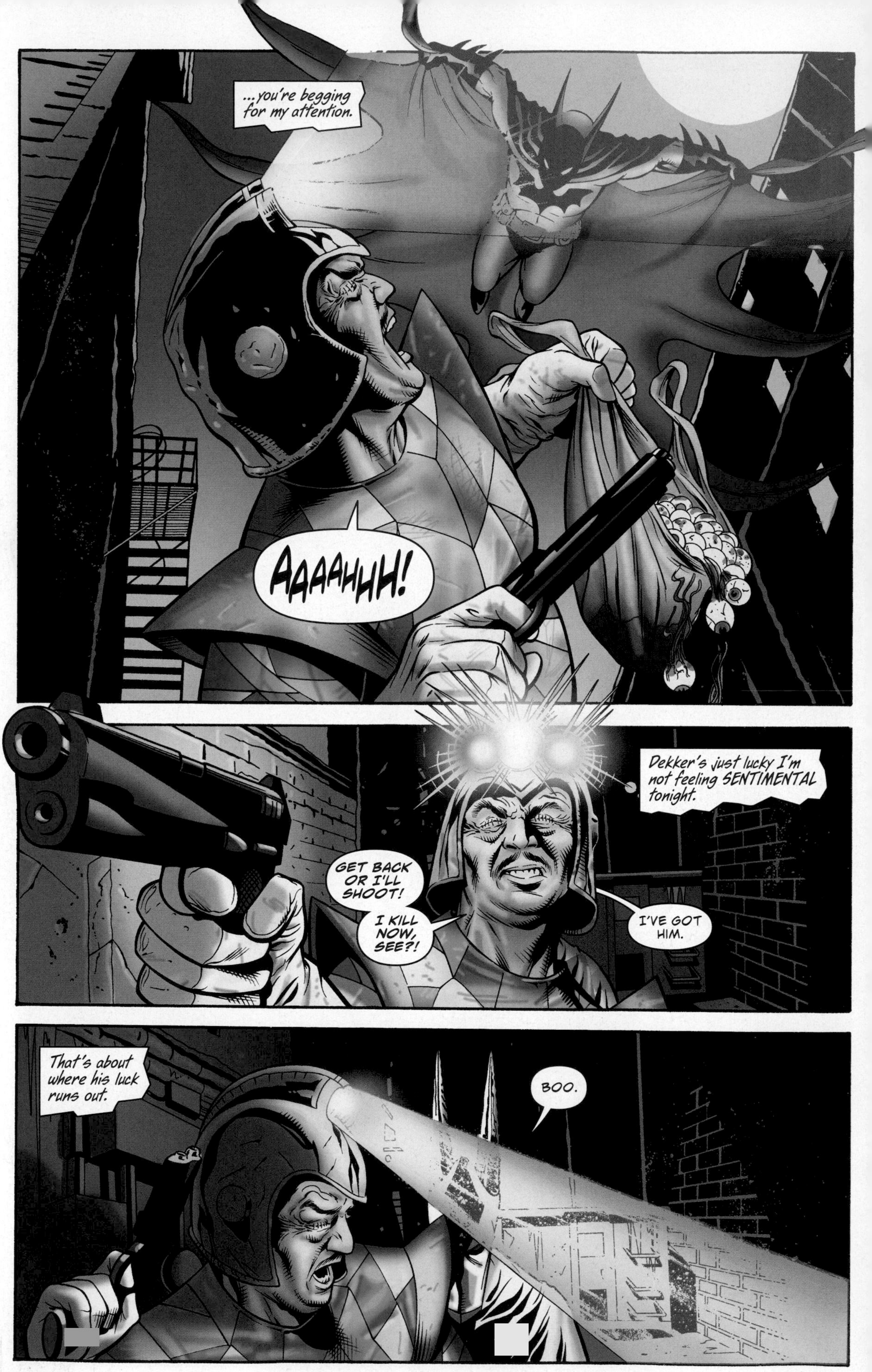
...you're begging for my attention.
AAAAHHH!
Dekker's just lucky I'm not feeling SENTIMENTAL tonight.
GET BACK OR I'LL SHOOT!
I KILL NOW, SEE?!
I'VE GOT HIM.
That's about where his luck runs out.
BOO.

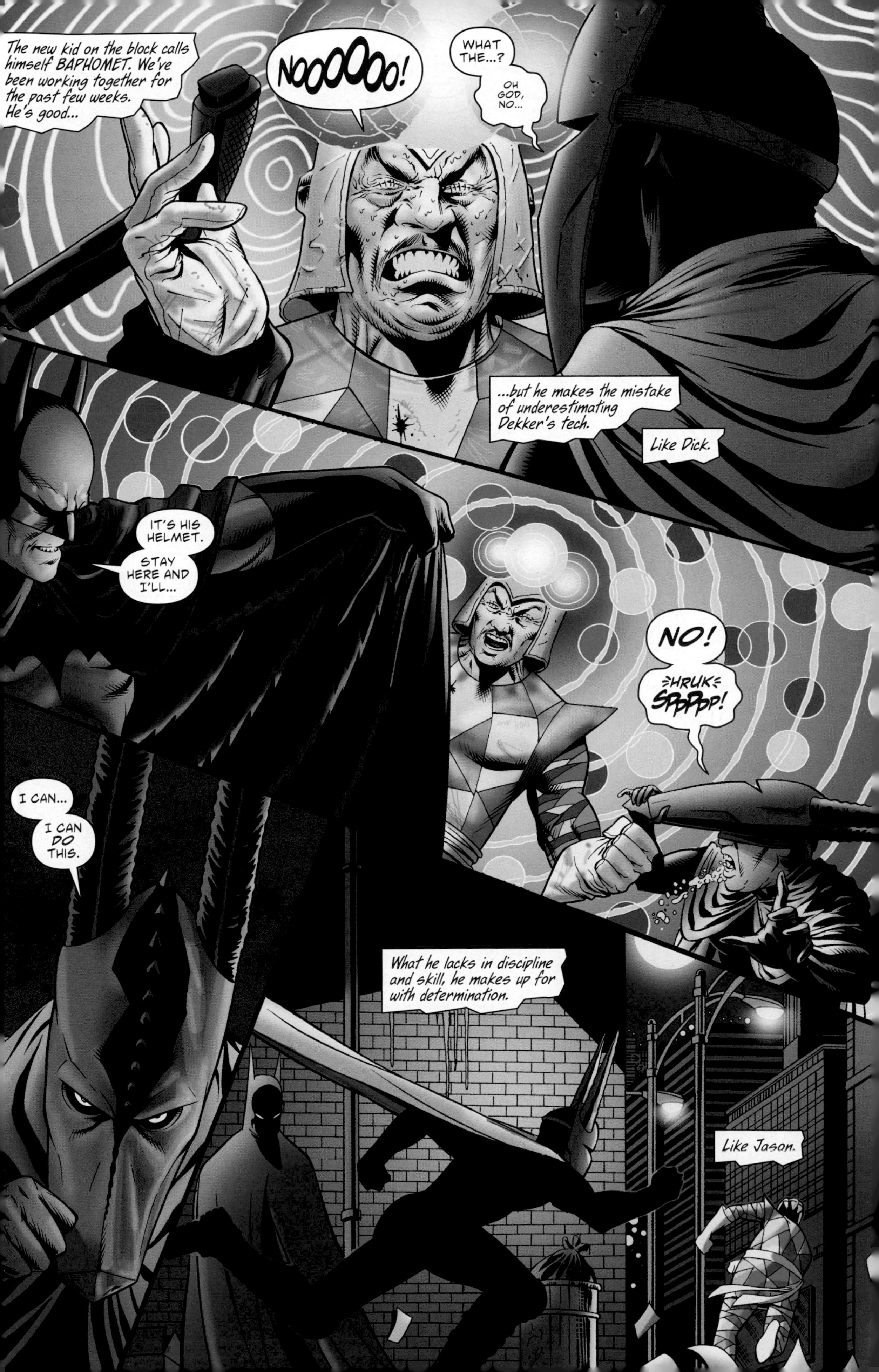
The new kid on the block calls himself BAPHOMET. We've been working together for the past few weeks. He's good...
NOOOOOO!
WHAT THE...?
OH GOD, NO...
...but he makes the mistake of underestimating Dekker's tech.
Like Dick.
IT'S HIS HELMET.
STAY HERE AND I'LL...
NO!
HRUK
SPPPPP!
I CAN...
I CAN DO THIS.
What he lacks in discipline and skill, he makes up for with determination.
Like Jason.

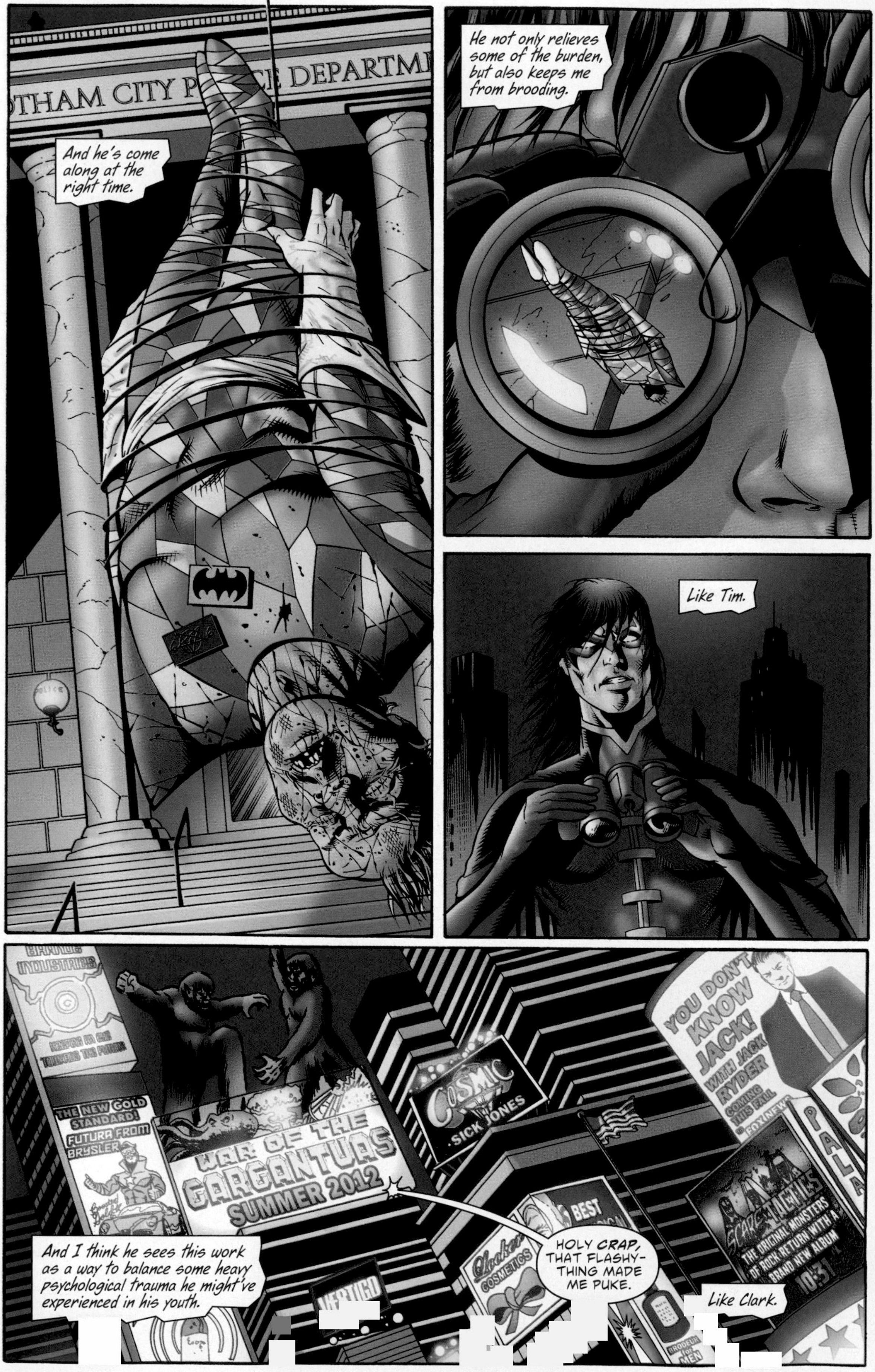

And he's come along at the right time.
He not only relieves some of the burden, but also keeps me from brooding.
Like Tim.
WAR OF THE GARGANTUAS
SUMMER 2012
THE NEW GOLD STANDARD! FUTURA FROM BRYSLER
COSMIC
SICK JONES
YOU DON'T KNOW JACK! WITH JACK RYDER
COMING THIS FALL
THE ORIGINAL MONSTERS OF ROCK RETURN WITH A BRAND NEW ALBUM
COSMETICS
And I think he sees this work as a way to balance some heavy psychological trauma he might've experienced in his youth.
HOLY CRAP, THAT FLASHY-THING MADE ME PUKE.
Like Clark.

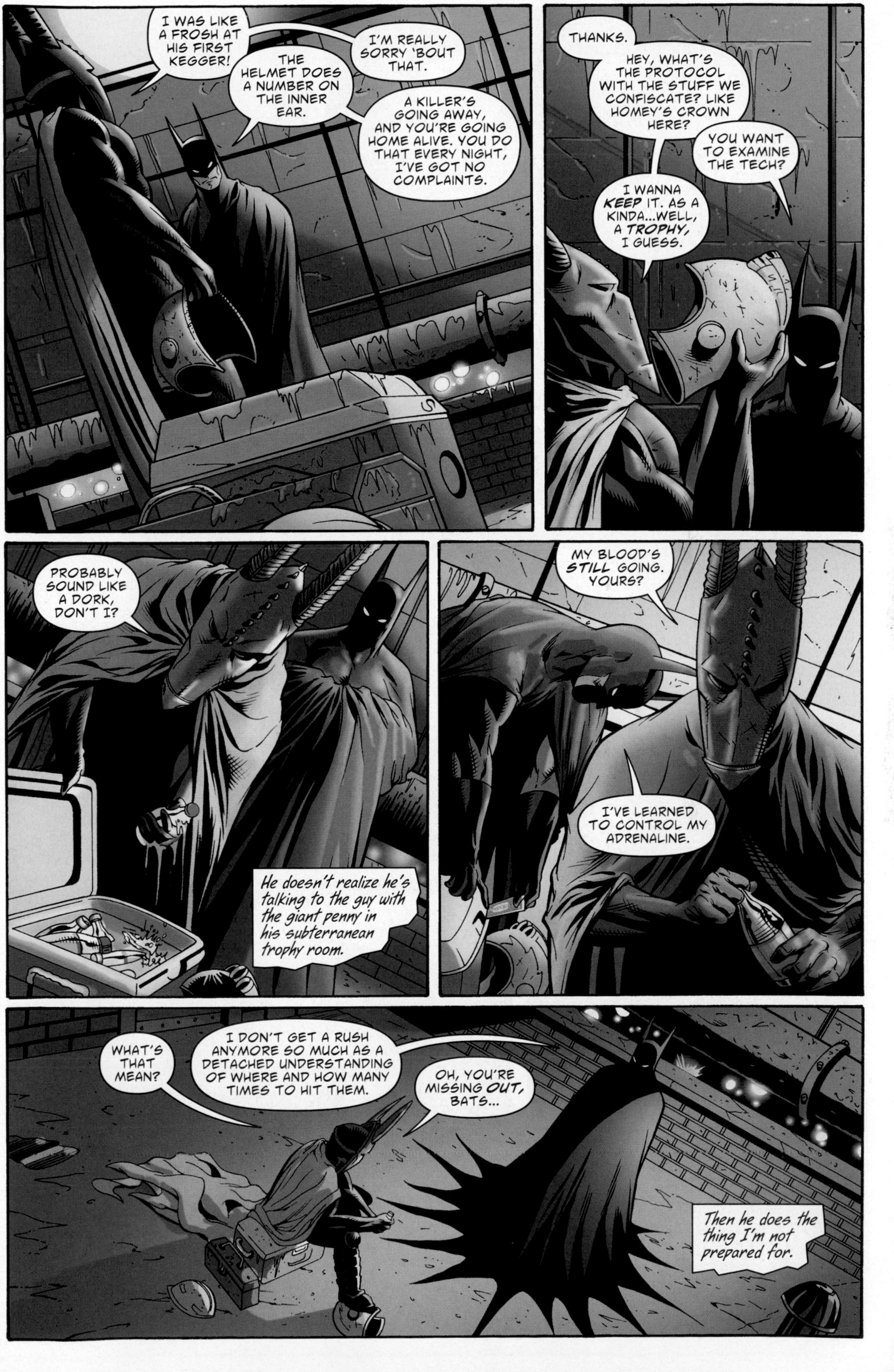
I WAS LIKE A FROSH AT HIS FIRST KEGGER!
I'M REALLY SORRY 'BOUT THAT.
THE HELMET DOES A NUMBER ON THE INNER EAR.
A KILLER'S GOING AWAY, AND YOU'RE GOING HOME ALIVE. YOU DO THAT EVERY NIGHT, I'VE GOT NO COMPLAINTS.
THANKS.
HEY, WHAT'S THE PROTOCOL WITH THE STUFF WE CONFISCATE? LIKE HOMEY'S CROWN HERE?
YOU WANT TO EXAMINE THE TECH?
I WANNA KEEP IT. AS A KINDA...WELL, A TROPHY, I GUESS.
PROBABLY SOUND LIKE A DORK, DON'T I?
He doesn't realize he's talking to the guy with the giant penny in his subterranean trophy room.
MY BLOOD'S STILL GOING. YOURS?
I'VE LEARNED TO CONTROL MY ADRENALINE.
WHAT'S THAT MEAN?
I DON'T GET A RUSH ANYMORE SO MUCH AS A DETACHED UNDERSTANDING OF WHERE AND HOW MANY TIMES TO HIT THEM.
OH, YOU'RE MISSING OUT, BATS...
Then he does the thing I'm not prepared for.

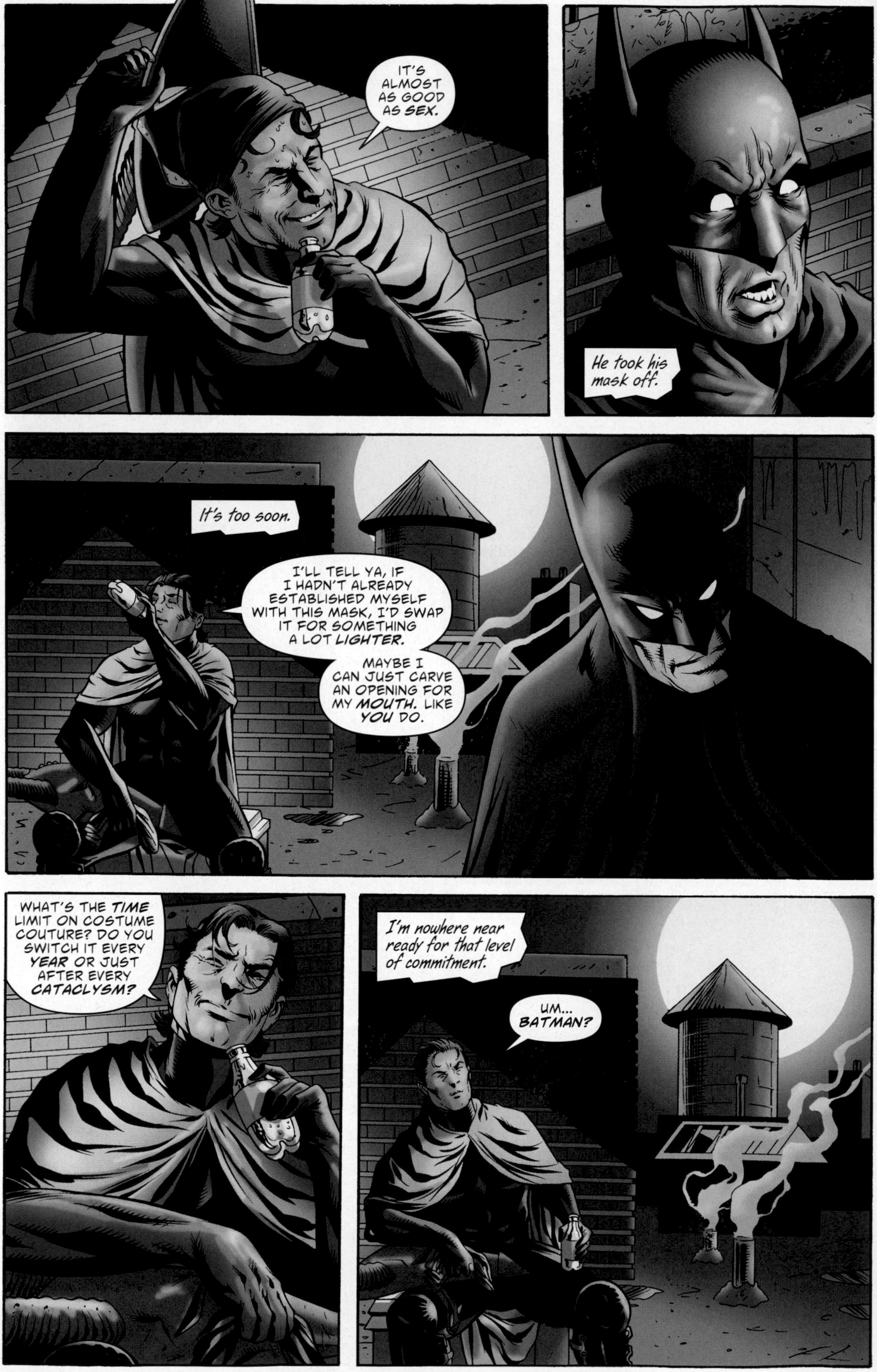
IT'S ALMOST AS GOOD AS SEX.
He took his mask off.
It's too soon.
I'LL TELL YA, IF I HADN'T ALREADY ESTABLISHED MYSELF WITH THIS MASK, I'D SWAP IT FOR SOMETHING A LOT LIGHTER.
MAYBE I CAN JUST CARVE AN OPENING FOR MY MOUTH. LIKE YOU DO.
WHAT'S THE TIME LIMIT ON COSTUME COUTURE? DO YOU SWITCH IT EVERY YEAR OR JUST AFTER EVERY CATACLYSM?
I'm nowhere near ready for that level of commitment.
UM... BATMAN?

SO, WAIT-- AM I *READING* THIS RIGHT?

YOU JUST *LEFT* HIM ALONE ON THE *ROOF?*

S'NOT A BIG DEAL. I DO IT TO EVERYONE.

SO THEN WHAT *WAS* THE BIG DEAL?

HE TOOK HIS *MASK* OFF, SILVER.

AND?

IT'S JUST NOT *DONE* LIKE THAT. ESPECIALLY THAT *SOON.*

I'VE KNOWN SUPERMAN FOR YEARS, AND I *STILL* DON'T TAKE MY MASK OFF IN FRONT OF HIM.

OKAY, BUT THAT'S *YOU.* THAT'S HOW *YOU* DO THINGS.

OBVIOUSLY, THIS GOAT MASK GUY...

BAPHOMET.

OBVIOUSLY THIS *BAPHOMET* DOESN'T HAVE ONE OF THE TEN MOST *RECOGNIZABLE* FACES IN THE WORLD--LIKE *SOME* CRIME FIGHTERS I KNOW.

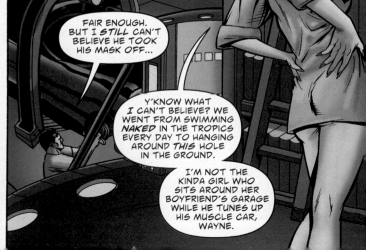

FAIR ENOUGH. BUT I *STILL* CAN'T BELIEVE HE TOOK HIS MASK OFF...

Y'KNOW WHAT *I* CAN'T BELIEVE? WE WENT FROM SWIMMING *NAKED* IN THE TROPICS EVERY DAY TO HANGING AROUND *THIS* HOLE IN THE GROUND.

I'M NOT THE KINDA GIRL WHO SITS AROUND HER BOYFRIEND'S GARAGE WHILE HE TUNES UP HIS MUSCLE CAR, WAYNE.

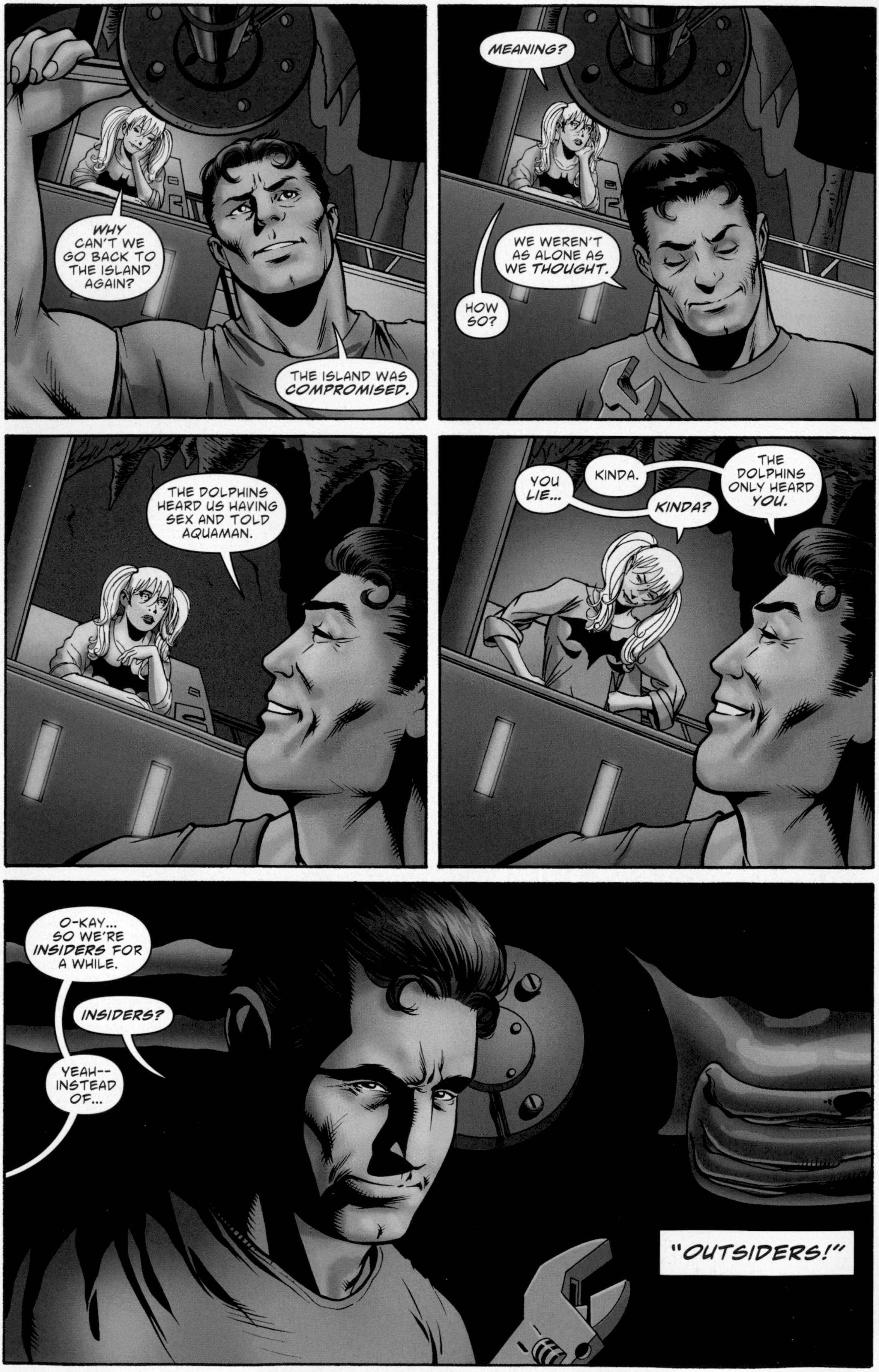
WHY CAN'T WE GO BACK TO THE ISLAND AGAIN?
THE ISLAND WAS COMPROMISED.
MEANING?
WE WEREN'T AS ALONE AS WE THOUGHT.
HOW SO?
THE DOLPHINS HEARD US HAVING SEX AND TOLD AQUAMAN.
YOU LIE...
KINDA.
KINDA?
THE DOLPHINS ONLY HEARD YOU.
O-KAY... SO WE'RE INSIDERS FOR A WHILE.
INSIDERS?
YEAH--INSTEAD OF...
"OUTSIDERS!"

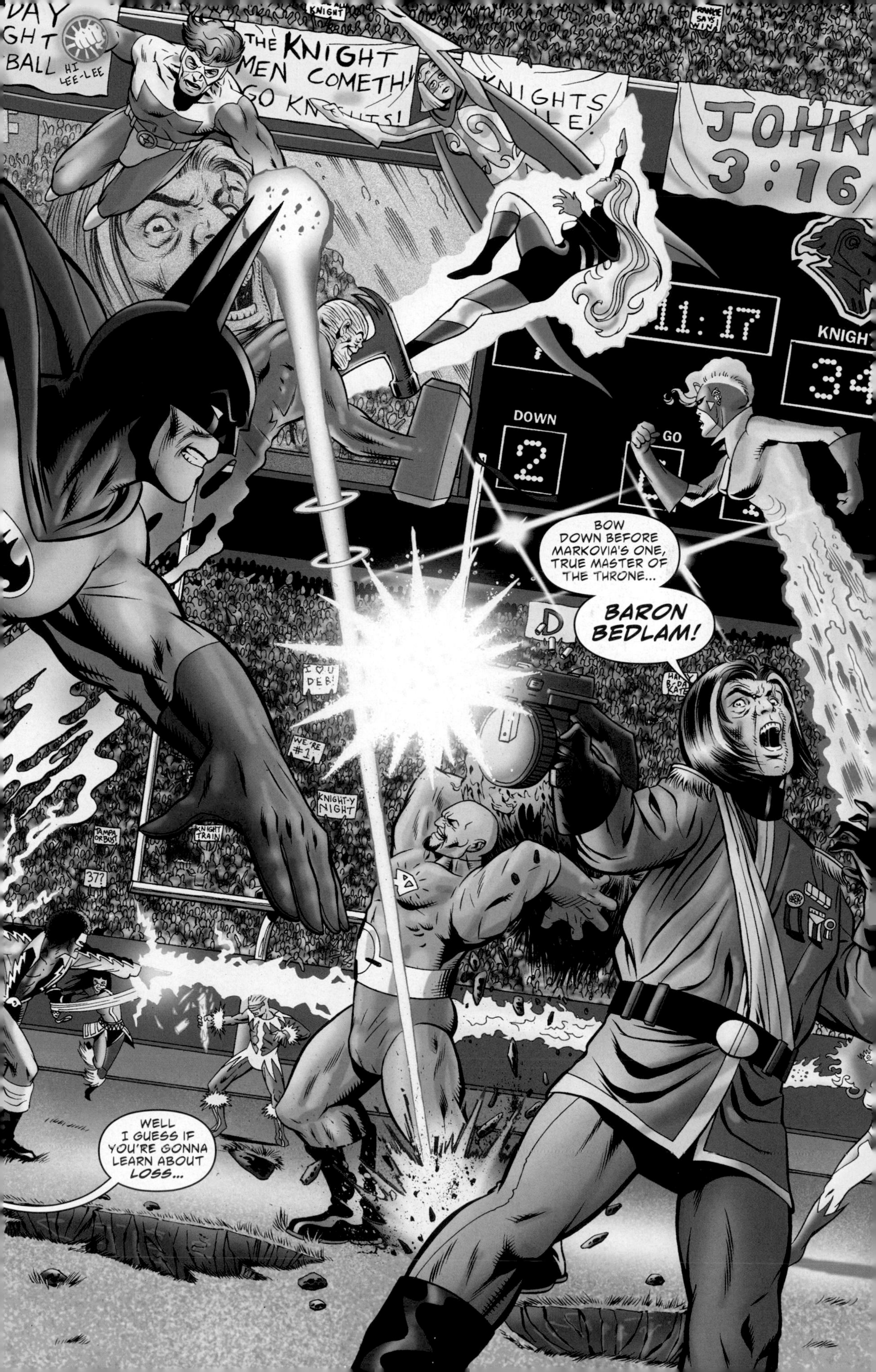
THE KNIGHT MEN COMETH! GO KNIGHTS!
KNIGHTS RULE!
JOHN 3:16
HI LEE-LEE
11:17
KNIGHTS
34
DOWN
2
GO
BOW DOWN BEFORE MARKOVIA'S ONE, TRUE MASTER OF THE THRONE...
BARON BEDLAM!
I ♥ U DEB!
WE'RE #1
KNIGHT-Y NIGHT
KNIGHT TRAIN
TAMPA OR BUST
37?
WELL I GUESS IF YOU'RE GONNA LEARN ABOUT LOSS...

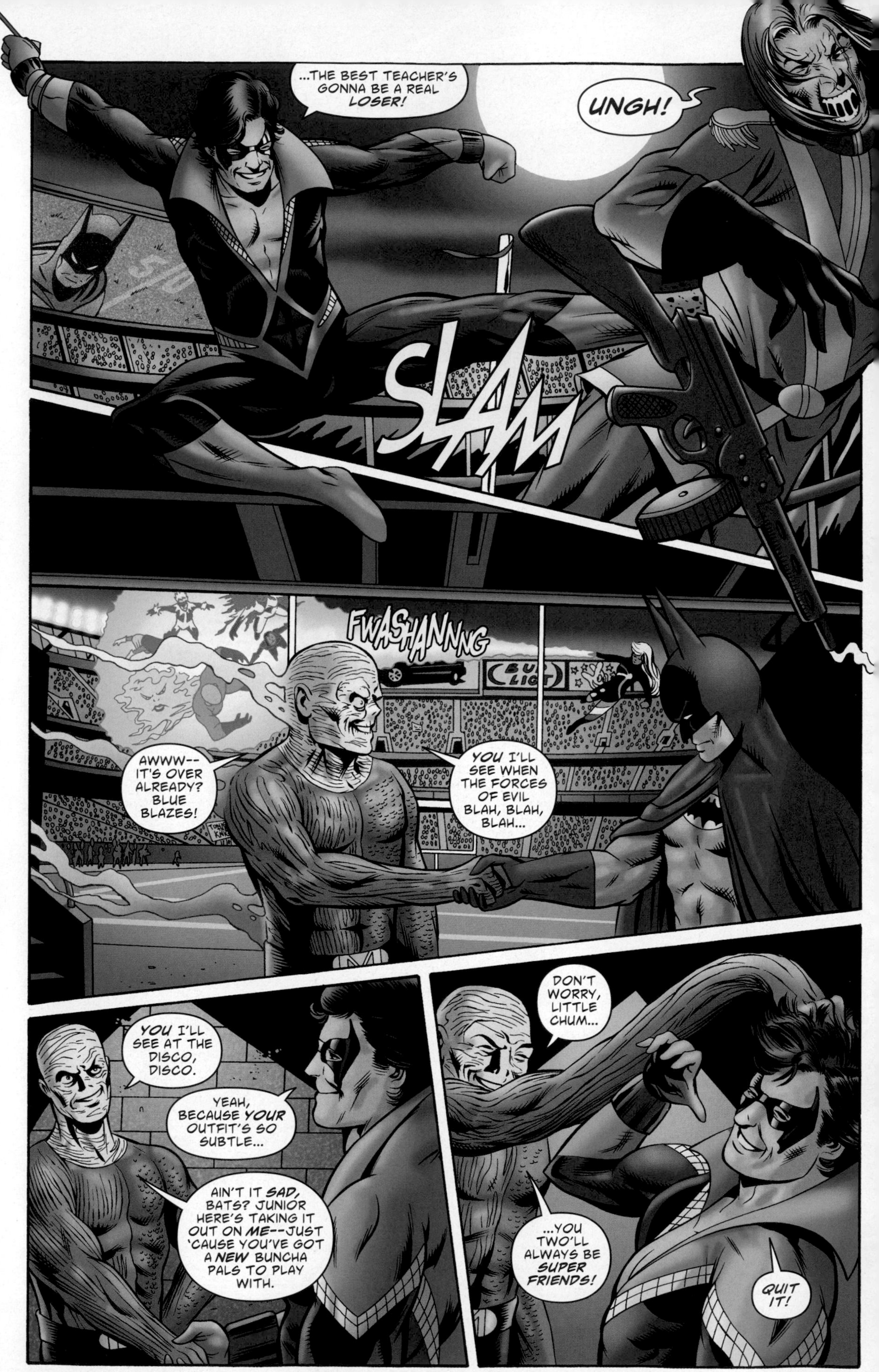
...THE BEST TEACHER'S GONNA BE A REAL LOSER!
UNGH!
SLAM
FWASHANNNG
AWWW-- IT'S OVER ALREADY? BLUE BLAZES!
YOU I'LL SEE WHEN THE FORCES OF EVIL BLAH, BLAH, BLAH...
YOU I'LL SEE AT THE DISCO, DISCO.
YEAH, BECAUSE YOUR OUTFIT'S SO SUBTLE...
AIN'T IT SAD, BATS? JUNIOR HERE'S TAKING IT OUT ON ME--JUST 'CAUSE YOU'VE GOT A NEW BUNCHA PALS TO PLAY WITH.
DON'T WORRY, LITTLE CHUM...
...YOU TWO'LL ALWAYS BE SUPER FRIENDS!
QUIT IT!

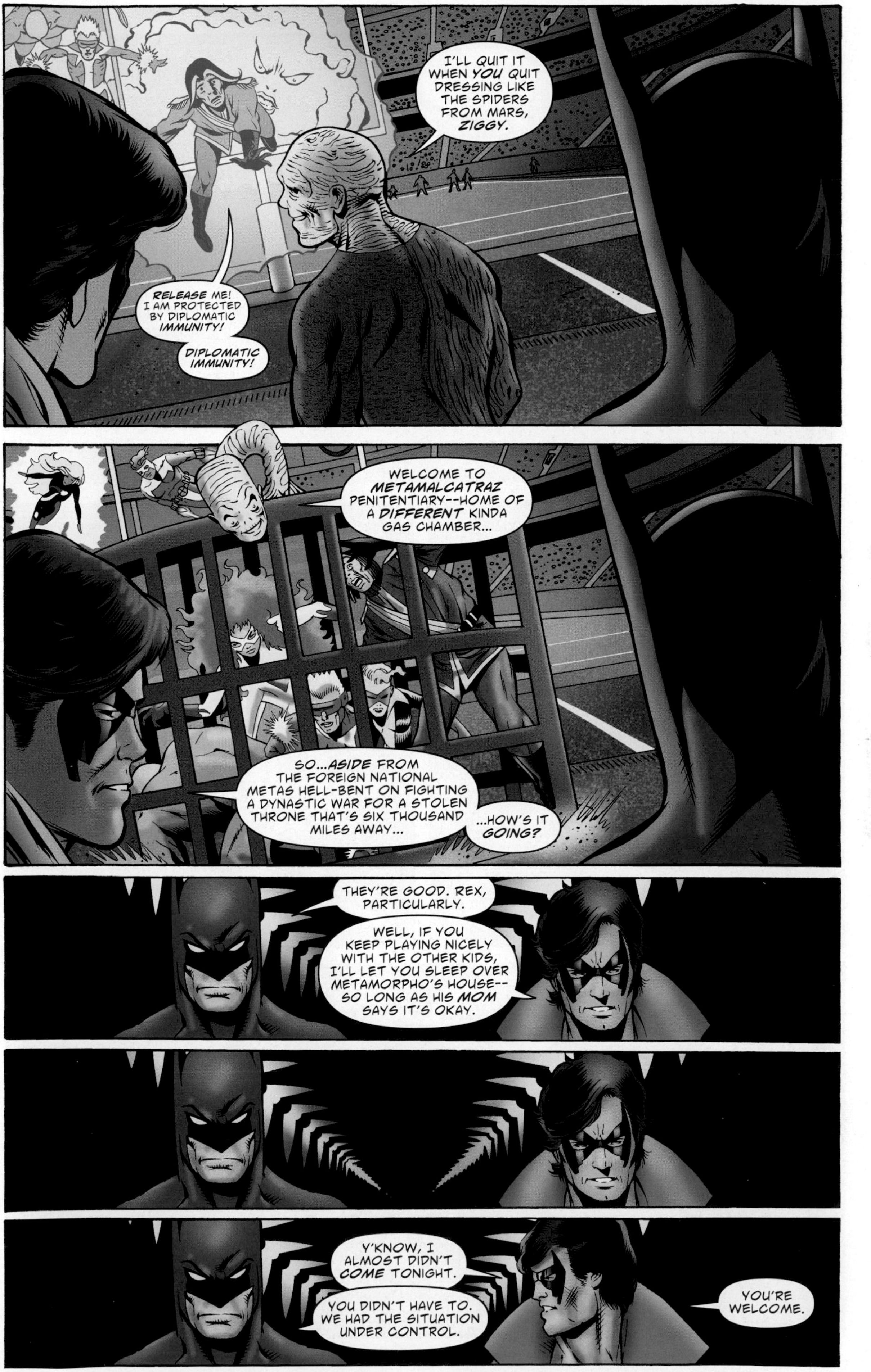
I'LL QUIT IT WHEN YOU QUIT DRESSING LIKE THE SPIDERS FROM MARS, ZIGGY.
RELEASE ME! I AM PROTECTED BY DIPLOMATIC IMMUNITY!
DIPLOMATIC IMMUNITY!
WELCOME TO METAMALCATRAZ PENITENTIARY--HOME OF A DIFFERENT KINDA GAS CHAMBER...
SO...ASIDE FROM THE FOREIGN NATIONAL METAS HELL-BENT ON FIGHTING A DYNASTIC WAR FOR A STOLEN THRONE THAT'S SIX THOUSAND MILES AWAY...
...HOW'S IT GOING?
THEY'RE GOOD. REX, PARTICULARLY.
WELL, IF YOU KEEP PLAYING NICELY WITH THE OTHER KIDS, I'LL LET YOU SLEEP OVER METAMORPHO'S HOUSE-- SO LONG AS HIS MOM SAYS IT'S OKAY.
Y'KNOW, I ALMOST DIDN'T COME TONIGHT.
YOU DIDN'T HAVE TO. WE HAD THE SITUATION UNDER CONTROL.
YOU'RE WELCOME.

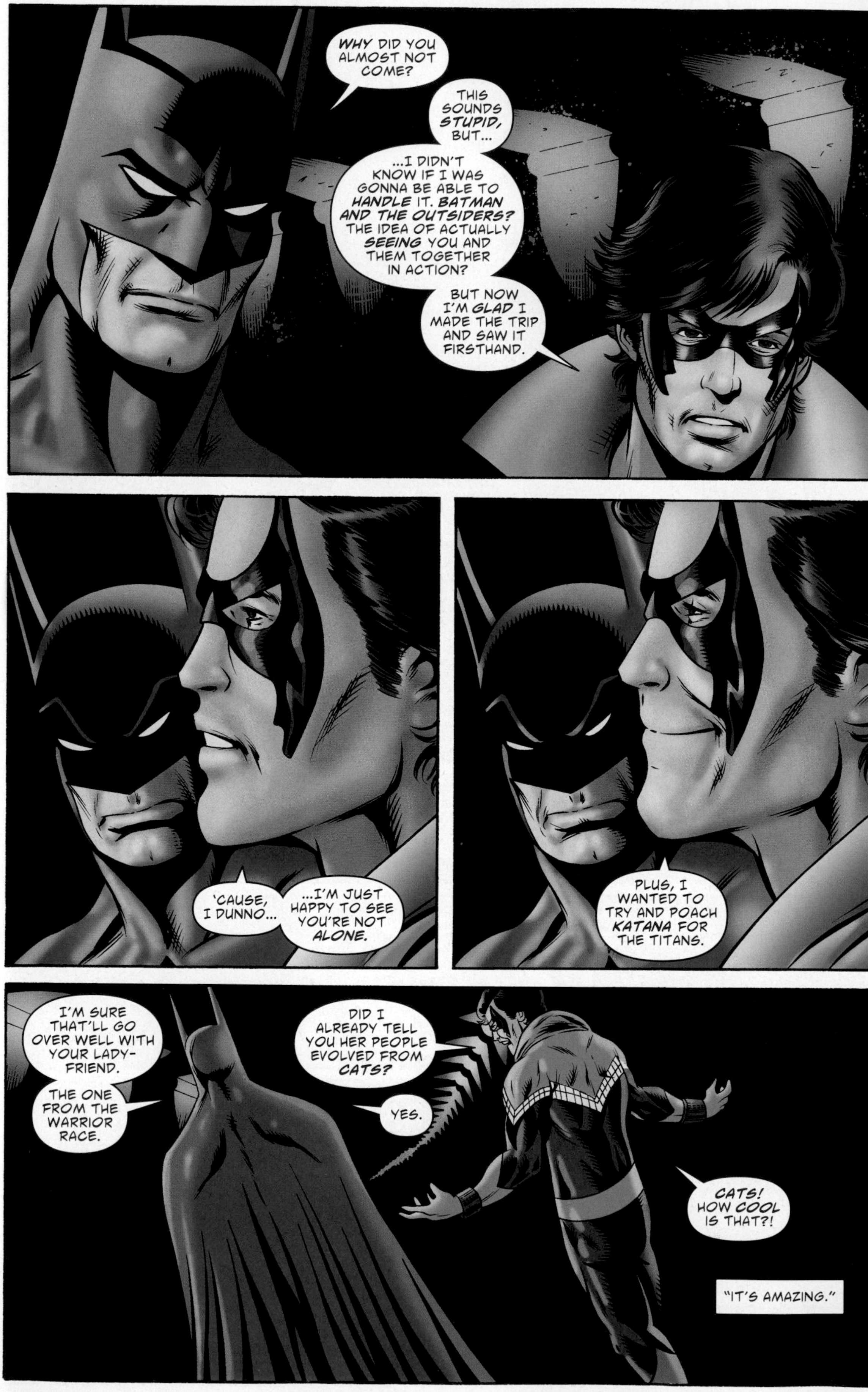
WHY DID YOU ALMOST NOT COME?
THIS SOUNDS STUPID, BUT...
...I DIDN'T KNOW IF I WAS GONNA BE ABLE TO HANDLE IT. BATMAN AND THE OUTSIDERS? THE IDEA OF ACTUALLY SEEING YOU AND THEM TOGETHER IN ACTION?
BUT NOW I'M GLAD I MADE THE TRIP AND SAW IT FIRSTHAND.
'CAUSE, I DUNNO...
...I'M JUST HAPPY TO SEE YOU'RE NOT ALONE.
PLUS, I WANTED TO TRY AND POACH KATANA FOR THE TITANS.
I'M SURE THAT'LL GO OVER WELL WITH YOUR LADY-FRIEND.
THE ONE FROM THE WARRIOR RACE.
DID I ALREADY TELL YOU HER PEOPLE EVOLVED FROM CATS?
YES.
CATS! HOW COOL IS THAT?!
"IT'S AMAZING."

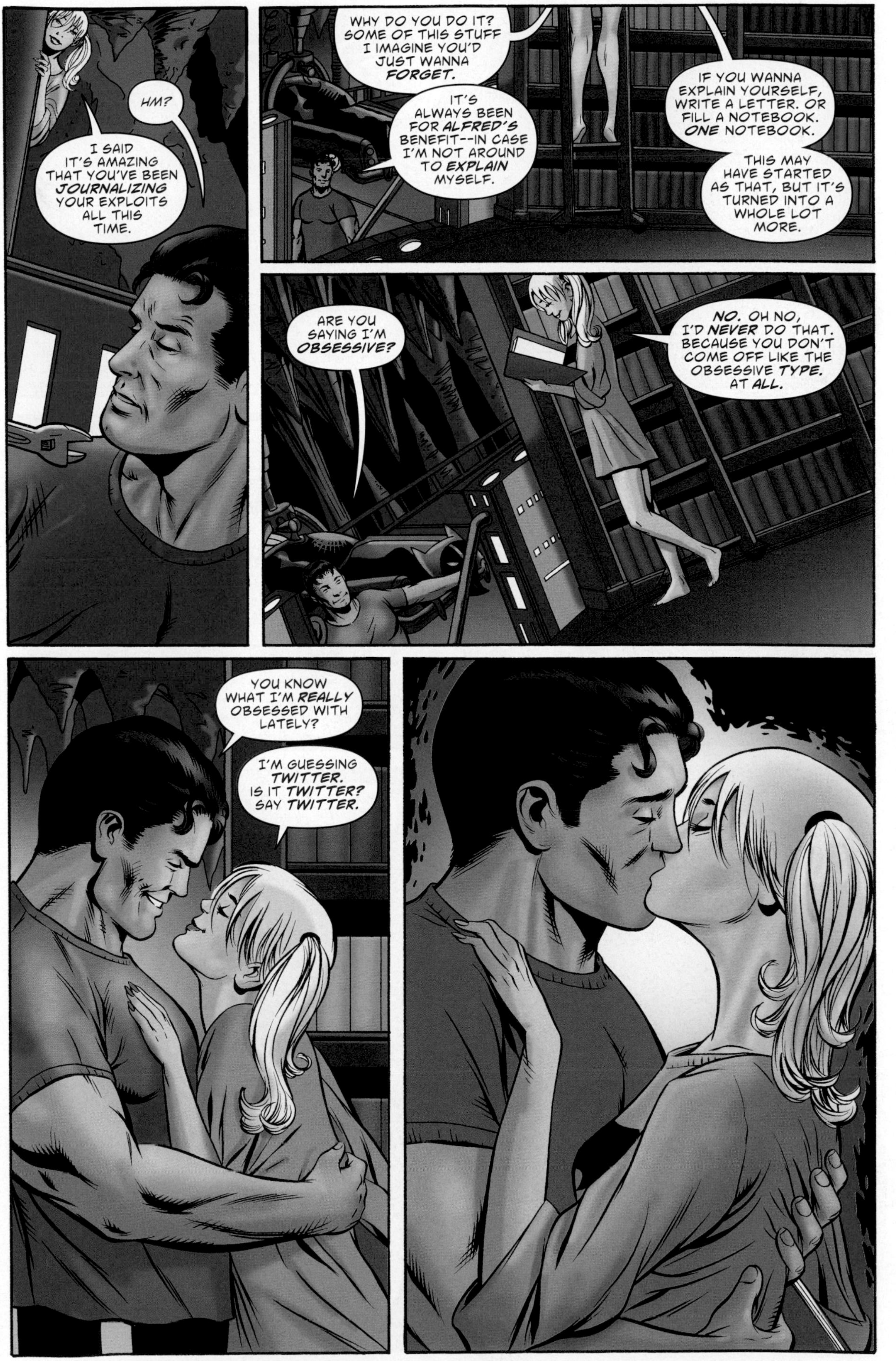
HM?
I SAID IT'S AMAZING THAT YOU'VE BEEN JOURNALIZING YOUR EXPLOITS ALL THIS TIME.
WHY DO YOU DO IT? SOME OF THIS STUFF I IMAGINE YOU'D JUST WANNA FORGET.
IT'S ALWAYS BEEN FOR ALFRED'S BENEFIT--IN CASE I'M NOT AROUND TO EXPLAIN MYSELF.
IF YOU WANNA EXPLAIN YOURSELF, WRITE A LETTER. OR FILL A NOTEBOOK. ONE NOTEBOOK.
THIS MAY HAVE STARTED AS THAT, BUT IT'S TURNED INTO A WHOLE LOT MORE.
ARE YOU SAYING I'M OBSESSIVE?
NO. OH NO, I'D NEVER DO THAT. BECAUSE YOU DON'T COME OFF LIKE THE OBSESSIVE TYPE. AT ALL.
YOU KNOW WHAT I'M REALLY OBSESSED WITH LATELY?
I'M GUESSING TWITTER. IS IT TWITTER? SAY TWITTER.

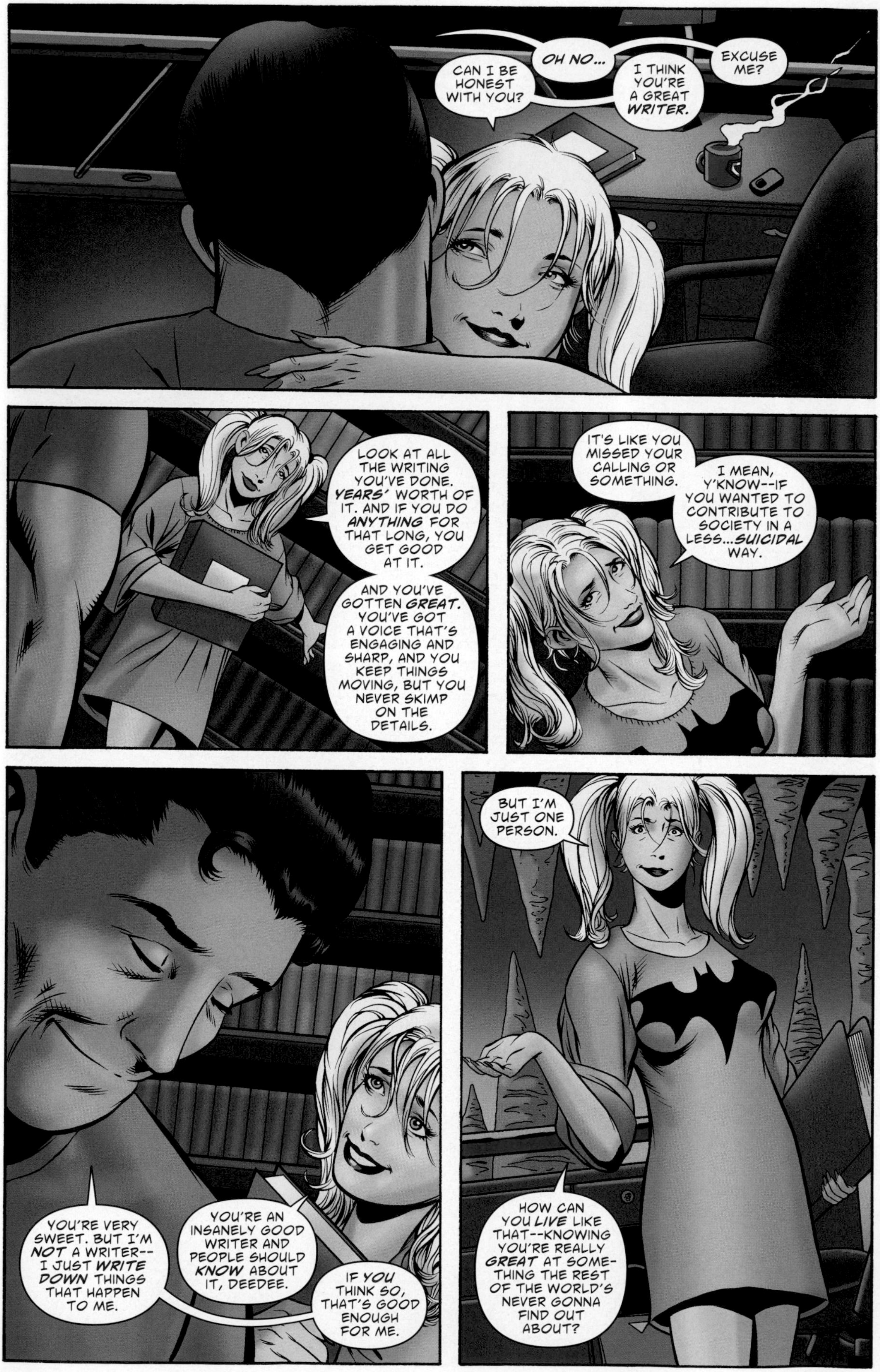
CAN I BE HONEST WITH YOU?
OH NO...
I THINK YOU'RE A GREAT WRITER.
EXCUSE ME?
LOOK AT ALL THE WRITING YOU'VE DONE. YEARS' WORTH OF IT. AND IF YOU DO ANYTHING FOR THAT LONG, YOU GET GOOD AT IT.
AND YOU'VE GOTTEN GREAT. YOU'VE GOT A VOICE THAT'S ENGAGING AND SHARP, AND YOU KEEP THINGS MOVING, BUT YOU NEVER SKIMP ON THE DETAILS.
IT'S LIKE YOU MISSED YOUR CALLING OR SOMETHING.
I MEAN, Y'KNOW--IF YOU WANTED TO CONTRIBUTE TO SOCIETY IN A LESS...SUICIDAL WAY.
YOU'RE VERY SWEET. BUT I'M NOT A WRITER-- I JUST WRITE DOWN THINGS THAT HAPPEN TO ME.
YOU'RE AN INSANELY GOOD WRITER AND PEOPLE SHOULD KNOW ABOUT IT, DEEDEE.
IF YOU THINK SO, THAT'S GOOD ENOUGH FOR ME.
BUT I'M JUST ONE PERSON.
HOW CAN YOU LIVE LIKE THAT--KNOWING YOU'RE REALLY GREAT AT SOME-THING THE REST OF THE WORLD'S NEVER GONNA FIND OUT ABOUT?

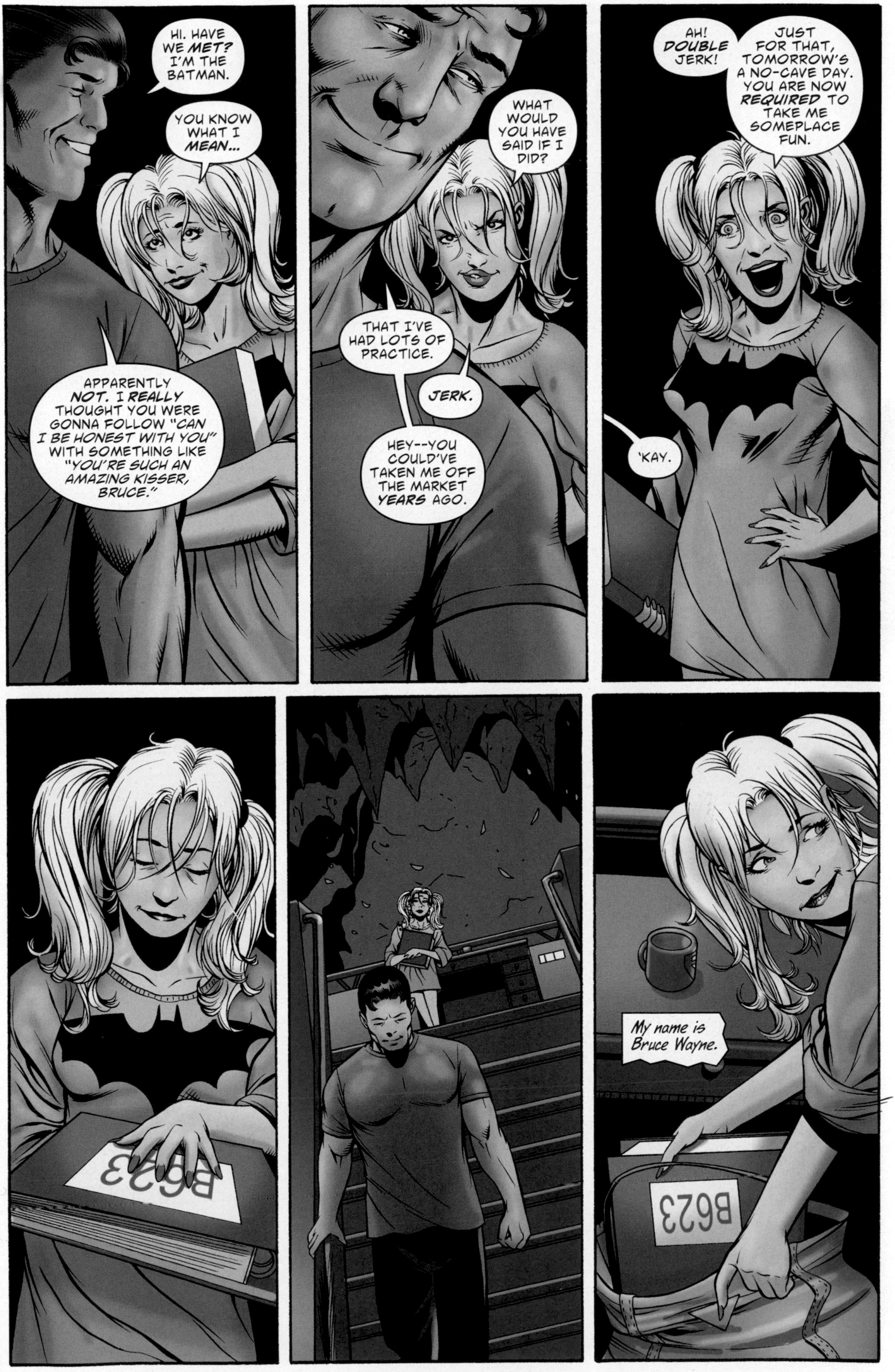
HI. HAVE WE MET? I'M THE BATMAN.
YOU KNOW WHAT I MEAN...
APPARENTLY NOT. I REALLY THOUGHT YOU WERE GONNA FOLLOW "CAN I BE HONEST WITH YOU" WITH SOMETHING LIKE "YOU'RE SUCH AN AMAZING KISSER, BRUCE."
WHAT WOULD YOU HAVE SAID IF I DID?
THAT I'VE HAD LOTS OF PRACTICE.
JERK.
HEY--YOU COULD'VE TAKEN ME OFF THE MARKET YEARS AGO.
AH! DOUBLE JERK!
JUST FOR THAT, TOMORROW'S A NO-CAVE DAY. YOU ARE NOW REQUIRED TO TAKE ME SOMEPLACE FUN.
'KAY.
B623
My name is Bruce Wayne.
B623

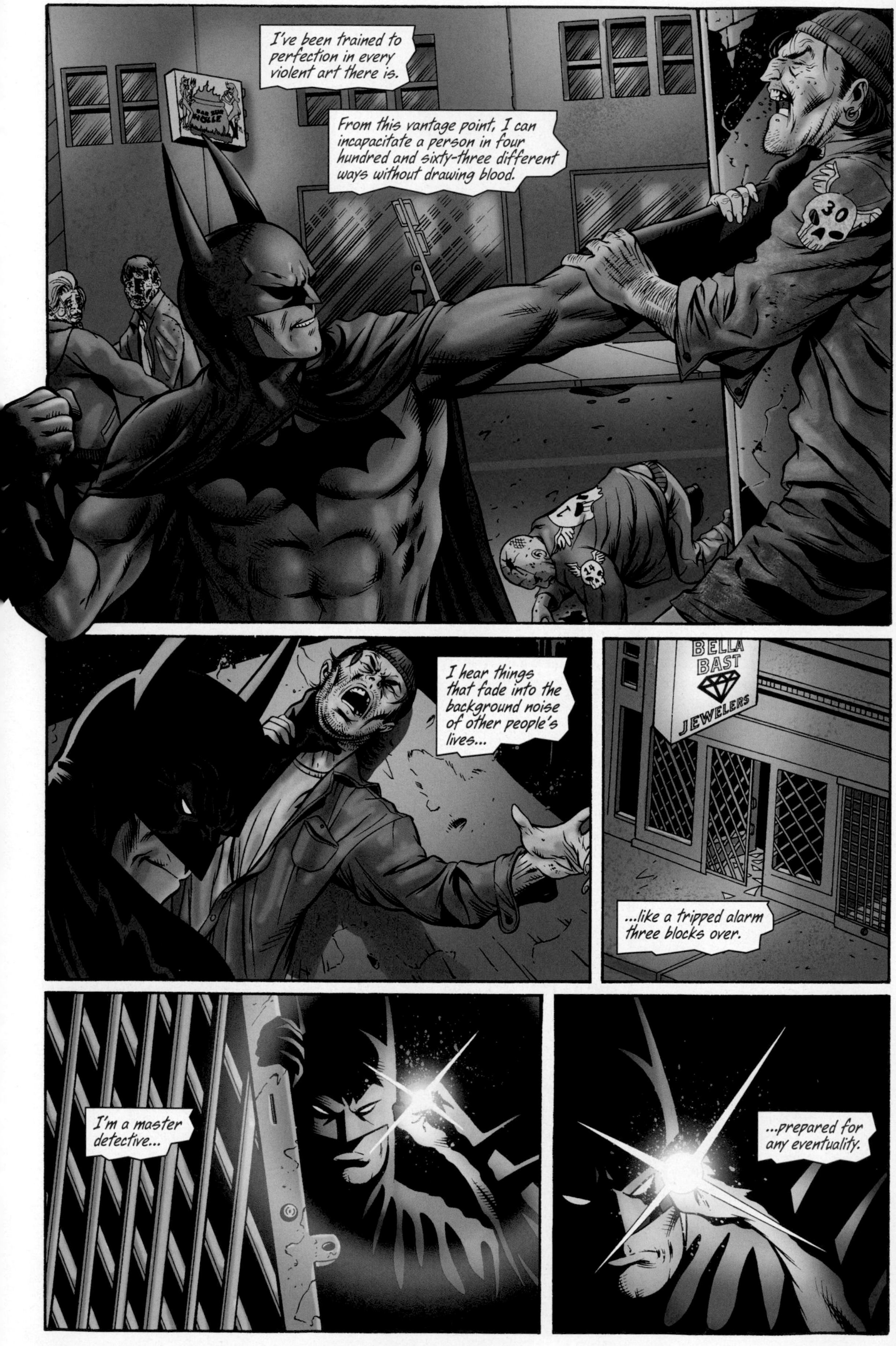
I've been trained to perfection in every violent art there is.
From this vantage point, I can incapacitate a person in four hundred and sixty-three different ways without drawing blood.
I hear things that fade into the background noise of other people's lives...
BELLA BAST JEWELERS
...like a tripped alarm three blocks over.
I'm a master detective...
...prepared for any eventuality.

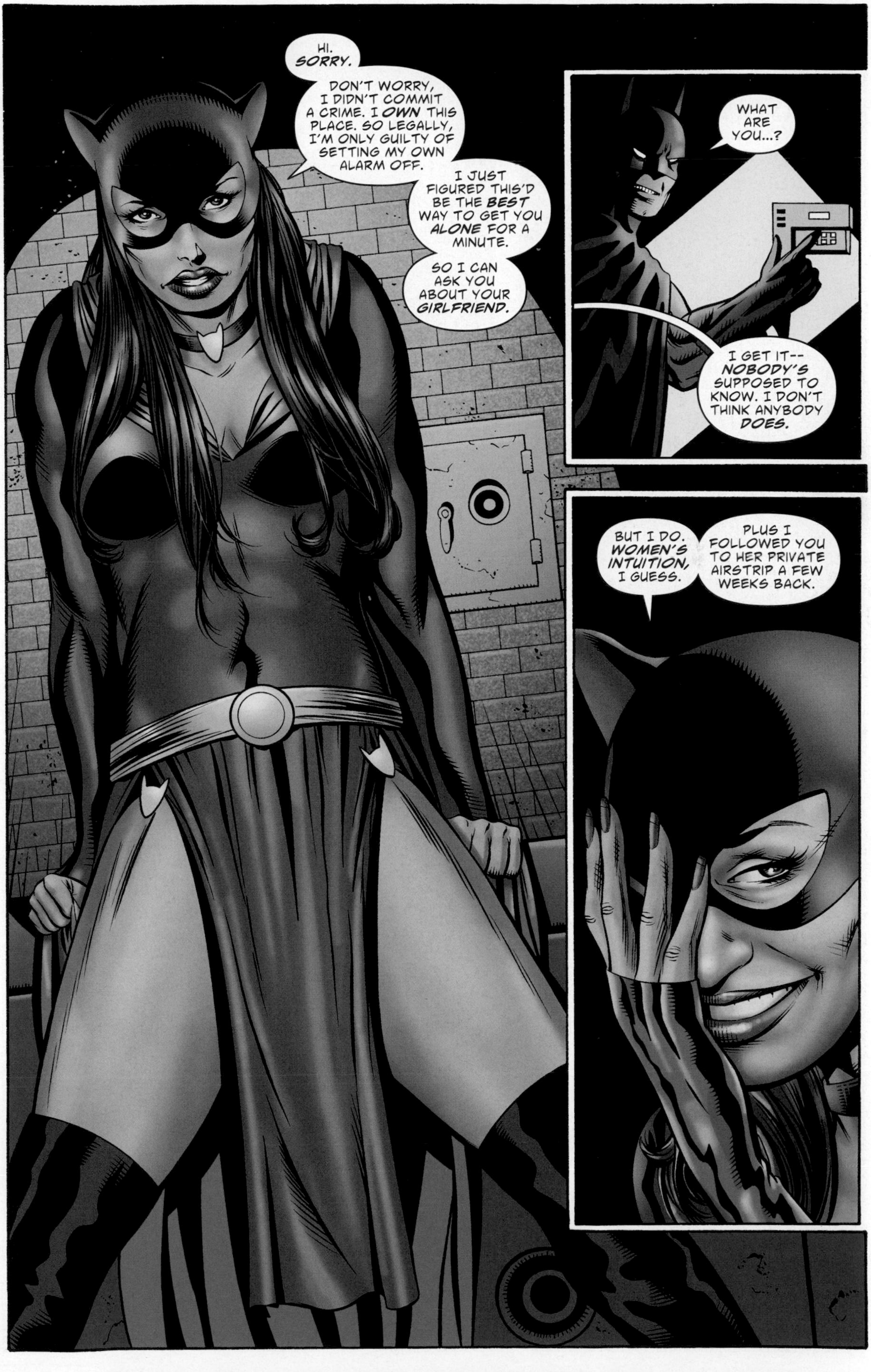
HI. SORRY.
DON'T WORRY, I DIDN'T COMMIT A CRIME. I OWN THIS PLACE. SO LEGALLY, I'M ONLY GUILTY OF SETTING MY OWN ALARM OFF.
I JUST FIGURED THIS'D BE THE BEST WAY TO GET YOU ALONE FOR A MINUTE.
SO I CAN ASK YOU ABOUT YOUR GIRLFRIEND.
WHAT ARE YOU...?
I GET IT--NOBODY'S SUPPOSED TO KNOW. I DON'T THINK ANYBODY DOES.
BUT I DO. WOMEN'S INTUITION, I GUESS.
PLUS I FOLLOWED YOU TO HER PRIVATE AIRSTRIP A FEW WEEKS BACK.

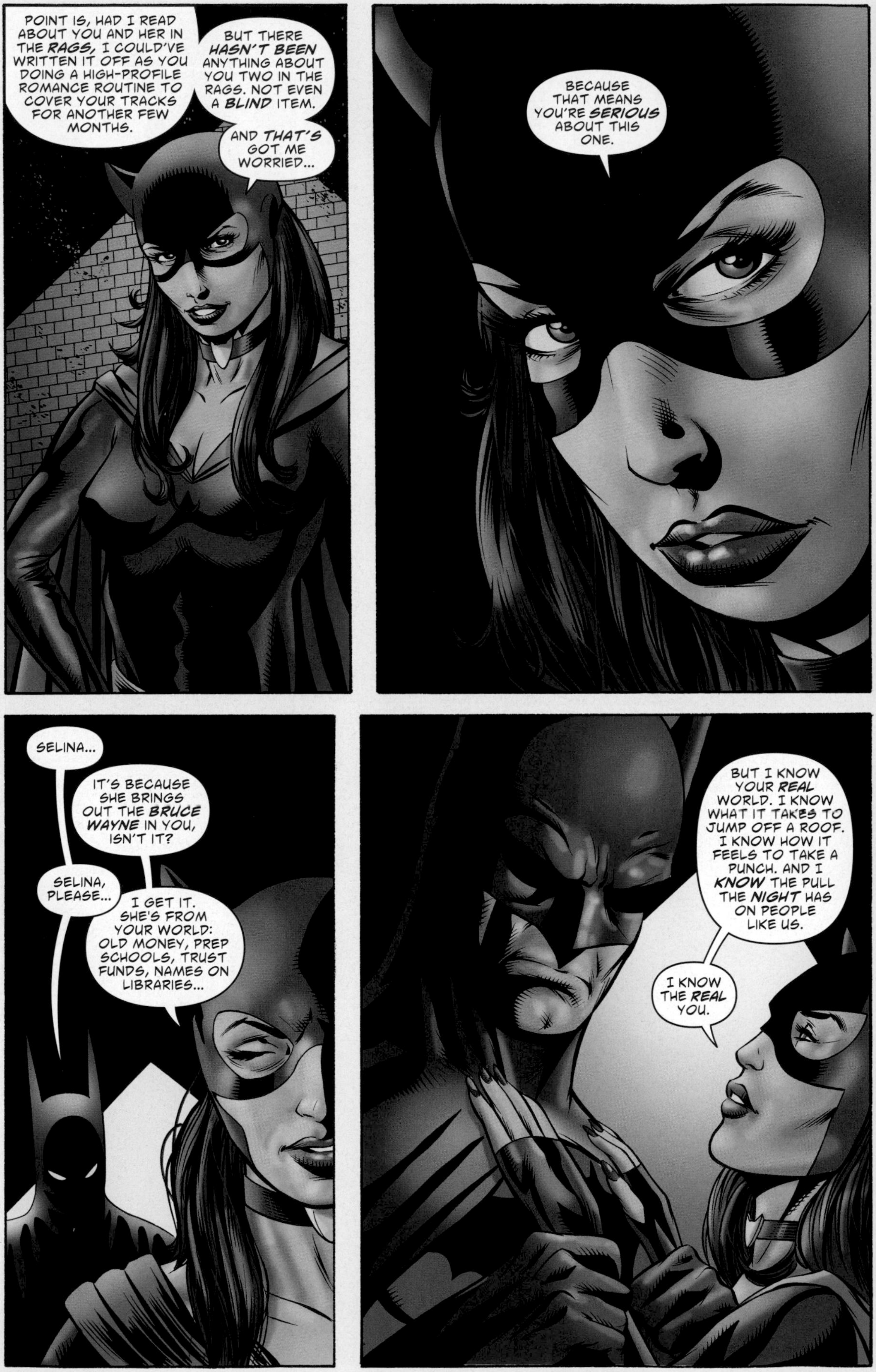
POINT IS, HAD I READ ABOUT YOU AND HER IN THE RAGS, I COULD'VE WRITTEN IT OFF AS YOU DOING A HIGH-PROFILE ROMANCE ROUTINE TO COVER YOUR TRACKS FOR ANOTHER FEW MONTHS.
BUT THERE HASN'T BEEN ANYTHING ABOUT YOU TWO IN THE RAGS. NOT EVEN A BLIND ITEM.
AND THAT'S GOT ME WORRIED...
BECAUSE THAT MEANS YOU'RE SERIOUS ABOUT THIS ONE.
SELINA...
IT'S BECAUSE SHE BRINGS OUT THE BRUCE WAYNE IN YOU, ISN'T IT?
SELINA, PLEASE...
I GET IT. SHE'S FROM YOUR WORLD: OLD MONEY, PREP SCHOOLS, TRUST FUNDS, NAMES ON LIBRARIES...
BUT I KNOW YOUR REAL WORLD. I KNOW WHAT IT TAKES TO JUMP OFF A ROOF. I KNOW HOW IT FEELS TO TAKE A PUNCH. AND I KNOW THE PULL THE NIGHT HAS ON PEOPLE LIKE US.
I KNOW THE REAL YOU.

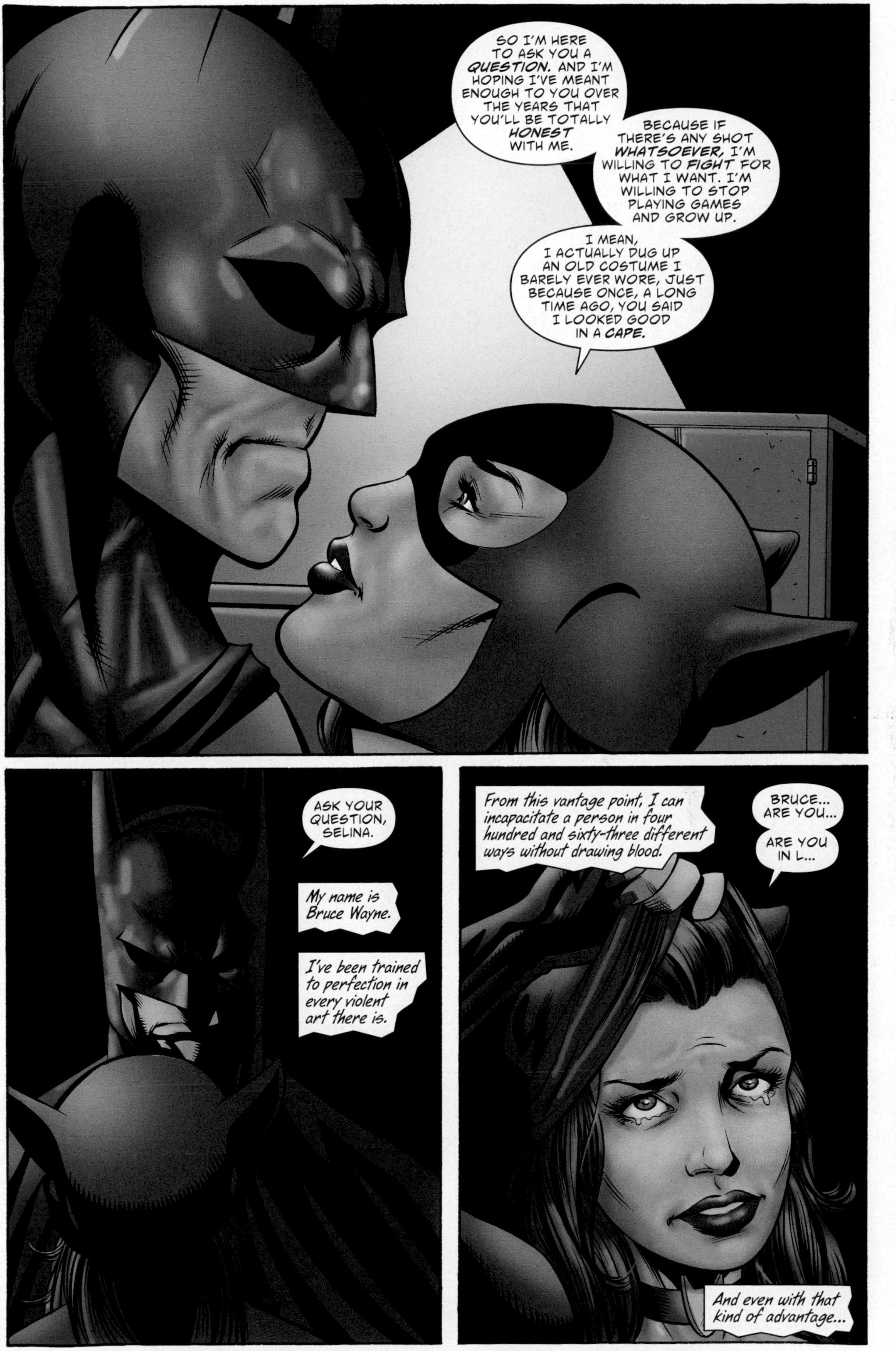
SO I'M HERE TO ASK YOU A QUESTION. AND I'M HOPING I'VE MEANT ENOUGH TO YOU OVER THE YEARS THAT YOU'LL BE TOTALLY HONEST WITH ME.
BECAUSE IF THERE'S ANY SHOT WHATSOEVER, I'M WILLING TO FIGHT FOR WHAT I WANT. I'M WILLING TO STOP PLAYING GAMES AND GROW UP.
I MEAN, I ACTUALLY DUG UP AN OLD COSTUME I BARELY EVER WORE, JUST BECAUSE ONCE, A LONG TIME AGO, YOU SAID I LOOKED GOOD IN A CAPE.
ASK YOUR QUESTION, SELINA.
My name is Bruce Wayne.
I've been trained to perfection in every violent art there is.
From this vantage point, I can incapacitate a person in four hundred and sixty-three different ways without drawing blood.
BRUCE... ARE YOU...
ARE YOU IN L...
And even with that kind of advantage...

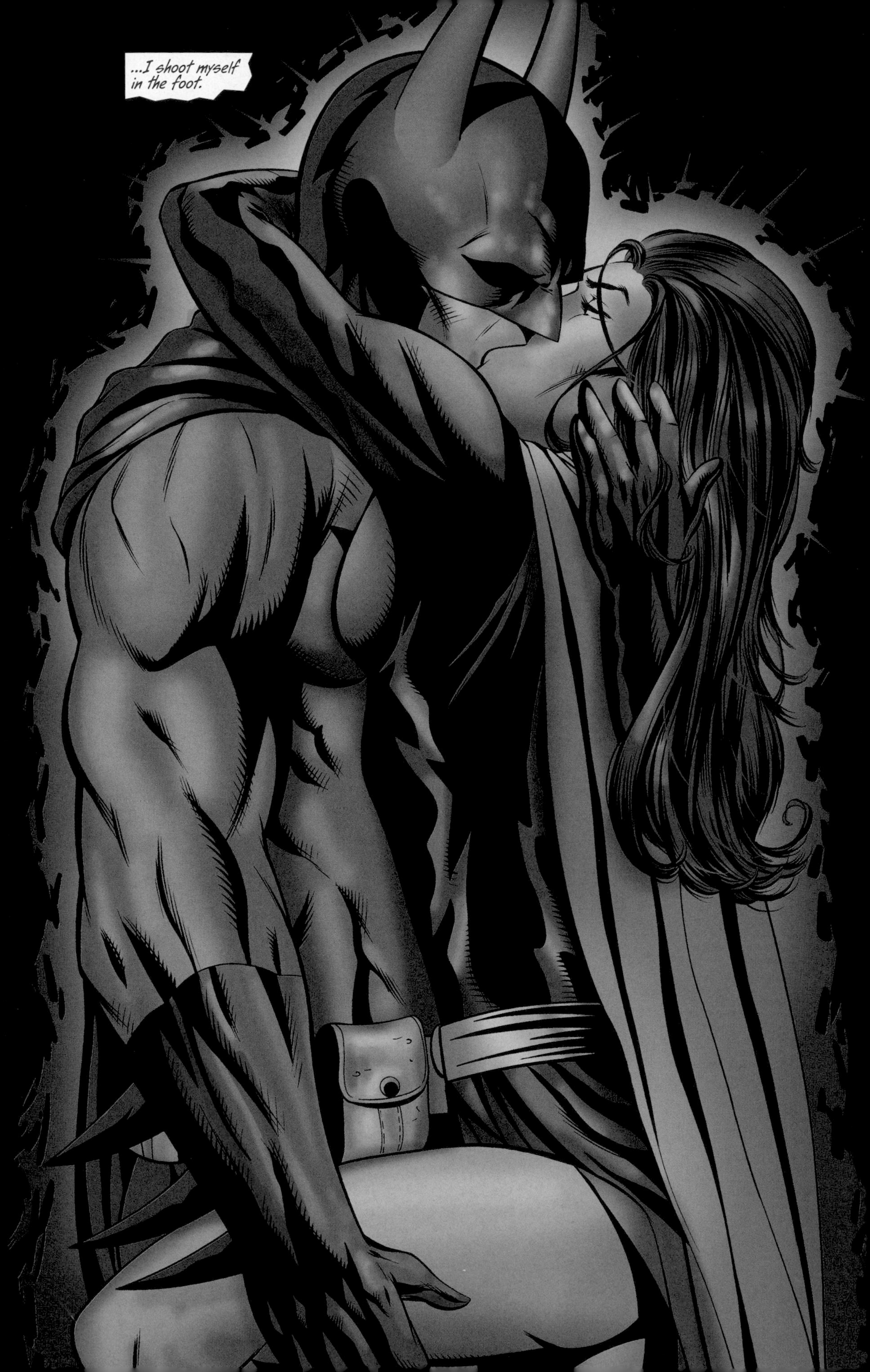
...I shoot myself in the foot.

Batman: The Widening Gyre #5 cover by BILL SIENKIEWICZ

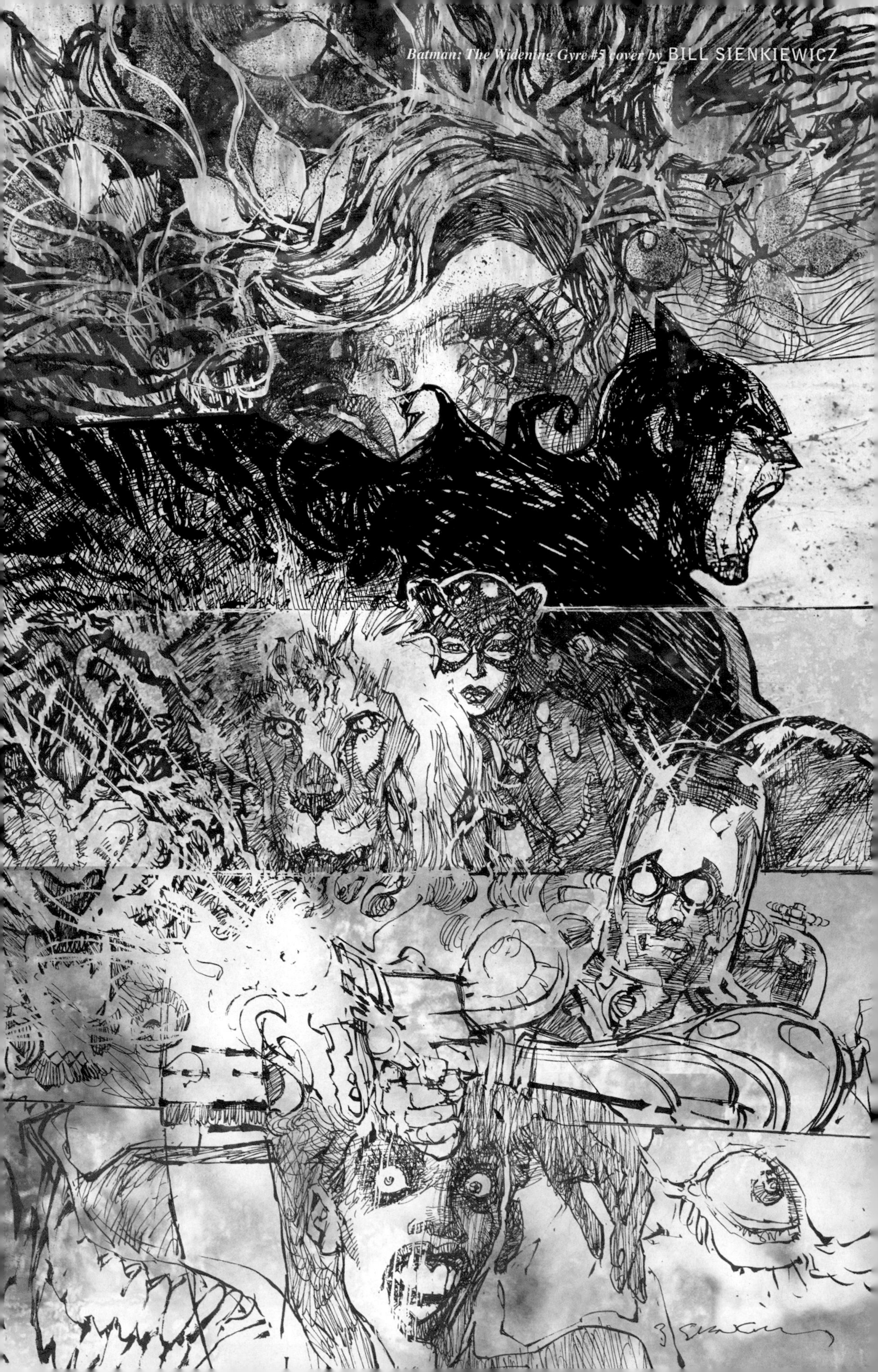

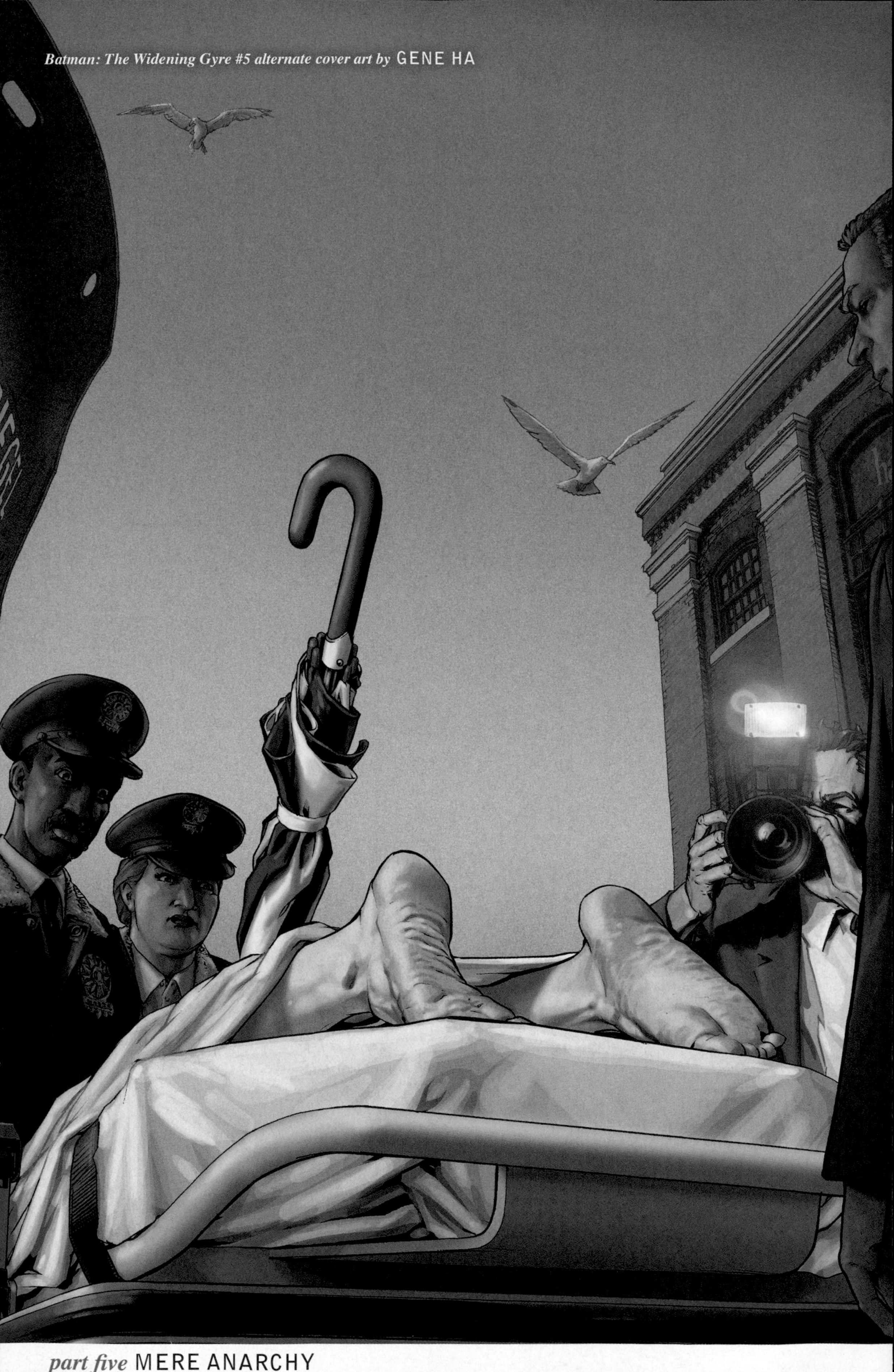

Batman: The Widening Gyre #5 alternate cover art by GENE HA

part five MERE ANARCHY

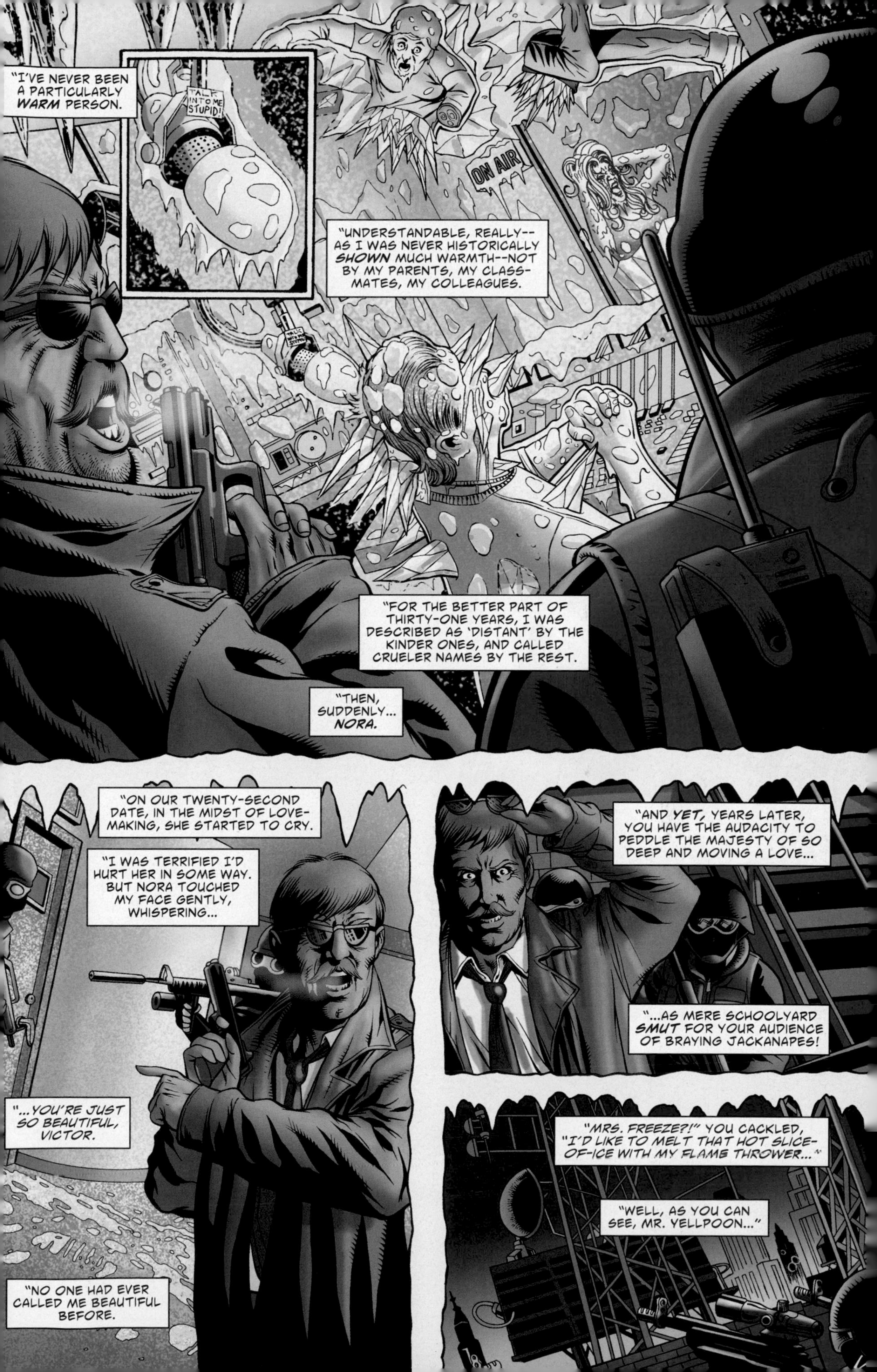
"I'VE NEVER BEEN A PARTICULARLY WARM PERSON.
TALK INTO ME STUPID!
ON AIR
"UNDERSTANDABLE, REALLY-- AS I WAS NEVER HISTORICALLY SHOWN MUCH WARMTH--NOT BY MY PARENTS, MY CLASS-MATES, MY COLLEAGUES.
"FOR THE BETTER PART OF THIRTY-ONE YEARS, I WAS DESCRIBED AS 'DISTANT' BY THE KINDER ONES, AND CALLED CRUELER NAMES BY THE REST.
"THEN, SUDDENLY... NORA.
"ON OUR TWENTY-SECOND DATE, IN THE MIDST OF LOVE-MAKING, SHE STARTED TO CRY.
"I WAS TERRIFIED I'D HURT HER IN SOME WAY. BUT NORA TOUCHED MY FACE GENTLY, WHISPERING...
"...YOU'RE JUST SO BEAUTIFUL, VICTOR.
"NO ONE HAD EVER CALLED ME BEAUTIFUL BEFORE.
"AND YET, YEARS LATER, YOU HAVE THE AUDACITY TO PEDDLE THE MAJESTY OF SO DEEP AND MOVING A LOVE...
"...AS MERE SCHOOLYARD SMUT FOR YOUR AUDIENCE OF BRAYING JACKANAPES!
"MRS. FREEZE?!" YOU CACKLED, "I'D LIKE TO MELT THAT HOT SLICE-OF-ICE WITH MY FLAME THROWER..."
"WELL, AS YOU CAN SEE, MR. YELLPOON..."

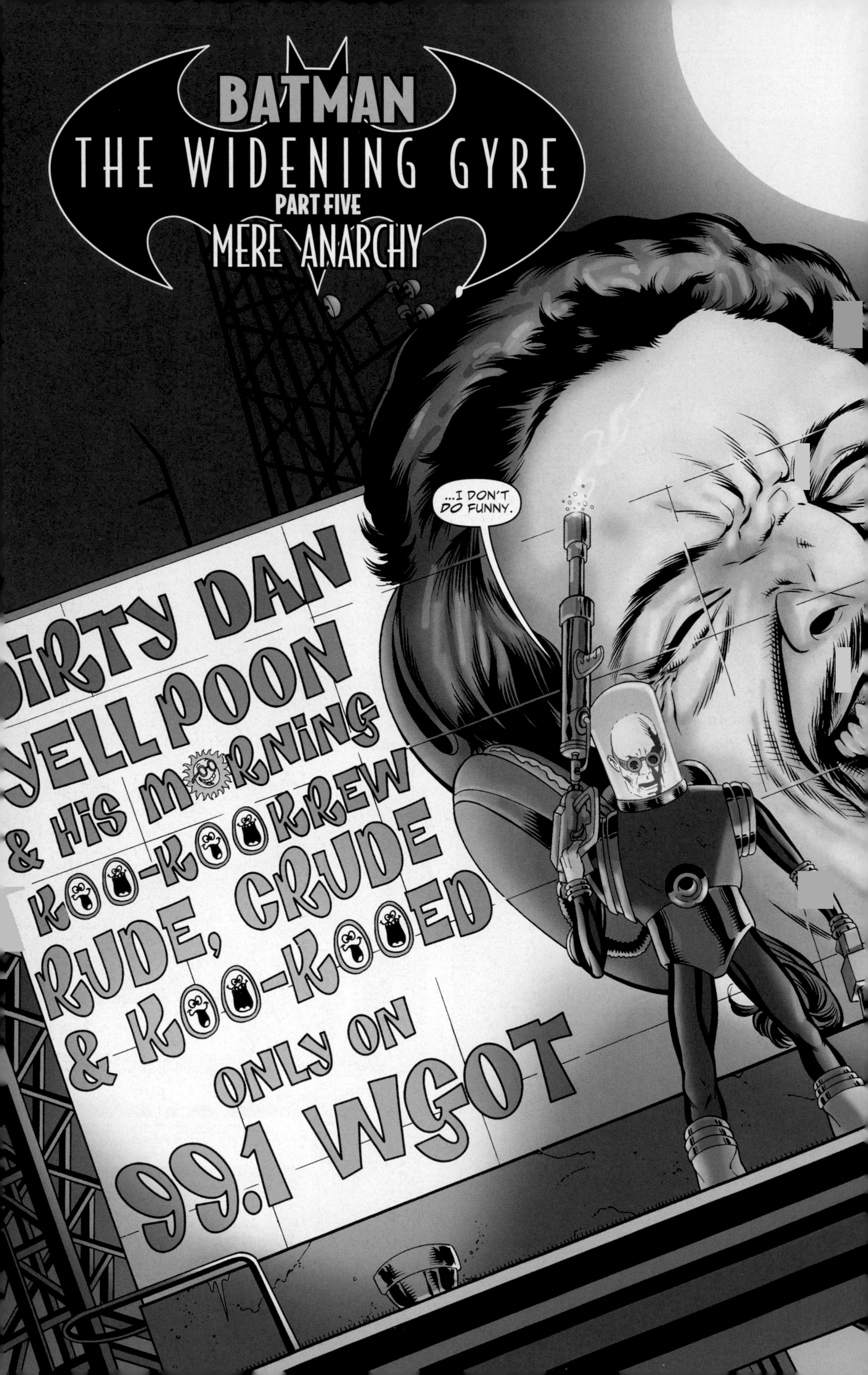
BATMAN
THE WIDENING GYRE
PART FIVE
MERE ANARCHY
...I DON'T DO FUNNY.
DIRTY DAN YELLPOON & HIS MORNING KOO-KOO KREW
RUDE, CRUDE & KOO-KOOED
ONLY ON 99.1 WGOT

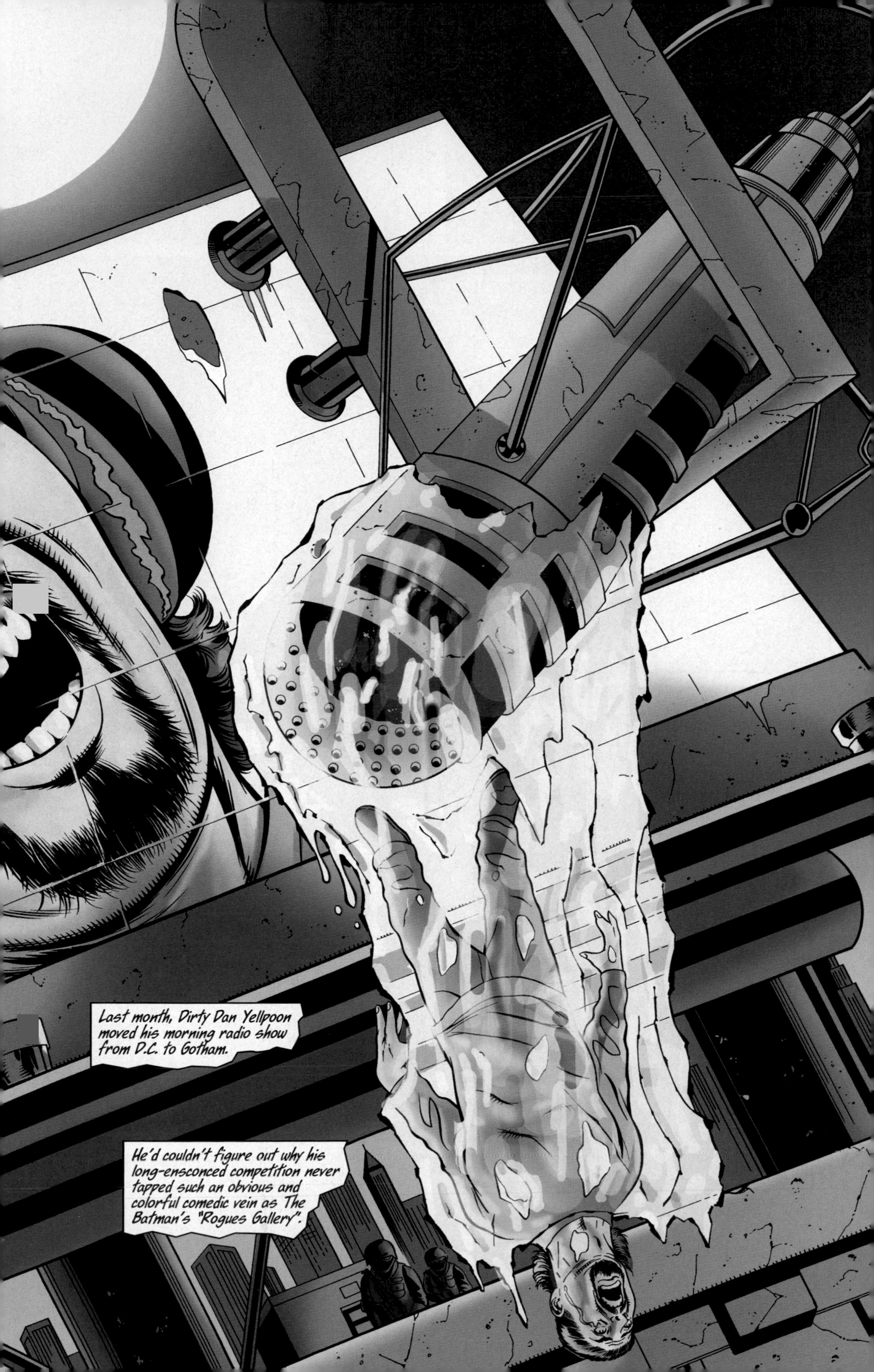
Last month, Dirty Dan Yellpoon moved his morning radio show from D.C. to Gotham.
He'd couldn't figure out why his long-ensconced competition never tapped such an obvious and colorful comedic vein as The Batman's "Rogues Gallery".

Neither did Frahnkus, the morning idiot for WBDH.

He thought calling out the Penguin as "lamer than Aquaman" was a real knee-slapper.

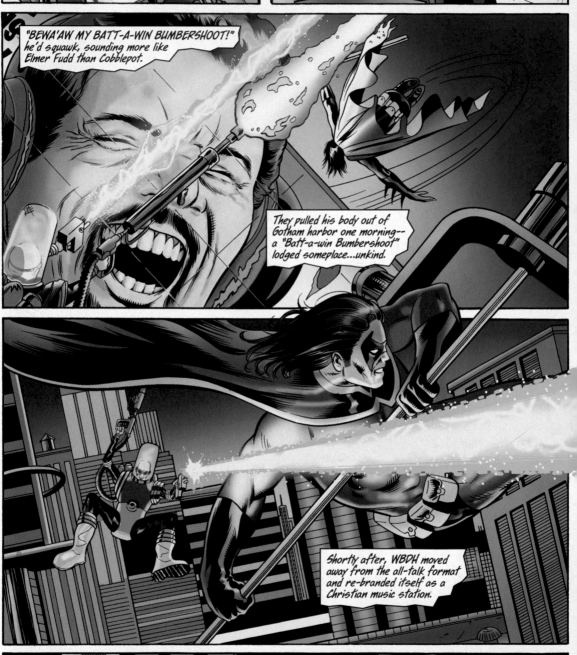

"BEWA'AW MY BATT-A-WIN BUMBERSHOOT!" he'd squawk, sounding more like Elmer Fudd than Cobblepot.

P-TINK

They pulled his body out of Gotham harbor one morning-- a "Batt-a-win Bumbershoot" lodged someplace...unkind.

Shortly after, WBDH moved away from the all-talk format and re-branded itself as a Christian music station.

Here is where I swoop in.

Or at least I would...

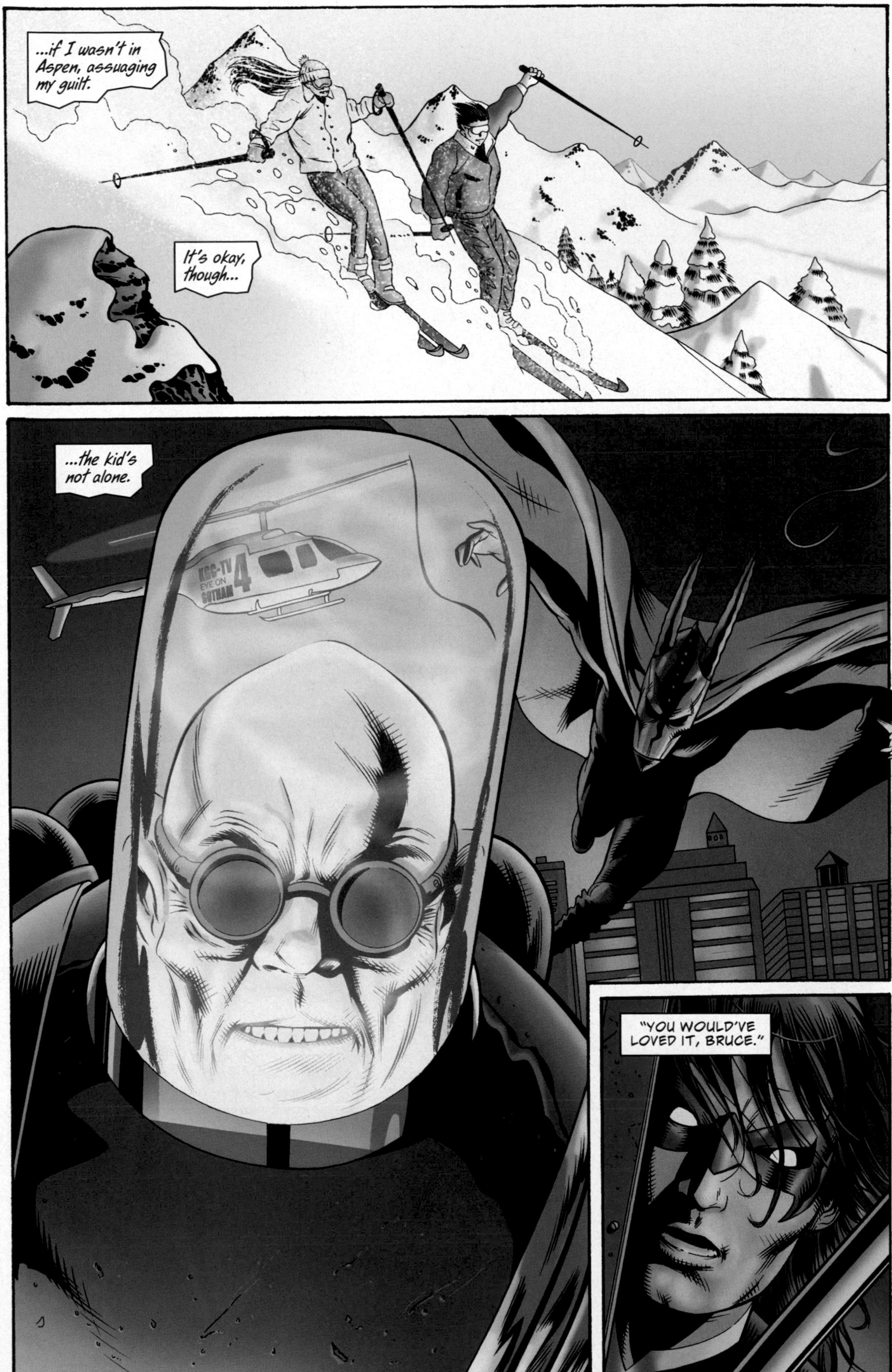
...if I wasn't in Aspen, assuaging my guilt.
It's okay, though...
...the kid's not alone.
KGC-TV 4 EYE ON GOTHAM
"YOU WOULD'VE LOVED IT, BRUCE."

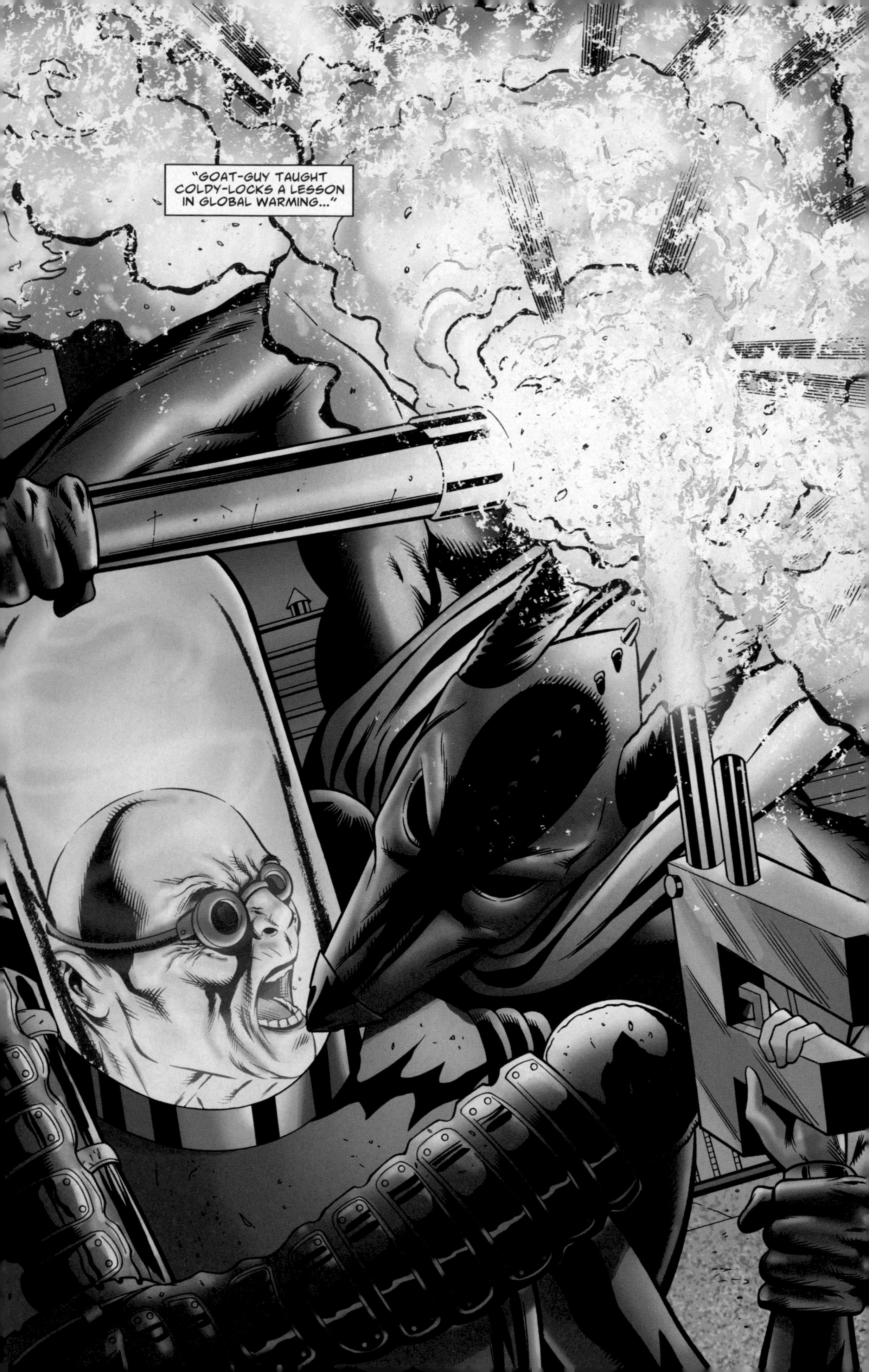
"GOAT-GUY TAUGHT
COLDY-LOCKS A LESSON
IN GLOBAL WARMING..."

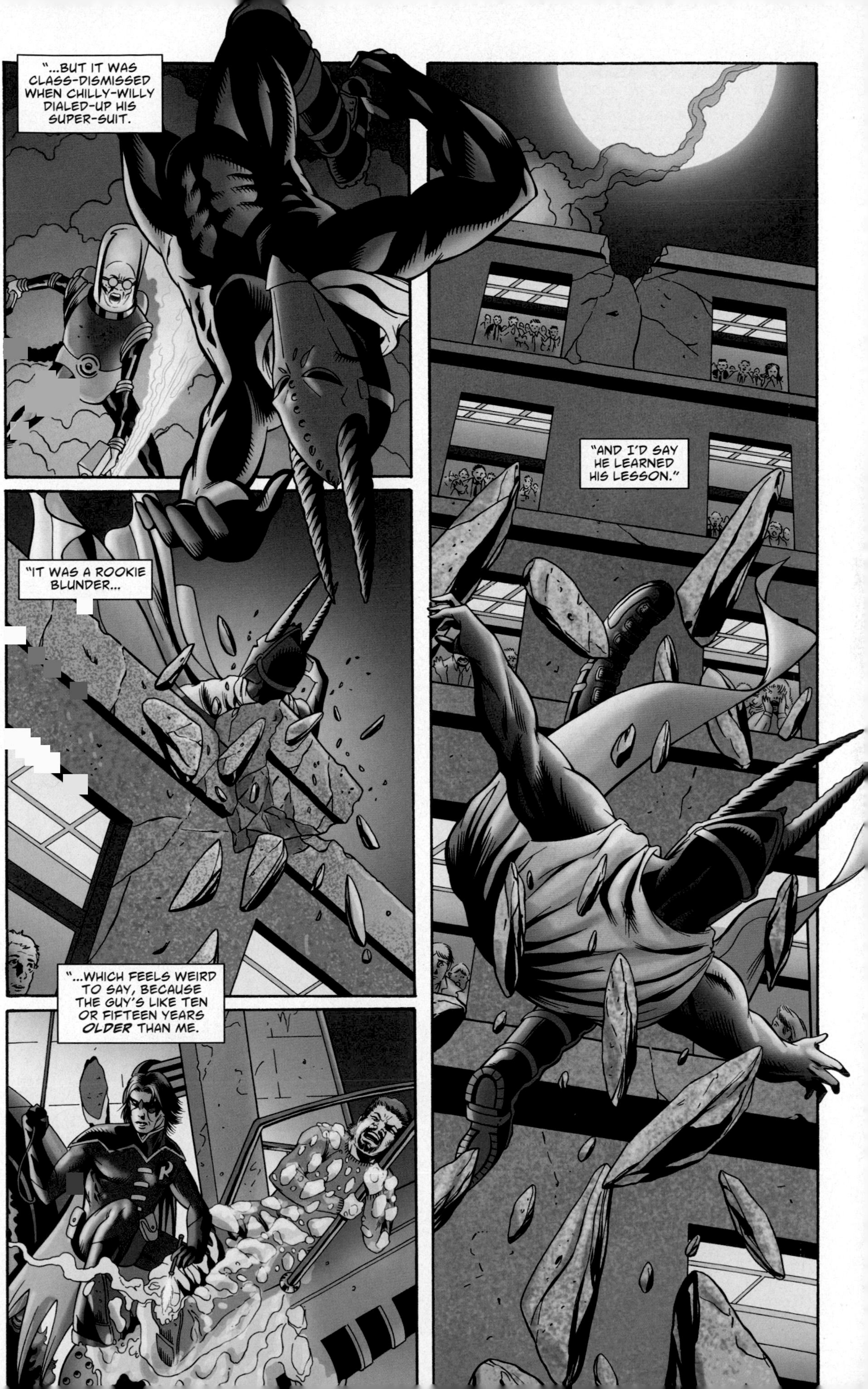
"...BUT IT WAS CLASS-DISMISSED WHEN CHILLY-WILLY DIALED-UP HIS SUPER-SUIT.
"IT WAS A ROOKIE BLUNDER...
"...WHICH FEELS WEIRD TO SAY, BECAUSE THE GUY'S LIKE TEN OR FIFTEEN YEARS OLDER THAN ME.
"AND I'D SAY HE LEARNED HIS LESSON."

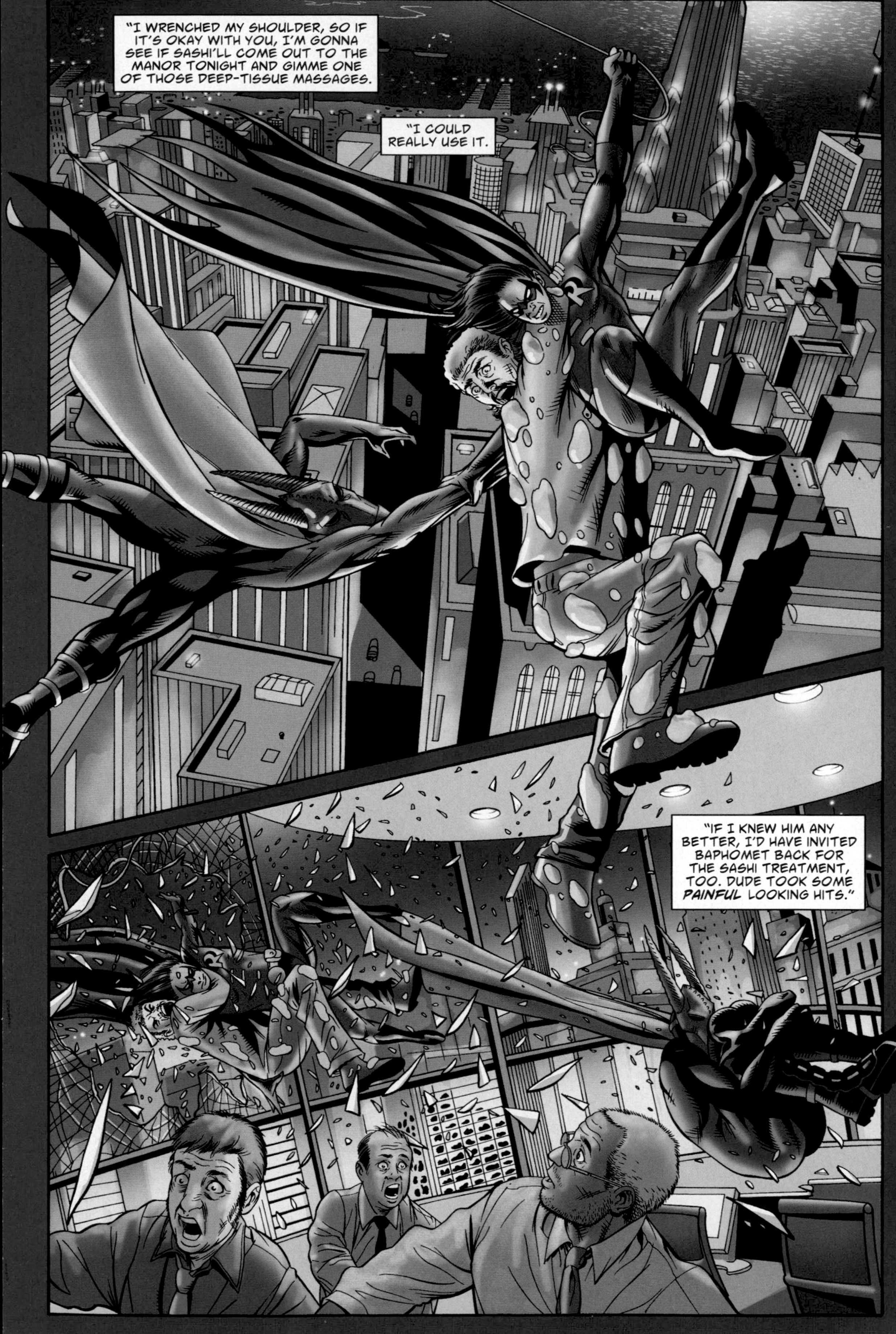
"I WRENCHED MY SHOULDER, SO IF IT'S OKAY WITH YOU, I'M GONNA SEE IF SASHI'LL COME OUT TO THE MANOR TONIGHT AND GIMME ONE OF THOSE DEEP-TISSUE MASSAGES.
"I COULD REALLY USE IT.
"IF I KNEW HIM ANY BETTER, I'D HAVE INVITED BAPHOMET BACK FOR THE SASHI TREATMENT, TOO. DUDE TOOK SOME *PAINFUL* LOOKING HITS."

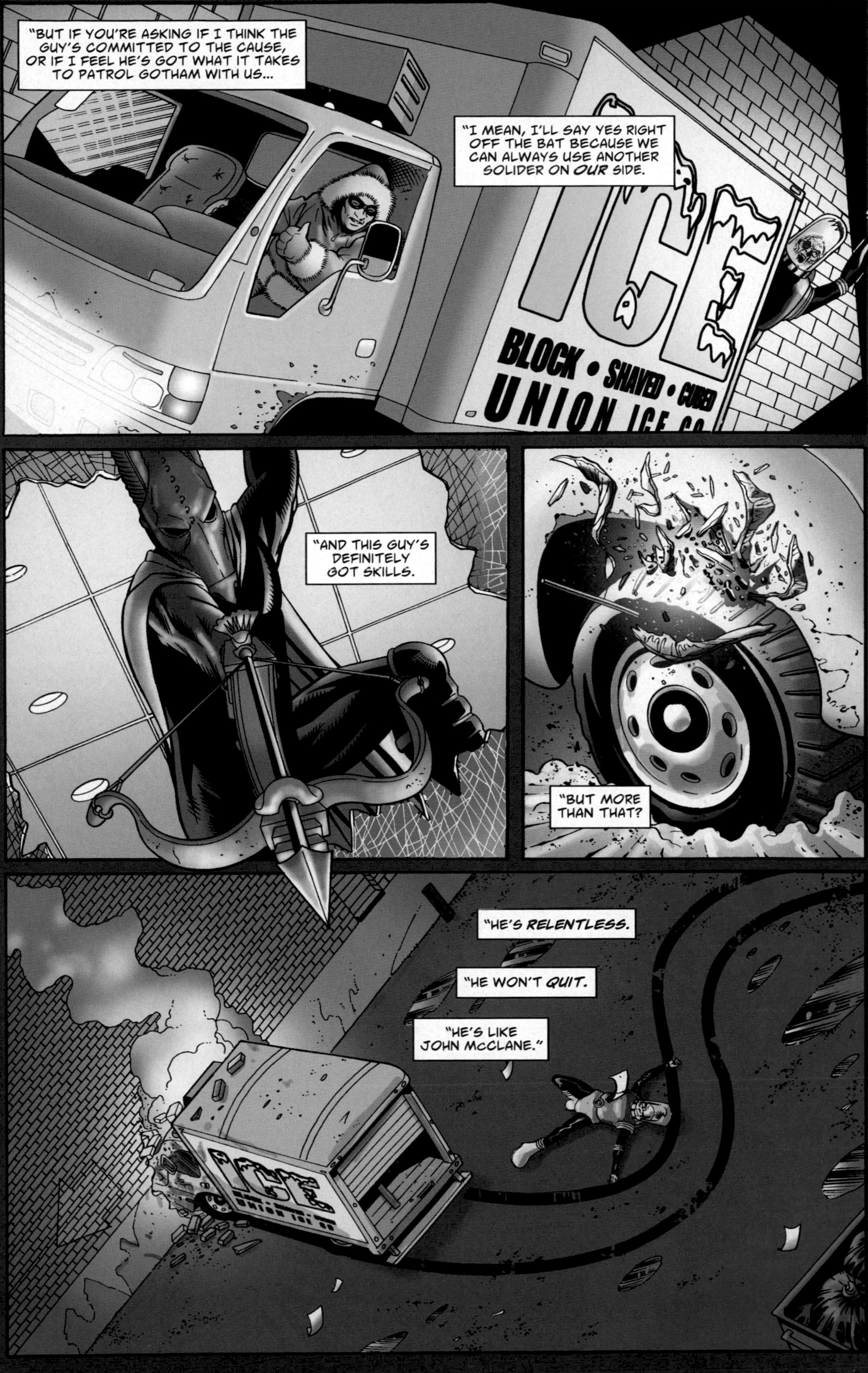
"BUT IF YOU'RE ASKING IF I THINK THE GUY'S COMMITTED TO THE CAUSE, OR IF I FEEL HE'S GOT WHAT IT TAKES TO PATROL GOTHAM WITH US...
"I MEAN, I'LL SAY YES RIGHT OFF THE BAT BECAUSE WE CAN ALWAYS USE ANOTHER SOLIDER ON *OUR* SIDE.
ICE
BLOCK • SHAVED • CUBED
UNION ICE CO.
"AND THIS GUY'S DEFINITELY GOT SKILLS.
"BUT MORE THAN THAT?
"HE'S *RELENTLESS.*
"HE WON'T *QUIT.*
"HE'S LIKE JOHN McCLANE."

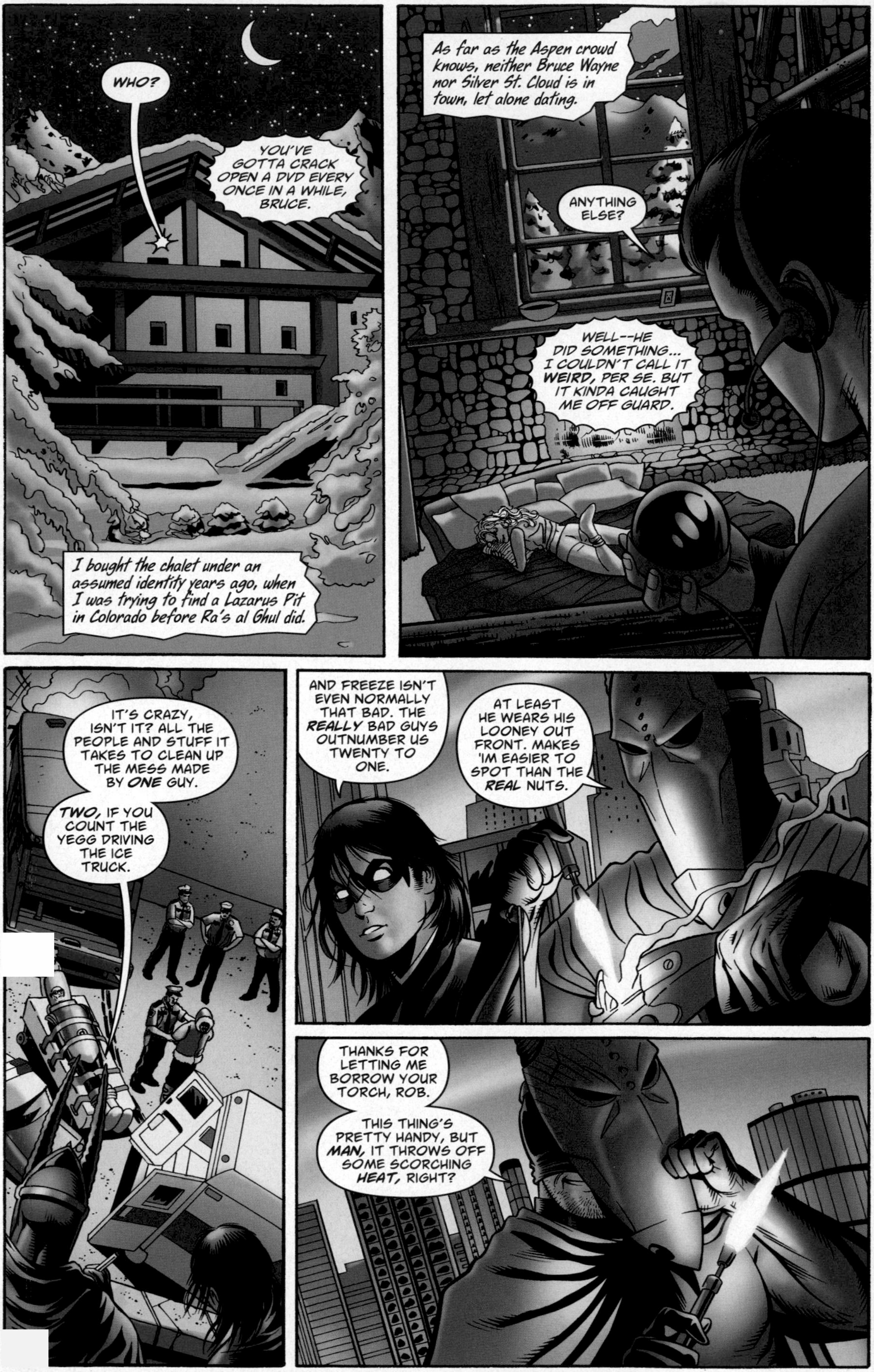
WHO?
YOU'VE GOTTA CRACK OPEN A DVD EVERY ONCE IN A WHILE, BRUCE.
I bought the chalet under an assumed identity years ago, when I was trying to find a Lazarus Pit in Colorado before Ra's al Ghul did.
As far as the Aspen crowd knows, neither Bruce Wayne nor Silver St. Cloud is in town, let alone dating.
ANYTHING ELSE?
WELL--HE DID SOMETHING... I COULDN'T CALL IT WEIRD, PER SE. BUT IT KINDA CAUGHT ME OFF GUARD.
IT'S CRAZY, ISN'T IT? ALL THE PEOPLE AND STUFF IT TAKES TO CLEAN UP THE MESS MADE BY ONE GUY.
TWO, IF YOU COUNT THE YEGG DRIVING THE ICE TRUCK.
AND FREEZE ISN'T EVEN NORMALLY THAT BAD. THE REALLY BAD GUYS OUTNUMBER US TWENTY TO ONE.
AT LEAST HE WEARS HIS LOONEY OUT FRONT. MAKES 'IM EASIER TO SPOT THAN THE REAL NUTS.
THANKS FOR LETTING ME BORROW YOUR TORCH, ROB.
THIS THING'S PRETTY HANDY, BUT MAN, IT THROWS OFF SOME SCORCHING HEAT, RIGHT?

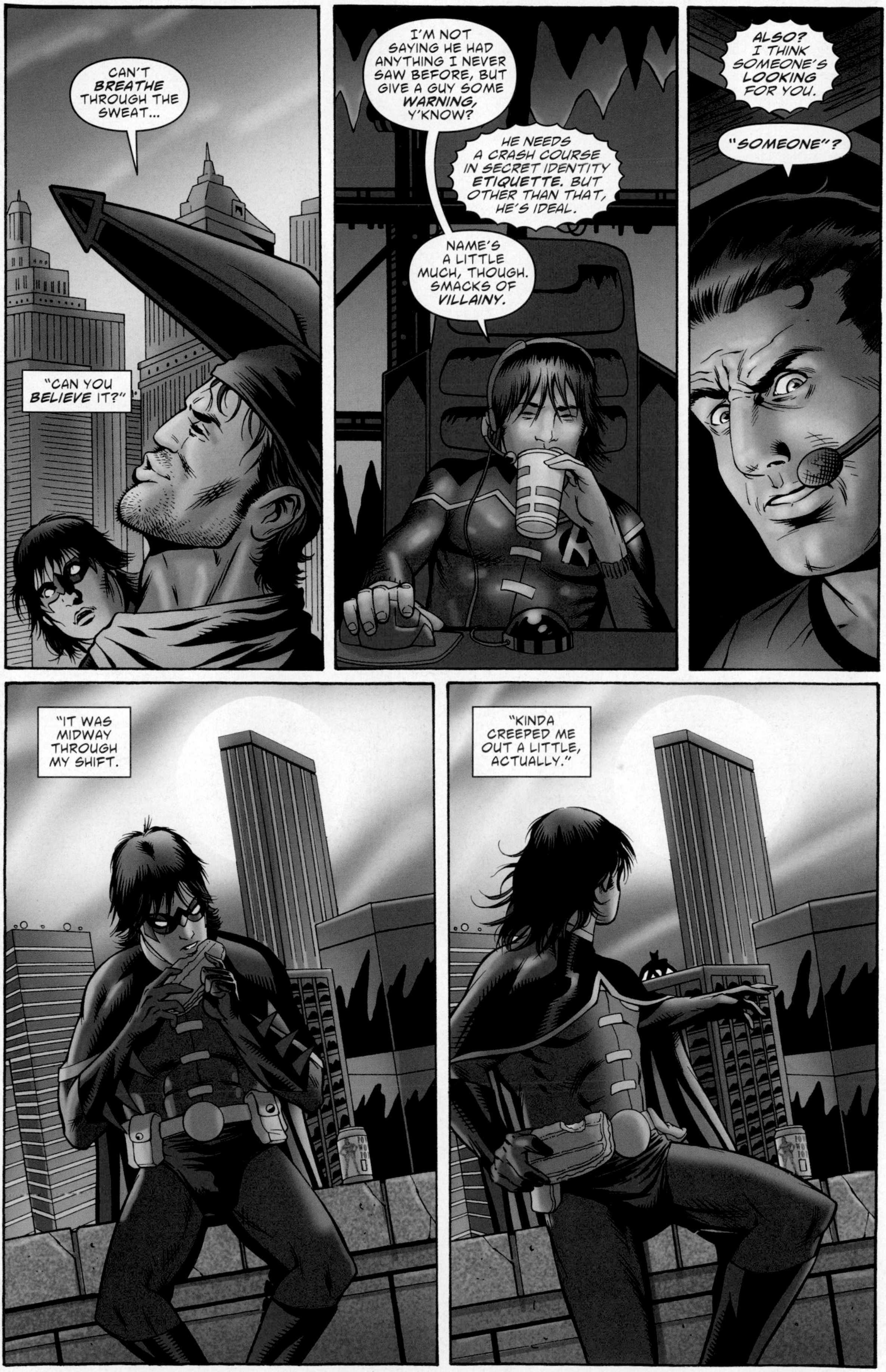
CAN'T BREATHE THROUGH THE SWEAT...
"CAN YOU BELIEVE IT?"
I'M NOT SAYING HE HAD ANYTHING I NEVER SAW BEFORE, BUT GIVE A GUY SOME WARNING, Y'KNOW?
HE NEEDS A CRASH COURSE IN SECRET IDENTITY ETIQUETTE. BUT OTHER THAN THAT, HE'S IDEAL.
NAME'S A LITTLE MUCH, THOUGH. SMACKS OF VILLAINY.
ALSO? I THINK SOMEONE'S LOOKING FOR YOU.
"SOMEONE"?
"IT WAS MIDWAY THROUGH MY SHIFT.
"KINDA CREEPED ME OUT A LITTLE, ACTUALLY."

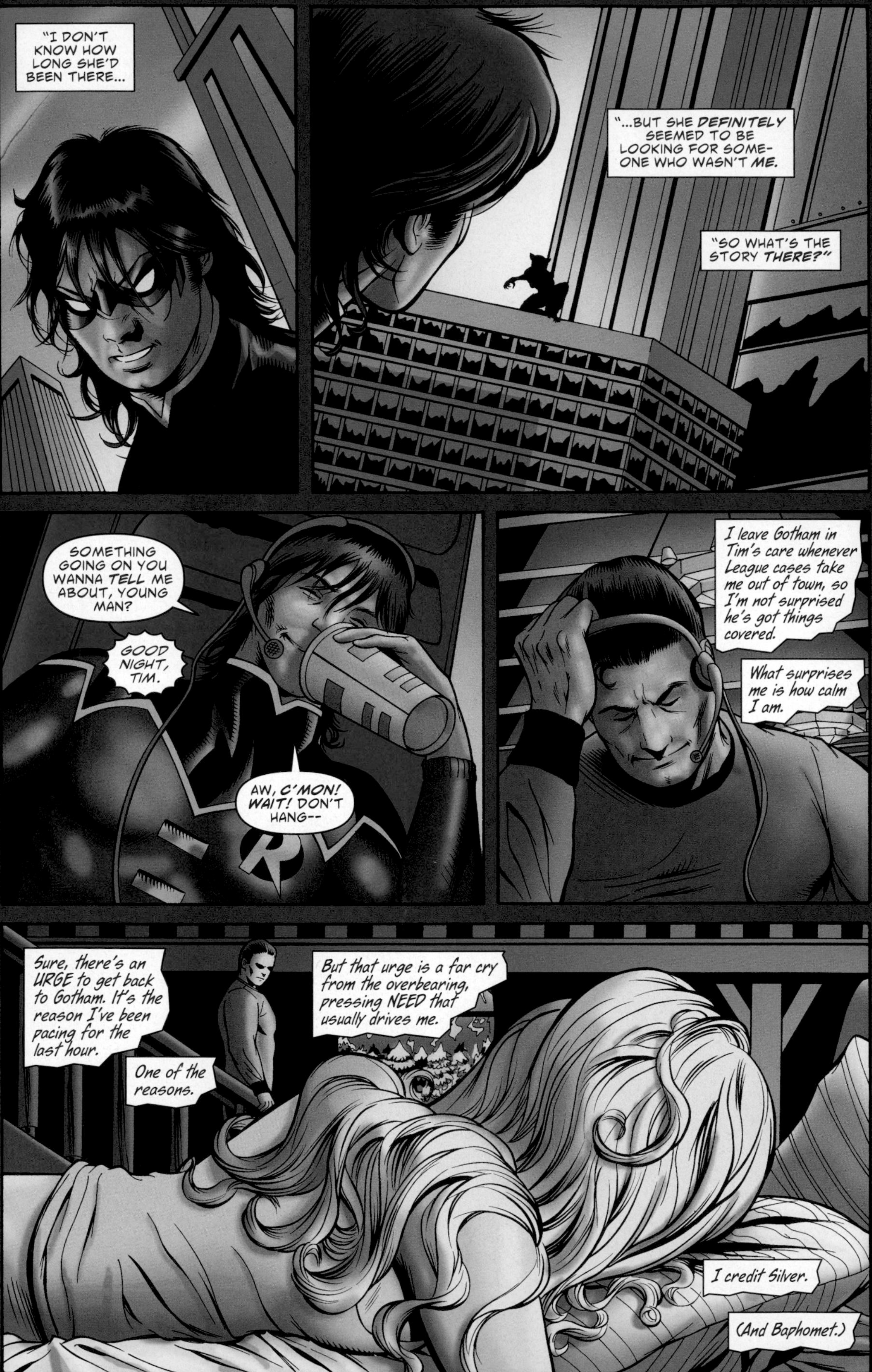
"I DON'T KNOW HOW LONG SHE'D BEEN THERE...
"...BUT SHE DEFINITELY SEEMED TO BE LOOKING FOR SOME-ONE WHO WASN'T ME.
"SO WHAT'S THE STORY THERE?"
SOMETHING GOING ON YOU WANNA TELL ME ABOUT, YOUNG MAN?
GOOD NIGHT, TIM.
AW, C'MON! WAIT! DON'T HANG--
I leave Gotham in Tim's care whenever League cases take me out of town, so I'm not surprised he's got things covered.
What surprises me is how calm I am.
Sure, there's an URGE to get back to Gotham. It's the reason I've been pacing for the last hour.
One of the reasons.
But that urge is a far cry from the overbearing, pressing NEED that usually drives me.
I credit Silver.
(And Baphomet.)

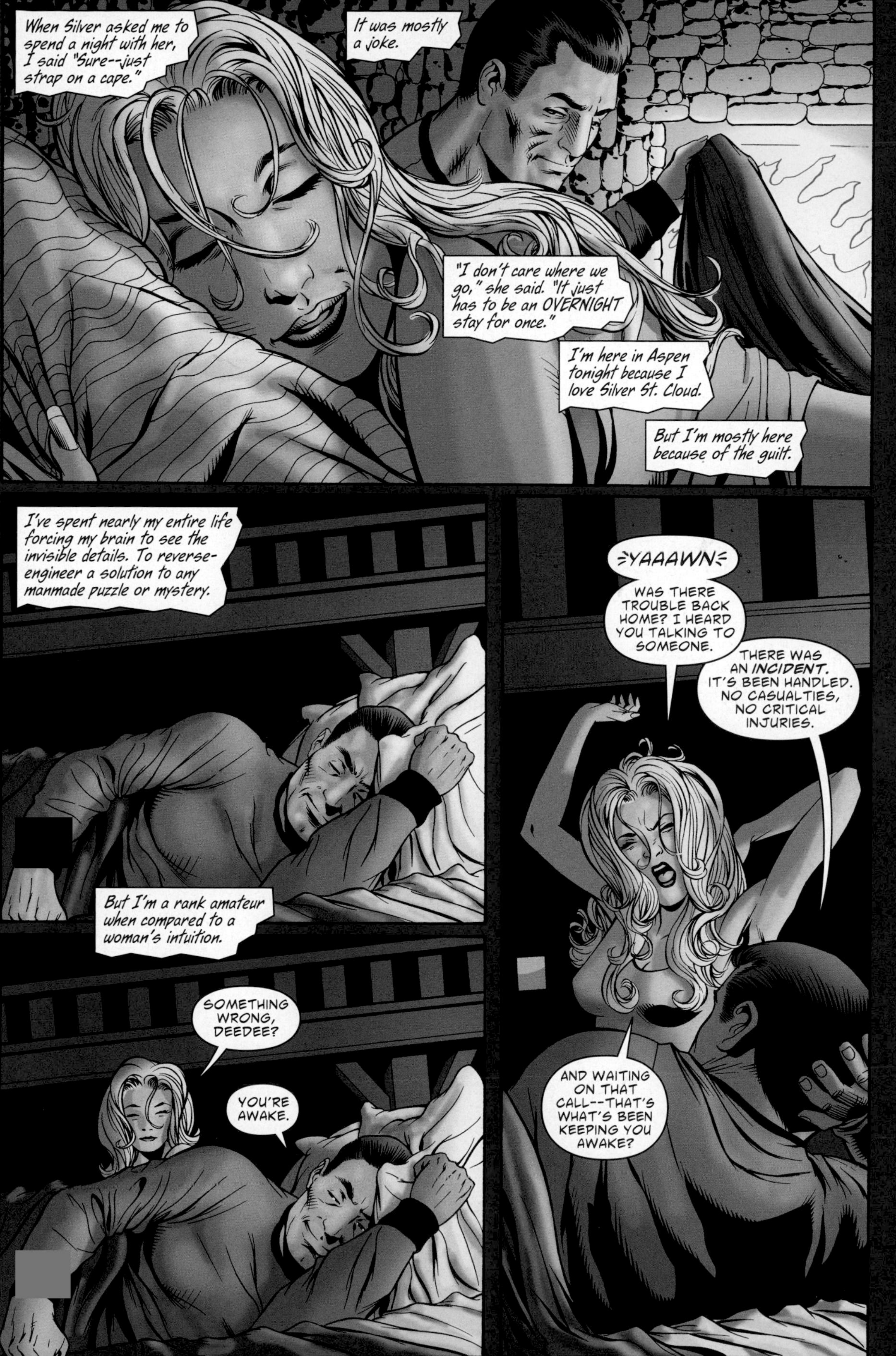
When Silver asked me to spend a night with her, I said "Sure--just strap on a cape."
It was mostly a joke.
"I don't care where we go," she said. "It just has to be an OVERNIGHT stay for once."
I'm here in Aspen tonight because I love Silver St. Cloud.
But I'm mostly here because of the guilt.
I've spent nearly my entire life forcing my brain to see the invisible details. To reverse-engineer a solution to any manmade puzzle or mystery.
But I'm a rank amateur when compared to a woman's intuition.
SOMETHING WRONG, DEEDEE?
YOU'RE AWAKE.
YAAAWN
WAS THERE TROUBLE BACK HOME? I HEARD YOU TALKING TO SOMEONE.
THERE WAS AN *INCIDENT.* IT'S BEEN HANDLED. NO CASUALTIES, NO CRITICAL INJURIES.
AND WAITING ON THAT CALL--THAT'S WHAT'S BEEN KEEPING YOU AWAKE?

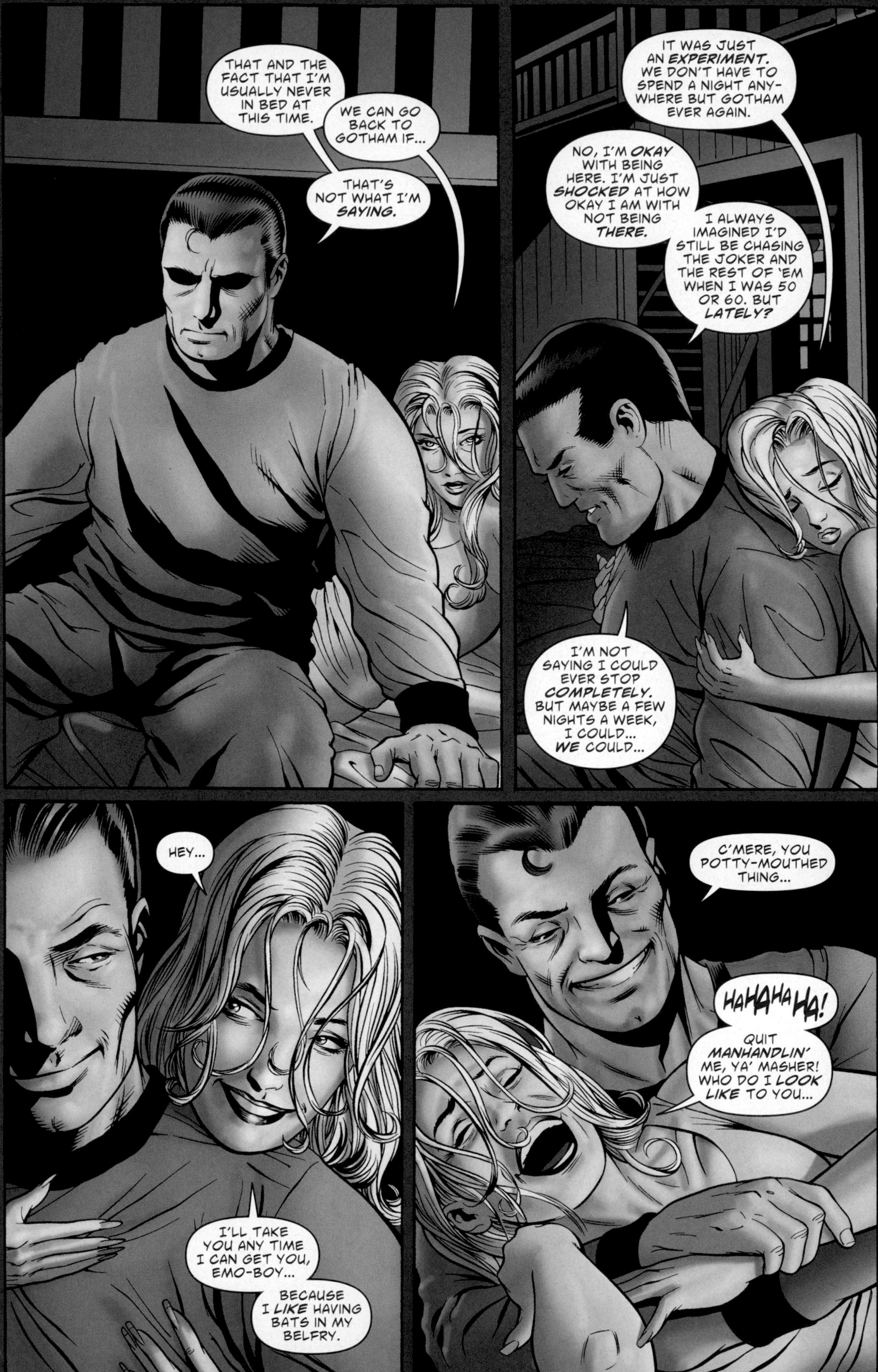

THAT AND THE FACT THAT I'M USUALLY NEVER IN BED AT THIS TIME.
WE CAN GO BACK TO GOTHAM IF...
THAT'S NOT WHAT I'M *SAYING.*
IT WAS JUST AN *EXPERIMENT.* WE DON'T HAVE TO SPEND A NIGHT ANY-WHERE BUT GOTHAM EVER AGAIN.
NO, I'M *OKAY* WITH BEING HERE. I'M JUST *SHOCKED* AT HOW OKAY I AM WITH NOT BEING *THERE.*
I ALWAYS IMAGINED I'D STILL BE CHASING THE JOKER AND THE REST OF 'EM WHEN I WAS 50 OR 60. BUT *LATELY?*
I'M NOT SAYING I COULD EVER STOP *COMPLETELY.* BUT MAYBE A FEW NIGHTS A WEEK, I COULD... ***WE*** COULD...
HEY...
I'LL TAKE YOU ANY TIME I CAN GET YOU, EMO-BOY...
BECAUSE I *LIKE* HAVING BATS IN MY BELFRY.
C'MERE, YOU POTTY-MOUTHED THING...
HAHAHAHA!
QUIT *MANHANDLIN'* ME, YA' MASHER! WHO DO I *LOOK LIKE* TO YOU...

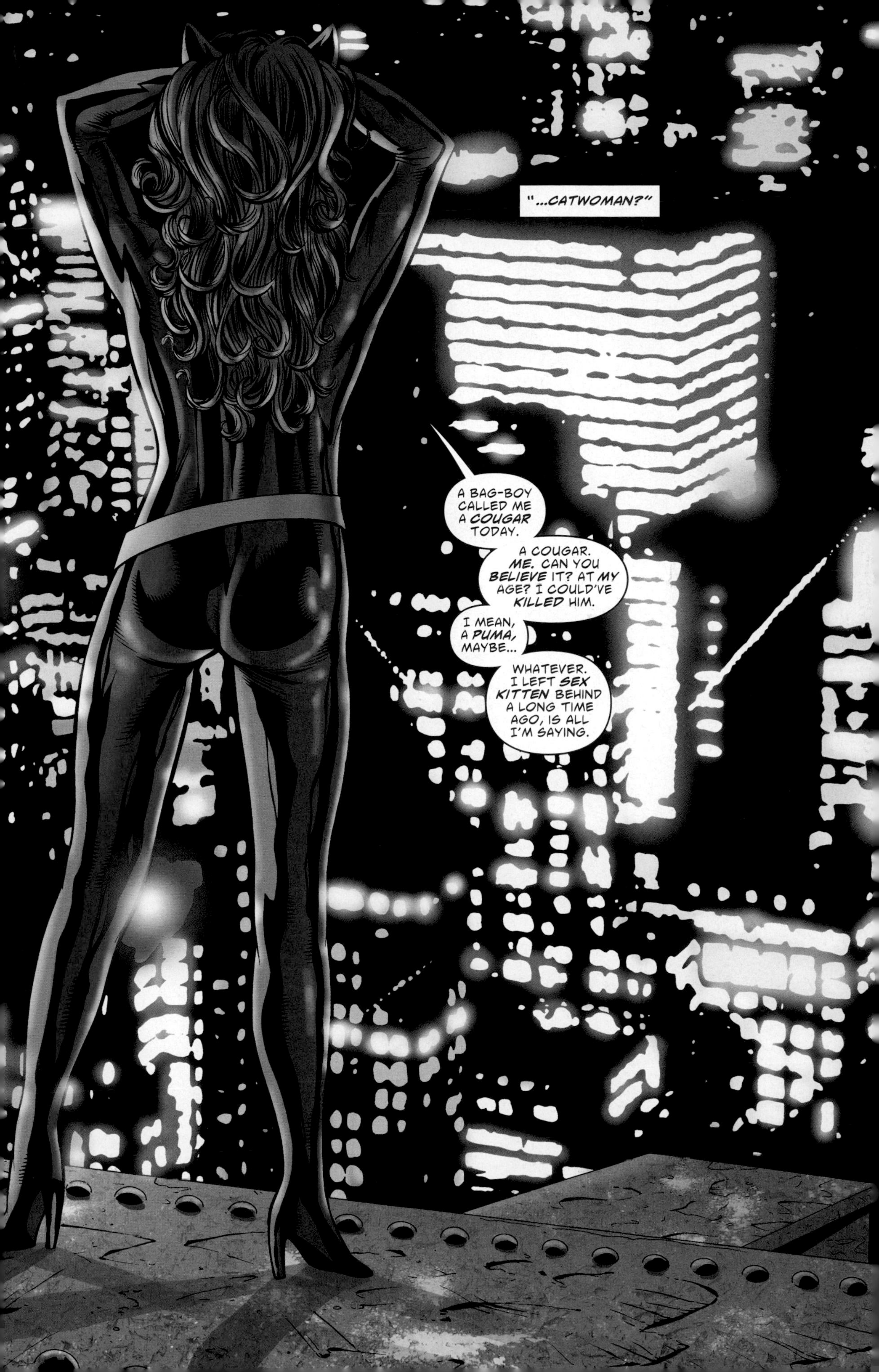
"...CATWOMAN?"
A BAG-BOY CALLED ME A COUGAR TODAY.
A COUGAR. ME. CAN YOU BELIEVE IT? AT MY AGE? I COULD'VE KILLED HIM.
I MEAN, A PUMA, MAYBE...
WHATEVER. I LEFT SEX KITTEN BEHIND A LONG TIME AGO, IS ALL I'M SAYING.

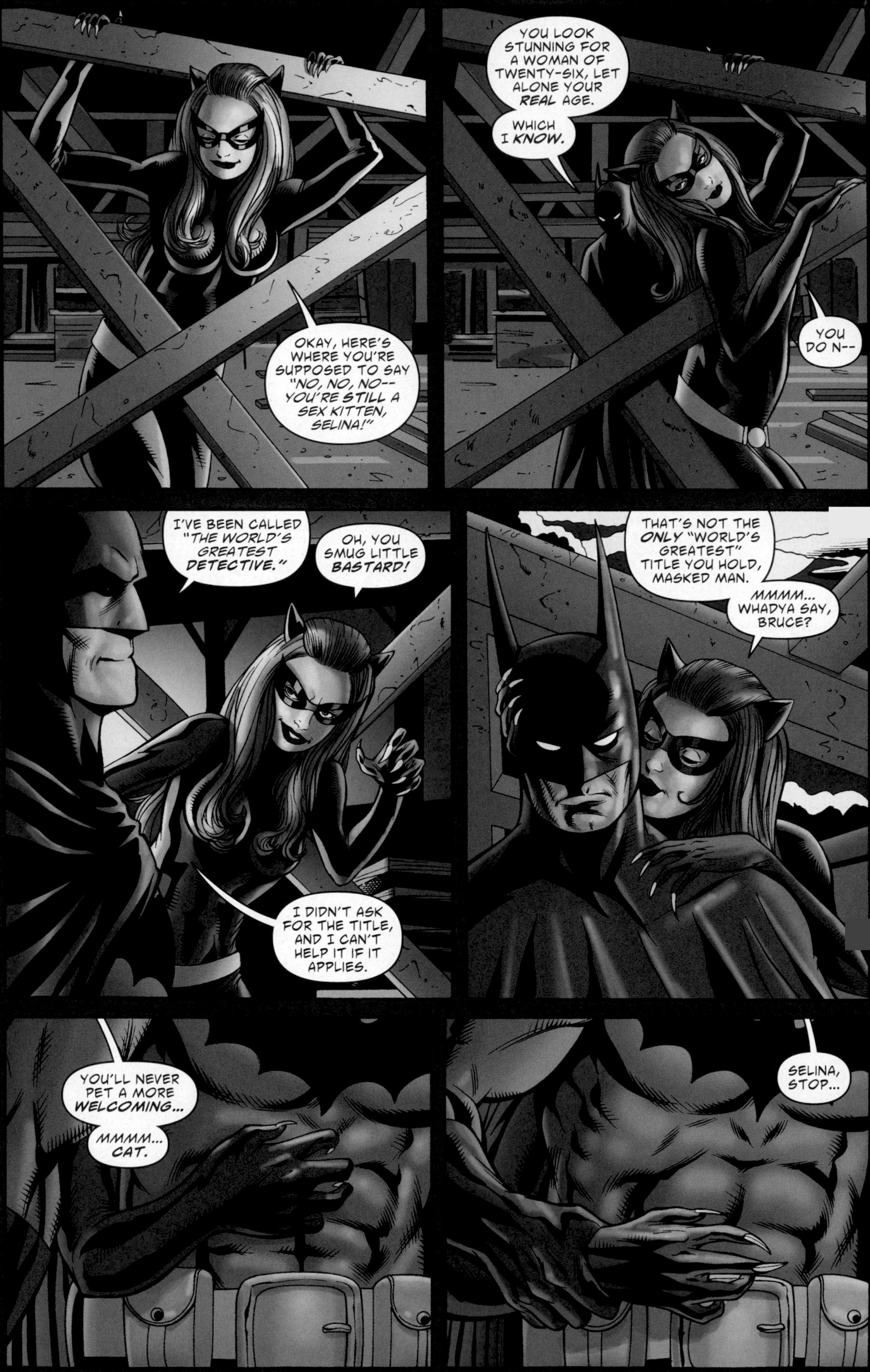
OKAY, HERE'S WHERE YOU'RE SUPPOSED TO SAY "NO, NO, NO-- YOU'RE STILL A SEX KITTEN, SELINA!"
YOU LOOK STUNNING FOR A WOMAN OF TWENTY-SIX, LET ALONE YOUR REAL AGE.
WHICH I KNOW.
YOU DO N--
I'VE BEEN CALLED "THE WORLD'S GREATEST DETECTIVE."
OH, YOU SMUG LITTLE BASTARD!
I DIDN'T ASK FOR THE TITLE, AND I CAN'T HELP IT IF IT APPLIES.
THAT'S NOT THE ONLY "WORLD'S GREATEST" TITLE YOU HOLD, MASKED MAN.
MMMM... WHADYA SAY, BRUCE?
YOU'LL NEVER PET A MORE WELCOMING...
MMMM... CAT.
SELINA, STOP...

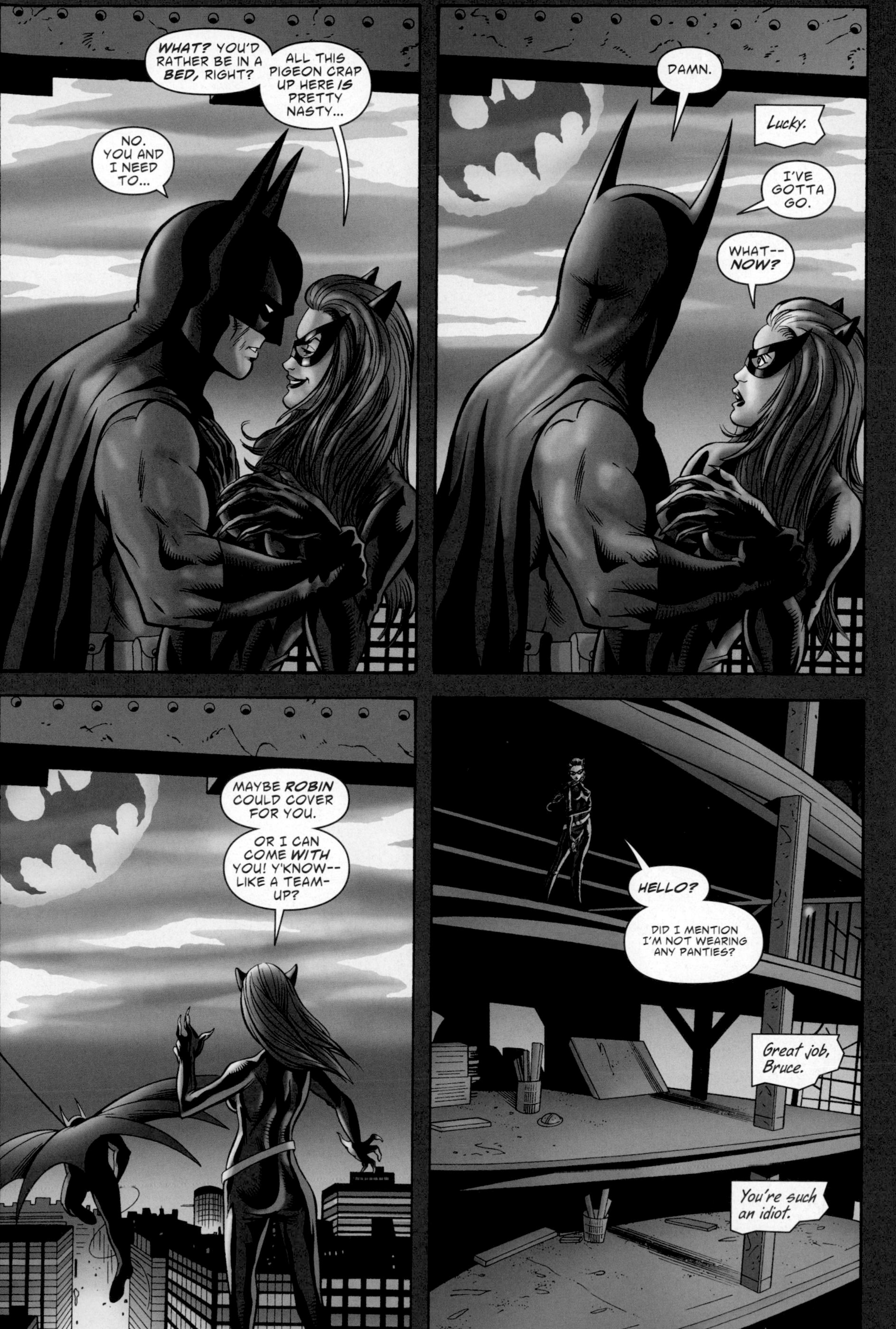

WHAT? YOU'D RATHER BE IN A BED, RIGHT?
ALL THIS PIGEON CRAP UP HERE IS PRETTY NASTY...
NO. YOU AND I NEED TO...
DAMN.
Lucky.
I'VE GOTTA GO.
WHAT-- NOW?
MAYBE ROBIN COULD COVER FOR YOU.
OR I CAN COME WITH YOU! Y'KNOW-- LIKE A TEAM-UP?
HELLO?
DID I MENTION I'M NOT WEARING ANY PANTIES?
Great job, Bruce.
You're such an idiot.

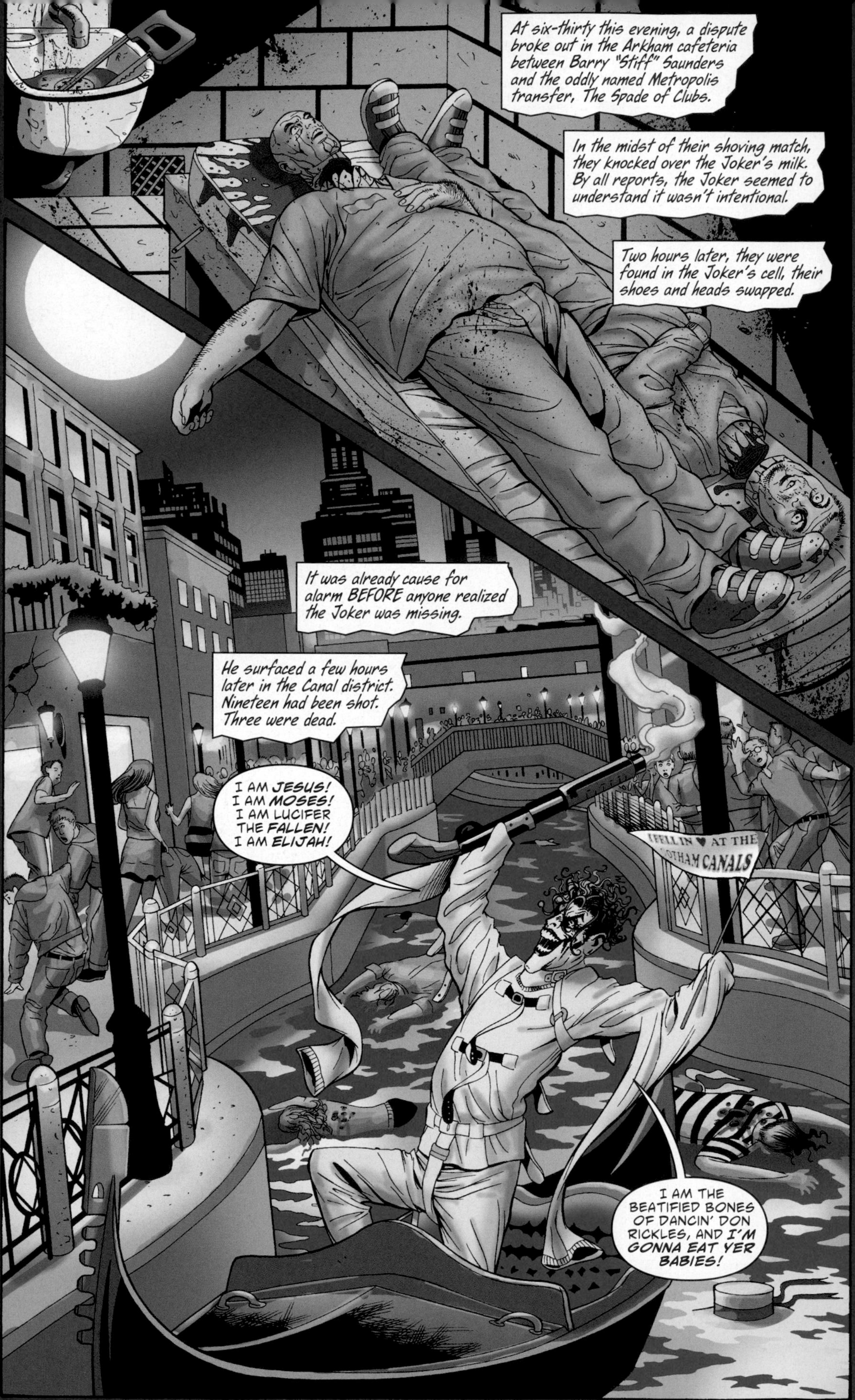
At six-thirty this evening, a dispute broke out in the Arkham cafeteria between Barry "Stiff" Saunders and the oddly named Metropolis transfer, The Spade of Clubs.
In the midst of their shoving match, they knocked over the Joker's milk. By all reports, the Joker seemed to understand it wasn't intentional.
Two hours later, they were found in the Joker's cell, their shoes and heads swapped.
It was already cause for alarm BEFORE anyone realized the Joker was missing.
He surfaced a few hours later in the Canal district. Nineteen had been shot. Three were dead.
I AM JESUS! I AM MOSES! I AM LUCIFER THE FALLEN! I AM ELIJAH!
I FELL IN ♥ AT THE
CANALS
I AM THE BEATIFIED BONES OF DANCIN' DON RICKLES, AND I'M GONNA EAT YER BABIES!

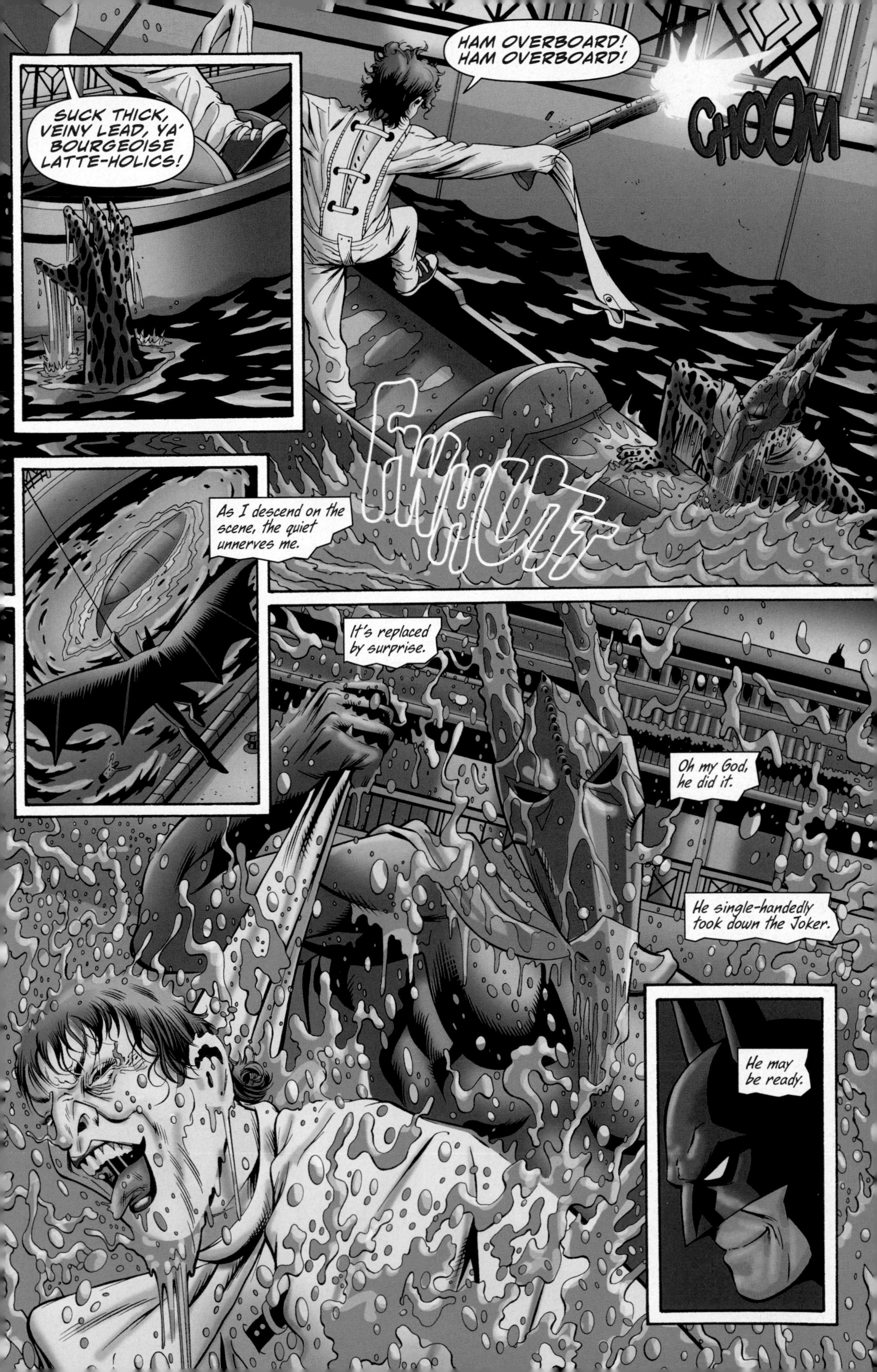
SUCK THICK, VEINY LEAD, YA' BOURGEOISE LATTE-HOLICS!
HAM OVERBOARD! HAM OVERBOARD!
CHOOM
As I descend on the scene, the quiet unnerves me.
It's replaced by surprise.
Oh my God, he did it.
He single-handedly took down the Joker.
He may be ready.

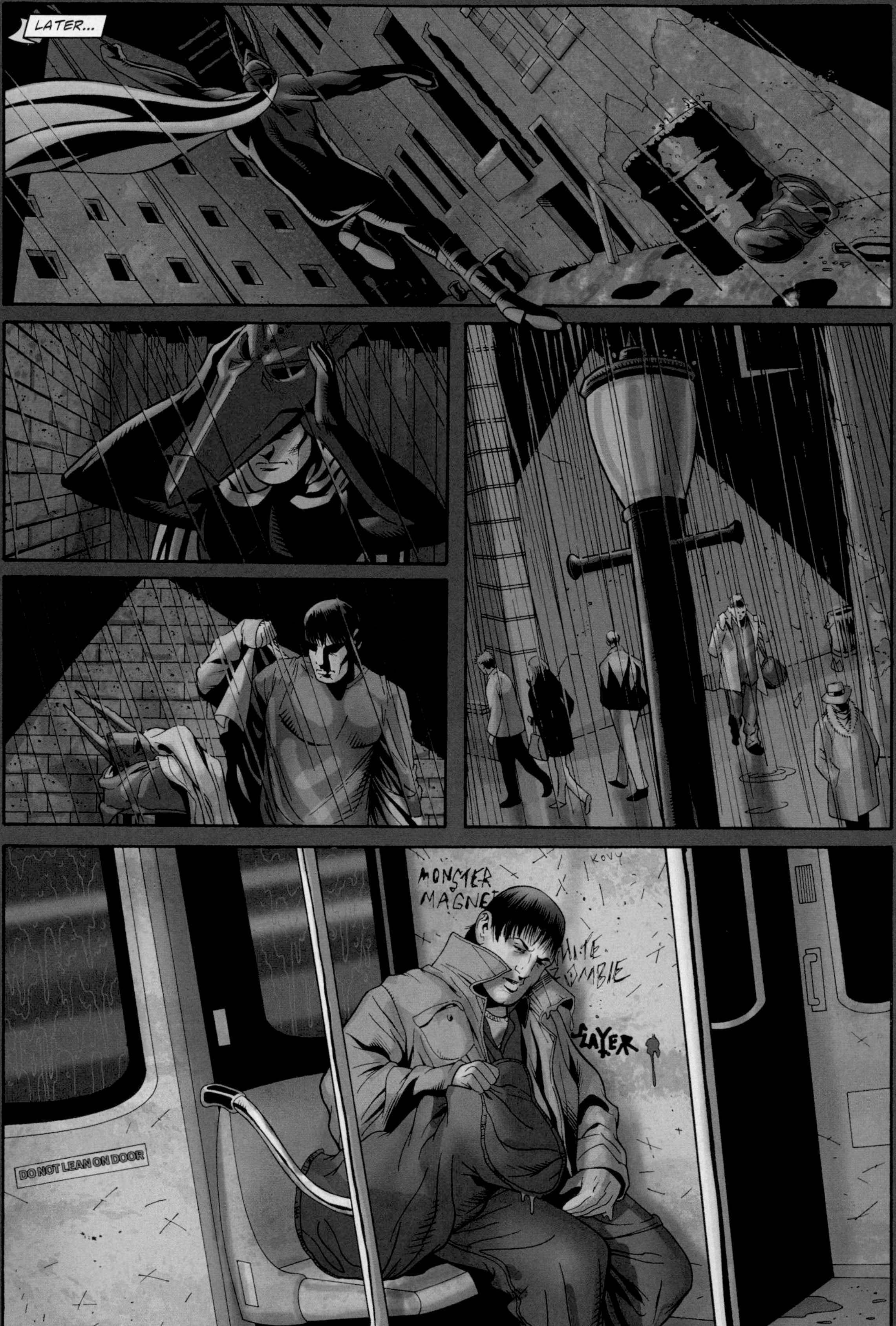
LATER...
MONSTER
KOVY
SLAYER
DO NOT LEAN ON DOOR

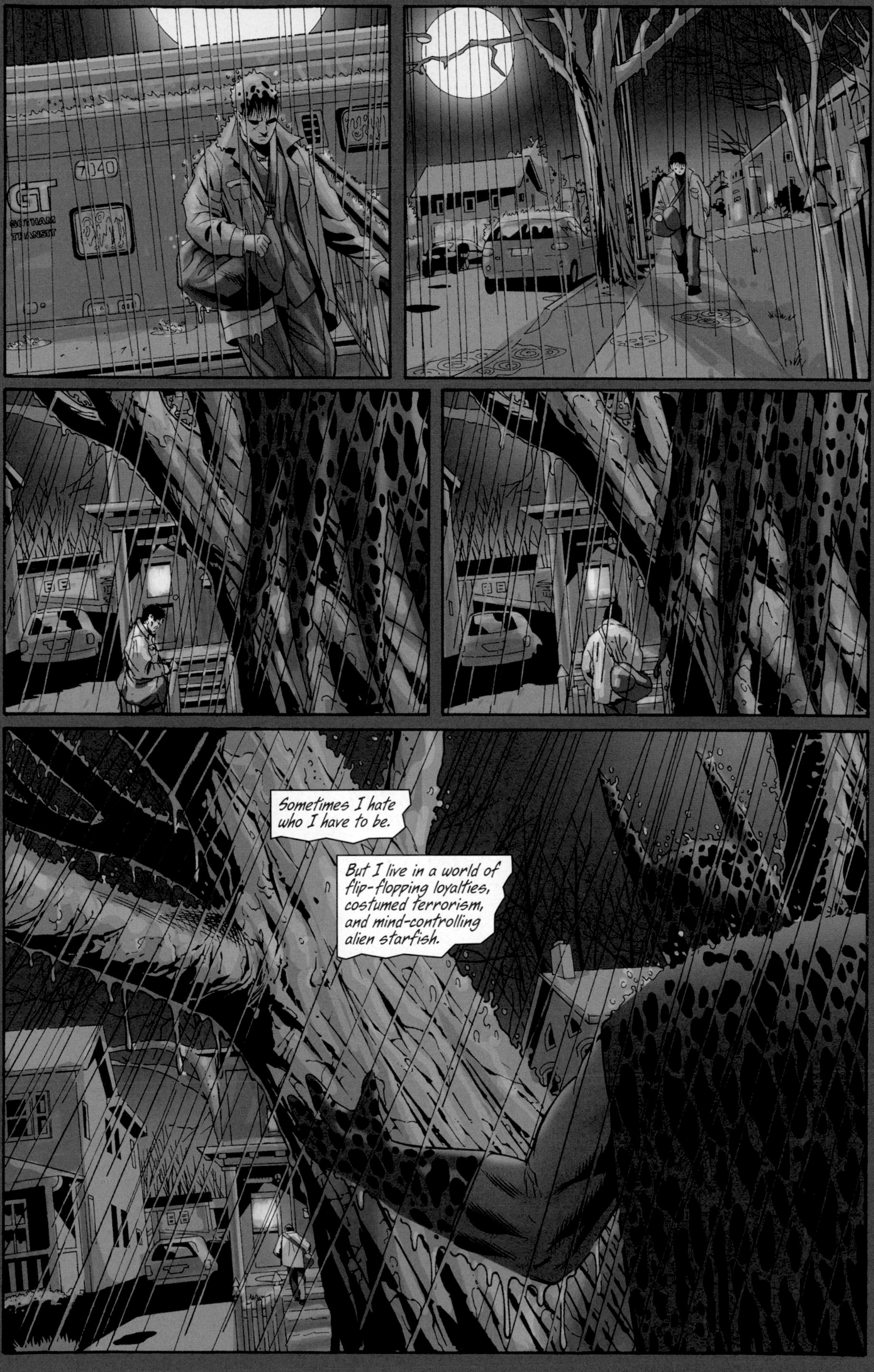
GT
GOTHAM TRANSIT
7040
Sometimes I hate who I have to be.
But I live in a world of flip-flopping loyalties, costumed terrorism, and mind-controlling alien starfish.

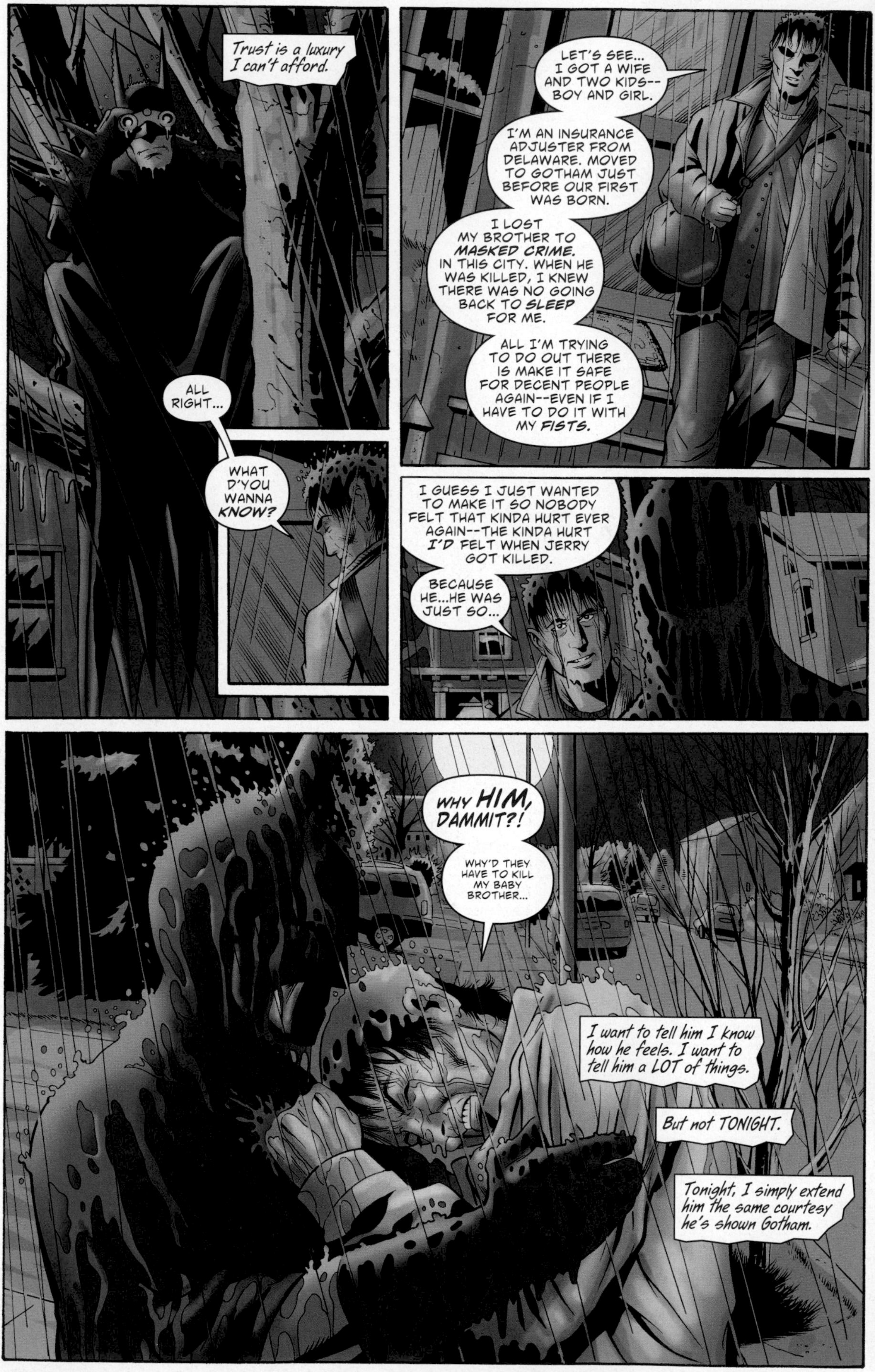
Trust is a luxury I can't afford.
LET'S SEE... I GOT A WIFE AND TWO KIDS-- BOY AND GIRL.
I'M AN INSURANCE ADJUSTER FROM DELAWARE. MOVED TO GOTHAM JUST BEFORE OUR FIRST WAS BORN.
I LOST MY BROTHER TO MASKED CRIME. IN THIS CITY. WHEN HE WAS KILLED, I KNEW THERE WAS NO GOING BACK TO SLEEP FOR ME.
ALL I'M TRYING TO DO OUT THERE IS MAKE IT SAFE FOR DECENT PEOPLE AGAIN--EVEN IF I HAVE TO DO IT WITH MY FISTS.
ALL RIGHT...
WHAT D'YOU WANNA KNOW?
I GUESS I JUST WANTED TO MAKE IT SO NOBODY FELT THAT KINDA HURT EVER AGAIN--THE KINDA HURT I'D FELT WHEN JERRY GOT KILLED.
BECAUSE HE...HE WAS JUST SO...
WHY HIM, DAMMIT?!
WHY'D THEY HAVE TO KILL MY BABY BROTHER...
I want to tell him I know how he feels. I want to tell him a LOT of things.
But not TONIGHT.
Tonight, I simply extend him the same courtesy he's shown Gotham.

Batman: The Widening Gyre #6 cover by BILL SIENKIEWICZ

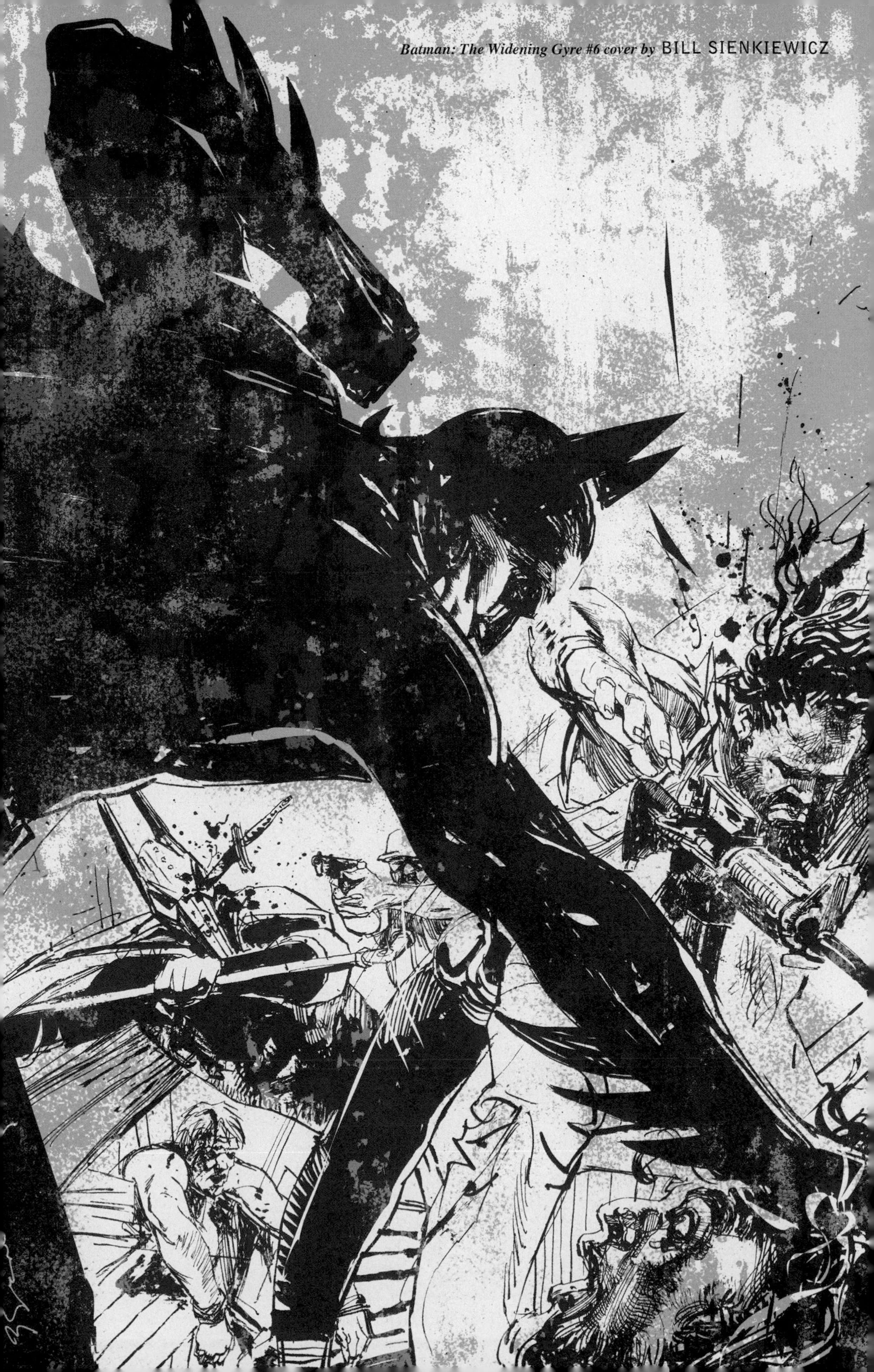

Batman: The Widening Gyre #6 alternate cover art by GENE HA

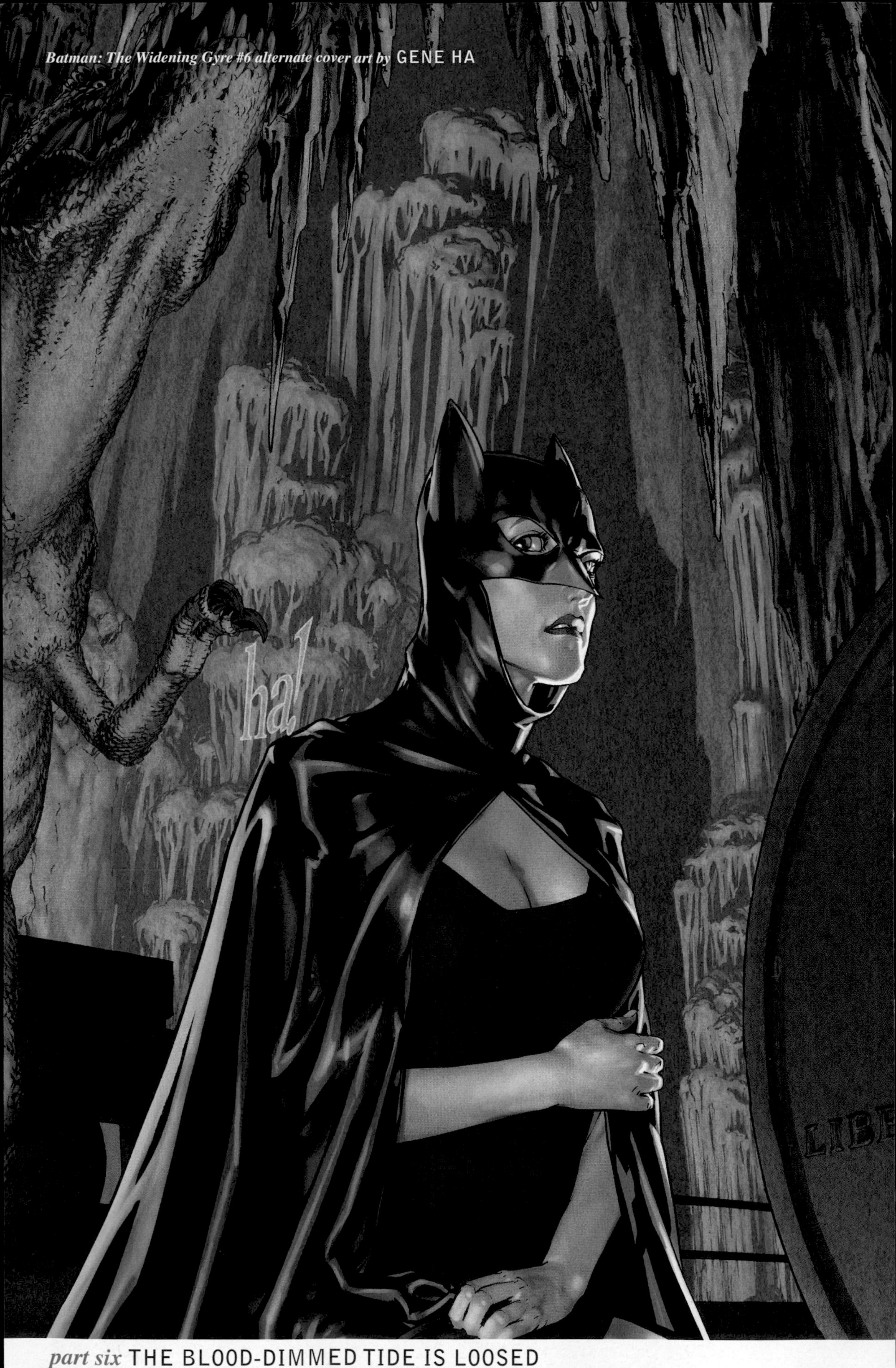
ha!

part six THE BLOOD-DIMMED TIDE IS LOOSED

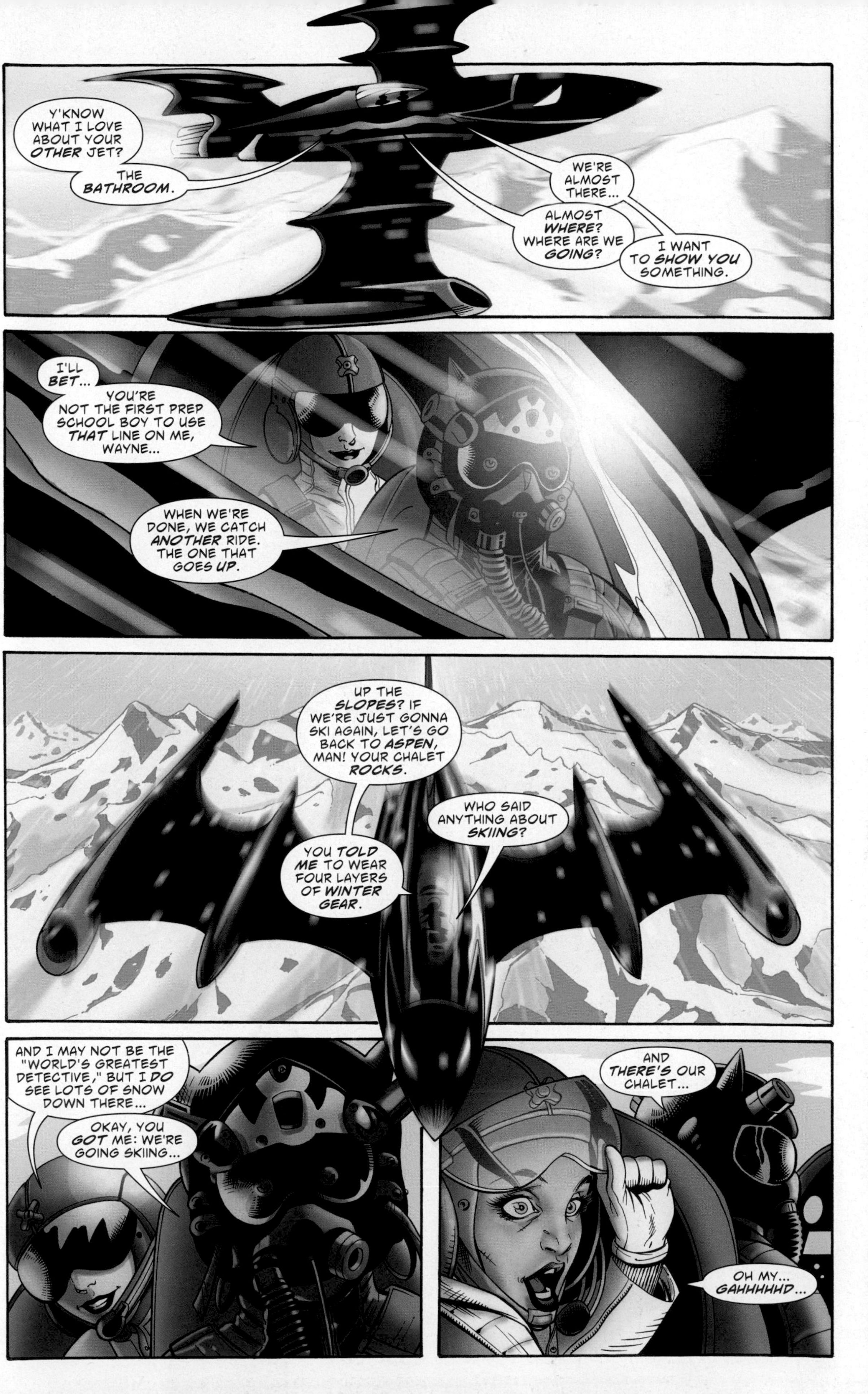
Y'KNOW WHAT I LOVE ABOUT YOUR OTHER JET?
THE BATHROOM.
WE'RE ALMOST THERE...
ALMOST WHERE? WHERE ARE WE GOING?
I WANT TO SHOW YOU SOMETHING.
I'LL BET...
YOU'RE NOT THE FIRST PREP SCHOOL BOY TO USE THAT LINE ON ME, WAYNE...
WHEN WE'RE DONE, WE CATCH ANOTHER RIDE. THE ONE THAT GOES UP.
UP THE SLOPES? IF WE'RE JUST GONNA SKI AGAIN, LET'S GO BACK TO ASPEN, MAN! YOUR CHALET ROCKS.
WHO SAID ANYTHING ABOUT SKIING?
YOU TOLD ME TO WEAR FOUR LAYERS OF WINTER GEAR.
AND I MAY NOT BE THE "WORLD'S GREATEST DETECTIVE," BUT I DO SEE LOTS OF SNOW DOWN THERE...
OKAY, YOU GOT ME: WE'RE GOING SKIING...
AND THERE'S OUR CHALET...
OH MY... GAHHHHHD...

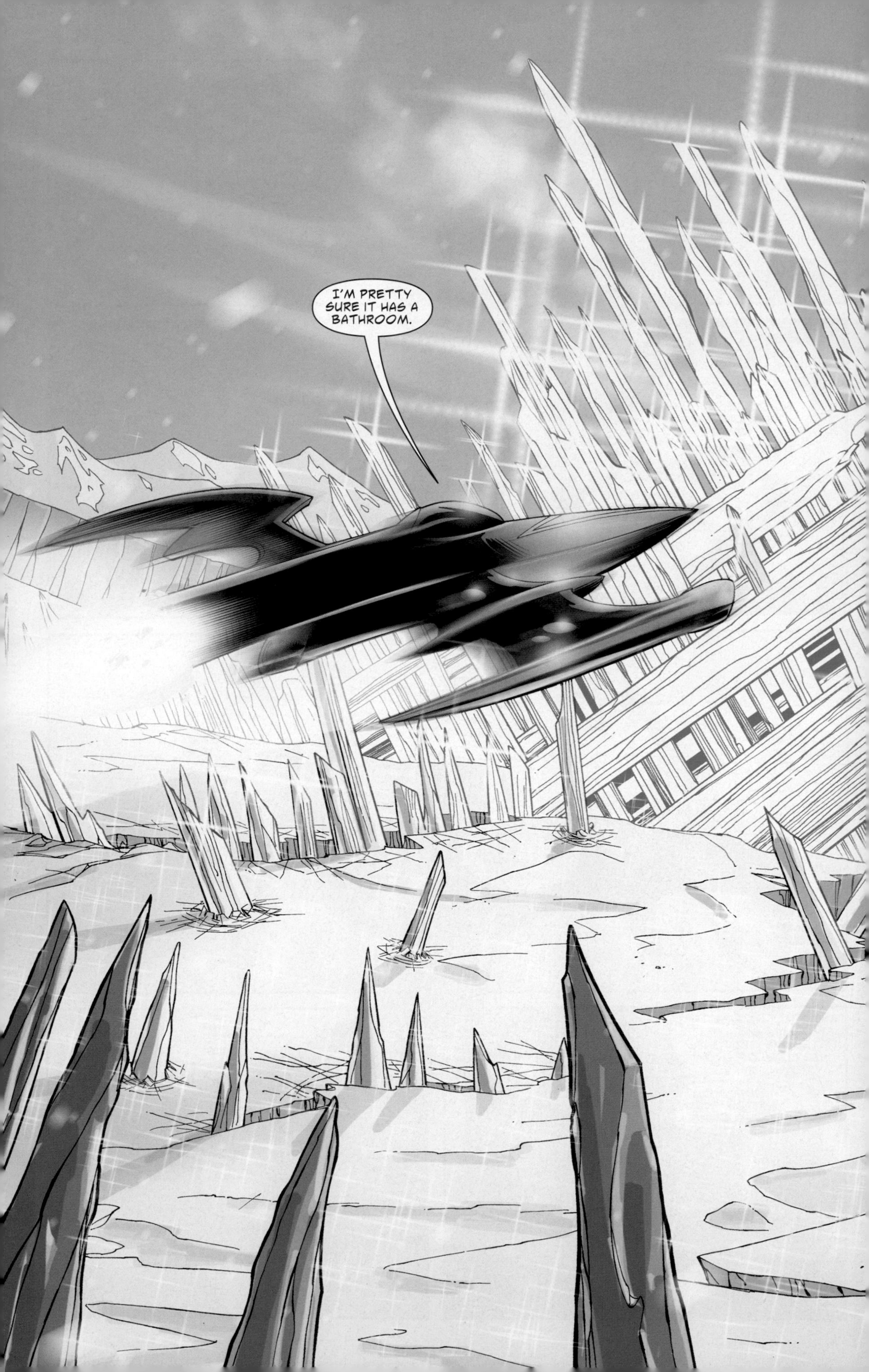
I'M PRETTY SURE IT HAS A BATHROOM.

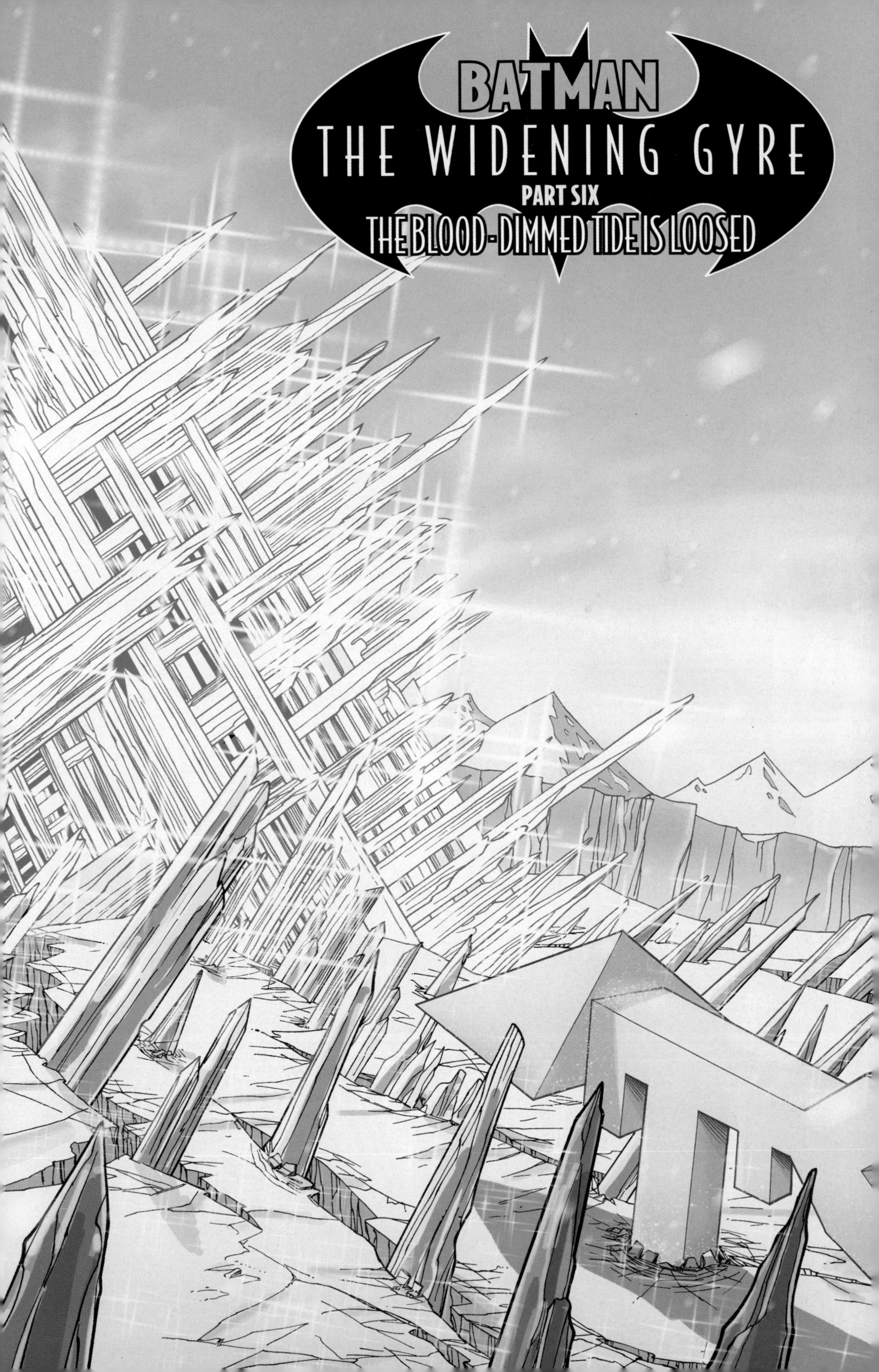
BATMAN
THE WIDENING GYRE
PART SIX
THE BLOOD-DIMMED TIDE IS LOOSED

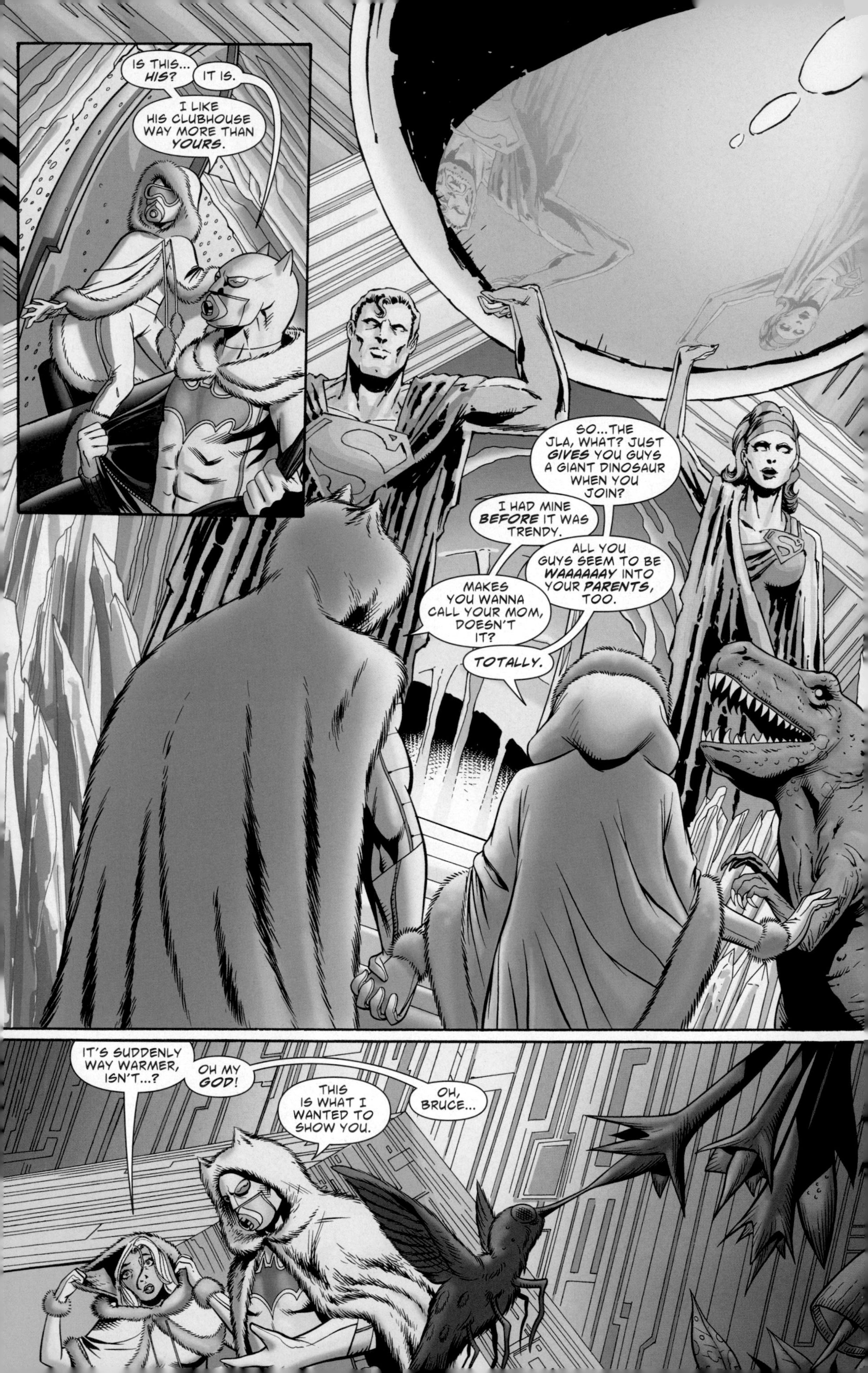
IS THIS... HIS?
IT IS.
I LIKE HIS CLUBHOUSE WAY MORE THAN YOURS.
SO...THE JLA, WHAT? JUST GIVES YOU GUYS A GIANT DINOSAUR WHEN YOU JOIN?
I HAD MINE BEFORE IT WAS TRENDY.
ALL YOU GUYS SEEM TO BE WAAAAAAY INTO YOUR PARENTS, TOO.
MAKES YOU WANNA CALL YOUR MOM, DOESN'T IT?
TOTALLY.
IT'S SUDDENLY WAY WARMER, ISN'T...?
OH MY GOD!
THIS IS WHAT I WANTED TO SHOW YOU.
OH, BRUCE...

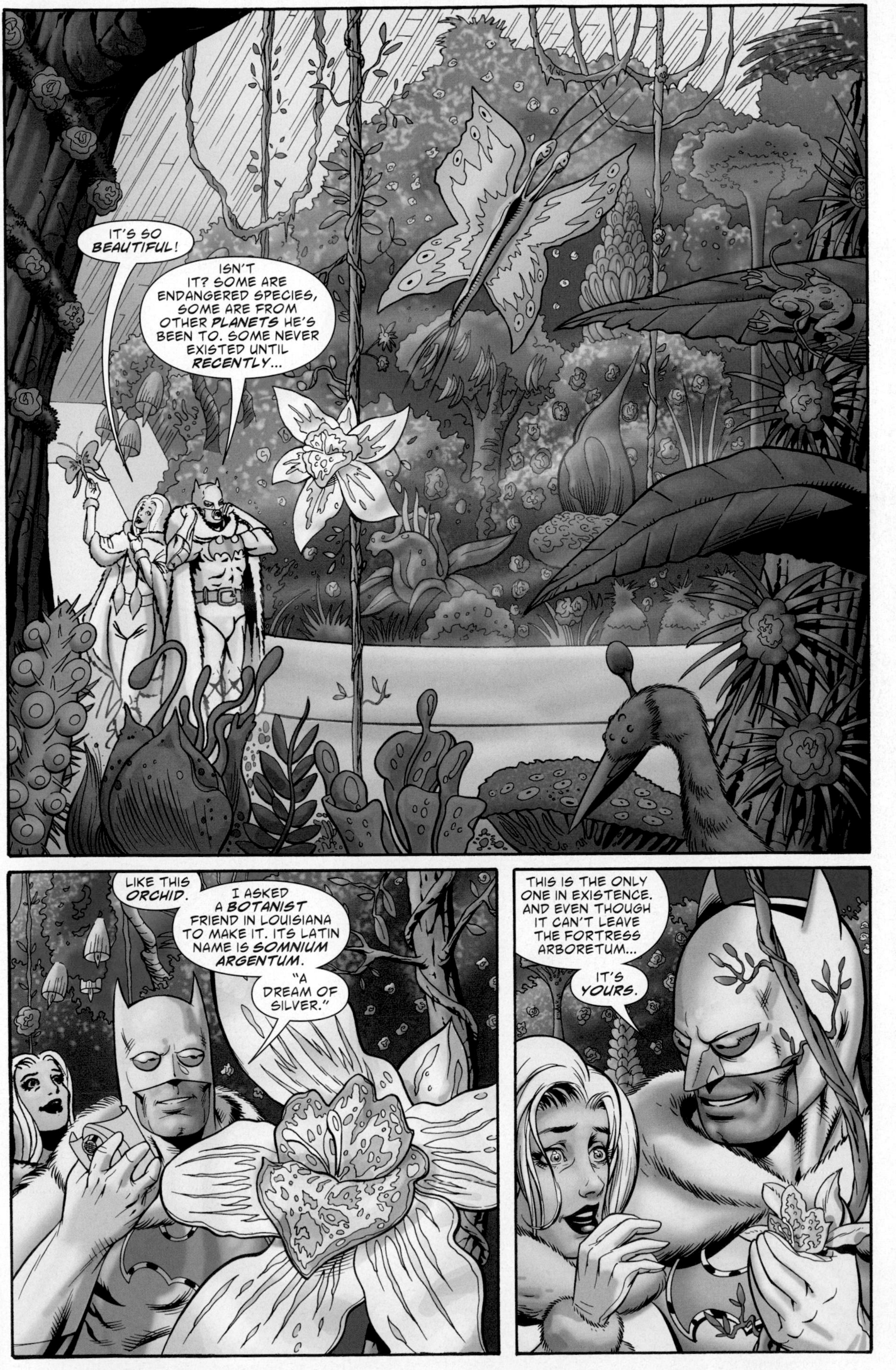
IT'S SO BEAUTIFUL!
ISN'T IT? SOME ARE ENDANGERED SPECIES, SOME ARE FROM OTHER PLANETS HE'S BEEN TO. SOME NEVER EXISTED UNTIL RECENTLY...
LIKE THIS ORCHID.
I ASKED A BOTANIST FRIEND IN LOUISIANA TO MAKE IT. ITS LATIN NAME IS SOMNIUM ARGENTUM.
"A DREAM OF SILVER."
THIS IS THE ONLY ONE IN EXISTENCE. AND EVEN THOUGH IT CAN'T LEAVE THE FORTRESS ARBORETUM...
IT'S YOURS.

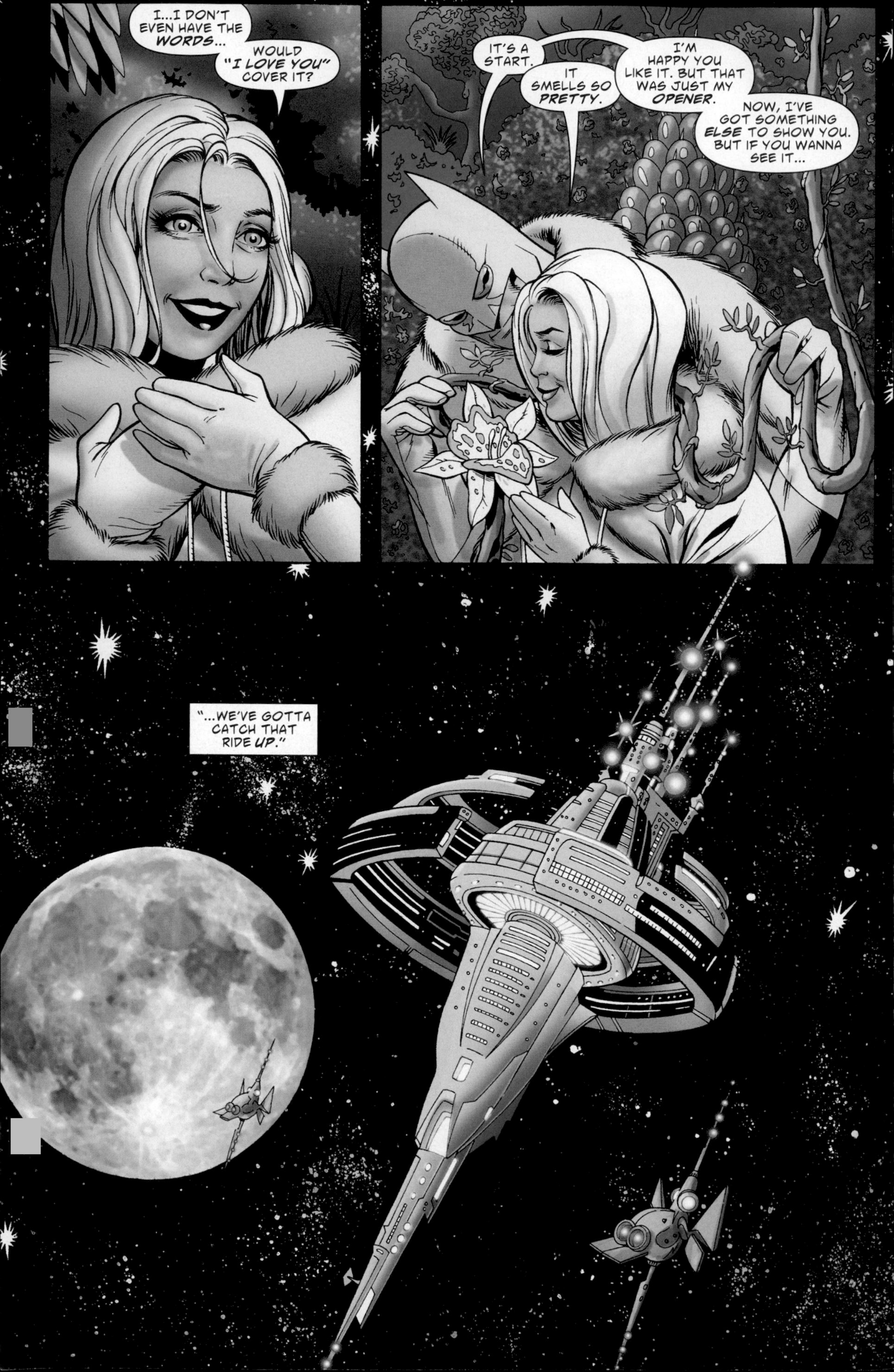
I...I DON'T EVEN HAVE THE *WORDS*...
WOULD *"I LOVE YOU"* COVER IT?
IT'S A START.
IT SMELLS SO *PRETTY*.
I'M HAPPY YOU LIKE IT. BUT THAT WAS JUST MY *OPENER*.
NOW, I'VE GOT SOMETHING *ELSE* TO SHOW YOU. BUT IF YOU WANNA SEE IT...
"...WE'VE GOTTA CATCH THAT RIDE *UP*."

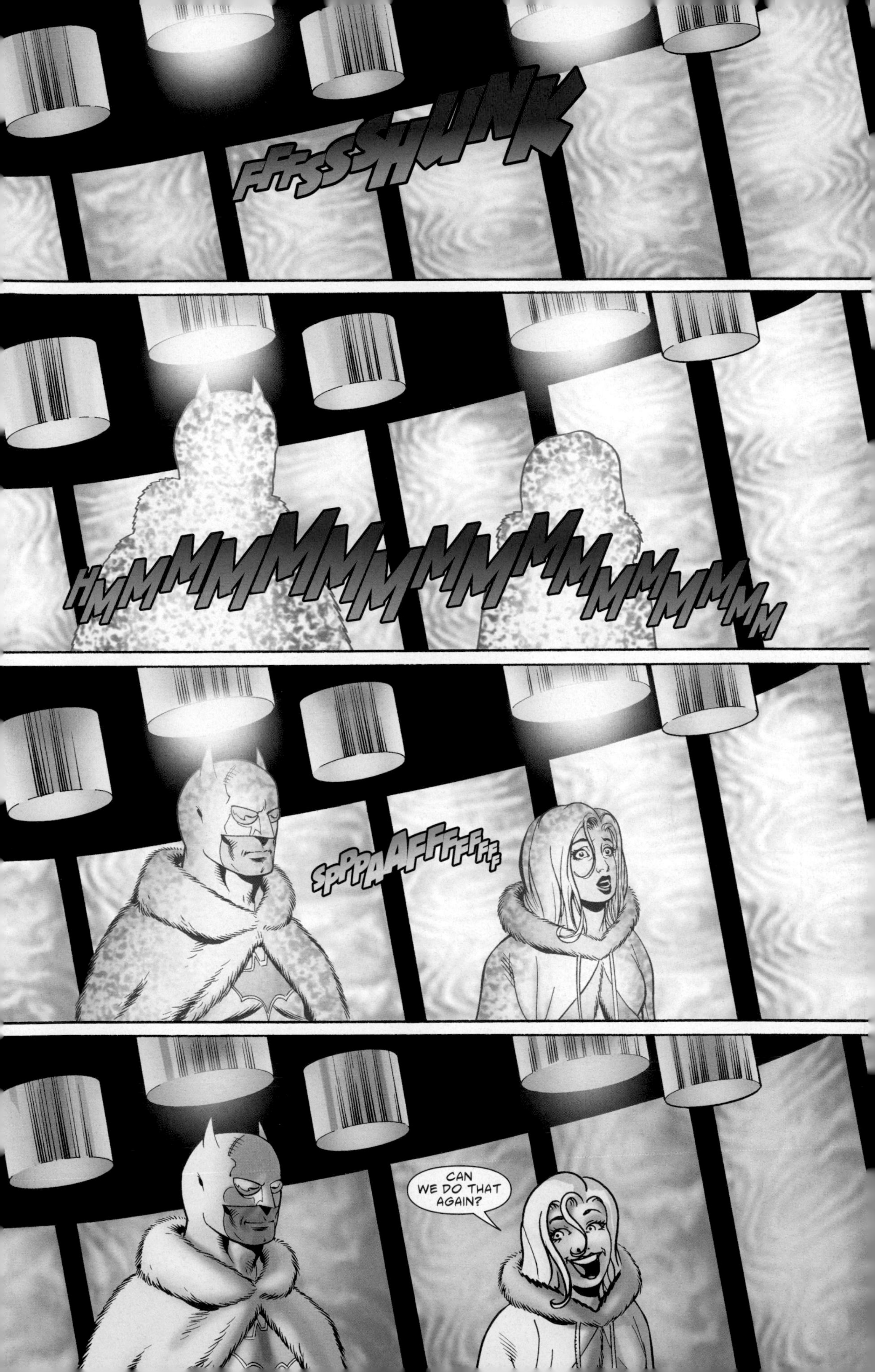
FFFSSSHUNK
HMMMMMMMMMMMMMMMMMMMMM
SPPPAAFFFFFFF
CAN WE DO THAT AGAIN?

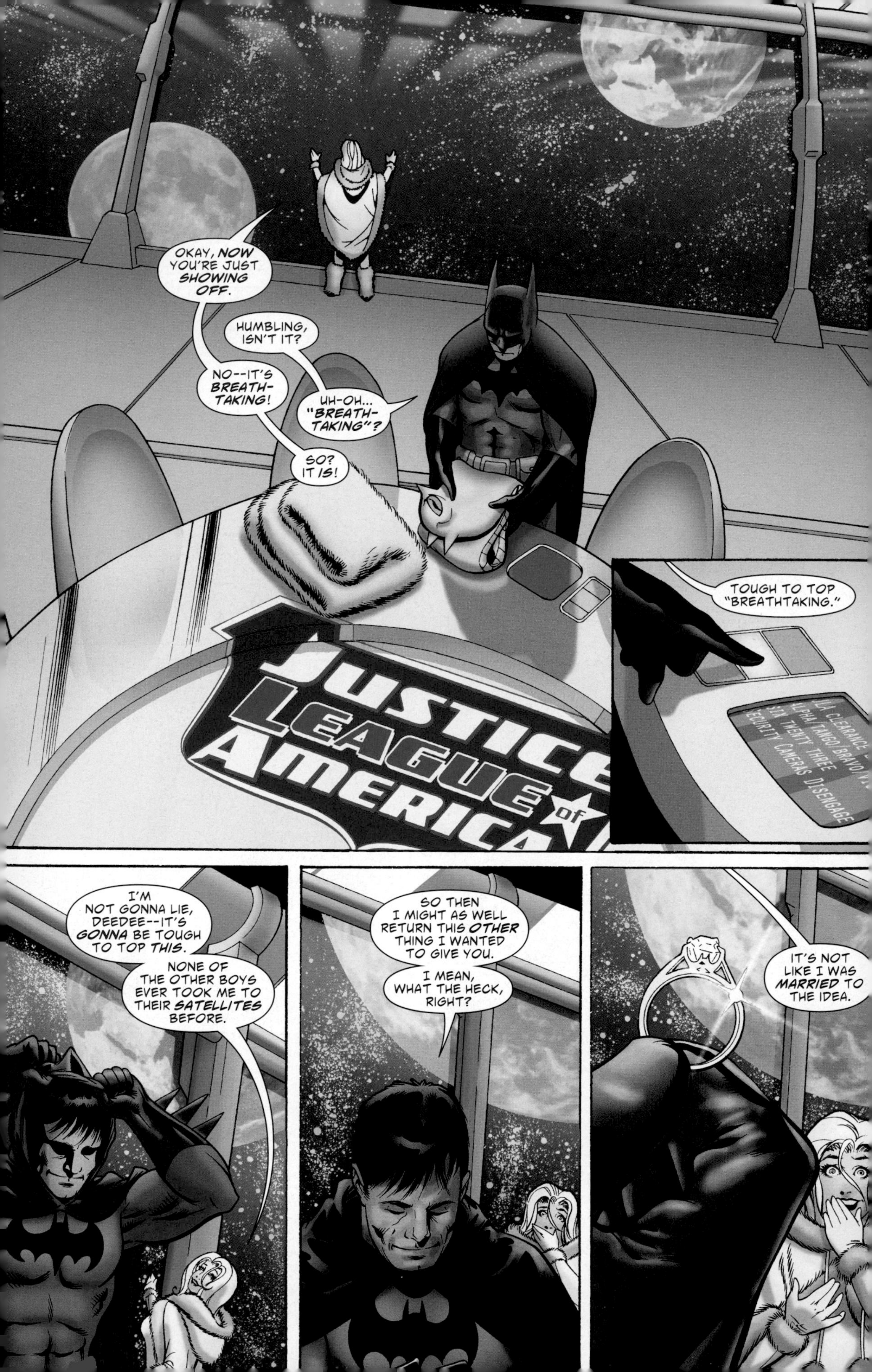
OKAY, NOW YOU'RE JUST SHOWING OFF.
HUMBLING, ISN'T IT?
NO--IT'S BREATH-TAKING!
UH-OH... "BREATH-TAKING"?
SO? IT IS!
JUSTICE LEAGUE of AMERICA
TOUGH TO TOP "BREATHTAKING."
JLA CLEARANCE
ALPHA/TANGO/BRAVO
SIX TWENTY THREE
SECURITY CAMERAS DISENGAGE
I'M NOT GONNA LIE, DEEDEE--IT'S GONNA BE TOUGH TO TOP THIS.
NONE OF THE OTHER BOYS EVER TOOK ME TO THEIR SATELLITES BEFORE.
SO THEN I MIGHT AS WELL RETURN THIS OTHER THING I WANTED TO GIVE YOU.
I MEAN, WHAT THE HECK, RIGHT?
IT'S NOT LIKE I WAS MARRIED TO THE IDEA.

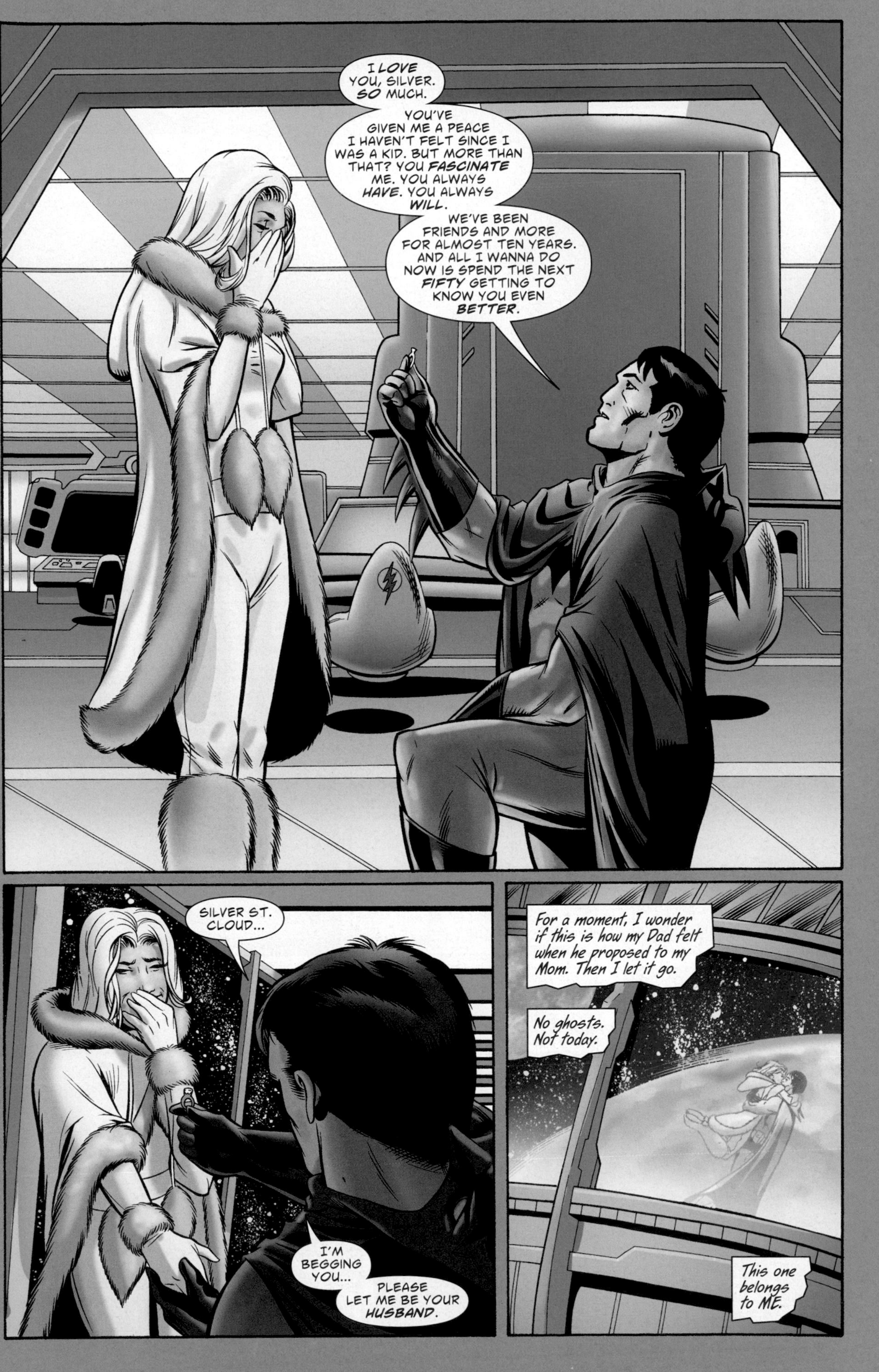
I LOVE YOU, SILVER. SO MUCH.
YOU'VE GIVEN ME A PEACE I HAVEN'T FELT SINCE I WAS A KID. BUT MORE THAN THAT? YOU FASCINATE ME. YOU ALWAYS HAVE. YOU ALWAYS WILL.
WE'VE BEEN FRIENDS AND MORE FOR ALMOST TEN YEARS. AND ALL I WANNA DO NOW IS SPEND THE NEXT FIFTY GETTING TO KNOW YOU EVEN BETTER.
SILVER ST. CLOUD...
I'M BEGGING YOU...
PLEASE LET ME BE YOUR HUSBAND.
For a moment, I wonder if this is how my Dad felt when he proposed to my Mom. Then I let it go.
No ghosts. Not today.
This one belongs to ME.

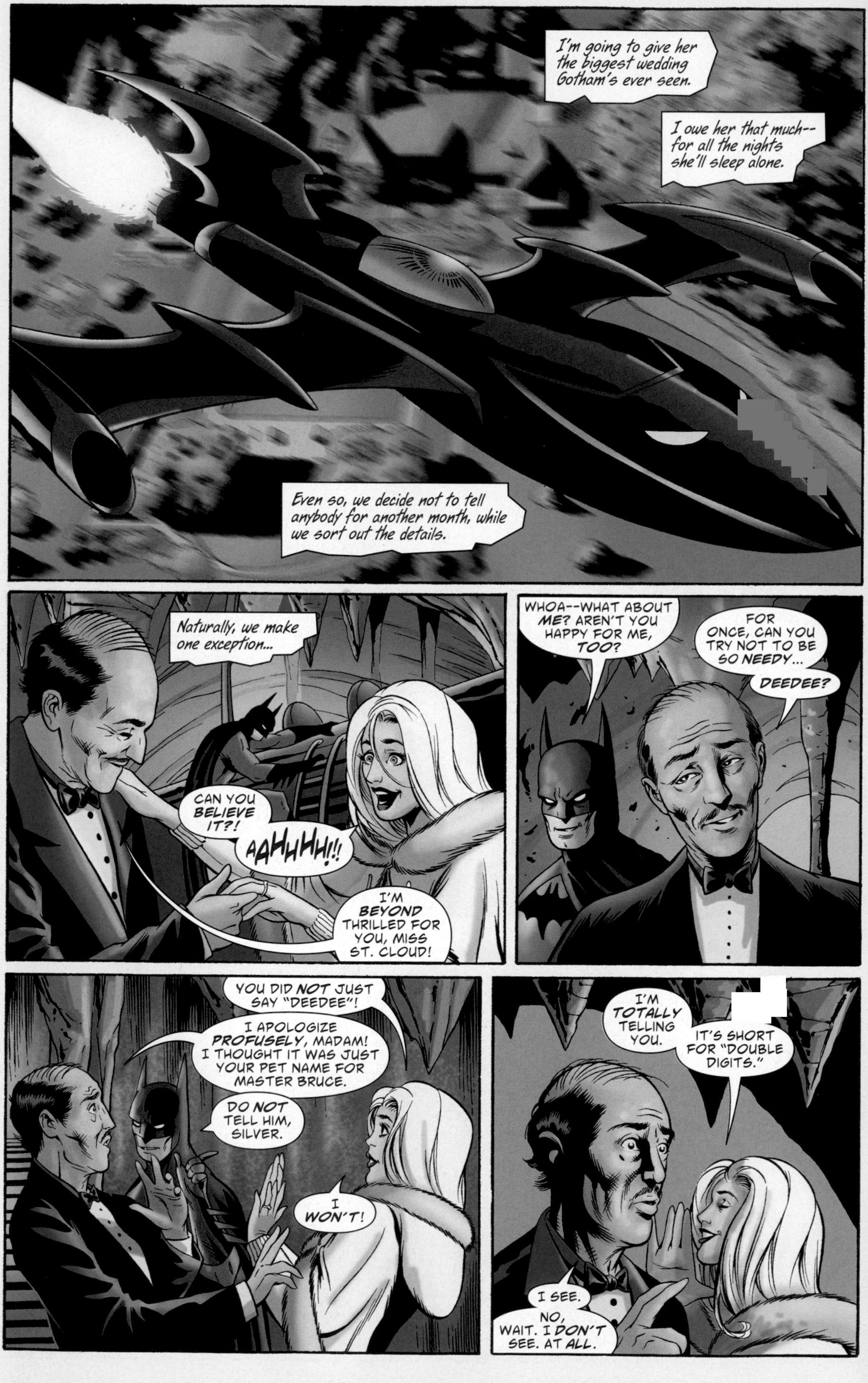
I'm going to give her the biggest wedding Gotham's ever seen.
I owe her that much--for all the nights she'll sleep alone.
Even so, we decide not to tell anybody for another month, while we sort out the details.
Naturally, we make one exception...
CAN YOU BELIEVE IT?!
AAHHHHH!!!
I'M BEYOND THRILLED FOR YOU, MISS ST. CLOUD!
WHOA--WHAT ABOUT ME? AREN'T YOU HAPPY FOR ME, TOO?
FOR ONCE, CAN YOU TRY NOT TO BE SO NEEDY...
DEEDEE?
YOU DID NOT JUST SAY "DEEDEE"!
I APOLOGIZE PROFUSELY, MADAM! I THOUGHT IT WAS JUST YOUR PET NAME FOR MASTER BRUCE.
DO NOT TELL HIM, SILVER.
I WON'T!
I'M TOTALLY TELLING YOU.
IT'S SHORT FOR "DOUBLE DIGITS."
I SEE.
NO, WAIT. I DON'T SEE. AT ALL.

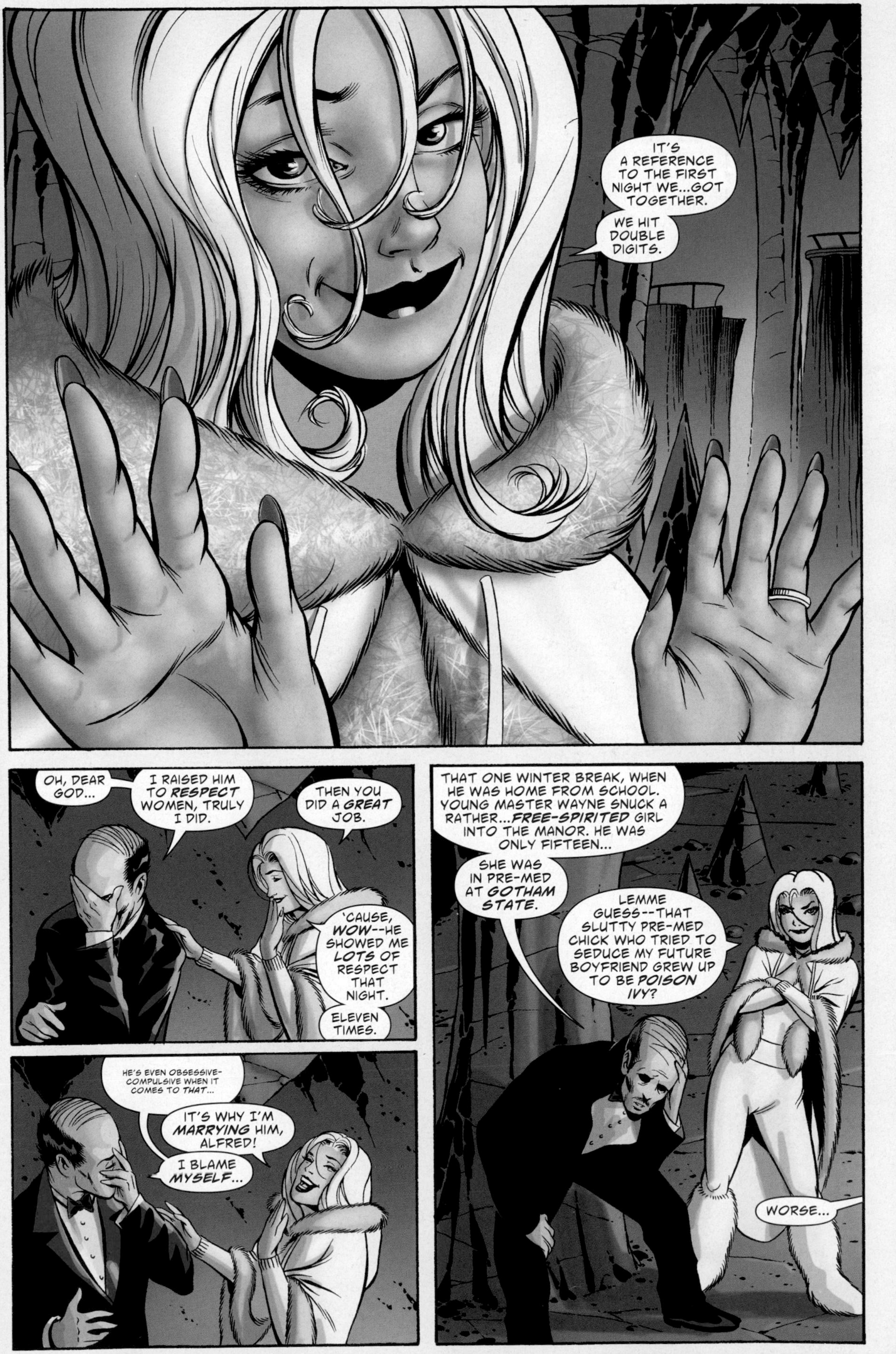
IT'S A REFERENCE TO THE FIRST NIGHT WE...GOT TOGETHER.
WE HIT DOUBLE DIGITS.
OH, DEAR GOD...
I RAISED HIM TO RESPECT WOMEN, TRULY I DID.
THEN YOU DID A GREAT JOB.
'CAUSE, WOW--HE SHOWED ME LOTS OF RESPECT THAT NIGHT.
ELEVEN TIMES.
HE'S EVEN OBSESSIVE-COMPULSIVE WHEN IT COMES TO THAT...
IT'S WHY I'M MARRYING HIM, ALFRED!
I BLAME MYSELF...
THAT ONE WINTER BREAK, WHEN HE WAS HOME FROM SCHOOL. YOUNG MASTER WAYNE SNUCK A RATHER...FREE-SPIRITED GIRL INTO THE MANOR. HE WAS ONLY FIFTEEN...
SHE WAS IN PRE-MED AT GOTHAM STATE.
LEMME GUESS--THAT SLUTTY PRE-MED CHICK WHO TRIED TO SEDUCE MY FUTURE BOYFRIEND GREW UP TO BE POISON IVY?
WORSE...

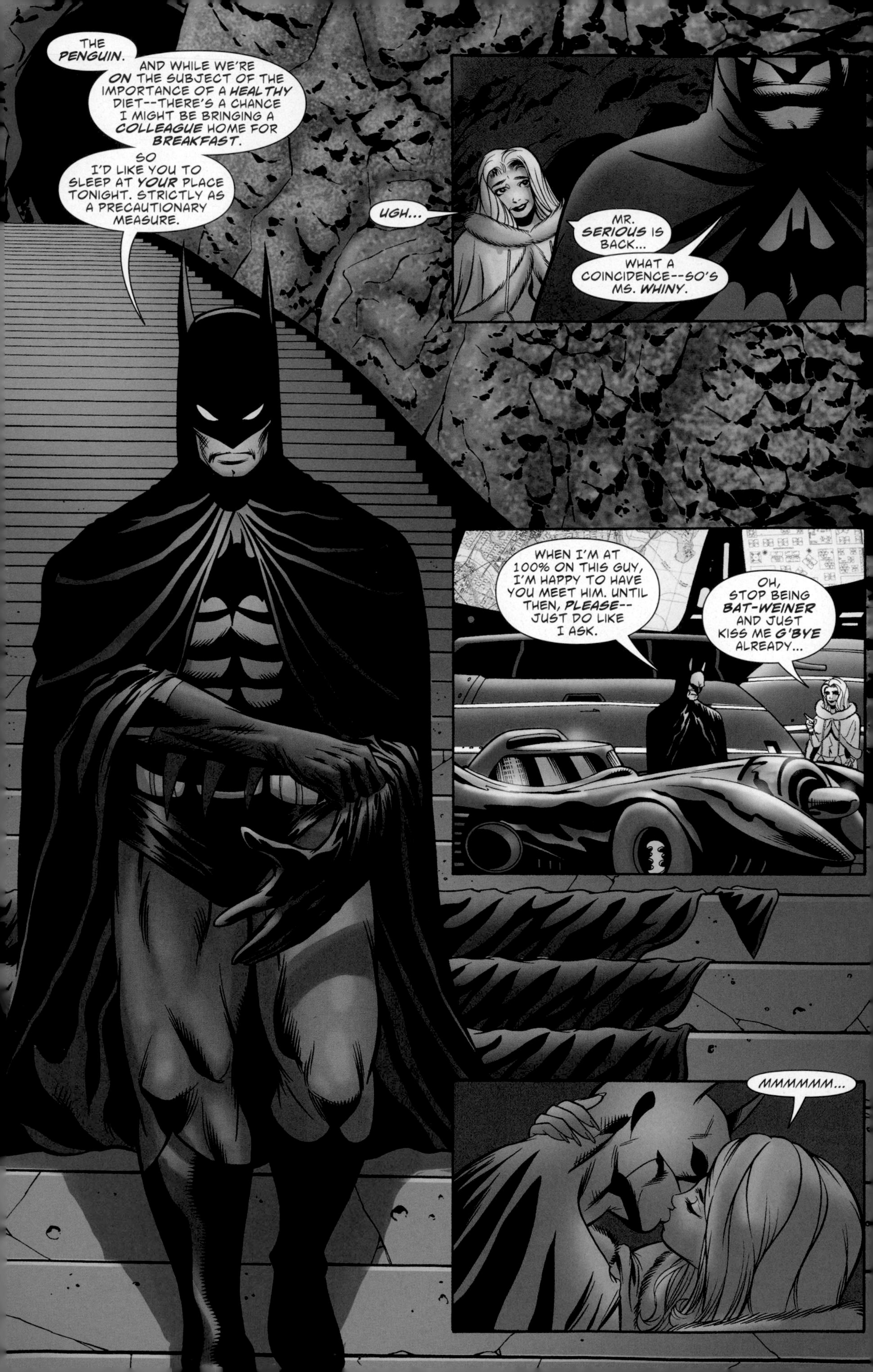
THE PENGUIN.
AND WHILE WE'RE ON THE SUBJECT OF THE IMPORTANCE OF A HEALTHY DIET--THERE'S A CHANCE I MIGHT BE BRINGING A COLLEAGUE HOME FOR BREAKFAST.
SO I'D LIKE YOU TO SLEEP AT YOUR PLACE TONIGHT. STRICTLY AS A PRECAUTIONARY MEASURE.
UGH...
MR. SERIOUS IS BACK...
WHAT A COINCIDENCE--SO'S MS. WHINY.
WHEN I'M AT 100% ON THIS GUY, I'M HAPPY TO HAVE YOU MEET HIM. UNTIL THEN, PLEASE--JUST DO LIKE I ASK.
OH, STOP BEING BAT-WEINER AND JUST KISS ME G'BYE ALREADY...
MMMMMM...

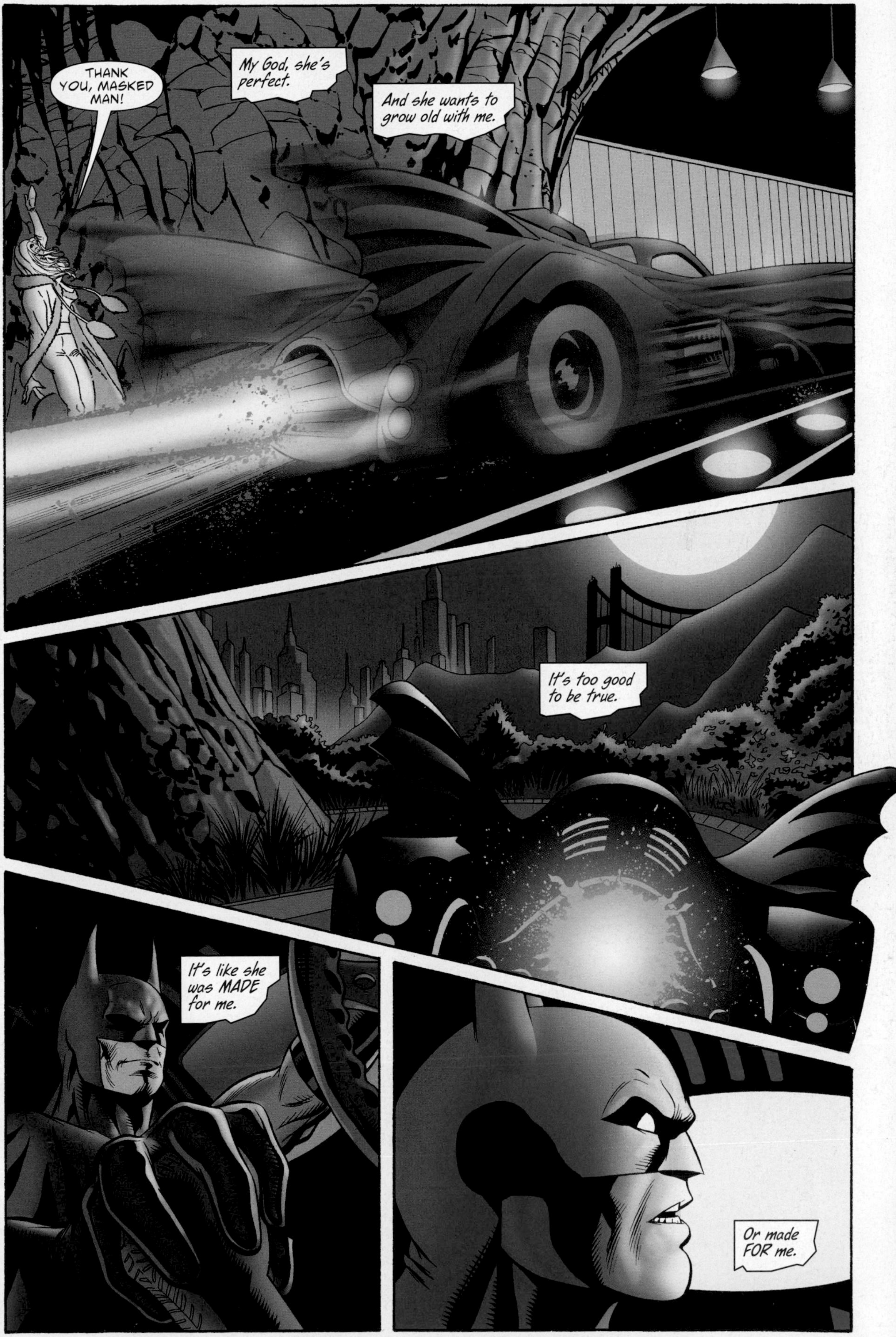
THANK YOU, MASKED MAN!
My God, she's perfect.
And she wants to grow old with me.
It's too good to be true.
It's like she was MADE for me.
Or made FOR me.

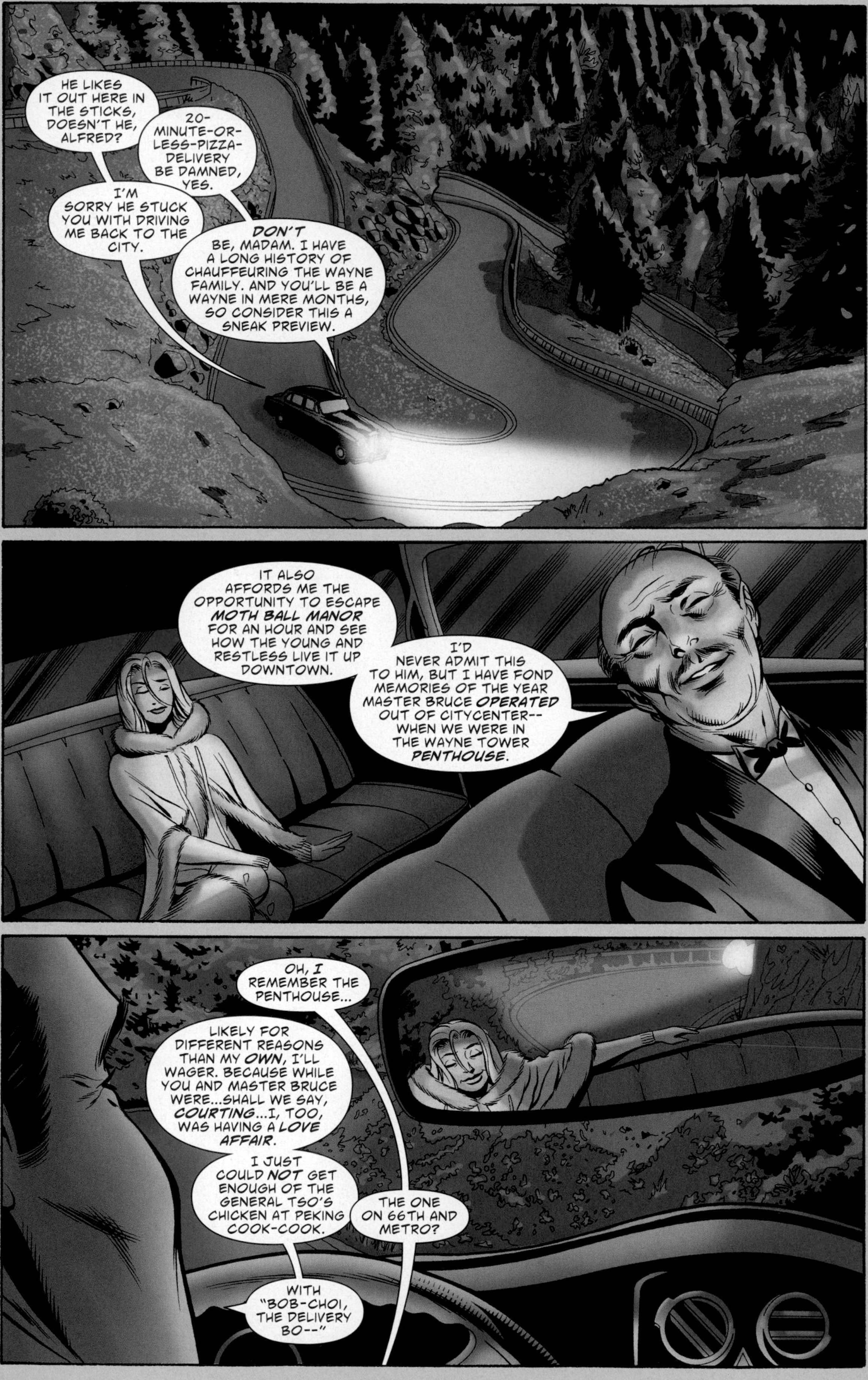
HE LIKES IT OUT HERE IN THE STICKS, DOESN'T HE, ALFRED?
20-MINUTE-OR-LESS-PIZZA-DELIVERY BE DAMNED, YES.
I'M SORRY HE STUCK YOU WITH DRIVING ME BACK TO THE CITY.
DON'T BE, MADAM. I HAVE A LONG HISTORY OF CHAUFFEURING THE WAYNE FAMILY. AND YOU'LL BE A WAYNE IN MERE MONTHS, SO CONSIDER THIS A SNEAK PREVIEW.
IT ALSO AFFORDS ME THE OPPORTUNITY TO ESCAPE *MOTH BALL MANOR* FOR AN HOUR AND SEE HOW THE YOUNG AND RESTLESS LIVE IT UP DOWNTOWN.
I'D NEVER ADMIT THIS TO HIM, BUT I HAVE FOND MEMORIES OF THE YEAR MASTER BRUCE *OPERATED* OUT OF CITYCENTER-- WHEN WE WERE IN THE WAYNE TOWER *PENTHOUSE*.
OH, *I* REMEMBER THE PENTHOUSE...
LIKELY FOR DIFFERENT REASONS THAN MY *OWN*, I'LL WAGER. BECAUSE WHILE YOU AND MASTER BRUCE WERE...SHALL WE SAY, *COURTING*...I, TOO, WAS HAVING A *LOVE AFFAIR*.
I JUST COULD *NOT* GET ENOUGH OF THE GENERAL TSO'S CHICKEN AT PEKING COOK-COOK.
THE ONE ON 66TH AND METRO?
WITH "BOB-CHOI, THE DELIVERY BO--"

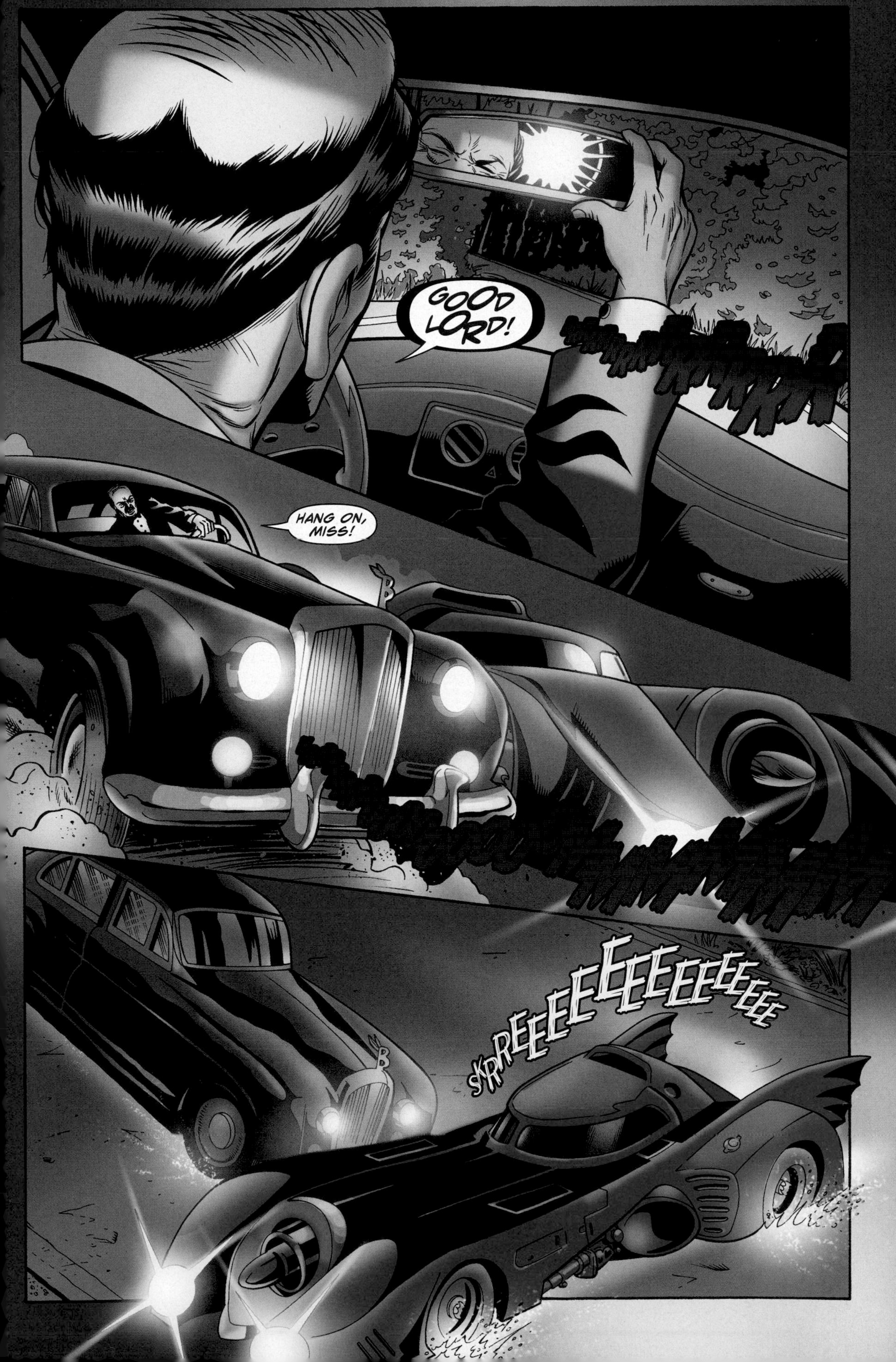
GOOD LORD!
HANG ON, MISS!
SKRREEEEEEEEEEEEEEE

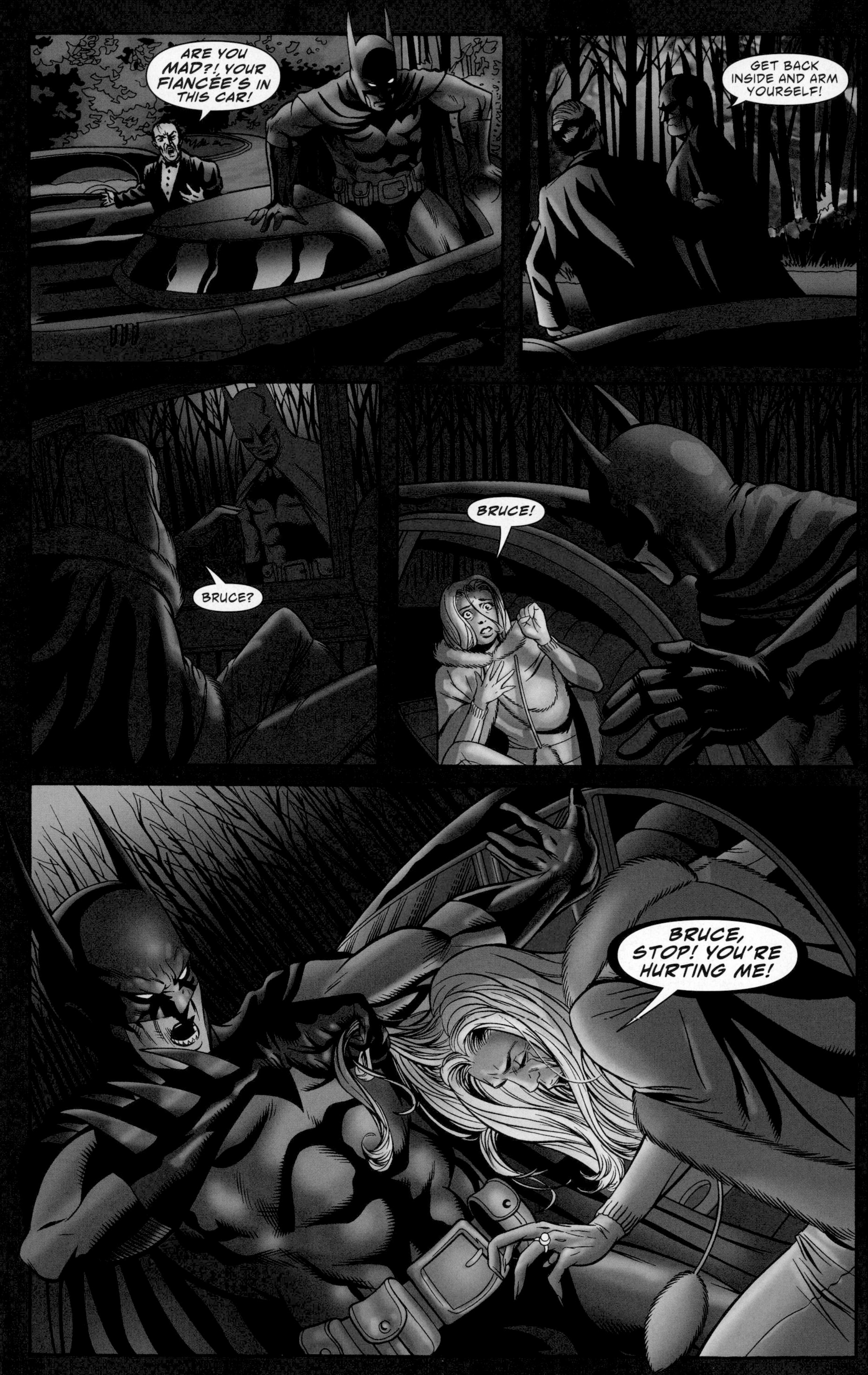
ARE YOU MAD?!, YOUR FIANCÉE'S IN THIS CAR!
GET BACK INSIDE AND ARM YOURSELF!
BRUCE?
BRUCE!
BRUCE, STOP! YOU'RE HURTING ME!

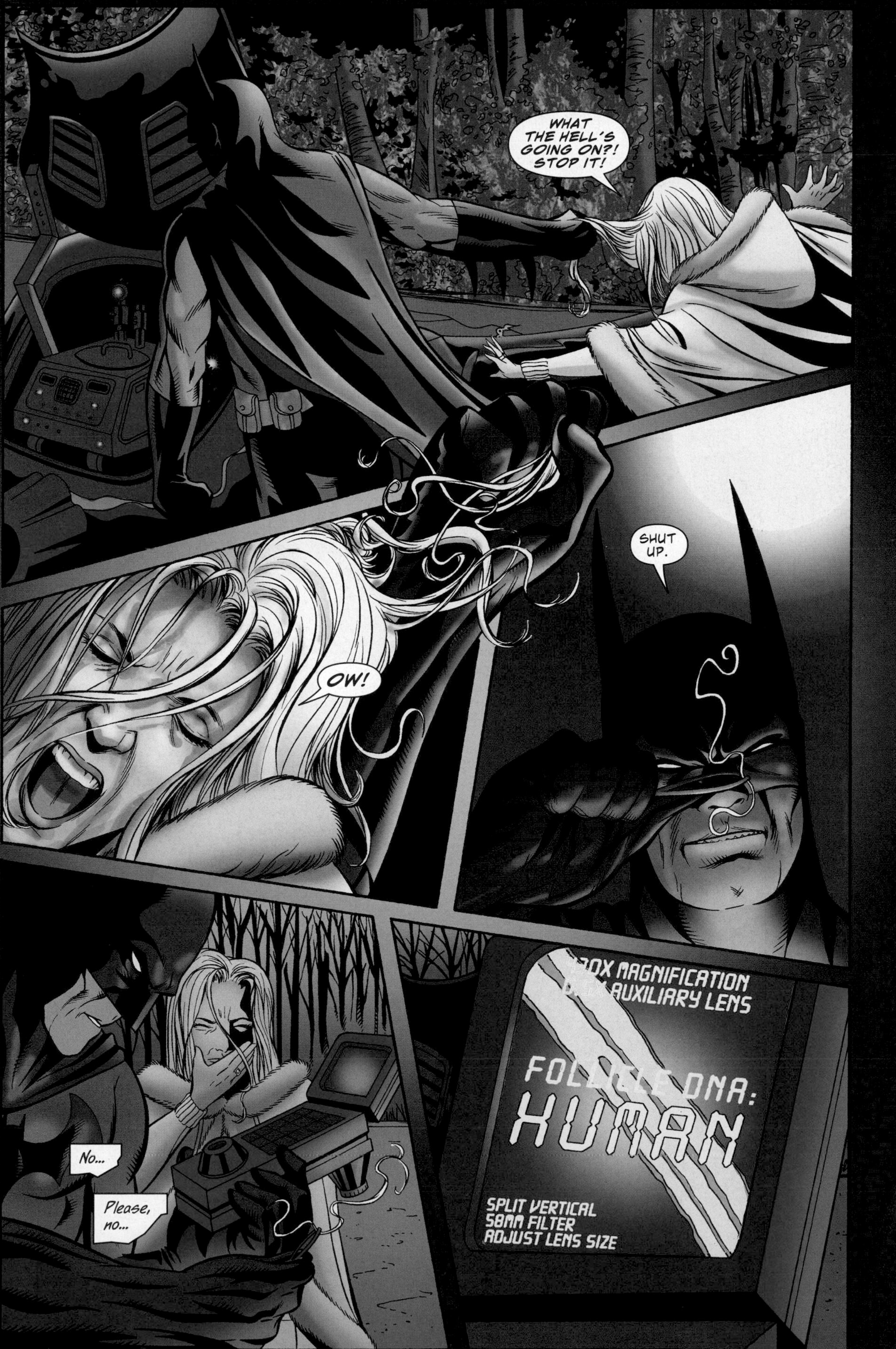
WHAT THE HELL'S GOING ON?! STOP IT!
SHUT UP.
OW!
No...
Please, no...
MAGNIFICATION
AUXILIARY LENS
FOLLICLE DNA:
HUMAN
SPLIT VERTICAL
58MM FILTER
ADJUST LENS SIZE

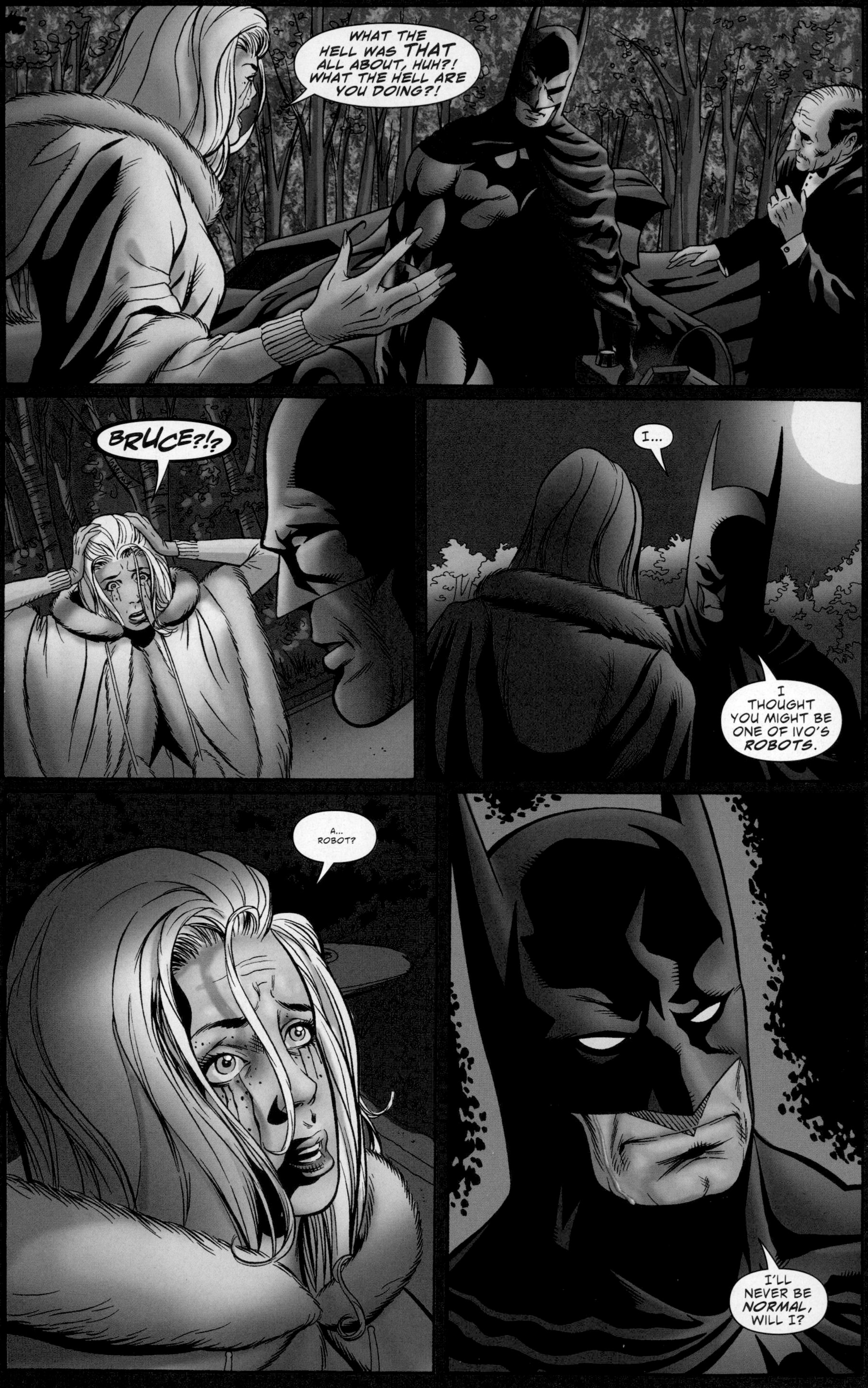

WHAT THE HELL WAS THAT ALL ABOUT, HUH?! WHAT THE HELL ARE YOU DOING?!
BRUCE?!?
I...
I THOUGHT YOU MIGHT BE ONE OF IVO'S ROBOTS.
A... ROBOT?
I'LL NEVER BE NORMAL, WILL I?

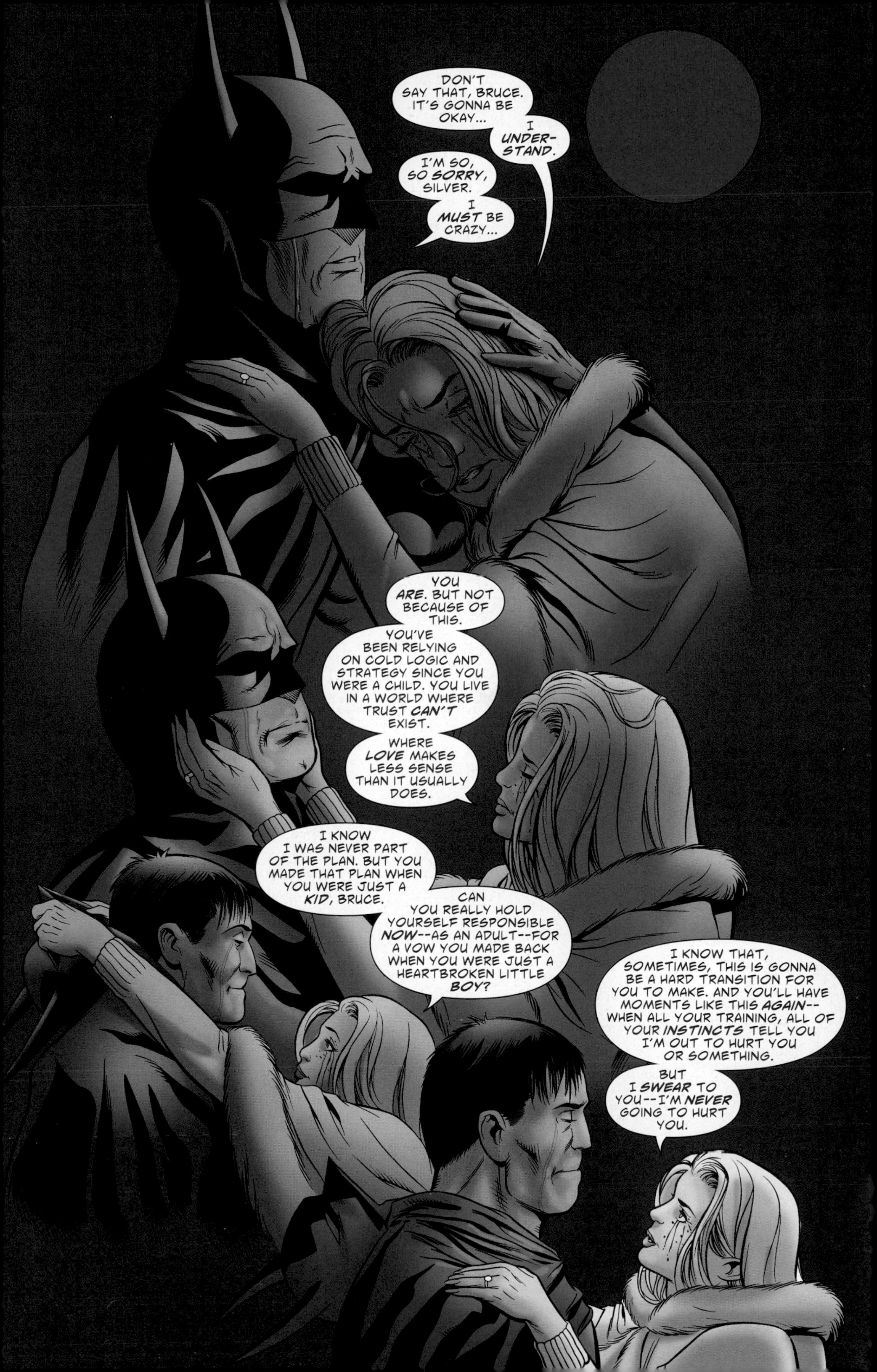
DON'T SAY THAT, BRUCE. IT'S GONNA BE OKAY...
I UNDERSTAND.
I'M SO, SO SORRY, SILVER.
I MUST BE CRAZY...
YOU ARE. BUT NOT BECAUSE OF THIS.
YOU'VE BEEN RELYING ON COLD LOGIC AND STRATEGY SINCE YOU WERE A CHILD. YOU LIVE IN A WORLD WHERE TRUST CAN'T EXIST.
WHERE LOVE MAKES LESS SENSE THAN IT USUALLY DOES.
I KNOW I WAS NEVER PART OF THE PLAN. BUT YOU MADE THAT PLAN WHEN YOU WERE JUST A KID, BRUCE.
CAN YOU REALLY HOLD YOURSELF RESPONSIBLE NOW--AS AN ADULT--FOR A VOW YOU MADE BACK WHEN YOU WERE JUST A HEARTBROKEN LITTLE BOY?
I KNOW THAT, SOMETIMES, THIS IS GONNA BE A HARD TRANSITION FOR YOU TO MAKE. AND YOU'LL HAVE MOMENTS LIKE THIS AGAIN--WHEN ALL YOUR TRAINING, ALL OF YOUR INSTINCTS TELL YOU I'M OUT TO HURT YOU OR SOMETHING.
BUT I SWEAR TO YOU--I'M NEVER GOING TO HURT YOU.

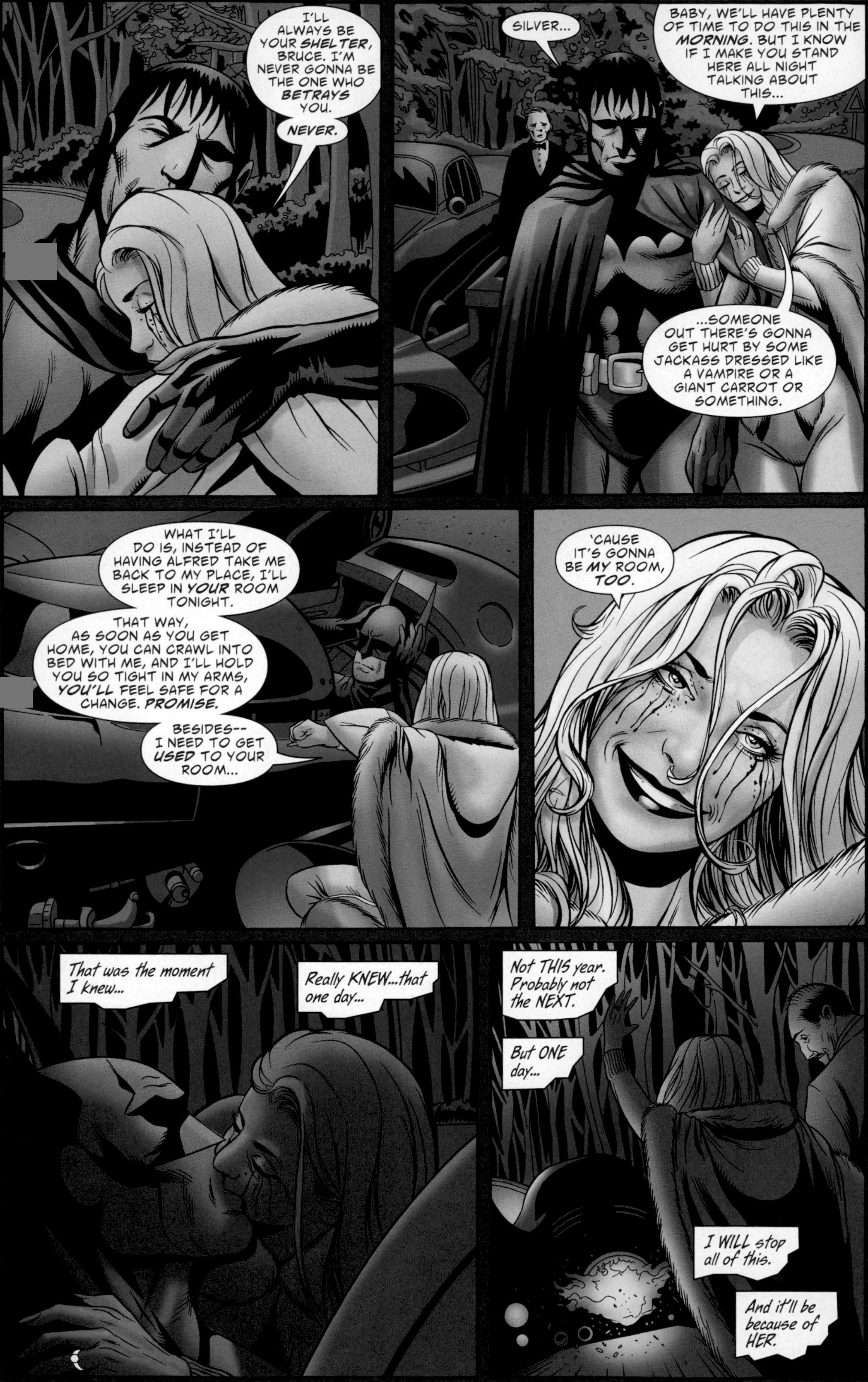
I'LL ALWAYS BE YOUR SHELTER, BRUCE. I'M NEVER GONNA BE THE ONE WHO BETRAYS YOU.
NEVER.
SILVER...
BABY, WE'LL HAVE PLENTY OF TIME TO DO THIS IN THE MORNING. BUT I KNOW IF I MAKE YOU STAND HERE ALL NIGHT TALKING ABOUT THIS...
...SOMEONE OUT THERE'S GONNA GET HURT BY SOME JACKASS DRESSED LIKE A VAMPIRE OR A GIANT CARROT OR SOMETHING.
WHAT I'LL DO IS, INSTEAD OF HAVING ALFRED TAKE ME BACK TO MY PLACE, I'LL SLEEP IN YOUR ROOM TONIGHT.
THAT WAY, AS SOON AS YOU GET HOME, YOU CAN CRAWL INTO BED WITH ME, AND I'LL HOLD YOU SO TIGHT IN MY ARMS, YOU'LL FEEL SAFE FOR A CHANGE. PROMISE.
BESIDES-- I NEED TO GET USED TO YOUR ROOM...
'CAUSE IT'S GONNA BE MY ROOM, TOO.
That was the moment I knew...
Really KNEW...that one day...
Not THIS year. Probably not the NEXT.
But ONE day...
I WILL stop all of this.
And it'll be because of HER.

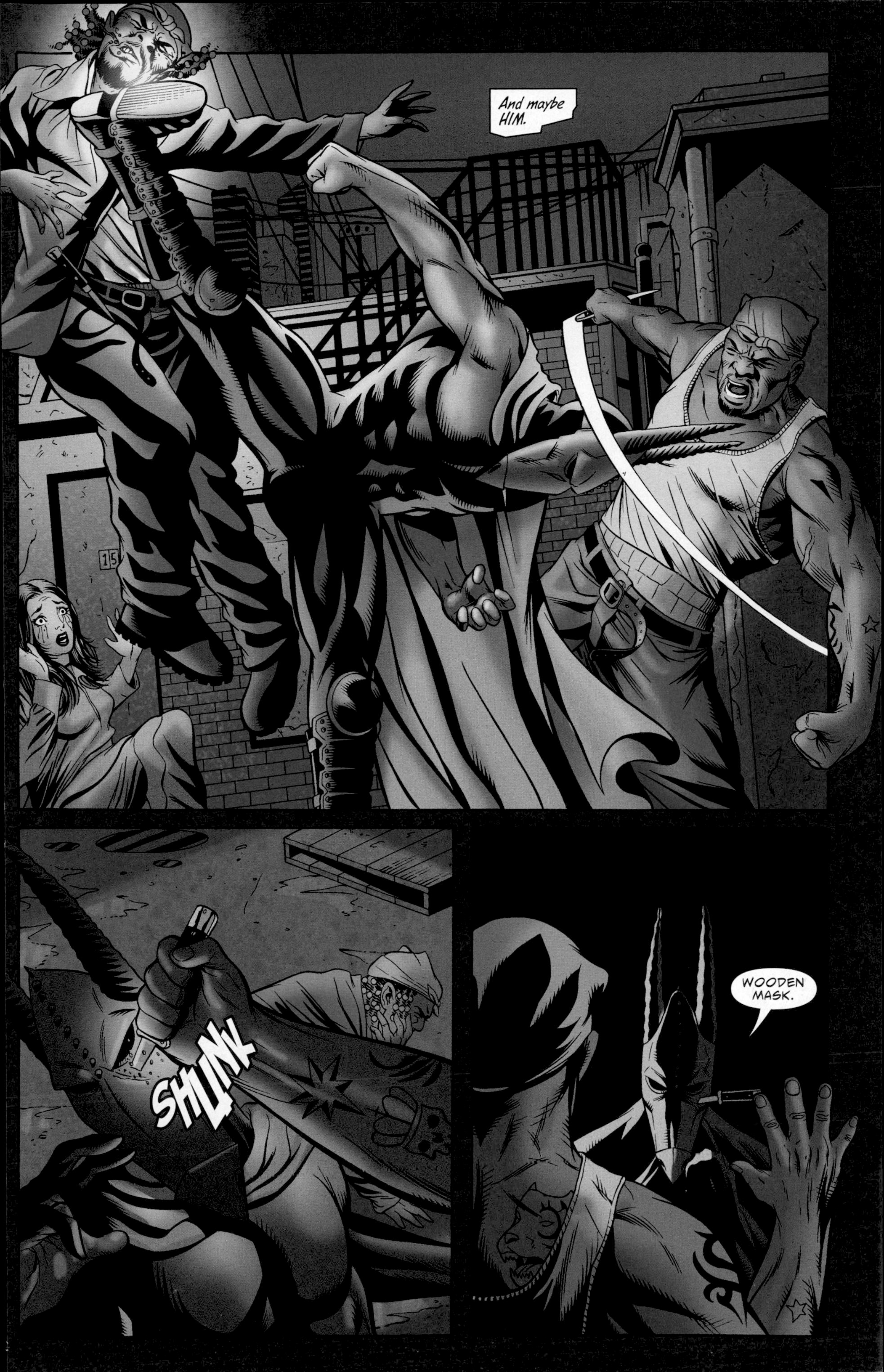
And maybe HIM.
SHUNK
WOODEN MASK.

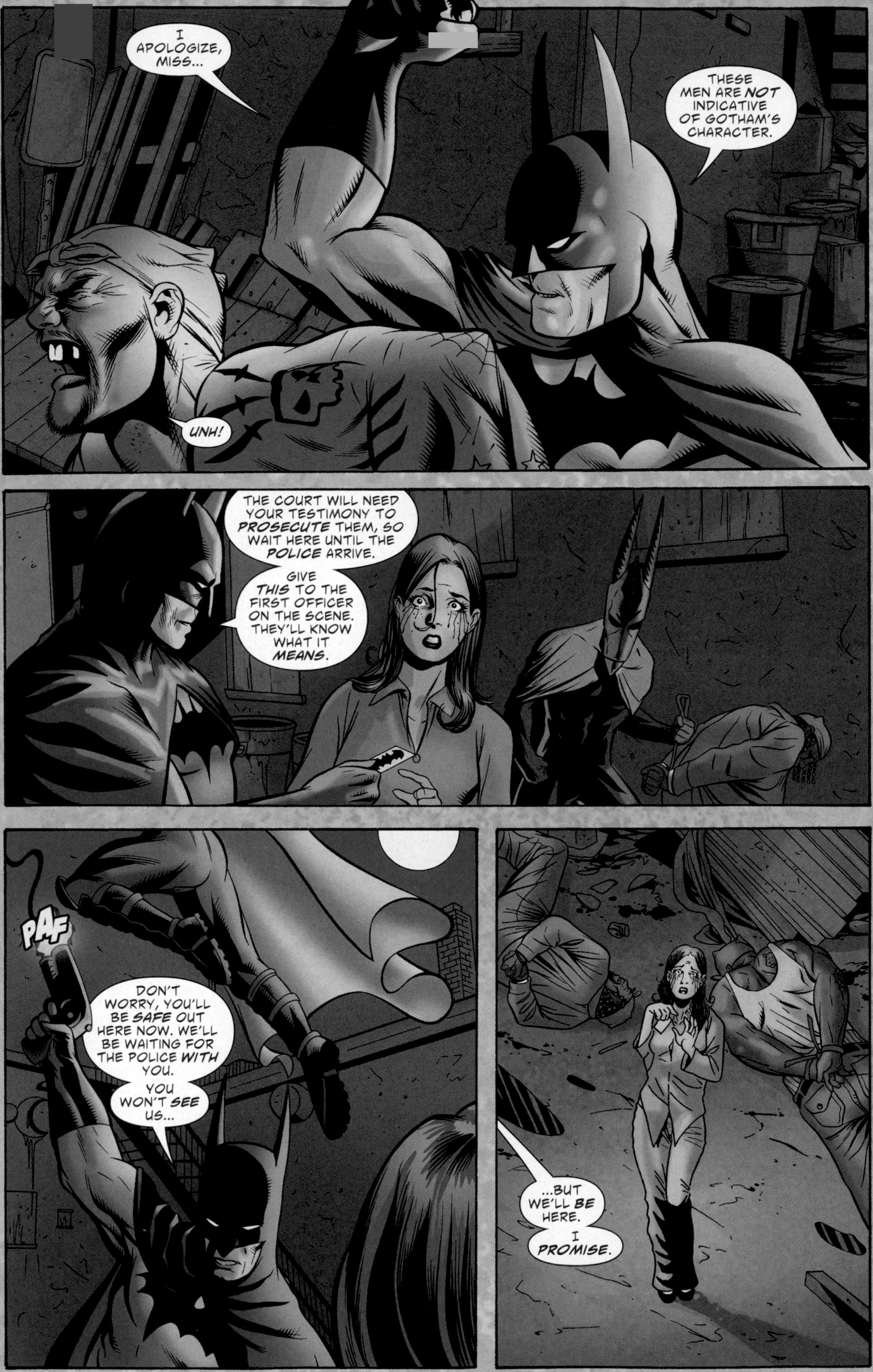
I APOLOGIZE, MISS...
THESE MEN ARE NOT INDICATIVE OF GOTHAM'S CHARACTER.
UNH!
THE COURT WILL NEED YOUR TESTIMONY TO PROSECUTE THEM, SO WAIT HERE UNTIL THE POLICE ARRIVE.
GIVE THIS TO THE FIRST OFFICER ON THE SCENE. THEY'LL KNOW WHAT IT MEANS.
PAF
DON'T WORRY, YOU'LL BE SAFE OUT HERE NOW. WE'LL BE WAITING FOR THE POLICE WITH YOU.
YOU WON'T SEE US...
...BUT WE'LL BE HERE.
I PROMISE.

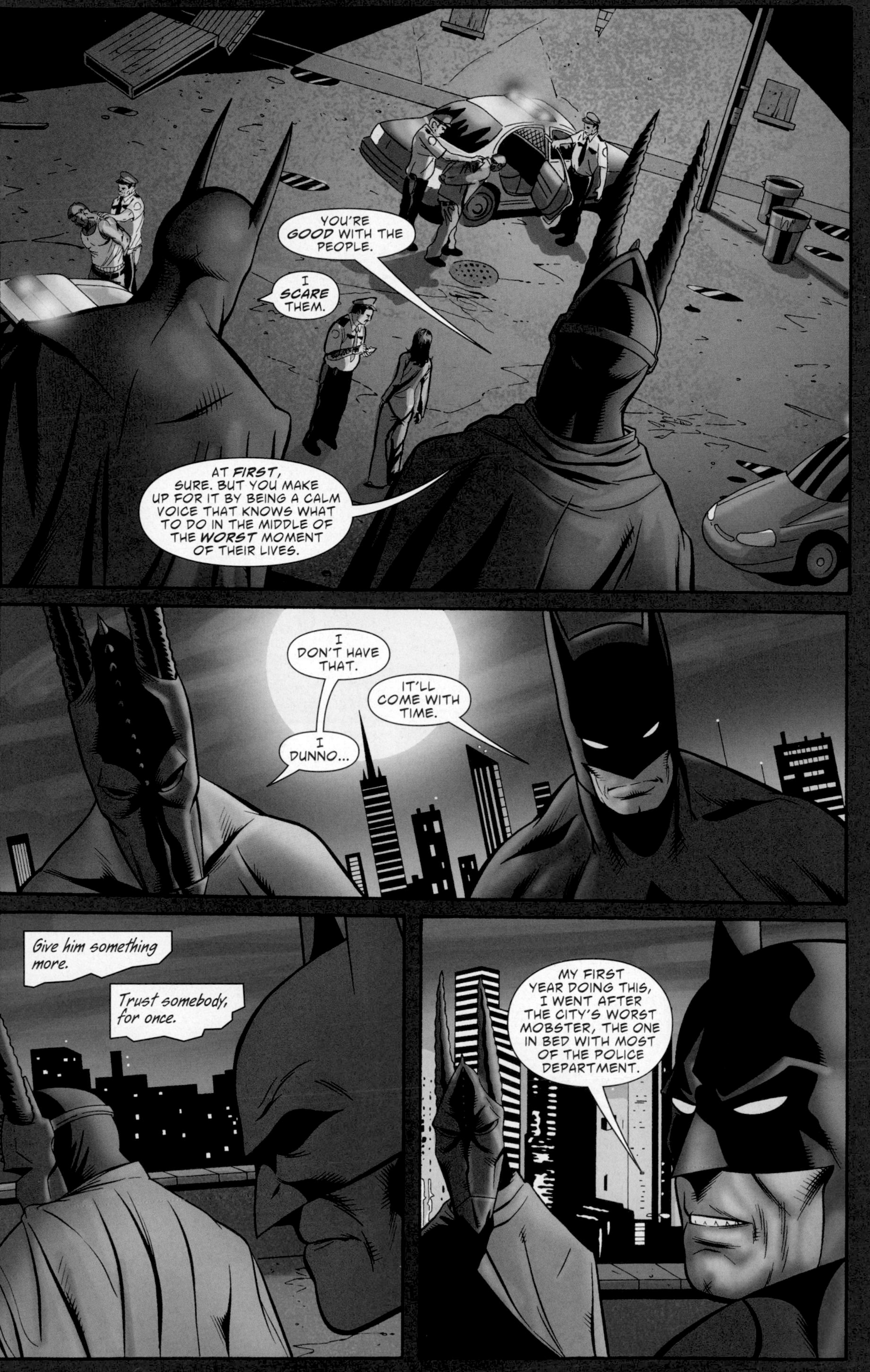
YOU'RE GOOD WITH THE PEOPLE.
I SCARE THEM.
AT FIRST, SURE. BUT YOU MAKE UP FOR IT BY BEING A CALM VOICE THAT KNOWS WHAT TO DO IN THE MIDDLE OF THE WORST MOMENT OF THEIR LIVES.
I DON'T HAVE THAT.
IT'LL COME WITH TIME.
I DUNNO...
Give him something more.
Trust somebody, for once.
MY FIRST YEAR DOING THIS, I WENT AFTER THE CITY'S WORST MOBSTER, THE ONE IN BED WITH MOST OF THE POLICE DEPARTMENT.

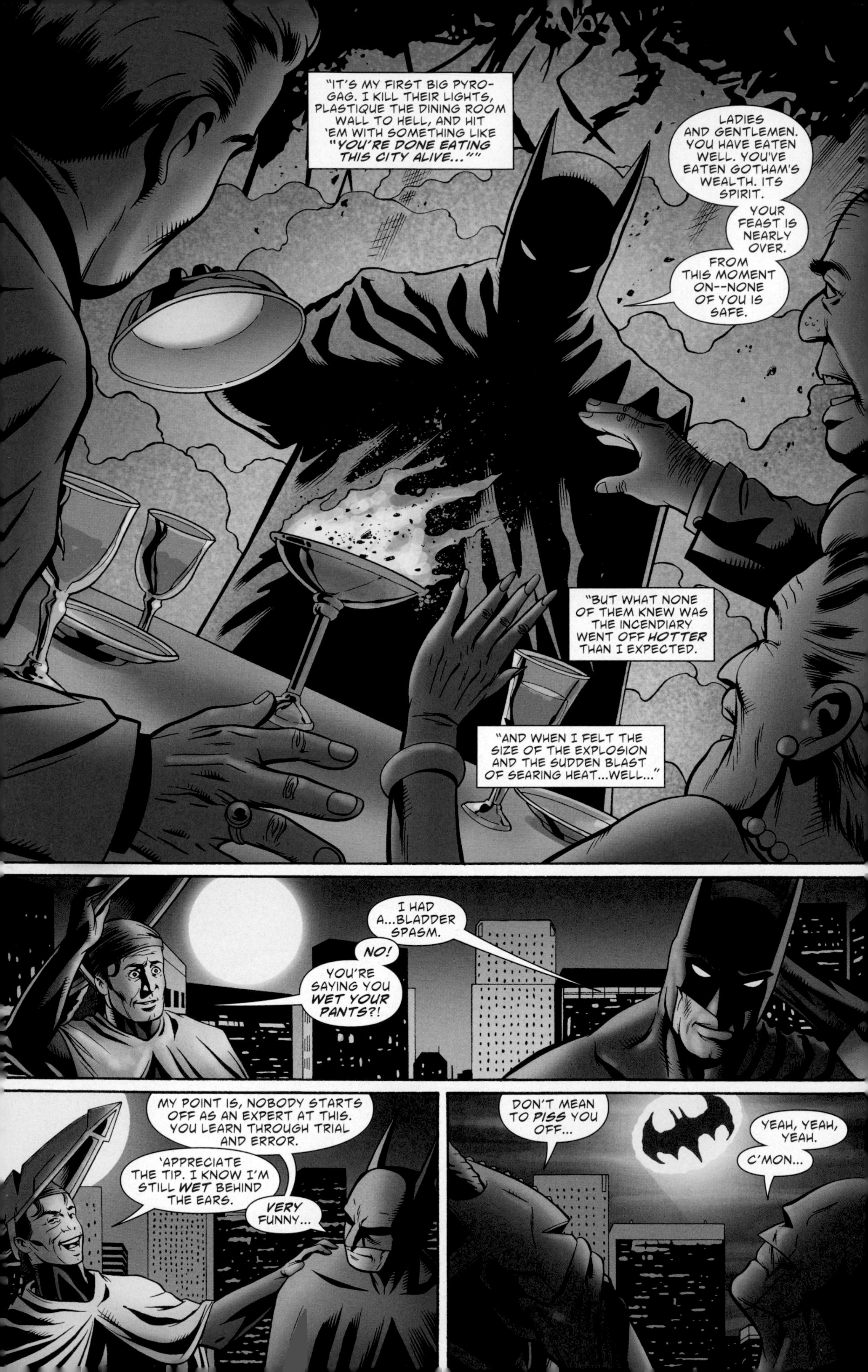
"IT'S MY FIRST BIG PYRO-GAG. I KILL THEIR LIGHTS, PLASTIQUE THE DINING ROOM WALL TO HELL, AND HIT 'EM WITH SOMETHING LIKE *"YOU'RE DONE EATING THIS CITY ALIVE..."*"
LADIES AND GENTLEMEN. YOU HAVE EATEN WELL. YOU'VE EATEN GOTHAM'S WEALTH. ITS SPIRIT.
YOUR FEAST IS NEARLY OVER.
FROM THIS MOMENT ON--NONE OF YOU IS SAFE.
"BUT WHAT NONE OF THEM KNEW WAS THE INCENDIARY WENT OFF *HOTTER* THAN I EXPECTED.
"AND WHEN I FELT THE SIZE OF THE EXPLOSION AND THE SUDDEN BLAST OF SEARING HEAT...WELL..."
I HAD A...BLADDER SPASM.
NO!
YOU'RE SAYING YOU *WET YOUR PANTS*?!
MY POINT IS, NOBODY STARTS OFF AS AN EXPERT AT THIS. YOU LEARN THROUGH TRIAL AND ERROR.
'APPRECIATE THE TIP. I KNOW I'M STILL *WET* BEHIND THE EARS.
VERY FUNNY...
DON'T MEAN TO *PISS* YOU OFF...
YEAH, YEAH, YEAH.
C'MON...

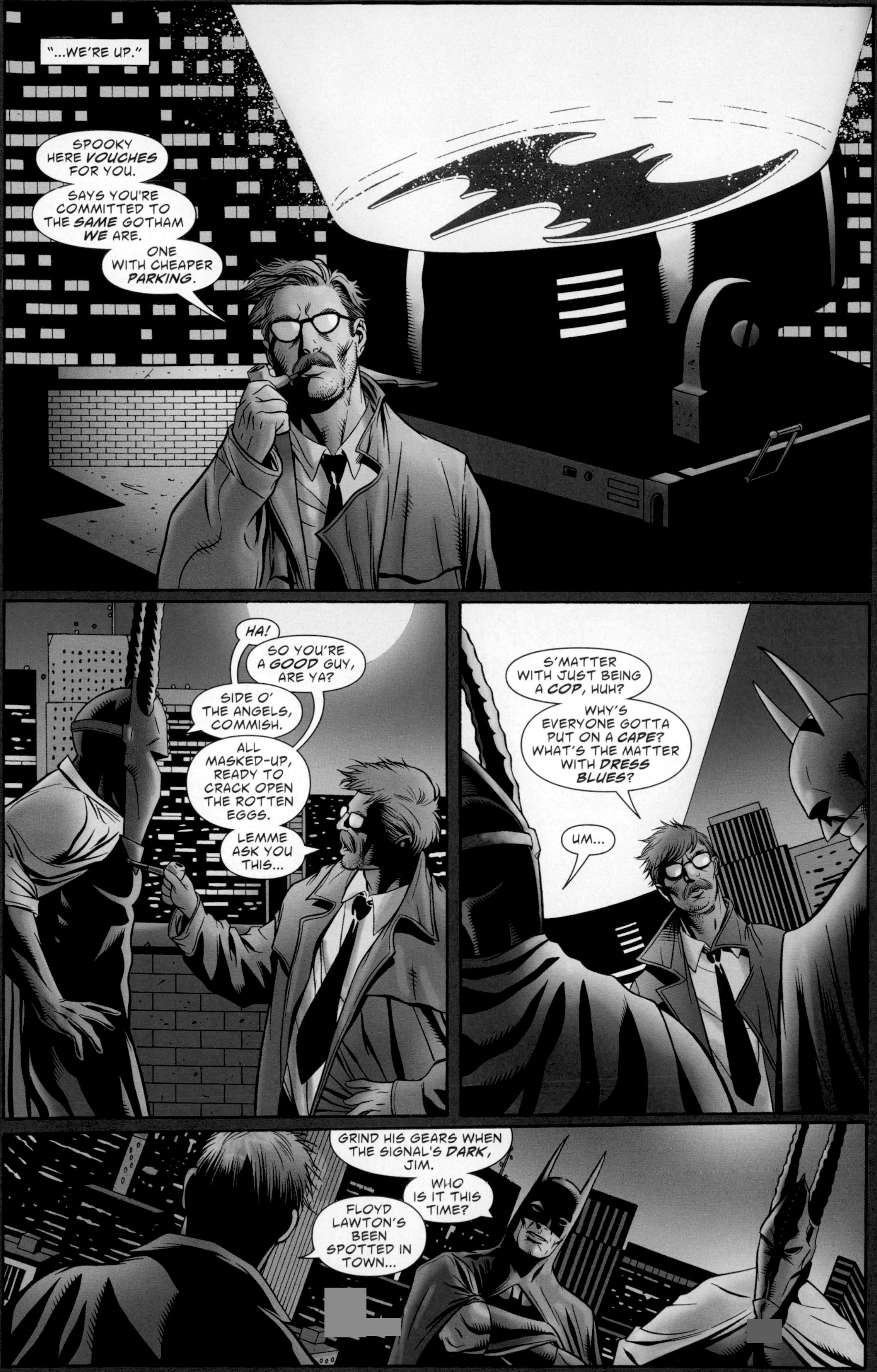
"...WE'RE UP."
SPOOKY HERE VOUCHES FOR YOU.
SAYS YOU'RE COMMITTED TO THE SAME GOTHAM WE ARE.
ONE WITH CHEAPER PARKING.
HA!
SO YOU'RE A GOOD GUY, ARE YA?
SIDE O' THE ANGELS, COMMISH.
ALL MASKED-UP, READY TO CRACK OPEN THE ROTTEN EGGS.
LEMME ASK YOU THIS...
S'MATTER WITH JUST BEING A COP, HUH?
WHY'S EVERYONE GOTTA PUT ON A CAPE? WHAT'S THE MATTER WITH DRESS BLUES?
UM...
GRIND HIS GEARS WHEN THE SIGNAL'S DARK, JIM.
WHO IS IT THIS TIME?
FLOYD LAWTON'S BEEN SPOTTED IN TOWN...

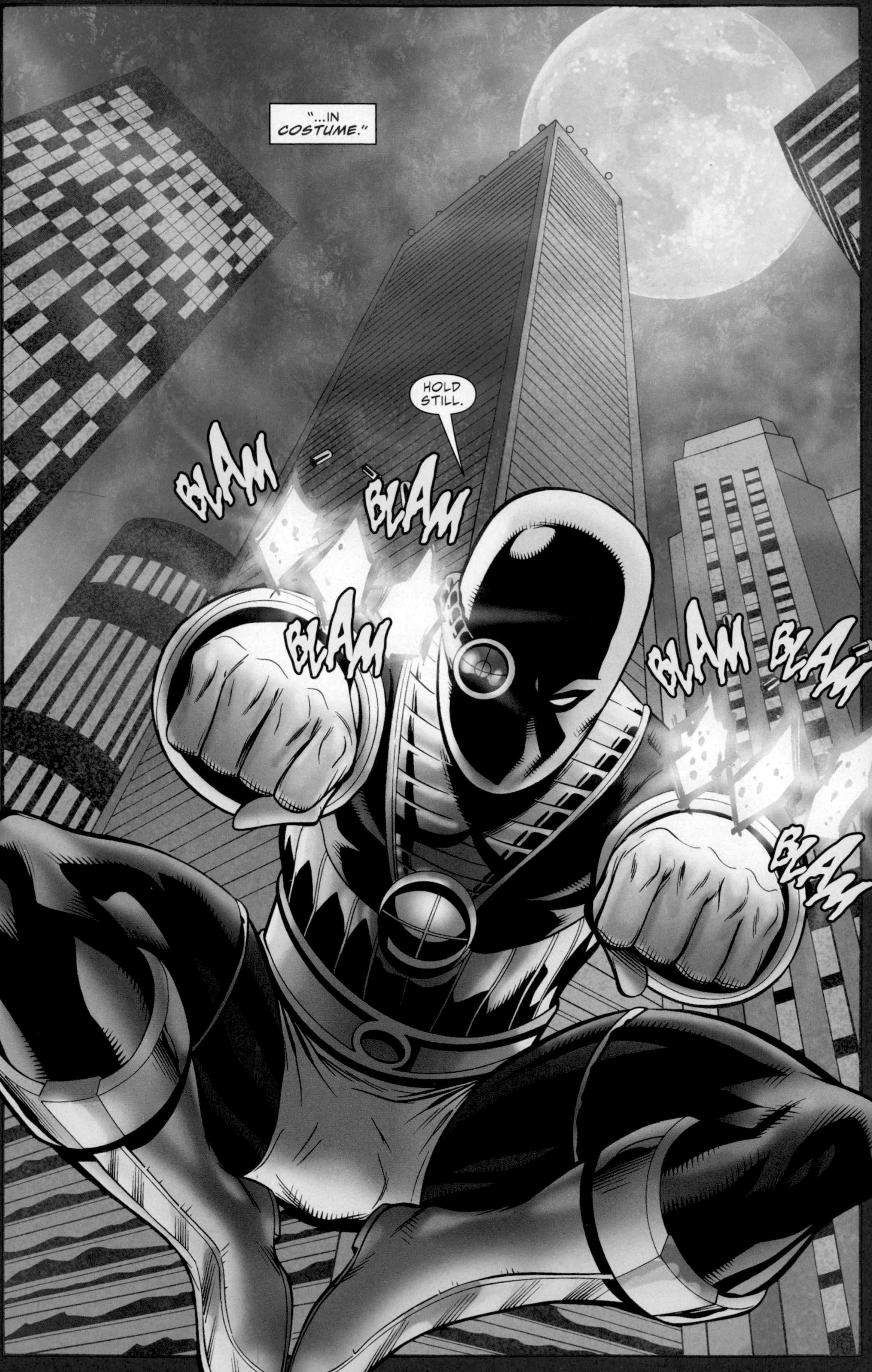
"...IN COSTUME."
HOLD STILL.
BLAM
BLAM
BLAM
BLAM
BLAM
BLAM

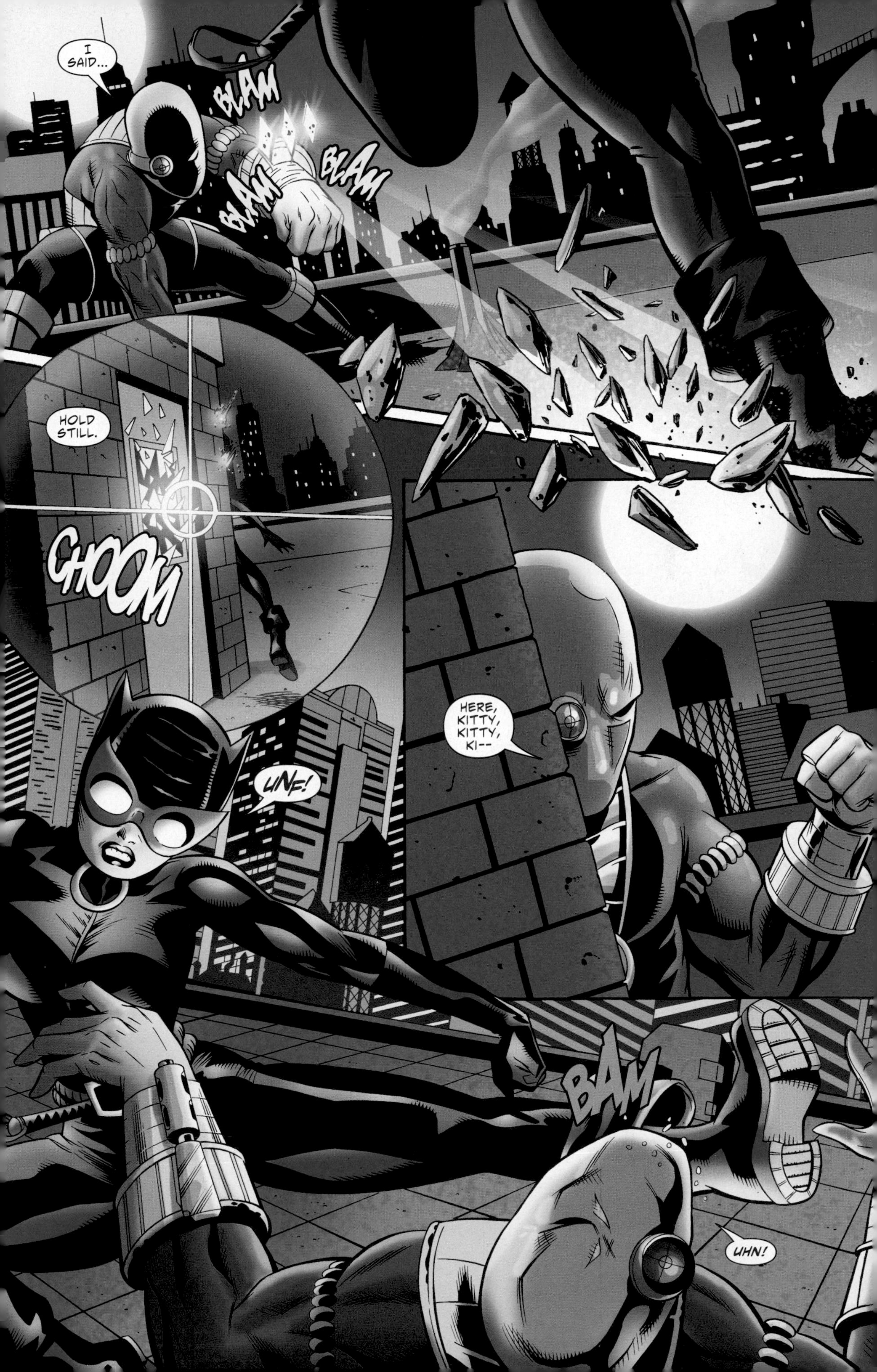
I SAID...
BLAM
BLAM
BLAM
HOLD STILL.
CHOOM
HERE, KITTY, KITTY, KI--
UNF!
BAM
UHN!

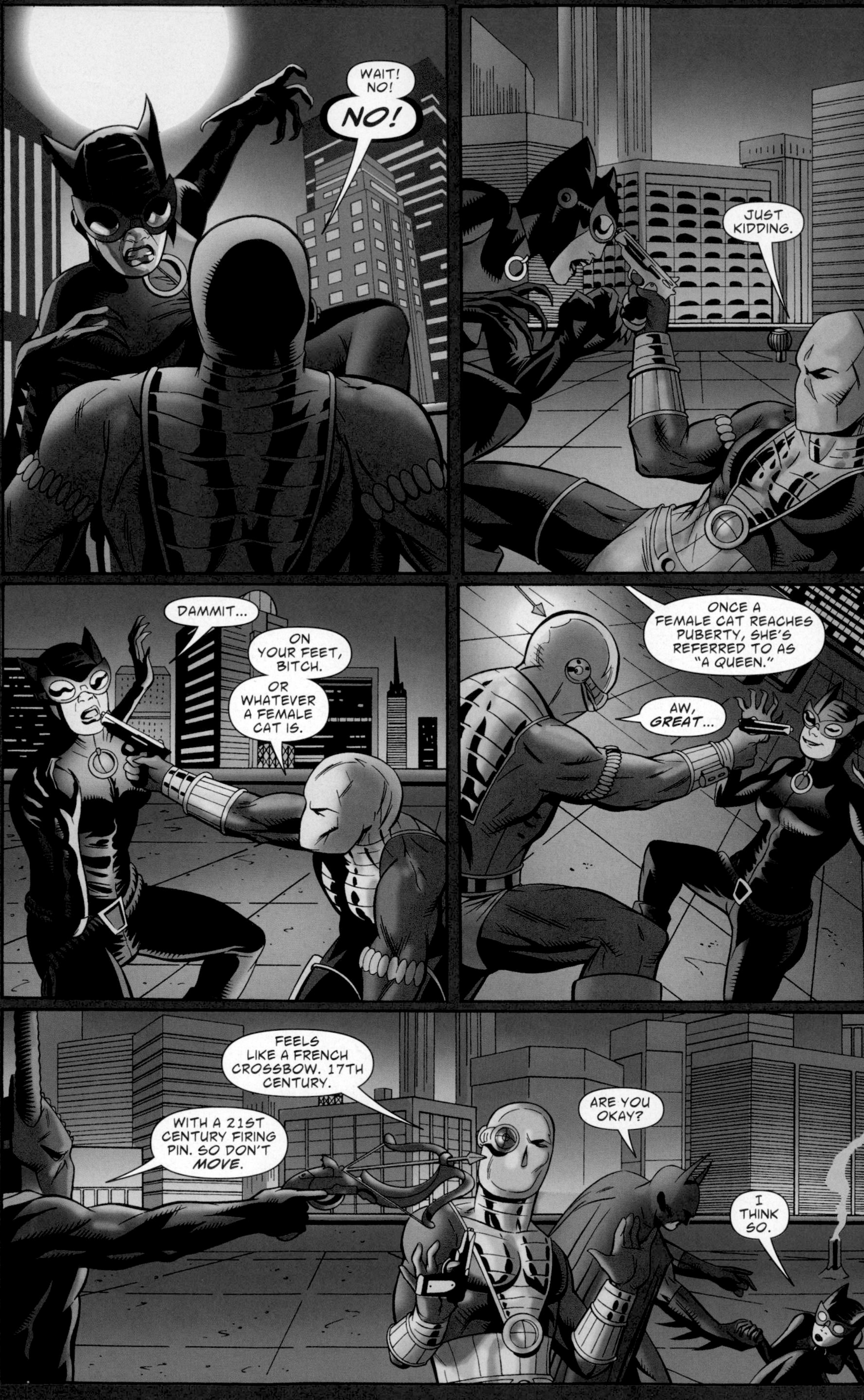
WAIT! NO! NO!
JUST KIDDING.
DAMMIT...
ON YOUR FEET, BITCH.
OR WHATEVER A FEMALE CAT IS.
ONCE A FEMALE CAT REACHES PUBERTY, SHE'S REFERRED TO AS "A QUEEN."
AW, GREAT...
FEELS LIKE A FRENCH CROSSBOW. 17TH CENTURY.
WITH A 21ST CENTURY FIRING PIN. SO DON'T MOVE.
ARE YOU OKAY?
I THINK SO.

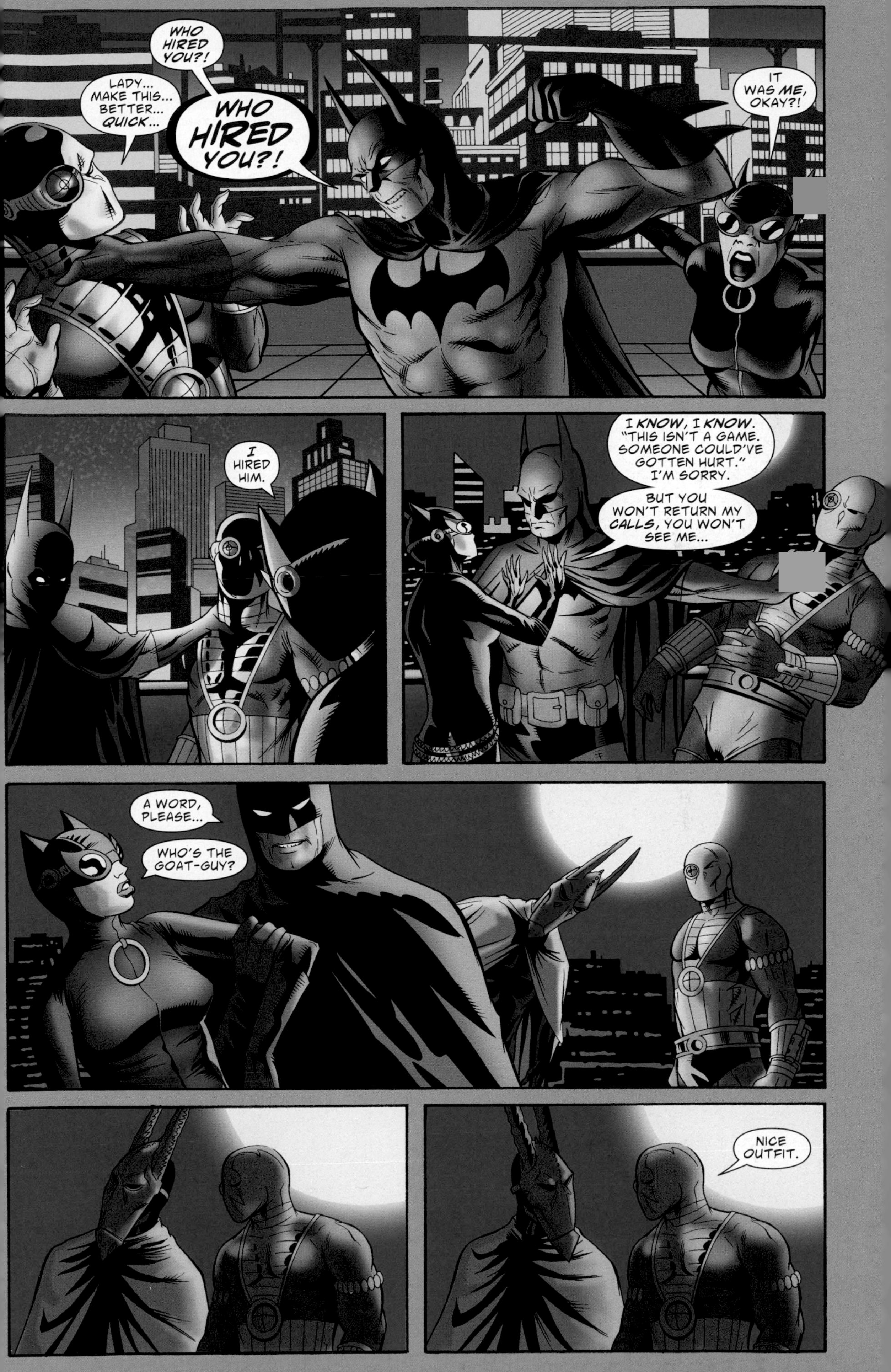
LADY... MAKE THIS... BETTER... QUICK...
WHO HIRED YOU?!
WHO HIRED YOU?!
IT WAS ME, OKAY?!
I HIRED HIM.
I KNOW, I KNOW. "THIS ISN'T A GAME. SOMEONE COULD'VE GOTTEN HURT." I'M SORRY.
BUT YOU WON'T RETURN MY CALLS, YOU WON'T SEE ME...
A WORD, PLEASE...
WHO'S THE GOAT-GUY?
NICE OUTFIT.

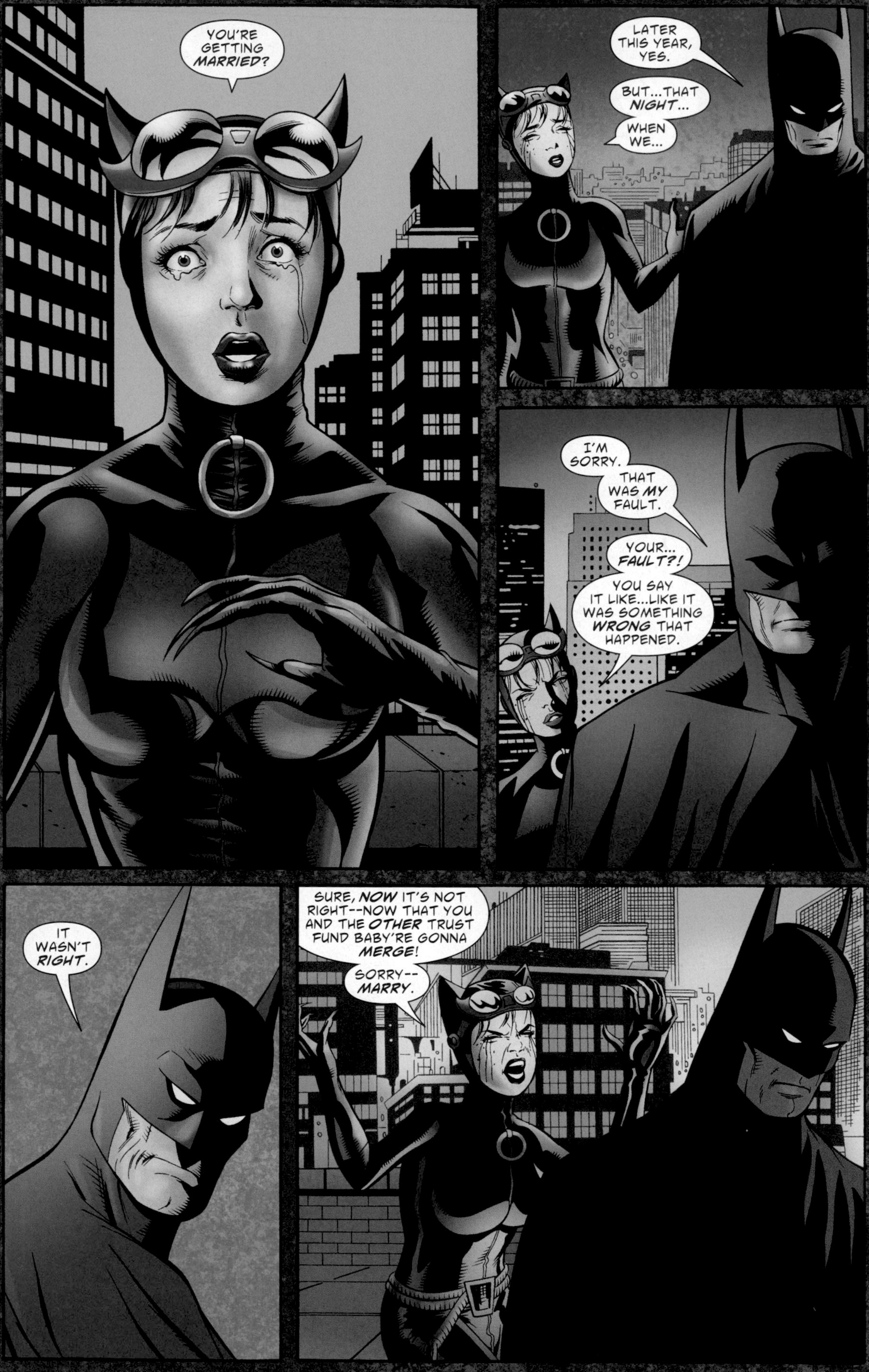
YOU'RE GETTING MARRIED?
LATER THIS YEAR, YES.
BUT...THAT NIGHT...
WHEN WE...
I'M SORRY.
THAT WAS MY FAULT.
YOUR... FAULT?!
YOU SAY IT LIKE...LIKE IT WAS SOMETHING WRONG THAT HAPPENED.
IT WASN'T RIGHT.
SURE, NOW IT'S NOT RIGHT--NOW THAT YOU AND THE OTHER TRUST FUND BABY'RE GONNA MERGE!
SORRY-- MARRY.

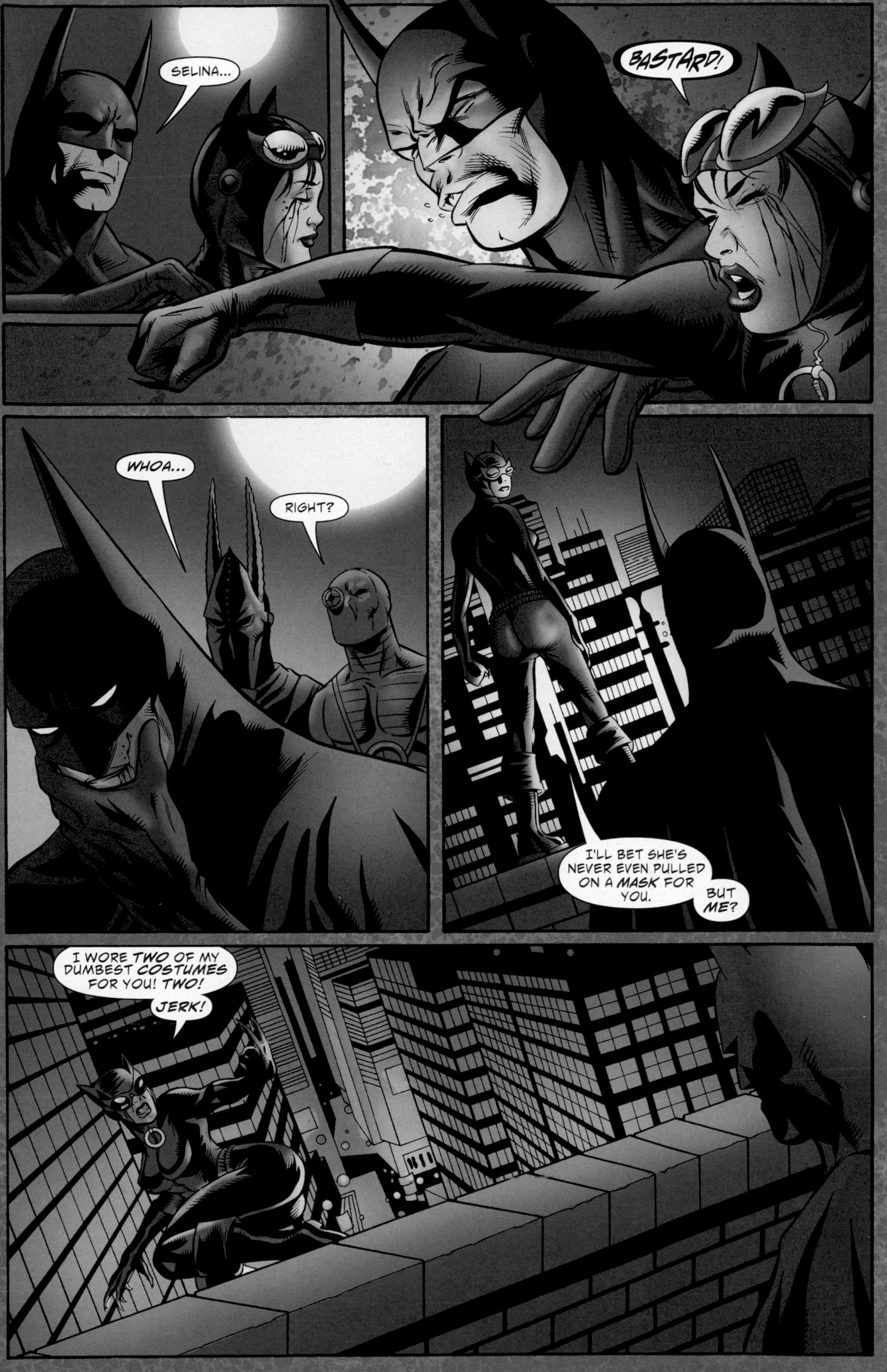
SELINA...
BASTARD!
WHOA...
RIGHT?
I'LL BET SHE'S NEVER EVEN PULLED ON A MASK FOR YOU.
BUT ME?
I WORE TWO OF MY DUMBEST COSTUMES FOR YOU! TWO!
JERK!

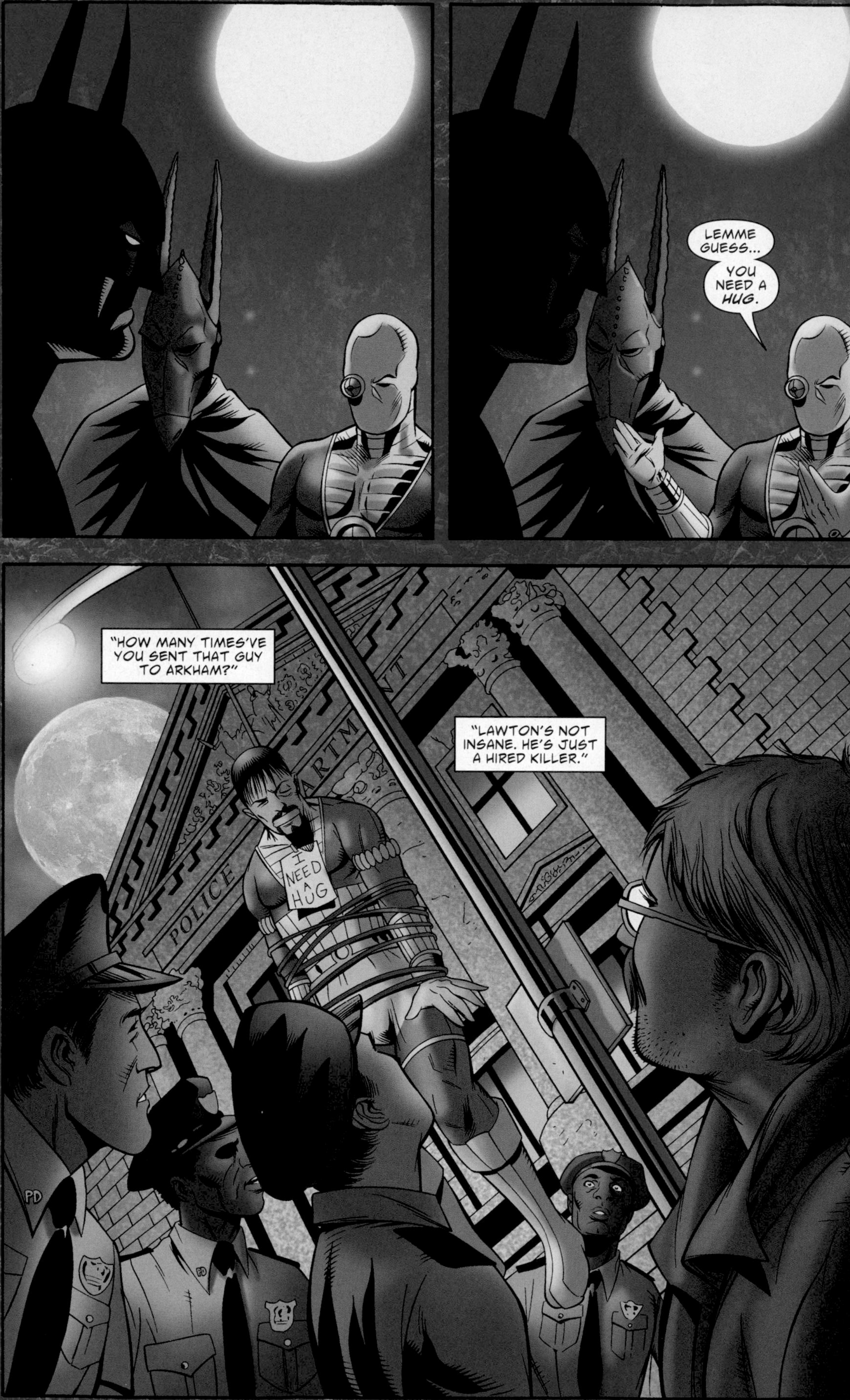
LEMME GUESS...
YOU NEED A HUG.
"HOW MANY TIMES'VE YOU SENT THAT GUY TO ARKHAM?"
"LAWTON'S NOT INSANE. HE'S JUST A HIRED KILLER."
I NEED A HUG
POLICE DEPARTMENT

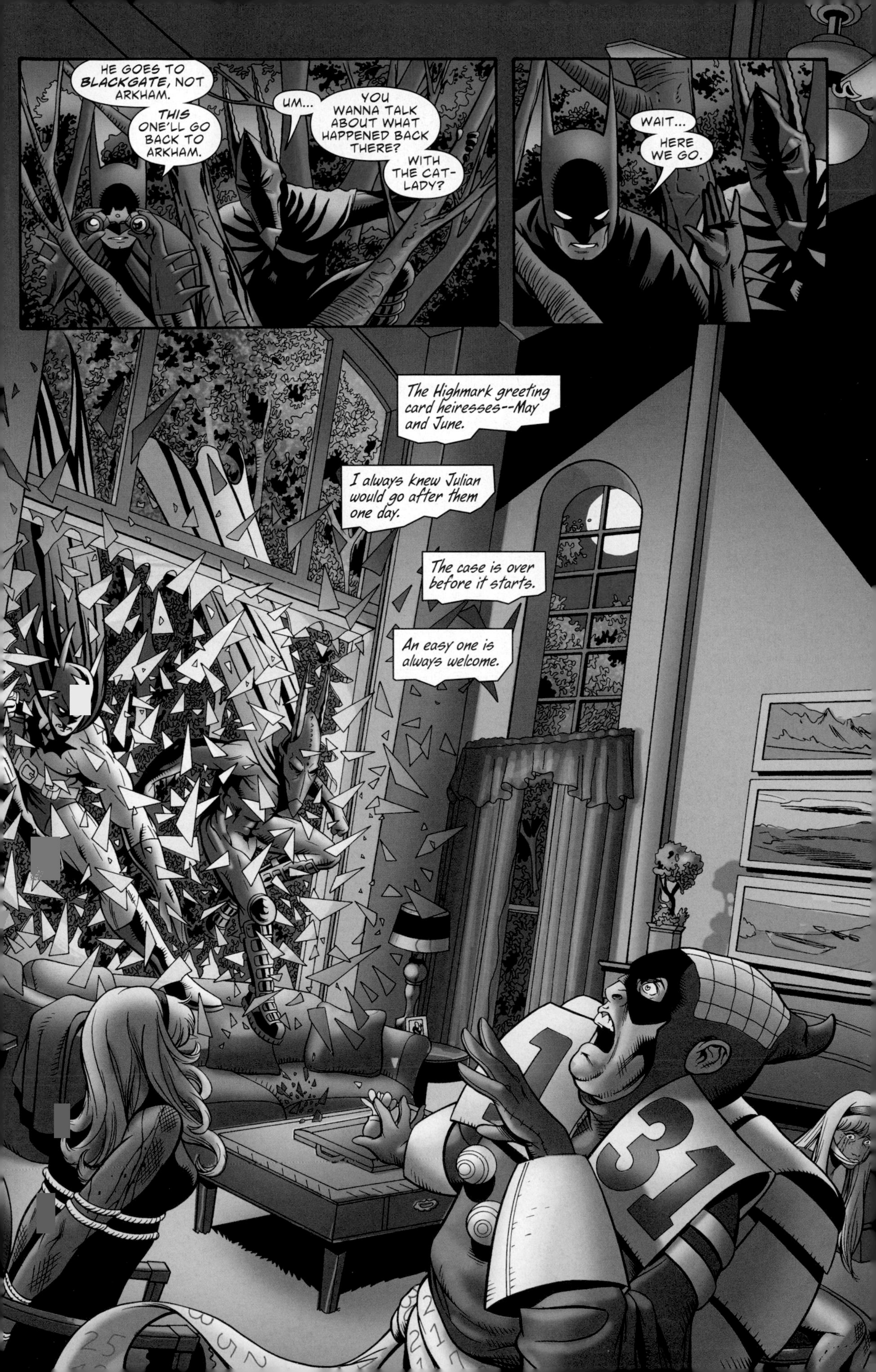
HE GOES TO BLACKGATE, NOT ARKHAM.
THIS ONE'LL GO BACK TO ARKHAM.
UM...
YOU WANNA TALK ABOUT WHAT HAPPENED BACK THERE?
WITH THE CAT-LADY?
WAIT...
HERE WE GO.
The Highmark greeting card heiresses--May and June.
I always knew Julian would go after them one day.
The case is over before it starts.
An easy one is always welcome.

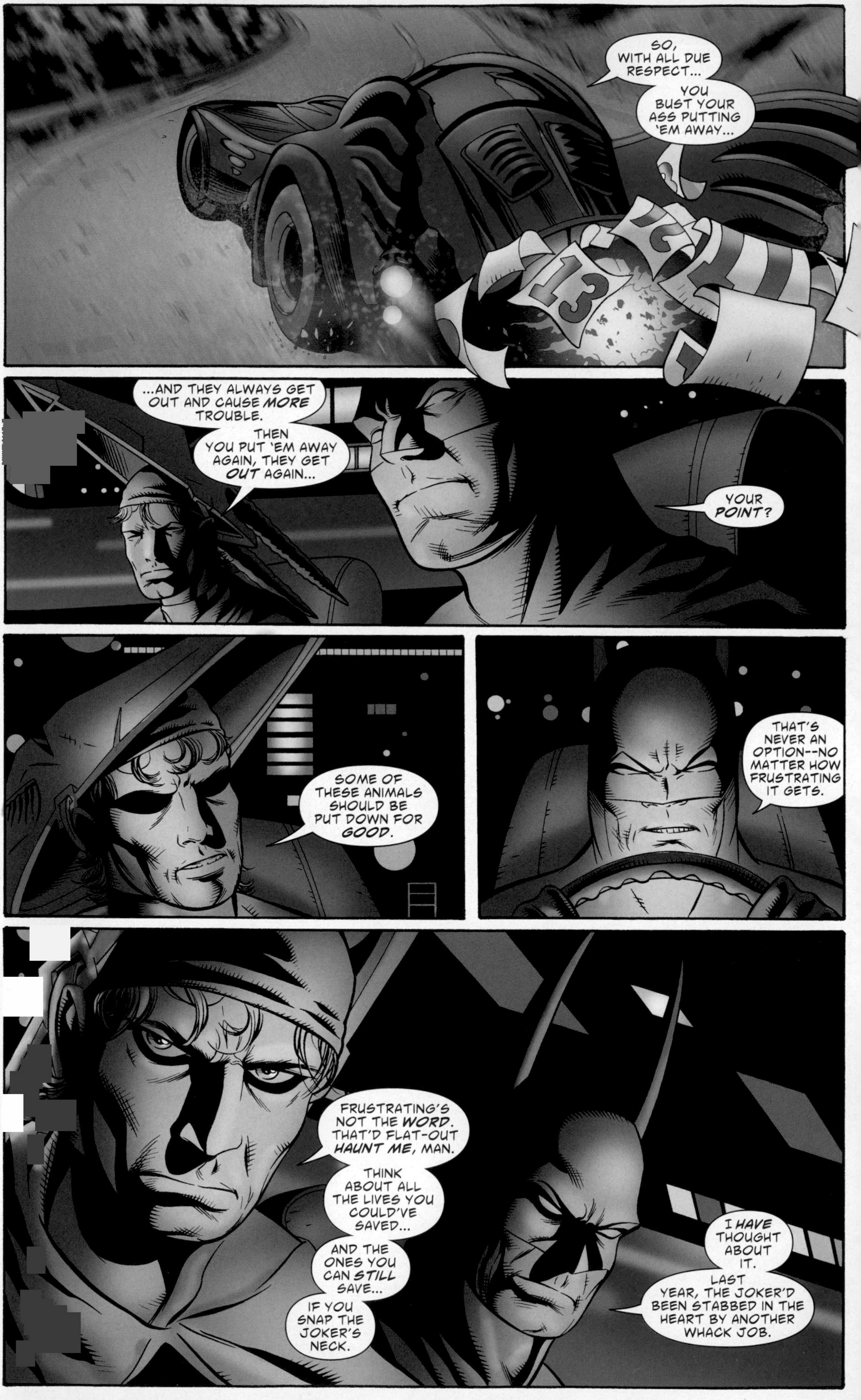
SO, WITH ALL DUE RESPECT...
YOU BUST YOUR ASS PUTTING 'EM AWAY...
...AND THEY ALWAYS GET OUT AND CAUSE MORE TROUBLE.
THEN YOU PUT 'EM AWAY AGAIN, THEY GET OUT AGAIN...
YOUR POINT?
SOME OF THESE ANIMALS SHOULD BE PUT DOWN FOR GOOD.
THAT'S NEVER AN OPTION--NO MATTER HOW FRUSTRATING IT GETS.
FRUSTRATING'S NOT THE WORD. THAT'D FLAT-OUT HAUNT ME, MAN.
THINK ABOUT ALL THE LIVES YOU COULD'VE SAVED...
AND THE ONES YOU CAN STILL SAVE...
IF YOU SNAP THE JOKER'S NECK.
I HAVE THOUGHT ABOUT IT.
LAST YEAR, THE JOKER'D BEEN STABBED IN THE HEART BY ANOTHER WHACK JOB.

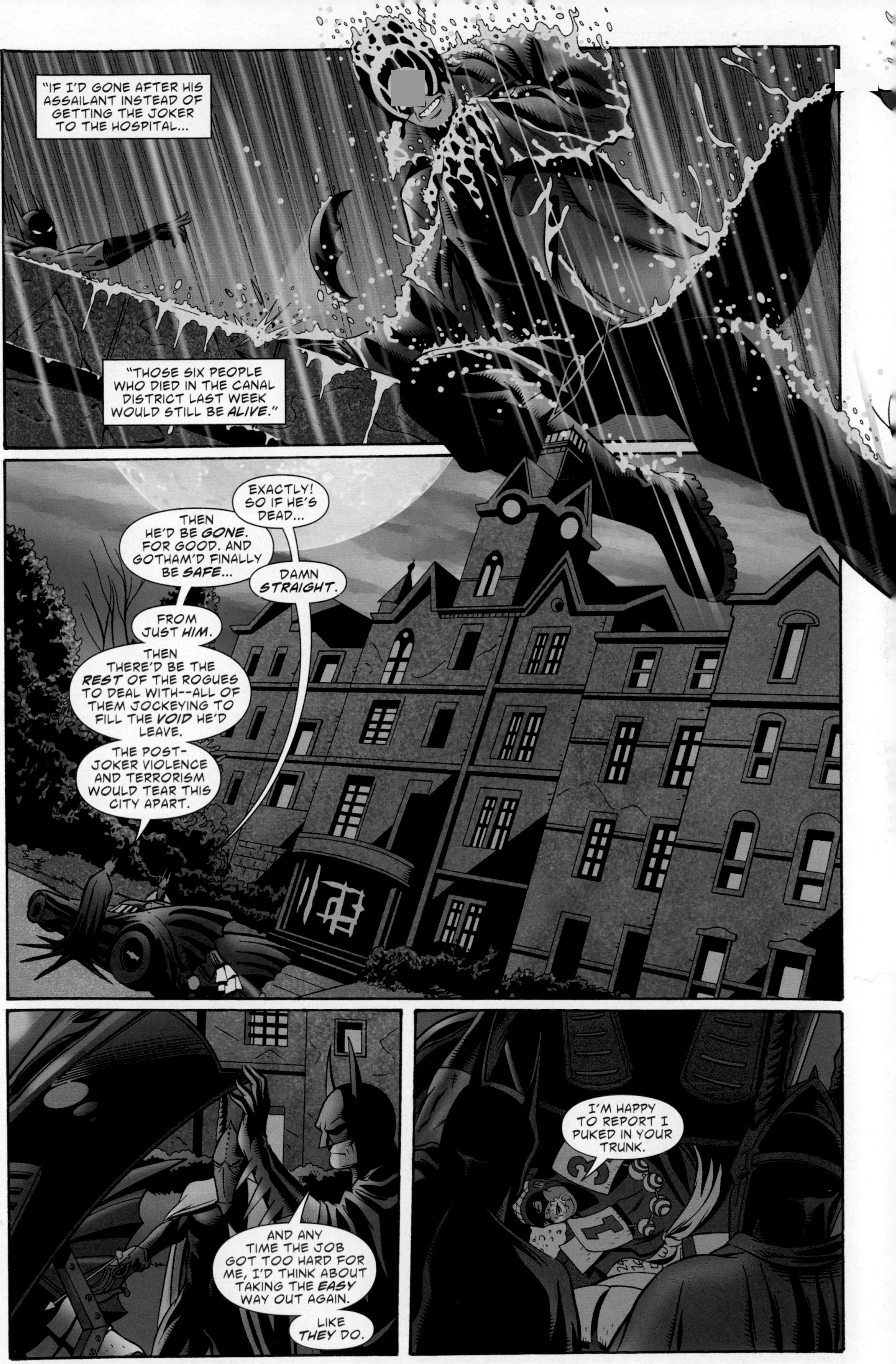
"IF I'D GONE AFTER HIS ASSAILANT INSTEAD OF GETTING THE JOKER TO THE HOSPITAL...
"THOSE SIX PEOPLE WHO DIED IN THE CANAL DISTRICT LAST WEEK WOULD STILL BE ALIVE."
THEN HE'D BE GONE. FOR GOOD. AND GOTHAM'D FINALLY BE SAFE...
EXACTLY! SO IF HE'S DEAD...
DAMN STRAIGHT.
FROM JUST HIM.
THEN THERE'D BE THE REST OF THE ROGUES TO DEAL WITH--ALL OF THEM JOCKEYING TO FILL THE VOID HE'D LEAVE.
THE POST-JOKER VIOLENCE AND TERRORISM WOULD TEAR THIS CITY APART.
AND ANY TIME THE JOB GOT TOO HARD FOR ME, I'D THINK ABOUT TAKING THE EASY WAY OUT AGAIN.
LIKE THEY DO.
I'M HAPPY TO REPORT I PUKED IN YOUR TRUNK.

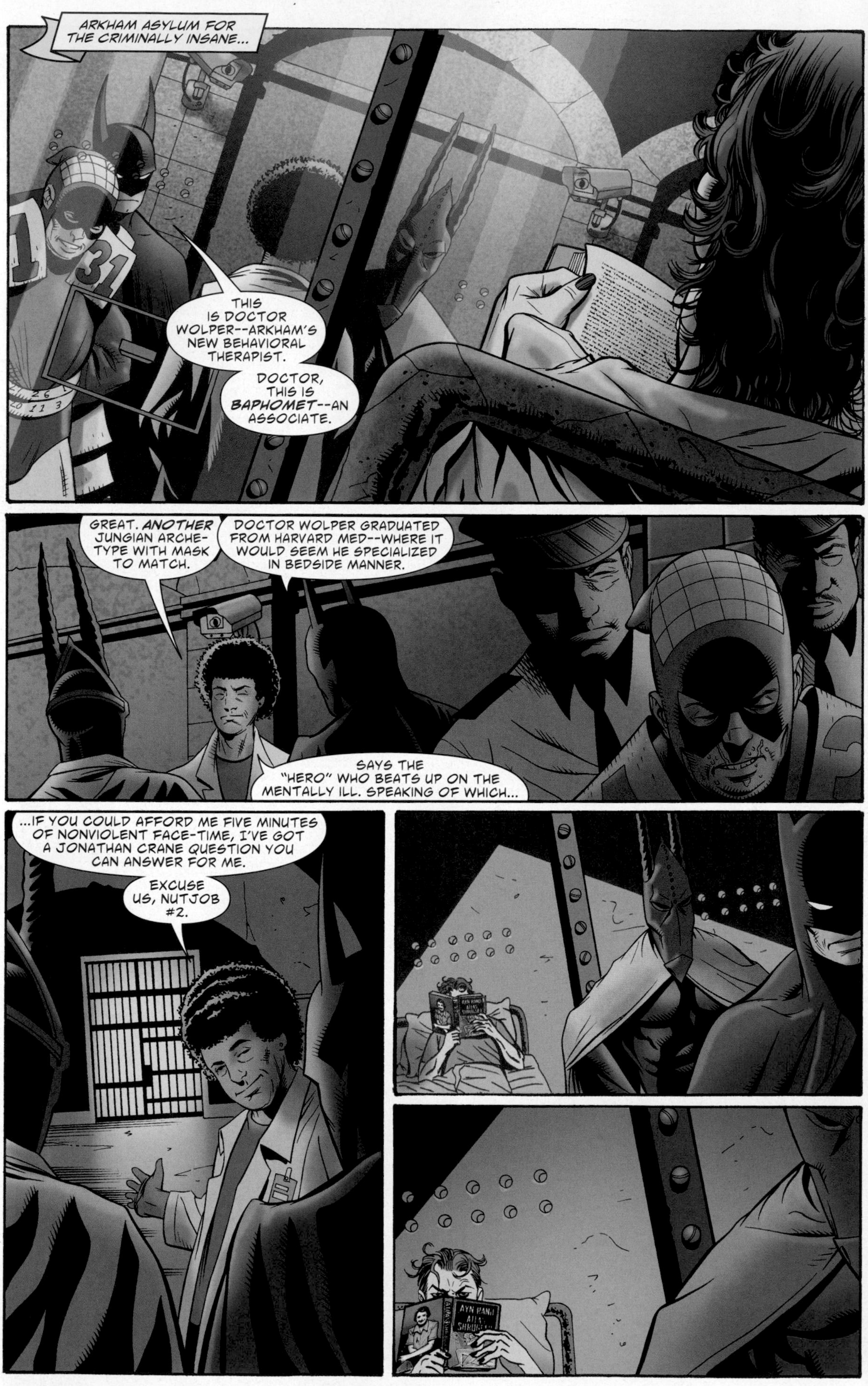
ARKHAM ASYLUM FOR THE CRIMINALLY INSANE...
THIS IS DOCTOR WOLPER--ARKHAM'S NEW BEHAVIORAL THERAPIST.
DOCTOR, THIS IS BAPHOMET--AN ASSOCIATE.
GREAT. ANOTHER JUNGIAN ARCHETYPE WITH MASK TO MATCH.
DOCTOR WOLPER GRADUATED FROM HARVARD MED--WHERE IT WOULD SEEM HE SPECIALIZED IN BEDSIDE MANNER.
SAYS THE "HERO" WHO BEATS UP ON THE MENTALLY ILL. SPEAKING OF WHICH...
...IF YOU COULD AFFORD ME FIVE MINUTES OF NONVIOLENT FACE-TIME, I'VE GOT A JONATHAN CRANE QUESTION YOU CAN ANSWER FOR ME.
EXCUSE US, NUTJOB #2.
AYN RAND ATLAS SHRUGGED

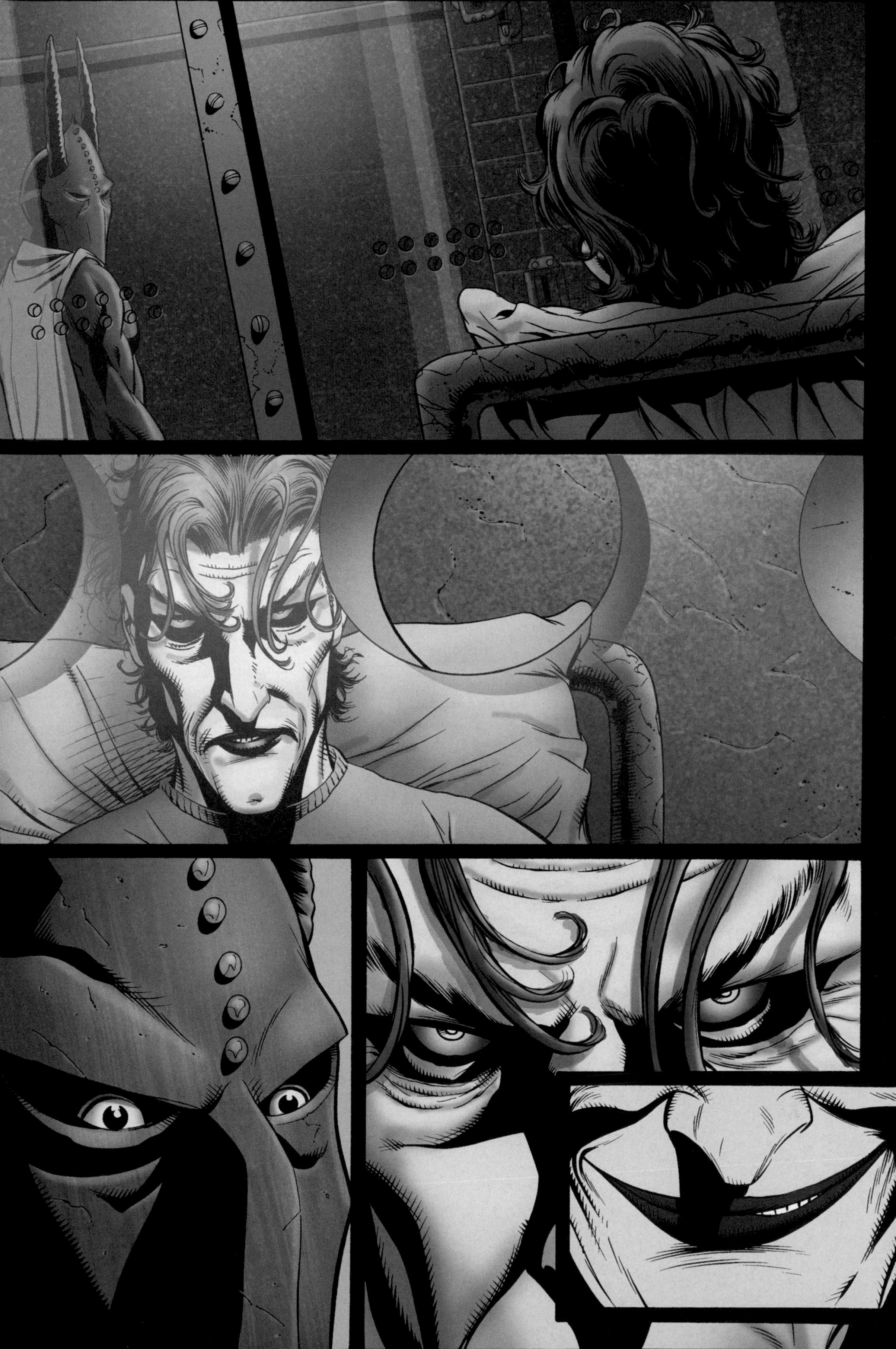

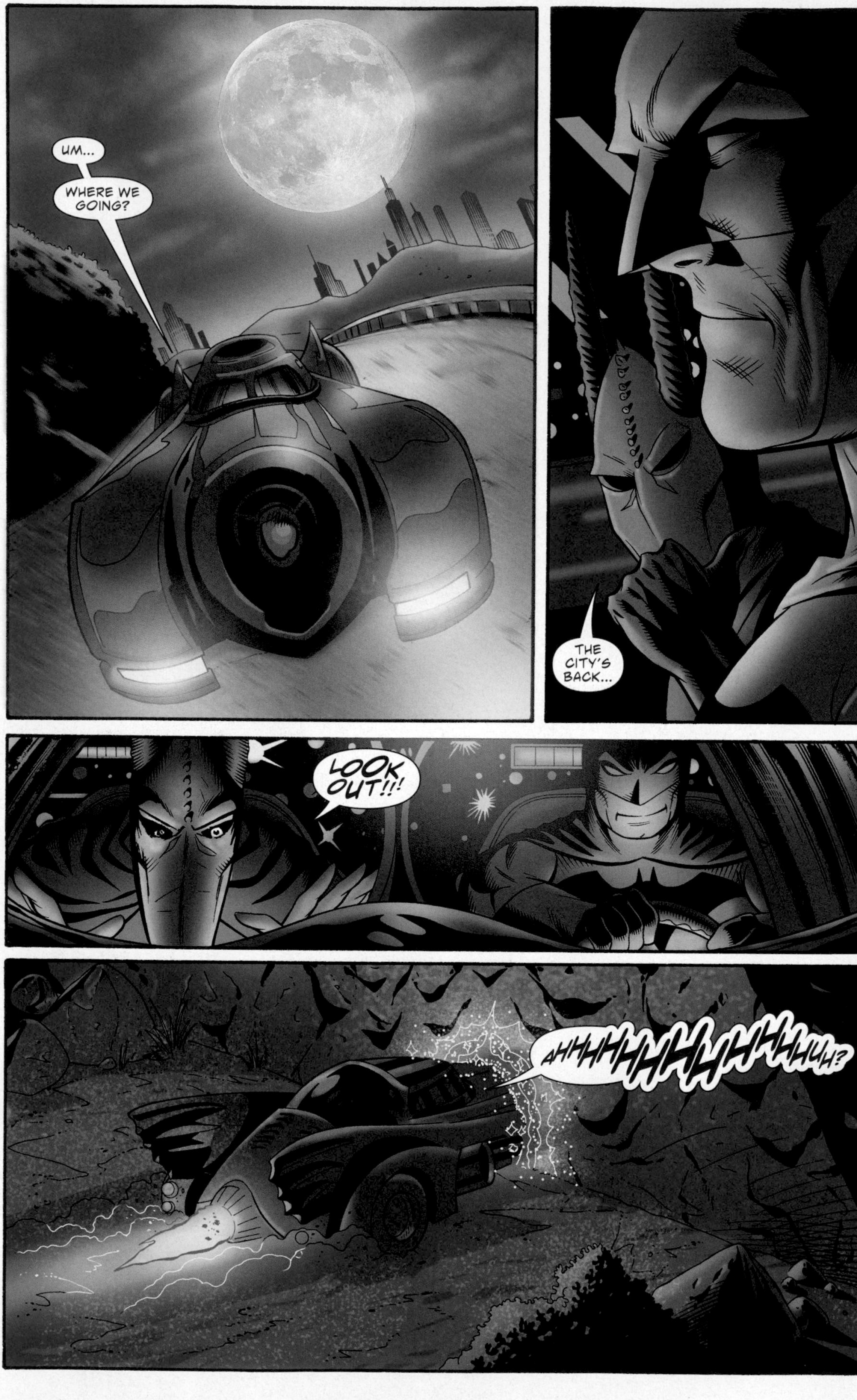
UM...
WHERE WE GOING?
THE CITY'S BACK...
LOOK OUT!!!
AHHHHHHHHHHHHHHHHUH?

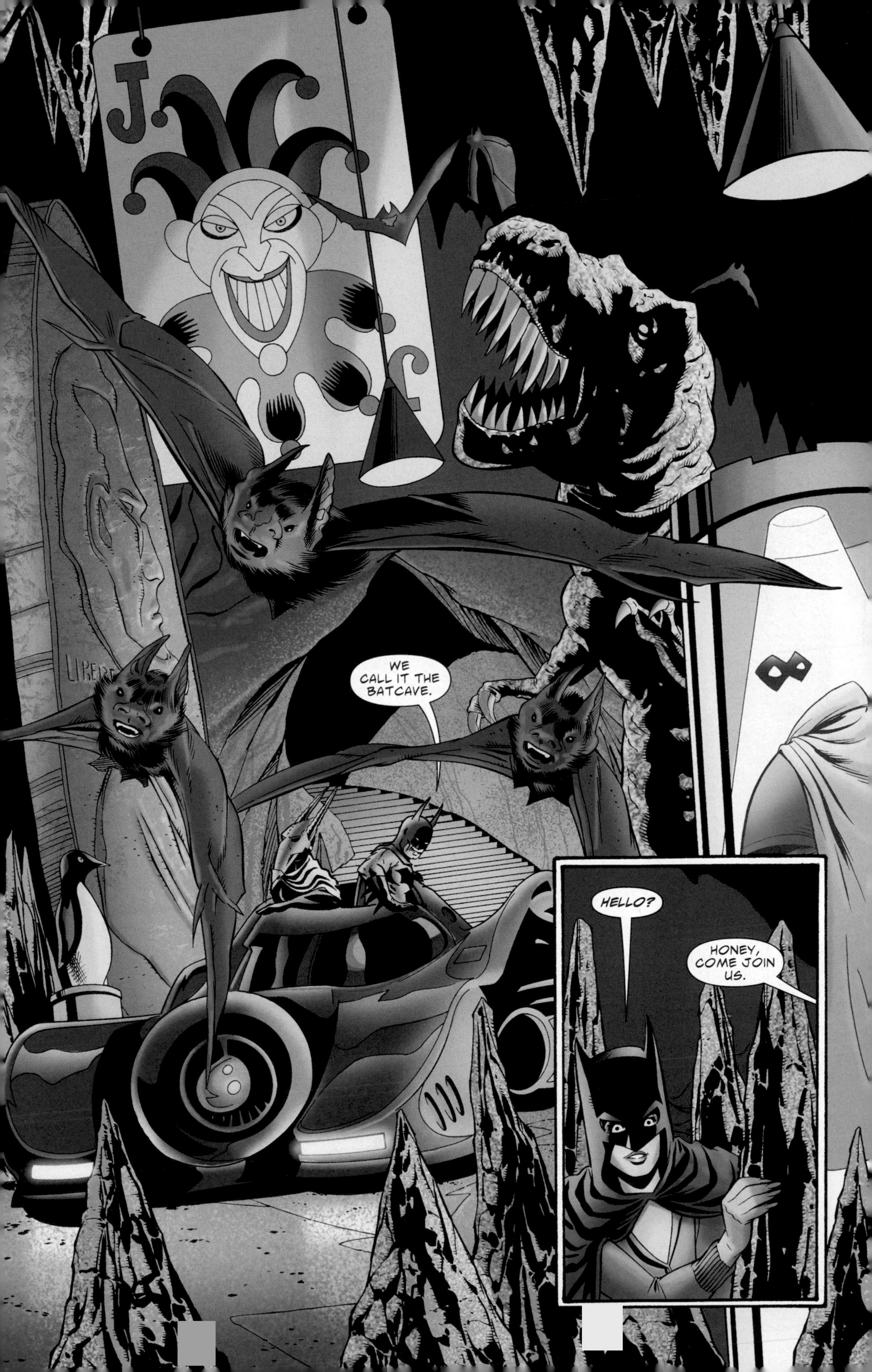
WE CALL IT THE BATCAVE.
HELLO?
HONEY, COME JOIN US.

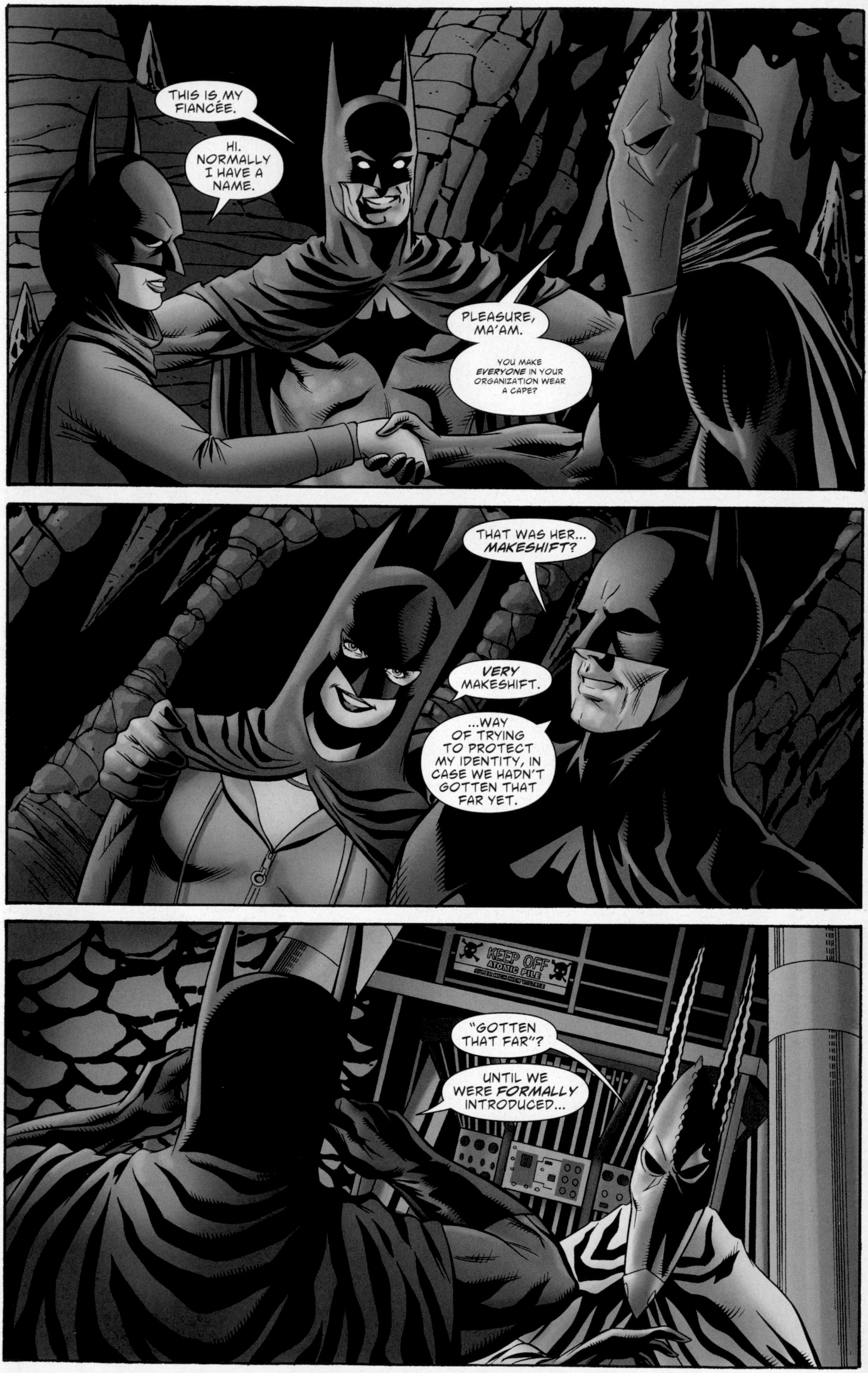

THIS IS MY FIANCÉE.
HI. NORMALLY I HAVE A NAME.
PLEASURE, MA'AM.
YOU MAKE EVERYONE IN YOUR ORGANIZATION WEAR A CAPE?
THAT WAS HER... MAKESHIFT?
VERY MAKESHIFT.
...WAY OF TRYING TO PROTECT MY IDENTITY, IN CASE WE HADN'T GOTTEN THAT FAR YET.
KEEP OFF
ATOMIC PILE
"GOTTEN THAT FAR"?
UNTIL WE WERE FORMALLY INTRODUCED...

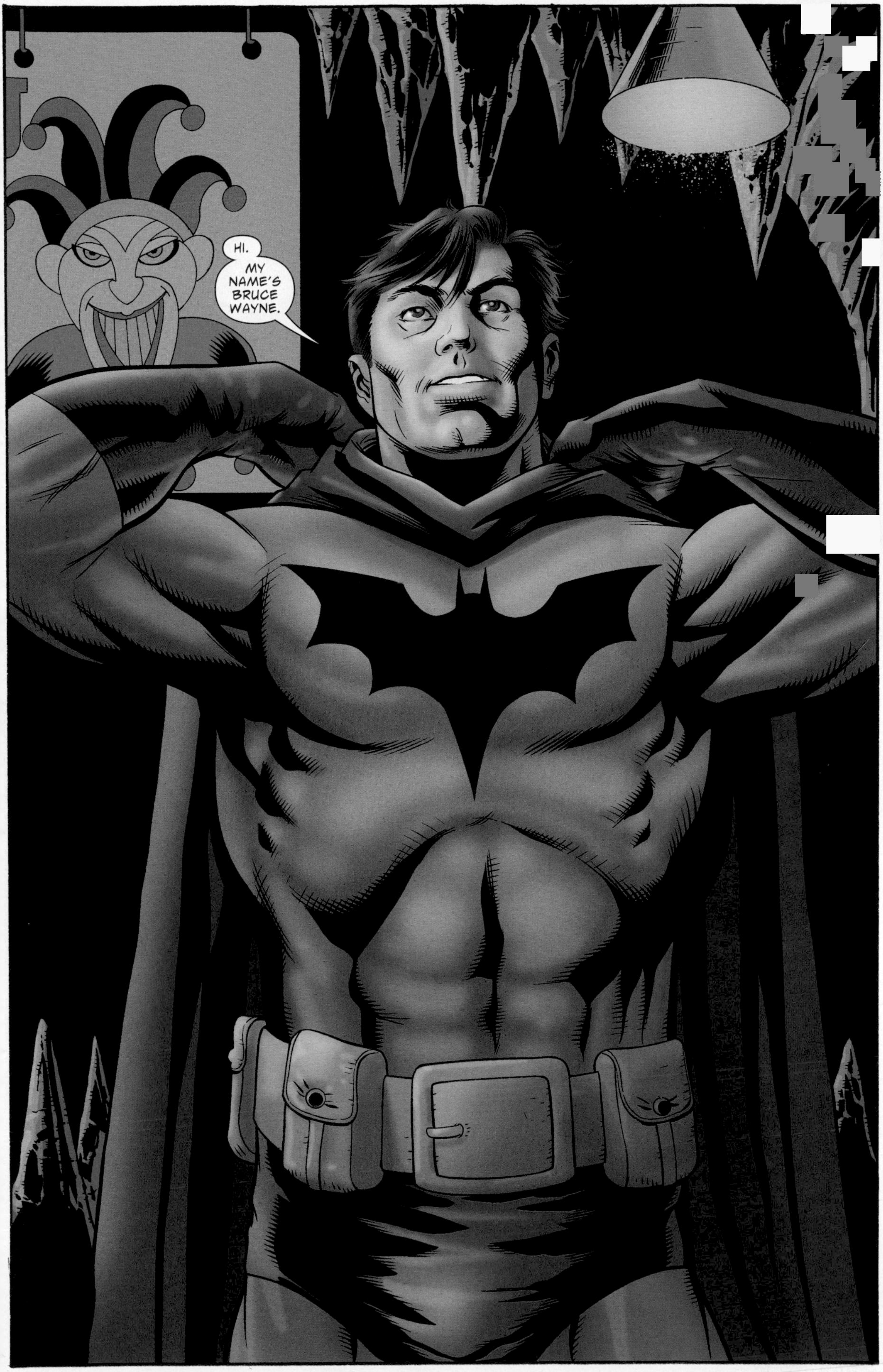
HI. MY NAME'S BRUCE WAYNE.

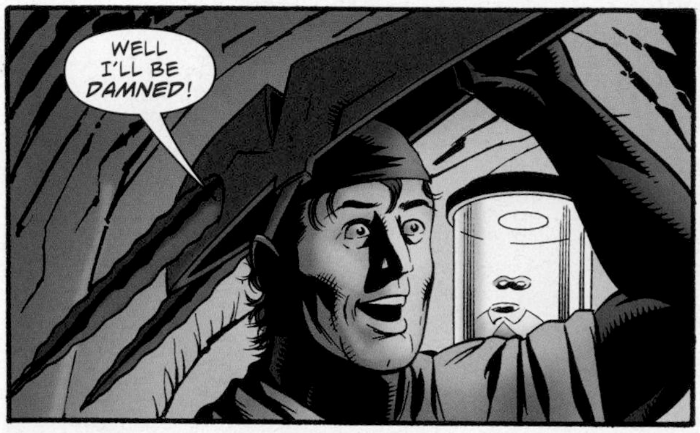
WELL I'LL BE DAMNED!

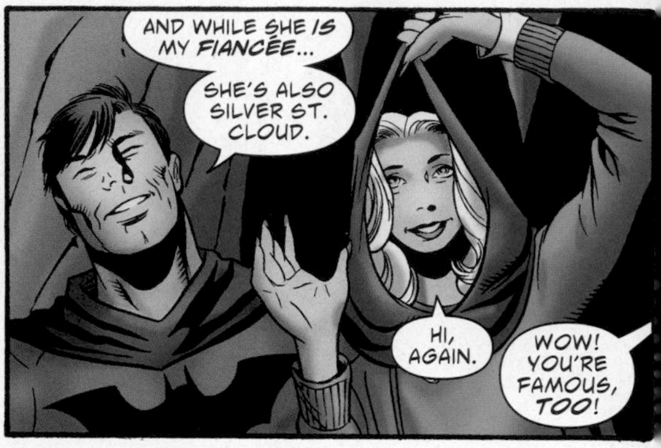
AND WHILE SHE IS MY FIANCÉE...
SHE'S ALSO SILVER ST. CLOUD.
HI, AGAIN.
WOW! YOU'RE FAMOUS, TOO!

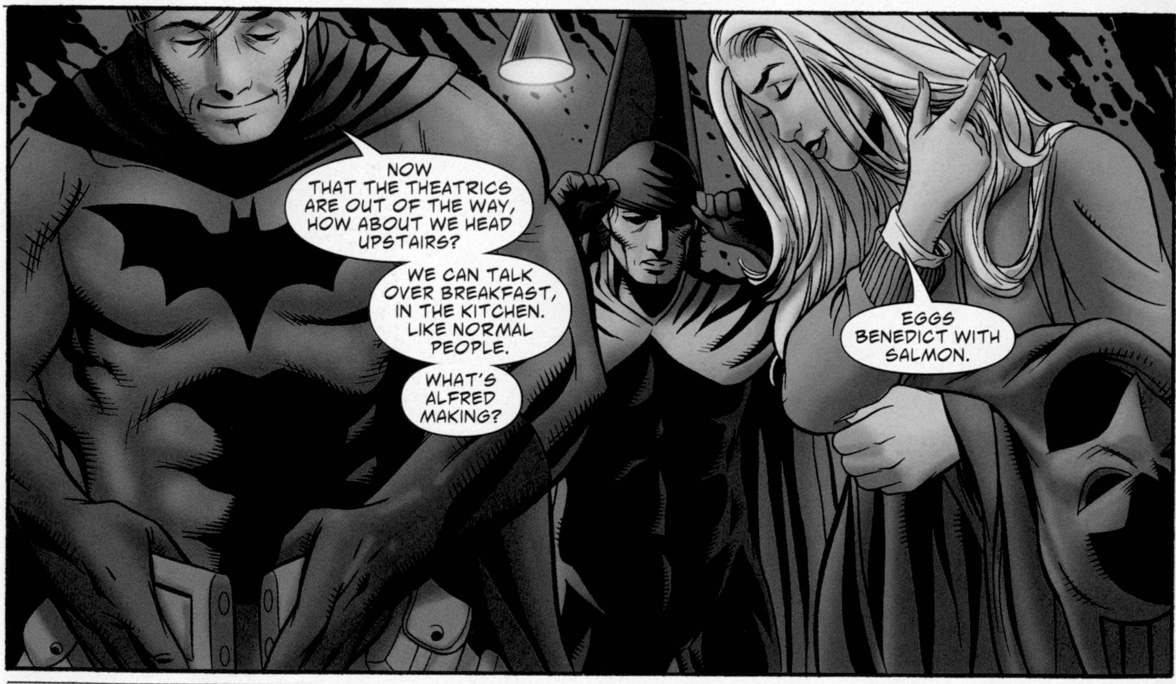
NOW THAT THE THEATRICS ARE OUT OF THE WAY, HOW ABOUT WE HEAD UPSTAIRS?
WE CAN TALK OVER BREAKFAST, IN THE KITCHEN. LIKE NORMAL PEOPLE.
WHAT'S ALFRED MAKING?
EGGS BENEDICT WITH SALMON.

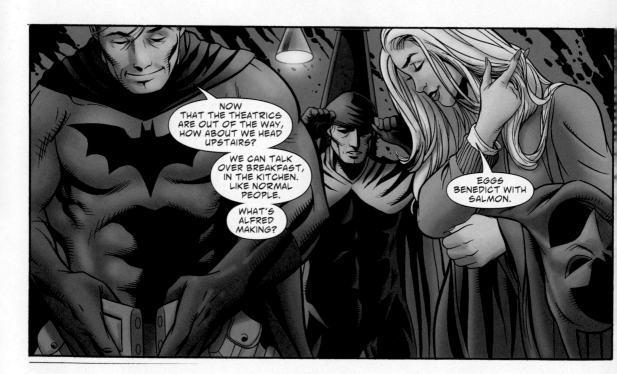

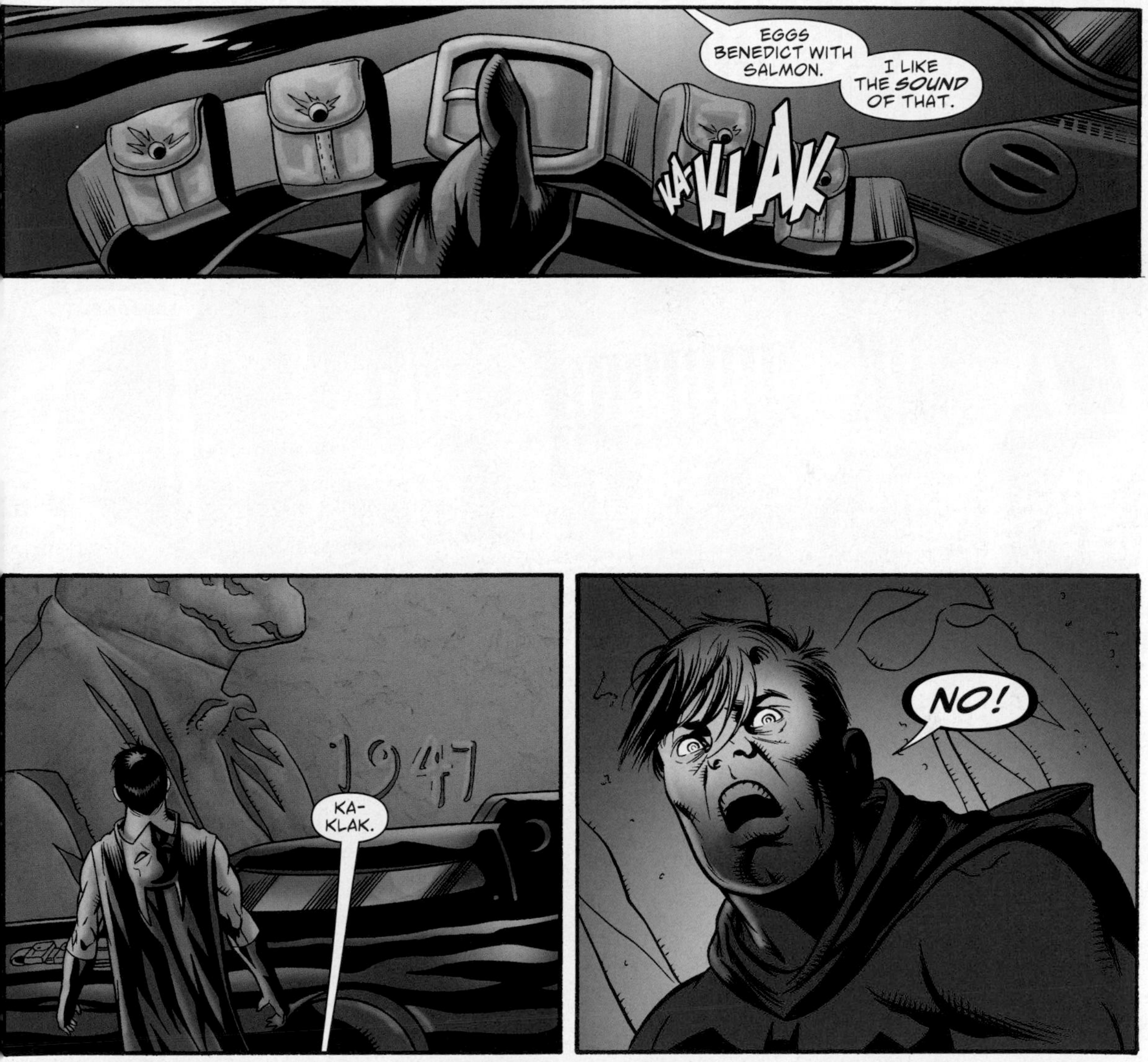
EGGS BENEDICT WITH SALMON.
I LIKE THE *SOUND* OF THAT.
KA-KLAK
1947
KA-KLAK.
NO!

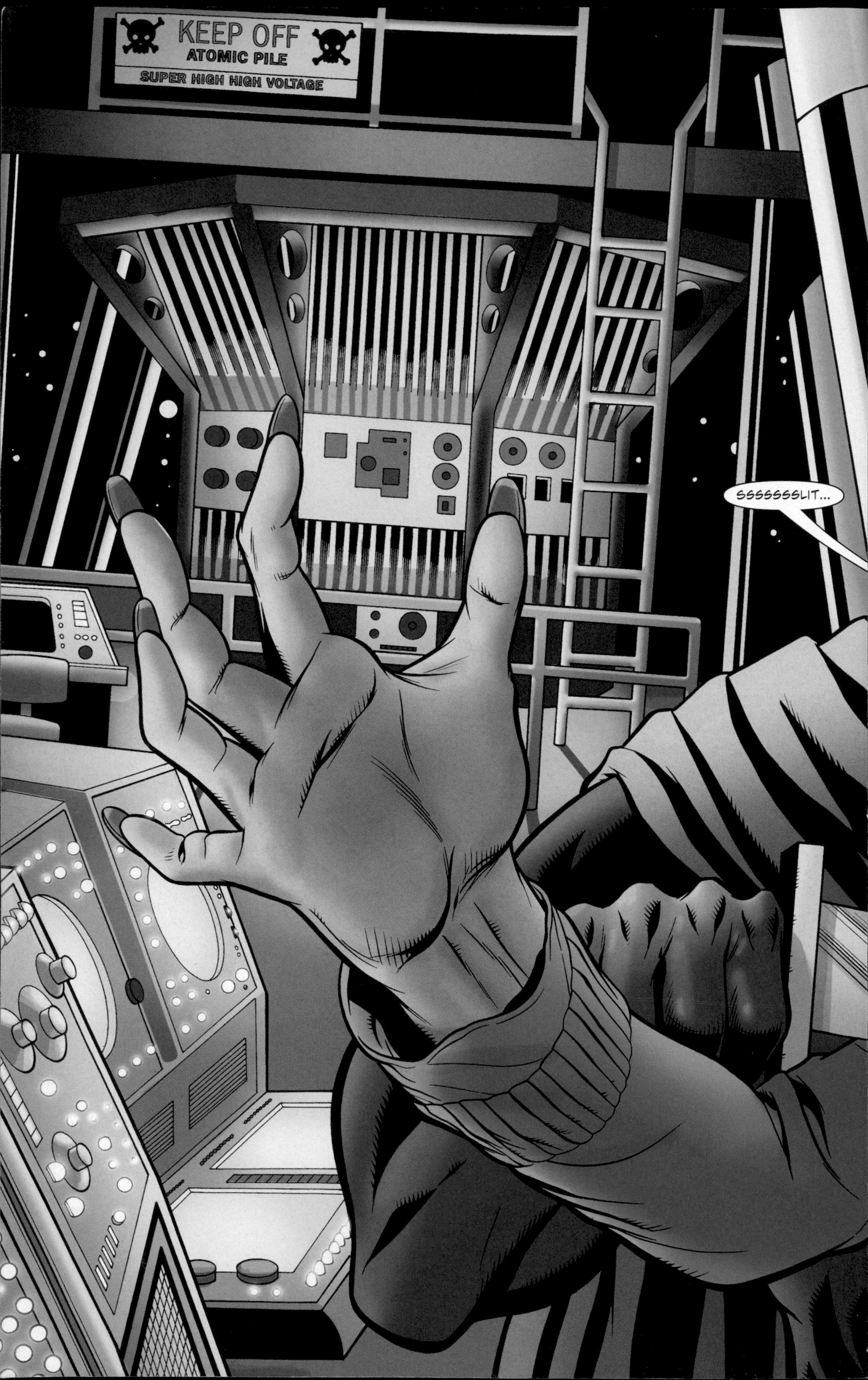
KEEP OFF
ATOMIC PILE
SUPER HIGH HIGH VOLTAGE
SSSSSSSLIT...

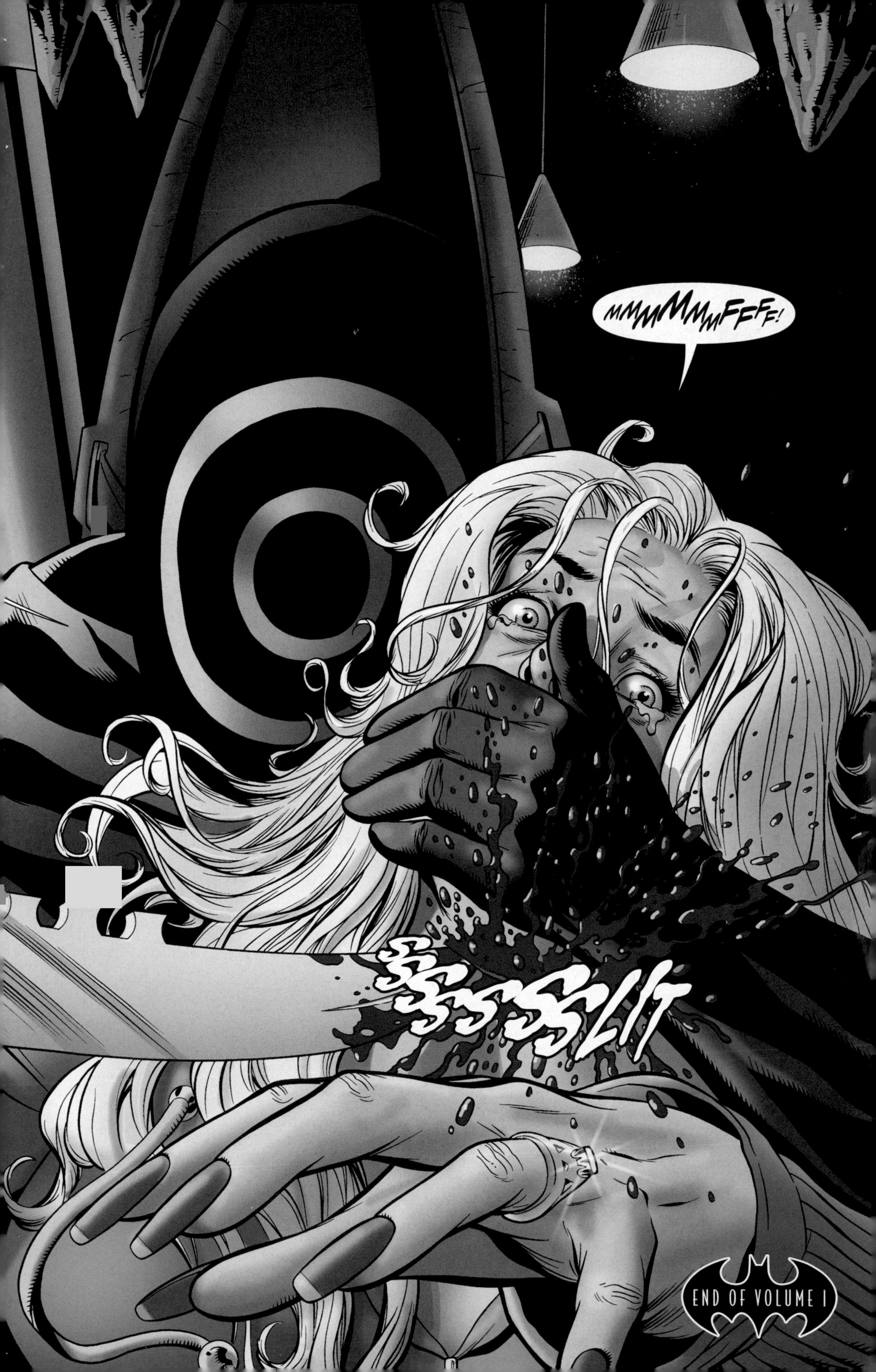
MMMMMMFFFF!
SSSSSLIT
END OF VOLUME 1

unused cover by BILL SIENKIEWICZ

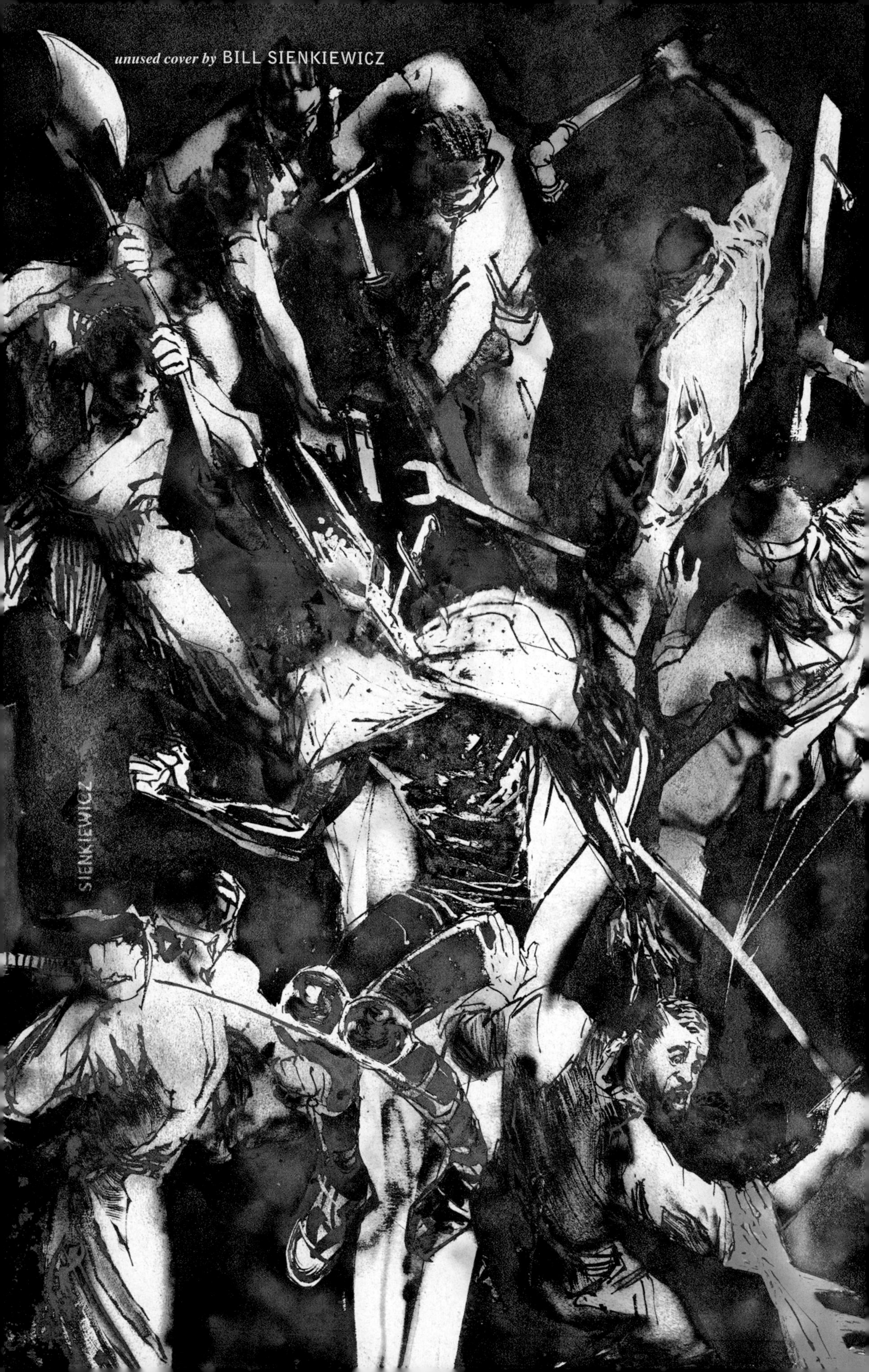
SIENKIEWICZ

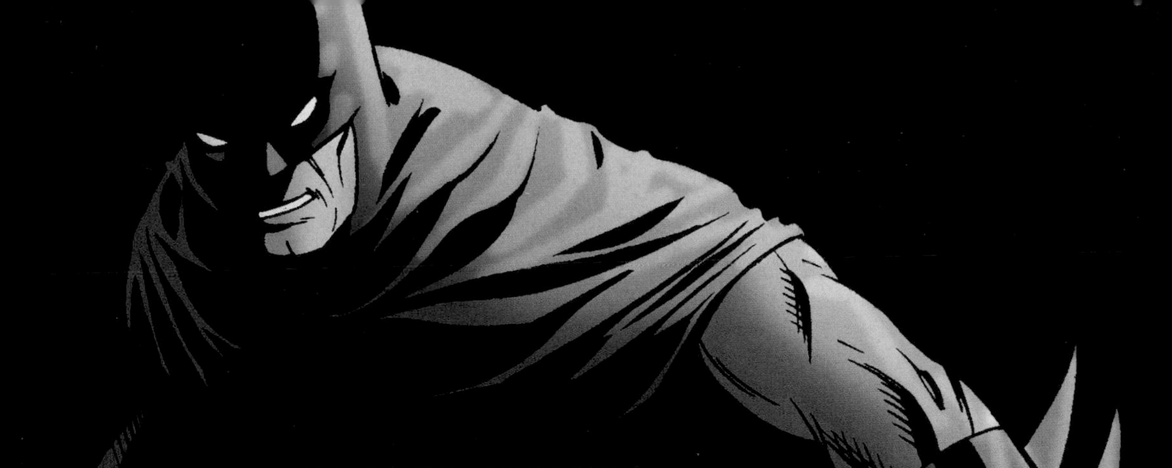

Crisis of INFINITE MIDLIFE!

A year.

Walt and I waited a full year for readers to turn that page to the big reveal splash (which I'm STILL not spoiling here, in case you're reading this before the actual story). We went to great lengths to keep the climax hidden from anybody who wasn't part of GYRE's creative team. I never even told my wife. Granted, she didn't care.

Not many did. The book didn't light the world on fire, saleswise. We knew it wouldn't going in, as GYRE was designed to be more like a wolf in sheep's clothing: a sleeper agent that wouldn't go active until issue six. So it sold well enough, buoyed mostly by the fact that there was an absolute absence of Bruce Wayne in the DCU at that time. By issue three, I started hearing some grousing (mostly from readers under 30) that I had Bruce Wayne giving piggy-backs and being far too happy.

Some folks started guessing that our new hero might not be so heroic. NEVER believe any jackass who tells you "I knew it was gonna be THAT guy under the mask" because NOBODY guessed at the villain's identity. Any time they even came close, I'd launch into a cover story Tweet about a Baphomet spinoff book called GOTHAM BABYLON, which I said we'd launch after GYRE six hit stands.

And by the time they turned the last page of issue six, the reader ultimately got that GYRE was more than just a midlife crisis tale about a lonely hero who finally tries to embrace his own humanity...

It was just Act II...

Twenty years ago, Walt and I had a dream about making a comic, taking it so far as to draw a few pages (seen following this afterword). 20 years later, it's mind-bending to me that Walt and I get to make comics that peple will actually see. For the biggest comics company on the planet. With the world's most well known comic book character. I assure you: it's a blessing I never take for granted.

It was a herculean effort to go spoiler-free in the information age, so I'd like to recognize the Gretzky-like assists we've had on this book — the folks who kept the secret.

On GYRE even more than CACOPHONY, artist Walt Flanagan was kind of a co-author — inasmuch as he'd write down the names of every DC character he ever wanted to draw and give them to me.

Crazy Quilt?" I remember asking incredulously when I laid eyes on his list. "You're kidding."
"How many chances am I ever gonna get to draw Crazy Quilt in a DC comic? Or in ANY comic?"

Flanagan's List forced me to be more creative than I would've been in GYRE, as I'd try to figure out ways with which to weave in the characters Walt wanted to pencil. The flashbacks exist because of Walt's list — and the flashbacks are ultimately the reason Batman allows himself to get to that ish six splash page.

And that was just Walt's contribution to the WRITING. His biggest contribution, naturally, was his art. I wrote the first six issues a year prior to issue six hitting the stands, so Walt was drawing long after I'd stopped writing — which led to one of my favorite pastimes: opening email from Walt and seeing some dopey situation I'd scripted fully realized as a drawing. And as I'd match the scripted dialogue to the pencils, I'd grin like the Joker — because one of my dearest friends was drawing this epic Batman arc and CRUSHING it.

This book had LOTS of Art, come to think of it: Art Thibert & Art Lyons, inker & colorist. You guys not only knocked it out of the park, you also kept the secret of the story, and honored any request for changes. Thanks for riding shotgun on something this important to me and Flanagan.

Thanks, too, to Dan DiDio (and later Jim Lee) for letting Walt and me continue our *New York Times* Best-Selling CACOPHONY storyline. Big thanks to Michael Marts (who not only edited our book but also gave life to a little human during the Vol. 1 run) and even bigger thanks to Janelle Siegel — who's about as patient with a stoner writer who gives overly meticulous lettering notes as I imagine she'd be with an infant (granted, the two aren't that dissimilar in the first place).

I loved every second I worked on THE WIDENING GYRE (the name of which, borrowed from Yeats, refers to the mask worn by the villain on that infamous ish-ending splash page), but more importantly, I LOVED that you didn't see that ending coming. Thanks for sticking with us through the Bat-Boyfriend arc of the story, but be sure to come back for the next six — when the unadulterated Bat-Brutality kicks in.

Walt? We're halfway to one of those big-ass Absolute editions...

Kevin Smith
3/30/2010

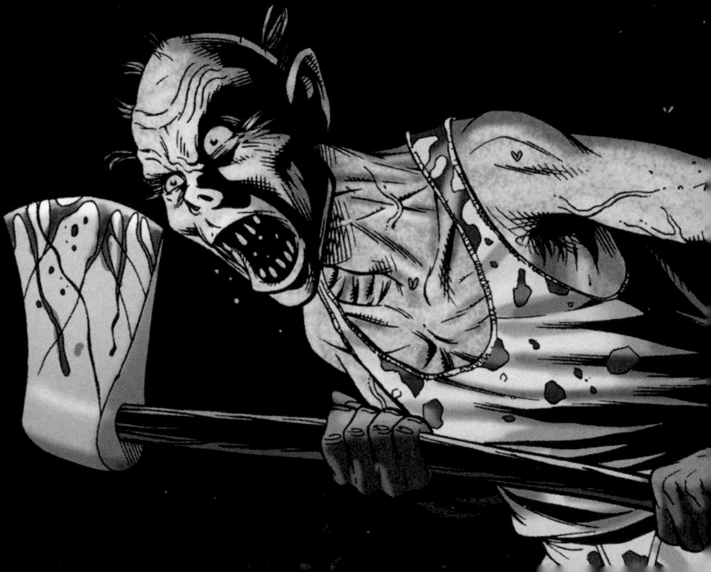

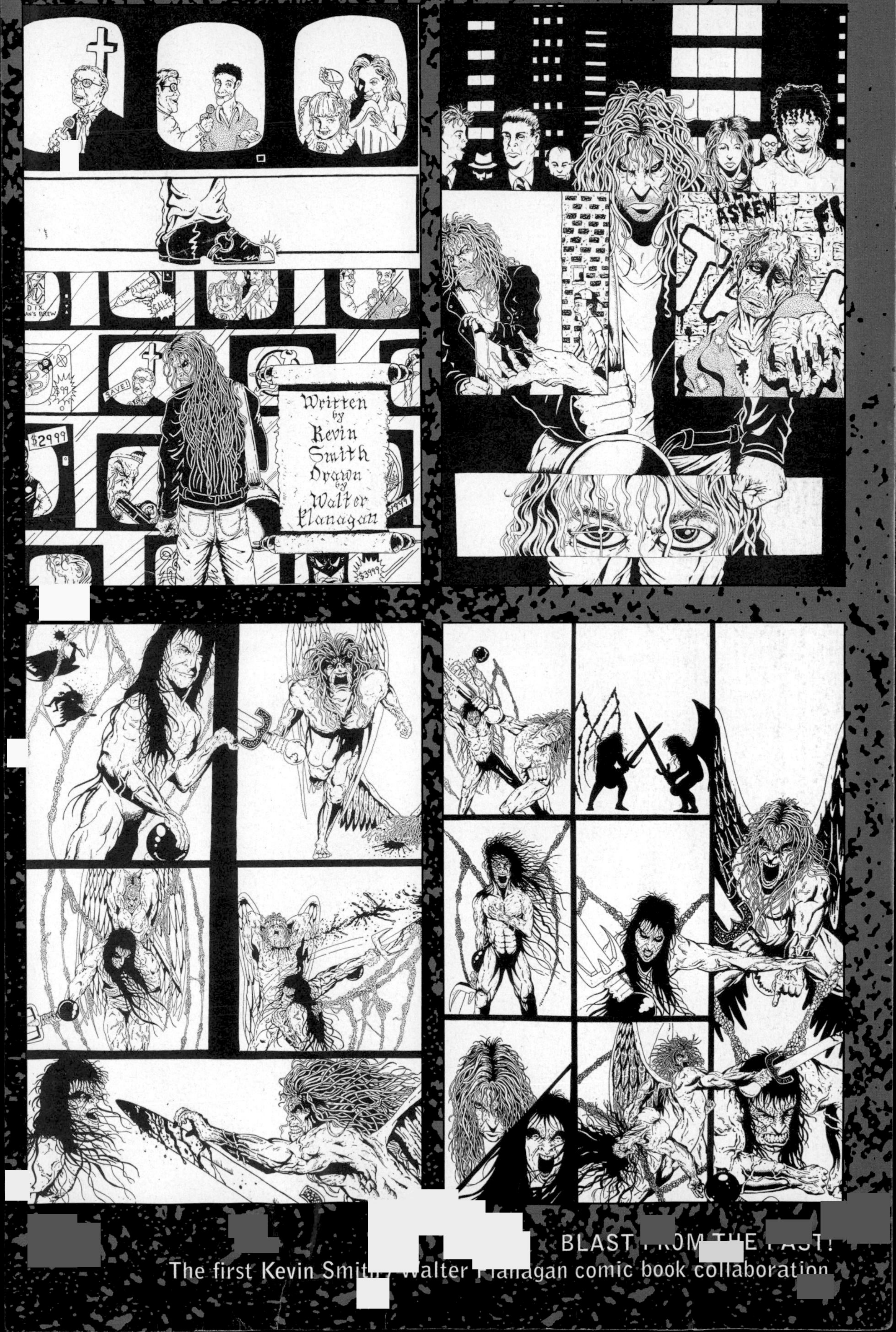
$29.99
SAVE!
SALE!
$39.99
Written by Kevin Smith Drawn by Walter Flanagan
ASKEW

BLAST FROM THE PAST!
The first Kevin Smith / Walter Flanagan comic book collaboration

Kevin Smith is the award-winning writer/director/producer of *Clerks*, *Chasing Amy*, *Zach and Miri Make a Porno* and other films. He's written comic books featuring his own characters (*Jay and Silent Bob*) as well as others (*Daredevil* for Marvel Comics and GREEN ARROW for DC), and even owns his own comic book store, Jay and Silent Bob's Secret Stash, in his hometown of Red Bank, New Jersey. He lives in LA with his wife and daughter. He still has a reputation for lateness.

Walter Flanagan is no stranger to comics fans. He drew the IDW series *Karney* and *War of the Undead*, manages Jay and Silent Bob's Secret Stash in Red Bank, NJ, and brought the first cinematic Fanboy to life ("Tell 'em, Steve-Dave."). BATMAN: CACOPHONY marked his DC debut. Flanagan lives in New Jersey with his wife, two daughters, and once legendarily fast dog.

Art Thibert has been both a penciller and an inker in the comics industry. He is best known for his work on various *X-Men* titles for Marvel. Most recently, his distinctive inking style has graced such titles as TRINITY and DOC SAVAGE.